# Lecture Notes in Artificial Intelligence     13033

## Subseries of Lecture Notes in Computer Science

Series Editors

Randy Goebel
*University of Alberta, Edmonton, Canada*
Yuzuru Tanaka
*Hokkaido University, Sapporo, Japan*
Wolfgang Wahlster
*DFKI and Saarland University, Saarbrücken, Germany*

Founding Editor

Jörg Siekmann
*DFKI and Saarland University, Saarbrücken, Germany*

More information about this subseries at http://www.springer.com/series/1244

Duc Nghia Pham · Thanaruk Theeramunkong ·
Guido Governatori · Fenrong Liu (Eds.)

# PRICAI 2021: Trends in Artificial Intelligence

18th Pacific Rim
International Conference on Artificial Intelligence, PRICAI 2021
Hanoi, Vietnam, November 8–12, 2021
Proceedings, Part III

Springer

*Editors*
Duc Nghia Pham
MIMOS Berhad
Kuala Lumpur, Malaysia

Guido Governatori (iD)
Data61
CSIRO
Brisbane, QLD, Australia

Thanaruk Theeramunkong
Sirindhorn International Institute of Science
and Technology
Thammasat University
Mueang Pathum Thani, Thailand

Fenrong Liu (iD)
Department of Philosophy
Tsinghua University
Beijing, China

ISSN 0302-9743          ISSN 1611-3349  (electronic)
Lecture Notes in Artificial Intelligence
ISBN 978-3-030-89369-9          ISBN 978-3-030-89370-5  (eBook)
https://doi.org/10.1007/978-3-030-89370-5

LNCS Sublibrary: SL7 – Artificial Intelligence

This Springer imprint is published by the registered company Springer Nature Switzerland AG
The registered company address is: Gewerbestrasse 11, 6330 Cham, Switzerland

# Preface

These three-volume proceedings contain the papers presented at the 18th Pacific Rim International Conference on Artificial Intelligence (PRICAI 2021) held virtually during November 8–12, 2021, in Hanoi, Vietnam.

PRICAI, which was inaugurated in Tokyo in 1990, started out as a biennial international conference concentrating on artificial intelligence (AI) theories, technologies, and applications in the areas of social and economic importance for Pacific Rim countries. It provides a common forum for researchers and practitioners in various branches of AI to exchange new ideas and share experience and expertise. Since then, the conference has grown, both in participation and scope, to be a premier international AI event for all major Pacific Rim nations as well as countries from all around the world. In 2018, the PRICAI Steering Committee decided to hold PRICAI on an annual basis starting from 2019.

This year, we received an overwhelming number of 382 submissions to both the Main track (365 submissions) and the Industry special track (17 submissions). This number was impressive considering that for the first time PRICAI was being held virtually during a global pandemic situation. All submissions were reviewed and evaluated with the same highest quality standard through a double-blind review process. Each paper received at least two reviews, in most cases three, and in some cases up to four. During the review process, discussions among the Program Committee (PC) members in charge were carried out before recommendations were made, and when necessary, additional reviews were sourced. Finally, the conference and program co-chairs read the reviews and comments and made a final calibration for differences among individual reviewer scores in light of the overall decisions. The entire Program Committee (including PC members, external reviewers, and co-chairs) expended tremendous effort to ensure fairness and consistency in the paper selection process. Eventually, we accepted 92 regular papers and 28 short papers for oral presentation. This gives a regular paper acceptance rate of 24.08% and an overall acceptance rate of 31.41%.

The technical program consisted of three tutorials and the main conference program. The three tutorials covered hot topics in AI from "Collaborative Learning and Optimization" and "Mechanism Design Powered by Social Interactions" to "Towards Hyperdemocary: AI-enabled Crowd Consensus Making and Its Real-World Societal Experiments". All regular and short papers were orally presented over four days in parallel and in topical program sessions. We were honored to have keynote presentations by four distinguished researchers in the field of AI whose contributions have crossed discipline boundaries: Mohammad Bennamoun (University of Western Australia, Australia), Johan van Benthem (University of Amsterdam, The Netherlands; Stanford University, USA; and Tsinghua University, China), Virginia Dignum (Umeå University, Sweden), and Yutaka Matsuo (University of Tokyo, Japan). We were grateful to them for sharing their insights on their latest research with us.

The success of PRICAI 2021 would not be possible without the effort and support of numerous people from all over the world. First, we would like to thank the authors, PC members, and external reviewers for their time and efforts spent in making PRICAI 2021 a successful and enjoyable conference. We are also thankful to various fellow members of the conference committee, without whose support and hard work PRICAI 2021 could not have been successful:

- Advisory Board: Hideyuki Nakashima, Abdul Sattar, and Dickson Lukose
- Industry Chair: Shiyou Qian
- Local/Virtual Organizing Chairs: Sankalp Khanna and Adila Alfa Krisnadhi
- Tutorial Chair: Guandong Xu
- Web and Publicity Chair: Md Khaled Ben Islam
- Workshop Chair: Dengji Zhao

We gratefully acknowledge the organizational support of several institutions including Data61/CSIRO (Australia), Tsinghua University (China), MIMOS Berhad (Malaysia), Thammasat University (Thailand), and Griffith University (Australia).

Finally, we thank Springer, Ronan Nugent (Editorial Director, Computer Science Proceedings), and Anna Kramer (Assistant Editor, Computer Science Proceedings) for their assistance in publishing the PRICAI 2021 proceedings as three volumes of its Lecture Notes in Artificial Intelligence series.

November 2021

Duc Nghia Pham<br>
Thanaruk Theeramunkong<br>
Guido Governatori<br>
Fenrong Liu

# Organization

## PRICAI Steering Committee

### Steering Committee

| | |
|---|---|
| Quan Bai | University of Tasmania, Australia |
| Tru Hoang Cao | The University of Texas Health Science Center at Houston, USA |
| Xin Geng | Southeast University, China |
| Guido Governatori | Data61, CSIRO, Australia |
| Takayuki Ito | Nagoya Institute of Technology, Japan |
| Byeong-Ho Kang | University of Tasmania, Australia |
| M. G. M. Khan | University of the South Pacific, Fiji |
| Sankalp Khanna | Australian e-Health Research Centre, CSIRO, Australia |
| Dickson Lukose | Monash University, Australia |
| Hideyuki Nakashima | Sapporo City University, Japan |
| Abhaya Nayak | Macquarie University, Australia |
| Seong Bae Park | Kyung Hee University, South Korea |
| Duc Nghia Pham | MIMOS Berhad, Malaysia |
| Abdul Sattar | Griffith University, Australia |
| Alok Sharma | RIKEN, Japan, and University of the South Pacific, Fiji |
| Thanaruk Theeramunkong | Thammasat University, Thailand |
| Zhi-Hua Zhou | Nanjing University, China |

### Honorary Members

| | |
|---|---|
| Randy Goebel | University of Alberta, Canada |
| Tu-Bao Ho | Japan Advanced Institute of Science and Technology, Japan |
| Mitsuru Ishizuka | University of Tokyo, Japan |
| Hiroshi Motoda | Osaka University, Japan |
| Geoff Webb | Monash University, Australia |
| Albert Yeap | Auckland University of Technology, New Zealand |
| Byoung-Tak Zhang | Seoul National University, South Korea |
| Chengqi Zhang | University of Technology Sydney, Australia |

## Conference Organizing Committee

### General Chairs

| | |
|---|---|
| Guido Governatori | Data61, CSIRO, Australia |
| Fenrong Liu | Tsinghua University, China |

## Program Chairs

| | |
|---|---|
| Duc Nghia Pham | MIMOS Berhad, Malaysia |
| Thanaruk Theeramunkong | Thammasat University, Thailand |

## Local/Virtual Organizing Chairs

| | |
|---|---|
| Sankalp Khanna | Australian e-Health Research Centre, CSIRO, Australia |
| Adila Alfa Krisnadhi | University of Indonesia, Indonesia |

## Workshop Chair

| | |
|---|---|
| Dengji Zhao | ShanghaiTech University, China |

## Tutorial Chair

| | |
|---|---|
| Guandong Xu | University of Technology Sydney, Australia |

## Industry Chair

| | |
|---|---|
| Shiyou Qian | Shanghai Jiao Tong University, China |

## Web and Publicity Chair

| | |
|---|---|
| Md Khaled Ben Islam | Griffith University, Australia |

## Advisory Board

| | |
|---|---|
| Hideyuki Nakashima | Sapporo City University, Japan |
| Abdul Sattar | Griffith University, Australia |
| Dickson Lukose | Monash University, Australia |

## Program Committee

| | |
|---|---|
| Eriko Aiba | The University of Electro-Communications, Japan |
| Patricia Anthony | Lincoln University, New Zealand |
| Chutiporn Anutariya | Asian Institute of Technology, Thailand |
| Mohammad Arshi Saloot | MIMOS Berhad, Malaysia |
| Yun Bai | University of Western Sydney, Australia |
| Chutima Beokhaimook | Rangsit University, Thailand |
| Ateet Bhalla | Independent Technology Consultant, India |
| Chih How Bong | Universiti Malaysia Sarawak, Malaysia |
| Poonpong Boonbrahm | Walailak University, Thailand |
| Aida Brankovic | Australian e-Health Research Centre, CSIRO, Australia |
| Xiongcai Cai | University of New South Wales, Australia |
| Tru Cao | University of Texas Health Science Center at Houston, USA |
| Hutchatai Chanlekha | Kasetsart University, Thailand |
| Sapa Chanyachatchawan | National Electronics and Computer Technology Center, Thailand |
| Siqi Chen | Tianjin University, China |

| | |
|---|---|
| Songcan Chen | Nanjing University of Aeronautics and Astronautics, China |
| Wu Chen | Southwest University, China |
| Yingke Chen | Sichuan University, China |
| Wai Khuen Cheng | Universiti Tunku Abdul Rahman, Malaysia |
| Boonthida Chiraratanasopha | Yala Rajabhat University, Thailand |
| Phatthanaphong Chomphuwiset | Mahasarakham University, Thailand |
| Dan Corbett | Optimodal Technologies, USA |
| Célia Da Costa Pereira | Université Côte d'Azur, France |
| Jirapun Daengdej | Assumption University, Thailand |
| Hoa Khanh Dam | University of Wollongong, Australia |
| Xuan-Hong Dang | IBM Watson Research, USA |
| Abdollah Dehzangi | Rutgers University, USA |
| Sang Dinh | Hanoi University of Science and Technology, Vietnam |
| Clare Dixon | University of Manchester, UK |
| Shyamala Doraisamy | University Putra Malaysia, Malaysia |
| Nuttanart Facundes | King Mongkut's University of Technology Thonburi, Thailand |
| Eduardo Fermé | Universidade da Madeira, Portugal |
| Somchart Fugkeaw | Thammasat University, Thailand |
| Katsuhide Fujita | Tokyo University of Agriculture and Technology, Japan |
| Naoki Fukuta | Shizuoka University, Japan |
| Marcus Gallagher | University of Queensland, Australia |
| Dragan Gamberger | Rudjer Boskovic Institute, Croatia |
| Wei Gao | Nanjing University, China |
| Xiaoying Gao | Victoria University of Wellington, New Zealand |
| Xin Geng | Southeast University, China |
| Manolis Gergatsoulis | Ionian University, Greece |
| Guido Governatori | Data61, CSIRO, Australia |
| Alban Grastien | Australian National University, Australia |
| Charles Gretton | Australian National University, Australia |
| Fikret Gurgen | Bogazici University, Turkey |
| Peter Haddawy | Mahidol University, Thailand |
| Choochart Haruechaiyasak | National Electronics and Computer Technology Center, Thailand |
| Hamed Hassanzadeh | Australian e-Health Research Centre, CSIRO, Australia |
| Tessai Hayama | Nagaoka University of Technology, Japan |
| Juhua Hu | University of Washington, USA |
| Xiaodi Huang | Charles Sturt University, Australia |
| Van Nam Huynh | Japan Advanced Institute of Science and Technology, Japan |
| Norisma Idris | University of Malaya, Malaysia |
| Mitsuru Ikeda | Japan Advanced Institute of Science and Technology, Japan |

| Masashi Inoue | Tohoku Institute of Technology, Japan |
| Takayuki Ito | Kyoto University, Japan |
| Sanjay Jain | National University of Singapore, Singapore |
| Guifei Jiang | Nankai University, China |
| Yichuan Jiang | Southeast University, China |
| Nattagit Jiteurtragool | Digital Government Development Agency, Thailand |
| Hideaki Kanai | Japan Advanced Institute of Science and Technology, Japan |
| Ryo Kanamori | Nagoya University, Japan |
| Natsuda Kaothanthong | Thammasat University, Thailand |
| Jessada Karnjana | National Electronics and Computer Technology Center, Thailand |
| C. Maria Keet | University of Cape Town, South Africa |
| Gabriele Kern-Isberner | Technische Universitaet Dortmund, Germany |
| Sankalp Khanna | Australian e-Health Research Centre, CSIRO, Australia |
| Nichnan Kittiphattanabawon | Walailak University, Thailand |
| Frank Klawonn | Ostfalia University, Germany |
| Sébastien Konieczny | CRIL-CNRS, France |
| Krit Kosawat | National Electronics and Computer Technology Center, Thailand |
| Alfred Krzywicki | University of New South Wales, Australia |
| Kun Kuang | Zhejiang University, China |
| Young-Bin Kwon | Chung-Ang University, South Korea |
| Weng Kin Lai | Tunku Abdul Rahman University College, Malaysia |
| Ho-Pun Lam | Data61, CSIRO, Australia |
| Nasith Laosen | Phuket Rajabhat University, Thailand |
| Vincent CS Lee | Monash University, Australia |
| Roberto Legaspi | KDDI Research Inc., Japan |
| Gang Li | Deakin University, Australia |
| Guangliang Li | Ocean University of China, China |
| Tianrui Li | Southwest Jiaotong University, China |
| Chanjuan Liu | Dalian University of Technology, China |
| Fenrong Liu | Tsinghua University, China |
| Michael Maher | Reasoning Research Institute, Australia |
| Xinjun Mao | National University of Defense Technology, China |
| Eric Martin | University of New South Wales, Australia |
| Maria Vanina Martinez | Instituto de Ciencias de la Computación, Argentina |
| Sanparith Marukatat | National Electronics and Computer Technology Center, Thailand |
| Michael Mayo | University of Waikato, New Zealand |
| Brendan McCane | University of Otago, New Zealand |
| Riichiro Mizoguchi | Japan Advanced Institute of Science and Technology, Japan |
| Nor Liyana Mohd Shuib | University of Malaya, Malaysia |
| M. A. Hakim Newton | Griffith University, Australia |

| | |
|---|---|
| Hung Duy Nguyen | Thammasat University, Thailand |
| Phi Le Nguyen | Hanoi University of Science and Technology, Vietnam |
| Kouzou Ohara | Aoyama Gakuin University, Japan |
| Francesco Olivieri | Griffith University, Australia |
| Mehmet Orgun | Macquarie University, Australia |
| Noriko Otani | Tokyo City University, Japan |
| Maurice Pagnucco | University of New South Wales, Australia |
| Laurent Perrussel | IRIT - Universite de Toulouse, France |
| Bernhard Pfahringer | University of Waikato, New Zealand |
| Duc Nghia Pham | MIMOS Berhad, Malaysia |
| Jantima Polpinij | Mahasarakham University, Thailand |
| Thadpong Pongthawornkamol | Kasikorn Business-Technology Group, Thailand |
| Yuhua Qian | Shanxi University, China |
| Joel Quinqueton | LIRMM, France |
| Teeradaj Racharak | Japan Advanced Institute of Science and Technology, Japan |
| Fenghui Ren | University of Wollongong, Australia |
| Mark Reynolds | University of Western Australia, Australia |
| Jandson S. Ribeiro | University of Koblenz-Landau, Germany |
| Kazumi Saito | University of Shizuoka, Japan |
| Chiaki Sakama | Wakayama University, Japan |
| Ken Satoh | National Institute of Informatics and Sokendai, Japan |
| Abdul Sattar | Griffith University, Australia |
| Nicolas Schwind | National Institute of Advanced Industrial Science and Technology, Japan |
| Nazha Selmaoui-Folcher | University of New Caledonia, France |
| Lin Shang | Nanjing University, China |
| Alok Sharma | RIKEN, Japan |
| Chenwei Shi | Tsinghua University, China |
| Zhenwei Shi | Beihang University, China |
| Mikifumi Shikida | Kochi University of Technology, Japan |
| Soo-Yong Shin | Sungkyunkwan University, South Korea |
| Yanfeng Shu | CSIRO, Australia |
| Tony Smith | University of Waikato, New Zealand |
| Chattrakul Sombattheera | Mahasarakham University, Thailand |
| Insu Song | James Cook University, Australia |
| Safeeullah Soomro | Virginia State University, USA |
| Tasanawan Soonklang | Silpakorn University, Thailand |
| Markus Stumptner | University of South Australia, Australia |
| Merlin Teodosia Suarez | De La Salle University, Philippines |
| Xin Sun | Catholic University of Lublin, Poland |
| Boontawee Suntisrivaraporn | DTAC, Thailand |
| Thepchai Supnithi | National Electronics and Computer Technology Center, Thailand |
| David Taniar | Monash University, Australia |

| | |
|---|---|
| Thanaruk Theeramunkong | Thammasat University, Thailand |
| Michael Thielscher | University of New South Wales, Australia |
| Satoshi Tojo | Japan Advanced Institute of Science and Technology, Japan |
| Shikui Tu | Shanghai Jiao Tong University, China |
| Miroslav Velev | Aries Design Automation, USA |
| Muriel Visani | Hanoi University of Science and Technology, Vietnam and La Rochelle University, France |
| Toby Walsh | University of New South Wales, Australia |
| Xiao Wang | Beijing University of Posts and Telecommunications, China |
| Paul Weng | Shanghai Jiao Tong University, China |
| Peter Whigham | University of Otago, New Zealand |
| Wayne Wobcke | University of New South Wales, Australia |
| Sartra Wongthanavasu | Khon Kaen University, Thailand |
| Brendon J. Woodford | University of Otago, New Zealand |
| Kaibo Xie | University of Amsterdam, The Netherlands |
| Ming Xu | Xi'an Jiaotong-Liverpool University, China |
| Shuxiang Xu | University of Tasmania, Australia |
| Hui Xue | Southeast University, China |
| Ming Yang | Nanjing Normal University, China |
| Roland Yap | National University of Singapore, Singapore |
| Kenichi Yoshida | University of Tsukuba, Japan |
| Takaya Yuizono | Japan Advanced Institute of Science and Technology, Japan |
| Chengqi Zhang | University of Technology Sydney, Australia |
| Du Zhang | California State University, USA |
| Min-Ling Zhang | Southeast University, China |
| Shichao Zhang | Central South University, China |
| Wen Zhang | Beijing University of Technology, China |
| Yu Zhang | Southern University of Science and Technology, China |
| Zhao Zhang | Hefei University of Technology, China |
| Zili Zhang | Deakin University, Australia |
| Yanchang Zhao | Data61, CSIRO, Australia |
| Shuigeng Zhou | Fudan University, China |
| Xingquan Zhu | Florida Atlantic University, USA |

## Additional Reviewers

Aitchison, Matthew
Akhtar, Naveed
Algar, Shannon
Almeida, Yuri
Boudou, Joseph
Burie, Jean-Christophe
Chandra, Abel

Cheng, Charibeth
Damigos, Matthew
Dong, Huanfang
Du Preez-Wilkinson, Nathaniel
Effendy, Suhendry
Eng, Bah Tee
Feng, Xuening

Fu, Keren
Gao, Yi
Geng, Chuanxing
Habault, Guillaume
Hang, Jun-Yi
He, Zhengqi
Hoang, Anh
Huynh, Du
Inventado, Paul Salvador
Jan, Zohaib
Jannai, Tokotoko
Jia, Binbin
Jiang, Zhaohui
Kalogeros, Eleftherios
Karim, Abdul
Kumar, Shiu
Lai, Yong
Laosen, Kanjana
Lee, Nung Kion
Lee, Zhiyi
Li, Weikai
Liang, Yanyan
Liu, Jiexi
Liu, Xiaxue
Liu, Yanli
Luke, Jing Yuan
Mahdi, Ghulam
Mayer, Wolfgang
Mendonça, Fábio
Ming, Zuheng
Mittelmann, Munyque
Nguyen, Duy Hung
Nguyen, Hong-Huy
Nguyen, Mau Toan
Nguyen, Minh Hieu
Nguyen, Minh Le
Nguyen, Trung Thanh
Nikafshan Rad, Hima
Okubo, Yoshiaki
Ong, Ethel
Ostertag, Cécilia

Phiboonbanakit, Thananut
Phua, Yin Jun
Pongpinigpinyo, Sunee
Preto, Sandro
Qian, Junqi
Qiao, Yukai
Riahi, Vahid
Rodrigues, Pedro
Rosenberg, Manou
Sa-Ngamuang, Chaitawat
Scherrer, Romane
Selway, Matt
Sharma, Ronesh
Song, Ge
Su Yin, Myat
Subash, Aditya
Tan, Hongwei
Tang, Jiahua
Teh, Chee Siong
Tettamanzi, Andrea
Tian, Qing
Tran, Vu
Vo, Duc Vinh
Wang, Deng-Bao
Wang, Kaixiang
Wang, Shuwen
Wang, Yuchen
Wang, Yunyun
Wilhelm, Marco
Wu, Linze
Xiangru, Yu
Xing, Guanyu
Xue, Hao
Yan, Wenzhu
Yang, Wanqi
Yang, Yikun
Yi, Huang
Yin, Ze
Yu, Guanbao
Zhang, Jianyi
Zhang, Jiaqiang

# Contents – Part III

# Reinforcement Learning

# Consistency Regularization for Ensemble Model Based Reinforcement Learning

Ruonan Jia[1,3], Qingming Li[2], Wenzhen Huang[2], Junge Zhang[2(✉)], and Xiu Li[3(✉)]

[1] Department of Automation, Tsinghua University, Beijing, China
jrn19@mails.tsinghua.edu.cn
[2] CRISE, Institute of Automation, Chinese Academy of Sciences, Beijing, China
chapnhan367383@gmail.com, huangwenzhen2014@ia.ac.cn,
jgzhang@nlpr.ia.ac.cn
[3] Tsinghua Shenzhen International Graduate School, Tsinghua University,
Shenzhen, China
li.xiu@sz.tsinghua.edu.cn

**Abstract.** It's generally believed that model-based reinforcement learning (RL) is more sample efficient than model-free RL. However, model-based RL methods typically suffer from model bias, which severely limits the asymptotic performance of the algorithm. Although previous model-based RL approaches use ensemble models to reduce the model error, we find that vanilla ensemble learning does not consider the model discrepancy. The discrepancy between different models is huge, which is not conducive to policy optimization. To alleviate the problem, this paper proposes an Ensemble Model Consistency Actor-Critic (EMC-AC) method to decrease the discrepancy between models while maintaining the model diversity. Specifically, we design ablation experiments to analyze the effects of the trade-off between diversity and consistency on the EMC-AC algorithm performance. Finally, extensive experiments on the continuous control benchmarks demonstrate that our approach achieves the significant performance to exceed the sample efficiency of prior model-based RL methods and to match the asymptotic performance of the state-of-the-art model-free RL algorithm.

**Keywords:** Model-based reinforcement learning · Ensemble model · Consistency · Sample efficiency

## 1 Introduction

Deep reinforcement learning (DRL) has achieved great success in recent years, including learning to play video games [24], mastering the game of Go [28,31,32], as well as learning robotic control [21–23,30]. DRL algorithms can be devided into two categories: model-based reinforcement learning (RL) which learns a predictive model of the environment and then utilizes this model to learn a policy, and model-free RL which directly learns a policy. Model-free RL algorithms

© Springer Nature Switzerland AG 2021
D. N. Pham et al. (Eds.): PRICAI 2021, LNAI 13033, pp. 3–16, 2021.
https://doi.org/10.1007/978-3-030-89370-5_1

require a tremendous number of interactions with environment, and suffer from sample complexity. The high sample complexity limits the application of such methods to real-world domain, e.g., robotics where data collection is expensive and time-consuming. In comparison, model-based RL algorithms learn to construct a dynamics model of real environment, interact with the learned model to produce imaginary samples and utilize these samples to train a policy. Therefore, model-based RL methods can potentially be much more sample efficient than model-free RL.

Model-based approaches tend to rely on accurate dynamics models to solve a task. However, learning an accurate dynamics model for a complex environment is very challenging. Inevitably, a learned model will not be perfectly precise. Small errors are compounded and can grow rapidly as we propagate our learned model to rollout imaginary trajectories further. Due to the inevitable errors of learned models, model-based methods fall into sub-optimal solutions and struggle to achieve the same asymptotic performance as model-free methods. Previous works have tried to alleviate model bias by characterizing the uncertainty of the models, often using ensemble probabilistic models to represent the posterior [35]. A detailed review could be found in Sect. 2.

Ensemble helps reduce the generalization error in unexplored states, and improves the uncertainty quantification. However, multiple inconsistent models will make the model usage full of uncertainty and likely lead to some inaccuracy for model transitions. In our paper, the difference between transition states of ensemble models is termed as model discrepancy. When the model discrepancy is not considered properly, the predictions of ensemble models will be unreliable and unstable, which are not conducive to policy optimization. We hope the next transition states output by ensemble models shall not be arbitrarily diverse, in the condition of the same input state-action pair. The consistency assumption is used in many regularizers [5]: "*Two points that are close in input space should have the same label*". Inspired by the assumption, we reckon that the states output by ensemble models should be similar. A natural concept that comes to mind is to add the consistency regularization and decrease the model discrepancy.

To solve this issue, in this paper, we propose an Ensemble Model Consistency framework built on the above insight. It utilizes semi-supervised learning to decrease the discrepancy between ensemble models while maintaining the model diversity to some extent. Additionally, we adopt Soft Actor-Critic (SAC) [13] as our policy optimization algorithm, which alternates between policy evaluation and policy improvement. We name this implementation as Ensemble-Model-Consistency Actor-Critic (EMC-AC). Experimental results demonstrate that our method outperforms the state-of-the-art model-based and model-free RL algorithms on multiple MuJoCo benchmarks.

The contributions of our work are as follows:

- Firstly, we analyze the problem of the distribution discrepancy of ensemble models, which could cause the model performance degradation.
- Secondly, we propose a simple but powerful algorithm named Ensemble Model Consistency Actor-Critic (EMC-AC) which constructs ensemble models with consistency regularization for model-based RL.

- Thirdly, our ablation study gives a meaningful insight that balancing discrepancy and consistency is helpful for ensemble model learning.
- Lastly, extensive experiments on the continuous control tasks show that EMC-AC has high asymptotic performance and low sample complexity. Our performance reaches comparable scores to the state-of-the-art model-free method with much fewer interactions.

## 2  Related Work

Recently, model-based RL shows a promising prospect of good performance with fewer environment interactions. There are two main research problems: how to learn an accurate model and how to utilize the learned model to train a policy. Our work mostly falls into the model learning.

**Model Learning.** The key of model-based RL is to address the problem of model inaccuracy. Previous methods are dedicated to combating the model error. Some exciting results with model-based RL have been obtained using simple linear models [1,3]. However, nonparametric models, like Gaussian Processes [9,20], are limited to the low dimensional domains. During recent years, neural network predictive models [7,25] are appealing because they could scale to complex high dimensional control problems. Ha et al. [12] and Hafner et al. [14] used VAE [17] to encode observation images into the latent vectors and trained a RNN [11] to model the next latent state vector. A major challenge when using neural network models is learning a reliable and accurate model of high dimensional dynamics.

Compared to the single model, ensemble learning has shown to be effective to boost the model accuracy [2]. Chua et al. [7] proposed a probabilistic ensemble model with trajectory sampling which uses an ensemble of bootstrapped probabilistic neural networks. Kurutach et al. [19] proposed to use an ensemble of models to maintain the model uncertainty and combine with TRPO [29] to stabilize policy learning. In contrast to prior ensemble methods, our method uses a consistent ensemble pattern to train a model with less model error.

**Model Usage.** It is natural to combine elements of model-based and model-free methods to attain high performance with low sample complexity. These methods compute gradients of the policy or value function through the learned dynamics model [8,15]. On the other hand, model-based value expansion (MVE) is a promising area. Feinberg et al. [10] used fixed depth model rollouts to improve value estimation and reduce sample complexity. Buckman et al. [6] extended MVE to interpolate between model rollouts of various horizon lengths. Additionally, dynamics model can also be used to help decision making when the agent interacts with environment [7,26]. Instead of using a learned dynamics model to plan, our method uses the model to gather fictitious data to train the policy and solve the task.

## 3   Background

**Markov Decision Process.** Reinforcement learning uses the formal framework of Markov Decision Process (MDP), defined by the tuple $(\mathcal{S}, \mathcal{A}, p, r, \gamma, \rho_0, H)$ [33]. We consider a discrete-time finite-horizon MDP that $\mathcal{S}$ and $\mathcal{A}$ are the state and action spaces, $\gamma \in (0, 1)$ is the discount factor, respectively, and $H$ is the horizon of the process. The dynamics or transition probability is denoted as $p(s'|s, a)$, the initial state distribution as $\rho_0(s)$, and the reward function as $r(s, a)$. We define the trajectory of states, actions, and rewards as $\tau = (s_0, a_0, r_0, s_1, \ldots, s_{H-1}, a_{H-1}, r_{H-1}, s_H)$. The goal of reinforcement learning is to find the optimal policy $\pi^*$ that maximizes the expected sum of discounted rewards, denoted by $J_\pi = \mathbb{E}_{\tau \sim \pi}\left[\sum_{t=0}^{H-1} \gamma^t r(s_t, a_t)\right]$.

**Policy Optimization.** Policy optimization is an effective RL approach to solve continuous control tasks. Soft Actor-Critic [13] is one of the state-of-the-art model-free methods, which optimizes a stochastic policy in an off-policy way. The major difference to other policy optimization methods is that SAC augments the objective with entropy regularization. The agent gets a bonus reward with the entropy of the policy at each time step. This changes the optimization objective into: $J_\pi = \mathbb{E}_{\tau \sim \pi}\left[\sum_{t=0}^{H-1} \gamma^t \left(r(s_t, a_t) + \alpha \mathcal{H}(\pi(\cdot|s_t))\right)\right]$, where the temperature parameter $\alpha$ is a trade-off coefficient.

The policy is trained to maximize a trade-off between expected return and entropy. This means policy is incentivized to explore more widely, while possibly giving up some anterior rewards. Especially, the entropy term could prevent the policy from prematurely converging to a bad local optimum. SAC follows the Actor-Critic framework [18]. The Critic estimates the action value (Q function), and the Actor updates the policy distribution in the direction suggested by the Critic. We consider a parameterized Q function $Q_\psi(s_t, a_t)$, Q-target function $\hat{Q}_{\hat{\psi}}(s_t, a_t)$ and a tractable policy $\pi_\phi$. The parameters of these networks are $\psi, \hat{\psi}$, and $\phi$.

The policy evaluation and policy improvement are trained alternately. SAC adopts Q function for policy evaluation which uses the MSE loss:

$$J_Q(\psi) = \mathbb{E}_{(s_t, a_t, a_{t+1}) \sim \mathcal{D}}\left[\frac{1}{2}\left(Q_\psi(s_t, a_t) - \hat{Q}_{\hat{\psi}}(s_t, a_t)\right)^2\right],$$
$$\hat{Q}_{\hat{\psi}}(s_t, a_t) = r(s_t, a_t) + \gamma\left(\hat{Q}_{\hat{\psi}}(s_{t+1}, a_{t+1}) + \alpha \mathcal{H}(\pi_\phi(a_{t+1}|s_{t+1}))\right). \tag{1}$$

Correspondingly, the policy improvement uses the Kullback-Leibler (KL) divergence loss:

$$J_\pi(\phi) = \mathbb{E}_{s_t \sim \mathcal{D}}\left[D_{KL}\left(\pi_\phi(\cdot|s_t) \| \exp\left(Q_\psi(s_t, \cdot) - \log Z(s_t)\right)\right)\right], \tag{2}$$

where $Z(s_t)$ is the partition function which normalizes the distribution.

**Model-Based Reinforcement Learning.** The standard model-based RL approaches alternate between model learning and policy optimization. The dynamics model $p(s'|s, a)$ is assumed to be unknown. Model-based RL methods aim to construct a model of the transition distribution, $p_\theta(s'|s, a)$, using data collected from interacting with the MDP. The learned model can be used to help for decision making when the agent interacts with environment.

Model-Based Policy Optimization (MBPO) [16] is one of the state-of-the-art model-based methods, which studies the role of model usage in policy optimization with theoretical guarantees. MBPO performs $k$-step rollouts from replay buffer states using a fixed number of policy updates.

## 4    Method

In this section, we aim to answer several questions related to model learning and implementation: (1) What is the dilemma of vanilla ensemble learning? (2) How to design our ensemble model in model-based RL? (3) How to implement the overall algorithm?

### 4.1    Model Discrepancy and Consistency

For the large and complex environments, when the training data is relatively scarce, the predictive model is likely to be inaccurate. Many recent model-based RL algorithms utilize ensemble models to capture epistemic uncertainty due to sparse knowledge of datas. However, these ensemble models could greatly differ from each other. It means that the different models would rollout much inconsistent states given the same initial state and action sequence. Although ensemble models could generate diverse samples, the model discrepancy will bring some inaccuracy for model transitions. For addressing this problem, we expect to reduce the disagreement between models while maintaining the model diversity to some extent. So we consider to make a trade-off between diversity and consistency.

Inspired by the consensus clustering [27] which improves the stability of clustering models by generation and integration, we introduce the consistency learning into the training of ensemble models. In this way, we can reduce the variance of predictive states rollouted by ensemble models. The reduction in variance is conducive to improve both the robustness and the stability of model-based RL.

### 4.2    Model Learning

It is general to use the probabilistic neural network to capture the aleatoric uncertainty and ensembles to capture the epistemic uncertainty. So we construct an ensemble of dynamics models by probabilistic neural networks, whose outputs simply parameterize the probability distribution functions. In our method, we define the predictive model to output a Gaussian distribution with diagonal covariances parameterized by $\theta$: $p_\theta(s_{t+1}|s_t, a_t) = \mathcal{N}(\mu_\theta(s_t, a_t), \Sigma_\theta(s_t, a_t))$. The overall framework of model learning in EMC-AC is shown in Fig. 1.

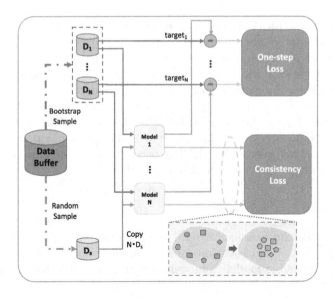

**Fig. 1.** The framework of model learning in EMC-AC. $N$ bootstrapped datasets and one random dataset are sampled from data buffer $\mathcal{D}_{env}$. We use semi-supervised learning to fit the ensemble models on the above two types of datasets with one-step loss and consistency loss. The arrows denote the different data flows.

**One-Step Prediction.** The basic objective of model learning is to find a parameter $\theta$ that minimizes the $\mathbf{L}_2$ one-step prediction loss. Given that the $N$ bootstrapped datasets are sampled from data buffer $\mathcal{D}_{env}$, i.e. $\{\mathcal{D}_1, \cdots, \mathcal{D}_N\}$, each model $p_{\theta_i}$ is trained on $\mathcal{D}_i$ with different initialization. We use the negative log prediction probability as the loss function for each individual model,

$$L_{one-step}(\theta) = -\sum_{n=1}^{N} \log p_\theta(s_{n+1}|s_n, a_n). \tag{3}$$

Take the above Gaussian models into Eq. (3). Then the loss becomes:

$$L_{one-step}(\theta) = \sum_{n=1}^{N} \Big[\mu_\theta(s_n, a_n) - s_{n+1}\Big]^{\mathsf{T}} \Sigma_\theta^{-1}(s_n, a_n)\Big[\mu_\theta(s_n, a_n) - s_{n+1}\Big] + \\ \log \det \Sigma_\theta(s_n, a_n). \tag{4}$$

**Consistency Regularization.** To improve consistency for ensemble models, we adopt the consistency regularization to constrain the structure error of model learning. Given that the data batch $D_s$ is randomly sampled from data buffer $\mathcal{D}_{env}$, each model $p_{\theta_i}$ predicts the next state transition for $D_s$. The overlap between any two transitions is used to measure the consistency of different models. Based on the discussion of Sect. 4.1, we use ensemble models with the consistency regularization. We measure the distance between different models by the KL divergence.

---

**Algorithm 1.** Ensemble Model Consistency Actor-Critic

---

1: **Initialization:** the policy $\pi_\phi$, Q function $\{Q_{\psi_1}, Q_{\psi_2}\}$, Q-target function $\{\hat{Q}_{\hat{\psi}_1} \leftarrow Q_{\psi_1}, \hat{Q}_{\hat{\psi}_2} \leftarrow Q_{\psi_2}\}$, predictive model $\{p_{\theta_i}\}_{i=1}^N$, environment dataset $\mathcal{D}_{env} \leftarrow \emptyset$, model dataset $\mathcal{D}_{model} \leftarrow \emptyset$

2: **for** E epochs **do**

3:     Bootstrap sample $\{\mathcal{D}_1, \cdots, \mathcal{D}_N\}$ and random sample $\mathcal{D}_s$ from $\mathcal{D}_{env}$

4:     Train ensemble models $\{p_{\theta_i}\}_{i=1}^N$ on $\{\mathcal{D}_1, \cdots, \mathcal{D}_N, \mathcal{D}_s\}$ via maximum likelihood and consistency regularization, by the Eq. (6)

5:     **for** K steps **do**

6:         Collect transitions from the real environment with the policy $\pi_\phi$

7:         Add the transitions to $\mathcal{D}_{env}$

8:         Sample $s_t$ from $\mathcal{D}_{env}$ and perform model rollouts starting from $s_t$ using $\pi_\phi$

9:         Add the imaginary transitions to $\mathcal{D}_{model}$

10:         **for** G gradient updates **do**

11:             Update $\psi_i \leftarrow \psi_i - \omega_Q \hat{\nabla}_{\psi_i} J_Q(\psi_i, \mathcal{D}_{model})$ for $i \in \{1, 2\}$, by the Eq. (1)

12:             Update $\phi \leftarrow \phi - \omega_\pi \hat{\nabla}_\phi J_\pi(\phi, \mathcal{D}_{model})$, by the Eq. (2)

13:             Update $\hat{\psi}_i \leftarrow \omega\psi_i + (1-\omega)\hat{\psi}_i$ for $i \in \{1, 2\}$

14: **return** Optimal policy parameters $\pi_\phi$

---

$$L_{KL} = \sum_{i=1}^{N-1} \sum_{j=i+1}^{N} D_{KL}\Big[p_{\theta_i}(s, a) \| p_{\theta_j}(s, a)\Big]. \tag{5}$$

By using the consistency loss in Eq. (5), the consistency of ensemble models can be improved.

**Overall Optimization Objective.** Our intuition is to leverage the ensemble models from generalization error and to improve consistency for the next transitions. Based on the ensemble models with one-step loss $L_{one-step}$ and consistency loss of model distribution $L_{KL}$, we obtain the overall optimization for the whole dynamics models. Thus the final learning objective of EMC-AC is:

$$L_{total} = L_{one-step} + \lambda * L_{KL}, \tag{6}$$

where $\lambda$ is a balance factor.

## 4.3   Implementation

Model learning and policy training are tightly coupled and jointly trained, while the stronger models learned by ensemble consistency help improve the policy, and the improved policy, in turn generates better transitions to continue improving the learned models.

To predict the next state transition from ensembles, we simply select a model uniformly at random. That is, we generate different transitions along a single model trajectory to be sampled from ensemble dynamics models. In addition, we adopt SAC [13] as our policy optimization algorithm, which alternates between policy evaluation and policy improvement. The procedure of EMC-AC is summarized in Algorithm 1.

## 5   Experiments

Our experiments are designed to address the following questions: (1) Compared with the prior model-free and model-based algorithms, does EMC-AC improve result in asymptotic performance and sample efficiency? (2) Are the ensemble models of EMC-AC more consistent than those without the consistency loss? (3) What is the relation between diversity and consistency in ensemble models?

**Fig. 2.** The screenshots of MuJoCo simulation environments used in our experiments. From left to right: Ant-v2, HalfCheetah-v2, Hopper-v2, Humanoid-v2, Walker2d-v2.

To answer the three questions, we evaluate our algorithm compared to various baselines on five continuous control benchmark tasks in the Mujoco simulator [34], which is commonly used to evaluate RL algorithms. The visualization of task environments is shown in Fig. 2. And our experimental environments are standard 1000-step versions of the benchmarks.

### 5.1   Comparative Evaluation

We compare our method EMC-AC with state-of-the-art model-free and model-based RL methods, including SAC [13], PETS [7], STEVE [6] and MBPO [16]. We run EMC-AC on the four tasks for 200 thousand timesteps, and on the Hopper task for 100 thousand timesteps where the algorithm is almost convergent. To ensure a fair comparison, we run EMC-AC and MBPO with the same network architectures and hyper-parameter configurations.

Figure 3 demonstrates the results in five complex continuous environments of MuJoCo-v2. To measure the sample efficiency of EMC-AC, we additionally run SAC 2 million timesteps on each task. We observe that EMC-AC achieves significant improvements in terms of both performance and sample efficiency across a wide range of environments. Specially, EMC-AC's performance on the HalfCheetah task at 200 thousand steps exceeds that of SAC at 2 million steps with about 10× fewer samples. On the most challenging tasks: Humanoid and Ant, our method significantly outperforms other baselines. However, on the task

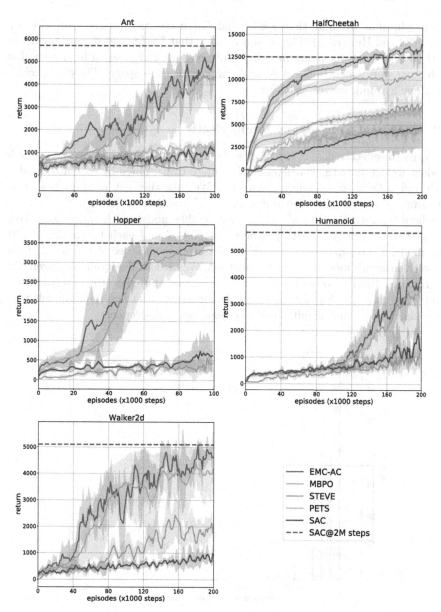

**Fig. 3.** Training curves on MuJoCo-v2 benchmarks. Solid curves depict the mean of four trials and shaded regions correspond to standard deviation among trials. The shaded area shows one standard deviation of scores in the region as defined above

of Walker2d, we observe that the return of EMC-AC drops at some timestep. We attribute the reason to the fact that Walker2d environment is unstable and sensitive to model bias.

In addition, we find that PETS fails to make any progress on Hopper, Walker2d and Humanoid. The reason is likely that PETS uses the cross-entropy method (CEM) [4] to maintain a distribution of actions yielding high reward at each time step which limits it to scale high-dimension space. Thus we exclude the three learning curves of PETS.

## 5.2   Effects of Consistency Regularization

To verify the effectiveness of the proposed consistency regularization for ensemble models, we compare the consistency of samples transitioned by ensemble models with and without consistency constraint. We take the task of HalfCheetah as an example. During the 50th round of model training, we sample two batches of rollout transitions $\{(s, a, s', r)\}_{i=1}^{N}$ by ensemble models with and without consistency constraint respectively, where the $N$ is 7 and each batch size is 100. The model discrepancy is computed by the average variance of predicted states between ensemble models for each transition. We use the histogram to present the discrepancy distribution of the average variance computed on the two batches of samples as shown in Fig. 4. The result demonstrates that ensemble models with consistency constraint significantly decrease model discrepancy.

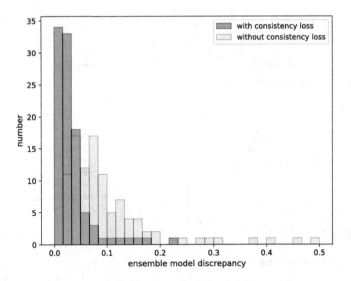

**Fig. 4.** The statistical histogram on the discrepancy of ensemble models with and without consistency loss. We compute the variance between the predicted states of ensemble model transitions as the model discrepancy. Compared to the approach without consistency loss, our method with consistency loss intuitively has the lower variance of the predicted states in transition samples.

## 5.3    Ablation Study

In order to understand the relationship between diversity and consistency in ensemble models, we conduct experiments to compare with different consensus coefficient $\lambda$. We examine several ablations on HalfCheetah and Hopper with a few interactions.

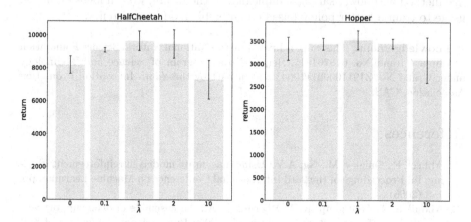

**Fig. 5.** Ablation studies on the coefficient $\lambda$ (50k steps for HalfCheetah and 100k steps for Hopper). The bars are average returns over 4 runs and error lines indicate one standard deviation.

As shown in Fig. 5, both results indicate that the trend between the performance and $\lambda$ looks like a parabola. This results also correspond to our intuition. On the consistency coefficient $\lambda$, we observed that EMC-AC with $\lambda = 1$ performs the best among [0, 0.1, 1, 2, 10]. In the case of $\lambda < 1$, the performance gradually improves as $\lambda$ increases. This means that our consistency loss (detail in Sect. 4.2) works and model errors are alleviated. However, too large $\lambda$ causes performance degradation, mainly because the excessive constrain of consistency loss discourages the diversity of ensemble models, which is not conductive to model learning. Therefore, a moderate choice such as $\lambda = 1$ can be better.

Note that our purpose is not to tune the best parameter, but to give a meaningful model learning discussion in model-based RL. That is, balancing diversity and consistency is important for ensemble model learning.

## 6    Conclusions

In this paper, we discuss the consistency problem in ensemble model methods from the perspective of model-based RL. We propose a simple but powerful algorithm, Ensemble Model Consistency Actor-Critic (EMC-AC), which learns an ensemble of dynamics models with the consistency regularization. Then we conduct experiments to analyze the effects of the trade-off between diversity and consistency in ensemble model learning and the result demonstrates that balancing diversity with consistency is helpful to learn a reasonable ensemble model. To our best knowledge, this paper makes a first attempt to analyze the consistency in ensemble model-based RL. Experimental results on the continuous control benchmarks demonstrate that ensemble consistency models provide the recipe for reaching the same level of performance as the state-of-the-art model-free method with lower sample complexity. In the future, we will focus on model usage to train a better policy based on ensemble model consistency.

**Acknowledgement.** This work is funded by the National Natural Science Foundation of China (Grand No. 61876181), Beijing Nova Program of Science and Technology under Grand No. Z191100001119043 and in part by the Youth Innovation Promotion Association, CAS.

# References

1. Abbeel, P., Quigley, M., Ng, A.Y.: Using inaccurate models in reinforcement learning. In: Proceedings of the 23rd International Conference on Machine Learning, pp. 1–8 (2006)
2. Abdullah, A., Veltkamp, R.C., Wiering, M.A.: An ensemble of deep support vector machines for image categorization. In: 2009 International Conference of Soft Computing and Pattern Recognition, pp. 301–306. IEEE (2009)
3. Bagnell, J.A., Schneider, J.G.: Autonomous helicopter control using reinforcement learning policy search methods. In: Proceedings 2001 ICRA. IEEE International Conference on Robotics and Automation (Cat. No. 01CH37164), vol. 2, pp. 1615–1620. IEEE (2001)
4. Botev, Z.I., Kroese, D.P., Rubinstein, R.Y., et al.: The cross-entropy method for optimization. In: Handbook of statistics, vol. 31, pp. 35–59. Elsevier (2013)
5. Bousquet, O., Chapelle, O., Hein, M.: Measure based regularization. In: Advances in Neural Information Processing Systems, pp. 1221–1228 (2004)
6. Buckman, J., Hafner, D., et al.: Sample-efficient reinforcement learning with stochastic ensemble value expansion. In: Proceedings of the 32nd International Conference on Neural Information Processing Systems, pp. 8234–8244 (2018)
7. Chua, K., Calandra, R., et al.: Deep reinforcement learning in a handful of trials using probabilistic dynamics models. In: Proceedings of the 32nd International Conference on Neural Information Processing Systems, pp. 4759–4770 (2018)
8. Clavera, I., Fu, Y., Abbeel, P.: Model-augmented actor-critic: backpropagating through paths. In: 8th International Conference on Learning Representations, ICLR 2020, Addis Ababa, Ethiopia, 26–30 April 2020. OpenReview.net (2020)
9. Deisenroth, M.P., Rasmussen, C.E.: PILCO: a model-based and data-efficient approach to policy search. In: Proceedings of the 28th International Conference on Machine Learning, ICML 2011, Bellevue, Washington, USA, pp. 465–472 (2011)
10. Feinberg, V., Wan, A., Stoica, I., Jordan, M.I., Gonzalez, J.E., Levine, S.: Model-based value estimation for efficient model-free reinforcement learning. CoRR abs/1803.00101 (2018). arXiv:1803.00101
11. Graves, A.: Generating sequences with recurrent neural networks. CoRR abs/1308.0850 (2013). arXiv:1308.0850

12. Ha, D., Schmidhuber, J.: Recurrent world models facilitate policy evolution. In: Proceedings of the 32nd International Conference on Neural Information Processing Systems, pp. 2455–2467 (2018)
13. Haarnoja, T., Zhou, A., Abbeel, P., Levine, S.: Soft actor-critic: off-policy maximum entropy deep reinforcement learning with a stochastic actor. In: International Conference on Machine Learning, pp. 1861–1870. PMLR (2018)
14. Hafner, D., et al.: Learning latent dynamics for planning from pixels. In: International Conference on Machine Learning, pp. 2555–2565. PMLR (2019)
15. Heess, N., Wayne, G., Silver, D., et al.: Learning continuous control policies by stochastic value gradients. In: Proceedings of the 28th International Conference on Neural Information Processing Systems-Volume 2, pp. 2944–2952 (2015)
16. Janner, M., Fu, J., Zhang, M., Levine, S.: When to trust your model: model-based policy optimization. In: Advances in Neural Information Processing Systems 32, pp. 12498–12509 (2019)
17. Kingma, D.P., Welling, M.: Auto-encoding variational bayes. In: 2nd International Conference on Learning Representations, ICLR 2014, Banff, AB, Canada, 14–16 April 2014, Conference Track Proceedings (2014)
18. Konda, V.R., Tsitsiklis, J.N.: Actor-critic algorithms. In: Advances in Neural Information Processing Systems, pp. 1008–1014. Citeseer (2000)
19. Kurutach, T., Clavera, I., Duan, Y., Tamar, A., Abbeel, P.: Model-ensemble trust-region policy optimization. In: International Conference on Learning Representations (2018)
20. Levine, S., Abbeel, P.: Learning neural network policies with guided policy search under unknown dynamics. In: Advances in Neural Information Processing Systems 27: Annual Conference on Neural Information Processing Systems 2014, 8–13 December 2014, Montreal, Quebec, Canada, pp. 1071–1079 (2014)
21. Levine, S., Finn, C., Darrell, T., Abbeel, P.: End-to-end training of deep visuomotor policies. J. Mach. Learn. Res. **17**, 39:1-39:40 (2016)
22. Lillicrap, T.P., et al.: Continuous control with deep reinforcement learning. In: ICLR (Poster) (2016)
23. Lyu, J., Ma, X., Yan, J., Li, X.: Efficient continuous control with double actors and regularized critics. arXiv preprint arXiv:2106.03050 (2021)
24. Mnih, V., et al.: Human-level control through deep reinforcement learning. Nature **518**(7540), 529–533 (2015)
25. Nagabandi, A., Kahn, G., Fearing, R.S., Levine, S.: Neural network dynamics for model-based deep reinforcement learning with model-free fine-tuning. In: 2018 IEEE International Conference on Robotics and Automation (ICRA), pp. 7559–7566. IEEE (2018)
26. Richards, A.G.: Robust constrained model predictive control. Ph.D. thesis, Massachusetts Institute of Technology (2005)
27. Sagi, O., Rokach, L.: Ensemble learning: a survey. Wiley Interdisc. Rev.: Data Min. Knowl. Discov. **8**(4), e1249 (2018)
28. Schrittwieser, J.,et al.: Mastering atari, go, chess and shogi by planning with a learned model. CoRR abs/1911.08265 (2019)
29. Schulman, J., Levine, S., Abbeel, P., Jordan, M.I., Moritz, P.: Trust region policy optimization. In: Proceedings of the 32nd International Conference on Machine Learning, ICML 2015, Lille, France, 6–11 July 2015, JMLR Workshop and Conference Proceedings, vol. 37, pp. 1889–1897. JMLR.org (2015)
30. Schulman, J., Moritz, P., Levine, S., Jordan, M.I., Abbeel, P.: High-dimensional continuous control using generalized advantage estimation. In: 4th International Conference on Learning Representations (2016)

31. Silver, D., et al.: Mastering the game of go with deep neural networks and tree search. Nature **529**(7587), 484–489 (2016)
32. Silver, D., et al.: Mastering the game of go without human knowledge. Nature **550**(7676), 354–359 (2017)
33. Sutton, R.S., Barto, A.G.: Reinforcement Learning: An Introduction. Adaptive Computation and Machine Learning. MIT Press, Cambridge (1998)
34. Todorov, E., Erez, T., Tassa, Y.: Mujoco: a physics engine for model-based control. In: 2012 IEEE/RSJ International Conference on Intelligent Robots and Systems, IROS 2012, Vilamoura, Algarve, Portugal, pp. 5026–5033. IEEE (2012)
35. Wang, T., Bao, X., Clavera, I., Hoang, J., et al.: Benchmarking model-based reinforcement learning. CoRR abs/1907.02057 (2019)

# Detecting and Learning Against Unknown Opponents for Automated Negotiations

Leling Wu, Siqi Chen(✉), Xiaoyang Gao, Yan Zheng, and Jianye Hao

College of Intelligence and Computing, Tianjin University, Tianjin, China
siqichen@tju.edu.cn

**Abstract.** Learning in automated negotiations, while successful for many tasks in recent years, is still hard when coping with different types of opponents with unknown strategies. It is critically essential to learn about the opponents from observations and then find the best response in order to achieve efficient agreements. In this paper, we propose a novel framework named Deep BPR+ (DBPR+) negotiating agent framework, which includes two key components: a learning module to learn a new coping policy when encountering an opponent using a previously unseen strategy, and a policy reuse mechanism to efficiently detect the strategy of an opponent and select the optimal response policy from the policy library. The performance of the proposed DBPR+ agent is evaluated against winning agents of ANAC competitions under varied negotiation scenarios. The experimental results show that DBPR+ agent outperforms existing state-of-the-art agents, and is able to make efficient detection and optimal response against unknown opponents.

**Keywords:** Automated negotiation · Multi-agent system · Policy reuse · Reinforcement learning

## 1 Introduction

Automated negotiations are a widely studied, emerging area in the field of autonomous agents and multi-agent systems. Research on agent-based negotiation not only significantly alleviates the efforts of human negotiators, but also aids humans in reaching better outcomes by compensating for the limited abilities of humans, e.g., from the computational, reasoning and cognitive perspective. At present, automated negotiation mechanism has been applied in many fields like e-commerce, laws and supply chain management. Automated negotiations may be rather complex, because there are many factors that characterize negotiations. These factors include the number of issues, dependency between issues, representation of the utility, negotiation protocol, negotiation form (e.g., bilateral or multi-party [10,30]), and time constraints [14,24]. Automated negotiations have been studied for a long time and there have been a large body of work concerning various settings [11,20,25,27,31].

This work is supported by National Natural Science Foundation of China (Grant Nos.: 61602391, 62106172).

D. N. Pham et al. (Eds.): PRICAI 2021, LNAI 13033, pp. 17–31, 2021.
https://doi.org/10.1007/978-3-030-89370-5_2

In a multi-agent system, the optimal decision of the auto-negotiation agent is contingent on the behaviors of co-existing agents. Especially, when faced with different types of opponents and the opponent's strategy is unknown, the agent is required to be able to detect opponent's strategy accurately and then adapt its own policy accordingly. Though a lot of research works already existed in the field of automated negotiation, none of these works explicitly categorizes the other agent's policy and then dynamically adjust their own coping strategies.

To address the above problem, we propose a novel framework, called Deep BPR+ negotiating agent framework, which leverages Bayesian policy reuse (BPR) [28] for responding to an unknown opponent by selecting among a number of policies available to the agent. BPR maintains a probability distribution (Bayesian belief) over a set of known opponents capturing their similarity to the new opponent that the agent is solving. The Bayesian belief is updated with observed signals which can be any information correlated with the performance of a policy. In this work, agreement utility, number of negotiation rounds and standard deviation of the utility received from opponents' offers are used as the signal. When an unknown opponent strategy comes, identified through moving average reward as in BPR+ [18], it switches to learning stage and starts to learn an optimal response policy using deep reinforcement learning algorithm, which learns to achieve efficient agreements by choosing a proper target utility at each step, conditioning on the timeline and offer exchange history.

The main contributions of the paper are as follows:

- We propose a general negotiation framework – Deep BPR+ negotiating agent framework – supports detection of an unlabeled opponent from observed signals and then adapts its own policy accordingly. Besides, our framework can automatically switch to learn new response policy when faced with a previously unseen opponent.
- We provide a RL-based formulation for automated negotiation, and the learnt policy can adapt to different negotiation domains without retraining.
- We validate this framework by evaluating it against ANAC winning agents under various negotiation scenarios.

## 2   Related Work

This work involves two research fields, one is automated negotiation, and the other is the detection and response of other agents in a multi-agent system (MAS). In this section we discuss work done in both fields.

Automated negotiation has been widely studied in the recent years owing to the growth in e-commerce and cloud-based applications. Artificial intelligence techniques [16], game theory [16,22], bayesian learning [20,31] and evolutionary programming [12,13] have all been used in automated negotiation. Baarslag et al. [6] proposes an architecture named BOA architecture which separates negotiation strategy to three components, namely, bidding strategy, opponent model and acceptance strategy. A comprehensive survey on opponent models is presented by

Baarslag et al. [4], which classified opponent models using a comprehensive taxonomy. [5] proposes an simple but efficient acceptance conditions which considers both time and utility gap to determine whether to accept an offer.

In recent years, the successful application of reinforcement learning algorithms in other fields has driven its application in the field of auto-negotiation. Bakker et al. [8] proposes an RLBOA framework based on the BOA architecture for auto-negotiation. The Tabular Q-learning algorithm is used to train the bidding strategy. So they map the offers to the utility space and discretize the utility space. But discretization can lead to information loss. Pallavi Bagga et al. [7] first pre-trains the model through supervised learning to accelerate the learning process, and then trains the DDPG [23] model. The disadvantage of this work is that it only addresses a single issue, and its RL agent's state and action are specific issue value, so it cannot work in other negotiation scenarios. [9] is limited to specific negotiation scenarios. In [29], SAC [17] algorithm is used to train the bidding strategy, whose input and output are utility values. So learned model can be used in other negotiation domains. But they do not consider the preferences of opponents.

In MAS, it is critically essential for agents to learn to cope with each other by taking the other agent's behaviors into account. But very little work has been done to explicitly categorize the other agent's policy. BPR+ algorithm [18, 19] can predict other agent's policy and learn a new response policy when previously unseen. But BPR+ is a tabular based algorithm that directly stores learned policies as Q-tables, which might be infeasible when handling large scale problems.

## 3    Preliminaries

### 3.1    Negotiation Settings

In this work, we consider bilateral negotiations which are negotiations between exactly two participants. The negotiation protocol we use in this paper is the stacked alternating offers protocol. During the negotiation, two parties will send alternating offers to each other until both sides agree on an offer together, or a deadline is reached [21].

A negotiation scenario consists of a negotiation domain and preference profiles of both parties. Both parties have certain preferences prescribed by a preference profile. These preferences can be modeled by means of a utility function that map a possible outcome $\omega$ to a real-valued number $u$ in the range $[0, 1]$, which indicates how satisfied the party is with an offer. The preference profiles and negotiation domain together constitute the utility space $\mathcal{U}$. In this paper we consider multi-issue negotiations and linear utility function.

### 3.2    Bayes Policy Reuse

BPR [28] is proposed as an efficient policy reuse framework for an agent to select the best policy from a policy library when facing unknown tasks. Formally, a task $\tau \in \mathcal{T}$ is defined as a MDP and a policy $\pi(s)$ outputs an appropriate action given state $s$. The return, which is also known as cumulative reward, is generated by interacting with the environment in the task over an episode of $k$ steps, $U = \sum_{i=1}^{k} r_i$, where $r_i$ is the immediate reward received at step $i - 1$. The agent is equipped with a policy library $\Pi$ which contains coping policies against previously seen tasks set $\mathcal{T}$. When facing an unseen task $\tau^*$, the agent is supposed to select the best coping policy $\pi^*$ from $\Pi$ within as small number of trials as possible. BPR uses the concept of $\beta(\tau)$ to measure the degree of similarity between current task $\tau^*$ and tasks seen before, where $\beta$ is a probability distribution over previous seen task $\mathcal{T}$. BPR uses performance model $P(U|\tau, \pi)$ to describe the performance of policy where $P(U|\tau, \pi)$ is a probability distribution over the return $U$ using $\pi$ on task $\tau$. The belief is initialized with a prior distribution (e.g. random distribution) as $\beta^0(\tau)$. Following the Bayes rule, the belief $\beta^{n-1}(\tau)$ is updated based on $P(U|\tau, \pi)$ as below:

$$\beta^n(\tau) = \frac{P\left(U^n|\tau, \pi^n\right)\beta^{n-1}(\tau)}{\sum_{\tau' \in \mathcal{T}} P\left(U^n|\tau', \pi^n\right)\beta^{n-1}\left(\tau'\right)} \tag{1}$$

Based on the belief $\beta(\tau)$, BPR selects the policy most likely to achieve any possible improvement of return $\bar{U} < U^+ < U^{max}$ as the best coping policy $\pi^*$:

$$\pi^* = \arg\max_{\pi \in \Pi} \int_{\bar{U}}^{U^{\max}} \sum_{\tau \in \mathcal{T}} \beta(\tau) P\left(U^+ \mid \tau, \pi\right) dU^+ \tag{2}$$

BPR+ extends BPR to handle non-stationary opponent with a learning mechanism, enabling it to continuously expand its policy library as needed. Deep. BPR+ [32] uses a refined belief model based on episode return and opponent behavior. Besides, it improves BPR+'s learning mechanism by using a distilled policy network for better and faster policy learning.

## 4   Agent Design

In this section we give the details of our proposed Deep BPR+ Negotiating Agent Framework, as shown in Algorithm 1. This framework is capable of identifying the opponent's strategy in real time, and select the best coping policy in the policy library. Besides, when encountering a previously unseen opponent and none of the policies in the policy library can achieve good performance, it will switch to learning module to learn the new coping policy using DRL algorithm. In Sect. 4.1, we will introduce the learning module of our proposed framework, and in Sect. 4.2, we will explain the policy reuse mechanism.

### 4.1   Deep Reinforcement Learning Based Learning Module

After detecting that the opponent is using a new strategy, the agent turns to the learning stage and begins to learn the best-response policy against it. We formulate the negotiation problem as a sequential decision making problem

---

**Algorithm 1.** Deep BPR+ Negotiating Agent

---

**Require:** Episodes $K$, performance model $P(U|T, \Pi)$, efficiency model $E(D|T, \Pi)$, behavior model $B(W|T, \Pi)$, policy library $\Pi$, known opponent policy set $T$, window $h$, threshold $\delta$

1: **for** $k = 1, 2, .., K$ **do**
2:     **if** stage is reuse **then**
3:         select a policy $\pi^k$ based on belief model $\beta^{k-1}$ and received utility $U^t$, agreement round $D^t$ and standard deviation $W^t$ (Eq. 2)
4:         update belief model using $U^t$, $D^t$ and $W^t$ (Eq. 7)
5:         calculated the average performance over past $h$ episodes $\bar{U} = \frac{\sum_{i-h}^{i} U}{h}$
6:         **if** $\bar{U} < \delta$ **then**
7:             switch stage to learn
8:         **end if**
9:     **else**
10:        Optimize $\pi$ using SAC
11:        **if** the policy is converged **then**
12:            update $P(U|T, \Pi)$, $E(D|T, \Pi)$, $B(W|T, \Pi)$, $\Pi$, $T$
13:        **end if**
14:        switch stage to reuse
15:     **end if**
16: **end for**

---

which can be solved with a RL agent. We first describe the environment and the method used in this paper to estimate the opponent's preference information as well as acceptance conditions. After that, we describe the policy-based RL agent and the training procedure of our RL agent. By interacting with the environment, the agent learns to pick the optimal target utility value.

**Environment - States, Actions, Transitions and Reward.** The classic framework of RL consists of two parts. The first part is the external environment $\varepsilon$ which specifies the dynamics of the interaction between the agent and the opponent. It is modeled as a Markov decision process (MDP) which can be represented by a 4-tuple $\langle \mathcal{S}, \mathcal{A}, \mathcal{P}, \mathcal{R} \rangle$. The second part is a policy network which maps the state vector to a stochastic policy. The neural network parameters $\theta$ are updated using stochastic gradient descent. For the sake of generalization, we design the output of the RL agent as the target utility value, which makes the action space continuous and large. Therefore, compared to value-based RL methods like Deep Q Network (DQN) [26], policy-based RL methods turn out to be more appropriate for our negotiation problem. Before we describe the structure of our policy network, we first elaborate each component (states, actions, rewards) of the RL environment.

*States.* In our negotiation setting, if an agreement cannot be achieved before the deadline, then the negotiation fails. So our agent's decision whether to compromise and the extent of the compromise depends in part on the timeline. Besides, the context during the negotiation process, that is, the historical bid trajectory, is crucial to the agent's decision-making. The state vector at step t is given as follows:

$$s_t = \left( \frac{t}{T_{max}}, u_o^{t-3}, u_s^{t-3}, u_o^{t-2}, u_s^{t-2}, u_o^{t-1}, u_s^{t-1} \right)$$

where $T_{max}$ denotes the maximum rounds of each negotiation session. $u_o^t$ denotes the utility of the bid received from the opponent at step t and $u_s^t$ denotes the utility of the bid proposed by our own agent at step t.

*Actions.* The set of possible actions from a state consists of all possible target utility values in the range $[u_r, 1]$, where $u_r$ denotes the reservation value. Formally, we define the action at step t as $a_t = u_s^t$. To get the actual offer from the utility value, we define an inverse utility function $\mathcal{F} : \mathcal{U} \rightarrow \Omega$ that maps a real-valued number $u$ to an outcome $\omega$, where $\Omega$ denotes the outcome space. Specifically, we obtain several offers whose utility value falls within $[u, u + \Delta_u]$, then select the one that the opponent may prefer the most according to the opponent model. In this work, we use the approach proposed by Niels van Galen Last [15] for estimating the opponents interests profile, whose main idea is issues that are important to the opponent shall not be adjusted as often. Formally, the inverse utility function $\mathcal{F} : \mathcal{U} \rightarrow \Omega$ is defined as

$$\mathcal{F}(u_s) = \arg\max_{\omega} U_o^{'}(\omega), \text{ where}$$
$$u_s \leq U_s(\omega) \leq u_s + \Delta_u \tag{3}$$

where $U_o^{'}$ denotes the opponent's utility function estimated by the opponent's historical bids, and $U_s$ represents our utility function. $\Delta_u$ denotes the window value. In practice, we set $\Delta_u = 0.05$.

*Rewards.* We only have a terminal reward. The agent is given a positive reward when two parties reach an agreement or reward of $-1$ when no agreement is achieved before the deadline. Our RL agent's acceptance condition is simple but effective. If our agent plans to propose a deal that is worse than the opponent's offer, we have reached a consensus with our opponent and we accept the offer. Formally, the reward function is defined as follows:

$$r_{t+1}(s_t, a_t) = \begin{cases} U_s(\omega), & \text{if there is an agreement } \omega \\ -1, & \text{if the deadline arrives and no agreement.} \\ 0, & \text{otherwise} \end{cases} \tag{4}$$

**Policy Network.** Any policy-based DRL algorithm can be used to solve the MDP modeled above. In this work, we consider Soft Actor Critic (SAC) algorithm [17] for learning the optimal target utility value. SAC is a maximum entropy DRL algorithm that optimizes a stochastic policy in an off-policy way.

The objective of SAC is to maximize the expected return and the entropy at the same time:

$$J(\theta) = \sum_{t=1}^{T} \mathbb{E}_{(s_t,a_t) \sim \rho_{\pi_\theta}} [r(s_t, a_t) + \alpha H(\pi_\theta(.|s_t))] \tag{5}$$

where $H(.)$ is the entropy measure and $\alpha$ controls how important the entropy term is, known as temperature parameter. The policy is trained to maximize a trade-off between expected return and entropy, a measure of randomness in the policy. This helps in improving robustness and generalization of the trained model. Soft Q-value that includes the entropy bonuses is defined as:

$$Q(s_t, a_t) = r(s_t, a_t) + \gamma \mathbb{E}_{(s_{t+1},a_{t+1}) \sim \rho_\pi} [Q(s_{t+1}, a_{t+1}) - \alpha \log \pi(a_{t+1} \mid s_{t+1})] \tag{6}$$

To reduce the overestimation of the value function, SAC uses two value networks. Both value networks are learned with MSBE minimization, by regressing to a single shared target. Since SAC is brittle with respect to the temperature parameter, in implementation, we use SAC with automatically adjusted temperature.

## 4.2   Policy Reuse Mechanism

It is difficult to find a policy that can deal with all opponents. In order to simplify the problem, we consider to reuse our existing policies in the policy library using a belief model that can match current opponent with previously seen opponents, this corresponds to the lines 2–8 in Algorithm 1. Every policy in our policy library is able to deal with a certain type of opponent. When encountering an unseen opponent, our policy reuse mechanism will distinguish the possibility that the previously unseen opponent belongs to a certain known negotiation style. The policy reuse mechanism is a very critical part, since higher detection accuracy can lead to more efficient strategy reuse. However, we cannot simply use the vanilla BPR+, which uses a performance model as the signal to detect different task. Since in the field of negotiation, opponents with different negotiation styles may lead to the same agreement utility. Here, we use three signals to evaluate an opponent's negotiation style: agreement utility, number of negotiation rounds, the changing trend of the utility received from opponent's offer. The changing trend of the utility received from opponent's offer can be measured with different criterion, here we use the standard deviation.

Similar to Deep BPR+, we can still using Bayes' Rule to update our belief model. Now the belief $\beta(\tau)$ can be regarded as the posterior probabilities measuring the opponent's policy, based on the agreement utility, number of negotiation rounds and the changing trend of the utility received from opponent's offer. Like the rectified belief model defined in Deep BPR+, we use performance model $P(U|\tau, \pi)$, efficiency model $E(D|\tau, \pi)$, behavior model $B(W|\tau, \pi)$ to describe the agreement performance, the negotiation efficiency and changes in opponent behavior where $P(U|\tau,\pi)$, $E(D|\tau,\pi)$, $B(W|\tau,\pi)$ are three probability distributions over the agreement utility $U$, number of negotiation rounds $D$ and the standard deviation of the utility received from opponent's offer $W$ using $\pi$ on task $\tau$ respectively. The belief is initialized with a prior distribution (e.g. random distribution) as $\beta^0(\tau)$ and is updated as below:

$$\beta^n(\tau) = \frac{P(U^n|\tau,\pi^n)\,E\,(D^n|\tau,\pi^n)\,B\,(W^n|\tau,\pi^n)\,\beta^{n-1}(\tau)}{\sum_{\tau'\in\mathcal{T}} P(U^n|\tau',\pi^n)\,E\,(D^n|\tau',\pi^n)\,B\,(W^n|\tau',\pi^n)\,\beta^{n-1}\,(\tau')} \quad (7)$$

Based on the belief $\beta(\tau)$, we selects the policy most likely to achieve any possible improvement of return $\bar{U} < U^+ < U^{max}$ as the best coping policy $\pi^*$, as is showed in Eq. 2.

For negotiation styles that have never been seen before, this refers to a brand-new style that does not match the policies in the policy library. It usually causes the agent to be at a lower agreement utility regardless of the strategy chosen for a period of time. Specifically, our agent calculates the average agreement utility $\bar{U}$ over $h$ episodes $\bar{U} = \frac{\sum_{i-h}^{i} U}{h}$ as the signal indicating the average performance over all policies till the current episode $i$. If the average agreement utility $\bar{U}$ is lower than a given threshold $\delta(\bar{U} < \delta)$, the agent will switch to learning module.

## 5   Experiments

In this section, we present experimental results of our agent based on the proposed Deep BPR+ negotiating agent framework. The goal of our experiments is to verify that our agent can efficiently detect the strategy of opponents and also supports the detection of previously unseen policies and learning a response policy accordingly. We first evaluate the performance of our agent against 8 ANAC winning agents. Secondly, we evaluate the performance of our agent against opponents using previously unseen strategies.

### 5.1   Experimental Setup

We evaluate the performance of our Deep BPR+ negotiating agent against the following 8 ANAC winning agents: Ponpoko, Caduceus, ParsCat, Atlas3, ParsAgent, The Fawkes, CUHKAgent and HardHeaded [1–3][1]. We conduct experiments on 20 domains from ANAC. The opposition of these domains ranges from 0.051 to 0.840 and the carnality of outcome space ranges from 3 to 56700. Table 1 shows the statistics of these 20 domains we conduct our experiments on.

In the training phase, the domain is randomly selected from these 20 domains for each negotiation session and the policy that the agent learns is evaluated in all 20 domains. The maximum rounds allowed per session is 60. In all experiments the agents are trained until convergence. Moreover, for simplicity all

---

[1] Ponpoko (2017 winner), Caduceus (2016 winner), ParsCat (2016 $2^{nd}$ position), Atlas3 (2015 winner), ParsAgent (2015 $2^{nd}$ position), The Fawkes (2013 winner), CUHKAgent (2012 winner) and HardHeaded (2011 winner).

**Table 1.** Statistics of 20 domains used in experiments.

| Domain | Opposition | Outcome space | Domain | Opposition | Outcome space |
|---|---|---|---|---|---|
| Acquisition | 0.117 | 384 | Icecream | 0.148 | 720 |
| Amsterdam-B | 0.223 | 3024 | Kitchen | 0.057 | 15625 |
| Animal | 0.110 | 1152 | Laptop | 0.160 | 27 |
| Barter-C | 0.492 | 80 | NiceOrDie | 0.840 | 3 |
| Camera | 0.212 | 3600 | Outfit | 0.198 | 128 |
| Coffee | 0.447 | 112 | Planes | 0.164 | 27 |
| DefensiveCharms | 0.322 | 36 | RentalHouse-B | 0.327 | 60 |
| DogChoosing | 0.051 | 270 | SmartPhone | 0.224 | 12000 |
| FiftyFifty2013 | 0.707 | 11 | Ultimatum | 0.545 | 9 |
| HouseKeeping | 0.272 | 384 | Wholesaler | 0.308 | 56700 |

hyperparameters of SAC algorithm are kept fixed while training against different opponents. Although we conduct our experiments on discrete domains, it is worth noting that our proposed framework works in continuous domains as well. When faced with different types of opponents and the opponent's strategy is unknown, an intuitive idea is to train a general agent, which we use as the baseline agent. Specifically, the baseline agent is trained using SAC algorithm with same hyperparameters. Both the scenarios and the opponents that the baseline agent encounters during training are randomly selected for each negotiation session. In our implementation, the baseline agent is trained for a total of 80,000 negotiation sessions.

All the experiments are conducted in our newly-developed negotiation environment. Among the negotiation settings, the reservation price is set as 0.1 and discount factor is ignored for all negotiations. Moreover, we used min-max normalisation for normalising the issue values to between 0 and 1. For performance comparisons, average utility values are calculated on negotiation data obtained in 1000 negotiation sessions between a pair of agents for each negotiation domain.

## 5.2 Performance Against ANAC Winning Agents

In this section, we present the empirical results of our agent against 8 ANAC winning agents. We pretrain our agent against each opponent for 10,000 negotiation sessions in succession. So our agent is equipped with the corresponding pre-trained response policies and aims at selecting the most appropriate policy in hand to reuse against the opponent by detecting its behaviors. Our experiments use the following metrics:

(1) Average utility benchmark: the mean utility acquired by the agent $a$ when negotiating with every other agent $b \in A$ in all negotiation domains $D$ where $A$ and $D$ denote the set of all agents and all domains respectively.
(2) Utility against opponent benchmark: the mean utility acquired by agents $b \in A/a$ while negotiating with agent $a$ in all negotiation scenarios.

(3) Domain utility benchmark: the mean utility obtained by all agents $a \in A$ in domain $d \in D$, while negotiating with every agent $b \in A$.

**Table 2.** Comparison of our proposed Deep BPR+ negotiator with 8 ANAC winning agents using average utility benchmark, average rounds per session and average agreement achievement rate.

| Agent | Avg utility | Avg round | Agreement achievement rate |
|---|---|---|---|
| Caduceus | $0.3461 \pm 0.0013$ | $48.98 \pm 0.12$ | $0.37 \pm 0.00$ |
| ParsAgent | $0.4570 \pm 0.0017$ | $51.73 \pm 0.01$ | $0.53 \pm 0.00$ |
| PonPokoAgent | $0.4880 \pm 0.0011$ | $48.65 \pm 0.23$ | $0.55 \pm 0.00$ |
| ParsCat | $0.5283 \pm 0.0003$ | $49.97 \pm 0.05$ | $0.64 \pm 0.00$ |
| Atlas3 | $0.5572 \pm 0.0026$ | $38.16 \pm 0.11$ | $0.84 \pm 0.00$ |
| HardHeadedAgent | $0.3900 \pm 0.0020$ | $51.75 \pm 0.15$ | $0.47 \pm 0.00$ |
| TheFawkes | $0.4369 \pm 0.0021$ | $49.81 \pm 0.01$ | $0.53 \pm 0.00$ |
| CUHKAgent | $0.4329 \pm 0.0007$ | $49.80 \pm 0.02$ | $0.51 \pm 0.00$ |
| Deep BPR+ Agent | $\mathbf{0.6106 \pm 0.0039}$ | $\mathbf{36.92 \pm 0.06}$ | $\mathbf{0.90 \pm 0.00}$ |

Table 2 shows the performance of our agent on the average utility benchmark, together with average rounds per negotiation session and average agreement achievement rate with standard deviation. Our Deep BPR+ negotiator outperforms all the ANAC winning agents, obtaining higher mean utility, higher agreement achievement rate and converging to an agreement in less rounds, which validates the effectiveness and efficiency of our proposed framework. On the contrary, the baseline agent fails to handle different types of opponents even though it trained with them[2]. In comparison with utility against opponent benchmark, the average utility obtained by our agent is 50% higher than the average benchmark over all ANAC winning agents as shown in Fig. 1(a). This means that when encountering each opponent, the agent is able to accurately detect the strategy of the opponent and act with the optimal policy in order to reach agreements. Figure 1(b) compares the average utility obtained by our agent with that of 8 ANAC winning agents in each domain. It can be seen that our agent performs best in 12 out of 20 domains. Although our agent doesn't obtain the highest utility in some domains with low opposition like Acquisition, its absolute utility is still high, exceeding 0.8. Therefore in terms of average utility across all domains, Deep BPR+ agent significantly outperforms other agents as depicted in Table 2.

---

[2] Due to the space limitation, we only present the statistics of baseline agent in this control experiment. Mean utility, average rounds and average agreement achievement rate are $0.4573 \pm 0.0040$, $49.54 \pm 0.07$ and $0.57 \pm 0.00$ respectively.

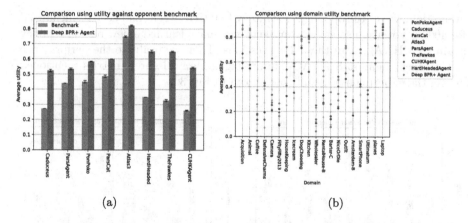

(a)                                      (b)

**Fig. 1.** (a) Comparison of our Deep BPR+ agent with utility against opponent benchmark consisting of 8 ANAC winning agents. (b) Comparison of Deep BPR+ agent with domain utility benchmark consisting of 20 domains.

## 5.3 New Opponent Detection and Learning

In this section, we evaluate the performance of Deep BPR+ agent against opponents using previously unseen strategy. Now assume that Deep BPR+ agent now is only equipped with 4 response policies against Ponpoko, ParsCat, The Fawkes and HardHeaded. Caduceus, ParsAgent, Atlas3 and CUHKAgent are unseen strategies to it. We first evaluate the performance of this agent against 8 ANAC winning agents by comparing with average utility benchmark and utility against opponent benchmark, the empirical results can be seen in Fig. 2. In this

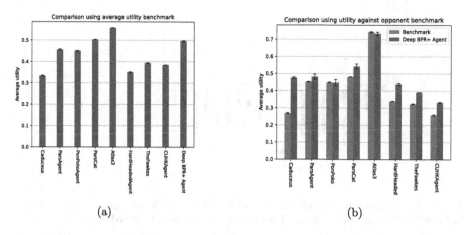

(a)                                      (b)

**Fig. 2.** The performance of our agent equipped with 4 response policy against 8 ANAC winning agents by comparing it with average utility benchmark and utility against opponent benchmark.

evaluation, we set the opponent's strategy to CUHKAgent and keep it unchanged for 4000 negotiation sessions. Our agent may have learned a new response policy against CUHKAgent in these 4000 sessions. Then we evaluate the performance of this agent against 8 ANAC winning agents on all three metrics mentioned above, the experimental results are shown in Fig. 3[3].

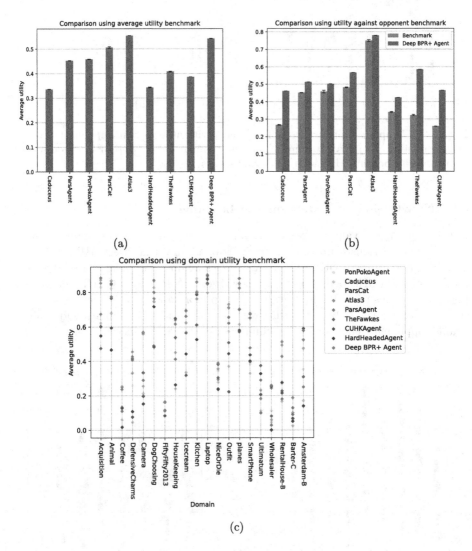

**Fig. 3.** The performance of our agent against 8 ANAC winning agents after encountering CUHKAgent opponent and learning the coping policy accordingly.

---

[3] We also conducted other configures and found similar results, so we only report this evaluation.

In Fig. 2(a), average utility obtained by our agent is lower than Atlas3 and perform comparably to the second place agent. In Fig. 2(b), although our agent never encounters Caduceus and CUHKAgent before, it achieves higher mean utility than utility against opponent benchmark when negotiating against Caduceus and CUHKAgent. This is because our agent can choose the optimal policy available in the policy library to act, which illustrates the importance of policy reuse mechanism.

After interacting with CUHKAgent opponent for 4000 sessions, our agent performs comparably to the Atlas3 and achieves performance improvements on all three metrics as shown in Fig. 3, which means that our agent can detect an previously unseen strategy, and successfully learn a response policy accordingly.

# 6   Conclusion

This paper presents a novel framework called Deep BPR+ negotiating agent framework, which responds to an unknown opponent by detecting the strategy of the opponent from received signals during negotiation and then acting with the best policy in the policy library. Besides, our framework enables online learning of new model when encountering an opponent using a new strategy and our policies available are not performing optimally. Experimental results show an efficient detection of the opponent based on observation signals, obtaining higher average utility than a baseline and ANAC winning agents.

The exceptional results justify to invest further research efforts into this deep BPR+ negotiating agent framework. As for future work, it is worth investigating how to accelerate the online new policy learning phase. Second, the extension of this framework to other negotiation settings, such as concurrent negotiation or multi-lateral negotiation, is another interesting avenue to exploit.

# References

1. Aydogan, R.: Anac 2016 - automated negotiating agents competition 2016. Website (2016). http://web.tuat.ac.jp/~katfuji/ANAC2016/
2. Aydoğan, R., Fujita, K., Baarslag, T., Jonker, C.M., Ito, T.: ANAC 2017: repeated multilateral negotiation league. In: Ito, T., Zhang, M., Aydoğan, R. (eds.) ACAN 2018. SCI, vol. 905, pp. 101–115. Springer, Singapore (2021). https://doi.org/10.1007/978-981-15-5869-6_7
3. Baarslag, T., Aydogan, R., Hindriks, K., Fujita, K., Ito, T., Jonker, C.: The automated negotiating agents competition, 2010–2015. AI Mag. **36**, 115–118 (2015). https://doi.org/10.1609/aimag.v36i4.2609
4. Baarslag, T., Hendrikx, M.J.C., Hindriks, K.V., Jonker, C.M.: Learning about the opponent in automated bilateral negotiation: a comprehensive survey of opponent modeling techniques. Auton. Agents Multi-Agent Syst. **30**(5), 849–898 (2015). https://doi.org/10.1007/s10458-015-9309-1
5. Baarslag, T., Hindriks, K., Jonker, C.: Effective acceptance conditions in real-time automated negotiation. Decis. Support Syst. **60**, 68–77 (2014)

6. Baarslag, T., Hindriks, K., Hendrikx, M., Dirkzwager, A., Jonker, C.: Decoupling negotiating agents to explore the space of negotiation strategies. In: Marsa-Maestre, I., Lopez-Carmona, M.A., Ito, T., Zhang, M., Bai, Q., Fujita, K. (eds.) Novel Insights in Agent-based Complex Automated Negotiation. SCI, vol. 535, pp. 61–83. Springer, Tokyo (2014). https://doi.org/10.1007/978-4-431-54758-7_4

7. Bagga, P., Paoletti, N., Alrayes, B., Stathis, K.: A deep reinforcement learning approach to concurrent bilateral negotiation. In: Proceedings of the Twenty-Ninth International Joint Conference on Artificial Intelligence, IJCAI-20, pp. 297–303 (2020)

8. Bakker, J., Hammond, A., Bloembergen, D., Baarslag, T.: RLBOA: a modular reinforcement learning framework for autonomous negotiating agents. In: Proceedings of the International Conference on Autonomous Agents and Multiagent Systems, pp. 260–268, May 2019

9. Chang, H.C.H.: Multi-issue bargaining with deep reinforcement learning. arXiv preprint arXiv:2002.07788 (2020)

10. Chen, S., Ammar, H.B., Tuyls, K., Weiss, G.: Using conditional restricted boltzmann machine for highly competitive negotiation tasks. In: Proceedings of the 23th International Joint Conference on Artificial Intelligence, pp. 69–75. AAAI Press (2013)

11. Chen, S., Weiss, G.: An intelligent agent for bilateral negotiation with unknown opponents in continuous-time domains. ACM Trans. Auton. Adapt. Syst. 9(3), 16:1-16:24 (2014). https://doi.org/10.1145/2629577

12. Choi, S.P., Liu, J., Chan, S.P.: A genetic agent-based negotiation system. Comput. Netw. 37(2), 195–204 (2001)

13. de Jonge, D., Sierra, C.: GANGSTER: an automated negotiator applying genetic algorithms. In: Fukuta, N., Ito, T., Zhang, M., Fujita, K., Robu, V. (eds.) Recent Advances in Agent-based Complex Automated Negotiation. SCI, vol. 638, pp. 225–234. Springer, Cham (2016). https://doi.org/10.1007/978-3-319-30307-9_14

14. Fujita, K., et al.: Modern Approaches to Agent-Based Complex Automated Negotiation. Springer, Cham (2017). https://doi.org/10.1007/978-3-319-51563-2

15. van Galen Last, N.: Agent smith: opponent model estimation in bilateral multi-issue negotiation. In: Ito, T., Zhang, M., Robu, V., Fatima, S., Matsuo, T. (eds.) New Trends in Agent-based Complex Automated Negotiations. Studies in Computational Intelligence, vol. 383, pp. 167–174. Springer, Heidelberg (2012). https://doi.org/10.1007/978-3-642-24696-8_12

16. Gerding, E.H., van Bragt, D.D.B., La Poutré, J.A.: Scientific approaches and techniques for negotiation: a game theoretic and artificial intelligence perspective. Centrum voor Wiskunde en Informatica (2000)

17. Haarnoja, T., Zhou, A., Abbeel, P., Levine, S.: Soft actor-critic: off-policy maximum entropy deep reinforcement learning with a stochastic actor. In: International Conference on Machine Learning, pp. 1861–1870. PMLR (2018)

18. Hernandez-Leal, P., Kaisers, M.: Learning against sequential opponents in repeated stochastic games. In: The 3rd Multi-disciplinary Conference on Reinforcement Learning and Decision Making, Ann Arbor, vol. 25 (2017)

19. Hernandez-Leal, P., Rosman, B., Taylor, M.E., Sucar, L.E., Munoz de Cote, E.: A bayesian approach for learning and tracking switching, non-stationary opponents. In: Proceedings of the 2016 International Conference on Autonomous Agents & Multiagent Systems, pp. 1315–1316 (2016)

20. Hindriks, K., Tykhonov, D.: Opponent modelling in automated multi-issue negotiation using bayesian learning. In: Proceedings of the 7th International Joint Conference on Autonomous Agents and Multiagent Systems-Volume 1, pp. 331–338 (2008)
21. Ito, T., Zhang, M., Robu, V., Fatima, S., Matsuo, T.: New Trends in Agent-based Complex Automated Negotiations, vol. 383. Springer, Heidelberg (2011). https://doi.org/10.1007/978-3-642-24696-8
22. Liang, Y.Q., Yuan, Y.: Co-evolutionary stability in the alternating-offer negotiation. In: 2008 IEEE Conference on Cybernetics and Intelligent Systems, pp. 1176–1180. IEEE (2008)
23. Lillicrap, T.P., et al.: Continuous control with deep reinforcement learning. In: 4th International Conference on Learning Representations, ICLR 2016, San Juan, Puerto Rico, 2–4 May 2016, Conference Track Proceedings (2016)
24. Marsa-Maestre, I., Lopez-Carmona, M.A., Ito, T., Zhang, M., Bai, Q., Fujita, K. (eds.): Novel Insights in Agent-based Complex Automated Negotiation. SCI, vol. 535. Springer, Tokyo (2014). https://doi.org/10.1007/978-4-431-54758-7
25. Matos, N., Sierra, C., Jennings, N.R.: Determining successful negotiation strategies: an evolutionary approach. In: Proceedings International Conference on Multi Agent Systems (Cat. No. 98EX160), pp. 182–189. IEEE (1998)
26. Mnih, V., et al.: Playing atari with deep reinforcement learning. arXiv preprint arXiv:1312.5602 (2013)
27. Robu, V., Somefun, D., La Poutré, J.A.: Modeling complex multi-issue negotiations using utility graphs. In: Proceedings of the Fourth International Joint Conference on Autonomous Agents and Multiagent Systems, pp. 280–287 (2005)
28. Rosman, B., Hawasly, M., Ramamoorthy, S.: Bayesian policy reuse. Mach. Learn. **104**(1), 99–127 (2016). https://doi.org/10.1007/s10994-016-5547-y
29. Sengupta, A., Mohammad, Y., Nakadai, S.: An autonomous negotiating agent framework with reinforcement learning based strategies and adaptive strategy switching mechanism. In: Proceedings of the 20th International Conference on Autonomous Agents and MultiAgent Systems, AAMAS '21, pp. 1163–1172 (2021)
30. Williams, C.R., Robu, V., Gerding, E.H., Jennings, N.R.: Negotiating concurrently with unkown opponents in complex, real-time domains. In: ECAI'12, pp. 834–839 (2012)
31. Zeng, D., Sycara, K.: Bayesian learning in negotiation. Int. J. Hum.-Comput. Stud. **48**(1), 125–141 (1998)
32. Zheng, Y., Meng, Z., Hao, J., Zhang, Z., Yang, T., Fan, C.: A deep bayesian policy reuse approach against non-stationary agents. In: Proceedings of the 32nd International Conference on Neural Information Processing Systems, pp. 962–972 (2018)

# Diversity-Based Trajectory and Goal Selection with Hindsight Experience Replay

Tianhong Dai[1(✉)], Hengyan Liu[1], Kai Arulkumaran[1,2], Guangyu Ren[1], and Anil Anthony Bharath[1]

[1] Imperial College London, London SW7 2AZ, UK
{tianhong.dai15,hengyan.liu15,g.ren19,a.bharath}@imperial.ac.uk
[2] Araya Inc., Tokyo 107-6024, Japan
kai_arulkumaran@araya.org

**Abstract.** Hindsight experience replay (HER) is a goal relabelling technique typically used with off-policy deep reinforcement learning algorithms to solve goal-oriented tasks; it is well suited to robotic manipulation tasks that deliver only sparse rewards. In HER, both trajectories and transitions are sampled uniformly for training. However, not all of the agent's experiences contribute equally to training, and so naive uniform sampling may lead to inefficient learning. In this paper, we propose diversity-based trajectory and goal selection with HER (DTGSH). Firstly, trajectories are sampled according to the diversity of the goal states as modelled by determinantal point processes (DPPs). Secondly, transitions with diverse goal states are selected from the trajectories by using $k$-DPPs. We evaluate DTGSH on five challenging robotic manipulation tasks in simulated robot environments, where we show that our method can learn more quickly and reach higher performance than other state-of-the-art approaches on all tasks.

**Keywords:** Deep reinforcement learning · Determinantal point processes · Hindsight experience replay

## 1 Introduction

Deep reinforcement learning (DRL) [3], in which neural networks are used as function approximators for reinforcement learning (RL), has been shown to be capable of solving complex control problems in several environments, including board games [27,28], video games [4,19,30], simulated and real robotic manipulation [2,9,15] and simulated autonomous driving [12].

However, learning from a *sparse* reward signal, where the only reward is provided upon the completion of a task, still remains difficult. An agent may rarely or never encounter positive examples from which to learn in a sparse-reward environment. Many domains therefore provide dense reward signals [5], or practitioners may turn to reward shaping [20]. Designing dense reward functions

© Springer Nature Switzerland AG 2021
D. N. Pham et al. (Eds.): PRICAI 2021, LNAI 13033, pp. 32–45, 2021.
https://doi.org/10.1007/978-3-030-89370-5_3

typically requires prior domain knowledge, making this approach difficult to generalise across different environments.

Fortunately, a common scenario is goal-oriented RL, where the RL agent is tasked with solving different goals within the same environment [11,25]. Even if each task has a sparse reward, the agent ideally *generalises* across goals, making the learning process easier. For example, in a robotic manipulation task, the goal during a single episode would be to achieve a specific position of a target object.

Hindsight experience replay (HER) [1] was proposed to improve the learning efficiency of goal-oriented RL agents in sparse reward settings: when past experience is replayed to train the agent, the desired goal is replaced (in "hindsight") with the achieved goal, generating many positive experiences. In the above example, the desired target position would be overwritten with the achieved target position, with the achieved reward also being overwritten correspondingly.

We note that HER, whilst it enabled solutions to previously unsolved tasks, can be somewhat inefficient in its use of uniformly sampling transitions during training. In the same way that prioritised experience replay [26] has significantly improved over the standard experience replay in RL, several approaches have improved upon HER by using data-dependent sampling [8,32]. HER with energy-based prioritisation (HEBP) [32] assumes semantic knowledge about the goal-space and uses the energy of the target objects to sample trajectories with high energies, and then samples transitions uniformly. Curriculum-guided HER (CHER) [8] samples trajectories uniformly, and then samples transitions based on a mixture of proximity to the desired goal and the diversity of the samples; CHER adapts the weighting of these factors over time. In this work, we introduce diversity-based trajectory and goal selection with HER (DTGSH; See Fig. 1), which samples trajectories based on the diversity of the goals achieved within the trajectory, and then samples transitions based on the diversity of the set of samples. In this paper, DTGSH is evaluated on five challenging robotic manipulation tasks. From extensive experiments, our proposed method converges faster and reaches higher rewards than prior work, without requiring domain knowledge [32] or tuning a curriculum [8], and is based on a single concept—determinantal point processes (DPPs) [14].

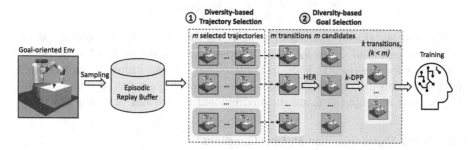

**Fig. 1.** Overview of DTGSH. Every time a new episode is completed, its diversity is calculated, and it is stored in the episodic replay buffer. During training, $m$ episodes are sampled according to their diversity-based priority, and then $k$ diverse, hindsight-relabelled transitions are sampled using a $k$-DPP [13].

## 2    Background

### 2.1    Reinforcement Learning

RL is the study of agents interacting with their environment in order to max-imise their reward, formalised using the framework of Markov decision processes (MDPs) [29]. At each timestep $t$, an agent receives a state $s_t$ from the environment, and then samples an action $a_t$ from its policy $\pi(a_t|s_t)$. Next, the action $a_t$ is executed in the environment to get the next state $s_{t+1}$, and a reward $r_t$. In the episodic RL setting, the objective of the agent is to maximise its expected return $\mathbb{E}[R]$ over a finite trajectory with length $T$:

$$\mathbb{E}[R] = \mathbb{E}\left[\sum_{t=1}^{T} \gamma^{t-1} r_t\right], \tag{1}$$

where $\gamma \in [0,1]$ is a discount factor that exponentially downplays the influence of future rewards, reducing the variance of the return.

### 2.2    Goal-Oriented Reinforcement Learning

RL can be expanded to the multi-goal setting, where the agent's policy and the environment's reward function $\mathcal{R}(s_t, a_t)$ are also conditioned on a goal $g$ [11,25]. In this work, we focus on the goal-oriented setting and environments proposed by OpenAI [23].

In this setting, every episode comes with a desired goal $g$, which specifies the desired configuration of a target object in the environment (which could include the agent itself). At every timestep $t$, the agent is also provided with the currently achieved goal $g_{t+1}^{ac}$. A transition in the environment is thus denoted as: $(s_t, a_t, r_t, s_{t+1}, g, g_{t+1}^{ac})$. The environment provides a sparse reward function, where a negative reward is given unless the achieved goal is within a small distance $\epsilon$ of the desired goal:

$$\mathcal{R}\left(g, g_{t+1}^{ac}\right) := \begin{cases} 0 & \text{if } \left\|g_{t+1}^{ac} - g\right\| \leq \epsilon \\ -1 & \text{otherwise.} \end{cases} \tag{2}$$

However, in this setting, the agent is unlikely to achieve a non-negative reward through random exploration. To overcome this, HER provides successful experiences for the agent to learn from by relabelling transitions during training: the agent trains on a hindsight desired goal $g'$, which is set to the achieved goal $g_{t+1}^{ac}$, with $r_t$ recomputed using the environment reward function (Eq. 2).

### 2.3    Deep Deterministic Policy Gradient

Deep deterministic policy gradient (DDPG) [16] is an off-policy actor-critic DRL algorithm for continuous control tasks, and is used as the baseline algorithm for HER [1,8,32]. The actor $\pi_\theta(s_t)$ is a policy network parameterised by $\theta$, and outputs the agent's actions. The critic $Q_\eta(s_t, a_t)$ is a state-action-value function approximator parameterised by $\eta$, and estimates the expected return following a given state-action pair. The critic is trained by minimising $\mathcal{L}_c = \mathbb{E}[(Q_\eta(s_t, a_t) - y_t)^2]$ where $y_t = r_t + \gamma Q_\eta(s_{t+1}, \pi_\theta(s_{t+1}))$. The actor is trained by maximising $\mathcal{L}_a = \mathbb{E}[Q_\eta(s_t, \pi_\theta(s_t))]$, backpropagating through the critic. Further implementation details can be found in prior work [1, 16].

### 2.4  Determinantal Point Processes

A DPP [14] is a stochastic process that characterises a probability distribution over sets of points using the determinant of some function. In machine learning it is often used to quantify the diversity of a subset, with applications such as video [18] and document summarisation [10].

Formally, for a discrete set of points $\mathcal{Y} = \{x_1, x_2, \cdots, x_N\}$, a point process $\mathcal{P}$ is a probability measure over all $2^{|\mathcal{Y}|}$ subsets. $\mathcal{P}$ is a DPP if a random subset $\mathbf{Y}$ is sampled with probability:

$$\mathcal{P}_L(\mathbf{Y} = Y) = \frac{\det(L_Y)}{\sum_{Y' \subseteq \mathcal{Y}} \det(L_{Y'})} = \frac{\det(L_Y)}{\det(L + I)}, \tag{3}$$

where $Y \subseteq \mathcal{Y}$, $I$ is the identity matrix, $L \in \mathbb{R}^{N \times N}$ is the positive semi-definite DPP kernel matrix, and $L_Y$ is the sub-matrix with rows and columns indexed by the elements of the subset $Y$.

The kernel matrix $L$ can be represented as the Gram matrix $L = X^T X$, where each column of $X$ is the feature vector of an item in $\mathcal{Y}$. The determinant, $\det(L_Y)$, represents the (squared) volume spanned by vectors $x_i \in Y$. From a geometric perspective, feature vectors that are closer to being orthogonal to each other will have a larger determinant, and vectors in the spanned subspace are more likely to be sampled: $\mathcal{P}_L(\mathbf{Y} = Y) \propto \det(L_Y)$. Using orthgonality as a measure of diversity, we leverage DPPs to sample diverse trajectories and goals.

## 3  Related Work

The proposed work is built on HER [1] as a way to effectively augment goal-oriented transitions from a replay buffer: to address the problem of sparse rewards, transitions from unsuccessful trajectories are turned into successful ones. HER uses an episodic replay buffer, with uniform sampling over trajectories, and uniform sampling over transitions. However, these samples may be redundant, and many may contribute little to the successful training of the agent.

In the literature, some efforts have been made to increase the efficiency of HER by prioritising more valuable episodes/transitions. Motivated by the work-energy principle in physics, HEBP [32] assigns higher probability to trajectories in which the target object has higher energy; once the episodes are sampled, the transitions are then sampled uniformly. However, HEBP requires knowing the semantics of the goal space in order to calculate the probability, which is proportional to the sum of the target's potential, kinetic and rotational energies.

CHER [8] dynamically controls the sampling of transitions during training based on a mixture of goal proximity and diversity. Firstly, $m$ episodes are uniformly sampled from the episodic replay buffer, and then a minibatch of $k < m$ is sampled according to the current state of the curriculum. The curriculum initially biases sampling to achieved goals that are close to the desired goal (requiring a distance function), and later biases sampling towards diverse goals, using a $k$-nearest neighbour graph and a submodular function to more efficiently sample a diverse subset of goals (using the same distance function).

Other work has expanded HER in orthogonal directions. Hindsight policy gradient [24] and episodic self-imitation learning [6] apply HER to improve the efficiency of goal-based on-policy algorithms. Dynamic HER [7] and competitive ER [17] expand HER to the dynamic goal and multi-agent settings, respectively.

The use of DPPs in RL has been more limited, with applications towards modelling value functions of sets of agents in multiagent RL [21,31], and most closely related to us, finding diverse policies [22].

## 4   Methodology

We now formally describe the two main components of our method, DTGSH: 1) a diversity-based trajectory selection module to sample valuable trajectories for the further goal selection; 2) a diversity-based goal selection module to select transitions with diverse goal states from the previously selected trajectories. Together, these select informative transitions from a large area of the goal space, improving the agent's ability to learn and generalise.

### 4.1   Diversity-Based Trajectory Selection

We propose a diversity-based prioritization method to select valuable trajectories for efficient training. Related to HEBP's prioritisation of high-energy trajectories [32], we hypothesise that trajectories that achieve diverse goal states $g_t^{ac}$ are more valuable for training; however, unlike HEBP, we do not require knowledge of the goal space semantics.

In a robotic manipulation task, the agent needs to move a target object from its initial position, $g_1^{ac}$, to the target position, $g$. If the agent never moves the object, despite hindsight relabelling it will not be learning information that would directly help in task completion. On the other hand, if the object moves a lot, hindsight relabelling will help the agent learn about meaningful interactions.

In our approach, DPPs are used to model the diversity of achieved goal states $g_t^{ac}$ in an episode, or subsets thereof. For a single trajectory $\mathcal{T}$ of length $T$, we divide it into several partial trajectories $\tau_j$ of length $b$, with achieved goal states $\{g_t^{ac}\}_{t=n:n+b-1}$. That is, with a sliding window of $b = 2$, a trajectory $\mathcal{T}$ can be divided into $N_p$ partial trajectories:

$$\mathcal{T}_i = \{\underbrace{\{g_1^{ac}, g_2^{ac}\}}_{\tau_1}, \underbrace{\{g_2^{ac}, g_3^{ac}\}}_{\tau_2}, \underbrace{\{g_3^{ac}, g_4^{ac}\}}_{\tau_3}, \cdots, \underbrace{\{g_{T-1}^{ac}, g_T^{ac}\}}_{\tau_{N_p}}\}. \tag{4}$$

The diversity $d_{\mathcal{T}_j}$ of each partial trajectory $\mathcal{T}_j$ can be computed as:

$$d_{\mathcal{T}_j} = \det(L_{\mathcal{T}_j}), \tag{5}$$

where $L_{\mathcal{T}_j}$ is the kernel matrix of partial trajectory $\mathcal{T}_j$:

$$L_{\mathcal{T}_j} = M^T M, \tag{6}$$

and $M = [\hat{g}_n^{ac}, \hat{g}_{n+1}^{ac}, \cdots, \hat{g}_{n+b-1}^{ac}]$, where each $\hat{g}^{ac}$ is the $\ell_2$-normalised version of the achieved goal $g^{ac}$ [13]. Finally, the diversity $d_{\mathcal{T}}$ of trajectory $\mathcal{T}$ is the sum of the diversity of its $N_p$ constituent partial trajectories:

$$d_{\mathcal{T}} = \sum_{j=1}^{N_p} d_{\mathcal{T}_j}. \tag{7}$$

Similarly to HEBP [32], we use a non-uniform episode sampling strategy. During training, we prioritise sampling episodes proportionally to their diversity; the probability $p(\mathcal{T}_i)$ of sampling trajectory $\mathcal{T}_i$ from a replay buffer of size $N_e$ is:

$$p(\mathcal{T}_i) = \frac{d_{\mathcal{T}_i}}{\sum_{n=1}^{N_e} d_{\mathcal{T}_n}}. \tag{8}$$

## 4.2  Diversity-Based Goal Selection

In prior work [1,32], after selecting the trajectories from the replay buffer, one transition from each selected trajectory is sampled uniformly to construct a minibatch for training. However, the modified goals $g'$ in the minibatch might be similar, resulting in redundant information. In order to form a minibatch with diverse goals for more efficient learning, we use $k$-DPPs [13] for sampling goals. Compared to the standard DPP, a $k$-DPP is a conditional DPP where the subset $Y$ has a fixed size $k$, with the probability distribution function:

$$\mathcal{P}_L^k(\mathbf{Y} = Y) = \frac{\det(L_Y)}{\sum_{|Y'|=k} \det(L_{Y'})}. \tag{9}$$

$k$-DPPs are more appropriate for goal selection with a minibatch of fixed size $k$. Given $m > k$ trajectories sampled from the replay buffer, we first uniformly sample a transition from each of the $m$ trajectories. Finally, a $k$-DPP is used to sample a diverse set of transitions based on the relabelled goals $g'$ (which, in this context, we denote as "candidate goals"). Figure 2a gives an example of uniform vs. $k$-DPP sampling, demonstrating the increased coverage of the latter. Figure 2b provides corresponding estimated density plots; note that the density of the $k$-DPP samples is actually more uniform over the *support* of the candidate goal distribution.

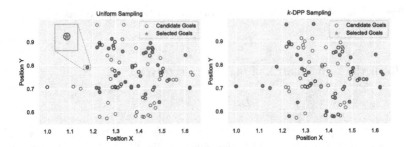

(a) Plot of candidate goals and selected goals. $k$-DPP sampling is more likely to sample points from the full span of the goal space.

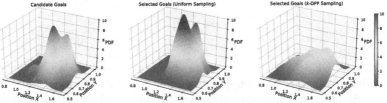

(b) Kernel density estimation of the distributions of goals. $k$-DPP leads to a more uniform selection of goals over the support of the goal space.

**Fig. 2.** Visualisation of $k = 32$ goals selected from $m = 100$ candidate goals of the Push task using either uniform sampling or $k$-DPP sampling, respectively. The candidate goals are distributed over a 2D ($xy$) space. Note that $k$-DPP sampling (right hand plots) results in a broader span of selected goals in $xy$ space compared to uniform sampling (left hand plots).

---

**Algorithm 1.** Diversity-based Goal Selection using $k$-DPP

---

**Require:** set of $m$ candidate goal states $\mathcal{G} := \{g_i\}_{i=1:m}$, minibatch size $k$

1: $J \leftarrow \varnothing$, $M \leftarrow [g_1, g_2, \cdots, g_m]$
2: Calculate the DPP kernel matrix $L_M$
3: $\{v_n, \lambda_n\} \leftarrow \text{EigenDecomposition}(L_M)$
4: $e_k(\lambda_1, \lambda_2, \ldots, \lambda_m) := \sum\limits_{\substack{J' \subseteq \{1,2,\ldots,m\} \\ |J'|=k}} \prod\limits_{n \in J'} \lambda_n$  $\quad \triangleright$ elementary symmetric polynomial: $e_k^m$

5: **for** n $= m, m - 1, \cdots, 1$ **do**
6:     **if** $u \sim \text{Uniform}[0, 1] < \lambda_n \dfrac{e_{k-1}^{n-1}}{e_k^n}$ **then**
7:        $J \leftarrow J \cup \{n\}$, $k \leftarrow k - 1$
8:        **if** $k = 0$ **then**
9:           **break**
10:        **end if**
11:     **end if**
12: **end for**
13: $V \leftarrow \{v_n\}_{n \in J}$, $B \leftarrow \varnothing$
14: **while** $|V| > 0$ **do**
15:     Select $g_i$ from $\mathcal{G}$ with $p(g_i) := \frac{1}{|V|} \sum_{v \in V} (v^T b_i)^2$  $\quad \triangleright b_i$ is the $i^{\text{th}}$ standard basis
16:     $B \leftarrow B \cup \{g_i\}$
17:     $V \leftarrow V_\perp$  $\quad \triangleright$ an orthonormal basis for the subspace of $V$ orthogonal to $b_i$
18: **end while**
19: **return** minibatch $B$ with size $k$

---

**Algorithm 2.** Diversity-based Trajectory and Goal Selection with HER

**Require:** RL environment with episodes of length $T$, number of episodes $N$, off-policy RL algorithm $\mathbb{A}$, episodic replay buffer $\mathcal{B}$, number of algorithm updates $U$, candidate transitions size $m$, minibatch size $k$

1: Initialize the parameters $\theta$ of all models in $\mathbb{A}$
2: $\mathcal{B} \leftarrow \varnothing$
3: **for** i $= 1, 2, \cdots, N$ **do**
4:     Sample a desired goal $g$ and an initial state $s_0$          ▷ start a new episode
5:     **for** t $= 1, 2, \cdots, T$ **do**
6:         Sample an action $a_t$ using the policy $\pi(s_t, g; \theta)$
7:         Execute action $a_t$ and get the next state $s_{t+1}$ and achieved goal state $g_{t+1}^{ac}$
8:         Calculate $r_t$ according to Eq. (2)
9:         Store transition $(s_t, a_t, r_t, s_{t+1}, g, g_{t+1}^{ac})$ in $\mathcal{B}$
10:    **end for**
11:    Calculate the diversity score of current episode $d_{\mathcal{T}_i}$ using Eq. (5) and Eq. (7)
12:    Calculate the diversity-based priority $p(\mathcal{T})$ of each episode in $\mathcal{B}$ using Eq. (8)
13:    **for** iteration $= 1, 2, \cdots, U$ **do**
14:        Sample $m$ trajectories from $\mathcal{B}$ according to priority $p(\mathcal{T})$
15:        Uniformly sample one transition from each of the $m$ trajectories
16:        Relabel goals in each transition and recompute the reward to get $m$ candidate transitions $\{(s_t, a_t, r'_t, s_{t+1}, g')_n\}_{n=1:m}$
17:        Sample minibatch $B$ with size $k$ from the $m$ candidates using Algorithm 1
18:        Optimise $\theta$ with minibatch $B$
19:    **end for**
20: **end for**

Algorithm 1 shows the details of the goal selection subroutine, and Algorithm 2 gives the overall algorithm for our method, DTGSH.

## 5  Experiments

We evaluate our proposed method, and compare it with current state-of-the-art HER-based algorithms [1,8,32] on challenging robotic manipulation tasks [23], pictured in Fig. 3. Furthermore, we perform ablation studies on our diversity-based trajectory and goal selection modules. Our code is based on OpenAI Baselines[1], and is available at: https://github.com/TianhongDai/div-hindsight.

### 5.1  Environments

The robotic manipulation environments used for training and evaluation include five different tasks. Two tasks use the 7-DoF Fetch robotic arm with two-fingers parallel gripper: Push, and Pick&Place, which both require the agent to move a cube to the target position. The remaining three tasks use a 24-DoF Shadow Dexterous Hand to manipulate an egg, a block and a pen, respectively. The sparse reward function is given by Eq. (2).

---

[1] https://github.com/openai/baselines.

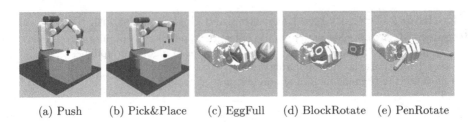

(a) Push     (b) Pick&Place     (c) EggFull     (d) BlockRotate     (e) PenRotate

**Fig. 3.** Robotic manipulation environments. (a–b) use the Fetch robot, and (c–e) use the Shadow Dexterous Hand.

In the Fetch environments, the state $s_t$ contains the position and velocity of the joints, and the position and rotation of the cube. Each action $a_t$ is a 4-dimensional vector, with three dimensions specifying the relative position of the gripper, and the final dimension specifying the state of the gripper (i.e., open or closed). The desired goal $g$ is the target position, and the achieved goal $g_t^{ac}$ is the position of the cube. Each episode is of length $T = 50$.

In the Shadow Dexterous Hand environments, the state $s_t$ contains the position and velocity of the joints. Each action $a_t$ is a 20-dimensional vector which specifies the absolute position of 20 non-coupled joints in the hand. The desired goal $g$ and achieved goal $g_t^{ac}$ specify the rotation of the object for the block and pen tasks, and the position + rotation of the object for the egg task. Each episode is of length $T = 200$.

## 5.2 Training Settings

We base our training setup on CHER [8]. We train all agents on minibatches of size $k = 64$ for 50 epochs using MPI for parallelisation over 16 CPU cores; each epoch consists of 1600 ($16 \times 100$) episodes, with evaluation over 160 ($16 \times 10$) episodes at the end of each epoch. Remaining hyperparameters for the baselines are taken from the original work [1,8,32]. Our method, DTGSH, uses partial trajectories of length $b = 2$ and $m = 100$ as the number of candidate goals.

## 5.3 Benchmark Results

We compare DTGSH to DDPG [16], DDPG+HER [1], DDPG+HEBP [32] and DDPG+CHER [8]. Evaluation results are given based on repeated runs with 5 different seeds; we plot the median success rate with upper and lower bounds given by the 75$^{th}$ and 25$^{th}$ percentiles, respectively.

Figure 4 and Table 1 show the performance of DDPG+DTGSH and baseline approaches on all five tasks. In the Fetch tasks, DDPG+DTGSH and DDPG+HEBP both learn significantly faster than the other methods, while in the Shadow Dexterous Hand tasks DDPG+DTGSH learns the fastest and achieves higher success rates than all other methods. In particular, DDPG cannot solve any tasks without using HER, and CHER performs worse in the Fetch

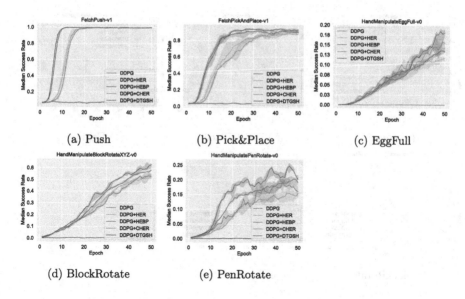

**Fig. 4.** Success rate of DTGSH and baseline approaches.

tasks. We believe the results highlight the importance of sampling both diverse trajectories *and* goals, as in our proposed method, DTGSH.

**Table 1.** Final mean success rate ± standard deviation, with best results in **bold**.

|  | Push | Pick&Place | EggFull | BlockRotate | PenRotate |
|---|---|---|---|---|---|
| DDPG [16] | $0.09 \pm 0.01$ | $0.04 \pm 0.00$ | $0.00 \pm 0.00$ | $0.01 \pm 0.00$ | $0.00 \pm 0.00$ |
| DDPG+HER [1] | $\mathbf{1.00 \pm 0.00}$ | $0.89 \pm 0.03$ | $0.11 \pm 0.01$ | $0.55 \pm 0.04$ | $0.15 \pm 0.02$ |
| DDPG+HEBP [32] | $\mathbf{1.00 \pm 0.00}$ | $0.91 \pm 0.03$ | $0.14 \pm 0.02$ | $0.59 \pm 0.02$ | $0.20 \pm 0.03$ |
| DDPG+CHER [8] | $\mathbf{1.00 \pm 0.00}$ | $0.91 \pm 0.04$ | $0.15 \pm 0.01$ | $0.54 \pm 0.04$ | $0.17 \pm 0.03$ |
| DDPG+DTGSH | $\mathbf{1.00 \pm 0.00}$ | $\mathbf{0.94 \pm 0.01}$ | $\mathbf{0.17 \pm 0.03}$ | $\mathbf{0.62 \pm 0.02}$ | $\mathbf{0.21 \pm 0.02}$ |

### 5.4 Ablation Studies

In this section, we perform the following experiments to investigate the effectiveness of each component in DTGSH: 1) diversity-based trajectory selection with HER (DTSH) and diversity-based goal selection with HER (DGSH) are evaluated independently to assess the contribution of each stage; 2) the performance using different partial trajectory lengths $b$; 3) the performance of using different candidate goal set sizes $m$.

Figure 5 shows the performance of using DTSH and DGSH independently. DDPG+DTSH outperforms DDPG+HER substantially in all tasks, which supports the view that sampling trajectories with diverse achieved goals can substantially improve performance. Furthermore, unlike DDPG+HEBP, DTSH does not require knowing the structure of the goal space in order to calculate the energy of the target object; DDPG+DGSH achieves better performance than

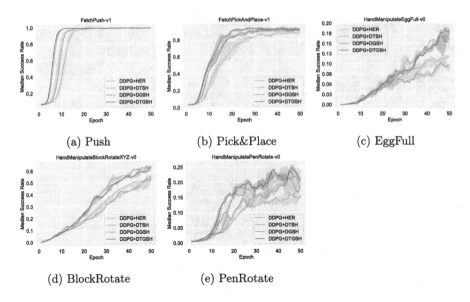

**Fig. 5.** Success rate of HER, DTGSH, and ablations DTSH and DGSH.

DDPG+HER in three environments, and is only worse in one environment. DGSH performs better in environments where it is easier to solve the task (e.g., Fetch tasks), and hence the trajectories selected are more likely to contain useful transitions. However, DTGSH, which is the combination of both modules, performs the best overall.

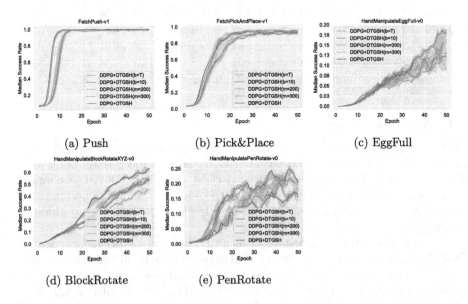

**Fig. 6.** Success rate of DTGSH with different partial trajectory lengths $b$ and different candidate goal set sizes $m$.

Figure 6 shows the performance of DDPG+DTGSH with different partial trajectory lengths $b$ and different candidate goal set sizes $m$. In this work, we use $b = 2$ and $m = 100$ as the defaults. Performance degrades with $b \gg 2$, indicating that pairwise diversity is best for learning in our method. $m \gg 100$ does not affect performance in the Fetch environments, but degrades performance in the Shadow Dexterous Hand environments.

## 5.5   Time Complexity

Table 2 gives example training times of all of the HER-based algorithms. DTGSH requires an additional calculation of the diversity score of $\mathcal{O}(N_p b^3)$ at the end of every training episode, and sampling of $\mathcal{O}(mk^2)$ for each minibatch.

**Table 2.** Training time (hours:minutes:seconds) of DTGSH and baseline approaches on the Push task for 50 epochs.

|      | DDPG+HER [1] | DDPG+HEBP [32] | DDPG+CHER [8] | DDPG+DTGSH |
|------|--------------|----------------|---------------|------------|
| Time | 00:55:08     | 00:56:32       | 03:02:18      | 01:52:30   |

## 6   Conclusion

In this paper, we introduced diversity-based trajectory and goal selection with hindsight experience replay (DTGSH) to improve the learning efficiency of goal-orientated RL agents in the sparse reward setting. Our method can be divided into two stages: 1) valuable trajectories are selected according to diversity-based priority, as modelled by determinantal point processes (DPPs) [14]; 2) $k$-DPPs [13] are leveraged to sample transitions with diverse goal states from previously selected trajectories for training. Our experiments empirically show that DTGSH achieves faster learning and higher final performance in five challenging robotic manipulation tasks, compared to previous state-of-the-art approaches [1,8,32]. Furthermore, unlike prior extensions of hindsight experience replay, DTGSH does not require semantic knowledge of the goal space [32], and does not require tuning a curriculum [8].

**Acknowledgements.** This work was supported by JST, Moonshot R&D Grant Number JPMJMS2012.

## References

1. Andrychowicz, M., et al.: Hindsight experience replay. In: Neural Information Processing Systems (2017)
2. Andrychowicz, O.M., et al.: Learning dexterous in-hand manipulation. Int. J. Robot. Res. **39**(1), 3–20 (2020)

3. Arulkumaran, K., Deisenroth, M.P., Brundage, M., Bharath, A.A.: Deep reinforcement learning: a brief survey. IEEE Signal Process. Mag. **34**(6), 26–38 (2017)
4. Berner, C., et al.: Dota 2 with large scale deep reinforcement learning. arXiv:1912.06680 (2019)
5. Brockman, G., et al.: Openai gym. arXiv preprint arXiv:1606.01540 (2016)
6. Dai, T., Liu, H., Bharath, A.A.: Episodic self-imitation learning with hindsight. Electronics **9**(10), 1742 (2020)
7. Fang, M., Zhou, C., Shi, B., Gong, B., Xu, J., Zhang, T.: DHER: Hindsight experience replay for dynamic goals. In: International Conference on Learning Representations (2018)
8. Fang, M., Zhou, T., Du, Y., Han, L., Zhang, Z.: Curriculum-guided hindsight experience replay. In: Neural Information Processing Systems (2019)
9. Gu, S., Holly, E., Lillicrap, T., Levine, S.: Deep reinforcement learning for robotic manipulation with asynchronous off-policy updates. In: International Conference on Robotics and Automation (2017)
10. Hong, K., Nenkova, A.: Improving the estimation of word importance for news multi-document summarization. In: Conference of the European Chapter of the Association for Computational Linguistics (2014)
11. Kaelbling, L.P.: Learning to achieve goals. In: International Joint Conference on Artificial Intelligence (1993)
12. Kiran, B.R., et al.: Deep reinforcement learning for autonomous driving: a survey. IEEE Trans. Intell. Transp. Syst. 1–18 (2021)
13. Kulesza, A., Taskar, B.: k-DPPs: fixed-size determinantal point processes. In: International Conference on Machine Learning (2011)
14. Kulesza, A., et al.: Determinantal Point Processes for Machine Learning. Foundations and Trends in Machine Learning (2012)
15. Levine, S., Finn, C., Darrell, T., Abbeel, P.: End-to-end training of deep visuomotor policies. J. Mach. Learn. Res. **17**, 1–40 (2016)
16. Lillicrap, T.P., et al.: Continuous control with deep reinforcement learning. In: International Conference on Learning Representations (2016)
17. Liu, H., Trott, A., Socher, R., Xiong, C.: Competitive experience replay. In: International Conference on Learning Representations (2019)
18. Mahasseni, B., Lam, M., Todorovic, S.: Unsupervised video summarization with adversarial lstm networks. In: IEEE Conference on Computer Vision and Pattern Recognition (2017)
19. Mnih, V., et al.: Human-level control through deep reinforcement learning. Nature **518**, 529–533 (2015)
20. Ng, A.Y., Harada, D., Russell, S.: Theory and application to reward shaping. In: International Conference on Machine Learning (1999)
21. Osogami, T., Raymond, R.: Determinantal reinforcement learning. In: AAAI Conference on Artificial Intelligence (2019)
22. Parker-Holder, J., Pacchiano, A., Choromanski, K.M., Roberts, S.J.: Effective diversity in population based reinforcement learning. In: Neural Information Processing Systems (2020)
23. Plappert, M., et al.: Multi-goal reinforcement learning: challenging robotics environments and request for research. arXiv:1802.09464 (2018)
24. Rauber, P., Ummadisingu, A., Mutz, F., Schmidhuber, J.: Hindsight policy gradients. In: International Conference on Learning Representations (2019)
25. Schaul, T., Horgan, D., Gregor, K., Silver, D.: Universal value function approximators. In: International Conference on Machine Learning (2015)

26. Schaul, T., Quan, J., Antonoglou, I., Silver, D.: Prioritized experience replay. In: International Conference on Learning Representations (2016)
27. Schrittwieser, J., et al.: Mastering Atari, go, chess and shogi by planning with a learned model. Nature **588**, 604–609 (2020)
28. Silver, D., et al.: Mastering the game of go without human knowledge. Nature **550**, 354–359 (2017)
29. Sutton, R.S., Barto, A.G.: Reinforcement Learning: An Introduction. The MIT Press, Cambridge (2018)
30. Vinyals, O., et al.: Grandmaster level in Starcraft ii using multi-agent reinforcement learning. Nature **575**, 350–354 (2019)
31. Yang, Y., et al.: Multi-agent determinantal q-learning. In: International Conference on Machine Learning (2020)
32. Zhao, R., Tresp, V.: Energy-based hindsight experience prioritization. In: Conference on Robot Learning (2018)

# Off-Policy Training for Truncated TD($\lambda$) Boosted Soft Actor-Critic

Shiyu Huang[1]([✉]), Bin Wang[2], Hang Su[1], Dong Li[2], Jianye Hao[2], Jun Zhu[1], and Ting Chen[1]

[1] Tsinghua University, Beijing 100084, China
hsy17@mails.tsinghua.edu.cn, {suhangss,dcszj,tingchen}@tsinghua.edu.cn
[2] Huawei Noah Ark's Lab, Beijing 100084, China
{wangbin158,lidong106,haojianye}@huawei.com

**Abstract.** TD($\lambda$) has become a crucial algorithm of modern reinforcement learning (RL). By introducing the trace decay parameter $\lambda$, TD($\lambda$) elegantly unifies Monte Carlo methods ($\lambda = 1$) and one-step temporal difference prediction ($\lambda = 0$), which can learn the optimal value significantly faster than extreme cases with an intermediate value of $\lambda$. However, it is mainly used in tabular or linear function approximation cases, which limits its practicality in large-scale learning and prevents it from adapting to modern deep RL methods. The main challenge of combining TD($\lambda$) with deep RL methods is the "deadly triad" problem between function approximation, bootstrapping and off-policy learning. To address this issue, we explore a new deep multi-step RL method, called SAC($\lambda$), to relieve this dilemma. Firstly, our method uses a new version of Soft Actor-Critic algorithm which stabilizes the learning of non-linear function approximation. Secondly, we introduce truncated TD($\lambda$) to reduce the impact of bootstrapping. Thirdly, we further use importance sampling as the off-policy correction. And the time complexity of the training process can be reduced via parallel updates and parameter sharing. Our experimental results show that SAC($\lambda$) can improve the training efficiency and the stability of off-policy learning. Our ablation study also shows the impact of changes in trace decay parameter $\lambda$ and emerges some insights on how to choose an appropriate $\lambda$.

**Keywords:** Deep reinforcement learning · TD($\lambda$) · Off-policy · Soft Actor-Critic

## 1 Introduction

The choice of the update target is an important part when designing reinforcement learning (RL) algorithms. It often influences the bias and the variance of the algorithm, as well as the convergence guarantees and learning speed. Earlier deep reinforcement learning algorithms [13,22,24] focus more on designing one-step return as the target, i.e., they utilize only one forward reward to update value

© Springer Nature Switzerland AG 2021
D. N. Pham et al. (Eds.): PRICAI 2021, LNAI 13033, pp. 46–59, 2021.
https://doi.org/10.1007/978-3-030-89370-5_4

functions. Recently, algorithms such as Retrace($\lambda$) [15], Rainbow [11], Reactor [6], IMPALA [4] and Ape-X [12] have achieved great success on various RL tasks. These algorithms are often designed with multi-step methods, which use trajectories of length $h$ to compute the target. Furthermore, a novel algorithm called TD($\lambda$) [19] elegantly combines the information of many multi-step targets to create a mixed target. By introducing the trace decay parameter $\lambda$, TD($\lambda$) is also a new way to unify Monte Carlo methods ($\lambda = 1$) and one-step temporal difference prediction ($\lambda = 0$).

Despite exhaustively studied, both theoretically and empirically, TD($\lambda$) is limited to tabular cases [27] or the semi-gradient method [18,28], preventing it from adapting to large-scale learning and modern deep RL methods. The main challenge of combining TD($\lambda$) with deep RL methods is the deadly triad problem [21] of function approximation, bootstrapping and off-policy learning. Despite the success of recent deep neural networks with temporal difference (TD) methods [4,6,11,12], the deadly triad problem makes the learning process diverging and the value estimates becoming unbounded.

In this paper, we introduce truncated TD($\lambda$) into deep reinforcement learning to relieve this problem. Firstly, we use the Soft Actor-Critic (SAC) algorithms [9] to stabilize the training of deep neural networks. Secondly, with multi-step returns of truncated TD($\lambda$), it reduces the impact of bootstrapping by increasing the number of steps. Thirdly, we apply a variant of importance sampling to the return, which can learn arbitrary target policies, and this off-policy correction introduces substantial variance to the training process. To sum up, we build a truncated TD($\lambda$) algorithm with a general function approximator (e.g., a neural network) to stabilize the training process and improve the learning efficiency of reinforcement learning tasks. To show the generalization of our algorithm, we evaluate our method on various types of reinforcement learning tasks. (with discrete action space, continuous action space, low-dimension vector input and high-dimension vision input) We compare our algorithm with normal multi-step TD algorithms, and the results show that our method has lower training variance and faster convergence speed. We also investigate the influence of the trace decay parameter $\lambda$ in our ablation study section, which emerges some insights on how to choose proper hyper-parameters for different tasks.

## 2    Related Work

### 2.1    TD Learning and Multi-step Methods

Temporal difference (TD) learning is a core learning technique in modern reinforcement learning [19], and there are a slew of TD control methods which have been proposed. Q-learning [25] is one of the most popular TD methods, and it is considered as an off-policy method. Sarsa [17] is a classical on-policy control method because the behaviour and target policies are the same. And Sarsa can also be extended to learn off-policy via importance sampling [16]. Expected Sarsa is an extension of Sarsa that has been studied as a strictly on-policy method [23]. All of these methods are described as the one-step case of TD methods, but they can be extended to the multi-step case. For example, Multi-step $Q(\sigma)$ [3] unifies multi-step Sarsa and multi-step Tree-backup, which creates a mixture of full-sampling and pure-expectation approach. Moreover, [27] propose a new algorithm $Q(\sigma, \lambda)$ that combines $Q(\sigma)$ with eligibility trace. It unifies Sarsa($\lambda$) [17] and $Q^\pi(\lambda)$ [10]. [28] further propose $GQ(\sigma, \lambda)$ that extends tabular $Q(\sigma, \lambda)$ with semi-gradient methods. However, their algorithm can not extend to non-linear function approximation, while our method can work with modern deep neural networks for large-scale learning.

## 2.2  TD($\lambda$) and Eligibility Traces

TD($\lambda$) [20] is a new TD algorithm that combines basic TD learning with $\lambda$-return for further speed learning. The forward view of TD($\lambda$) is that the estimate at each time step is moved toward the $\lambda$-return after the trajectory data been collected. The forward version of TD($\lambda$) is also named off-line TD($\lambda$). The backward view of TD($\lambda$) [19] is also introduced for online learning with a small cost in computation. A new variable called eligibility trace is used during the online learning process. [18] introduce a new variant of the backward view of TD($\lambda$) called True Online TD($\lambda$), which takes into account the possibility of changing estimates. However, their algorithm can only work with the linear function approximation and under the online setting. Our algorithm brings TD($\lambda$) into modern RL frameworks, which often rely on non-linear function approximation and off-line training. [6] bring Retrace($\lambda$) [15], a method similar to TD($\lambda$), into a distributional reinforcement learning setting. Their method focuses more on discrete action space, while our method can be applied to both discrete and continuous action spaces. [2] bring multi-step methods into an actor-critic framework, but their method focuses more on how to store and use data in the replay memory, and they do not deal with the difference between behavior policy and target policy. Our method applies importance sampling as the off-policy correction, which reduces the bias of training data.

## 3  Preliminaries

### 3.1  MDPs and Temporal Difference Learning

RL problems are modeled as Markov decision processes (MDPs), in which an agent interacts with the environment during a sequence of discrete-time steps. At each time step $t$, the agent receives the observation about the environment's current state, $s_t \in \mathcal{S}$, where $\mathcal{S}$ is the set of states in the MDP. The agent selects an action, $a_t \in \mathcal{A}$, based on current state, where $\mathcal{A}$ is the action space. Based on the current state and the selected action, the agent receives next state $s_{t+1}$ from the environment according to the state-transition function $P_T(s_t, a_t, s_{t+1})$, and also a scalar reward $r_{t+1}$ according to the reward function $r_{t+1} = r(s_t, a_t, s_{t+1})$. The action $a_t$ is selected according to a policy $\pi(a_t|s_t)$, which gives the probability of taking action $a_t$ at $s_t$. The target return is defined as:

$$G_t = \sum_{k=t}^{T-1} \gamma^{k-t} r_{k+1}, \tag{1}$$

where $\gamma \in [0, 1]$ is the discount factor and $T$ is the final time step, which can be infinite in a continuing task.

In policy evaluation, the goal is to estimate the policy's expected return. And a state-value function is learned:

$$v_\pi(s_t) = \mathbb{E}_\pi[G_t|s_t]. \tag{2}$$

In control, the goal is to learn a policy which maximizes the expected return. And an action-value function is learned:

$$q_\pi(s_t, a_t) = \mathbb{E}_\pi[G_t|s_t, a_t]. \tag{3}$$

In one-step temporal difference methods, we need to approximate value functions by expressing Eqs. 2 and 3 in terms of successor values (the Bellman equation). The Bellman equation for $v_\pi$ is:

$$v_\pi(s_t) = \sum_a \pi(a|s_t) \sum_{s_{t+1}} P_T(s_{t+1}|s_t, a)[r(s_t, a, s_{t+1})$$
$$+ \gamma v_\pi(s_{t+1})]. \tag{4}$$

In a control task, the agent takes an action according to the policy, gets immediate reward and successor state from the environment, and bootstraps off of the current estimated value of the next state. The difference between this TD target and the value of the previous state is denoted as the TD error $\delta$. For example, the TD error of Expected Sarsa is defined as:

$$\delta_t^{ES} = r_{t+1} + \gamma V(s_{t+1}) - Q(s_t, a_t), \tag{5}$$

where the expected action-value $V(s_{t+1}) = \sum_a \pi(a|s_{t+1})Q(s_{t+1}, a)$. And the value function is iteratively updated by taking a step proportional to the TD error with $\xi \in (0, 1]$:

$$Q(s_t, a_t) \leftarrow Q(s_t, a_t) + \xi \delta_t^{ES}. \tag{6}$$

## 3.2 Multi-step Algorithms and TD($\lambda$)

TD methods presented in the previous section can be extended to longer time intervals. In practical applications, RL algorithms [4,6,11] with longer backup length usually achieve better performance than one-step methods. These algorithms which make use of a multi-step backup are denoted as multi-step algorithms. Just like one-step methods, multi-step algorithms also need to approach a target return (the multi-step return). For multi-step Sarsa, the multi-step return is:

$$G_{t:t+n} = r_{t+1} + \gamma r_{t+2} + \gamma^2 r_{t+3} + \dots + \gamma^{n-1} r_{t+n} + \gamma^n Q(s_{t+n}, a_{t+n})$$
$$= \sum_{k=0}^{n-1} \gamma^k r_{t+k+1} + \gamma^n Q(s_{t+n}, a_{t+n}), \tag{7}$$

where the subscript range $t : t + n$ denotes the length of the backup. The target return is biased when the trajectory is collected by other policies. To deal with the off-policy learning, the importance sampling ratio [16] is introduced:

$$\rho_{t:t+n} = \prod_{k=t}^{\tau} \frac{\pi(a_k|s_k)}{b(a_k|s_k)}, \tag{8}$$

where $\tau = \min(t + n - 1, T - 1)$ is the time step before the end of the update or the end of the episode, and $b(a_k|s_k)$ is the behavior policy, which differs from the target policy $\pi(a_k|s_k)$. It will then be multiplied with the TD error to get the update rule:

$$Q(s_t, a_t) \leftarrow Q(s_t, a_t) + \xi \rho_{t+1:t+n} \left[ G_{t:t+n} - Q(s_t, a_t) \right]. \tag{9}$$

This update rule is not only applicable for off-policy multi-step Sarsa, but is also general for some other multi-step algorithms. Moreover, Tree-backup (TB) [16] is a multi-step algorithm which does not require importance sampling during off-policy learning and the target return of the Tree-backup is defined as:

$$G_{t:t+n}^{TB} = Q(s_t, a_t) + \sum_{k=t}^{\tau} \delta_k^{ES} \prod_{i=t+1}^{k} \gamma \pi(a_i|s_i), \tag{10}$$

where $\delta_k^{ES}$ is the TD error of Expected Sarsa from Eq. 5. When designing multi-step algorithms, the backup length should be designated and different tasks may need different backup lengths. There is a novel algorithm which can mix many multi-step TD learning algorithms through weighting $n$-step returns, which is referred to as $\lambda$-return algorithm [25]. In $\lambda$-return algorithms, different $n$-step returns are weighted proportionally to $\lambda^{n-1}$, $\lambda \in [0, 1]$. For example, the definition of $\lambda$-return of Sarsa($\lambda$) [20] is as follows:

$$G_t^{\lambda} = (1 - \lambda) \sum_{n=1}^{\infty} \lambda^{n-1} G_{t:t+n}, \tag{11}$$

where $G_{t:t+n}$ is $n$-step return of Sarsa from time $t$. And the TD($\lambda$) algorithm also applies temporal difference learning update to the value function:

$$Q(s_t, a_t) \leftarrow Q(s_t, a_t) + \xi[G_t^{\lambda} - Q(s_t, a_t)]. \tag{12}$$

TD ($\lambda$) reduces to the one-step TD method and Monte Carlo method when $\lambda = 0$ and $\lambda = 1$ respectively.

# 4 Soft Actor-Critic with Truncated TD ($\lambda$)

## 4.1 Off-Policy Truncated TD($\lambda$)

Truncated TD($\lambda$), first introduced by [18], is a variant of TD($\lambda$) and takes into account the possibility of changing estimates. Correspondingly, the truncated $\lambda$-return is defined as:

$$G_{t:t+h}^{\lambda} = (1 - \lambda) \sum_{n=1}^{h-1} \lambda^{n-1} G_{t:t+n} + \lambda^{h-1} G_{t:t+h}, \tag{13}$$

where $G_{t:t+n}$ is the $n$-step return of Sarsa as showed in Eq. 7, and $h$ is the length of the horizon. Because $h$ is fixed and finite, we can sample a batch of data with length $h$ from the replay memory conveniently during off-policy training. In Eq. 13, rewards values will appear in $G_{t:t+n}$ multiple times. To make calculation convenient, we derive a recursive version of the truncated $\lambda$-return:

$$G_{t:t+h}^{\lambda} = r_{t+1} + (1 - \lambda)\gamma Q(s_{t+1}, a_{t+1}) + \lambda\gamma G_{t+1:t+h}^{\lambda}, \tag{14}$$

so that rewards and value functions will only be used once when calculating the return.

In modern model-free RL learning, we often need to evaluate a policy from the trajectory data from older policies, which is biased and needs to incorporate the off-policy correction. The direct way for the off-policy correction is using important sampling outside the target return as showed in Eq. 9. However, it can not be applied to truncated TD($\lambda$), whose return is a mixture of many $n$-step Sarsa returns. Instead, we can use the form of per-decision importance sampling, which could have lower variance [20]:

$$G_{t:t+h}^{\lambda_{IS}} = \rho_t[r_{t+1} + (1 - \lambda)\gamma Q(s_{t+1}, a_{t+1}) + \lambda\gamma G_{t+1:t+h}^{\lambda}] + (1 - \rho_t)Q(s_t, a_t), \tag{15}$$

where $\rho_t = \frac{\pi(a_t|s_t)}{b(a_t|s_t)}$ is the importance sampling ratio at time step $t$, $\pi(a_t|s_t)$ is the policy to be evaluated and $b(a_t|s_t)$ is the behavior policy which maybe differs from $\pi(a_t|s_t)$. To prevent the variance explosion of importance sampling ratios, we truncate the sampling ratio at 1:

$$\rho_t = \min\left(1, \frac{\pi(a_t|s_t)}{b(a_t|s_t)}\right). \tag{16}$$

In deep RL, we often use a parameterized Q-function $Q_\theta(s_t, a_t)$, where $\theta$ is the function parameter, which can be updated by minimizing the TD error loss. The update rule for truncated TD($\lambda$) is:

$$\theta \leftarrow \theta + \xi\left[G_{t:t+h}^{\lambda_{IS}} - Q_\theta(s_t, a_t)\right]\nabla Q_\theta(s_t, a_t), \tag{17}$$

where $\xi$ is the learning rate. Learning an action-based value function is sufficient for control tasks with a discrete action space, but this is inapplicable for tasks with continuous action space. We will present how to involve truncated TD($\lambda$) into a flexible actor-critic framework in the following section.

## 4.2   Soft Actor-Critic with Truncated TD($\lambda$)

Soft Actor-Critic (SAC) [8] is an Actor-Critic algorithm based on the maximum entropy RL framework, which provides a substantial improvement in exploration and robustness [7,29]. We utilize the SAC algorithm as the basic architecture in our method. As an Actor-Critic algorithm, there are separate policy and value function networks. The policy is referred to as the *Actor*, and the value network as the *Critic*. In this case, we consider a parameterized $Q$-function $Q_\theta(s_t, a_t)$ and a policy network $\pi_\phi(a_t|s_t)$, whose parameters are $\theta$ and $\phi$ respectively. The Actor-Critic algorithm is jointly trained via policy evaluation and policy improvement.

In policy evaluation, we need to update the value function $Q_\theta(s_t, a_t)$. Instead of using standard Bellman backup, SAC uses a soft value update function. For a one-step value iteration, the soft $Q$-value is computed as:

$$Q_\theta(s_t, a_t) \leftarrow r_{t+1} + \gamma \mathbb{E}_{s_{t+1} \sim P_T} V_{soft}(s_{t+1}), \tag{18}$$

where

$$V_{soft}(s_t) = \mathbb{E}_{a_t \sim \pi}[Q_\theta(s_t, a_t) - \beta \log \pi(a_t|s_t))] \tag{19}$$

is the soft value function, and $\beta$ is the temperature parameter. Similar to Eq. 18, our truncated $\lambda$-return with importance sampling can be modified to:

$$G_{t:t+h}^{\lambda_{IS}} = \rho_t[r_{t+1} + (1-\lambda)\gamma V_{soft}(s_{t+1}) + \lambda\gamma G_{t+1:t+h}^{\lambda}] + (1-\rho_t)Q_\theta(s_t, a_t), \tag{20}$$

and the $Q$-function parameters are trained via the update rule in Eq. 17. The loss function of the $Q$-function is the mean squared error (MSE):

$$J_Q(\theta) = \mathbb{E}_{(s_{t:t+h+1}, a_{t:t+h}) \sim \mathcal{D}}\left[\frac{1}{2}(Q_\theta(s_t, a_t) - G_{t:t+h}^{\lambda_{IS}})^2\right], \tag{21}$$

where $G_{t:t+h}^{\lambda_{IS}}$ the soft $\lambda$-return in Eq. 20 and the gradient of $G_{t:t+h}^{\lambda_{IS}}$ is stopped. The loss can be optimized with stochastic gradient descent.

As for the policy improvement, we need to use the value function to obtain a better policy. The main idea for policy improvement is to minimize the Kullback-Leibler divergence between the policy and the soft value function. The final loss function for policy network is:

$$J_\pi(\phi) = \mathbb{E}_{s_t \sim \mathcal{D}, \epsilon_t \sim \mathcal{N}}[\beta \log \pi_\phi(f_\phi(\epsilon_t; s_t)) - Q_\theta(s_t, f_\phi(\epsilon_t; s_t))], \tag{22}$$

where $\epsilon_t$ is an input noise sampled from the Gaussian distribution, and $a_t = f_\phi(\epsilon_t; s_t)$ is an action sampler in line with current policy.

## 4.3   SAC($\lambda$) Training

The learning process of deep RL algorithms is often unstable, we describe how SAC($\lambda$) is trained in detail in this section. As introduced in twin delayed DDPG

---

**Algorithm 1:** SAC($\lambda$) with Off-policy Training

---

1 **Initialize:** value network parameters $\theta^1$ and $\theta^2$, policy network parameters $\phi$, temperature parameter $\beta$, replay memory $\mathcal{M}$, training sequential length $h$, training batch size $N$, target network update parameter $\sigma$. Set target network parameters equal to main parameters: $\hat{\theta}^1 \leftarrow \theta^1$, $\hat{\theta}^2 \leftarrow \theta^2$ and $\hat{\phi} \leftarrow \phi$.

2 **for** $t = 1, 2, 3, ...$ **do**

3      Sample action $a_t$ from policy $\pi_\phi(\cdot|s_t)$.

4      Observe next state $s_{t+1}$ and reward $r_{t+1}$.

5      Store the transition $(s_t, a_t, r_{t+1}, s_{t+1}, \pi_\phi(a_t|s_t))$ into the replay memory $\mathcal{M}$

6      If $s_{t+1}$ is terminal, reset environment state.

7      Randomly sample a batch of sequential data $(s_{1:h+1}, r_{1:h+1}, a_{1:h}, \pi(a|s)_{1:h})_{1:N}$ from $\mathcal{M}$ and use target networks to compute the $\lambda$-return as Equation 20.

8      Update parameters of $Q$-value functions, policy network and temperature.

9      Update target networks.

10 **end**

---

(TD3) [5], we use a pair of $Q$-value functions $(Q_{\theta^1}, Q_{\theta^2})$ to reduce the overestimation bias. Thus, the loss function of the policy network is changed to the average of losses with respect to these two value functions:

$$J_\pi(\phi) = \mathbb{E}_{s_t \sim \mathcal{D}, \epsilon_t \sim \mathcal{N}}[\beta \log \pi_\phi(f_\phi(\epsilon_t; s_t))$$
$$- \frac{1}{2}[Q_{\theta^1}(s_t, f_\phi(\epsilon_t; s_t)) + Q_{\theta^2}(s_t, f_\phi(\epsilon_t; s_t))]]. \tag{23}$$

The target network [14] is a standard approach in many RL algorithms, which can provide a stable objective in the learning procedure. In our algorithm, there are three sets of target network parameters $(\hat{\theta}^1, \hat{\theta}^2, \hat{\phi})$, which correspond to parameters of two value functions and parameters of the policy network. The target network parameters are updated via an exponentially moving average of original parameters. The $Q$-value $Q_\theta(s_t, a_t)$ used in Eq. 20 is replaced by the minimum between the two target values:

$$Q_{\min}(s_t, a_t) = \min_{i=1,2} Q_{\hat{\theta}^i}(s_t, a_t). \tag{24}$$

The temperature parameter $\beta$ can be manually set or learned automatically. Usually, an adaptive temperature is more flexible to different tasks and different learning periods. The loss function for temperature parameter $\beta$ is defined as:

$$J(\beta) = \mathbb{E}_{a_t \sim \pi, s_t \sim \mathcal{D}}[-\beta \log \pi(a_t|s_t) - \mathcal{H}], \tag{25}$$

where $\mathcal{H}$ is the desired minimum expected entropy. The temperature is usually set to 1 at the beginning of training and gradually decreases along with the learning process. A greater temperature in the early stage of learning can help the exploration of the agent.

Our algorithm can be applied to both discrete and continuous action space. When the action space is discrete, $\pi_\phi(a_t|s_t)$ is a softmax policy, whose outputs are probabilities of different actions. And an $\epsilon$-greedy policy is used to help the exploration. When the action space is continuous, the output of $\pi_\phi(a|s)$ is a Gaussian distribution with mean and covariance. Constant action noises are also added every time step to help the exploration.

Because of the off-policy training, the training data is generated by past policies and stored in a replay memory. At each training step, a batch of sequence data is sampled from the replay memory and parameters of both value networks and the policy network are updated by minimizing losses of Eq. 21, Eq. 23 and Eq. 25. Value functions in the $\lambda$-return are computed by the same target networks, which can execute in parallel. Algorithm 1 shows the overall training procedure of our algorithm.

## 5   Experiments

To show the generalization of our method, we evaluate our algorithm on three types of OpenAI gym benchmarks [1], i.e., a task with a discrete action space named CartPole, a task with a continuous space named BipedalWalker and a task with a high-dimension input vector named Pong. We also investigate the impact of hyper-parameter $\lambda$ and the off-policy correction in the ablation study section.

### 5.1   Evaluation of SAC($\lambda$)

We apply five multi-step RL algorithms as our baselines:

**Multi-step DQN (MS+DQN):** a method which uses deep $Q$-learning [14] and uses multi-step returns estimation as described in Eq. 7.
**Tree-backup (TB)** [16]: a method which takes an expectation at every step and does not require importance sampling as described in Sect. 3.2.
**Multi-step Soft Actor-Critic (MS+SAC):** a method which uses multi-step returns estimation and a vanilla Soft Actor-Critic framework.
**Multi-step TD3 (MS+TD3)** [5]: a method which uses multi-step returns estimation and a TD3 framework.
**Retrace($\lambda$)** [15]: a method which uses TD($\lambda$) for control tasks with discrete action space.

All the methods use the same hyper-parameters and the same basic neural architecture for each task. The horizon length $h$ is set to four for all algorithms. As for SAC($\lambda$), we set $\lambda$ to an intermediate value, i.e., $\lambda = 0.5$. For each algorithm, we conduct 10 independent runs and report means and variances of their results.

**SAC($\lambda$) with Discrete Action Space.** We choose CartPole [1] as the test benchmark for the agent with discrete action space. In the environment, a pole is attached by an un-actuated joint to a cart, which moves along a frictionless

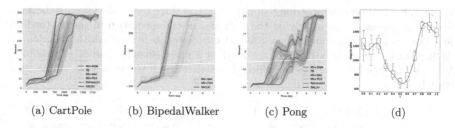

(a) CartPole          (b) BipedalWalker          (c) Pong          (d)

**Fig. 1.** (a)–(c) Learning curves of different algorithms on three tasks. The shaded region represents half a standard deviation of the average evaluation over 10 independent runs. Results show that SAC($\lambda$) converges faster than other baselines on all three tasks. (d) Impact of the trace decay parameter $\lambda$. $\lambda$ ranges from 0 to 1 with step size 0.1 (10 independent runs for each scenario). We draw boxplots [26] for each value of $\lambda$ and also draw the smoothed curve of average steps of solving Cartpole. The result shows that $\lambda$ with an intermediate value performs better than extreme values.

track. The system is controlled by applying a force of $+1$ or $-1$ to the cart. The goal is to prevent the pendulum from falling over. A reward of $+1$ is provided for every time step that the pole remains upright. The episode ends when the pole is more than 15 degrees from vertical, or the cart moves more than 2.4 units from the center. CartPole defines "solving" as getting an average reward of 195 over 100 consecutive trials.

We use a deep architecture with four hidden layers with 128 hidden units for both Actor and Critic in this task. The batch size is set to 64, the learning rate is 0.001 for both Actor and Critic networks and 0.0001 for temperature parameter. The discount factor is set to 0.9. Actions will be randomly sampled during training with the probability of 0.1 to help the exploration. Figure 1(a) shows the training curves of baselines and SAC($\lambda$), and SAC($\lambda$) converges faster than other baselines. We also report the average steps of solving the task in Table 1, which shows that SAC($\lambda$) is more stable than other baselines.

**SAC($\lambda$) with Continuous Action Space.** We choose BipedalWalker [1] as the test benchmark for the agent with continuous action space. A four-dimension action vector is required to control the agent walk through the rough terrain. A positive reward is given for moving forward, total more than 300 points up to the far end. If the robot falls, it gets $-100$. The episode ends when the robot body touches the ground or the robot reaches the far right side of the environment. BipedalWalker defines "solving" as getting an average reward of 300 over 100 consecutive trials. Because multi-step DQN, Tree-backup and Retrace($\lambda$) can only work with the discrete action space, we skip these methods for this task.

We use multi-layer neural networks in this task. The batch size is set to 200, the learning rate is 0.001 for both actor and critic networks and 0.0001 for temperature parameter. The discount factor is set to 0.99. Action noises uniformly sampled from $[-0.3, 0.3]$ are added during training for better exploration. Figure 1(b) shows the training curves of baselines and SAC($\lambda$), and SAC($\lambda$) converges faster than other baselines. We also report the average steps of

**Table 1.** Evaluation results of different algorithms on three tasks (the lower the better). We report average steps of solving the task and $\pm$ corresponds to a single standard deviation over 10 independent runs. SAC($\lambda$) uses fewer steps to reach the solution on all three tasks, which indicates that our method is more efficient than other baselines. And SAC($\lambda$) has lower variances, which shows that the SAC($\lambda$) is more stable than other baselines.

|  | **SAC** ($\lambda$) | Retrace ($\lambda$) | MS+TD3 | MS+SAC | TB | MS+DQN |
|---|---|---|---|---|---|---|
| CartPole | **694 $\pm$ 71** | 768 $\pm$ 122 | 944 $\pm$ 153 | 810 $\pm$ 165 | 1960 $\pm$ 117 | 1056 $\pm$ 161 |
| Walker($\times 10^4$) | **2.95 $\pm$ 0.41** | – | 4.40 $\pm$ 0.47 | 5.01 $\pm$ 0.47 | – | – |
| Pong($\times 10^5$) | **5.85 $\pm$ 0.43** | 6.42 $\pm$ 0.41 | 6.84 $\pm$ 0.22 | 6.12 $\pm$ 0.27 | 6.60 $\pm$ 0.35 | 6.78 $\pm$ 0.43 |

solving the task in Table 1, which shows that SAC($\lambda$) is also more stable than other baselines.

**SAC($\lambda$) with High-dimension Vector Input.** We use Pong [1] as the test benchmark for the agent with high-dimension vector input. In the environment, the observation is an RGB image of the screen, which is an array of shape $(210, 160, 3)$. Pong is not an MDP task, because it can not obtain the velocity of the moving ball from a single observation. As introduced in [14], we resize the gray-scaled image to $84 \times 84$ and stack four frames as the input for the neural network. Pong defines "solving" as getting an average reward of 18 over 100 consecutive trials.

We use deep convolution neural networks in this task to handle image inputs. The batch size is set to 32, the learning rate is 0.0001 for both actor and critic networks and 0.0001 for temperature parameter. The discount factor is set to 0.99. We use an $\epsilon$-greedy policy with $\epsilon$ annealing linearly from 1.0 to 0.02 over $100,000$ frames. Figure 1(c) shows the training curves of different algorithms, and SAC($\lambda$) converges faster than other baselines. We also report the average steps of solving the task in Table 1, which also shows that SAC($\lambda$) is more efficient than other baselines.

## 5.2 Ablation Study

We investigate the impact of the hyper-parameter $\lambda$ and the off-policy correction in this section.

**Impact of Trace Decay Parameter $\lambda$:** TD($\lambda$) is a method which unifies Monte Carlo methods ($\lambda = 1$) and one-step temporal difference prediction ($\lambda = 0$). We study how the performance changes when increasing the value of $\lambda$ from 0 to 1 with step size 0.1. Figure 1(d) shows the curve of how performance changes with $\lambda$. The result shows that $\lambda$ with an intermediate value performs better than extreme values.

**Impact of Off-Policy Corrections:** Some deep multi-step RL algorithms [2, 12] have achieved remarkable results without using off-policy corrections.

We study whether off-policy corrections have a positive effect on off-policy training. We report the evaluation results of three versions of training strategies in Table 2, i.e., without importance sampling, with normal importance sampling and with truncated importance sampling as proposed in this paper. SAC($\lambda$) with truncated importance sampling achieves the best performance on Bipedal-Walker and Pong, but performs slightly worse on CartPole. This is reasonable because the policy converges fast on CartPole and the newest policy is close to older policy, which weakens the demand of the off-policy correction. However, algorithms on BipedalWalker and Pong have a long training period, which makes the newest policy differs from older ones. The truncated importance sampling outperforms normal importance sampling on three tasks, which indicates that the truncated importance sampling can prevent the variance explosion and stabilize the learning process.

**Table 2.** Impact of off-policy corrections. We report evaluation results (average scores of 10 independent runs) of three versions of training strategies, i.e., without importance sampling (No IS), with normal importance sampling (With IS) and with truncated importance sampling (With Truncated IS).

|  | CartPole | BipedalWalker $\times 10^4$ | Pong $\times 10^5$ |
|---|---|---|---|
| No IS | **685** | 3.44 | 6.28 |
| With IS | 726 | 3.52 | 6.09 |
| With Truncated IS | 694 | **2.95** | **5.85** |

# 6 Discussion

In this paper, we explore a new algorithm called SAC($\lambda$), which boosts Soft Actor-Critic with truncated TD($\lambda$). SAC($\lambda$) relieves the dilemma of deadly triad problem via using SAC and TD3 to stabilize the training of deep neural networks, incorporating truncated TD($\lambda$) to reduce the impact of bootstrapping and applying truncated importance sampling to deal with the off-policy. Our algorithm has the generalization ability to various types of control tasks and is easy to adapt to other deep RL algorithms. Experimental results on three types of control tasks show that our algorithm is more efficient and stable than other multi-step RL algorithms. Our ablation study shows that appropriate parameter $\lambda$ is crucial in performance improvement. And our experimental results also show that off-policy corrections in SAC($\lambda$) can improve the performance of off-policy training. In the future, we will try to develop algorithms for automatically tuning the parameter $\lambda$.

# References

1. Brockman, G., et al.: Openai gym. arXiv preprint arXiv:1606.01540 (2016)
2. Chen, G., Li, D., Xu, R.: Context-aware active multi-step reinforcement learning. arXiv preprint arXiv:1911.04107 (2019)
3. De Asis, K., Hernandez-Garcia, J.F., Holland, G.Z., Sutton, R.S.: Multi-step reinforcement learning: a unifying algorithm (2017)
4. Espeholt, L., et al.: IMPALA: scalable distributed deep-RL with importance weighted actor-learner architectures. arXiv: Learning (2018)
5. Fujimoto, S., Van Hoof, H., Meger, D.: Addressing function approximation error in actor-critic methods (2018)
6. Gruslys, A., Dabney, W., Azar, M.G., Piot, B., Bellemare, M.G., Munos, R.: The reactor: a fast and sample-efficient actor-critic agent for reinforcement learning. arXiv:ArtificialIntelligence (2017)
7. Haarnoja, T., Tang, H., Abbeel, P., Levine, S.: Reinforcement learning with deep energy-based policies. arXiv preprint arXiv:1702.08165 (2017)
8. Haarnoja, T., Zhou, A., Abbeel, P., Levine, S.: Soft actor-critic: Off-policy maximum entropy deep reinforcement learning with a stochastic actor. arXiv preprint arXiv:1801.01290 (2018)
9. Haarnoja, T., et al.: Soft actor-critic algorithms and applications (2018)
10. Harutyunyan, A., Bellemare, M.G., Stepleton, T., Munos, R.: Q($\lambda$) with off-policy corrections. In: Ortner, R., Simon, H.U., Zilles, S. (eds.) ALT 2016. LNCS (LNAI), vol. 9925, pp. 305–320. Springer, Cham (2016). https://doi.org/10.1007/978-3-319-46379-7_21
11. Hessel, M., et al.: Rainbow: combining improvements in deep reinforcement learning, pp. 3215–3222 (2018)
12. Horgan, D., et al.: Distributed prioritized experience replay. arXiv:Learning (2018)
13. Mnih, V., et al.: Playing atari with deep reinforcement learning. arXiv preprint arXiv:1312.5602 (2013)
14. Mnih, V., et al.: Human-level control through deep reinforcement learning. Nature 518(7540), 529 (2015)
15. Munos, R., Stepleton, T., Harutyunyan, A., Bellemare, M.G.: Safe and efficient off-policy reinforcement learning, pp. 1054–1062 (2016)
16. Precup, D., Sutton, R.S., Singh, S.P.: Eligibility traces for off-policy policy evaluation. In: Proceedings of the Seventeenth International Conference on Machine Learning. ICML 2000, pp. 759–766. Morgan Kaufmann Publishers Inc., San Francisco, CA, USA (2000)
17. Rummery, G.A., Niranjan, M.: On-line Q-learning Using Connectionist Systems, vol. 37. University of Cambridge, Department of Engineering Cambridge, UK (1994)
18. Seijen, H., Sutton, R.: True online td (lambda). In: International Conference on Machine Learning, PMLR, vol. 32, pp. 692–700 (2014)
19. Sutton, R.S.: Learning to predict by the method of temporal differences. Mach. Learn. 3(1), 9–44 (1988)
20. Sutton, R.S., Barto, A.G.: Reinforcement Learning: An Introduction. MIT Press, Cambridge (2018)
21. Van Hasselt, H., Doron, Y., Strub, F., Hessel, M., Sonnerat, N., Modayil, J.: Deep reinforcement learning and the deadly triad (2018)
22. Van Hasselt, H., Guez, A., Silver, D.: Deep reinforcement learning with double q-learning. Computer Ence (2015)

23. Van Seijen, H., Van Hasselt, H., Whiteson, S., Wiering, M.: A theoretical and empirical analysis of expected Sarsa. In: 2009 IEEE Symposium on Adaptive Dynamic Programming and Reinforcement Learning, pp. 177–184 (2009)
24. Wang, Z., Schaul, T., Hessel, M., Van Hasselt, H., Lanctot, M., De Freitas, N.: Dueling network architectures for deep reinforcement learning (2015)
25. Watkins, C.J.C.H.: Learning from delayed rewards. Ph.D. thesis, Cambridge University (1989)
26. Wickham, H., Stryjewski, L.: 40 years of boxplots. American Statistician (2011)
27. Yang, L., Shi, M., Zheng, Q., Meng, W., Pan, G.: A unified approach for multi-step temporal-difference learning with eligibility traces in reinforcement learning (2018)
28. Yang, L., Zhang, Y., Zheng, Q., Li, P., Pan, G.: Gradient q($\sigma, \lambda$): a unified algorithm with function approximation for reinforcement learning. arXiv: Learning (2019)
29. Ziebart, B.D.: Modeling purposeful adaptive behavior with the principle of maximum causal entropy (2010)

# Adaptive Warm-Start MCTS in AlphaZero-Like Deep Reinforcement Learning

Hui Wang[✉], Mike Preuss, and Aske Plaat

Leiden Institute of Advanced Computer Science, Leiden University,
Leiden, The Netherlands
h.wang.13@liacs.leidenuniv.nl
http://www.cs.leiden.edu

**Abstract.** AlphaZero has achieved impressive performance in deep reinforcement learning by utilizing an architecture that combines search and training of a neural network in self-play. Many researchers are looking for ways to reproduce and improve results for other games/tasks. However, the architecture is designed to learn from scratch, tabula rasa, accepting a cold-start problem in self-play. Recently, a warm-start enhancement method for Monte Carlo Tree Search was proposed to improve the self-play starting phase. It employs a fixed parameter $I'$ to control the warm-start length. Improved performance was reported in small board games. In this paper we present results with an adaptive switch method. Experiments show that our approach works better than the fixed $I'$, especially for "deep", tactical, games (Othello and Connect Four). We conjecture that the adaptive value for $I'$ is also influenced by the size of the game, and that on average $I'$ will increase with game size. We conclude that AlphaZero-like deep reinforcement learning benefits from adaptive rollout based warm-start, as Rapid Action Value Estimate did for rollout-based reinforcement learning 15 years ago.

**Keywords:** MCTS · AlphaZero · Deep reinforcement learning

## 1 Introduction

The combination of online Monte Carlo Tree Search (MCTS) [1] in self-play and offline neural network training has been widely applied as a deep reinforcement learning technique, in particular for solving game-related problems by AlphaGo series programs [9–11]. The approach of this paradigm is to use game playing records from self-play by MCTS as training examples to train the neural network, whereas this trained neural network is used to inform the MCTS value and policy. Note that in contrast to AlphaGo Zero or AlphaZero, the original AlphaGo also uses large amounts of expert data to train the neural network and a fast rollout policy together with the policy provided by neural network to guide the MCTS.

© Springer Nature Switzerland AG 2021
D. N. Pham et al. (Eds.): PRICAI 2021, LNAI 13033, pp. 60–71, 2021.
https://doi.org/10.1007/978-3-030-89370-5_5

However, although the transition from a combination of using expert data and self-play (AlphaGo) to only using self-play (AlphaGo Zero and AlphaZero) appears to have only positive results, it does raise some questions.

The first question is: 'should all human expert data be abandoned?' In other games we have seen that human knowledge is essential for mastering complex games, such as StarCraft [14]. Then when should expert data be used?

The second question is: 'should the fast rollout policy be abandoned?' Recently, Wang et al. [19] have proposed to use warm-start search enhancements **at the start phase** in AlphaZero-like self-play, which improves performance in 3 small board games. Instead of only using the neural network for value and policy, in the first few iterations, classic rollout (or RAVE etc.) can be used.

In fact, the essence of the warm-start search enhancement is to re-generate expert knowledge in the start phase of self-play training, to reduce the cold-start problem of playing against untrained agents. The method uses rollout (which can be seen as experts) instead of a randomly initialized neural network, up until a number of $I'$ iterations, when it switches to the regular value network. In their experiments, the $I'$ was fixed at 5. Obviously, a fixed $I'$ may not be optimal. Therefore, in this work, we propose an adaptive switch method. The method uses an **arena** in the self-play stage (see Algorithm 2), where the search enhancement and the default MCTS are matched, to judge whether to switch or not. With this mechanism, we can dynamically switch off the enhancement if it is no longer better than the default MCTS player, as the neural network is being trained.

Our main contributions can be summarized as follows:

1. Warm-start method improves the Elo [2] of AlphaZero-like self-play in small games, but it introduces a new hyper-parameter. Adaptive warm-start further improves performance and removes the hyper-parameter.
2. For deep games (with a small branching factor) warm-start works better than for shallow games. This indicates that the effectiveness of warm-start method may increase for larger games.

The rest of paper is designed as follows. An overview of the most relevant literature is given in Sect. 2. Before proposing our adaptive switch method in Sect. 4, we describe the warm-start AlphaZero-like self-play algorithm in Sect. 3. Thereafter, we set up the experiments in Sect. 5 and present their results in Sect. 6. Finally, we conclude our paper and discuss future work.

## 2  Related Work

There are a lot of early successful works in reinforcement learning [12], e.g. using temporal difference learning with a neural network to play backgammon [13]. MCTS has also been well studied, and many variants/enhancements were designed to solve problems in the domain of sequential decisions, especially on games. For example, enhancements such as Rapid Action Value Estimate (RAVE) and All Moves as First (AMAF) have been conceived to improve MCTS [3,4]. The AlphaGo series algorithms replace the table based model with a deep neural network based model, where the neural network has a policy head (for evaluating of a state) and a value head (for learning a best action) [16], enabled by the GPU hardware development. Thereafter, the structure that combines MCTS with neural network training has become a typical approach for reinforcement learning tasks [8,18] of this kind model-based deep reinforcement learning [6,7]. Comparing AlphaGo with AlphaGo Zero and AlphaZero, the latter did not use any expert data to train neural network, and abandoned the fast rollout policy for improving MCTS on the trained neural network.

Within a general game playing framework, in order to improve training examples efficiency, [15] assessed the potential of classic Q-learning by introducing Monte Carlo Search enhancements. In an AlphaZero-like self-play framework, [20] used domain-specific features and optimizations, starting from random initialization and no preexisting data, to accelerate the training. We also base our work on an open reimplementation of AlphaZero, AlphaZero General [5].

However, AlphaStar, which defeated human professionals at StarCraft [14], went back to utilize human expert data, thereby suggesting that this is still an option at the start phase of training. Apart from this, [19] proposed a warm-start search enhancement method, pointed out the promising potential of utilizing MCTS enhancements to re-generate expert data at the start phase of training. Our approach differs from AlphaStar, as we generate expert data using MCTS enhancements other than collecting it from humans; further, compared to the static warm-start of [19], we propose an adaptive method to control the iteration length of using such enhancements instead of a fixed $I'$.

## 3    Warm-Start AlphaZero Self-play

### 3.1    The Algorithm Framework

Based on [10,16,19], the core of AlphaZero-like self-play (see Algorithm 1) is an iterative loop which consists of three stages (self-play, neural network training and arena comparison) within the single iteration. The detail description of these 3 stages can be found in [19]. Note that in the Algorithm 1, line 5, a fixed $I'$ is employed to control whether to use MCTS or MCTS enhancements, the $I'$ should be set as relatively smaller than $I$, which is known as warm-start search.

### 3.2    MCTS

Classic MCTS has shown successful performance to solve complex games, by taking random samples in the search space to evaluate the state value. Basically, the classic MCTS can be divided into 4 stages, which are known as *selection, expansion, rollout* and *backpropagate* [1]. However, for the default MCTS in AlphaZero-like self-play (e.g. our Baseline), the neural network directly informs the MCTS state policy and value to guide the search instead of running a rollout.

**Algorithm 1.** Warm-start AlphaZero-like Self-play Algorithm

---

1: Randomly initialize $f_\theta$, assign retrain buffer $D$
2: **for** iteration=1, ...,$I'$, ..., $I$ **do**
3:     **for** episode=1,..., $E$ **do**                                  ▷ self-play
4:         **for** t=1, ..., $T'$, ..., $T$ **do**
5:             **if** $I \le I'$ **then** $\pi_t \leftarrow$ **MCTS Enhancement**
6:             **else** $\pi_t \leftarrow$ **default MCTS**
7:             **if** $t \le T'$ **then** $a_t =$ randomly select on $\pi_t$
8:             **else** $a_t = \arg\max_a(\pi_t)$
9:             executeAction($s_t, a_t$)
10:            $D \leftarrow (s_t, \pi_t, z_t)$ with outcome $z_{t \in [1,T]}$
11:        Sample minibatch $(s_j, \pi_j, z_j)$ from $D$                  ▷ training
12:        Train $f_{\theta'} \leftarrow f_\theta$
13:        $f_\theta = f_{\theta'}$ if $f_{\theta'}$ is better, using **default MCTS**     ▷ arena
14: **return** $f_\theta$;

---

### 3.3   MCTS Enhancements

In this paper, we adopt the same two individual enhancements and three combinations to improve neural network training as were used by [19].

**Rollout** runs a classic MCTS random rollout to get a value that provides more meaningful information than a value from random initialized neural network.

**RAVE** is a well-studied enhancement to cope with the cold-start of MCTS in games like Go [3], where the playout-sequence can be transposed. The core idea of RAVE is using AMAF to update the state visit count $N_{rave}$ and Q-value $Q_{rave}$, which are written as: $N_{rave}(s_{t_1}, a_{t_2}) \leftarrow N_{rave}(s_{t_1}, a_{t_2}) + 1$, $Q_{rave}(s_{t_1}, a_{t_2}) \leftarrow \frac{N_{rave}(s_{t_1}, a_{t_2}) * Q_{rave}(s_{t_1}, a_{t_2}) + v}{N_{rave}(s_{t_1}, a_{t_2}) + 1}$, where $s_{t_1} \in VisitedPath$, and $a_{t_2} \in A(s_{t_1})$, and for $\forall t < t_2, a_t \ne a_{t_2}$.

**RoRa** is the combination which adds the random rollout to enhance RAVE.

**WRo** introduces a weighted sum of rollout value and the neural network value as the return value to guide MCTS [9].

**WRoRa** also employs a weighted sum to combine the values from the neural network and the RoRa.

Different from [19], since there is no pre-determined $I'$, in our work, *weight* is simply calculated as $1/i, i \in [1, I]$, where $i$ is the current iteration number.

## 4   Adaptive Warm-Start Switch Method

The fixed $I'$ to control the length of using warm-start search enhancements as suggested by [19] works, but seems to require different parameter values for different games. In consequence, a costly tuning process would be necessary for each game. Thus, an adaptive method would have multiple advantages.

We notice that the core of the warm-start method is re-generating expert data to train the neural network at the start phase of self-training to avoid learning

---

**Algorithm 2.** Adaptive Warm-Start Switch Algorithm

---

1: Randomly initialize $f_\theta$; Initialize retrain buffer $D$, Switch←False, $r_{mcts}$ ← 0
2: **for** iteration=1, ..., $I$ **do**                                                        ▷ no $I'$
3:   **if** not Switch **then**                                                      ▷ not switch
4:     **for** episode=1,..., $E$ **do**                              ▷ arena with enhancements
5:       **for** t=1, ..., $T'$, ..., $T$ **do**
6:         **if** *episode* $\leq E/2$ **then**
7:           **if** t is odd **then** $\pi_t$ ← **MCTS Enhancement**
8:           **else** $\pi_t$ ← **default MCTS**
9:         **else**
10:           **if** t is odd **then** $\pi_t$ ← **default MCTS**
11:           **else** $\pi_t$ ← **MCTS Enhancement**
12:         **if** $t \leq T'$ **then** $a_t$ = randomly select on $\pi_t$
13:         **else** $a_t = \arg\max_a(\pi_t)$
14:         executeAction($s_t$, $a_t$)
15:         $D \leftarrow (s_t, \pi_t, z_t)$ with outcome $z_{t\in[1,T]}$
16:         $r_{mcts}$+= reward of **default MCTS** in this episode
17:   **else**                                                                           ▷ switch
18:     **for** episode=1,..., $E$ **do**                                         ▷ purely self-play
19:       **for** t=1, ..., $T'$, ..., $T$ **do**
20:         $\pi_t$ ← **default MCTS**
21:         **if** $t \leq T'$ **then** $a_t$ = randomly select on $\pi_t$
22:         **else** $a_t = \arg\max_a(\pi_t)$
23:         executeAction($s_t$, $a_t$)
24:         $D \leftarrow (s_t, \pi_t, z_t)$ with outcome $z_{t\in[1,T]}$
25:   Set Switch←True if $r_{mcts}$ >0, and set $r_{mcts}$ ← 0
26:   Sample minibatch $(s_j, \pi_j, z_j)$ from $D$                              ▷ training
27:   Train $f_{\theta'} \leftarrow f_\theta$
28:   $f_\theta = f_{\theta'}$ if $f_{\theta'}$ is better, using **default MCTS**              ▷ arena
29: **return** $f_\theta$;

---

from weak (random or near random) self-play. We suggest to stop the warm-start when the neural network is on average playing stronger than the enhancements. Therefore, in the self-play, we employ a tournament to compare the standard AlphaZero-like self-play model (Baseline) and the enhancements (see Algorithm 2). The switch occurs once the Baseline MCTS wins more than 50%. In order to avoid spending too much time on this, these arena game records will directly be used as training examples, indicating that the training data is played by the enhancements and the Baseline. This scheme enables to switch at individual points in time for different games and even different training runs.

## 5  Experimental Setup

Since [19] only studied the winrate of single rollout and RAVE against a random player, this can be used as a test to check whether rollout and RAVE work.

**Table 1.** Default parameter setting

| Para | Description | Value | Para | Description | Value |
|------|-------------|-------|------|-------------|-------|
| $I$ | Number of iterations | 100 | $lr$ | Learning rate | 0.005 |
| $rs$ | Number of retrain iterations | 20 | $m$ | MCTS simulation times | 100 |
| $ep$ | Number of epochs | 10 | $d$ | Dropout probability | 0.3 |
| $E$ | Number of episodes | 50 | $c$ | Weight in UCT | 1.0 |
| $bs$ | Batch size | 64 | $n$ | Number of comparison games | 40 |
| $T'$ | Step threshold | 15 | $u$ | Update threshold | 0.6 |

However, it does not reveal any information about relative playing strength, which is necessary to explain how good training examples provided by MCTS enhancements actually are. Therefore, at first we let all 5 enhancements and the baseline MCTS play 100 repetitions with each other on the same 3 games ($6 \times 6$ Connect Four, Othello and Gobang, game description can be found in [19]) in order to investigate the relative playing strength of each pair.

In the second experiment, we tune the fixed $I'$, where $I' \in \{1, 3, 5, 7, 9\}$, for different search enhancements, based on Algorithm 1 to play $6 \times 6$ Connect Four.

In our last experiment, we use new adaptive switch method Algorithm 2 to play $6 \times 6$ Othello, Connect Four and Gobang. We set parameters values according to Table 1. The parameter choices are based on [17]. The detail introduction of these parameters can be found in [17].

Our experiments are run on a high-performance computing (HPC) server, which is a cluster consisting of 20 CPU nodes (40 TFlops) and 10 GPU nodes (40 GPU, 20 TFlops CPU + 536 TFlops GPU). We use small versions of games ($6 \times 6$) in order to perform a medium number of repetitions. Each single run is deployed in a single GPU which takes several days for different games.

## 6 Results

### 6.1 MCTS Vs MCTS Enhancements

Here, we compare the Baseline player (the neural network is initialized randomly which can be regarded as an arena in the first iteration self-play) to the other 5 MCTS enhancements players on 3 different games. Each pair performs 100 repetitions. In Table 2, for Connect Four, the highest winrate is achieved by WRoRa, the lowest by Rave. Except Rave, others are all higher than 50%, showing that the enhancements (except Rave) are better than the untrained Baseline. In Gobang, it is similar, Rave is the lowest, RoRa is the highest. But the winrates are relatively lower than that in other 2 games. It is interesting that in Othello, all winrates are relatively the highest compared to the 2 other games (nearly 100%), although Rave still achieves the lowest winrate which is higher than 50%.

One reason that enhancements work best in Othello is that the Othello game tree is the longest and narrowest (low branching factor). Enhancements like Rollout can provide relatively accurate estimations for these trees. In contrast,

**Table 2.** Results of comparing default MCTS with Rollout, Rave, RoRa, WRo and WRoRa, respectively on the three games with random neural network, weight as $1/2$, $T' = 0$, win rates in percent (row vs column), 100 repetitions each.

| | Default MCTS | | |
|---|---|---|---|
| | ConnectFour | Othello | Gobang |
| Rollout | 64 | 93 | 65 |
| Rave | 27.5 | 53 | 43 |
| RoRa | 76 | 98 | 70 |
| WRo | 82 | 96 | 57 |
| WRoRa | 82.5 | 99 | 62 |

Gobang has the shortest game length and the most legal action options. Enhancements like Rollout do not contribute much to the search in short but wide search tree with limited MCTS simulation. As in shorter games it is more likely to reach a terminal state, both Baseline and enhancements get the true result. Therefore, in comparison to MCTS, enhancements like Rollout work better while it does not terminate too fast. Rave is filling more state action pairs based on information from the neural network, its weaknesses at the beginning are more emphasized. After some iterations of training, the neural network becomes smarter, and Rave can therefore enhance the performance as shown in [19].

### 6.2 Fixed $I'$ Tuning

Taking Connect Four as an example, in this experiment we search for an optimal fixed $I'$ value, utilizing the warm-start search method proposed in [19]. We set $I'$ as 1, 3, 5, 7, 9 respectively (the value should be relatively small since the enhancement is only expected to be used at the start phase of training). The Elo ratings of each enhancements using different $I'$ are presented in Fig. 1.

The Elo ratings are calculated based on the tournament results using a Bayesian Elo computation system [2], same for Fig. 2. We can see that for Rave and WRoRa, it turns out that $I' = 7$ is the optimal value for fixed $I'$ warm-start framework, for others, it is still unclear which value is the best, indicating that the tuning is inefficient and costly.

### 6.3 Adaptive Warm-Start Switch

In this final experiment, we train models with the parameters in Table 1 and then let them compete against each other in different games. In addition, we record the specific iteration number where the switch occurs for every training run and the corresponding self-play arena rewards of MCTS before this iteration. A statistic of the iteration number for the 3 games is shown in Table 3. The table shows that, generally, the iteration number is relatively small compared to the total length of the training (100 iterations). Besides, not only for different

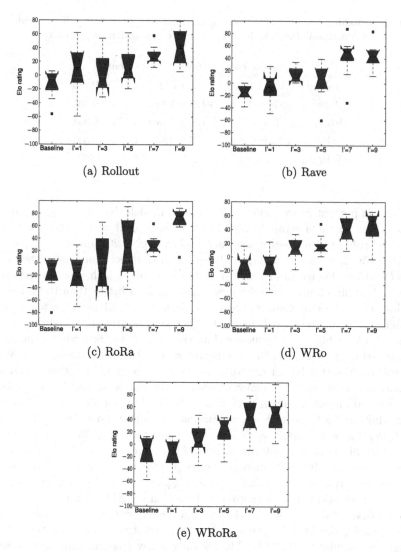

**Fig. 1.** Elo ratings for different warm-start phase iterations with different search enhancement on 6 × 6 Connect Four

games, but also for different training runs on the same game, the switch iteration varies. This is because for different training runs, the neural network training progresses differently. Therefore, a fixed $I'$ can not be used for each specific training. Note that for Gobang, a game with a large branching factor, with the default setting, it always switches at the first iteration. Therefore, we also test with larger $m = 200$, thereby providing more time to the MCTS. With this change, there are several runs keeping the enhancements see Table 3, but it still shows a small influence on this game.

**Table 3.** Switching iterations for training on different games with different enhancements over 8 repetitions (average iteration number ± standard deviation)

|        | Connect Four   | Othello         | Gobang          |
|--------|----------------|-----------------|-----------------|
| Rollout | $6.625 \pm 3.039$ | $5.5 \pm 1.732$  | $1.375 \pm 0.484$ |
| Rave    | $2.375 \pm 1.218$ | $3.125 \pm 2.667$ | $1.125 \pm 0.331$ |
| RoRa    | $7.75 \pm 4.74$   | $5.125 \pm 1.364$ | $1.125 \pm 0.331$ |
| WRo     | $4.25 \pm 1.561$  | $4.375 \pm 1.654$ | $1.125 \pm 0.331$ |
| WRoRa   | $4.375 \pm 1.576$ | $4.0 \pm 1.0$    | $1.25 \pm 0.433$  |

More importantly, we collect all trained models based on our adaptive method, and let them compete with the models trained using fixed $I' = 5$ in a full round-robin tournament where each 2 players play 20 games.

From Fig. 2, we see that, generally, on both Connect Four and Othello, all fixed $I'$ achieve higher Elo ratings than the Baseline, which was also reported in [19]). And all adaptive switch models also perform better than the Baseline. Besides, for each enhancement, the Elo ratings of the adaptive switch models are higher than for the fixed $I'$ method, which suggests that our adaptive switch method leads to better performance than the fixed $I'$ method when controlling the warm-start iteration length. Specifically, we find that for Connect Four, WRo and RoRa achieve the higher Elo Ratings (see Fig. 2(a)) and for Othello, WRoRa performs best (see Fig. 2(b)), which reproduces the consistent conclusion (at least one combination enhancement performs better in different games) as [19]).

In addition, for Connect Four, comparing the tuning results in Fig. 1 and the *switch iterations* in Table 3, we find that our method generally needs a shorter warm-start phase than employing a fixed $I'$. The reason could be that in our method, there are always 2 different players playing the game, and they provide more diverse training data than a pure self-play player. In consequence, the neural network also improves more quickly, which is highly desired.

Note that while we use the default parameter setting for training in the Gobang game, the *switch* occurs at the first iteration. And even though we enlarge the simulation times for MCTS, only a few training runs shortly keep using the enhancements. We therefore presume that it is meaningless to further perform the tournament comparison for Gobang.

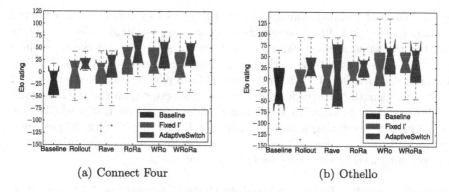

(a) Connect Four                    (b) Othello

**Fig. 2.** Comparison of adaptive switch method versus fixed $I'$ based on a full tournament for $6 \times 6$ Connect Four and Othello

## 7    Discussion and Conclusion

Since AlphaGo Zero' results, self-play has become a default approach for generating training data tabula rasa, disregarding other information for training. However, if there is a way to obtain better training examples from the start, why not use them, as has been done recently in StarCraft (see DeepMind's AlphaStar [14]). In addition [19] investigate the possibility of utilizing MCTS enhancements to improve AlphaZero-like self-play. They embed Rollout, RAVE and combinations as enhancements at the start period of iterative self-play training and tested this on small board games.

Confirming [19], we find that finding an optimal value of fixed $I'$ is difficult, therefore, we propose an adaptive method for deciding when to switch. We also use Rollout, RAVE, and combinations with network values to quickly improve MCTS tree statistics (using RAVE) with meaningful information (using Rollout) before we switch to Baseline-like self-play training. We employed the same games, namely the $6 \times 6$ versions of Gobang, Connect Four, and Othello. In these experiments, we find that, for different games, and even different training runs for the same game, the new adaptive method generally switches at different iterations. This indicates the noise in the neural network training progress for different runs. After 100 self-play iterations, we still see the effects of the warm-start enhancements as playing strength has improved in many cases, and for all enhancements, our method performs better than the method proposed in [19] with $I'$ set to 5. In addition, some conclusions are consistent to [19], for example, there is also at least one combination that performs better.

The new adaptive method works especially well on Othello and Connect Four, "deep" games with a moderate branching factor, and less well on Gobang, which has a larger branching factor. In the self-play arena, the default MCTS is already quite strong, and for games with a short and wide episode, the MCTS enhancements do not benefit much. Short game lengths reach terminal states early, and MCTS can use the true reward information more often, resulting in a higher chance of winning. Since, Rollout still needs to simulate, with a limited simulation count it is likely to not choose a winning terminal state but a state that has the same average value as the terminal state. In this situation, in a short game episodes, MCTS works better than the enhancement with $T' = 15$. With ongoing training of the neural network, both players become stronger, and as the game length becomes longer, $I' = 5$ works better than the the Baseline.

Our experiments are with small games. Adaptive warm-start works best in deeper games, suggesting a larger benefit for bigger games with deeper lines. Future work includes larger games with deeper lines, and using different but stronger enhancements to generate training examples.

**Acknowledgments.** Hui Wang acknowledges financial support from the China Scholarship Council (CSC), CSC No.201706990015.

# References

1. Browne, C.B., et al.: A survey of Monte Carlo tree search methods. IEEE Trans. Comput. Intell. AI Games **4**(1), 1–43 (2012)
2. Coulom, R.: Whole-history rating: a Bayesian rating system for players of time-varying strength. In: van den Herik, H.J., Xu, X., Ma, Z., Winands, M.H.M. (eds.) CG 2008. LNCS, vol. 5131, pp. 113–124. Springer, Heidelberg (2008). https://doi.org/10.1007/978-3-540-87608-3_11
3. Gelly, S., Silver, D.: Combining online and offline knowledge in UCT. In: Proceedings of the 24th International Conference on Machine Learning, pp. 273–280 (2007)
4. Gelly, S., Silver, D.: Monte-Carlo tree search and rapid action value estimation in computer go. Artif. Intell. **175**(11), 1856–1875 (2011)
5. Nair, S.: Alphazero general (2018). https://github.com/suragnair/alpha-zero-general. Accessed May 2018
6. Plaat, A.: Learning to Play: Reinforcement Learning and Games. Springer, Cham (2020). https://doi.org/10.1007/978-3-030-59238-7
7. Schmidhuber, J.: Deep learning in neural networks: an overview. Neural Netw. **61**, 85–117 (2015)
8. Segler, M.H., Preuss, M., Waller, M.P.: Planning chemical syntheses with deep neural networks and symbolic AI. Nature **555**(7698), 604–610 (2018)
9. Silver, D., et al.: Mastering the game of go with deep neural networks and tree search. Nature **529**(7587), 484–489 (2016)
10. Silver, D.: A general reinforcement learning algorithm that masters chess, shogi, and go through self-play. Science **362**(6419), 1140–1144 (2018)
11. Silver, D., et al.: Mastering the game of go without human knowledge. Nature **550**(7676), 354–359 (2017)
12. Sutton, R.S., Barto, A.G.: Reinforcement learning: An Introduction. MIT Press, Cambridge (2018)
13. Tesauro, G.: Temporal difference learning and TD-Gammon. Commun. ACM **38**(3), 58–68 (1995)
14. Vinyals, O.: Grandmaster level in starcraft II using multi-agent reinforcement learning. Nature **575**(7782), 350–354 (2019)

15. Wang, H., Emmerich, M., Plaat, A.: Assessing the potential of classical Q-learning in general game playing. In: Atzmueller, M., Duivesteijn, W. (eds.) BNAIC 2018. CCIS, vol. 1021, pp. 138–150. Springer, Cham (2019). https://doi.org/10.1007/978-3-030-31978-6_11

16. Wang, H., Emmerich, M., Preuss, M., Plaat, A.: Alternative loss functions in alphazero-like self-play. In: 2019 IEEE Symposium Series on Computational Intelligence (SSCI), pp. 155–162. IEEE (2019)

17. Wang, H., Emmerich, M., Preuss, M., Plaat, A.: Analysis of hyper-parameters for small games: Iterations or epochs in self-play? arXiv preprint arXiv:2003.05988 (2020)

18. Wang, H., Preuss, M., Emmerich, M., Plaat, A.: Tackling morpion solitaire with alphazero-like ranked reward reinforcement learning. arXiv preprint arXiv:2006.07970 (2020)

19. Wang, H., Preuss, M., Plaat, A.: Warm-start alphazero self-play search enhancements. In: Proceedings of the Parallel Problem Solving from Nature - PPSN XVI, pp. 528–542 (2020)

20. Wu, D.J.: Accelerating self-play learning in go. arXiv preprint arXiv:1902.10565 (2019)

# Batch-Constraint Inverse Reinforcement Learning

Mao Chen[1], Li Wan[1(✉)], Chunyan Gou[2], Jiaolu Liao[2], and Shengjiang Wu[1]

[1] College of Computer Science, Chongqing University, Chongqing, China
{chenmao,wanli,shengjiangwu}@cqu.edu.cn
[2] Department of Acupuncture and Moxibustion, Chongqing Traditional Chinese Medicine Hospital, Chongqing, China

**Abstract.** We consider a completely offline inverse reinforcement learning setup, i.e., where the reward function is unknown and the interaction with the environment is not possible. This typically occurs in situations where data collection is risky or costly, such as healthcare or industrial controls. Establishing explainable rewards for decision-making is critical to quantifying and adapting policy. However, existing methods hardly learn an interpretable reward in offline setting. In this paper, we introduce an offline inverse reinforcement learning algorithm, BCIRL, to recover the implicit reward function and optimal policy from expert demonstrations in off-policy model-free settings. To address challenges in offline settings, we restrict the action space to behave close to the policy on the given data. We demonstrate that BCIRL performs strongly on control environment, that recovered rewards provide useful insights on experts' preferences.

**Keywords:** Inverse reinforcement learning · Offline reinforcement learning · Interpretable rewards

## 1 Introduction

For applications in risky and complicated environments, there is hardly access to appropriate rewards here, nor to the environment dynamics to interact and test policies. In this case, we can only get trajectories based on expert that record states visited and actions taken in each state. For example, in clinical decision-making, we want to learn policies from medical experts, but it is unreasonable to implement policies on patients during the training process. Further, we are interested in the trade-offs and preferences related to expert actions, and therefore we need to obtain interpretable rewards of expert behavior so that we can quantify and adapt policies.

Given the trajectories made by an expert, imitation learning (IL) [10] simply learns an imitator policy to match the expert. However, to further understand expert motivation, we can recourse to inverse reinforcement learning (IRL) [21]. IRL attempts to obtain the expert policy by recovering the expert's hidden

© Springer Nature Switzerland AG 2021
D. N. Pham et al. (Eds.): PRICAI 2021, LNAI 13033, pp. 72–82, 2021.
https://doi.org/10.1007/978-3-030-89370-5_6

reward function. Abbeel et al. [1] proposes max-margin IRL to find a reward function that maximizes the margin between feature expectations (the expected discounted accumulated feature value) obtained by the expert decision and the candidate policy, and execute forward reinforcement learning (RL) [23] to optimize candidate policy for recovered reward function. Both estimating feature expectation and forward RL are performed by interacting with the environment online[1]. To operate IRL in the offline setting, Lee et al. [16] proposes Deep Successor Feature Networks (DSFN) which picks the neural network to approximate the feature expectation and performs forward RL with off-policy evaluation. But off-policy methods in offline setting suffers from distributional shift (the distribution of data in the buffer and that generated by the learning policy differ significantly) which is also known as "cold-start" problem. DSFN constrains state distribution shifts by limiting the extent to which learned policies deviate from expert policies, i.e., initial policy must be close to the expert's policy. Moreover, features need to be carefully designed in DSFN which uses hidden layers of the network to extract the features, so that the recovered reward of unknown features cannot explain expert motivation. Instead, we replace the off-policy evaluation with the batch reinforcement learning (BRL) approach [17], which works to solve the problem of distribution shift with no additional online data collection. The off-policy methods select the action with the largest value function, while our method first excludes those actions with small probability and then selects the action based on the value function.

The main contribution of our work is a method for advancing DSFN beyond the cold-start problem and unexplainable reward. First, our constraints on actions during policy optimization adapt BCIRL to the completely offline setting. This allows us to no more need warm-start and features-design. Using raw states as features making us better interpret the recovered reward. Second, Experiments demonstrate that our recovered policy outperforms the rest of the baseline. Our algorithm Batch-Constraint Inverse Reinforcement

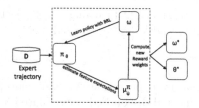

**Fig. 1. Overview.** BCIRL is a framework that output an optimal policy $\pi_{\theta*}$ and reward weights $\omega^*$, leveraging only expert trajectory without interacting with the environment.

Learning (BCIRL) are depicted in Fig. 1, which iteratively executes the following steps to recover reward weights and optimal policy: (1) estimate feature expectations of current policy $\pi$, (2) update reward weights $\omega$ by maximizing the distance of feature expectation between the expert and current policy, (3) optimize $\pi$ using linearly reward function $R = \omega \cdot \phi$, $\phi$ is feature mapping.

In the following, we review modern approaches to offline IL/IRL (Sect. 2), and present our algorithm in three sub-blocks (Sect. 3). Through experiments applied

---

[1] The online learning mentioned in this paper refers to the need to interact with the environment. Offline learning or batch learning refers to no interaction with the environment at all.

to control tasks and healthcare, we verified that the BCIRL algorithm is effective in acquiring policies and recovering rewards (Sect. 4). Lastly, we summarize the paper and propose our future research directions (Sect. 5).

## 2    Offline Inverse Reinforcement Learning

**Preliminaries.** We use the standard Markov decision process (MDP) setup, which is defined as a five-tuple $(S, A, P, R, \gamma)$, with the state set $S$, action set $A$ (discrete[2]), transfer probability matrix $P$ (which we don't know), a reward function $R$, and a discount factor $\gamma$. The policy $\pi(a \mid s)$ denotes the probability of performing an action $a(\in A)$ at state $s(\in S)$. To measure the performance of state $s$ and action $a$ under policy $\pi$, the value function is defined as:

$$V^\pi(s) = \mathbb{E}_\pi \left[ \sum_{t=0}^{T} \gamma^t R(s_t, a_t) \mid s_0 = s \right], \tag{1}$$

where $s_0 \in S_0$, denotes the initial state and $\mathbb{E}_\pi$ denotes the expectation under policy $\pi$. We consider a finite MDP, with T being the terminal step. The state-action value function is defined as:

$$Q^\pi(s, a) = R(s, a) + \mathbb{E}_\pi \left[ \sum_{t=1}^{T} \gamma^t R(s_t, a_t) \mid s_0 = s, a_0 = a \right]. \tag{2}$$

Reinforcement Learning (RL) objective is to find a policy $\pi_*$ such that the values of Q and V are maximized, i.e.,

$$\pi_* = \arg \max_\pi V^\pi(s), \forall s \in S. \tag{3}$$

Feature expectation is a core concept in IRL algorithm which is defined as the expected discounted accumulated feature:

$$\mu^\pi(s, a) = \phi(s, a) + \mathbb{E}_\pi \left[ \sum_{t=1}^{T} \gamma^t \phi(s_t, a_t) \right], \tag{4}$$

where $\phi(s, a)$ is a feature map $S, A \to [0, 1]^k$. We assume that the reward function is linear, i.e., $R(s, a) = \omega \cdot \phi(s, a)$. Note, from Eq. (2) and Eq. (4) we can get: $Q^\pi(s, a) = \omega \cdot \mu^\pi(s, a)$, $\mu^\pi$ can be regarded as a component of the action value function $Q^\pi$. To get the reward function for the raw features, the mapping: $\phi(s, a) = \text{concat}(s, a)$ or $\phi(s, a) = s$ is used in our algorithm.

In our setting, reward function $R(s, a)$ is unknown, and we cannot interact with the environment in the training process. All we can get is the expert data $\mathcal{D} = \left\{ \left( s_1^{(i)}, a_1^{(i)}, \ldots, s_{T^{(i)}}^{(i)}, a_{T^{(i)}}^{(i)} \right) \right\}_{i=1}^{m}$ which is generated from experts(we denote the implicit expert policy as $\pi_e$).

---

[2] The derivations and the experiments in this paper are in discrete case examples, and our algorithm can be easily generalized to a continuous setting by changing Q-learning to Actor-Critic model.

**Imitation Learning.** The goal of imitation learning is to learn a policy $\pi_*$ which is as close as possible to the expert policy $\pi_e$, i.e., to match the action. This can be formulated as $\pi_* = \operatorname{argmin}_\pi \mathbb{E}_{s \sim D} \mathcal{L} (\pi_e(\cdot \mid s), \pi(\cdot \mid s))$, where $\mathcal{L}$ represents some loss function. Behavior Cloning (BC) [2] is an efficient but very simple approach that ignores the valuable information of states transition and uses only supervised learning for classification. Since BC does not take long-term planning into account, which leads to it being subject to compounding errors and drifting away from expert data [20]. Once drifted to these out-of-distribution states, the agents are unable to make correct decisions.

**Inverse Reinforcement Learning.** To use the information of states transition, the inverse reinforcement learning algorithm [19] was proposed, which not only obtains the optimal policy but also recovers a reward. IRL assumes that a reward function the expert always does better than any learning policies which have been found previously and IRL uses forward RL repeatedly to optimize policy in an inner loop. Forward RL can be executed according to Eq. 3. Reward $R$ is calculated by the following:

$$R = \operatorname{argmin}_R \left( V^{\pi_e} - \max_\pi V^\pi \right). \tag{5}$$

The value function of the learning policy and the expert policy value function are closest given the learned reward $R$. Adversarial imitation learning [9] interprets the above two processes as generators and discriminators in GAN [7] and proves the convergence of the results. This type of learning method we mentioned above is online learning, and forward RL requires access to the environment for training.

**Offline IRL.** However, in many cases we can't interact with the environment to train the agent, either because data collection is costly (e.g., in robotics or educational agents) or risky (e.g., in autonomous driving or healthcare). A simple approach is to learn a simulator of the environment dynamics [8], but this approach is only applicable to low-dimensional environments and requires a large amount of data collection. DSFN [16] uses an off-policy approach with a fixed expert buffer to execute forward RL, but the ensuing problem is to warm-start the initial policy and to carefully design the feature functions. In contrast, some excellent off-line methods in recent years, AVRIL [5], EDM [11], ValueDice [14], do not explicitly learn the reward function.

## 3   Method

We use the max-margin apprenticeship learning [1,16] as a framework, minimizing the distance of feature expectation between the expert and candidate policy. We modify the interactive forward RL to offline learning and use a neural network to approximate the feature expectations. We iteratively execute the following steps to recover reward weights and optimal policy: (1) estimate feature expectations of current policy $\pi$, (2) update reward weighs $\omega$ by solving quadratic program(QP), (3) optimize $\pi$ using recovered reward with Batch Reinforcement Learning(BRL) [17]. As depicted in Fig. 1, the feature expectation is estimated by a deep neural network, which is an off-policy evaluation method, as detailed in Sect. 3.1. In contrast to DSFN, which uses the DQN [18] with a fixed buffer to optimize the current policy, we use the BRL approach which constrains action choice in the policy. Our approach no longer requires the initial policy $\pi_0$ to be similar to the expert policy $\pi_e$, and an additional network to learn a suitable feature representation, as detailed in Sect. 3.2. Finally, the algorithm Batch-Constraint Inverse Reinforcement Learning (BCIRL) is introduced in Sect. 3.3.

### 3.1 Feature Expectation Approximation

As mentioned before, the feature expectation is actually a component of the value function. So all methods of optimizing value function are applicable to train feature expectation, such as Monte Carlo (MC) or temporal difference (TD) methods. Similar to [16], We estimate the feature expectation using a neural network parameterized with $\psi$ and use an additional target network parameterized by $\psi'$ to find the target value, and $\psi$ replaces $\psi'$ at certain step intervals. Given policy $\pi$, feature mapping $\phi$, the Bellman target value is as follows:

$$
y_{\psi'}^{\pi} = \begin{cases} \phi(s, a) & \text{if trajectory terminates at } s' \\ \phi(s, a) + \gamma \mathbb{E}_{a' \sim \pi}\left[\mu_{\psi'}^{\pi}(s', a')\right] & \text{otherwise} \end{cases}, \quad (6)
$$

where $(s, a)$ is sampled from the fixed buffer(expert demonstration), $a'$ is generated by the current policy $\pi$ following the $\epsilon$-greedy policy. We train the network using mean square error between estimated values and target values:

$$
\mathcal{L}_{\psi} = \frac{1}{2}\mathbb{E}_{(s,a,s') \sim D_e}\left[\left\|\mu_{\psi}^{\pi}(s, a) - y_{(\psi')}^{\pi}\right\|^2\right] \quad (7)
$$

Gradient descent is used to update the parameters:

$$
\psi \leftarrow \psi - \alpha \nabla \mathcal{L}_{\psi} \quad (8)
$$

In the offline setting, cross-validation is used to determine whether the training converges. We divide the expert demonstration into a training set and a validation set, and training ends when the validation loss $L_{val}$ is less than a fixed threshold $\delta$ or the iterations reaches the set maximum number. Algorithm 1 describes feature expectation approximation method.

### 3.2 Policy Optimization with BRL

When the weights $\omega$ of the reward function are updated, the optimal policy is trained for the current reward. The existing methods [1,3,16] use off-policy optimization directly. However, offline policy optimization is challenging because it

---

**Algorithm 1:** Feature Expectation Approximation Network(FEAN)

---

    **Input**   : Expert demonstration $D$, Maximum number of iterations $N$
    **Output**: $\mu_\psi^\pi$

1 **while** $L_{val} > \delta$ *and* $n < N$ **do**
2      Sample batch $B$ $\{(s, a, s')\}$ from $D$;
3      Compute feature expectation target with Equation 6;
4      Compute loss for batch $B$ with Equation 7;
5      Update $\psi$ with Equation 8;
6      Compute $L_{val}$ on the validation set;
7 **end**

---

only relies on a fixed set of expert demonstration. Distribution drift occurs in the truly offline setting. That means, the value function approximation networks and policy networks we use are trained only on a fixed distribution, while applying or testing the optimal policy will encounter a different distribution, as the policy will visit new states. The value function generates erroneous estimations for state-action pairs that do not appear in the expert set. This issue has been thoroughly studied in [17]. By constraining the degree of difference between the learned policy $\pi(a \mid s)$ and the expert policy $\pi_e(a \mid s)$, the state distribution drift can be controlled to a certain upper limit [22].

The constraint we use refers to BCQ [6]. The training procedure is described in Algorithm 2. The algorithm is a modification of DQN [18], approximating the state action value function with a neural network $Q$ Parameterized with $\theta$, using TD-error with 1-step bootstrapping. The learning policy still chooses the action with the largest Q value, but the constraint is that the probability of selected actions is above a threshold $\tau$. The threshold $Pr(a)$ of discrete actions can be calculated as follows: $Pr(a) = p_b(a \mid s)/\max_{\hat{a}} p_b(\hat{a} \mid s)$, where $p_b$ is BC network trained on expert data $D$, it simply classifies actions with supervised learning, using cross-entropy loss. Policy $\pi$ can be described as:

$$\pi(s) = \underset{Pr(a) > \tau}{\mathrm{argmax}} Q_\theta(s, a). \tag{9}$$

The training loss of the Q network is as follows,

$$\mathcal{L}(\theta) = l\left(r + \gamma Q_{\theta', a' \mid Pr(a') > \tau}\left(s', a'\right) - Q_\theta(s, a)\right), \tag{10}$$

where $l$ is Huber loss. The algorithm shrinks to Q-learning when $\tau = 0$ and to complete BC when $\tau = 1$.

### 3.3 Batch-Constraint Inverse Reinforcement Learning Algorithm (BCIRL)

Algorithm 3 shows our proposed Batch-Constraint Inverse Reinforcement Learning Algorithm (BCIRL) method for completely offline setup. BCIRL uses deep

---

**Algorithm 2:** Batch Constraint Q-Learning

---

    **Input**   : Expert demonstration $D$, reward weights $\omega$, maximum iterations $T$,
               threshold $\tau$
    **Output**: optimal policy $\pi_\theta$

1  Random Initial:$Q$-network $\theta$,probability network $p_b$;
2  **for** $t = 0$ **to** $T$ **do**
3      Sample batch B $\{(s, a, s')\}$ from $D$;
4      Compute reward $r_i(s, a) = \omega_i^T \phi(s, a)$;
5      Choose next action using Equation 9;
6      Update $Q$ network using loss in Equation 10;
7      Update $P_b$ network using loss $-\sum_{(s,a)\in B} \log p_b(a \mid s)$;
8  **end**

---

neural networks to estimate feature expectations (described in Sect. 3.1) for intermediate policies with an off-policy approach suitable for offline settings. Then it updates the reward weights to minimize the difference of feature expectation between the experts and intermediate policies. This optimization step can be seen as an inverse reinforcement learning process where we attempt to guess the reward function that the expert is optimizing. Let $\mu_e$ be the expert feature expectation, $\mu_i$ be the intermediate feature expectation. Maximizing the margin is equivalent to solving a quadratic program:

$$\max_{t,\omega} t \quad \text{s.t.} \quad \omega^T \mu_e \geq \omega^T \mu_i + t, i = 0, \ldots, i - 1 \quad \text{and} \quad \|w\|_2 \leq 1, \qquad (11)$$

where $t$ denotes the value function margin between expert and intermediate policy. Abbeel et al. [1] proves that the algorithm will end at finite step (assumed to be n) and that the algorithm's performance under the returned reward differs from the expert performance by no more than $t^{(n)}$. We record the intermediate results, the final output are the policy and reward weights corresponding to the minimum margin $t_{min}$.

---

**Algorithm 3:** Batch-Constraint Inverse Reinforcement Learning

---

    **Input**   : convergence threshold $\epsilon$, maximum iterations $n$
    **Output**: reward weights $\omega^*$, optimal policy $\pi^*$(parameterized by $\theta$)

1  **for** $i = 0$ **to** $n$ **do**
2      Estimate $\mu_\psi^{\pi_i}$ using Algorithm 1;
3      Compute reward weights $\omega_i$ using Equation 11;
4      **if** $t < \epsilon$ **then** break Update $\pi_{i+1}$ with reward $r_i(s, a) = \omega_i^T \phi(s, a)$ using
      Algorithm 2;
5  **end**

---

# 4   Experiments

We verify the effectiveness of our method in two aspects: (1) whether it can obtain near-optimal policies, and (2) whether it can recover a reasonable reward function. To evaluate (1), we perform experiments on the simulated environment the OpenAI gym [4]. (2) is not easy to verify because there are few explicit reward functions about the features in the simulation environment. And the true rewards in the real world are even more unavailable for us. Therefore, we perform the demonstration in a toy grid world environment to explicitly see the recovered rewards.

## 4.1   Standard Control Environments

**Benchmarks.** We consider the following four baselines: LSTD-$\mu$+LSPI [12], SCIRL [13], DSFN [16], which recover reward and optimal policy in an offline setting, and Behavior Cloning(BC). LSTD-$\mu$ estimates feature expectations by off-policy evaluation using LSTD and solves MDP with Least-Squares Policy Iteration (LSPI). SCIRL approximates the Q-function offline directly by a linear score metric classifier, it still estimates feature expectations using LSTD. DSFN uses a deep neural network to estimate feature expectations and uses DQN to get an optimal policy. Since DSFN does not converge if there is no warm-start and feature extraction, we still initialize the policy and extract features for DSFN.

**Training Details.** Three neural networks are used to approximate: feature expectation $\mu$, state action value function $Q$, and supervised classification network $Pr$, respectively. Since the first two networks are modifications of the DQN, they have common hyper-parameters. We adopt 3-layered full-connected network with a hidden layer of 256 for each network. In addition, a 80–20 training-validation split is used in feature expectation network, the training termination threshold $\delta$ is set to 0.01. In Q network, action selection threshold $\tau$ is set to 0.1. We choose three control tasks: CartPole-v0, MountainCar-v0, Acrobot-v1. We first use DQN to obtain the best policy and then utilize this policy to produce demonstration data. We collect in total 1000 demonstration episodes and then use 1, 10, 100, and 1000 episodes as training input respectively. We do not access the simulator anymore once the data has been collected.

Figure 2 shows the test results of the learned policies on the three control tasks. Our model outperforms the benchmark in all tasks, reaching near-optimal performance even when the amount of data is small (except in the case of episodes of 1 under the MountainCar-v0 task, we conjecture that the agent car experiences the same location several times in the MountainCar-v0 environment, and the expert actions may be inconsistent at each experience, the learning policy cannot determine the optimal action with very little expert data). LSTD-$\mu$ and SCIRL perform poorly because least squares estimation is highly sensitive to data distribution and basis features. And the state-of-art method DSFN will not converge at all if there is no warm-start. We attempt to explain the meaning of the recovered reward. There are four raw features of the CartPole-v0 environment: cart position, cart velocity, pole angle and pole velocity at tip. The normalized parameters recovered by the algorithm are: –0.3, –0.3, –0.8, –0.3. The episode will end when the angle of the pole reaches ±41.8°, therefore the reward function has the largest penalty factor for this feature.

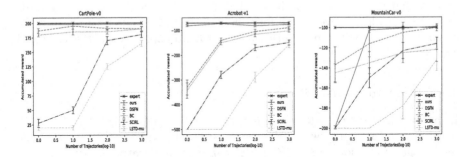

**Fig. 2.** The performance is the average of 5 random seeds and the error bars show a standard error, showing results for 1, 10, 100 and 1000 demonstration episodes. All the baselines were initialized with TRIL [16], the numerical results are identical to those in Lee et al. [16].

We split the expert data into train-test sets of 80-20. Table 1 shows action matching accuracy over 1000 expert trajectories. Action matching is calculated as the proportion of same actions selected by the expert policy and the learning policy on the test set. The policies learned by BCIRL can best match the behavior of the experts.

**Table 1.** Action matching accuracy in control environment

|         | CartPole-v0 | MountainCar-v0 | Acrobot-v1 |
|---------|-------------|----------------|------------|
| BCIRL   | **94 ± 1%** | **81 ± 3%**    | **90 ± 1%** |
| DSFN    | 89 ± 3%     | 80 ± 2%        | 83 ± 3%    |
| BC      | 83 ± 3%     | 75 ± 3%        | 80 ± 4%    |
| LSTD-mu | 65 ± 5%     | 45 ± 4%        | 55 ± 4%    |
| SCIRL   | 66 ± 4%     | 40 ± 4%        | 61 ± 3%    |

### 4.2  Gridworld Example

We learn the optimal policy with value iteration and generate 100 episodes of expert trajectories, then apply BCIRL to the grid world environment with the reward discount of 0.5. The raw state of gridworld (vertical coordinates $x$, horizontal coordinate $y$ ) is treated as the feature, and the final recovered reward function is $r = -0.54x + 0.84y$ when we put sparse reward endpoint at the top right corner, $r = 0.65x + 0.76y$ when the sparse reward endpoint is put at the bottom right corner. Figure 3 plots heat-maps of the ground truth reward and the recovered reward. The recovered linear reward replaces the original sparse reward, both of which can guide the RL algorithm to the optimal policy. Our algorithm establishes whether rewards and features are positively or negatively correlated, while assigning certain reward weights to features.

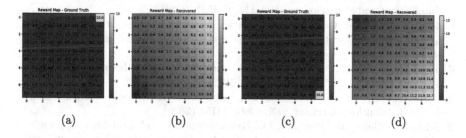

(a)                  (b)                  (c)                  (d)

**Fig. 3.** (a) and (c) depict the ground truth reward, (b) and (d) are the recovered reward map. The BCIRL recovers the sparse reward with a linear reward function approximation.

## 5   Conclusion

In this paper, we introduce an offline IRL algorithm, BCIRL, to recover the implicit reward function from expert demonstrations and to obtain near-expert policies. BCIRL constrains the probability of actions selection in off-policy evaluation to mitigate the drift of the state distribution. We demonstrate that BCIRL performs strongly in control environments, that recovered rewards provide useful insights on experts' preferences. However, our approach still has some limitations that will be improved in the future. For example, we assume that the reward function is linear which should be extended to a more flexible functional form in the future. For future works, It seems promising to explore the connection of the batch reinforcement learning and the inverse reinforcement learning. The data-driven approach batch reinforcement learning has attracted extensive research, such as [15,24].

## References

1. Abbeel, P., Ng, A.Y.: Apprenticeship learning via inverse reinforcement learning. In: Proceedings of the Twenty-First International Conference on Machine learning, p. 1 (2004)
2. Bain, M., Sammut, C.: A framework for behavioural cloning. Mach. Intell. **15**, 103–129 (1995)
3. Bica, I., Jarrett, D., Hüyük, A., Schaar, M.: Batch inverse reinforcement learning using counterfactuals for understanding decision making. arXiv:abs/2007.13531 (2020)

4. Brockman, G., et al.: Openai gym. arXiv:1606.01540 (2016)
5. Chan, A.J., van der Schaar, M.: Scalable bayesian inverse reinforcement learning. arXiv:2102.06483 (2021)
6. Fujimoto, S., Meger, D., Precup, D.: Off-policy deep reinforcement learning without exploration. In: International Conference on Machine Learning, pp. 2052–2062. PMLR (2019)
7. Goodfellow, I.J., et al.: Generative adversarial nets. In: NIPS (2014)
8. Herman, M., Gindele, T., Wagner, J., Schmitt, F., Burgard, W.: Inverse reinforcement learning with simultaneous estimation of rewards and dynamics. In: Artificial Intelligence and Statistics, pp. 102–110. PMLR (2016)
9. Ho, J., Ermon, S.: Generative adversarial imitation learning. In: Proceedings of the 30th International Conference on Neural Information Processing Systems, pp. 4572–4580 (2016)
10. Hussein, A., Gaber, M.M., Elyan, E., Jayne, C.: Imitation learning: a survey of learning methods. ACM Compu. Surv. **50**(2), 1–35 (2017)
11. Jarrett, D., Bica, I., van der Schaar, M.: Strictly batch imitation learning by energy-based distribution matching. arXiv:2006.14154 (2020)
12. Klein, E., Geist, M., Pietquin, O.: Batch, off-policy and model-free apprenticeship learning. In: European Workshop on Reinforcement Learning. pp. 285–296. Springer (2011). https://doi.org/10.1007/978-3-642-29946-9_28
13. Klein, E., Piot, B., Geist, M., Pietquin, O.: A cascaded supervised learning approach to inverse reinforcement learning. In: Joint European Conference on Machine Learning and Knowledge Discovery in Databases, pp. 1–16. Springer (2013). https://doi.org/10.1007/978-3-642-40988-2_1
14. Kostrikov, I., Nachum, O., Tompson, J.: Imitation learning via off-policy distribution matching. In: International Conference on Learning Representations (2019)
15. Kumar, A., Fu, J., Tucker, G., Levine, S.: Stabilizing off-policy q-learning via bootstrapping error reduction. arXiv:1906.00949 (2019)
16. Lee, D., Srinivasan, S., Doshi-Velez, F.: Truly batch apprenticeship learning with deep successor features. arXiv:1903.10077 (2019)
17. Levine, S., Kumar, A., Tucker, G., Fu, J.: Offline reinforcement learning: tutorial, review, and perspectives on open problems. arXiv:2005.01643 (2020)
18. Mnih, V., et al.: Human-level control through deep reinforcement learning. Nature **518**(7540), 529–533 (2015)
19. Ng, A.Y., Russell, S.J., et al.: Algorithms for inverse reinforcement learning. In: Icml, vol. 1, p. 2 (2000)
20. Ross, S., Gordon, G., Bagnell, D.: A reduction of imitation learning and structured prediction to no-regret online learning. In: Proceedings of the Fourteenth International Conference on Artificial Intelligence and Statistics, pp. 627–635. JMLR Workshop and Conference Proceedings (2011)
21. Russell, S.: Learning agents for uncertain environments. In: Proceedings of the Eleventh Annual Conference on Computational Learning Theory, pp. 101–103 (1998)
22. Schulman, J., Levine, S., Abbeel, P., Jordan, M., Moritz, P.: Trust region policy optimization. In: International Conference on Machine Learning, pp. 1889–1897. PMLR (2015)
23. Sutton, R.S., Barto, A.G.: Reinforcement Learning: An Introduction. MIT press (2018)
24. Wu, Y., Tucker, G., Nachum, O.: Behavior regularized offline reinforcement learning. arXiv:1911.11361 (2019)

# KG-RL: A Knowledge-Guided Reinforcement Learning for Massive Battle Games

Shiyang Zhou[1,2]🆔, Weiya Ren[1,2(✉)]🆔, Xiaoguang Ren[1,2], Xianya Mi[1,2], and Xiaodong Yi[1,2]

[1] Artificial Intelligence Research Center, Defense Innovation Institute, Beijing 100072, China
[2] Tianjin Artificial Intelligence Innovation Center, Tianjin 300457, China

**Abstract.** In a multi-agent game, the complexity of the environment increases exponentially as the number of agents increases. Learning becomes difficult when there are so many agents. Mean field multi-agent reinforcement learning (MFRL) uses the average action of the neighbors to increase the input of the value network, which can be applied in the environment with hundreds of agents. However, inefficient exploration and slow convergence speed limit the performance of the algorithm. In this article, we propose a new **K**nowledge-**G**uided **R**einforcement Learning (KG-RL) method, which can be divided into *rule-mix* and *plan-extend*. We use the *rule-mix* to encode knowledge into plans which can reduce redundant information and invalid actions in the state. And the *plan-extend* can combine the result of *rule-mix* with reinforcement learning to achieve more efficient joint exploration. Through experiments in Magent environment, we prove that the win rate of our proposed KG-RL is 22% higher than that of knowledge-based decision tree and 39% higher than that of MFRL. Thus, the KG-RL can perform well in massive battle games due to its high exploration efficiency and fast convergence.

**Keywords:** Knowledge-guided · Reinforcement learning · Multi-agent · Massive battle games

## 1 Introduction

In recent years, multi-agent reinforcement learning (MARL) has made remarkable progress in various tasks [3,6,18]. However, learning in an environment of multiple agents is still fundamentally difficult, because agents not only interact with the environment, but also with each other [12]. With the increase number of agents, the policy space expands rapidly, and the simultaneous learning of multiple agents makes the environment non-stationary, which brings great difficulties for each agent to find the convergence policy [6], especially when the number of agents is huge.

Due to the limitation of the network size which increases linearly when the number of agents increases [11], the current popular methods, such as MADDPG [12],

© Springer Nature Switzerland AG 2021
D. N. Pham et al. (Eds.): PRICAI 2021, LNAI 13033, pp. 83–94, 2021.
https://doi.org/10.1007/978-3-030-89370-5_7

QMIX [15], etc., are often limited by the number of agents. Thus, the algorithm represented by Independent Q-learning [17] directly treats other agents and the environment as a whole. However, due to the instability caused by the other agents' changing policies, the algorithm cannot converge stably. MFRL [21] proposes a provably-converged mean-field formulation to scale up the actor-critic framework by feeding the state and the average value of nearby agents' actions to the critic, enhancing the stability of learning. However, the average actions of other agents in the execution process will be obtained by communication, which is not easy.

In addition, incorporating human knowledge into reinforcement learning is a good way. Purely knowledge-based approaches, such as decision trees, often require a mass of human labor and expertise knowledge, while reinforcement learning (RL) has a strong ability of sustainable learning. Recently, there has been a lot of work in this area. DARLING [8] proposes a method in which candidate solutions are generated by the planner and then merged and passed to the reinforcement learning module to learn the final approximate policy. However, the effect of this method has a lot to do with the design of the planner. Bougie [1] used additional knowledge as a supervision signal for network learning, and enhanced the information provided to the agent by introducing human expertise, but this supervision signal would interfere with the original training target of the network. Xie [20] proposed to train an additional network to make decisions from knowledge-based policy or the policy learned by the DDPG [9] algorithm. However, adding a network means increasing training difficulty and training time, which runs counter to the original intention of using human knowledge. In addition, these methods all need to provide a complete solution covering all states based on human knowledge, and do not consider about the situation when the number of agents is huge.

In this article, we define the knowledge that can only give actions in some states as *rules*, and the knowledge that has corresponding actions in all states as *plan*. Then we propose a new **K**nowledge-**G**uided **R**einforcement **L**earning (KG-RL) method for massive battle games, which includes Rule-Mix and Plan-Extend modules. The difference from the previous method is that we only need to design some effective rules instead of manually designing a complete solution. We designed a rule-mix module based on the hypernetwork structure in Qmix [15], which can learn more complex logical relationships than manually designed decision trees and reduce subjective bias of people. Then a plan-extend module is designed by extending the exploration policy of Actor-Critic (AC) [14] algorithm. It uses actor's policy and plan policies for joint exploration through a selector, which increases the exploration efficiency of reinforcement learning and accelerates the convergence speed of the algorithm. Through experiments in the Magent environment, we prove that the win rate of KG-RL is 22% higher than rule-based decision tree and 39% higher than the best-performing MFAC in pure reinforcement learning. The main contributions of this paper can be summarized as follows.

- We innovatively propose the rule-mix module, which uses a hypernetwork structure to learn more complex logical relationships between rules. It improves the win rate by 17% over the rule-based decision tree;

- We innovatively propose the plan-extend module. It combines rule-mix with actor-critic for joint exploration and enhances the exploration efficiency of the algorithm. The model with plan-extend improves the win rate by 22%;
- The KG-RL (rule-mix+plan-extend) method we proposed achieves the highest win rate in the Magent environment, which is 39% higher than the previous best method MFRL in this environment.

## 2   Related Work

An important cluster of related research is the research on the scalability of MARL. Based on graph convolutional neural network, [13] divided agents into different domains, and the impact of dimensional explosion is reduced by reducing the number of agents in the domain; [10] combine the attention mechanism with reinforcement learning, so that the agent can only consider about a part of the agent which is most relevant to itself, rather than all of them. However, these methods are all learned from scratch, and the number of agents that can support is limited [11], which cannot be applied to the environment where there are hundreds of agents.

Recent years, there has been a lot of research on combining human domain knowledge with RL, such as [2,19] combine knowledge graph with reinforcement learning in recommendation. PROLONETS [16] proposes a new network structure by embedding human knowledge, and realizes the dynamic change of network depth by adding random decision nodes. This method needs to design the structure of decision tree manually, which requires a high level of human technology. Based on QMix, RMLPE [5] expands the action space of RL with the selection of rules, leverages the Q-value in RL as a uniform criterion to judge the value of rules and original actions. The method is convenient to implement, but the expansion of the action space increases the difficulty of learning.

## 3   Method

In many tasks, the state returned by the environment contains a lot of redundant information, and the original action space also contains many invalid and illegal action options. Therefore, it is necessary to encode some rules from the original state space and action space through people's understanding of the task. By mixing these rules through the rule-mix module, we can quickly get some strategies based on human knowledge, called *plan 1*, *plan 2*.... In order to enhance their exploration capability, we combine them with the Actor-Critic [14] algorithm to reduce the invalid exploration, and accelerate the convergence speed of the algorithm. This method is collectively called KG-RL, and the overall structure is shown in Fig. 1.

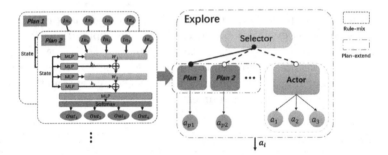

**Fig. 1.** The overall structure of KG-RL. Rules is combined into *plan* through rule-mix, and then plan-extend combine the *plan* with actor in RL for more efficient joint exploration.

### 3.1   Rule-Mix

The original input often contains a lot of information and is not easy to process. For example, for image input, we often only care about the content of the picture, and it is quite time-consuming to directly input the entire image into the network for end-to-end training. Besides we can use existing algorithms or common sense to get some information that is helpful for decision-making. We first form the method of extracting these more valuable information into decision modules, which is represented by the function $In_i(s)$, as shown in Table 1.

Similarly, the original action space directly uses the most direct actions like up, down, left, right and attack, which does not contain any knowledge. Therefore, in some cases, many invalid or illegal actions are often selected. Especially in some environments, the cost of illegal actions is high. However, these invalid and illegal actions are intuitive and easy to judge for humans in many problems, such as suicide operations in games. Thus, we can embed human knowledge into simple actions and form rules. We call these nodes which finally determine the output action as action modules. They are represented by the function $Out_i(s)$, as shown in Table 1.

Inspired by QMix, we also design a hypernetwork in rule-mix, which uses state $s$ to generate weight $W_i$ and bias $B_i$ through MLP, as shown in the left part of Fig. 1. We combine $W_i$ and $B_i$ with the decision module, which can be calculated as Eq. (1). This hypernetwork structure correlates the state $s$ with the decision module $In_i$ through multiplication, by which an additional representation of the current state is integrated into the gradient of $In_i$, so that more information can be provided [23].

$$Hypernet\_out = Relu((W_i * in_i(s)) + B_i), \tag{1}$$

Then, the output of the hypernetwork is processed through a Softmax layer, and the probability of each action module is output of the latter. Finally, the AC algorithm is used to train the network, and the goal is to maximize the long-term return. The role of the hypernetwork is to generate a logical structure similar to a decision tree. With the powerful representation ability of deep neural network, the hypernetwork designed by us can represent a more complex logical structure than decision tree. This is an important reason why rule-mix performs better than regular manual rules.

## 3.2   Plan-Extend

Actor-critic algorithm uses a stochastic policy for discrete actions, and actor output the probability of each action. It is explored by sampling distribution of the actor. In the early stage of training, the actor network contains less information. The exploration based on the actor is almost equivalent to random exploration, which is inefficient. Due to the low probability of success, rewards are often sparse. This seriously affects the learning speed of the network. Therefore, we can combine a actor policy with the rule-based policies for joint exploration. Furthermore, we design a *selector* to choose the exploration policy.

We call the rule-based strategies obtained by rule-mix as *Planj*. *Selector* decides to choose *Planj* or the current actor's policy to interact with the environment. Specifically, the *selector* determines the final action interaction with the environment, as shown in Fig. 1. We can make a selection at each step or at the end of each episode. The goal of selection is to choose the current better policy, so that better samples can be generated and the convergence speed of the algorithm can be accelerated.

Our goal is to use *Planj* to explore when the actor's policy is not as good as *Planj*. Thus *selector* can be a predefined function, or an adaptive variable. In this article, we define it as a variable, which is selected by evaluation after each round of training. When the win rate of the actor's policy is lower than that of the *Planj* in the last 30 evaluations, the *Planj* is selected for exploration. Otherwise, the current actor's policy is selected.

It is important to note that the *selector* and *Planj* here are only used to interact with the environment to generate trajectories $T(s_t, a_t, r_t, s_{t+1}, done)$, which is not included in the final reinforcement learning training model. Secondly, the *Planj* uses deterministic rules, which means $P(a_t^p|s_t) = 1.0, \forall s_t$. So that the importance sampling rate $c$ can be represented as $c = \frac{\pi(a_t|s_t)}{P(a_t|s_t)} = \pi(a_t|s_t)$. Therefore, the trajectory got by *Planj* can directly be used for Actor-Critic algorithm updates. We call this method plan-extend which is shown in the right part of Fig. 1.

# 4   Experiment Setup

## 4.1   Environment

We conduct experiments in the Magent [22] environment, which is a confrontation environment of large-scale agents. In the experiment, we use a $40 \times 40$ map. At the beginning, there are 64 agents on each side, and they will not be supplemented after death in battle. The termination condition is that one party is completely wiped out or the maximum step of episode is reached. When the terminal state is reached, the one with more surviving agents wins.

There are two parts in the agent's observation. One is a 7-channel $13 \times 13$ matrix representing obstacles, teammates, teammates' HP, own mini map, opponent location, opponent's HP, opponent's mini map, the other is a 34 dimensional feature vector including ID embedding, last action, last reward and position. The 21 actions of the agent include 13 movable positions and 8 attackable positions around the agent. The reward setting in learning is the same as in MFRL[1].

## 4.2 Human Knowledge Based Module Design

In the Magent environment, we use the rules of human experience in the battle problem: attack only when there is an enemy within the attack range; give priority to attacking the enemy with the least HP or the nearest distance; in order to strengthen cooperation, people will approach teammates; for better survive, humans will pay attention to their blood volume in time. Based on the above human knowledge, we abstract the reules into the decision module $In_i$ and action module $Out_i$ as shown in Table 1.

**Table 1.** The decision modules and action modules we used in the experiment.

| $i$ | $In_i(s)$ | $Out_i(s)$ |
|---|---|---|
| 1 | Are there any opponents in attack range | Attack the enemy with the least health |
| 2 | Are there any opponents in observation | Move to the nearest opponent |
| 3 | Are there any teammates in view | Move to the teammate with the least health |
| 4 | Is my current health more than half | Move to the opponent with the least health |
| 5 | Whether the number of our agents is greater than that of the opponent | Move to the opponent with the least health |
| 6 | Whether the last action is an attack action | Attack any one within range |

## 4.3 Experiment Settings

In the experiment, agents in the same team share parameters. We use Adam optimizer with a learning rate of $1 \times 10^{-4}$. The discount factor $\gamma$ is 0.95. For value-based methods (MFQ, DQN, RMLPE [5]), the batch size is set to 64, and the buffer contains the most recent 80000 transitions. All models are trained for 2000 rounds of self-plays, and then are used for battles.

Through the combination of human knowledge modules (rules), we can manually design a decision tree based on human knowledge as shown in Fig. 3 as **Baseline**. Experiments have proved that even this simple rule-base decision tree performs better than other algorithms which are trained from scratch. In addition, we also selected MFRL and RMLPE [5] for comparison. The MFRL is the current state-of-the-art method in this environment and the RMLPE is another practical method based on human domain knowledge.

---

[1] https://github.com/mlii/mfrl

# 5   Experimental Results

Winning or losing is a good condition for judging in the battle environment, and it is also the most valuable indicator. Therefore, we first use the models trained by each algorithm to play against each other. Then, with the Baseline as the opponent, the model improvement speed of each model was compared in the training phase. In addition, we also compared the output policies of rule-mix and the Baseline to show the differences between them. Furthermore, we study the influence of different decisions and action modules. Finally, we analyzed the behavior of the model combined with the battle playback.

## 5.1   Battle Game

In this experiment, we directly use the models trained by each algorithm for comparison. In order to reduce random errors, we trained three models for each algorithm, named Algo 1, Algo 2, and Algo 3. In each round we randomly choose two from all the models to have a battle. At the end of the experimentation, we get a total of 200,000 duels. In addition to the number of wins for each model, we also record the number of kills and be killed by each model.

**Table 2.** Result of battle

|            | Elo score | Wins   | Draws | Totalls | Win rate | Killed  | Be_killed | Kill_ratio |
|------------|-----------|--------|-------|---------|----------|---------|-----------|------------|
| KG-RL 1    | **2521**  | 15104  | 79    | 16792   | 90.42%   | **1039159** | 634900  | **1.64**   |
| KG-RL 2    | 2498      | 15070  | 72    | 16715   | 90.59%   | 1034676 | 636241    | 1.63       |
| KG-RL 3    | 2409      | **15208** | 66  | 16766   | **91.10%** | 1038573 | 637606  | 1.63       |
| Rule_Mix 3 | 2351      | 14539  | 71    | 16807   | 86.93%   | 1031148 | 653521    | 1.58       |
| Rule_Mix 2 | 2322      | 14348  | 85    | 16677   | 86.54%   | 1022675 | 650434    | 1.57       |
| Rule_Mix 1 | 2242      | 14430  | 85    | 16732   | 86.75%   | 1025922 | 654432    | 1.57       |
| Baseline 1 | 1848      | 11257  | 101   | 16496   | 68.85%   | 909402  | 620709    | 1.47       |
| Baseline 3 | 1769      | 11454  | 106   | 16809   | 68.77%   | 926807  | 635147    | 1.46       |
| Baseline 2 | 1749      | 11413  | 114   | 16558   | 69.62%   | 913718  | 621215    | 1.47       |
| MFAC 3     | 1344      | 8407   | 131   | 16596   | 51.45%   | 869221  | 755577    | 1.15       |
| MFAC 1     | 1299      | 8570   | 132   | 16638   | 52.30%   | 874899  | 748140    | 1.17       |
| AC 3       | 1288      | 7770   | 159   | 16615   | 47.72%   | 835245  | 781361    | 1.07       |
| MFAC 2     | 1268      | 8688   | 160   | 16857   | 52.49%   | 886280  | 760472    | 1.17       |
| AC 1       | 1227      | 7866   | 161   | 16751   | 47.92%   | 843229  | 785245    | 1.07       |
| AC 2       | 1169      | 7670   | **170** | 16554 | 47.36%   | 830664  | 778978    | 1.07       |
| MFQ 3      | 842       | 3824   | 44    | 16414   | 23.57%   | 623389  | 931098    | 0.67       |
| MFQ 1      | 804       | 3849   | 46    | 16470   | 23.65%   | 625485  | 934899    | 0.67       |
| MFQ 2      | 802       | 4078   | 53    | 16528   | 24.99%   | 632251  | 931803    | 0.68       |
| RMLPE 1    | 774       | 2910   | 6     | **16942** | 17.21% | 380365  | 939619    | 0.40       |
| RMLPE 2    | 655       | 2786   | 3     | 16715   | 16.69%   | 368833  | 929389    | 0.40       |
| DQN 1      | 633       | 2269   | 96    | 16622   | 14.23%   | 480286  | 863041    | 0.56       |
| DQN 3      | 617       | 2293   | 121   | 16715   | 14.44%   | 485276  | 867214    | 0.56       |
| DQN 2      | 614       | 2266   | 111   | 16543   | 14.37%   | 481625  | 856605    | 0.56       |
| RMLPE 3    | 552       | 2842   | 6     | 16688   | 17.07%   | 374305  | 925787    | 0.40       |

In addition, learning from [4,7], we also use ELO ratings to describe the performance of each agent, as commonly used in both traditional games like chess and in competitive video game ranking and matchmaking services. Assuming that the current grade scores of agent $A$ and agent $B$ are $R_A$ and $R_B$ respectively, then the expected win rate of agent $A$ to $B$, according to Logistic distribution, should be:

$$E_A = \frac{1}{1 + 10^{(R_A - R_B)/400}}. \tag{2}$$

If agent's grade is adjusted accordingly, the specific mathematical formula is $R'_A = R_A + K(S_A - E_A)$. At the masters level $K$ is usually 16. In order to create a gap between agents, we set it to 32 here.

The result of the battle is shown in Table 2. It shows that the KG-RL (rule-mix+plan-extend) we proposed is better than other methods in terms of ELO scoring, win rate, or KD ratio. In particular, KG-RL and rule-mix are better than the Baseline. On the contrary, other methods starting from scratch is not as good as the Baseline. This illustrates the huge potential of embedding human knowledge into RL.

### 5.2   Comparison of Training Process

Because each algorithm is trained by self-play. The model itself is constantly changing when it is updated. In order to evaluate the convergence speed of each algorithm, we let the model play a round against the Baseline after each round of training. Then we calculate the win rate of the last 30 rounds. It can be seen from Fig. 2 that KG-RL converges the fastest, and stably reaching a win rate of 1.0 at 500 steps. In the end, only rule-mix and KG-RL have a winning percentage of 1.0. This shows the good performance of reinforcement learning based on human knowledge.

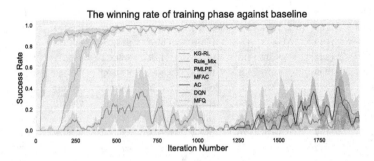

**Fig. 2.** The win rate of each algorithm when Baseline is used as opponent. We calculate the win rate of the last 30 rounds after each round of training.

### 5.3   Model Differences

We count the output frequency of rule-mix and the Baseline on different action modules. Through the different selection actions of each model in Table 3, we can find that the network after learning is quite different from the decision tree we manually designed. This is because the neural network can learn more complex logical relationships, corresponding to better strategies.

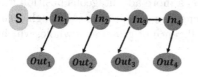

**Fig. 3.** Decision tree built from human knowledge, which we used as Baseline in experiment.

**Table 3.** Selection ratio of each action module

|         | Baseline | | Rule_Mix | |
|---------|----------|--------|----------|--------|
|         | Times | Rate | Times | Rate |
| $Out_1$ | 13925 | 32.60% | 13561 | 34.16% |
| $Out_2$ | 17726 | 41.50% | 14316 | 36.06% |
| $Out_3$ | 840 | 1.96% | 10659 | 26.85% |
| $Out_4$ | 10214 | 23.91% | 1165 | 2.93% |

## 5.4 The Influence of Different Decisions and Action Modules

The different choices of the decision module and the action module have different effects on the algorithm. We named the models that used the decision modules $(In_1, In_2, In_3, In_4)$, $(In_1, In_2)$ and the model without the decision module as *rule_mix_in4*, *rule_mix_in2* and *rule_mix_in0* respectively. Figure 4 shows their training curve. It can be seen that the more input modules used, the faster the convergence the algorithm will be. The added decision-making module reduces the redundant information in the original state, providing more concise and more valuable information for the network, which accelerates the learning speed of the network.

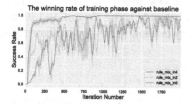

**Fig. 4.** Comparison of models using different decision modules.

**Table 4.** Comparison of models using different action modules.

| Models | ELO score | Win rate |
|--------|-----------|----------|
| rule_mix_out 1 | 1586 | 82% |
| rule_mix_out 2 | 1268 | 21% |
| rule_mix_out 3 | 1369 | 43% |
| rule_mix_out 4 | 1479 | 51% |

We named the models that used action modules $(Out_1, Out_2, Out_3, Out_4)$, $(Out_1, Out_2, Out_3, Out_5)$, $(Out_2, Out_3, Out_4, Out_5)$, $(Out_2, Out_3, Out_4, Out_6)$ as *rule_mix_out1*, *rule_mix_out2*, *rule_mix_out3*, *rule_mix_out4*, respectively. Table 4 shows a comparison of the win rate of the trained models. It can be seen that choosing different output modules will have different effects on the final models. In this article, *rule_mix_out1* performs best, so its corresponding action modules are also used in other experiments.

## 5.5   Discussion

As shown in Fig. 5, these are screenshots of a battle between KG-RL and MFAC. It can be seen that KG-RL (in red) formed a semi-encircled state of the opponent from the beginning. This semi-encirclement is a more advantageous position for agents to concentrate their firepower and strengthen cooperation. Although each agent is trained separately, it shows the intelligence of group as a whole, which is meaningful.

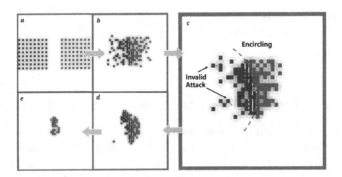

**Fig. 5.** These are screenshots of a battle between KG-RL (red) and MFAC (blue). At the beginning of battle, two group are initialized in a symmetrical position on the left and right. In order to show the details, *c*) enlarges one of the screenshots. (Color figure online)

Secondly, by observing the local actions of agents, we can see that MFAC (in blue) has more ineffective attacks (attacks no-one's areas) than KG-RL. Taking advantage of human rules, KG-RL directly shields those invalid and illegal actions through rule-mix, which reduces the exploration space of the algorithm.

## 6   Conclusion

In this article, we propose a knowledge-guided reinforcement learning method for massive agent battle games, named KG-RL, which can be divided into rule-mix and plan-extend. The hypernetwork structure in the rule-mix can obtain more complex logical relationships than manually designed decision trees. The plan-extend can combine the result of rule-mix with reinforcement learning to achieve more efficient joint exploration. In fact, the experimental results has proved it. In the Magent environment, it shows that the win rate of KG-RL is 22% higher than rule-based decision tree and 39% higher than the best-performing MFAC in pure reinforcement learning. In the future, it will be meaningful to study the design and evaluation of rule modules. In addition, we will continue to conduct research on the automation of rule module design.

**Acknowledgment.** This work was partly supported by both National Key Research and Development Program of China (Grant No.2019AAA0104800) and NSFC under grant No. 91648204.

# References

1. Bougie, N., Ichise, R.: Deep reinforcement learning boosted by external knowledge. In: Proceedings of the 33rd Annual ACM Symposium on Applied Computing, pp. 331–338 (2018)
2. Chen, X., Huang, C., Yao, L., Wang, X., Zhang, W., et al.: Knowledge-guided deep reinforcement learning for interactive recommendation. In: 2020 International Joint Conference on Neural Networks (IJCNN), pp. 1–8. IEEE (2020)
3. Ecoffet, A., Huizinga, J., Lehman, J., Stanley, K.O., Clune, J.: First return, then explore. Nature **590**(7847), 580–586 (2021)
4. Elo, A.E.: The rating of chessplayers, past and present. Arco Pub. (1978)
5. Han, X., Tang, H., Li, Y., Kou, G., Liu, L.: Improving multi-agent reinforcement learning with imperfect human knowledge. In: International Conference on Artificial Neural Networks, pp. 369–380. Springer (2020). https://doi.org/10.1007/978-3-030-61616-8_30
6. Hernandez-Leal, P., Kartal, B., Taylor, M.E.: A survey and critique of multiagent deep reinforcement learning
7. Jaderberg, M., Czarnecki, W., Dunning, I., Marris, L., Lever, G., Castaneda, A., et al.: Human-level performance in first-person multiplayer games with population-based deep reinforcement learning. arXiv:1807.01281 (2018)
8. Leonetti, M., Iocchi, L., Stone, P.: A synthesis of automated planning and reinforcement learning for efficient, robust decision-making. Artif. Intell. **241**, 103–130 (2016)
9. Lillicrap, T.P., et al.: Continuous control with deep reinforcement learning. arXiv:1509.02971 (2015)
10. Liu, Y., Wang, W., Hu, Y., Hao, J., Chen, X., Gao, Y.: Multi-agent game abstraction via graph attention neural network. In: Proceedings of the AAAI Conference on Artificial Intelligence, vol. 34, pp. 7211–7218 (2020)
11. Long, Q., Zhou, Z., Gupta, A., Fang, F., Wu, Y., Wang, X.: Evolutionary population curriculum for scaling multi-agent reinforcement learning. arXiv:2003.10423 (2020)
12. Lowe, R., Wu, Y., Tamar, A., Harb, J., Abbeel, P., Mordatch, I.: Multi-agent actor-critic for mixed cooperative-competitive environments. NIPS (2017)
13. Mao, H., et al.: Neighborhood cognition consistent multi-agent reinforcement learning. In: Proceedings of the AAAI Conference on Artificial Intelligence, vol. 34, pp. 7219–7226 (2020)
14. Mnih, V., et al.: Asynchronous methods for deep reinforcement learning. In: International Conference on Machine Learning, pp. 1928–1937. PMLR (2016)
15. Rashid, T., Samvelyan, M., Schroeder, C., Farquhar, G., Foerster, J., Whiteson, S.: Qmix: monotonic value function factorisation for deep multi-agent reinforcement learning. In: International Conference on Machine Learning, pp. 4295–4304. PMLR (2018)
16. Silva, A., Gombolay, M.: Neural-encoding human experts' domain knowledge to warm start reinforcement learning. arXiv:1902.06007 (2019)

17. Tan, M.: Multi-agent reinforcement learning: Independent vs. cooperative agents. In: Proceedings of the Tenth International Conference on Machine Learning. pp. 330–337 (1993)
18. Tang, Z., et al.: Discovering diverse multi-agent strategic behavior via reward randomization. arXiv:2103.04564 (2021)
19. Wang, P., Fan, Y., Xia, L., Zhao, W.X., Niu, S., Huang, J.: Kerl: a knowledge-guided reinforcement learning model for sequential recommendation. In: Proceedings of the 43rd International ACM SIGIR Conference on Research and Development in Information Retrieval, pp. 209–218 (2020)
20. Xie, L., et al.: Learning with stochastic guidance for navigation. arXiv:1811.10756 (2018)
21. Yang, Y., Rui, L., Li, M., Ming, Z., Wang, J.: Mean field multi-agent reinforcement learning (2018)
22. Zheng, L., et al.: Magent: A many-agent reinforcement learning platform for artificial collective intelligence. In: Proceedings of the AAAI Conference on Artificial Intelligence, vol. 32 (2018)
23. Zhou, M., Liu, Z., Sui, P., Li, Y., Chung, Y.Y.: Learning implicit credit assignment for cooperative multi-agent reinforcement learning (2020)

# Vision and Perception

# A Semi-supervised Defect Detection Method Based on Image Inpainting

Huibin Cao[1], Yongxuan Lai[1(✉)], Quan Chen[2], and Fan Yang[3]

[1] School of Informatics/Shenzhen Research Institute, Xiamen University,
Xiamen, China
bboyhb@stu.xmu.edu.cn, laiyx@xmu.edu.cn
[2] Department of Computer Science, Xiamen University Malaysia, Sepang, Malaysia
[3] Department of Automation, Xiamen University, Xiamen, China
yang@xmu.edu.cn

**Abstract.** Defect detection plays an important role in the industrial field. Because the defective images are often insufficient and defects can be various, defective image synthesis is commonly used and models always tend to learn the distribution of defects. However, the complexity of defective image synthesis and difficulty of detecting unseen defects are still the main challenges. To solve these problems, this paper proposes a semi-supervised defect detection method based on image inpainting, denoted as SDDII, which combines the training strategies of CycleGAN and Pix2Pix. First, we train a defect generator unsupervisedly to generate defective images. Second, we train the defect inpaintor supervisedly using the generated images. Finally, the defect inpaintor is used to inpainting the defects, and the defective areas can be segmented by comparing images before and after inpainting. Without ground truth for training, SDDII achieves better results than the naive CycleGAN, and comparable results with UNET which is supervised learning. In addition, SDDII learns the distribution of contents in defect-free images so it has good adaptability for defects unseen before.

**Keywords:** Defect detection · Automated optical inspection · Generative adversarial networks

## 1 Introduction

The defect detection is an important part to ensure product quality. Traditionally, this complex task is completed by manpower which is time-consuming and labor-consuming, where the accuracy is affected by subjective judgments of

This work was supported in part by the Natural Science Foundation of Guangdong under Grant 2021A1515011578; in part by the Natural Science Foundation of China under Grant 61672441 and Grant 61673324; in part by the Natural Science Foundation of Fujian under Grant 2018J01097; in part by the Shenzhen Basic Research Program under Grant JCYJ20170818141325209 and Grant JCYJ20190809161603551.

D. N. Pham et al. (Eds.): PRICAI 2021, LNAI 13033, pp. 97–108, 2021.
https://doi.org/10.1007/978-3-030-89370-5_8

workers and the efficiency depends on the physical condition of workers. In recent years, with the development of deep learning, more and more defect detection methods based on deep learning have been used to assist or even replace the traditional manpower to improve the accuracy and efficiency [1,3,15].

In industrial scenes, it cost a lot to collect and label defective images so the defective image synthesis is often used to help generate more data. However, defective image synthesis [8] is complicated and not general-purpose which needs to design exclusive method. Additionally, it is still challenging for model to recognize unseen defects even though the data is sufficient.

Recently, to reduce complexity of defective image synthesis, CycleGAN [26] is often used to generate defective images in an image-to-image manner by inputting defect-free images [18]. Through this method, the defective images can be inpainted back to defect-free images conveniently. By comparing the images before and after inpainting, the defective areas can be segmented. This method would make the model to learn the distribution of contents in defect-free images, instead of learning the distribution of defects. It is like to make the model to generate "mind-set", where the unseen contents in images will be inpainted. So this method can be good at detecting unseen defects. However, CycleGAN is trained in an unsupervised manner and the generated defective images are not utilized. It still has improvement space.

The main contribution of this paper is that we propose a semi-supervised method utilizing the generated defective images to further improve inpainting performance of CycleGAN [26]. Our method is denoted as SDDII, which stands for "Semi-supervised Defect Detection based on Image Inpainting". Firstly, CycleGAN is trained to generate the defective images and inpaint the defective images. Secondly, we introduce the training strategy of Pix2pix [7], which utilizes the generated defective images to supervisedly train the defect inpainting. Finally, the defects are segmented by comparing the images before and after inpainting. Experiments show that SDDII can achieve better results than the naive CycleGAN, and comparable results with the UNET which is supervised learning.

The rest of the paper is structured as follows: in Sect. 2, we review the literature examining the applications of GAN on defect detection. In Sect. 3 we outline the methodology employed, while in Sect. 4 we report the experiments and results. In Sect. 5, we make a brief summary of this paper.

## 2   Related Work

GAN [6] is a network proposed by Ian Goodfellow in 2014. Compared with other applications of convolutional network, such as image classification [19], object detection [4], semantic segmentation [16], GAN can generate new data by inputting random noise. Applications of GAN include face generation [23], super-resolution generation [25], image inpainting [10], etc. To some extent, GAN is a way of using reinforcement learning [9] to realize generative tasks. The ideas of GAN and the "Actor-Critic" algorithm in reinforcement learning [12] are similar, where actors are like generators in GAN, and critics are like discriminators in GAN, maintaining a game between actors (generators) and critics (discriminators) to achieve Nash equilibrium [20].

As GAN becomes more and more popular, GAN is gradually introduced into the field of defect detection [2,14,24]. The common application is defective image synthesis where defects are generated through GAN and pasted into the defect-free image. Defective image synthesis has the following disadvantages: the design process is complicated and the pasted images look fake. To overcome these, we use CycleGAN [26] to generate the defective images in an image-to-image manner where a forward mapping flow and a backward mapping flow form a circle. In this method [18], a generator in a CycleGAN is adopted to generate defective images first, then the other generator is used to inpaint defective images, finally the defective areas can be segmented by comparing the images before and after inpainting (as shown in Fig. 1). However, consistency loss ($LossF2$) and the adversarial loss ($LossB1$) are in two separated mapping flows which leads to an imbalance in the training of $DI$ (Defect Inpaintor). The performance of $DI$ has a direct impact on defect detection, so we aim to further improve the defect inpainting. At this research, we introduce the supervised training strategy of Pix2pix [7], where the consistency loss ($LossF4$) and the adversarial loss ($LossF3$) are combined together in forward mapping flow (as shown in Fig. 2) to improve the defect inpainting.

## 3 Methodology

### 3.1 Architecture

This paper proposes a semi-supervised defect detection method, denoted as SDDII, which combines the training strategies of CycleGAN [26] and Pix2Pix [7]. The training strategy of SDDII can be divided into two phases: the first phase is unsupervised phase which contains unsupervised defect generation and unsupervised defect inpainting. The second phase is supervised phase in which we train additional supervised defect inpainting.

The unsupervised phase is implemented with CycleGAN, as shown in Fig. 1. Through CycleGAN, data do not need to be collected in pairs [26]. Two generators in CycleGAN are defined as $DG$ (Defect Generator) and $DI$ (Defect Inpaintor), which are responsible for defect generation and defect inpainting respectively. We define the defect-free dataset as $X$ and the defective dataset as $Y$. As shown in Fig. 1, a defect-free image $x$ in $X$ is used to generate a defective image $DG(x)$ by $DG$, then $DG(x)$ is inpainted back to a defect-free image $DI(DG(x))$ by $DI$. In the same way, a defective image $y$ in $Y$ is inpainted to a defect-free image $DI(y)$ by $DI$, then the $DI(y)$ is used to generate a defective image $DG(DI(y))$ by $DG$.

It is worth noting that in the actual operation process, the performance of defect generation is often better than that of defect inpainting. That is because the generated defects do not need too many constraints generally. The generated content can be considered as defects as long as it can "destroy" the defect-free images to some extent. As for the defect inpainting, we not only need to inpaint

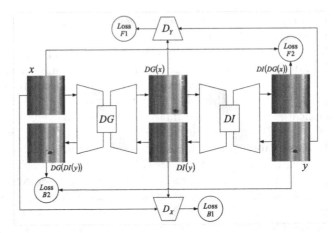

**Fig. 1.** The unsupervised training phase of SDDII. We train CycleGAN to generate defective images and inpaint defects. Two generators in CycleGAN are defined as $DG$ (Defect Generator) and $DI$ (Defect Inpaintor), which are responsible for defect generation and defect inpainting respectively. The loss functions in the forward mapping flow are defined as $LossF$x, while those in the backward mapping flow are defined as $LossB$x.

the defective content in local area, but also need to make the content distribution of the whole image close to that of the defect-free images. So in practice, the difficulty of defect inpainting is greater than that of defect generation.

Since CycleGAN [26] can use unpaired data to generate paired data, we introduce an additional supervised training phase to improve the defect inpainting. As shown in Fig. 2, we fix the parameters of $DG$ and then input a defect-free image $x$ to generate a defective images $DG(x)$. $x$ and $DG(x)$ are used for supervised training of $DI$. In addition, a new discriminator $D_Z$ is added to form adversarial training. The $S$ operation is channel stacking, where the defective images $DG(x)$ are stacked with the defect-free images $x$ or inpainted images $DI(DG(x))$, the stacked images will be inputted to the discriminator for comparison. In essence, it is an implementation of conditional GAN [17], which is also used in the famous Pix2pix [7] and has achieved good results.

In terms of model structure, we adapt both $DG$ and $DI$ from UNET [21]. $D_X$, $D_Y$ and $D_Z$ use modules of the discriminator structure of patchGAN [7] while the number of input channels of $D_Z$ is twice that of $D_X$ and $D_Y$. For example, for RGB color images, the number of input channels of $D_X$ and $D_Y$ is 3, and that of $D_Z$ is 6 because the $S$ operation stacks two images with channel number of 3 into a feature map with channel number of 6.

In the test phase, as shown in Fig. 3. The defective images $y$ are inpainted to defect-free images $DI(y)$ by $DI$. Then the images before and after the inpainting, $y$ and $DI(y)$, are compared pixel by pixel and the pixels whose absolute

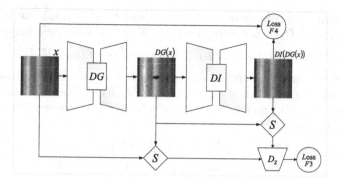

**Fig. 2.** The supervised training phase of SDDII. We introduce an additional supervised training phase which aims to improve defect inpainting. The parameters of $DG$ are fixed to generate defective images for $DI$'s training. $S$ denotes image channel stacking.

difference is greater than the threshold will be segmented to form a binary image $D\&T(y, DI(y))$. The binary image $D\&T(y, DI(y))$ represents the locations and shapes of the defects, where $D\&T$ denotes pixel-level difference computing and thresholding.

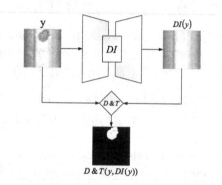

**Fig. 3.** The test phase of SDDII. $DI$ is used to inpaint the images in testset. And then we compare the images before and after inpainting pixel by pixel to get the defective area, that is to calculate the prediction mask $D\&T(y, DI(y))$. $D\&T$ denotes pixel-level difference computing and thresholding.

### 3.2 Loss Function

**Unsupervised Phase.** In the unsupervised phase, which contains defect generation and inpainting, the loss is divided into two parts, the adversarial loss and the consistency loss. As shown in Fig. 1, there are the forward $(X \to Y \to X)$ mapping flow and the backward $(Y \to X \to Y)$ mapping flow. Among them, $X \to Y$ in the forward mapping flow is completed by $DG$ cooperating with the discriminator $D_Y$, and the loss function is shown in the Equation LossF1. $DG$

tries to minimize this function against $D_Y$ who tries to maximize it, that is, $\min_{DG} \max_{D_Y} L_{F1}(DG, D_Y)$. Similarly, for $Y \rightarrow X$ in the backward mapping flow, the loss function is shown in the Eq. 2, i.e., $\min_{DI} \max_{D_X} L_{B1}(DI, D_X)$. The loss functions in the forward mapping flow are defined as $LossFx$, and those in the backward mapping flow are defined as $LossBx$. We define the data distribution as $x \sim Pdata(x)$ and $y \sim Pdata(y)$ where $Pdata$ denotes the empirical distribution of dataset.

$$L_{F1}(DG, D_Y) = E_{y \sim Pdata(y)}[\log D_Y(y)] \\ + E_{x \sim Pdata(x)}[\log(1 - D_Y(DG(x)))] \tag{1}$$

$$L_{B1}(DI, D_X) = E_{x \sim Pdata(x)}[\log D_X(x)] \\ + E_{y \sim Pdata(y)}[\log(1 - D_X(DI(y)))] \tag{2}$$

$Y \rightarrow X$ in the forward mapping flow is mapped by $DI$. And $X \rightarrow Y$ in the backward mapping flow is mapped by $DG$. The consistency loss of each of them corresponds to $LossF2$ and $LossB2$ in Fig. 1 respectively. The loss functions are shown in the Eq. 3 and the Eq. 4.

$$L_{F2}(DG, DI) = E_{x \sim Pdata(x)}[\|DI(DG(x)) - x\|_1] \tag{3}$$

$$L_{B2}(DG, DI) = E_{y \sim Pdata(y)}[\|DG(DI(y)) - y\|_1] \tag{4}$$

The total loss function of the unsupervised phase is shown in the Eq. 5, where $\alpha$ is a balance parameter between adversarial loss and consistency loss. In this phase, we aim to solve $DG^*, DI^* = \arg \min_{DG, DI} \max_{D_X, D_Y} L_{phase1}(DG, DI, D_X, D_Y)$.

$$L_{phase1}(DG, DI, D_X, D_Y) = L_{F1}(DG, D_Y) + L_{B1}(DI, D_X) \\ + \alpha(L_{F2}(DG, DI) + L_{B2}(DG, DI)) \tag{5}$$

**Supervised Phase.** In the supervised phase, the parameters of $DG$ are fixed and only the $DI$ are trained because we aim to improve the defect inpainting. As shown in Fig. 2, the defect-free image $x$ is inputted to $DG$ to generate the defective image $DG(x)$, which is then inpainted by $DI$ to obtain $DI(DG(x))$. The discriminator $D_Z$ compares and judges the images before and after inpainting, so as to assist $DI$ to optimize the inpainting performance. In the training phase, the discriminator label is true for the stacking input of $x$ and $DG(x)$, and false for the stacking input of $DI(DG(x))$ and $DG(x)$. And the loss is also divided into adversarial loss and consistency loss. The adversarial loss corresponds to $LossF3$ in Fig. 2, as shown in the Eq. 6 where $z$ and $Pz$ denote Gaussian noise and Gaussian distribution respectively. According to cGAN [17], we should provide Gaussian noise $z$ as an input to the generator in addition to original input. If $z$ is ignored, the mapping still can be learned, however, deterministic outputs will be produced and $DI$ can not learn a whole distribution.

$$L_{F3}(DI, D_Z) = E_{x \sim Pdata(x)}[\log D_Z(DG(x), x)] \\ + E_{x \sim Pdata(x), z \sim Pz(z)}[\log(1 - D_Z(DG(x), DI(DG(x), z)))] \tag{6}$$

The consistency loss can be calculated according to the pixel difference between the defect-free image $x$ and the inpainted image $DI(DG(x))$, corresponding to $LossF4$ in Fig. 2, as shown in the Eq. 7.

$$L_{F4}(DI) = E_{x \sim Pdata(x), z \sim Pz(z)}[\|DI(DG(x), z) - x\|_1] \tag{7}$$

The total loss function of the supervised phase is shown in the Eq. 8, in which $\beta$ is a balance parameter between the adversarial loss and the consistency loss. In this phase, we aim to solve $DI^* = \arg\min_{DI}\max_{D_Z} L_{phase2}(DI, D_Z)$.

$$L_{phase2}(DI, D_Z) = L_{F3}(DI, D_Z) + \beta L_{F4}(DI) \tag{8}$$

## 4    Experiments

### 4.1    Preparations

We evaluate SDDII on the RSDDs (Rail Surface Defect Datasets) [5] which contains two types of datasets. The first is a Type-I RSDDs captured from express rails, which contains 67 challenging images. The second is a Type-II RSDDs captured from common/heavy haul rails, which contains 128 challenging images. Each image contains at least one defect, and there is a corresponding ground truth, which is a binary mask image with the same size that shows the locations and shapes of the defects.

For evaluation, we choose IOU (Intersection over Union), pixel-level precision, pixel-level recall, and pixel-level F1 score as the evaluation metrics which are commonly used in semantic segmentation. As shown in Eq. 9, $TP$, $FP$, and $FN$ denote the numbers of correctly detected pixels, falsely detected pixels, and undetected defect pixels. The values in following experiments are averaged over the whole testset.

$$
\begin{aligned}
IOU &= TP/(TP + FP + FN) \\
Pre &= TP/(TP + FP) \\
Rec &= TP/(TP + FN) \\
F1 &= 2 \times Pre \times Rec/(Pre + Rec)
\end{aligned}
\tag{9}
$$

For comparison, on these datasets we also implement naive CycleGAN [26] for ablation study, and UNET [21] which needs binary mask images for supervised training while SDDII does not need. To be fair, no pre-trained model is used in our experiments.

### 4.2    Implementation Details

For Type-I RSDDs, the width of each image is 160 $px$, and the height can be from 1000 to 1282 $px$. And for Type-II RSDDs, all images share the same size of $55 \times 1250$ $px^2$. To save GPU memory, we crop the original images and mask images via sliding windows. What's more, by this trick we can get more training images although the number of images in original dataset is small. In our experiments, the window size is set to $160 \times 160$ $px^2$ and $55 \times 55$ $px^2$, and the sliding stride is set to 80 and 27 $px$, for Type-I and Type-II RSDDs respectively. All the cropped images will be resized to $256 \times 256$ $px^2$ before being inputted. As for labelling, if a cropped binary image contains any TRUE pixels(pixel value equals 1), we label the corresponding cropped image as defective image, otherwise, defect-free image.

During the unsupervised training phase, we input the cropped images to train our model with Adam [11] solver from scratch. The $\alpha$ is set to 10 and the batchsize is set to 1. In the first 100 epoch we keep the learning rate at 0.0002 and in the next 100 epoch we decay the learning rate to zero linearly.

During the supervised training phase, we randomly pick a image $x$ from $X$ and input it to $DG$ to generate defective image $DG(x)$, where $x$ and $DG(x)$ make up the paired images for supervised training of $DI$. In theory, we can generate training paired images infinitely. In our experiments, we generate 10000 paired images for $DI$'s further training and we set $\beta = 100$ then keep other training options the same as those of the unsupervised training phase.

In the test phase, we crop each image into an image-set and input the cropped images into $DI$, like what we do in the training phase. For each cropped image and its output, we compute the difference of each pixel between them and get a pixel-level difference image. After inference of each image-set, we gather the difference images and rebuild the whole prediction binary image which is used to be compared with ground truth for evaluation.

### 4.3  Results

We train our model on a machine with a GPU of NVIDIA GTX 1660 Ti @ 6GB and a CPU of Intel(R) Core(TM) i7-3770 CPU @ 3.40 GHz. It takes 2–3 days to complete all the trainings. Then we implement the inference and the results are shown in the Table 1 and Table 2. In addition, we also refer to the results of CFE [5] which is proposed by the RSDDs publisher. By now, CFE still achieves the best results. However, CFE is an exclusive system which is specially designed for RSDDs, which contains lots of designs of feature extracting. That is, if we change the dataset, we should design the method again, which is complicated and not general-purpose.

Due to the complexity of analyzing the performance of inpainting, we directly analyze the performance of segmentation instead. Besides, the performance of segmentation is representative of the performance of inpainting.

As for UNET, we can see its performance differs a lot between two datasets. On Type-I RSDDs the most of defects tend to be oval-shaped but on Type-II RSDDs the shapes of defects are various. UNET is good at learning invariant patterns so it get better results than SDDII on Type-I RSDDs, but get worse

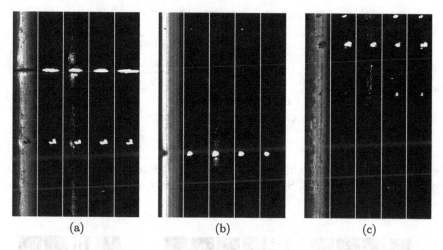

**Fig. 4.** The results of Rail 40 (a), 54 (b), and 55 (c) in Type-I RSDDs. The sequence of images for each rail is the original image, result of UNET, result of CycleGAN, result of SDDII, ground truth.

*IOU*, *Pre* and *F*1 than SDDII on Type-II RSDDs. Relatively, SDDII get more stable performances on both Type-I and Type-II RSDDs. SDDII detects defects by comparing images before and after inpainting, so it is adaptive for those unseen defects and can handle defects with various shapes in Type-II RSDDs. Besides, UNET is supervised learning which needs ground truth for training while SDDII does not need. Some representative results are picked and shown in Fig. 4 and Fig. 5. We can see that SDDII output comparable mask with UNET on Type-I RSDDs in Fig. 4 and get more stable and accurate outputs of Type-II RSDDs in Fig. 5.

**Table 1.** Results on Type-I RSDDs

| Method | IOU(%) | Pre(%) | Rec(%) | F1(%) |
|---|---|---|---|---|
| CFE [5] | – | 87.54 | 85.63 | 85.12 |
| UNET [21] | 45.73 | 89.25 | 58.33 | 68.86 |
| CycleGAN [26] | 27.18 | 60.25 | 46.40 | 48.45 |
| SDDII (Ours) | **36.50** | **83.42** | **48.15** | **57.04** |

Compared to CycleGAN which is unsupervised learning, SDDII is semi-supervised learning where we additionally implement the supervised training by utilizing the generated paired data. And as shown in Table 1 and Table 2, SDDII outperforms CycleGAN on both Type-I RSDDs and Type-II RSDDs, which shows that our proposed supervised training phase can significantly improve

**Table 2.** Results on Type-II RSDDs

| Method | IOU(%) | Pre(%) | Rec(%) | F1(%) |
|---|---|---|---|---|
| CFE [5] | – | 83.88 | 83.58 | 82.11 |
| UNET [21] | 24.57 | 63.49 | 52.72 | 50.91 |
| CycleGAN [26] | 21.11 | 64.48 | 37.57 | 42.57 |
| SDDII (Ours) | **26.82** | **70.72** | 49.75 | **54.48** |

the defect inpainting and then improve the defect detection of CycleGAN. As shown in Fig. 4 and Fig. 5, SDDII's outputs are more stable and accurate than that of CycleGAN.

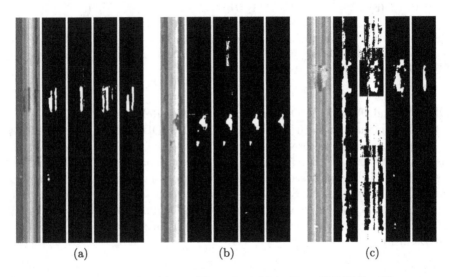

Fig. 5. The results of Rail 6 (a), 11 (b), and 40 (c) in Type-II RSDDs. The sequence of images is the same as Fig. 4.

## 5    Conclusions

Aiming at reducing the complexity of defective image synthesis and difficulty of detecting unseen defects, we proposed a semi-supervised method, denoted as SDDII, which combines the training strategy of CycleGAN and Pix2Pix. First, through unsupervised training phase, $DG$ and $DI$ would get the abilities of defect generation and defect inpainting respectively. Second, through supervised training phase, we further improve the defect inpainting of $DI$. Finally, experiments show that SDDII can indeed achieve better results than naive CycleGAN. In addition, SDDII is practical in many industrial scenes, since SDDII has good adaptability for unseen defects and we do not need to label the segmentation masks for training.

# References

1. Cao, W., Liu, Q., He, Z.: Review of pavement defect detection methods. IEEE Access **8**, 14531–14544 (2020)
2. Cui, Z., Zhang, M., Cao, Z., Cao, C.: Image data augmentation for sar sensor via generative adversarial nets. IEEE Access **7**, 42255–42268 (2019)
3. Czimmermann, T., Ciuti, G., Milazzo, M., Chiurazzi, M., Roccella, S., Oddo, C.M., Dario, P.: Visual-based defect detection and classification approaches for industrial applications–a survey. Sensors **20**(5), 1459 (2020)
4. Dhillon, A., Verma, G.K.: Convolutional neural network: a review of models, methodologies and applications to object detection. Prog. Artif. Intell. **9**(2), 85–112 (2019). https://doi.org/10.1007/s13748-019-00203-0
5. Gan, J., Li, Q., Wang, J., Yu, H.: A hierarchical extractor-based visual rail surface inspection system. IEEE Sens. J. **17**(23), 7935–7944 (2017)
6. Goodfellow, I.J., et al.: Generative adversarial networks. arXiv:1406.2661 (2014)
7. Isola, P., Zhu, J.Y., Zhou, T., Efros, A.A.: Image-to-image translation with conditional adversarial networks. In: Proceedings of the IEEE Conference on Computer Vision and Pattern Recognition, pp. 1125–1134 (2017)
8. Jain, S., Seth, G., Paruthi, A., Soni, U., Kumar, G.: Synthetic data augmentation for surface defect detection and classification using deep learning. J. Intell. Manuf. 1–14 (2020). https://doi.org/10.1007/s10845-020-01710-x
9. Kaelbling, L.P., Littman, M.L., Moore, A.W.: Reinforcement learning: a survey. J. Artif. Intelli. Res. **4**, 237–285 (1996)
10. Kim, J., Tae, D., Seok, J.: A survey of missing data imputation using generative adversarial networks. In: 2020 International Conference on Artificial Intelligence in Information and Communication (ICAIIC), pp. 454–456. IEEE (2020)
11. Kingma, D.P., Ba, J.: Adam: a method for stochastic optimization. arXiv:1412.6980 (2014)
12. Konda, V.R., Tsitsiklis, J.N.: Actor-critic algorithms. In: Advances in Neural Information Processing Systems, pp. 1008–1014. Citeseer (2000)
13. Li, X., Su, H., Liu, G.: Insulator defect recognition based on global detection and local segmentation. IEEE Access **8**, 59934–59946 (2020)
14. Lian, J., Jia, W., Zareapoor, M., Zheng, Y., Luo, R., Jain, D.K., Kumar, N.: Deep-learning-based small surface defect detection via an exaggerated local variation-based generative adversarial network. IEEE Trans. Industr. Inf. **16**(2), 1343–1351 (2019)
15. Luo, Q., Fang, X., Liu, L., Yang, C., Sun, Y.: Automated visual defect detection for flat steel surface: a survey. IEEE Trans. Instrum. Meas. **69**(3), 626–644 (2020)
16. Minaee, S., Boykov, Y.Y., Porikli, F., Plaza, A.J., Kehtarnavaz, N., Terzopoulos, D.: Image segmentation using deep learning: a survey. IEEE Transactions on Pattern Analysis and Machine Intelligence (2021)
17. Mirza, M., Osindero, S.: Conditional generative adversarial nets. arXiv:1411.1784 (2014)
18. Niu, S., Li, B., Wang, X., Lin, H.: Defect image sample generation with gan for improving defect recognition. IEEE Trans. Autom. Sci. Eng. **17**(3), 1611–1622 (2020)
19. Obaid, K.B., Zeebaree, S., Ahmed, O.M., et al.: Deep learning models based on image classification: a review. Int. J. Sci. Bus. **4**(11), 75–81 (2020)
20. Pfau, D., Vinyals, O.: Connecting generative adversarial networks and actor-critic methods. arXiv:1610.01945 (2016)

21. Ronneberger, O., Fischer, P., Brox, T.: U-net: convolutional networks for biomedical image segmentation. In: International Conference on Medical Image Computing And Computer-assisted Intervention, pp. 234–241. Springer (2015). https://doi.org/10.1007/978-3-319-24574-4_28

22. Suh, S., Lukowicz, P., Lee, Y.O.: Fusion of global-local features for image quality inspection of shipping label. arXiv:2008.11440 (2020)

23. Tolosana, R., Vera-Rodriguez, R., Fierrez, J., Morales, A., Ortega-Garcia, J.: Deepfakes and beyond: a survey of face manipulation and fake detection. Inf. Fus. **64**, 131–148 (2020)

24. Wang, G., Kang, W., Wu, Q., Wang, Z., Gao, J.: Generative adversarial network (gan) based data augmentation for palmprint recognition. In: 2018 Digital Image Computing: Techniques and Applications (DICTA), pp. 1–7. IEEE (2018)

25. Wang, Z., Chen, J., Hoi, S.C.: Deep learning for image super-resolution: a survey. IEEE transactions on pattern analysis and machine intelligence (2020)

26. Zhu, J.Y., Park, T., Isola, P., Efros, A.A.: Unpaired image-to-image translation using cycle-consistent adversarial networks. In: Proceedings of the IEEE International Conference on Computer Vision, pp. 2223–2232 (2017)

# ANF: Attention-Based Noise Filtering Strategy for Unsupervised Few-Shot Classification

Guangsen Ni[1], Hongguang Zhang[2], Jing Zhao[1], Liyang Xu[1(✉)],
Wenjing Yang[1], and Long Lan[1]

[1] Institute for Quantum Information and State Key Laboratory of High Performance Computing, College of Computer, National University of Defense Technology, Changsha 410073, China
xuliyang08@nudt.edu.cn
[2] Systems Engineering Institute, AMS, Beijing, China

**Abstract.** How to learn concepts from few-shot samples remains an open challenge in the deep learning era. The previous meta-learning methods require a large number of annotated samples in the training phase, which still contributes to high manual-labeling costs. In this paper, we propose a unsupervised few-shot learning framework and pointed out that negative queue constructed via randomly sampling contains many false-negative samples (noise), which has negative impacts on the model's generalized performance especially when only few samples are available. Specially, we propose an Attention-based Noise Filtering (ANF) strategy to make momentum contrastive loss more applicable to few-shot learning scenario. In addition, we also propose a dynamic momentum update method, which can greatly improve the classification accuracy. Our evaluations demonstrate state-of-the-art unsupervised few-shot learning performance, which is comparable to supervised baseline models.

**Keywords:** Self-supervised · Unsupervised few-shot learning · Attention mechanism · Computer vision

## 1 Introduction

Deep learning [13] has been a powerful tool to significantly advance the performance of many computer vision tasks [15,17,20,22,23,33], *e.g.*, image classification, action recognition, person re-identification, semantic segmentation, *etc.*, in recent years. However, deep learning models generally rely on large-scale annotated training samples to achieve promising generalized performance. In other

This work was partially supported by the National Natural Science Foundation of China (No. 12002380, 91948303, 91648204, 62106282 and 61803375), the National Key Research and Program of China (No. 2017YFB1001900 and 2017YFB1301104), the National University of Defense Technology Foundation (No. ZK20-52), and the National Science and Technology Major Project.

D. N. Pham et al. (Eds.): PRICAI 2021, LNAI 13033, pp. 109–123, 2021.
https://doi.org/10.1007/978-3-030-89370-5_9

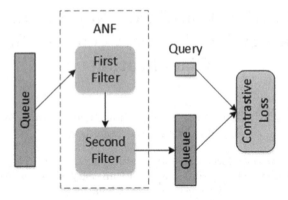

**Fig. 1.** We eliminate noise in the negative queue through the filter.

word, these models are not capable of learning from few-shot samples, which is inconsistent with human's learning process. To illustrate, human beings can easily understand novel concepts via very limited samples, and such a learning process is achievable as we can transfer knowledge obtained from previous tasks. Consequently, few-shot learning is proposed to study how to make machine learn like a human, and can adopt previous knowledge (parameters of pretrained model) to solve new problems [3].

The meta-learning framework, in which models learn upon tasks to learn, has been the most popular choice to study the knowledge transfer process. Most of the recent few-shot learning works [9,24,34,36,37,39,40] are build upon meta-learning architecture. Though its usefulness has been verified, the meta-training tasks require plentiful manual annotations as supervision for gradient descent optimization, thus the manual-labeling costs cannot be ignored under the current few-shot learning setting. Recently the self-supervised learning strategies, i. e., instance discrimination and transformation prediction, have demonstrated strong performance in representation learning and shown an opportunity to achieve unsupervised few-shot learning without any annotated samples. The objective of metric-based few-shot learning works [9,24,34,36,37] is to learn discriminative representations and making prediction by measuring the Euclidean or Cosine distance, thus the quality of learnt representations apparently has significant impacts. From this viewpoint, the self-supervised methods can be naturally applied in few-shot learning pipelines as they share the same goal. Among all self-supervised methods, the contrastive learning [3,14,28] has a closer formulation to metric-based few-shot learning methods, thus it is the first learning method to be applied in few-shot learning scenario.

In this paper, we first apply the most powerful contrastive learning method *Momentum Contrast* (MoCo) [14] in few-shot setting to develop an unsupervised few-shot learning framework. Though it is observed that MoCo achieves strong few-shot classification accuracy, one issue existed in the dictionary (negative queue) may lead to significant performance loss. In fact, the key contribution of MoCo is to construct a large dictionary that covers a rich set of negative

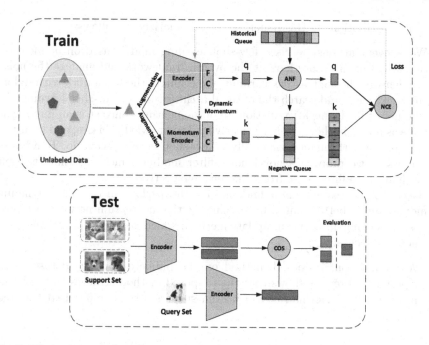

**Fig. 2.** The training and testing processes of our unsupervised few-shot learning framework. Noise filter is capable of filtering the keys from the same class of data $q$ in the historical queue. The model is trained to learn the relations between q and 1 positive sample and $N$ negative samples. We apply the infoNCE [28] (NCE in picture) as our training loss function to achieve the gradients for parameters' updating, and lastly use the encoder's parameters to update the Momentum Encoder with a dynamic rate.

samples while the encoder for dictionary keys is kept as consistent as possible. However, as the dictionary is constructed via randomly sampling, it may contain many false-negative samples and lead to parameter biases in contrastive learning. This drawback is especially important in few-shot setting as the model's generalized performance can be very sensitive to such biases when only very few samples are available.

To solve the above problem, we propose a novel attention-based two-stage noise filter strategy as shown in Fig. 1, which can be easily embedded into MoCo and other dictionary-based contrastive learning models to neglect the false-negative samples in dictionary keys and reduce the knowledge biases. Our unsupervised few-shot learning framework is shown in Fig. 2. It is obviously that the historical queue is not directly used for contrastive learning, but it first fed into the noise filter module to denoise the false-negative samples. In such a way, the false-negative samples in the dictionary can be neglected and the overall quality of contrastive knowledge is significantly improved. We calculate the similarities between query data and filtered negative queue, then use the infoNCE [28] to calculate loss, which is used to update encoder's parameters. And following we use dynamic momentum update method to update the momentum encoder.

Our contributions in this paper can be summarized as follows:

- We reinvent an unsupervised few-shot learning model based on momentum contrast, take a deeper look at the overall framework and analyze the noise problems in the contrastive learning. We evaluate the framework with different backbones, and search the optimal architecture for few-shot learning.
- The noises in the negative dictionary of momentum contrast is an important issue as noises in the dictionary clearly lead to knowledge biases, and limit the recognition performance, especially in few-shot learning scenario. To address this issue, we propose a novel noise filter module which use the attention mechanism to filter noise from different perspective.
- Based on our experimental finding that the performance with a dynamic momentum is better than a fixed value for the momentum network, we propose a dynamic momentum update method, which greatly improves the classification accuracy.

We evaluate our proposed method on the publicly available dataset, and the experimental results shows that the proposed method achieves state-of-the-art unsupervised performance, which even surpasses some supervised baseline models.

## 2   Related Work

**One and Few-Shot Learning.** The one- and few-shot learning has been studied widely in computer vision in both shallow [2,6,8,21] and deep learning scenarios [10,19,34,38]. Early works [6,21] propose one-shot learning methods motivated by the observation that humans can learn new concepts from very few samples. These two works employ a generative model with an iterative inference for transfer.

Matching Network [38] introduces the concept of support set and $L$-way $Z$-shot learning protocols. It captures the similarity between one testing and several support images, thus casting the one-shot learning problem as set-to-set learning. Such a network works with test classes unobserved at the training time without any modifications. Prototypical Networks [34] learn a model that computes distances between a datapoint and prototype representations of each class. Model-Agnostic Meta-Learning (MAML) [10] introduces a meta-learning model which can be considered a form of transfer learning method. MAML is trained on a variety of different learning tasks and falls into the category of meta-learning approaches, and this results in a good initial condition for the solver to generalize to other novel tasks.

A large family of meta-learning approaches apply some form of the gradient correction. Algorithms such as Meta-SGD [25], MAML++ [1], CAVIA [41] and LEO [31] adaptively alter the step-size of the gradient updates.

**Self-supervised Learning.** The self-supervised learning is a recent popular learning strategy between unsupervised and supervised learning. It includes two types of learning strategies: 1) transformation prediction; 2) instance discrimination (contrastive learning).

Transformation prediction learns to predict self-information as auxiliary objective to improve the performance and reduce the uncertainty on many tasks, e.g., object recognition [12], video representation learning [7,32], and also few-shot image classification [11,35]. To demonstrate, [12] learns to predict random image rotations, [5] learns to discriminate a set of surrogate classes, and [11,35] propose to improve the few-shot performance by predicting image rotations and jigsaw patterns.

Contrastive self-supervised learning does not focus on the details of samples, but learn features that distinguish it from others. DeepMind proposes the infoNCE loss function in CPC [28], which builds the foundation for Contrastive self-supervised learning. CPC learns representations by predicting the future in latent space by using autoregressive models. They employ a probabilistic contrastive loss which induces the latent space to capture information that is maximally useful to predict future samples. It also makes the model tractable by using negative sampling. MoCo [14] proposes to expand the number of negative samples as a large dynamic dictionary with a queue and a moving-averaged encoder. This enables building a large and consistent dictionary on-the-fly that facilitates contrastive unsupervised learning.

**Unsupervised Few-Shot Learning.** Unsupervised few-shot learning is a new field combining few-shot learning and unsupervised learning. It assumes that the training set does not contain any label information. In unsupervised few-shot learning, the simplest idea is to put a pseudo-label for unlabeled data through a certain method, so that unlabeled data can be trained in the same way as labeled data. Many scholars have followed this line of thinking and proposed a series of methods. The CACTU [16] method proposed by Kyle et al. is the pioneer of this type of method. CACTU first uses an unsupervised representation learning method (such as BiGAN [4]) to obtain feature representations from the unlabeled training set, and then uses clustering methods to divide the features into multiple subsets and randomly add pseudo-labels to them, and finally uses Pseudo-label data to train MAML [9], ProtoNet [34] and other FSL models. In the pre-training process of CACTU, it need to obtain pseudo labels by clustering. The process of this method is relatively complicated and the additional cost is relatively large. To solve this problem, UMTRA [18] provides an end-to-end solution. UMTRA first randomly samples $N$ pictures from the unlabeled training set. These $N$ pictures are considered to be from different categories, then use data augmentation to enhance each picture by $K$ and divide the support set and query set, and finally use the few-shot learning method (such as MAML [9]) to train.

## 3    Approach

The causes of noise is analyzed in this part first, and the detail of the attention-based noise filtering strategy will be introduced then.

### 3.1   Dictionary Noises

***The Causes of Noise.*** In order to reduce the noises in the dictionary keys, we first clarify the origin and the proportion of noises in the queue. Ideally, all dictionary keys should differ from the positive query data, so that the contrastive loss will not push intra-class samples farther. However, if the number of classes is much smaller than the training batch size or the number of samples per class, there is a very big possibility that the dictionary keys contain samples from the same class and these samples are called false-negative keys.

***The Proportion of False-Negative Keys.*** Currently, there are two main ways to construct negative samples: 1) Taking historical samples as the negative queue. Assuming the probability of each category data appearing in the queue is equal, the queue length is $L$, the number of classes is $C$, then the average number of false-negative keys in the dictionary is $\frac{L}{C}$; 2) Randomly sampling a batch of data points, and for every data point in the mini-batch, treating the rest data points as negative samples [3]. Assuming the batch size is $B$ and the number of training classes is $C$, then the amount of noise in each batch is $\frac{B}{C}$. Therefore, it is consistent with our analysis that as long as the queue length and batch size is larger than the number of classes, there are definitely false-negative samples existed in the queue. Regrettably, there are no works considering to address this issue in self-supervised learning.

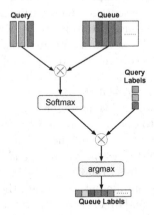

**Fig. 3.** We annotate the data in the history queue using the attention-based method. For each sample in the historical queue, we find the most similar to each input batch, and then mark it as the same category.

**Table 1.** The effect of cosine noise filtering, attention noise filtering and dynamic momentum updating. We apply the trained model to novel class 5-way 1-shot few-shot learning and 5-way 5-shot few-shot learning. ResNet-18 is used as backbone on *mini*Imagenet.

| Case | Cos | Att. | Dyn. | Acc. (%) | |
|------|-----|------|------|----------|--------|
|      |     |      |      | (5, 1)   | (5, 5) |
| (a)  | –   | –    | –    | 50.04    | 69.87  |
| (b)  | ✓   | –    | –    | 52.11    | 71.17  |
| (c)  | ✓   | ✓    | –    | 52.77    | 71.25  |
| (d)  | ✓   | ✓    | ✓    | 54.69    | 73.36  |

## 3.2 Direct Noise Filter

To address the above-mentioned issue, we first propose a simple solution named *Direct Noise Filter* (DNF) to reduce the number of false-negative keys in the dictionary. As the core task of the filter is to find the data points which are close to $x_q$ and $x_k$ in feature space, we first calculate the similarities $s$ between the positive sample $x_q$ and all dictionary keys, and then simply remove the data points with top-k highest similarity scores from the dictionary in contrastive learning. For a dictionary key $x_i$, the similarity between it and $x_q$ can be calculated as follows,

$$s_i = f_q(x_q)^T \cdot f_q(x_i), \tag{1}$$

where $f_q(\cdot)$ denotes the feature extractor in the network model and the notes $T$ refers the transpose of the feature vector $x_q$. The top $k$ results which mean most similar to a positive sample will be removed from the dictionary queue.

Theoretically, the ratio of false-negative samples in the queue should be close to $p = \frac{1}{C}$, so we search the optimal discarding ratio around $p$. We conduct numbers of experiments on *mini*Imagenet. We find that the best performance is achieved when the discard ratio is set to 1% for 5-way 1-shot learning task. Due to the limited quality of feature space, there are some misclassifications in the filtering, so that the best discarding ratio is slightly lower than $p$. If the discarding ratio is high, some discriminative negative samples will be discarded, which makes the losses outweigh the gains.

**Table 2.** Comparison with previous results. 'Clustering' represents the clustering algorithms used by that model. 5-1 represents 5-way 1-shot few-shot learning, 5-5 represents 5-way 5-shot few-shot learning, no special note, same in the following.

| Methods | Backbones | Clustering | *mini*Imagenet | | Omniglot | |
|---|---|---|---|---|---|---|
| | | | 5-1(%) | 5-5(%) | 5-1(%) | 5-5(%) |
| Supervised models | | | | | | |
| MAML [9] | ConvNet-4 | N/A | 46.81 | 62.13 | 94.46 | 98.83 |
| PN [34] | ConvNet-4 | N/A | 46.56 | 62.29 | 98.35 | 99.58 |
| RN [36] | ConvNet-4 | N/A | 50.44 | 65.32 | 97.6 | 99.1 |
| SoSN [40] | ConvNet-4 | N/A | 52.96 | 65.32 | 99.8 | 99.9 |
| MetaOptNet [24] | ResNet-12 | N/A | 62.64 | 78.63 | – | – |
| DeepEMD [39] | ResNet-12 | N/A | **65.91** | **82.41** | – | – |
| Unsupervised models | | | | | | |
| MLP with dropout [4] | – | BiGAN | 22.91 | 29.06 | 40.54 | 62.56 |
| CACTUs-MAML [16] | ConvNet-4 | BiGAN | 36.24 | 51.28 | 58.18 | 78.66 |
| CACTUs-ProtoNets [16] | ConvNet-4 | BiGAN | 36.62 | 50.16 | 54.74 | 71.69 |
| MLP with dropout [4] | – | DC/ACAI | 29.03 | 39.67 | 51.95 | 77.20 |
| CACTUs-MAML [16] | ConvNet-4 | DC/ACAI | 39.90 | 53.97 | 68.84 | 87.78 |
| CACTUs-ProtoNets [16] | ConvNet-4 | DC/ACAI | 39.18 | 53.36 | 68.12 | 83.58 |
| UMTRA [18] | ConvNet-4 | N/A | 39.93 | 50.73 | 83.80 | 95.43 |
| Unsupervised-RN | ConvNet-4 | N/A | 35.14 | 44.10 | – | – |
| MoCo | ResNet-18 | N/A | 50.10 | 69.81 | 91.08 | 97.64 |
| Ours (ANF) | ResNet-18 | N/A | **54.69** | **73.36** | **91.78** | **97.73** |

### 3.3    Attention-Based Noise Filter

Though the DNF proposed initially by us has achieved some promising results, it is easy to misjudge when only relying on transverse noise filtering. Inspired by some recent work [37], we propose the *Attention-based Noise Filter* (ANF). In general, the method contains two stages. **The first stage** is to use the attention mechanism to label the data in the historical queue. The label $\hat{y}$ is calculated by Eq. (2),

$$\hat{y} = \sum_{i=1}^{N} S(x, x_i) \cdot y_i, \tag{2}$$

where $y$ is the real label existed in the dataset. As shown in Fig. 3, for each sample in the historical queue, we find the most similar to each input batch, and then mark it as the same category. The similarity is calculated by Eq. (3),

$$S(x, x_i) = \frac{e^{f(x) \cdot g(x_i)}}{\sum_{k=1}^{N} e^{f(x) \cdot g(x_k)}}, \tag{3}$$

where $f(\cdot)$ and $g(\cdot)$ represent encoder and moment encoder respectively. **The second stage** is to change the similarity of the same label to zero when calculating the similarity between the query data and the negative sample. Then we use DNF filter the noise. The proposed ANF filter the noise in negative samples from different perspective. From the perspective of input data, DNF searches the historical queue for the data with the highest similarity to the query sample and then removes it. This method focuses on each individual input data. ANF reflects a kind of reverse thinking, which starts from the perspective of historical queues. ANF searches each round of input data and uses the label of the input sample with the highest similarity as the historical data label. This method focuses on the overall data sampled in each round.

### 3.4  Dynamic Momentum Updating

Table 1 shows the performance improvement of the model by cosine filtering, attention filtering and dynamic momentum updating. In MoCo, momentum encoder can be regarded as a historical version of encoder. We believe that when the momentum encoder and encoder feature extraction capabilities are high, the greater the gap between them, the better the filtering accuracy. This is actually a dilemma. When the momentum update is high, the momentum encoder and encoder parameters are similar, and when the momentum update is low, the feature extraction ability of the momentum encoder will be poor. We have designed a dynamic update mechanism to solve this problem. The calculations of dynamic momentum is given by Eq. (4), $\delta$ is used to control the growth rate.

$$m = m_{base} + \delta \cdot \frac{epoch_{now}}{epoch_{all}}, \tag{4}$$

In the early stage of training, the encoder performance is poor. At this time, we choose a higher momentum update ratio. As the training progresses, the performance of the model gradually improves. Reducing the momentum update ratio can improve the accuracy of similarity calculation and improve the accuracy of filtering.

## 4  Experiments

In this section we empirically study the noise filter behaviors. We pay special attention to how to improve filtering performance.

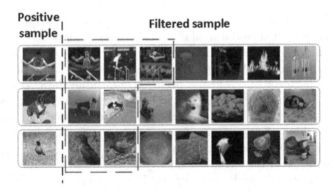

**Fig. 4.** The comparison of filtered samples and positive samples. We selected some of the filtered samples in the experiment as shown in this figure, where the samples in the red dashed box represent samples of the same category as the positive samples. (Color figure online)

### 4.1  Datasets

We evaluate our unsupervised model on two benchmarks, *mini*Imagenet [37] and Omniglot [21]. Our models are trained from scratch in unsupervised manner, and do not require pre-training on any large-scale dataset.

**mini*Imagenet*** is the most popular dataset for few-shot classification. It contains 100 classes sampled from ILSVRC-2012 [30], and every class has 600 images with 84 × 84 resolution. It is randomly split to 64, 16, 20 classes for training, validation and testing respectively.

**Omniglot** is a character image dataset containing 1623 handwritten characters from 50 alphabets. Every character in Omniglot has 20 different instances written by different people. In Omniglot, 1200 characters are used for training, 100 characters are used for validation and 323 characters are used for testing.

**Table 3.** The performance of noise filter on different backbones without dynamic momentum. ANF represents attention-based noise filter. 5-1 represents 5-way 1-shot few-shot learning, 5-5 represents 5-way 5-shot few-shot learning

| Methods | Backbones | 5-1(%) | 5-5(%) |
| --- | --- | --- | --- |
| MoCo | ConvNet4 | 42.78 | 58.98 |
| Ours (ANF) | ConvNet4 | 43.46 | 59.03 |
| MoCo | ResNet-12 | 50.33 | 68.20 |
| Ours (ANF) | ResNet-12 | 51.87 | 68.90 |
| MoCo | ResNet-18 | 50.10 | 69.81 |
| Ours (ANF) | ResNet-18 | 52.86 | 71.91 |

## 4.2    Implementation Details

The experiments are built on PyTorch platform. The ResNet-18 [15] is used as backbone in our unsupervised few-shot learning framework. We use SGD solver as the optimizer, in which the initial learning rate is 0.03, weight decay is set to 0.0001 and the momentum is 0.9. The training batchsize is 128. We train the model for 200 epochs with 4 GPUs, and the learning rate is decayed by 0.1 at the 120-th and the 160-th epochs. During training phase, we randomly augment the training data, e.g., random resized crop ($224 \times 224$), random color jitter, random vertical and horizontal flips. The fully-connected layer in ResNet-18 is modified to produce 128-dimension image features.

We set dynamic momentum update from 0.1 to 0.001. Following MoCo [14], we apply shuffling BN [14] to further improve the discrimination of feature space.The negative sample queue length is set to 6144 and the discarding ratio to 1% respectively.

In the testing phase, the model is evaluated for 2000 episodes in 5-way 1-shot setup to achieve the final performance. For fair comparisons between baselines and our models, we use random seeds to control the generation of few-shot learning tasks. We remove the fully-connected layer from the encoder for feature extraction and all parameters are frozen.

## 4.3    Experimental Results

Following the standard few-shot setup [27], we conduct extensive experiments on miniImageNet and Omniglot, whose results are shown in Table 2. It is observed that the proposed method, i.e., Attention-based Noise Filter (ANF) significantly outperforms all previous unsupervised baseline models with a large-margin. The top-1 accuracy of Ours ANF on miniImagenet is up to 54.69% and 73.36% under 5-way 1-shot and 5-way 5-shot respectively, which surpasses MoCo by 4.59% and 3.55% respectively and become the new state-of-the-art method. In addition, Our ANF even surpasses part of supervised methods, e.g., MAML [9] and ProtoNet [34] and narrows the gap between the performance of the best supervised method to a certain extent.

## 4.4    Visualization of Filter Results

To verify the filtering quality of ANF, we randomly select several mini-batch of query samples and visualize their corresponding false-negative keys and classes. We observe in the visualization that many true false-negative keys can be indeed selected as shown in Fig. 4. These experimental results verify our assumption that there are noises existed in the dictionary, and reducing such noises can effectively improve the performance.

## 4.5    Ablation Studies

***Different Backbones.*** We further evaluate our methods on different backbones as show in Table 3. The experimental results show that our method can improve

**Table 4.** The performance of different distance metric on *mini*Imagenet without dynamic momentum, where Cos denotes Cosine distance and L2 denotes Euclidean distance.

| Metric | Backbones | 5-1(%) | 5-5(%) |
|--------|-----------|--------|--------|
| Cos    | ResNet-18 | 52.86  | 71.91  |
| L2     | ResNet-18 | 51.13  | 69.52  |

performance under different backbones. At the same time, we find an interesting phenomenon: the simpler the backbone, the smaller the performance improvement. We believe that this phenomenon occurs because the filter depends on the features extracted by the backbone. We mainly filter the noise in negative samples based on the cosine distance between sample feature vectors. When the backbone is complex, the extracted feature vector is more accurate, so the filtered noise is also more accurate. In other words, the more complex the backbone, the more accurate the noise filtering and the higher the performance improvement.

**Different Metrics.** How to properly design the similarity measurement is also an important factor in the filtering process. A better metric can bring higher detecting accuracy. For example, in Prototypical Networks [34], the authors find that using Euclidean distance instead of cosine distance can get better results. In order to find the optimal distance metric, we perform experiments on replacing the cosine similarity with squared Euclidean distance in filter as shown in Table 4. While in [34] they analyze that squared Euclidean distance is a Bregman divergence which is suitable for taking average, we observe cosine distance is a better choice for noise filter. A possible reason is that in contrast learning the direction of the high-dimensional vector reflects category information better than the squared distance. Another possible reason is that different backbones apply different distance metrics.

**Queue Length and Remove Ratio.** As shown in the Table 5, we experiment on miniImageNet and find that the model has a larger tolerance interval for the queue length. And the effect is best when the dropped data is 1%.

**Table 5.** The effect of queue length and discard ratio on 5-way 1-shot classification performance. The distance measure for the following experiment is cos.

| Queue size | Remove | Acc. (%) |
|------------|--------|----------|
| 00256      | 0      | 50.04    |
| 06144      | 0      | 50.06    |
| 65536      | 0      | 49.26    |
| 06144      | 0.1    | 49.93    |
| 06144      | 0.01   | 52.11    |
| 06144      | 0.001  | 50.32    |

**Table 6.** We use traditional methods to extract features and use this to filter noise. This part of the experiment was based on ResNet-50.

| Methods | Queue size | Remove | Acc. (%) |
|---------|-----------|--------|----------|
| sift    | 6144      | 0.01   | 48.36    |
| orb     | 6144      | 0.01   | 49.12    |
| cos     | 6144      | 0.01   | 50.88    |

### 4.6  Traditional Feature Descriptor

In Table 6, we use traditional methods to extract features to filter noise. We believe that traditional feature description operators (such as orb [29], sift [26]) can learn different features from neural networks, and noise filtering with traditional feature description operators can supplement the features learned by neural networks. In order to verify this method, we used traditional methods to extract image features and constructed a mapping table to map the features extracted by neural network one by one. Unfortunately, we find that the features extracted by traditional methods are much worse than neural networks, and filtering with this scheme is not as good as directly relying on features extracted by neural networks.

## 5  Conclusions

In this paper, we propose a novel unsupervised few-shot learning framework based on momentum contrast. We are the first to point out the noise problem in momentum contrast, and present simple yet effective attention-based noise filter (ANF) methods to reduce the noise in the contrastive dictionary. The experimental results shows that our method outperforms recent state-of-the-art methods with a large margin. Besides, we also designed a dynamic momentum update method that can greatly improve model's classification performance. The ablation studies shows that our method can improve the performance with different backbones, and get better effect of noise filtering with cosine distance. We hope our study will attract the community's attention to effect of noise filter in contrastive learning.

## References

1. Antoniou, A., Edwards, H., Storkey, A.: How to train your MAML. In: International Conference on Learning Representations (ICLR) (2019)
2. Bart, E., Ullman, S.: Cross-generalization: learning novel classes from a single example by feature replacement. In: CVPR, pp. 672–679 (2005)
3. Chen, T., Kornblith, S., Norouzi, M., Hinton, G.E.: A simple framework for contrastive learning of visual representations. CoRR abs/2002.05709 (2020)
4. Donahue, J., Krähenbühl, P., Darrell, T.: Adversarial feature learning. In: ICLR (Poster). OpenReview.net (2017)

5. Dosovitskiy, A., Springenberg, J.T., Riedmiller, M., Brox, T.: Discriminative unsupervised feature learning with convolutional neural networks. In: Advances in Neural Information Processing Systems, pp. 766–774 (2014)
6. Fei-Fei, L., Fergus, R., Perona, P.: One-shot learning of object categories. PAMI **28**(4), 594–611 (2006)
7. Fernando, B., Bilen, H., Gavves, E., Gould, S.: Self-supervised video representation learning with odd-one-out networks. In: Proceedings of the IEEE Conference on Computer Vision and Pattern Recognition, pp. 3636–3645 (2017)
8. Fink, M.: Object classification from a single example utilizing class relevance metrics. In: NIPS, pp. 449–456 (2005)
9. Finn, C., Abbeel, P., Levine, S.: Model-agnostic meta-learning for fast adaptation of deep networks. In: ICML Proceedings of Machine Learning Research, vol. 70, pp. 1126–1135. PMLR (2017)
10. Finn, C., Abbeel, P., Levine, S.: Model-agnostic meta-learning for fast adaptation of deep networks. In: ICML, pp. 1126–1135 (2017)
11. Gidaris, S., Bursuc, A., Komodakis, N., Pérez, P., Cord, M.: Boosting few-shot visual learning with self-supervision. arXiv preprint arXiv:1906.05186 (2019)
12. Gidaris, S., Singh, P., Komodakis, N.: Unsupervised representation learning by predicting image rotations. arXiv preprint arXiv:1803.07728 (2018)
13. Goodfellow, I., Bengio, Y., Courville, A., Bengio, Y.: Deep Learning, vol. 1. MIT Press Cambridge (2016)
14. He, K., Fan, H., Wu, Y., Xie, S., Girshick, R.B.: Momentum contrast for unsupervised visual representation learning. In: CVPR, pp. 9726–9735. IEEE (2020)
15. He, K., Zhang, X., Ren, S., Sun, J.: Deep residual learning for image recognition. In: CVPR, June 2016
16. Hsu, K., Levine, S., Finn, C.: Unsupervised learning via meta-learning. In: ICLR (Poster). OpenReview.net (2019)
17. Huang, G., Liu, Z., Van Der Maaten, L., Weinberger, K.Q.: Densely connected convolutional networks. In: Proceedings of the IEEE Conference on Computer Vision and Pattern Recognition, pp. 4700–4708 (2017)
18. Khodadadeh, S., Bölöni, L., Shah, M.: Unsupervised meta-learning for few-shot image classification. In: NeurIPS, pp. 10132–10142 (2019)
19. Koch, G., Zemel, R., Salakhutdinov, R.: Siamese neural networks for one-shot image recognition. In: ICML Deep Learning Workshop, vol. 2 (2015)
20. Krizhevsky, A., Sutskever, I., Hinton, G.E.: ImageNet classification with deep convolutional neural networks. In: NIPS, pp. 1106–1114 (2012)
21. Lake, B.M., Salakhutdinov, R., Gross, J., Tenenbaum, J.B.: One shot learning of simple visual concepts. CogSci (2011). cognitivesciencesociety.org
22. Lan, L., Wang, X., Hua, G., Huang, T.S., Tao, D.: Semi-online multi-people tracking by re-identification. Int. J. Comput. Vis. **128**(7), 1937–1955 (2020)
23. Lan, L., Wang, X., Zhang, S., Tao, D., Gao, W., Huang, T.S.: Interacting tracklets for multi-object tracking. IEEE Trans. Image Process. **27**(9), 4585–4597 (2018)
24. Lee, K., Maji, S., Ravichandran, A., Soatto, S.: Meta-learning with differentiable convex optimization. In: Proceedings of the IEEE Conference on Computer Vision and Pattern Recognition, pp. 10657–10665 (2019)
25. Li, Z., Zhou, F., Chen, F., Li, H.: Meta-SGD: learning to learn quickly for few shot learning. arXiv preprint arXiv:1707.09835 (2017)
26. Lowe, D.G.: Distinctive image features from scale-invariant keypoints. Int. J. Comput. Vis. **60**(2), 91–110 (2004)
27. Munkhdalai, T., Yu, H.: Meta networks. In: ICML. Proceedings of Machine Learning Research, vol. 70, pp. 2554–2563. PMLR (2017)

28. van den Oord, A., Li, Y., Vinyals, O.: Representation learning with contrastive predictive coding. CoRR abs/1807.03748 (2018)

29. Rublee, E., Rabaud, V., Konolige, K., Bradski, G.R.: ORB: an efficient alternative to SIFT or SURF. In: ICCV, pp. 2564–2571. IEEE Computer Society (2011)

30. Russakovsky, O., et al.: ImageNet large scale visual recognition challenge. Int. J. Comput. Vis. 115(3), 211–252 (2015)

31. Rusu, A.A., et al.: Meta-learning with latent embedding optimization. In: International Conference on Learning Representations (2019)

32. Sermanet, P., et al.: Time-contrastive networks: self-supervised learning from pixels (2017)

33. Simonyan, K., Zisserman, A.: Very deep convolutional networks for large-scale image recognition. ICLR abs/1409.1556 (2015)

34. Snell, J., Swersky, K., Zemel, R.: Prototypical networks for few-shot learning. In: NIPS, pp. 4077–4087 (2017)

35. Su, J.C., Maji, S., Hariharan, B.: Boosting supervision with self-supervision for few-shot learning. arXiv preprint arXiv:1906.07079 (2019)

36. Sung, F., Yang, Y., Zhang, L., Xiang, T., Torr, P.H.S., Hospedales, T.M.: Learning to compare: Relation network for few-shot learning. In: CVPR, pp. 1199–1208. IEEE Computer Society (2018)

37. Vinyals, O., Blundell, C., Lillicrap, T., Kavukcuoglu, K., Wierstra, D.: Matching networks for one shot learning. In: NIPS, pp. 3630–3638 (2016)

38. Vinyals, O., Blundell, C., Lillicrap, T., Wierstra, D., et al.: Matching networks for one shot learning. In: NIPS, pp. 3630–3638 (2016)

39. Zhang, C., Cai, Y., Lin, G., Shen, C.: DeepEMD: few-shot image classification with differentiable earth mover's distance and structured classifiers. In: Proceedings of the IEEE/CVF Conference on Computer Vision and Pattern Recognition, pp. 12203–12213 (2020)

40. Zhang, H., Koniusz, P.: Power normalizing second-order similarity network for few-shot learning. In: 2019 IEEE Winter Conference on Applications of Computer Vision (WACV), pp. 1185–1193. IEEE (2019)

41. Zintgraf, L., Shiarli, K., Kurin, V., Hofmann, K., Whiteson, S.: Fast context adaptation via meta-learning. In: International Conference on Machine Learning, pp. 7693–7702 (2019)

# Asymmetric Mutual Learning for Unsupervised Cross-Domain Person Re-identification

Danyang Huang, Lei Zhang, Qishuai Diao, Wei Wu, and Zhong Zhou[✉]

State Key Laboratory of Virtual Reality Technology and Systems,
Beihang University, Beijing, People's Republic of China
zz@buaa.edu.cn

**Abstract.** Unsupervised domain adaptation in person re-identification is a challenging task. The performance of models trained on a specific domain generally degrades significantly on other domains due to the domain gaps. State-of-the-art clustering-based cross-domain methods inevitably introduce noisy labels. The negative effects of noisy labels gradually accumulate during iterative training. Besides, optimizing with conventional triplet loss could make the model stuck in local optima in the late stage of domain adaptation. To mitigate the effects of noisy labels, this paper proposes an asymmetric mutual learning framework which cooperates two models with asymmetric labels. The learned asymmetric information is helpful for the two models to complement with each other. Specifically, we propose a merging clusters algorithm to generate asymmetric labels. We also introduce a similarity weighted loss which can further adapt the model to target domain. Extensive experiments demonstrate that our approach outperforms the state-of-the-art methods on three popular person re-identification datasets.

**Keywords:** Person re-identification · Asymmetric mutual learning · Unsupervised · Cross-domain

## 1 Introduction

Person re-identification (re-id) aims to find the matched person in a candidate gallery given a query person image. Although existing supervised deep learning methods of person re-id have made great achievements, most of them require accurate labels which are time-consuming to annotate. Besides, these models perform poorly when the training dataset and the test dataset distribute in different domains. Unsupervised Domain Adaptation (UDA) approaches are proposed to alleviate above issues. UDA aims to transfer the knowledge learned on a source dataset with accurate identity labels to a target dataset without annotated labels. State-of-the-art UDA methods [3,15] alternatively generate pseudo labels on target domain with clustering algorithm and fine-tune the model with pseudo labels. Nevertheless, noisy labels are introduced into the iterative training since

ⓒ Springer Nature Switzerland AG 2021
D. N. Pham et al. (Eds.): PRICAI 2021, LNAI 13033, pp. 124–137, 2021.
https://doi.org/10.1007/978-3-030-89370-5_10

clustering algorithm can not classify images accurately. The noise will accumulate continuously and then hinder the improvement of the model. To address above issue, some recent works [4,5] adopt mutual learning framework to mitigate the negative effects of noise. Mutual learning framework can make remarkable improvement in cross-domain person re-id.

Mutual learning generally utilizes two collaborative models to solve a task together [4,5,14,17]. The two collaborative models usually start from different initial conditions. Diverse knowledge learned by two models can be combined in various ways to improve the discriminative capability of the whole network. For example, [17] utilizes KL divergence based loss to match the probability estimate of two peer networks. [5] makes the two models select the reliable samples from each other. Both of them use identical labels for two models, which restricts the diversity of information learned by the whole network and thus hinders the models from further adapting to the target domain. To address this issue, we propose an asymmetric mutual learning framework (AML) which uses asymmetric pseudo labels for two collaborative models. As shown in Fig. 1, one model uses original labels generated by clustering algorithm, the other uses the new labels augmented by our proposed algorithm of processing the original labels. When generating pseudo labels with clustering algorithm, images of the same person could be divided into different classes, these images will be separated further during iterative training. In light of this, we generate augmented pseudo labels by merging clusters based on k-nearest neighbors relationship. The augmented pseudo labels can make the model learn more generative information compared to original labels, while the model trained with original labels learns relatively discriminative information. Both augmented labels and original labels can be regarded as information complement to each other.

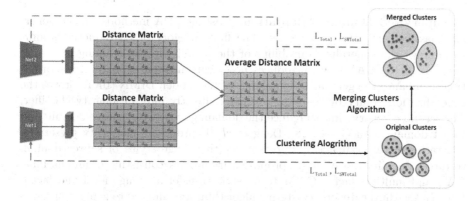

**Fig. 1.** The proposed asymmetric mutual learning framework (AML). $L_{total}$ refers to the normal loss. $L_{SWtotal}$ refers to the similarity weighted loss. The distance matrix of two branches refers to the distance between features of all training images which is computed with re-ranking in [21]. The average distance matrix is the average of two distance matrix from two branches. Clustering algorithm takes the average distance as the input and generates original clustering results. Our proposed merging clusters algorithm merges part of the original clusters to get new labels.

Triplet loss is commonly used in person re-identification. It focuses on the difference between positive pairs and negative pairs. In the fully-supervised scenario, since the identity labels are accurate, the expansion of the gap between the distributions of positive pairs and negative pairs can enhance the discrimination ability of the model. However, the pseudo labels are inaccurate in unsupervised cross-domain scenario. The large gap between the inaccurate positive pairs and negative pairs makes the model stuck in local optima and hinders the model from further improving in the target domain. To address above issue, we utilize the triplets which become invalid due to the large gap between positive pairs and negative pairs. In this way, we propose a similarity weighted loss which can further bring dissimilar positive pairs closer despite the large gap mentioned above. We argue that similarity weighted loss allows the model to escape local optima and continue adapting to target domain in late training stage. The main contributions of our work are summarized as follows:

- We propose an asymmetric mutual learning framework (AML). AML utilizes asymmetric pseudo labels to optimize models on the target domain, which makes the whole network capable to learn more diverse information.
- We propose a similarity weighted loss which can further adapt the model to the target domain in late training stage. It mines dissimilar positive samples despite the difference between the distributions of positive pairs and negative pairs.
- To evaluate our method, we conduct experiments on three large-scale datasets. Experimental results show that our method outperforms state-of-the-art methods for unsupervised cross-domain person re-identification.

## 2    Related Work

**Unsupervised Domain Adaptation.** Existing UDA methods can be generally classified into three categories. The first category of UDA methods aims to improve the generalization ability of the model without training on target domain [6,10]. EANet [6] introduces pose segmentation as auxiliary information to enhance the generalization ability of the model. DIMN [10] improves the generalization ability by mapping an image directly into an identity classifier. The second category aims to reduce the domain gap between source domain and target domain with GAN [1,8]. Deng *et al.* [1] propose a similarity preserving generative adversarial network to transfer the image styles of source domain to target domain. Liu *et al.* [8] propose a framework consisting of an ensemble GAN and multiple factor GANs to do style transfer at image level and factor level. In the third category, clustering algorithms are adopted to generate pseudo labels on the target domain, and then pseudo labels are used to fine-tune the re-identification models. SSG [3] obtains multiple pseudo labels by clustering global and local features of persons respectively. Zhai *et al.* [15] present an augmented discriminative clustering method to enforce the discrimination ability of models in the target domain. Zhang *et al.* [16] propose a two-stage framework which consists of conservative stage and promoting stage, the conservative stage aims to capture the local structure of target-domain data, while the promoting stage aims to utilize of global information about the data distribution. The results of the first and second kinds of methods are generally poor compared to the third category. However, clustering-based algorithms are troubled by noisy labels and the results are still unsatisfactory compared to supervised approaches.

**Supervised Mutual Learning.** Mutual learning generally refers to the idea that two or more models learn from each other and stimulate each other. DML [17] utilizes a pool of networks to solve the task collaboratively rather than single network. Co-Teaching [5] makes two models select reliable samples for each other. Both of them were originally designed for supervised tasks. Different from them, we mainly focus on the unsupervised cross-domain task.

**Unsupervised Mutual Learning.** MMT [4] introduces mutual learning into cross-domain person re-identification and proposes an alternative training manner that combines hard pseudo labels and soft refined labels. Zhao *et al.* [18] propose a noise resistible mutual learning method which performs collaborative clustering and mutual instance selection during training. Most of the existing mutual learning works use symmetric structure, which makes the models learn similar information. Yang *et al.* [14] propose an asymmetric co-teaching framework (ACT) to make the models see hard examples.

We mainly focus on unsupervised mutual learning in this paper. Similar but different from above works, our proposed AML aims to combine generative information and discriminative information. Our work differs from ACT in the following two aspects: (1) Our work does mutual learning without complicated sample selection process, the two models interact in a simpler way. (2) While ACT mainly focuses on effective usage of unreliable outliers, our work makes two models learn more diverse information by utilizing reliable inliers effectively.

# 3 Proposed Method

## 3.1 Structure of Asymmetric Mutual Learning

Our proposed asymmetric mutual framework (AML) consists of two stages: (1) Supervised training in the source domain. (2) Unsupervised clustering-based adaptation to the target domain. In the supervised stage, we train two models with same architecture on the source dataset. In the unsupervised adaptation stage, we adapt the trained models to target domain with asymmetric pseudo labels as shown in Fig. 1. To generate asymmetric labels, we propose a merging clusters algorithm which will be discussed in Sect. 3.2. We train two models with normal triplet loss and cross-entropy loss at first, and then utilize similarity weighted loss in Sect. 3.3 to further adapt two models to target domain.

## 3.2 Merging Clusters Algorithm

Existing clustering algorithms generally need to set the number of clusters except those based on density. Density-based clustering algorithms can generate

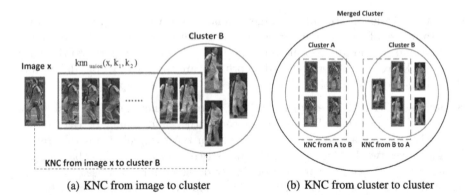

(a) KNC from image to cluster    (b) KNC from cluster to cluster

**Fig. 2.** Our proposed merging clusters algorithm. (a) We consider a image x has a KNC connection to cluster B if the union set of $k_1$ normal nearest neighbors and $k_2$ cross-camera nearest neighbors of x intersects with cluster B. (b) For two clusters A and B, we compute KNC connection between two classes according to Eq. 2 and merge then if both condition 3 and condition 4 satisfy.

the number of clusters by themselves. Since the number of clusters is usually unknown in UDA tasks, we adopt a density-based clustering algorithm [2] to cluster images. Density-based clustering algorithms generally consider points from the same continuous high-density region as a cluster. However, in cross-camera person re-identification scenario, the image distribution of the same person may be sparse due to the difference of pose and camera view. Thus the images belonging to the same person could be divided into different clusters. In contrast, $k$-nearest neighbors are less affected by the density, sparse points can also have $k$-nearest neighbors relationship. Accordingly, we propose a method to merge clusters by calculating $k$-nearest connection (KNC) between two clusters.

Given a data point $x_a$ in cluster $C_a$, we look for two kinds of k-nearest neighbors of it. One kind is normal k-nearest neighbors $knn_{normal}(x_a, k_1)$ obtained by sorting distance matrix computed with [21]. The other kind is cross-camera k-nearest neighbors $knn_{crosscam}(x_a, k_2)$ which contains the nearest $k_2$ neighbors selected from samples of different cameras from $x_a$. Note that $knn_{crosscam}(x_a, k_2)$ is utilized to bridge the gap between images across cameras since the camera ID is easy to obtain in real scenes and has effective supervised information. As shown in Fig. 2(a), we consider that $x_a$ is connected to cluster $C_b$ if the union set of $k_1$ normal nearest neighbors and $k_2$ cross-camera nearest neighbors contains at least one sample in cluster $C_b$, i.e.,

$$KNC_{x_a->C_b} = \begin{cases} 1 & \text{if } |knn_{union}(x_a, k_1, k_2) \cap C_b| > 0 \\ 0 & \text{otherwise} \end{cases}, \qquad (1)$$

where $knn_{union}(x_a, k_1, k_2)$ denotes the union set mentioned above. Hence, as shown in Fig. 2(b), we define the asymmetric k-nearest connection (KNC) from cluster $C_a$ to cluster $C_b$ as:

$$KNC_{C_a->C_b} = \sum_{x_a \in C_a} KNC_{x_a->C_b}, \tag{2}$$

which represents the number of samples that have k-nearest connection (KNC) to cluster $C_b$ in cluster $C_a$. Finally, we merge $C_a$ and $C_b$ if

$$\frac{KNC_{C_a->C_b}}{|C_a|} > thresh \tag{3}$$

and

$$\frac{KNC_{C_b->C_a}}{|C_b|} > thresh, \tag{4}$$

where $thresh$ is a threshold that controls the proportion of $KNC_{C_a->C_b}$ to the number of samples in cluster $C_a$.

Our merging clustering algorithm tends to merge small clusters which usually do not contain all the images belonging to the same person. Although our algorithm merges some images belonging to different persons during the merging process, it should be noted that our purpose is not to improve the clustering accuracy. The key point is that the merged clusters contain relatively generative information compared to original clusters. Training with merged clusters can prevent the model from further separating some images belonging to the same person. Thus the two models can complement with each other, which is effective in mutual learning.

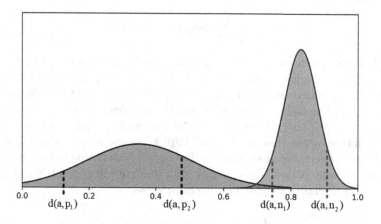

**Fig. 3.** A illustration of the motivation of similarity weighted loss. $d(a, p_1)$ and $d(a, p_2)$ denote the distance between anchor $a$ and its positive samples, while $d(a, n_1)$ and $d(a, n_2)$ denote the distance between anchor $a$ and its negative samples. When there is a large gap between the distributions of the distance of negative pairs and the distance of positive pairs, the triplet loss can not further narrow the distance between positive pairs.

## 3.3  Similarity Weighted Loss

Triplet loss and cross-entropy loss are two widely-used losses in person re-identification. The purpose of triplet loss is to bring positive pairs closer and push away the negative pairs. Typically, the triplet loss is defined as:

$$L_{Tri} = [d_p - d_n + \alpha]_+, \tag{5}$$

where $d_p$ represents the distance between the anchor $x^a$ and its positive samples $x_i^p$, $d_n$ represents the distance between the anchor $x^a$ and its negative samples $x_i^n$, $\alpha$ is the margin between $d_p$ and $d_n$, $[x]_+$ means $max(x, 0)$. The triplet loss will expand the gap between $d_p$ and $d_n$. When using triplet loss to fine-tune re-id model, the triplet loss tends to be zero at the end of training because $d_n$ is much larger than $d_p$. However, it doesn't mean that $d_p$ is nearly zero. As shown in Fig. 3, when $d_n$ is too large, $[d_p - d_n + \alpha]_+$ can still be zero while $d_p$ is a large value as long as $d_p \leq d_n - \alpha$. When $L_{tri}$ is zero, the gradient of $L_{tri}$ is zero, which makes the triplet invalid and the effect of $d_p$ ignored. To address this issue, we adapt triplet loss to focus more on dissimilar positive pairs, which we call similarity weighted triplet loss. Our similarity weighted triplet loss is computed as:

$$L_{SWTri} = [d_p - s_p d_n + \alpha]_+, \tag{6}$$

where $\alpha$ is the margin between $d_p$ and $s_p d_n$, $s_p$ is the average cosine similarity of the anchor and its positive samples in a mini-batch, i.e., for an anchor $x^a$, its $s_p$ is computed as:

$$s_p = \frac{1}{K} \sum_{i=1}^{K} cos(f(x^a), f(x_i^p)), \tag{7}$$

where $K$ is the number of positive samples of anchor $x^a$ in a mini-batch, $f(x^a)$ is the feature of anchor anchor $x^a$, $x_i^p$ denotes the $i$th positive sample of $x^a$. For dissimilar positive samples, their $s_p$ are smaller compared to similar positive samples. According to Eq. 6, dissimilar positive samples have lower weight of $d_n$, which means that $L_{SWTri}$ is less likely to be zero while the positive pairs are not similar. Thus we argue that our adapted triplet loss can avoid the problem that the distance between the dissimilar positive samples can not be further narrowed in the late training period. To cooperate with similarity weighted triplet loss, we also design a similarity weighted cross-entropy loss:

$$L_{SWID} = \frac{1}{max(\beta, s_p)} L_{ID}, \tag{8}$$

where $L_{ID}$ is the cross-entropy loss with label smoothing in [9], $\beta$ is a factor controlling the range of similarity weight. $L_{SWID}$ gives more weight to those samples which have low average cosine similarity with positive samples in a mini-batch compared to $L_{ID}$. Since $L_{SWTri}$ could be larger for those dissimilar positive samples, $L_{SWID}$ ensures that the proportion of triplet loss and cross-entropy loss will not change greatly. In summary, the normal total loss function is:

$$L_{total} = L_{Tri} + \lambda L_{ID},\tag{9}$$

while the total similarity weighted loss is:

$$L_{SWtotal} = L_{SWTri} + \lambda L_{SWID},\tag{10}$$

where $\lambda$ is the balanced weight of cross-entropy loss.

## 4 Experiments

Market-1501 [19], DukeMTMC-reID [20] and MSMT17 [13] are three large-scale person re-identification datasets. We evaluate our method on four domain adaptation tasks: Duke-to-Market, Market-to-Duke, Market-to-MSMT17, Duke-to-MSMT17. We take Rank-1 accuracy and mean average precision (mAP) as evaluation metrics. As shown in Table 1, experimental results show that our method outperforms most of existing methods.

### 4.1 Datasets

**Market-1501 [19].** The training set of Market-1501 contains 12936 annotated images of 751 person identities shot from 6 cameras in total. The testing set contains 3368 query images of 750 identities and 15913 gallery images of 751 identities.

**DukeMTMC-reID [20].** The training set of DukeMTMC-reID contains 12936 annotated images of 751 person identities shot from 6 cameras in total. The testing set contains 3368 query images of 750 identities and 15913 gallery images of 751 identities.

**MSMT17 [13].** As the largest and most challenging person re-ID dataset, MSMT17 contains 32621 images of 1041 person identities for training and 93820 images of 3060 identities for testing. In the testing set, 11659 images of 3060 identities are used for query and the gallery contains 82161 images of 3060 identities.

### 4.2 Implementation Details

**Stage 1: Supervised Training in Source Domain.** Previous works [3,6] have proved that focusing on local features can improve the cross-domain capabilities of the model. In view of this, we adopt PCB [12] to extract global features and local features of images and a semantic segmentation network to extract the masks of the upper and lower parts of the body. Hence, we apply the upper-part mask and lower-part mask to the global feature to get upper-part feature and lower-part feature which are used as local features. Then the global feature is used to calculate the triplet loss and all features are used to calculate the cross-entropy loss. We take ResNet-50 as backbone of PCB [12] and adopt SCHP [7] as our semantic segmentation network. SCHP is initialized with the weights trained on LIP dataset and does not update parameters during training. We adopt the Adam optimizer to optimize two re-id models separately. The learning rate is initially set to $3 \times 10^{-4}$, and decreased by 0.1 at the 35th epoch, 55th epoch and 70th epoch respectively. In addition, we use same warmup strategy following [9]. In the end of this stage, we get two feature extraction models with different weights.

**Stage 2: Unsupervised Clustering-Based Adaptation to Target Domain.** Given two models with different weights, we use them to extract features of person images. As mentioned in Sect. 3.2, we adopt DBSCAN [2] to cluster extracted global features, setting density radius $eps = 1.6 \times 10^{-3}$ and minimum size of a cluster to 4. The distance matrix between features is calculated separately using re-ranking in [21] and the average of them is given to DBSCAN [2]. With pseudo labels $\gamma_{origin}$ generated by DBSCAN [2], we use the method in Sect. 3.2 to get the new pseudo labels $\gamma_{new}$ with $thresh = 0.5$, $k_1 = 3$ and $k_2 = 15$. Then one of the two models is fine-tuned on target domain with $\gamma_{origin}$ and the other with $\gamma_{new}$. Different from stage 1, the learning rate is initially set to $3 \times 10^{-5}$ and decreased by 0.1 at the 10th epoch, and the warmup strategy is not used at this stage. Note that our proposed similarity weighted loss is not utilized until the training with Eq. 9 converges, since the proposed loss is to solve the problem that it is difficult to optimize the models in the late training period. In practice, we set $\beta$ to 0.7 and $\lambda$ to 0.01 when the model is transferred between Market1501 [19] and DukeMTMC-reID [20]. When the model is transferred to MSMT17 [13], we change $\beta$ to 0.9 to get best result.

### 4.3    Comparison with State-of-the-Art Methods

In this section, we compare our proposed method with state-of-the-art unsupervised cross-domain methods for person re-identification including: (1) EANet [6] that uses auxiliary information (2) SPGAN [1], ATNet [8] and ECN [22] that use GANs (3) SSG [3], UDAP [11], PCB-R-PAST [16], ACT [14], AD-Cluster [15], MMT [4], NRMT[18] that use pseudo labels. Among above methods, ACT, MMT and NRMT adopt mutual learning for unsupervised cross-domain person re-identification, which is highly relevant to our work. Specifically, our proposed method combines asymmetric mutual learning with similarity weighted loss to improve performance of cross-domain person re-id.

**Table 1.** Comparisons with state-of-the-art unsupervised cross-domain person re-id methods on Duke-to-Market, Market-to-Duke, Market-to-MSMT17, Duke-to-MSMT17.

| Methods | Duke → Market | | Market → Duke | |
|---|---|---|---|---|
| | mAP | Rank-1 | mAP | Rank-1 |
| SPGAN [1] | 22.8 | 51.5 | 22.3 | 41.1 |
| ATNet [8] | 25.6 | 55.7 | 24.9 | 45.1 |
| EANet [6] | 35.8 | 66.1 | 36.0 | 56.1 |
| ECN [22] | 43.0 | 75.1 | 40.4 | 63.3 |
| UDAP [11] | 53.7 | 75.8 | 49.0 | 68.4 |
| SSG$^{++}$ [3] | 68.7 | 86.2 | 60.3 | 76.0 |
| PCB-R-PAST[16] | 54.6 | 78.4 | 54.3 | 72.4 |
| ACT [14] | 60.6 | 80.5 | 54.5 | 72.4 |
| Co-Teaching [5] | 65.1 | 82.5 | 55.7 | 71.9 |
| AD-Cluster [15] | 68.3 | 86.7 | 54.1 | 72.6 |
| MMT-500 [4] | 71.2 | 87.7 | 63.1 | 76.8 |
| NRMT [18] | 71.7 | 87.8 | 62.2 | 77.8 |
| Ours | **75.5** | **88.7** | **64.5** | **78.6** |
| Methods | Market → MSMT17 | | Duke → MSMT17 | |
| | mAP | Rank-1 | mAP | Rank-1 |
| ECN [22] | 8.5 | 25.3 | 10.2 | 30.2 |
| SSG$^{++}$ [3] | 16.6 | 37.6 | 18.3 | 41.6 |
| MMT-500 [4] | 16.6 | 37.5 | 19.9 | 41.3 |
| Ours | **19.4** | **46.8** | **22.2** | **51.5** |

As shown in Table 1, our method outperforms all compared methods. For Duke → Market, our method outperforms state-of-the-art NRMT [18] by 3.8% in mAP and 0.9% in rank-1 accuracy. For Market → Duke, our method outperforms NRMT [18] by 2.3% in mAP and 0.8% in rank-1 accuracy. For Market → MSMT17, our method outperforms MMT-500 [4] by 2.8% in mAP and 9.3% in rank-1 accuracy. For Duke → MSMT17, our method outperforms MMT-500 [4] by 2.3% in mAP and 10.2% in rank-1 accuracy.

### 4.4 Ablation Study

In order to prove the effectiveness of our method, we create a baseline that optimize two models with original labels and normal loss function. As shown in Table 2, we perform ablation studies based on this baseline.

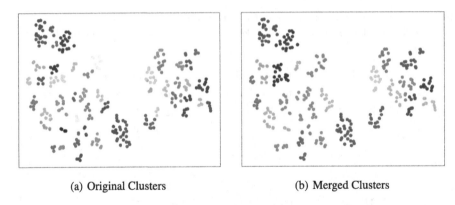

      (a) Original Clusters                          (b) Merged Clusters

**Fig. 4.** Visualization of some original clusters generated by DBSCAN and the corresponding merged clusters generated by our proposed algorithm.

**Effectiveness of Asymmetric Labels.** For better clarity, we visualize some original clusters and the corresponding merged clusters in Fig. 4. As shown in Fig. 4, small clusters are merged with their adjacent clusters. To show the effectiveness of new augmented labels generated by our proposed merging clusters algorithm, we train the two models with augmented labels, the result is denoted as "Baseline+Merged Clusters" in Table 2. As shown in the table, we improve the performance on Duke-to-Market by 9.7% in mAP and 6.6% in rank-1 accuracy with augmented labels. When testing on Market-to-Duke, "Baseline+Merged Clusters" surpass "Baseline" by 4.7% in mAP and 3.0% in rank-1 accuracy. To investigate the necessity of using asymmetric labels generated by our proposed merging clusters algorithm, we create mutual learning baseline models that only use original pseudo labels generated by DBSCAN [2]. As shown in Table 2, with asymmetric labels, we improve the performance by 11.3% in mAP and 6.8% in rank-1 accuracy compared to baseline on Duke-to-Market. Similarly, when the model is transferred from Market-1501 to DukeMTMC-reID, the performance gain becomes 5.8% in mAP and 3.1% in rank-1 accuracy. Besides, "AML" beats "Baseline+Merged Clusters" by 1.6% and 1.1% in mAP when testing on Duke-to-Market and Market-to-Duke respectively, which shows asymmetric labels performs better than symmetric augmented labels.

**Effectiveness of Similarity Weighted Loss.** To show the performance of similarity weighted loss, we train the baseline with similarity weighted loss after the training with normal loss converges, the result is denoted as "Baseline*" in Table 2. When testing on Duke-to-Market, "Baseline*" surpass "Baseline" by 1.6% in mAP and 0.9% in rank-1 accuracy. When testing on Market-to-Duke, "Baseline*" surpass "Baseline" by 2.3% in mAP and 1.3% in rank-1 accuracy. To prove the similarity weighted loss can work on AML, we also train the model with asymmetric labels by optimizing Eq. 10 after the training with Eq. 9 converges. As shown in Table 2, the combination of similarity weighted triplet loss and similarity weighted cross-entropy loss surpasses the combination of normal triplet

**Table 2.** Ablation studies of our proposed methods on Duke-to-Market and Market-to-Duke. "Direct Transfer" refers to directly applying the model trained on source domain to the target domain, "Baseline" refers to symmetric mutual learning with original labels and normal loss function $L_{total}$, "Baseline*" refers to symmetric mutual learning with similarity weighted loss function $L_{SWtotal}$, "Baseline+Merged Clusters" refers to symmetric mutual learning with augmented labels and $L_{total}$, "AML" denotes our proposed asymmetric mutual learning framework in Sect. 3 optimized with $L_{total}$, "AML*" stands for proposed AML enhanced by similarity weighted loss $L_{SWtotal}$.

| Methods | Duke → Market | | Market → Duke | |
|---|---|---|---|---|
| | mAP | rank-1 | mAP | rank-1 |
| Direct transfer | 25.4 | 55.6 | 24.6 | 42.9 |
| Baseline | 62.5 | 81.5 | 56.8 | 74.1 |
| Baseline* | 64.1 | 82.4 | 59.1 | 75.4 |
| Baseline+Merged Clusters | 72.2 | 88.1 | 61.5 | 77.1 |
| AML | 73.8 | 88.3 | 62.6 | 77.2 |
| AML* | **75.5** | **88.7** | **64.5** | **78.6** |

loss and cross-entropy loss by 1.7% in mAP and 0.4% in rank-1 accuracy on Duke-to-Market. The performance testing on Market-to-Duke also boosts by 1.9% in mAP and 1.4% in rank-1 accuracy.

## 5   Conclusion

In this paper, we propose a novel asymmetric mutual learning framework for unsupervised cross-domain person re-identification. Our framework consists of two models which utilize asymmetric labels. We propose a merging clusters algorithm to generate new pseudo labels which contain different information from original pseudo labels. Furthermore, a similarity weighted loss is proposed to mine dissimilar positive samples so that the two models can continue adapting to target domain in late training stage. Comprehensive experimental results demonstrate that the performance of our approach outperforms the most of existing methods on three large-scale datasets. In the future, we will explore how to integrate camera information into the network more reasonably.

**Acknowledgment.** This work is supported by National Key R&D Program of China (Grant No. 2018YF B2100603) and National Natural Science Foundation of China (Grant No. 61872024).

## References

1. Deng, W., Zheng, L., Ye, Q., Kang, G., Yang, Y., Jiao, J.: Image-image domain adaptation with preserved self-similarity and domain-dissimilarity for person re-identification. In: Proceedings of the IEEE Conference on Computer Vision and Pattern Recognition, pp. 994–1003 (2018)

2. Ester, M., Kriegel, H.P., Sander, J., Xu, X., et al.: A density-based algorithm for discovering clusters in large spatial databases with noise. In: Proceedings of the Knowledge Discovery and Data Mining, pp. 226–231 (1996)
3. Fu, Y., Wei, Y., Wang, G., Zhou, Y., Shi, H., Huang, T.S.: Self-similarity grouping: a simple unsupervised cross domain adaptation approach for person re-identification. In: Proceedings of the IEEE International Conference on Computer Vision, pp. 6112–6121 (2019)
4. Ge, Y., Chen, D., Li, H.: Mutual mean-teaching: pseudo label refinery for unsupervised domain adaptation on person re-identification. In: International Conference on Learning Representations (2020)
5. Han, B., et al.: Co-teaching: Robust training of deep neural networks with extremely noisy labels. In: Proceedings of the 32nd International Conference on Neural Information Processing Systems, pp. 8536–8546 (2018)
6. Huang, H., et al.: Eanet: enhancing alignment for cross-domain person re-identification. arXiv preprint arXiv:1812.11369 (2018)
7. Li, P., Xu, Y., Wei, Y., Yang, Y.: Self-correction for human parsing. arXiv preprint arXiv:1910.09777 (2019)
8. Liu, J., Zha, Z.J., Chen, D., Hong, R., Wang, M.: Adaptive transfer network for cross-domain person re-identification. In: Proceedings of the IEEE Conference on Computer Vision and Pattern Recognition, pp. 7202–7211 (2019)
9. Luo, H., Gu, Y., Liao, X., Lai, S., Jiang, W.: Bag of tricks and a strong baseline for deep person re-identification. In: Proceedings of the IEEE Conference on Computer Vision and Pattern Recognition Workshops, pp. 1487–1495 (2019)
10. Song, J., Yang, Y., Song, Y.Z., Xiang, T., Hospedales, T.M.: Generalizable person re-identification by domain-invariant mapping network. In: Proceedings of the IEEE Conference on Computer Vision and Pattern Recognition, June 2019
11. Song, L., et al.: Unsupervised domain adaptive re-identification: Theory and practice. Pattern Recognition **102**, 107173 (2020)
12. Sun, Y., Zheng, L., Yang, Y., Tian, Q., Wang, S.: Beyond part models: person retrieval with refined part pooling (and a strong convolutional baseline). In: Proceedings of the European Conference on Computer Vision, pp. 480–496 (2018)
13. Wei, L., Zhang, S., Gao, W., Tian, Q.: Person transfer GAN to bridge domain gap for person re-identification. In: Proceedings of the IEEE Conference on Computer Vision and Pattern recognition, pp. 79–88 (2018)
14. Yang, F., et al.: Asymmetric co-teaching for unsupervised cross-domain person re-identification. In: Proceedings of the AAAI Conference on Artificial Intelligence, pp. 12597–12604 (2020)
15. Zhai, Y., et al.: Ad-cluster: augmented discriminative clustering for domain adaptive person re-identification. In: Proceedings of the IEEE Conference on Computer Vision and Pattern Recognition, pp. 9021–9030 (2020)
16. Zhang, X., Cao, J., Shen, C., You, M.: Self-training with progressive augmentation for unsupervised cross-domain person re-identification. In: Proceedings of the IEEE International Conference on Computer Vision, pp. 8222–8231 (2019)
17. Zhang, Y., Xiang, T., Hospedales, T.M., Lu, H.: Deep mutual learning. In: Proceedings of the IEEE Conference on Computer Vision and Pattern Recognition, pp. 4320–4328 (2018)
18. Zhao, F., Liao, S., Xie, G.-S., Zhao, J., Zhang, K., Shao, L.: Unsupervised domain adaptation with noise resistible mutual-training for person re-identification. In: Vedaldi, A., Bischof, H., Brox, T., Frahm, J.-M. (eds.) ECCV 2020. LNCS, vol. 12356, pp. 526–544. Springer, Cham (2020). https://doi.org/10.1007/978-3-030-58621-8_31

19. Zheng, L., Shen, L., Tian, L., Wang, S., Wang, J., Tian, Q.: Scalable person re-identification: a benchmark. In: Proceedings of the IEEE International Conference on Computer Vision, pp. 1116–1124 (2015)
20. Zheng, Z., Zheng, L., Yang, Y.: Unlabeled samples generated by GAN improve the person re-identification baseline in vitro. In: Proceedings of the IEEE International Conference on Computer Vision, pp. 3754–3762 (2017)
21. Zhong, Z., Zheng, L., Cao, D., Li, S.: Re-ranking person re-identification with k-reciprocal encoding. In: Proceedings of the IEEE Conference on Computer Vision and Pattern Recognition, pp. 1318–1327 (2017)
22. Zhong, Z., Zheng, L., Luo, Z., Li, S., Yang, Y.: Invariance matters: exemplar memory for domain adaptive person re-identification. In: Proceedings of the IEEE Conference on Computer Vision and Pattern recognition, pp. 598–607 (2019)

# Collaborative Positional-Motion Excitation Module for Efficient Action Recognition

Tamam Alsarhan[1] and Hongtao Lu[1,2(✉)]

[1] Key Lab of Shanghai Education Commission for Intelligent Interaction
and Cognitive Engineering, Department of Computer Science and Engineering,
Shanghai Jiao Tong University, Shanghai, China
{tamamhazza,htlu}@sjtu.edu.cn
[2] MOE Key Lab of Artificial Intelligence, AI Institute, Shanghai Jiao Tong
University, Shanghai, China

**Abstract.** Massive progress for vision-based action recognition has been made in the last few years, owing to the advancement of deep convolutional neural networks (CNNs). In contrast with 2D CNN-based approaches, 3D CNN-based approaches can effectively capture spatial and temporal features. However, they are computationally intensive. To boost 2D-CNN performance, most of the existing methods leverage channel attention (e.g. squeeze and excitation), which despite its strong impact on the model performance, operates only on the channel space and ignores the spatial space. In this work, we design a generic and collaborative excitation module, namely the Collaborative Positional-Motion Excitation Module (CPME) for action recognition. CPME is a dual-pathway excitation module designed to embed the crucial types of information, mainly the positional information and the motion information, for efficient action recognition. Positional Enhancement Pathway (PEP), the first pathway of CPME, considers encoding direction-aware and position-sensitive information. Motion Enhancement Pathway (MEP), the second pathway, encodes the motion information by emphasizing the informative features in each frame and excite motion-sensitive channels. We integrate the proposed CPME into 2D CNNs to form a simple yet effective CPME-Net with limited extra computational cost. Finally, a discriminative and diverse video-level representation for action recognition is generated by end-to-end training. Experiments on two popular action recognition datasets demonstrate that CPME blocks bring performance improvements on 2D CNN baseline, and our method achieves competitive results against the state-of-the-art methods.

**Keywords:** Video action recognition · Motion encoding · Spatio-temporal learning

© Springer Nature Switzerland AG 2021
D. N. Pham et al. (Eds.): PRICAI 2021, LNAI 13033, pp. 138–151, 2021.
https://doi.org/10.1007/978-3-030-89370-5_11

# 1   Introduction

Considering the fact that video-based action recognition task has an essential role in various real-world applications such as security and human-computer interaction [1,2], designing an effective architecture for understanding video contents, and hence recognizing the human actions became a persistence need. The key to this task lies in learning powerful joint spatio-temporal and motion representations from large-scale video datasets. Spatial features mainly describe the scene containing the objects involved in an action in each video frame, while temporal features capture motion cues embedded in the evolving frames over time. Generally, human actions are classified into spatial-related actions and temporal-related actions. Spatial-related actions (e.g. "Brush hair" and "Kick ball") can be interpreted based on the scene itself, while temporal-related actions contain similar "spatial" features and the only way to differentiate them is to capture temporal features. For example, "Moving something up" and "Moving something down" are temporal-related actions which have similar 'spatial' features with exactly 'reversed' temporal information, see Fig. 1. The same thing is true for other actions like 'rotate something clockwise' and 'rotate something counterclockwise'. Therefore, studying action recognition comprehensively involves temporal modeling and spatial modeling together.

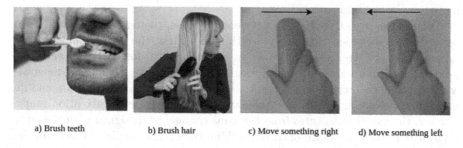

a) Brush teeth          b) Brush hair          c) Move something right          d) Move something left

**Fig. 1.** Illustration of scene-based actions (a and b) and temporal-based actions (c and d).

Research into the wide spectrum of action recognition problems has been highly dependent on 3D-CNN based approaches and 2D-CNN based approaches, with each line of research attempting to tackle this problem effectively and efficiently. 3D-CNN based approaches have been shown to be effective due to their ability in jointly learning spatial and temporal features of video clips [3–6] by employing 3D convolution kernels. However, some challenging issues such as the inadequate modeling of information contained in videos as well as the computational burdens limit their deployment in real-world applications.

The recent progress of 2D CNN-based approaches [7–10] is impressive, owing to the remarkable capability of CNN in capturing spatial features from video frames. Despite that, such approaches do not bear the ability of temporal modeling. Hence, weak performance in recognizing temporal-based actions is noticed.

In addition to modeling the appearance information using 2D CNN, another line of research, which is integrating optical flow as an additional stream to model the temporal cues, is investigated [11, 12]. The flow stream, which is usually called the temporal stream, along with the RGB image stream (appearance stream) form two stream architecture. To date, these two-stream approaches have emerged as a dominant paradigm in video-based action recognition.

In recent years, the view has been shifting towards adopting the aspect of channel attention to strengthen the power of discrimination of deep learning models, which is a critical aspect in deep vision models. This shift in the view was brought about by the recently proposed modules e.g. Squeeze and Excitation (SE) [13] and Efficient Channel Attention (ECA) [14], which are proved to enhance the model learning capability. To date, various action recognition methods employed enhancement modules based on self attention and channel attention to learn better representation [8, 15]. The essential idea of SE is utilizing the attention mechanism in a channel-wise manner, SE is a self-gating mechanism, designed to embed two stages (1) Squeeze and (2) Excitation, before they are fed into the next transformation. Motion information is another research line focused on studying moving objects or people for each input video, aiming to better modeling the temporal information. The importance of motion modeling originates from the fact that the temporal evolution of visual features enables us to capture dynamic variation in videos and relate adjacent frame-level features for action recognition.

Despite the recent progress of previous methods, there are still several open issues in this direction that deserve rethinking. First, the term channel attention module is better thought of as an umbrella term for a way of encoding inter-channel information, in which features from the same channel are assigned with the same coefficient. This definition neglects positional information and its importance, which is critical for generating spatially selective attention maps. Further, the fact that features from the same channel are assigned with the same coefficient leads to a failure of distinguishing the crucial moving objects on the spatial dimension.

Inspired by the previous analysis and to build a robust architecture for video action recognition capable of capturing diverse information from video frames, we focus on two complementary and crucial aspects including the positional information and the motion encoding. Our proposed module is a Collaborative Positional-Motion Excitation Module (CPME) consisting of two parallel pathways, mainly the Motion Enhancement Pathway (MEP), which is designed to emphasize the informative features in each frame then calculate and excite motion-sensitive channels. The second pathway is the Positional Enhancement Pathway (PEP), which embeds the positional information into the channel attention and captures long-range dependencies along the two spatial directions. In this way, the motion-wise and long-range dependencies provided in one module with the help of encoding positional and motion features, can offer a fine-grained description for the motion clues collaboratively.

The main contributions of this paper can be summarized as follows:

1) We propose a learning representational module, the Collaborative Positional-Motion Excitation Module (CPME), to effectively and jointly capture appropriate channel-wise features and motion information for vision-based action recognition.
2) We propose a simple yet effective 2D-CNN based module, namely CPME-Net to learn a discriminative video-level representation for action recognition.
3) Our approach is a plug and play module, which allows it to be served as a plug-in operation for a wide range of 2D CNN-based action recognition architectures.
4) By end to end training, the proposed CPME-Net achieves promising action recognition results on two benchmarks, UCF101 and HMDB51 datasets.

## 2   Related Work

In this section, we briefly review previous works regarding action recognition in general, CNN-based action recognition approaches, temporal modeling in action recognition and the attention mechanisms.

### 2.1   Action Recognition

Action recognition has attracted much attention in recent years. Most of the previous works leverage convolutional networks to model video clips [4,16–19]. Two-stream methods are also investigated for this task. For instance, Simonyan and Zisserman [11] proposed a two-stream ConvNet architecture, incorporating spatial stream ConvNet and temporal stream ConvNet. This architecture exploits motion cues and significantly improves the model accuracy. Similarly, in [20] the two streams are fused by a 3D filter which is able to learn correspondences between highly abstract features of both streams.

### 2.2   CNN-Based Approaches

3D CNN has the ability to capture spatio-temporal features. Slowfast networks [5] involved two branches, a slow pathway to model spatial semantics and a fast path to model motion at fine temporal resolution. I3D [3] inflated the ImageNet pre-trained 2D kernel into 3D to capture spatiotemporal features and modeled motion features with another flow stream. STCNet [21] inserted its STC block into 3D ResNet to capture both spatial-channels and temporal-channels correlation information throughout network layers. To avoid the heavy computations of 3D CNNs, several works proposed 2D CNN-based frameworks for video action recognition. TSN [9] was the first framework introduced the concept of 'segment' to process videos by extracting short snippets over a long video sequence with a uniform sparse sampling scheme. STM block [22] is proposed to encode spatiotemporal and motion features together. The original residual blocks in the

ResNet architecture is replaced with STM blocks to form a simple yet effective STM network with limited extra computation cost. Other works such as TEINet [23] and TEA [8] are proposed to augment state-of-the-art 2D CNNs with temporal aggregation modules, aiming to effectively capture the spatiotemporal features at a low cost.

### 2.3 Temporal Modeling in Action Recognition

Various schemes have been proposed specifically to explore the temporal dimension, adopting the fact that temporal modeling is considered to be crucial for action recognition [5,7,24]. In [7], authors proved that shifting the channels along the temporal dimension yields a good performance gain fully based on 2D CNNs. Several existing temporal modeling modules focus on capturing discriminative features from the spatio-temporal vector by exciting the motion-sensitive channels features. For instance, in [8], a temporal excitation and aggregation (TEA) block is proposed to capture both short and long-range temporal evolution. In this module, the motion modeling and the spatio-temporal features learning are incorporated into a unified framework. Additionally, authors in [23] propose an adaptive temporal modeling module composed of a motion enhanced module, designed to excite channel features and a temporal interaction module, designed to capture contextual features. To avoid the redundant information utilization, authors in [25] proposed a sequential channel filtering mechanism which is especially designed to excite the discriminative features channels from different frames.

### 2.4 Attention Mechanisms

Attention mechanisms emerged as one of the most influential ideas in deep learning field, with a massive usage in various vision applications. The intensive exploration of these mechanisms concludes that they boost the learning capability of deep learning methods. CBAM [26] is an attention mechanism composed of Channel Attention Module (CAM) and Spatial Attention Module (SAM), which are integrated sequentially. Squeeze and Excitation blocks (abbreviated as SE-block) [13] is an easy-to-plug-in attention module, designed to computes channel attention. SE has gained remarkable performance at considerably low computational cost. However, it only considers encoding inter-channel information and ignores the importance of spatial information, which is proved to be crucial to capturing object structures in vision tasks. Coordinate Attention [27], on the other hand, factorizes channel attention into two parallel 1D feature encoding processes. Hence, spatial coordinate information are embedded into the generated attention maps.

## 3   Approach

### 3.1   Architecture of CPME

The main insight of CPME is the dual encoding of the positional and motion information in one module, in which the adaptively enhanced motion-related channels as well as the positional information are complementary encoded in two parallel pathways i.e., Positional Enhancement Pathway (PEP) and Motion Enhancement Pathway (MEP) as illustrated in Fig. 2.

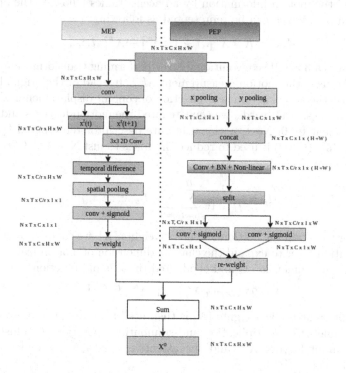

**Fig. 2.** A detailed view of the Collaborative Positional-Motion Excitation Module (CPME). The enhanced feature map $(x^o)$ is obtained through the fusion of the result of both PEP and PEM, which both share the same input vector. On MEP side, several steps started with convolution, and ended with broadcasting the channel attention vector to the original input tensor, are conducted. On PEP side, 1D horizontal global pooling and 1D vertical global pooling are conducted then a series of concatenation, batch normalization and convolution is also conducted. Finally, the output vector is obtained by using a fusion operation.

$X^{in}$, which is a 5-dimensional vector of the shape (N, C, T, W, H) is fed into both PEP and MEP. N represents the batch size, C represents the number of channels, and T, H, W are the spatiotemporal dimensions. $X^o$, the output of CPME module, is also a 5-D tensor of the same shape. MEP adopts the idea of exciting motion sensitive features as normally different channels tend to capture different features. For instance, some channels concerns motion information while the others are tend to capture scene information. Motion excitation aspect has been previously explored by [8,22], where they proposed a whole block for extracting motion. Different from them, we use the MEP collaboratively with PEP in on block.

First, a $1 \times 1$ 2D convolutional layer with channel reduction is conducted. Channel reduction is used for efficiency. We reduced the spatial channels by a factor of r, which is set to 16 in our experiments and obtained $X^r$. Next, we modeled the motion information by adjacent frames following the operation proposed in [22], which can be represented as following:

$$M_{exc} = K * X^r[:, t+1, :, :, :] - X^r[:, t, :, :, :]$$ (1)

where K is a $3 \times 3$ 2D convolutional layer performing transformation for each channel. We used the motion measurement $M_{exc}$ instead of the original feature map because the actual action is a reflection of content displacements of the two successive frames. Afterwards, we concatenated the motion features and padded the last element by 0. Next, a global feature descriptor represented by spatial average pooling (GAP) is used to reduce the space to just N $\times$ T $\times$ C/r $\times$ 1 $\times$ 1, as illustrated in Eq. 2:

$$M_p = \frac{1}{H \times W} \sum_{i=1}^{H} \sum_{j=1}^{W} M_{exc}[:, :, :, i, j]$$ (2)

In order to obtain the motion-attentive weights (A), we conduct another $1 \times 1$ 2D convolution layer to expand the channel dimension of motion features to the original channel dimension C and conducted the sigmoid function.

$$A = 2\delta(conv * M_p) - 1, A^{N \times T \times C \times 1 \times 1}$$ (3)

The motion-attentive weights (A) is then used to re-weight the input tensor $X^{in}$ by channel-wise multiplication and summation operation. As illustrated in Eq. 4, the input feature $X^{in}$ and the attentive weight A are multiplied in a residual manner.

$$X^o = A \cdot X^{in} + X^{in}$$ (4)

The idea behind using the residual connection is to enhance the spatio-temporal features meanwhile preserve scene information.

The main insight of MEP was exciting the motion features, which is crucial aspect for vision recognition. As noticed in Eq. 2, we used a global spatial pooling to focus on which channels are important. In PEP, from the other hand, we are incorporating positional information into channel attention. Different from PEP and to preserve positional information, we factorized the global pooling into 1D horizontal global pooling and 1D vertical global pooling as illustrated in Eq. 5 and 6. To this end, we obtained direction-aware feature maps.

$$V^h = \frac{1}{W} \sum_{i=1}^{W} X_{in}[:, :, :, :, i]$$ (5)

$$V^w = \frac{1}{H} \sum_{j=1}^{H} X_{in}[:, :, :, j, :] \tag{6}$$

The direction-aware feature maps are then concatenated and fed into $1 \times 1$ convolution layer followed by batch normalization and non-linear activation as illustrated in Eq. 7. Channel reduction with (r) ratio is conducted in this stage to reduce the overhead model complexity.

$$V_t = \delta(conv * [v^w, v^h]), V_t^{N \times T \times C/r \times 1 \times (H+W)} \tag{7}$$

$V^h$ and $V^w$ are again obtained by splitting $V_t$ along the spatial dimension into two separate tensors. Next, another transformation is needed in this stage to restore the number of channels as in the input tensor $X^{in}$. See Eq. 8 and Eq. 9.

$$A_h = \delta(conv * V^h) \tag{8}$$

$$A_w = \delta(conv * V^w) \tag{9}$$

The Positional attentive vectors $A^h$ and $A^w$ are then used to re-weight the input tensor $X_{in}$.

## 3.2   CPME Network

We integrate the proposed CPME module into the existing ResNet [28] to form CPME Network. The overall design of the CPME-Net is illustrated in Fig. 3.

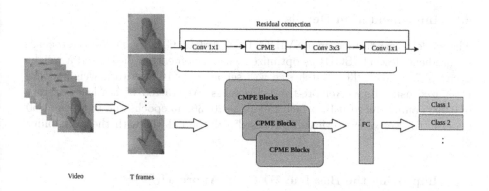

**Fig. 3.** The overall architecture of CPME network

A $(1 \times 1)$ 2D convolution layer is applied for channel reduction purpose. Then, the compressed feature maps are fed into CPME block to encode positional and motion features together. Adding CPME block does not require any modification for the original design. The action recognition network can be constructed by stacking the CPME blocks.

We train our CPME-Net architecture on both RGB and optical flow inputs and fuse the prediction scores at the end, following the two-stream framework [11]. We use TVL1 optical flow algorithm [29] to compute optical flow because of its efficiency.

## 4    Experiments

### 4.1    Experimental Settings

We conducted extensive experiments to demonstrate that the proposed CPME-Net can enhance the performance of 2D CNN-based approaches compared to previous models. The baseline method in our experiments is Temporal Segment Networks (TSN) [9] where we use the same backbone (ResNet-50) for fair comparison. We conducted our experiments on two large scale human motion datasets HMDB51 [30] and UCF101 [31]. HMDB51 includes 6.8K videos of 51 actions taken from movies and web videos. UCF-101 includes 13K videos of 101 action classes. We followed the original evaluation scheme using three training/testing splits. Also, we reported average accuracy over these splits. To conduct our experiments on video action recognition tasks, we followed the sampling strategy in TSN [9]. Given an input video, we firstly divided it into T segments of equal duration. Then one frame from each segment is randomly selected to obtain a clip with T frames. Additionally, we utilize random scaling and corner cropping during training for data augmentation. Each cropped frame was finally resized to 224 × 224, which was used for training the model.

### 4.2    Implementation Details

The models were trained on a NVIDIA RTX 2080 Ti GPU. We adopted stochastic gradient descent (SGD) as optimizer with a momentum of 0.9 and a weight decay of $5 \times 10^{-4}$. The Batch size was set as N = 16. Network weights were initialized using ImageNet pre-trained weights. We started with a learning rate of 0.0005 and reduced it by a factor of 10 at 20, 30, 45 epochs and stopped at 50 epochs. To overcome overfitting, we used a dropout layer with the probability of 0.5.

### 4.3    Improving the Baseline 2D CNN-Approach

To highlight the effectiveness of CPME module, we showed the improvement of its performance over 2D CNN based method. To do so, we conducted extensive experiments on split 1 of HMDB51 dataset comparing the baseline with different CPME-Net architectures. First, we attached CPME's components, PEP and MEP in sequential manner, Fig. 4(b). Then, we used sum operation to fuse CPME components, Fig. 4 (c). A shift module is added to both architectures, Fig. 4 (d) and (e). The results are mentioned in Table 1.

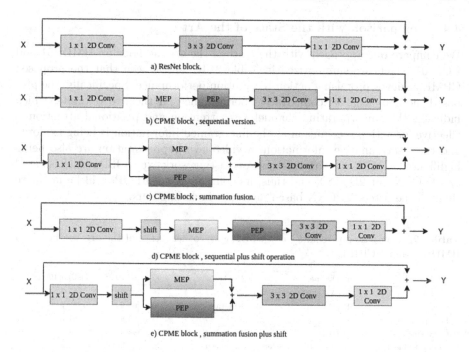

**Fig. 4.** The altered blocks of different architectures based on standard ResNet block.

As illustrated in Table 1, CPME module brings performance improvement on 2D CNN baseline by 0.8%. Temporal shift operation, embedded to a part of channels in TSM [7], encodes some temporal information to the network. However, it lacks explicit temporal modeling and inter-channel information, which both are included in CPME. Moreover, adding shift module boosts the model performance. Further, summation fusion was better than sequential. Overall, results demonstrate that exploring fine-grained key information by focusing on motion and positional information makes the video-level representation more discriminative for action recognition. To conclude, CPME block verifies that fine-grained motion and positional attention scores benefit for boosting the action recognition performance.

**Table 1.** Evaluation of key components on HMDB51 split 1.

| Methods | Top-1% |
|---|---|
| TSN (our implementation) | 54.3 |
| Baseline+CPME (summation) | 55.0 |
| Baseline+CPME (Sequential) | 54.7 |
| Baseline+CPME+Shift (summation) | **55.1** |
| Baseline+CPME+Shift (sequential) | 54.8 |

### 4.4    Comparison with the State of the Art

We compare our approach with the state-of-the-art methods on HMDB51 and UCF101 which are summarized in Table 2. It can be seen that the proposed CPME achieves promising action recognition performance. Specifically, the proposed method achieves comparative performance on the two datasets, which indicates that incorporating channel-wise attention and positional attention is effective for action recognition as the fine-grained information is being explored and the discriminative information in video-level representation are also being highlighted. CMPE outperforms most of existing work except I3D, which is based on 3D CNN not 2D CNN and thus, its computational FLOPs will be far more than all the listed 2D CNN based methods, including ours.

**Table 2.** Comparison results of CPME with other state-of-the-art methods on HMDB51 and UCF101.

| Method | Backbone | Pre-train | Flow | HMDB51 (%) | UCF101 (%) |
|---|---|---|---|---|---|
| C3D [4] | 3D VGG-11 | Sports-1M | No | 51.6 | 82.3 |
| STC [21] | ResNet101 | Kinetics | No | 66.8 | 93.7 |
| LTC [12] | – | – | Yes | 64.8 | 91.7 |
| Conv Fusion [20] | VGG-16 | ImageNet | Yes | 65.4 | 92.5 |
| ST-Multiplier [33] | ResNet-50 & ResNet-152 | ImageNet | No | 68.9 | 94.2 |
| ST-Pyramid [34] | ResNet-50 | ImageNet | Yes | 66.5 | 93.8 |
| ARTNet with TSN [35] | 3D ResNet-18 | Kinetics | Yes | 70.9 | 94.3 |
| TSN [9] | ResNet-50 | ImageNet | No | 54.7 | 86.2 |
| TSN two-Stream [9] | BNInception | ImageNet+Kinetics | Yes | – | 97.0 |
| TSN RGB [9] | | | | | 91.0 |
| StNet [36] | ResNet-50 | ImageNet+Kinetics | No | – | 93.5 |
| I3D [3] | 3D Inception | ImageNet+Kinetics | Yes | **80.7** | **98.0** |
| TSM [7] | ResNet-50 | ImageNet+Kinetics | Yes | 70.7 | 94.5 |
| Disentangling [32] | BNInception | ImageNet+Kinetics | No | – | 95.9 |
| Ours (RGB) | ResNet-50 | ImageNet | No | 55.1 | 86.5 |
| Ours (RGB + Flow) | ResNet-50 | ImageNet | Yes | 72.3 | 95.1 |

## 5    Conclusion

In this paper, we presented a simple yet effective network for action recognition by encoding positional and motion features together in a unified 2D CNN network. We replace the original residual blocks with CPME blocks in ResNet architecture to build the CPME network. CPME block contains a MEP to model channel-wise motion features and a PEP to capture long-range dependencies with precise positional information together. Without any 3D convolution, our CPME achieves promising results on both UCF101 and HMDB51. Despite that, our method still has a drawback. Computing the optical flow is a bit expensive. In future work, we will try to explore more efficient ways to model temporal features.

**Acknowledgement.** This paper is supported by NSFC (No. 61772330, 62176155, 61876109), Shanghai Municipal Science and Technology Major Project (2021SHZ DZX0102), the Shanghai Key Laboratory of Crime Scene Evidence (no. 2017XC WZK01), and the Interdisciplinary Program of Shanghai Jiao Tong University (no. YG2019QNA09).

# References

1. Wu, A.D., Sharma, N., Blumenstein, M.: Recent advances in video-based human action recognition using deep learning: a review. In: 2017 International Joint Conference on Neural Networks (IJCNN), Anchorage, AK, USA, pp. 2865–2872 (2017). https://doi.org/10.1109/IJCNN.2017.7966210
2. Coşar, S., Donatiello, G., Bogorny, V., Garate, C., Alvares, L.O., Brémond, F.: Toward abnormal trajectory and event detection in video surveillance. IEEE Trans. Circuits Syst. Video Technol. **27**(3), 683–695 (2017). https://doi.org/10.1109/TCSVT.2016.2589859
3. Carreira, J., Zisserman, A.: Quo vadis, action recognition? A new model and the kinetics dataset. In: 2017 IEEE Conference on Computer Vision and Pattern Recognition (CVPR), Honolulu, HI, USA, pp. 4724–4733 (2017). https://doi.org/10.1109/CVPR.2017.502
4. Tran, D., Bourdev, L., Fergus, R., Torresani, L., Paluri, M.: Learning spatiotemporal features with 3D convolutional networks. In: 2015 IEEE International Conference on Computer Vision (ICCV), Santiago, Chile, pp. 4489–4497 (2015). https://doi.org/10.1109/ICCV.2015.510
5. Feichtenhofer, C., Fan, H., Malik, J., He, K.: SlowFast networks for video recognition. In: IEEE/CVF International Conference on Computer Vision, ICCV, pp. 6201–6210 (2019)
6. Chen, Y., Kalantidis, Y., Li, J., Yan, S., Feng, J.: $A^2$-nets: double attention networks. In: Advances in Neural Information Processing Systems, pp. 350–359 (2018)
7. Lin, J., Gan, C., Han, S.: TSM: temporal shift module for efficient video understanding. In: Proceedings of the IEEE International Conference on Computer Vision, pp. 7083–7093 (2019)
8. Li, Y., Ji, B., Shi, X., Zhang, J., Kang, B., Wang, L.: TEA: temporal excitation and aggregation for action recognition. In: 2020 IEEE/CVF Conference on Computer Vision and Pattern Recognition (CVPR), Seattle, WA, USA, pp. 906–915 (2020). https://doi.org/10.1109/CVPR42600.2020.00099
9. Wang, L., et al.: Temporal segment networks for action recognition in videos. IEEE Trans. Pattern Anal. Mach. Intell. **41**(11), 2740–2755 (2019). https://doi.org/10.1109/TPAMI.2018.2868668
10. Weng, J., et al.: Temporal distinct representation learning for action recognition. In: Vedaldi, A., Bischof, H., Brox, T., Frahm, J.-M. (eds.) ECCV 2020. LNCS, vol. 12352, pp. 363–378. Springer, Cham (2020). https://doi.org/10.1007/978-3-030-58571-6_22
11. Simonyan, K., Zisserman, A.: Two-stream convolutional networks for action recognition in videos. In: Advances in Neural Information Processing Systems, pp. 568–576 (2014)
12. Varol, G., Laptev, I., Schmid, C.: Long-term temporal convolutions for action recognition. IEEE Trans. Pattern Anal. Mach. Intell. **40**(6), 1510–1517 (2018). https://doi.org/10.1109/TPAMI.2017.2712608

13. Hu, J., Shen, L., Sun, G.: Squeeze-and-excitation networks. In: 2018 IEEE/CVF Conference on Computer Vision and Pattern Recognition, Salt Lake City, UT, USA, pp. 7132–7141 (2018). https://doi.org/10.1109/CVPR.2018.00745
14. Wang, Q., Wu, B., Zhu, P., Li, P., Zuo, W., Hu, Q.: ECA-Net: efficient channel attention for deep convolutional neural networks. In: IEEE Conference on Computer Vision and Pattern Recognition, pp. 11534–11542 (2020)
15. Li, J., Zhang, S., Wang, J., Gao, W., Tian, Q.: Global-local temporal representations for video person re-identification. In: 2019 IEEE/CVF International Conference on Computer Vision (ICCV), pp. 3957–3966 (2019). https://doi.org/10.1109/ICCV.2019.00406
16. Karpathy, A., Toderici, G., Shetty, S., Leung, T., Sukthankar, R., Fei-Fei, L.: Large-scale video classification with convolutional neural networks. In: 2014 IEEE Conference on Computer Vision and Pattern Recognition, Columbus, OH, USA, pp. 1725–1732 (2014). https://doi.org/10.1109/CVPR.2014.223
17. Zhou, B., Andonian, A., Oliva, A., Torralba, A.: Temporal relational reasoning in videos. In: Ferrari, V., Hebert, M., Sminchisescu, C., Weiss, Y. (eds.) ECCV 2018. LNCS, vol. 11205, pp. 831–846. Springer, Cham (2018). https://doi.org/10.1007/978-3-030-01246-5_49
18. Sun, L., Jia, K., Yeung, D., Shi, B.E.: Human action recognition using factorized spatio-temporal convolutional networks. In: 2015 IEEE International Conference on Computer Vision (ICCV), pp. 4597–4605 (2015). https://doi.org/10.1109/ICCV.2015.522
19. Wang, X., Gupta, A.: Videos as space-time region graphs. In: Ferrari, V., Hebert, M., Sminchisescu, C., Weiss, Y. (eds.) ECCV 2018. LNCS, vol. 11209, pp. 413–431. Springer, Cham (2018). https://doi.org/10.1007/978-3-030-01228-1_25
20. Feichtenhofer, C., Pinz, A., Zisserman, A.: Convolutional two-stream network fusion for video action recognition. In: Proceedings of the IEEE Conference on Computer Vision and Pattern Recognition (CVPR), June 2016
21. Diba, A., et al.: Spatio-temporal channel correlation networks for action classification. In: Ferrari, V., Hebert, M., Sminchisescu, C., Weiss, Y. (eds.) ECCV 2018. LNCS, vol. 11208, pp. 299–315. Springer, Cham (2018). https://doi.org/10.1007/978-3-030-01225-0_18
22. Jiang, B., Wang, M., Gan, W., Wu, W., Yan, J.: STM: spatiotemporal and motion encoding for action recognition. In: Proceedings of the IEEE International Conference on Computer Vision, pp. 2000–2009 (2019)
23. Liu, Z., et al.: TEINet: towards an efficient architecture for video recognition. In: Proceedings of the AAAI Conference on Artificial Intelligence, vol. 34, no. 7, pp. 11669–11676 (2020)
24. Wu, C.Y., Feichtenhofer, C., Fan, H., He, K., Krahenbuhl, P., Girshick, R.: Long-term feature banks for detailed video understanding. In: Proceedings of the IEEE Conference on Computer Vision and Pattern Recognition, pp. 284–293 (2019)
25. Weng, J., et al.: Temporal distinct representation learning for action recognition. In: Vedaldi, A., Bischof, H., Brox, T., Frahm, J.-M. (eds.) ECCV 2020. LNCS, vol. 12352, pp. 363–378. Springer, Cham (2020). https://doi.org/10.1007/978-3-030-58571-6_22
26. Woo, S., Park, J., Lee, J.-Y., Kweon, I.S.: CBAM: convolutional block attention module. In: Ferrari, V., Hebert, M., Sminchisescu, C., Weiss, Y. (eds.) ECCV 2018. LNCS, vol. 11211, pp. 3–19. Springer, Cham (2018). https://doi.org/10.1007/978-3-030-01234-2_1
27. Hou, Q., Zhou, D., Feng, J.: Coordinate attention for efficient mobile network design. In: CVPR (2021)

28. He, K., Zhang, X., Ren, S., Sun, J.: Deep residual learning for image recognition. In: CVPR, pp. 770–778 (2016)
29. Zach, C., Pock, T., Bischof, H.: A duality based approach for realtime TV-$L^1$ optical flow. In: Hamprecht, F.A., Schnörr, C., Jähne, B. (eds.) DAGM 2007. LNCS, vol. 4713, pp. 214–223. Springer, Heidelberg (2007). https://doi.org/10.1007/978-3-540-74936-3_22
30. Kuehne, H., Jhuang, H., Garrote, E., Poggio, T.A., Serre, T.: HMDB: a large video database for human motion recognition. In: ICCV, pp. 2556–2563 (2011)
31. Soomro, K., Zamir, A.R., Shah, M.: UCF101: a dataset of 101 human actions classes from videos in the wild. arXiv preprint arXiv:1212.0402 (2012)
32. Zhao, Y., Xiong, Y., Lin, D.: Recognize actions by disentangling components of dynamics. In: Proceedings of the IEEE Conference on Computer Vision and Pattern Recognition, pp. 6566–6575 (2018)
33. Feichtenhofer, C., Pinz, A., Wildes, R.P.: Spatiotemporal multiplier networks for video action recognition. In: Proceedings of IEEE International Conference on Computer Vision and Pattern Recognition, pp. 7445–7454 (2017)
34. Wang, Y., Long, M., Wang, J., Yu, P.S.: Spatiotemporal pyramid network for video action recognition. In: Proceedings of IEEE International Conference on Computer Vision and Pattern Recognition, pp. 2097–2106 (2017)
35. Wang, L., Li, W., Li, W., Van Gool, L.: Appearance-and-relation networks for video classification. In: Proceedings of the IEEE Conference on Computer Vision and Pattern Recognition, pp. 1430–1439 (2018)
36. He, D., et al.: StNet: local and global spatial-temporal modeling for action recognition. In: AAAI (2019)

# Graph Attention Convolutional Network with Motion Tempo Enhancement for Skeleton-Based Action Recognition

Ruwen Bai[1,2], Xiang Meng[1], Bo Meng[1,3], Miao Jiang[1,2], Junxing Ren[1], Yang Yang[1,2], Min Li[1,2(✉)], and Degang Sun[1,2]

[1] Institute of Information Engineering, Chinese Academy of Sciences, Beijing, China
{bairuwen,mengxiang,jiangmiao,renjunxing,yangyang,limin}@iie.ac.cn
[2] School of Cyber Security, University of Chinese Academy of Sciences, Beijing, China
[3] Beijing Institute of Technology, Beijing, China

**Abstract.** Graph convolutional network (GCN) exhibits advantages in handling non-Euclidean data. Previous works using spatio-temporal graph convolution for skeleton action recognition achieve good performance. However, several limitations still exist. First, the uniform modeling of joint motion assumes that the motion tempo of different joints remains constant, which ignores the dynamic changes in the position offset of each joint during the action. In this work, we propose a robust action feature extractor, graph attention convolutional network with motion tempo enhancement (MTEA-GCN), which captures different joint motion tempos with two streams. Second, the dependencies among bone-connected and spatially separated joints cannot be adequately considered from the graph topology based on the human physical connections. For this reason, we propose a multi-neighborhood graph attention convolution module that fully considers the dependencies among each joint and different neighborhood joints while focusing on discriminative joints. This study experiments on two large-scale skeleton datasets, including Kinetics-Skeleton and NTU RGB+D. Our proposed *MTEA-GCN* shows good performance with comparable computational complexity and fewer parameters.

**Keywords:** Skeleton-based action recognition · Graph convolution network · Human motion

## 1 Introduction

Human action recognition is widely used in many applications such as intelligent video surveillance and smart retail. In the last few years, low-cost depth sensors like the Microsoft Kinect [27] and advanced estimation algorithms [1] have brought about a considerable increase in available skeleton data. Data are always the driving force behind the development of deep learning methods, which enables skeleton action recognition to make great progress. Skeleton data consist of 2D or 3D

© Springer Nature Switzerland AG 2021
D. N. Pham et al. (Eds.): PRICAI 2021, LNAI 13033, pp. 152–165, 2021.
https://doi.org/10.1007/978-3-030-89370-5_12

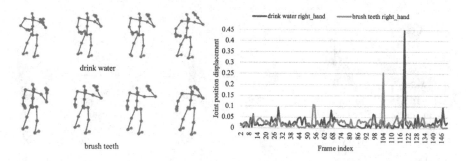

**Fig. 1.** Similar single-frame skeletal poses (left) and motion tempo variations along the time series (right) in the two actions of "drink water" and "brush teeth".

coordinate positions of human joints, which are a high-level abstract representations of the human body. Compared with RGB videos, skeleton data are free from activity-independent uncertainties (e.g. complex backgrounds, lighting, and human appearance changes), allowing skeleton-based methods to compute efficiently due to the low-dimensional feature representation.

GCNs generalize convolution operations to graph data in non-Euclidean space. The human skeleton appears as a natural topological graph, with joints as vertices and bones as edges. Existing GCNs [11,13,15,17,24] for action recognition are devoted to utilizing the topological information of the graph to access rich spatial correlations among joints and temporal dependencies in skeleton sequences. However, the uniform spatio-temporal modeling of skeleton sequences by GCNs ignores the motion tempo variations implied in sequences. The motion tempo represents the displacement magnitude variations of the joint in the space-time direction, which is an important factor to describe an action and distinguishing between actions with similar postures.

Taking Fig. 1 as an example, the two actions "drink water" and "brush teeth" have similar spatial configurations of joints on a single-frame skeleton graph, which differ significantly in the displacement variations of hand joints. Inspired by this, we preprocess the raw skeleton sequences following two different frame rates and input them to two branches of the relative static motion feature extractor (RSM) and the relative dynamic motion feature extractor (RDM), as shown in Fig. 2. The RSM branch extracts high-dimensional feature maps from sparse skeleton sequences to focus on the feature responses of joints on the graph topology. The RDM branch extracts low-dimensional feature maps from dense skeleton sequences to focus on the temporal motion variations of joints. Thereby, the RSM and RDM branches model relatively static and relatively dynamic joint motion tempos, respectively. Additional motion state migration channels integrate the relatively dynamic motion tempo into the relatively static motion tempo. The attention mechanisms in deep learning draw on the human attentional mindset and are effective for many tasks [20,21,23]. Previous studies [16,18] have extended the GCN into a graph convolutional

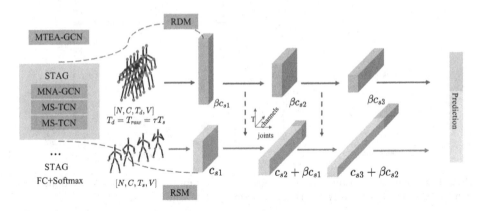

**Fig. 2.** Overview of our proposed *MTEA-GCN*.

long short-term memory (LSTM) network and added spatio-temporal attention with a self-supervised gating mechanism. The LSTM gating mechanism improves the skeleton recognition performance, but leads to a large number of additional parameters. The recursive structure of LSTM cannot support parallel computation, limiting the efficiency of model learning. The purpose of this study is to enhance the graph representation by adding a self-supervised attention mechanism, while bringing about an improvement in model performance with few additional parameters.

In this work, we present a two-stream network *MTEA-GCN* for skeleton action recognition. One branch is designed to capture relatively static motion tempos of joints with sparse skeletal sequences of inputs and high-dimensional representations of features. The other branch is designed to capture relatively dynamic motion tempos of joints with dense skeletal sequences of inputs and low-dimensional representations of features. Besides, we apply various single neighborhood adjacency matrices to construct a powerful multi-neighborhood graph convolution, which simultaneously learns the correlation between each joint and its different neighborhood joints. A joint gating mechanism is proposed to learn the self-attention weights of each joint and enhances joint feature information with significant responses. The main contributions in this work are as follows:

1. We construct a two-stream GCN consisting of RSM and RDM, which model different joint motion tempos. The state migration channels are used between the two branches for the temporal alignment and feature fusion.
2. We propose a multi-neighborhood graph attention module (MNA-GCN) to highlight discriminative joints, which can efficiently learn inter-joint dependencies, including locally bone connected and physically unconnected joints.
3. We explicitly explore the complementary roles of the joint motion tempos for action recognition. The proposed *MTEA-GCN* is lightweight, but robust and effective for action feature representation.

4. We conduct exhaustive ablation studies on two large-scale skeleton datasets, Kinetics-Skeleton and NTU RGB+D, to demonstrate the effectiveness of *MTEA-GCN*.

## 2    Related Work

### 2.1    GCN for Skeleton Action Recognition

GCN-based methods for skeleton action recognition conform to the original topology of the human skeleton and does not rely on any artificial pre-defined rules to analyze the spatial patterns of data. Yang *et al.* [24] first apply graph convolution to action recognition and verify the effectiveness of GCNs in modeling human motion patterns spatially and temporally. To construct relationships of non-physically connected joints, Li *et al.* [13] introduce a link inference module to construct action-related potential relationships between joints and apply a higher-order adjacency matrix to learn the dependencies of long-range joints. Shi *et al.* [17] construct an adaptive graph and adds bone information to form a two-stream framework for learning action features. Liu *et al.* [15] consider the information flow across space-time by the decomposed multi-scale graph convolution and space-time graph convolution operators. These works continuously enhance the representational capabilities of the human skeletal graph and model human skeletal sequences uniformly following the paradigm of 2D spatial relationship extraction and 1D temporal dependency learning. The process of co-encoding of spatio-temporal features ignores the variation of motion tempo involved in the human skeletal sequences.

### 2.2    Motion Tempo Modeling

Several methods for RGB video-based activity recognition [5,22,25] consider the effect of tempo changes in visual appearance. These attempts for extracting the dynamic visual tempos of action instances mainly rely on constructing a frame pyramid with different temporal resolutions. Feichtenhofer *et al.* [5] believe that different dimensions of feature maps imply different degrees of visual change information on the image. The traditional 3D convolution [2,19] indicates that the motion of the two spatial dimensions x and y of the image along all spatio-temporal directions are equally possible and displacement invariant, but this condition is impractical. Modeling different visual tempos using branches with different temporal resolutions allows for asymmetric treatment of spatial-temporal features. On this basis, the variable displacement of individual joints in the space-time direction is not equally possible for skeleton recognition. Many daily actions involve rapid dynamic changes in joints on local body parts, such as "eating", "reading" and "writing". Statistically, we find that approximately 70% actions in the NTU RGB+D dataset involve large dynamic changes only in the local body parts. Therefore, the human joints are likely to move relatively statically (slowly). We split the joint motion into relatively static and dynamic branches to increase the flexibility of joint shifting in different space-time directions by capturing different motion tempos of each joint for each action instance.

## 3    Method

The overview of our proposed *MTEA-GCN* is shown in Fig. 2. Here, $c$ denotes the feature dimensions. $\tau$ is the frame rate ratio of the two branches, and $\beta$ is the channel ratio. We follow a two-stream framework to build two branches, RSM and RDM, which process different frame rates of skeleton sequences and model motion tempo variations of joints. The RDM branch is lightweight. The state migration channels between two branches are used to fuse different motion tempos of joints. Each branch consists of STAG operators. The STAG operator is a robust spatio-temporal motion feature extractor that contains a multi-neighborhood graph attention enhancement module (MNA-GCN) and multi-scale temporal convolution modules (MS-TCN).

### 3.1    Multi-neighborhood Graph Attention Module

The raw skeleton data are a series of vectors consisting of the single-frame skeleton, where each vector represents 2D or 3D coordinates of human joints at a time stamp. If $V = \{v_0, v_1, v_2, \ldots, v_N\}$ denotes $N$ joints, C denotes the dimensions of feature maps, the single-frame skeleton graph at time $t$ can be represented by the joint feature $X_t \in X^{C \times N}$ and the adjacency matrix $A \in R^{N \times N}$. $A$ represents the topology of the graph, where if $v_i$ and $v_j$ are connected, $A_{i,j} = 1$, otherwise $A_{i,j} = 0$. The update mechanism of the graph convolution layer $l$ at time $t$ can be formulated as Eq. 1

$$X_t^{l+1} = \sigma(\tilde{D}^{-\frac{1}{2}} \tilde{A} \tilde{D}^{-\frac{1}{2}} X_t^l W^l) \tag{1}$$

Here, $\tilde{A} = A + I$, the self-loop constant matrix $I$ considers the influence of the node itself. $\sigma(\cdot)$ is the activation function. $\tilde{D}^{-\frac{1}{2}} \tilde{A} \tilde{D}^{-\frac{1}{2}}$ is the normalization of the adjacency matrix, which is used to weaken the influence of neighbor nodes on the current node. $W^l \in R^{C_l \times C_{l+1}}$ is the weight matrix that can be learned by the $l$th layer of the network.

As Liu *et al.* explored in [15], the dependencies captured by the adjacency matrix of higher-order polynomials are still dominated by the bone-connected joints. In our work, a multi-neighborhood graph convolution is used similar to MS-G3D [15], where its adjacency matrix is a powerful matrix of $k$ one-order adjacency matrices concatenated (Fig. 3(a)) This adjacency matrix can effectively access the dependencies between each joint and its $k$-neighborhood joints by removing the redundant dependencies of close neighbors. *Mask* is a learnable matrix initialized with random values around 0. Equation 2 shows the definition of the $k$th adjacency matrix $A_k$ according to MS-G3D [15]. However, the complete non-differential treatment of different distance joints in MS-G3D [15] is inconsistent with a common sense of the action.

$$A_{(k)} = \begin{cases} 1 & \text{if } d(v_i, v_j) = k, \\ 1 & \text{if } i = j, \\ 0 & otherwise \end{cases} \tag{2}$$

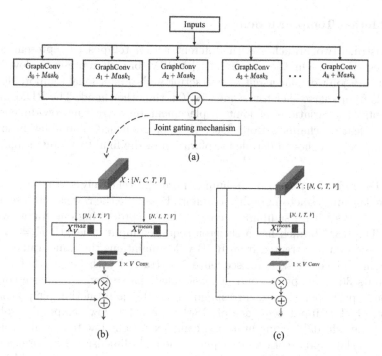

**Fig. 3.** Schematic illustration of Multi-neighborhood graph attention module (MNA-GCN). (a) is a multi-neighborhood graph convolution. (b) and (c) are two joint gating solutions considered in our work.

Our MNA-GCN module introduces the joint gating mechanism, which globally considers all joints and explicitly measures the importance of each joint. We consider two joint gating solutions as shown in Fig. 3(b) and (c), which are calculated as in Eq. 3, where $f^{1 \times V}$ denotes the convolution operation with filter size $1 \times V$. $G_{Sa}$ is the attention weights to assign different importance for joints, which is updated iteratively as the training process. The fine-tuned features represent more power. The additional joint gating mechanism introduces only a few parameters. We use a MS-TCN to model the inter-frame association of skeletons as in MS-G3D [15].

$$X_V^{mean} = Avgpool(X_{in})$$
$$X_V^{max} = Maxpool(X_{in})$$
$$G_{Sa} = Sigmoid(f^{1 \times V}(X_V^{max}, X_V^{mean})) \quad in \ (b)$$
$$G_{Sa} = Sigmoid(f^{1 \times V}(X_V^{mean})) \quad in \ (c)$$
$$X_{out} = G_{Sa} * X_{in} + X_{in}$$

(3)

## 3.2  Motion Tempo Modeling

We construct two branches with different action tempos to represent action instances (Fig. 2). On the one hand, the RSM branch represents slow variations of each joint displacement by extracting high-dimensional temporal feature channels from sparse skeleton sequences. On the other hand, The RDM branch represents fast variations of joint displacement by extracting low-dimensional temporal feature channels from dense skeleton sequence. The ablation experiments in Sect. 4.3 show a detailed exploration of the final two-stream model.

**RSM Branch.** To focus on the human pose and relatively static joint motion on a single-frame skeleton graph, we uniformly sample the raw skeleton sequence of $T_{raw}$ frames with a sampling factor $\tau$, that is, processing one frame every $\tau$ frame. The RSM branch has a skeleton sequence input of length $T_s = T_{raw}/\tau$. The skeleton data extracted from RGB video maintains the same frame rate as the original video. A skeleton sequence is extracted with 30 fps, that is, each joint shifts 30 times per second. The sampled sparse frame sequence contains $30/\tau$ body poses per second, corresponding to $30/\tau$ joint motion tempo changes per second. The input sequence of RSM branch has low temporal resolution and thus an affordable computational complexity. The low temporal resolution indicates a slow update of the body pose. The high-dimensional feature channels characterize the detailed joint features in the graph topology. The RSM branch thereby focuses on inter-joint dependencies spatially and captures the relatively static motion tempo of each joint temporally.

**RDM Branch.** RDM and RSM are two parallel branches. The RDM branch inputs dense skeleton sequences with a high frame rate, where the human pose is rapidly updated. The full skeleton sequence is fed into the RDM branch to ensure that the model observes the full human action, i.e. $T_d = T_{raw} = \tau T_s$. $\tau$ denotes the sampling factor of the RSM branch and the frame rate ratio of skeleton sequence processed by the two branches. The RDM branch is similar to the RSM branch, but with a lower dimensions of extracted features. The number of feature channels is only $\beta(\beta < 1)$ times than that of the RSM branch. $\beta$ defines the channel ratio of features in two branches. Considering the intrinsic mechanism of convolution, higher dimensional feature representations have stronger spatial semantic representation. Each dimension of the feature map corresponds to the response of a convolutional kernel with trainable weights to the input features. A higher dimensionality of the feature map indicates that the convolutional layer uses more filters with different weights to extract various types of detailed features across space. The representation of low-dimensional features in the RDM branch weakens the ability to represent the structural information of the human pose spatially, but is sensitive to the motion changes of the joints in time. The low-dimensional feature representation makes the branch lightweight and computationally efficient. The good performance of the model validates our idea.

**Dynamic and Static Tempo Fusion.** The features extracted from the two branches represent different joint motion tempos, where the difference depends on the frame rate ratio $\tau$ and the channel ratio $\beta$. The feature fusion in two branches allows the two-stream model to integrate the feature representations of joints at each stage of learning. We add *state migration channels* between the two branches, which are implemented by convolution operations. The convolution operations have been used to fuse features in two-stream networks [3,6]. Here, we use 2D convolution for temporal feature alignment and migrate the aligned relative dynamic features to the RSM branch in a concatenated manner.

## 4  Experiments

We evaluate the *MTEA-GCN* on two large-scale skeleton datasets, Kinetics-Skeleton [24] and NTU RGB+D [16]. To demonstrate the validity of our final model, we perform extensive ablation experiments on the NTU RGB+D dataset.

### 4.1  Datasets

**NTU RGB+D.** NTU RGB+D [16] is a human action dataset collected by Microsoft Kinect V2 at 30 fps, which contains 3D joint coordinates of 25 body joints. The dataset collects 60 action categories from 40 subjects, which contains daily actions, interactive actions and health-related actions. A total of 56,880 video samples and 4 million images are available. The dataset has two benchmarks: Cross-subject (X-Sub) and Cross-view (X-View). The former training and validation set contain actions performed by the subjects in the two subsets. The latter training set contains videos captured by cameras 2 and 3, and the validation set contains videos captured by camera 1. Top-1 accuracy is reported on two benchmarks.

**Kinetics-Skeleton.** The Kinetics-skeleton dataset is a collection of skeleton data extracted from the Kinetics-400 dataset using OpenPose toolbox [1]. The Kinetics video dataset [8] published by DeepMind is a high-quality collection of YouTube videos and contains a wide variety of human actions. All videos are first adjusted to a resolution of $340 \times 256$ at 30 fps before extracting the joints. The OpenPose toolbox estimates the 2D coordinates of the 18 body joints of each person and their corresponding confidence. If more than two individuals are present, the ones with lower confidence are ignored. We report Top-1 and Top-5 recognition accuracies.

### 4.2  Training Details

All models contain 3 STAG operators and are trained with the same batch size (32). For NTU RGB+D and Kinetics-Skeleton, the learning rate is initialized to 0.05 and 0.01, respectively, and reduce by a factor of 10 at epoch $\{30, 40\}$

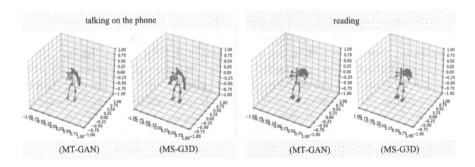

**Fig. 4.** Visualization of MTEA-GCN and MS-G3D extracted features.

and {45, 55}. Weight decay is set to 0.0005. The optimization scheme applies stochastic gradient descent with momentum (0.9). Cross-entropy is selected as the loss function to backpropagate gradients. The raw inputs are preprocessed with normalization and translation following [15,17,24]. All action samples are padded with skeleton sequences to 300 frames, where 256 consecutive frames are randomly selected as inputs.

### 4.3   Ablation Study

To verify the rationality and validity of the two-stream model setup, we conduct a series of ablation experiments on the NTU-RGBD dataset by using a single variable. The performances of models are compared with the X-Sub benchmark. If not specified, the neighborhood scale of the graph convolution in all models is set to $k = 5$, the tempo ratio $\tau = 2$, and the channel ratio $\beta = 4$ for two streams.

**Appropriate Neighborhood-Scale Settings.** Experiments on different scales of sparse graph convolution in MS-G3D [15] suggest that different neighborhoods of joints should be considered by the maximum diameter (12) of the skeletal graph in the NTU RGB+D dataset. However, we experimentally found that such a consideration is unsuitable, and considering each scale indiscriminately aggregates excessive useless joint dependencies (Fig. 4). A similar intensity of attention to many distant joints unrelated to action can be observed for the MS-G3D. We reconsider the different neighborhood settings on our proposed model MTEA-GCN as shown in Fig. 5. When $k = 2$, it means that the adjacency matrix contains self-loop with $1st$ order neighborhood. Figure 5 shows the accuracy, computational complexity and parameters for the model using different neighborhood-scale $k$. We observe that the model achieves the best performance for each joint with its $5th$ order neighborhood considered.

**Joint Gating Mechanism Configuration.** Pooling operations along the channels can effectively highlight more discriminative feature regions [7]. We perform experiments on the two configurations of joint gating mechanisms.

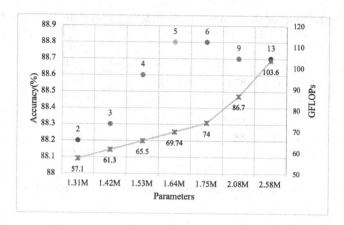

**Fig. 5.** Comparisons of the recognition accuracy (%), number of parameters (M), and computational complexity (GFLOPs) for MTEA-GCN using different neighborhood-scale $k$.

The results are shown in Table 1. The joint features fine-tuned by the maximum pooling operation and average pooling operation can greatly represent human actions. We believe that the maximum pooling operation highlight the most salient responses of joint features and the average pooling operation is the comprehensive consideration of individual joint features. Thus, we suggest using both pooling operations in our joint gating mechanism.

**Modeling Different Joint Motion Tempo.** This study aims to explore the joint feature representations of different motion tempos that are more discriminative and lead to the robust characterization of human actions. Therefore, we perform a series of ablation studies for the two-stream RSM and RDM with different frame rate ratio $\tau$ and channel ratio $\beta$. We use the factorized pathway MS-GCN from MS-G3D as the baseline. The baseline model has one branch without motion tempo variations and inputs the raw skeletal frames. We first observe that all settings outperform the baseline due to the modeling of the motion tempo variations of joints from the Table 2 and 3.

**Table 1.** Comparisons of the recognition accuracy (%) for different joint gating configurations

| Gating set | Params | Accuracy& |
|---|---|---|
| None | 16.0M | 88.5 |
| Avg | 1.62M | 88.7 |
| Max+Avg | 1.64M | 88.8 |

**Table 2.** Comparisons of the recognition accuracy (%) for different frame rate ratio settings

|         | Accuracy (%) | RSM-input | GFLOPs |
|---------|--------------|-----------|--------|
| MS-GCN  | 87.8         | 300f      | 9.76   |
| =1      | 88.5         | 256f      | 13.46  |
| 2       | **88.8**     | 128f      | 6.97   |
| 4       | 88.5         | 64f       | 3.73   |
| 8       | 88.0         | 32f       | 2.11   |

**Table 3.** Comparisons of the recognition accuracy (%) for different channel ratio settings

|             | Accuracy (%) | Params |
|-------------|--------------|--------|
| $\beta = 1$ | 88.3         | 5.48M  |
| 1/2         | 88.5         | 2.59M  |
| 1/4         | **88.8**     | 1.64M  |
| 1/8         | 88.6         | 1.37M  |

Table 2 shows the different frame rate ratio settings between the two streams. The frame rate ratio is related to the length of the skeletal sequence processed by the RSM branch, where a larger $\tau$ leads to fewer frames processed and lower computational complexity. The frame rate ratio $\tau = 2$ results in 1.0% improvement to the MS-GCN with lower computational complexity. Table 3 shows that the channel ratio has a significant effect on the number of model parameters. The RDM branches with low channel capacity ($\beta = 1/4, 1/8$) improve the performance without capturing the detailed features of the joints in the topology. A 4-fold reduction in channel capacity results in the best performance of our model.

### 4.4    Comparisons with the State-of-the-Art Methods

We compare our model with state-of-the-art methods in Table 4, Table 5, including RNN-based methods, CNN-based methods, and GCN-based methods. Our model shows superior performance on two large-scale skeleton datasets, Kinetics-Skeleton and NTU RGB+D, with improvements of 6% and 9%, respectively, compared to the basic GCN method [24]. Compared to most existing methods, *MTEA-GCN* consists of only three stacked layers of the spatio-temporal feature extraction operator STAG, which is shallow and lightweight, but achieves a good performance improvement. Our model gains 0.3% higher accuracy than 2s-AGCN [17] by only using joint data. The model performance is slightly lower than MS-G3D [15], but the amount of parameters is 50% less (1.6M vs 3.2M) and the computational consumption is greatly reduced. MS-G3D considers oversized joint neighborhoods, resulting in slight overfitting in its training on the NTU RGB+D dataset.

**Table 4.** Comparisons of the recognition accuracy (%) on the NTU RGB+D dataset.

| Methods | X-Sub (%) | X-View (%) |
|---|---|---|
| HBRNN [4] | 59.1 | 64.0 |
| ST-LSTM [14] | 69.2 | 77.7 |
| STA-LSTM [18] | 73.4 | 81.2 |
| VA-LSTM [26] | 79.2 | 87.7 |
| TCN [10] | 74.3 | 83.1 |
| Clips+CNN+MTLN [9] | 79.6 | 84.8 |
| CNN+Motion+Trans [12] | 83.2 | 89.3 |
| ST-GCN [24] | 81.5 | 88.3 |
| AS-GCN [13] | 86.8 | 94.2 |
| ST-GR [11] | 86.9 | 92.3 |
| 2s-AGCN [17] | 88.5 | 95.1 |
| MS-G3D [15] | 91.5 | 96.2 |
| MTEA-GCN (Joint-only) | 88.8 | 94.9 |
| MTEA-GCN (Bone-only) | 88.9 | 95.0 |
| MTEA-GCN (Ours) | **90.5** | **95.6** |

**Table 5.** Comparisons of the recognition accuracy (%) on the Kinetics-Skeleton.

| Methods | Top-1 (%) | Top-5 (%) |
|---|---|---|
| TCN [10] | 20.3 | 40.0 |
| ST-GCN [24] | 30.7 | 52.8 |
| AS-GCN [13] | 34.8 | 56.5 |
| ST-GR [11] | 33.6 | 56.1 |
| Js-AGCN [17] | 35.1 | 57.1 |
| 2s-AGCN [17] | 36.1 | 58.7 |
| MS-G3D [15] | 38.0 | 60.9 |
| MTEA-GCNOurs | **36.7** | **59.6** |

## 5    Conclusion

In this work, we propose a multi-neighborhood motion tempo-enhanced graph attention network (MTEA-GCN) for skeleton-based action recognition. We add a lightweight RDM branch to form a two-stream framework and model the tempo variation of joint motion. Detailed ablations validate the complementary role of motion tempo in identifying human actions. The multi-neighborhood graph attention module can effectively capture the dependencies between the current joint and neighboring and distant joints, and automatically select the more discriminative joints through the joint gating mechanism. Experiments show that our model represents human action features robustly. In future work, we will further explore the rich and exact dependencies among joints in each action.

# References

1. Cao, Z., Hidalgo, G., Simon, T., Wei, S.E., Sheikh, Y.: OpenPose: realtime multi-person 2D pose estimation using part affinity fields. IEEE Trans. Pattern Anal. Mach. Intell. **43**(1), 172–186 (2019)
2. Carreira, J., Zisserman, A.: Quo vadis, action recognition? A new model and the kinetics dataset. In: Proceedings of the IEEE Conference on Computer Vision and Pattern Recognition, pp. 6299–6308 (2017)
3. Christoph, R., Pinz, F.A.: Spatiotemporal residual networks for video action recognition. In: Advances in Neural Information Processing Systems, pp. 3468–3476 (2016)
4. Du, Y., Fu, Y., Wang, L.: Representation learning of temporal dynamics for skeleton-based action recognition. IEEE Trans. Image Process. **25**(7), 3010–3022 (2016)
5. Feichtenhofer, C., Fan, H., Malik, J., He, K.: SlowFast networks for video recognition. In: Proceedings of the IEEE/CVF International Conference on Computer Vision, pp. 6202–6211 (2019)
6. Feichtenhofer, C., Pinz, A., Zisserman, A.: Convolutional two-stream network fusion for video action recognition. In: Proceedings of the IEEE Conference on Computer Vision and Pattern Recognition, pp. 1933–1941 (2016)
7. Hu, J., Shen, L., Sun, G.: Squeeze-and-excitation networks. In: Proceedings of the IEEE Conference on Computer Vision and Pattern Recognition, pp. 7132–7141 (2018)
8. Kay, W., et al.: The kinetics human action video dataset. arXiv preprint arXiv:1705.06950 (2017)
9. Ke, Q., Bennamoun, M., An, S., Sohel, F., Boussaid, F.: A new representation of skeleton sequences for 3D action recognition. In: Proceedings of the IEEE Conference on Computer Vision and Pattern Recognition, pp. 3288–3297 (2017)
10. Kim, T.S., Reiter, A.: Interpretable 3D human action analysis with temporal convolutional networks. In: 2017 IEEE Conference on Computer Vision and Pattern Recognition Workshops (CVPRW), pp. 1623–1631. IEEE (2017)
11. Li, B., Li, X., Zhang, Z., Wu, F.: Spatio-temporal graph routing for skeleton-based action recognition. In: Proceedings of the AAAI Conference on Artificial Intelligence, pp. 8561–8568 (2019)
12. Li, C., Zhong, Q., Xie, D., Pu, S.: Skeleton-based action recognition with convolutional neural networks. In: 2017 IEEE International Conference on Multimedia & Expo Workshops (ICMEW), pp. 597–600. IEEE (2017)
13. Li, M., Chen, S., Chen, X., Zhang, Y., Wang, Y., Tian, Q.: Actional-structural graph convolutional networks for skeleton-based action recognition. In: Proceedings of the IEEE/CVF Conference on Computer Vision and Pattern Recognition, pp. 3595–3603 (2019)
14. Liu, J., Shahroudy, A., Xu, D., Wang, G.: Spatio-temporal LSTM with trust gates for 3D human action recognition. In: Leibe, B., Matas, J., Sebe, N., Welling, M. (eds.) ECCV 2016. LNCS, vol. 9907, pp. 816–833. Springer, Cham (2016). https://doi.org/10.1007/978-3-319-46487-9_50

15. Liu, Z., Zhang, H., Chen, Z., Wang, Z., Ouyang, W.: Disentangling and unifying graph convolutions for skeleton-based action recognition. In: Proceedings of the IEEE/CVF Conference on Computer Vision and Pattern Recognition, pp. 143–152 (2020)
16. Shahroudy, A., Liu, J., Ng, T.T., Wang, G.: NTU RGB+D: a large scale dataset for 3D human activity analysis. In: Proceedings of the IEEE Conference on Computer Vision and Pattern Recognition, pp. 1010–1019 (2016)
17. Shi, L., Zhang, Y., Cheng, J., Lu, H.: Two-stream adaptive graph convolutional networks for skeleton-based action recognition. In: Proceedings of the IEEE/CVF Conference on Computer Vision and Pattern Recognition, pp. 12026–12035 (2019)
18. Song, S., Lan, C., Xing, J., Zeng, W., Liu, J.: An end-to-end spatio-temporal attention model for human action recognition from skeleton data. In: Proceedings of the AAAI Conference on Artificial Intelligence, vol. 31 (2017)
19. Tran, D., Bourdev, L., Fergus, R., Torresani, L., Paluri, M.: Learning spatiotemporal features with 3D convolutional networks. In: Proceedings of the IEEE International Conference on Computer Vision, pp. 4489–4497 (2015)
20. Vaswani, A., et al.: Attention is all you need. arXiv preprint arXiv:1706.03762 (2017)
21. Wang, F., et al.: Residual attention network for image classification. In: Proceedings of the IEEE Conference on Computer Vision and Pattern Recognition, pp. 3156–3164 (2017)
22. Wang, Y., Long, M., Wang, J., Yu, P.S.: Spatiotemporal pyramid network for video action recognition. In: Proceedings of the IEEE conference on Computer Vision and Pattern Recognition, pp. 1529–1538 (2017)
23. Xu, K., et al.: Show, attend and tell: neural image caption generation with visual attention. In: International Conference on Machine Learning, pp. 2048–2057. PMLR (2015)
24. Yan, S., Xiong, Y., Lin, D.: Spatial temporal graph convolutional networks for skeleton-based action recognition. In: Proceedings of the AAAI Conference on Artificial Intelligence (2018)
25. Zhang, D., Dai, X., Wang, Y.-F.: Dynamic temporal pyramid network: a closer look at multi-scale modeling for activity detection. In: Jawahar, C.V., Li, H., Mori, G., Schindler, K. (eds.) ACCV 2018. LNCS, vol. 11364, pp. 712–728. Springer, Cham (2019). https://doi.org/10.1007/978-3-030-20870-7_44
26. Zhang, P., Lan, C., Xing, J., Zeng, W., Xue, J., Zheng, N.: View adaptive recurrent neural networks for high performance human action recognition from skeleton data. In: Proceedings of the IEEE International Conference on Computer Vision, pp. 2117–2126 (2017)
27. Zhang, Z.: Microsoft kinect sensor and its effect. IEEE Multimedia 19(2), 4–10 (2012)

# Learning to Synthesize and Remove Rain Unsupervisedly

Yinhe Qi[1], Meng Pan[1], and Zhi Jin[1,2,3(✉)]

[1] School of Intelligent Systems Engineering, Sun Yat-sen University, Shenzhen, China
{qiyh6,panm9}@mail2.sysu.edu.cn, jinzh26@mail.sysu.edu.cn
[2] Guangdong Provincial Key Laboratory of Fire Science and Technology,
Guangzhou 510006, China
[3] Guangdong Provincial Key Laboratory of Robotics and Digital Intelligent
Manufacturing Technology, Guangzhou 510535, China

**Abstract.** Most existing single image deraining networks are trained in a supervised way, which relies on paired images including one clean image and one rain image. In most cases, the rain images are synthesized from the clean ones manually to obtain sufficient paired images. However, not only huge time costs but expert knowledge are needed to ensure the synthesized images are realistic enough. In addition, the superior performance of these deraining networks trained on manually synthesized rain images is hard to be maintained when testing on real rain images. To address these issues, we propose a scene adaptive asymmetric CycleGAN (SAA-CycleGAN) which transfers clean images to their rainy counterparts automatically so that adequate realistic rain images can be obtained for training deraining networks in a supervised way. Moreover, SAA-CycleGAN can both remove rain from rainy images and synthesize rain on clean images benefiting from the cycle consistency strategy. Since the information is not symmetric during the rain synthesis process and the deraining process, the generators are designed with different architecture accordingly for these two processes. Comprehensive experiments show that the SAA-CycleGAN is able to synthesize more lifelike rain images and achieve similar deraining performance compared with the state-of-the-art deraining methods.

**Keywords:** Rain synthesis · Image deraining · CycleGAN · Attention mechanism

## 1 Introduction

Rain is common to see in daily life, while rain streaks and rain mist can reduce visibility and thus degrade the performance of various high-level vision tasks, including image classification, object detection in surveillance, etc. Single image deraining aims to remove unpleasant rain streaks and rain mist from rain images and provide the recovered background for subsequent high-level vision tasks, which attracts lots of attention and has become an important topic in computer vision fields [3].

© Springer Nature Switzerland AG 2021
D. N. Pham et al. (Eds.): PRICAI 2021, LNAI 13033, pp. 166–181, 2021.
https://doi.org/10.1007/978-3-030-89370-5_13

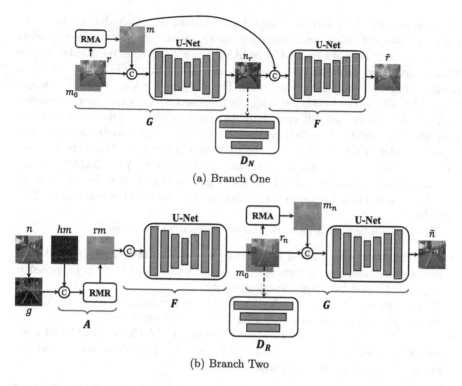

(a) Branch One

(b) Branch Two

**Fig. 1.** The framework of SAA-CycleGAN: (a) branch one performs the deraining process first and then the rain synthesis process; (b) branch two performs the rain synthesis process first and then the deraining process. (Color figure online)

The existing single image deraining methods can be mainly divided into traditional optimization-based methods [19] and deep learning-based methods [4,5,10,18,23,28,29]. The traditional optimization-based deraining methods firstly enforce handcrafted priors on both background and rain layers, then design a deraining loss function and optimize it. However, due to the complexity of rain streaks and background texture, the handcrafted priors are not adaptable to the complex and changing rain images.

Since Fu *et al.* [4] first proposed to use convolutional neural networks (CNNs) for single image deraining, deep learning-based methods have gradually replaced traditional optimization-based methods. Remarkably, most existing deep learning-based deraining algorithms are supervised ones whose training depends on paired rain datasets where each image pair contains one clean image and one rain image under the same scene. As we know that the image pairs captured under the same real scenes are hard to be directly obtained, most of the existing deraining works are trained on synthetic datasets. However, the synthetic rain images look unreal from the real rain images and limit the performance of single image deraining algorithms when applied to real rain images.

To automatically generate a large-scale paired rain image dataset for training supervised deraining networks, we propose a novel unsupervised scene adaptive asymmetric network (SAA-CycleGAN) (see Fig. 1) to better synthesize rain streaks and rain mist on the clean images, and meanwhile to obtain clean images from the rain images as well. The proposed SAA-CycleGAN adopts CycleGAN [31] as the backbone, which is proposed for unpaired image-to-image translation between two different domains, and modifies two default symmetric generators in CycleGAN to be asymmetric. The generator adopted for deraining in SAA-CycleGAN is divided into the rain mask attention (RMA) module and an U-Net. The generator adopted for rain synthesis in SAA-CycleGAN consists of a rain mask refinement (RMR) module and another U-Net. In addition, we introduce a novel loss function called mask loss to constrain the training of RMR module.

The contributions of this work can be summarized as three-fold:

- To address the information asymmetry in rain synthesis and image deraining, a scene adaptive asymmetric network (SAA-CycleGAN) is proposed to implement these two tasks simultaneously.
- As an unsupervised adaptively rain synthesis method, SAA-CycleGAN can obtain good visual performance without human intervention.
- In order to extract more information, we design RMA module and RMR module for the rain synthesis process and the deraining process, and introduced mask loss to constrain RMR module.

The remaining sections of this paper are organized as follows. Section 2 mainly reviews the image deraining and rain synthesis works as well as generative adversarial networks. In Sect. 3, the proposed SAA-CycleGAN is introduced in detail, including the framework and objective function. Experimental results including quantitative and qualitative evaluation are presented in Sect. 4, followed by the conclusion in Sect. 5.

## 2    Related Work

Our target is to implement an efficient rain image synthesis method to produce more natural rain images, with which single image deraining and other high-level vision tasks can be trained in a supervised manner. To this end, we first survey some closely related deraining and image synthesis works in this section. Considering the architecture of SAA-CycleGAN, we also give a brief introduction to the development of generative adversarial networks (GANs) [7].

### 2.1    Single Image Deraining Methods

Generally, a rain image can be modeled as a linear superposition of a rain layer and a background layer, and the goal of the deraining task is to decompose the rain image into these two layers and drop the rain layer. In [4] and [5], Fu *et al.* creatively applied a low-pass filter to decompose a rain image into a high-frequency detail layer and a low-frequency background layer, then a CNN was employed to remove the rain from the high-frequency detail layer. Deep residual networks [8] have been demonstrated to be successful in different tasks, inspired by this, some works adopted residual learning to predict the rain layer and obtained the background image by element-wise subtraction between the rain image and the predicted rain layer. Zhang et al. [29] predict the rain density by a residual-aware classifier and further estimate the rain layer by several densely-connected networks. Li et al. [18] designed a contextual dilated network using squeeze-and-excitation to predict the rain layer stage by stage. Ren et al. [23] deploy residual blocks with iterative training procedures to predict the rain layer. However, only rain streaks are taken into account but rain mist is neglected in those methods due to existing datasets. Hu et al. [10] observed that the rain mist is intimately related to the scene depth. Based on this observation, they designed a network to extract depth-attention features, which were further used for subsequent image deraining.

### 2.2 Rain Synthesis Methods

Some early works have synthesized rain image datasets by manual methods in order to train their supervised deraining networks, such as Rain100L [28], Rain100H [28] Rain12000 [29], etc. Rain12 [19] and Rain100L [28] were synthesized by the photo-realistic rendering techniques designed by Garg et al. [6]. Different from those datasets mentioned above, Rain100H [28], Rain800 [30], Rain14000 [5] and Rain12000 [29] were synthesized by adding noise first and then a gaussian blur filter was applied to the noise in Photoshop[1]. The synthetic rain images from these datasets only contain rain streaks ignoring the physical properties of rain and no rain mist. Both Hu et al. [10] and Li et al. [17] proposed to synthesize rain images combining scene depth information and released their synthetic datasets, i.e., RainCityscapes and NYU-Rain, respectively. Due to containing both depth-related rain streaks and rain mist, the rain images synthesized based on depth information have a more natural visual effect. However, this kind of synthesis method requires manual participation to choose appropriate parameters for different scenarios to achieve more natural effects. A method with a simple, standard, end-to-end procedure for rain image synthesis is urgently needed. Therefore, in this paper, we propose an automatic method to synthesize natural rain images.

### 2.3 Generative Adversarial Networks

GANs [7] have been demonstrated by many works to achieve great success in many fields, e.g., image inpainting [13], image generation [15,25], image-to-image translation [1,12,14,20,31]. GANs are intended to train a pair of generator and discriminator based on the min-max game. In the training stage, the generator

---

[1] http://www.photoshopessentials.com/photo-effects/rain/.

tries to generate real enough images to fool the discriminator while the discriminator tends to distinguish the synthesis images and real images. CycleGAN [31] was proposed to translate images from a source domain $X$ to a target domain $Y$ in the absence of paired samples. CycleGAN contains a generator $G : X \to Y$ and a generator $F : Y \to X$, where $G$ and $F$ are inverses of each other. In addition, a cycleGAN is constrained by a cycle consistency loss, which is introduced to encourage $F(G(x)) \approx x$ and $G(F(y)) \approx y$. An attention mechanism was proposed by Wei et al. [26] to help generators of CycleGAN to improve the performance of deraining. However, they paid little attention to the information asymmetry of the rain synthesis process and the deraining process, which made the visual effect of the synthetic rain images still unreal.

## 3   SAA-CycleGAN

In this section, an overview of SAA-CycleGAN is firstly provided. Then, we present the deraining process and the rain synthesis process in SAA-CycleGAN in detail, respectively. At the end of the section, the objective function used to train SAA-CycleGAN is introduced.

### 3.1   Overview

SAA-CycleGAN is proposed for rain synthesis and image deraining, which consists of two branches (see Fig. 1). Branch one first performs the deraining process on the rain image $r$ to obtain the deraining image $n_r$, and then performs the rain synthesis process on $n_r$ to obtain a new synthetic rain image $\tilde{r}$, i.e., $r \to n_r \to \tilde{r}$. The procedure of branch two is the inverse version of branch one, which is to perform the rain synthesis process and deraining process in order, i.e., $n \to r_n \to \tilde{n}$, where $n$, $r_n$, and $\tilde{n}$ are the clean image, synthetic rain image and reconstructed clean image, respectively. These two branches are based on adversarial learning. Furthermore, to realize the unsupervised training of SAA-CycleGAN, the cycle-consistency loss is implemented by ensuring that $\tilde{r}$ is as close as $r$ and $\tilde{n}$ is as close as $n$.

### 3.2   Deraining Process

On the premise that $R$ represents the rain image domain and $N$ represents the no-rain clean image domain, the deraining process can be considered as a mapping from the rain image domain to no-rain clean image domain, i.e., $G : R \to N$, as shown in the orange brace $G$ in Fig. 1. To extract the features of rain from the input rain image $r$, the RMA module is designed to output a rain mask map $m$, which mainly contains the background texture information obscured by rain mist and the appearance and location information of rain streaks. To obtain the clean background image $n_r$, the rain mask is inputted to the subsequent U-Net as an attention map with the rain image $r$.

Inspired by [26], our RMA module extracts the rain mask in multiple stages (see Fig. 3(a), where each stage includes four parts: 1) a convolutional layer $f_{in}$ receives the network inputs; 2) a dual-path residual dense block (DPRDB) unit [27] $f_{dprdb}$ extracts the deep representation; 3) a LSTM unit [9] $f_{lstm}$ propagates feature dependencies across stages; 4) a convolutional layer $f_{out}$ outputs the rain mask. The inference of RMA module at stage $t$ can be formulated as

$$m^{t-0.5} = f_{dprdb}(f_{in}(r, m^{t-1})),$$
$$s^t = f_{lstm}(s^{t-1}, m^{t-0.5}),$$
$$m^t = f_{out}(s^t) \tag{1}$$

where $f_{in}$, $f_{dprdb}$, $f_{lstm}$, and $f_{out}$ are stage-invariant, $i.e.$, the parameters reused across different stages, $m^t$ denotes the output rain mask of stage $t$, $m^0$ is set to 0.5 as the initial input, $s^t$ denotes the LSTM state of stage $t$, and $r$ denotes the input rain image.

DPRDB has been proven effective by [27] in obtaining the deep feature representation of rain streaks and rain mist. As shown in Fig. 3(b), the structure of DPRDB is divided into two paths named residual path and dense path, which are realized by skip connections. The skip connections can overcome the drawback of gradient vanishing of deep layers. The residual path is inspired by ResNet [8], which realizes the feature re-usage ability through a residual add operation between the input and conducted feature maps. The dense path completes the function of new features exploration of DenseNet [11] by the concatenation of the input and conducted feature maps.

### 3.3   Rain Synthesis Process

In two branches of SAA-CycleGAN, the information passed to the rain synthesis process is different. Thus, we design different network architectures for the rain synthesis process in two branches.

In branch one, the generator used for rain synthesis receives the deraining image $n_r$ and its corresponding rain mask $m$, which is generated by the RMA module in $G$ (see the blue brace $F$ in Fig. 1(a)). We adopt the U-Net as the generator to fuse them to reconstruct the rain image $\tilde{r}$.

Branch two first performs the rain synthesis process $n \rightarrow r_n$ and then the deraining process $r_n \rightarrow \tilde{n}$. However, the rain synthesis process in branch two only receives the clean images from domain $N$ as the input, which does not contain any rain information. To provide the rain information, we synthesize a hand-made rain mask (see Fig. 2(b)) using photoshop (See Footnote 1) as another input of the rain synthesis process. However, the distribution of rain from the hand-made rain mask has a simpler pattern ($i.e.$ only rain streaks) compared with the real rain pattern. Thus, we further design an RMR module to refine the hand-made rain mask, referring to the green brace $A$ in Fig. 1(b). The RMR module receives the gradient map of the clean image and the hand-made rain mask as inputs, where the gradient image provides texture information and the hand-made rain mask provides rain streaks information. The RMR module fuses

(a) Rain mask from $G$

(b) Hand-made rain mask

**Fig. 2.** The comparison of the rain mask generated by RMA module and the hand-made rain mask made by photoshop referring to the existing method (See Footnote 1).

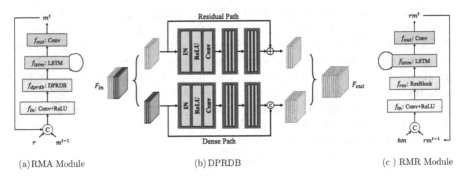

(a) RMA Module          (b) DPRDB          (c) RMR Module

**Fig. 3.** The architecture of modules in SAA-CycleGAN: (a) the architecture of the RMA module, where Conv represents the convolutional layer, ReLU is the activation function and LSTM is a convolutional long short-term memory block; (b) the structure of dual-path residual dense block (DPRDB), where IN represents the instance normalization layer; (c) the architecture of the RMR module, where ResBlock represents the ResNet block [8].

$g$ and $hm$ and outputs a refined rain mask $rm$, which is used to provide rain information for the subsequent rain synthesis module $F$ to obtain the synthesized rain image $r_n$.

The RMR module refines the rain mask in multiple stages just like the RMA module in $G$, except that the DPRDB in RMA is replaced with several more lightweight residual blocks [8] (see Fig. 3(c)). The inference of the RMA module at stage $t$ can be formulated as

$$
\begin{aligned}
rm^{t-0.5} &= f_{res}(f_{in}(hm, rm^{t-1})), \\
s^t &= f_{lstm}(s^{t-1}, rm^{t-0.5}), \\
rm^t &= f_{out}(s^t)
\end{aligned}
\tag{2}
$$

where $f_{in}$, $f_{res}$, $f_{lstm}$, and $f_{out}$ are stage-invariant, *i.e.*, the parameters reused across different stages, $rm^t$ denotes the output refined rain mask of stage $t$, $rm^0$ is set to 0.5 as the initial input, $s^t$ denotes the LSTM state of stage $t$, and $hm$ denotes the input hand-made rain mask.

### 3.4 Objective Function

The objective function used for the unsupervised training of SAA-CycleGAN is presented as follows:

$$\mathcal{L}_{total} = \lambda_{adv}\mathcal{L}_{adv} + \lambda_{cc}\mathcal{L}_{cc} + \lambda_p\mathcal{L}_p + \lambda_{idt}\mathcal{L}_{idt} + \lambda_{rm}\mathcal{L}_{rm} + \lambda_{rmc}\mathcal{L}_{rmc}, \qquad (3)$$

where $\lambda_{adv}$, $\lambda_{cc}$, $\lambda_p$, $\lambda_{idt}$, $\lambda_{rm}$, and $\lambda_{rmc}$ are trade-off parameters.

**Adversarial Loss.** Following the least-square GAN [21], the adversarial losses are applied to both the deraining process and the rain synthesis process as:

$$\mathcal{L}_{adv} = \mathcal{L}_{adv}(G, D_N, R, N) + \mathcal{L}_{adv}(F, D_R, N, R) \qquad (4)$$

For the deraining process $G : R \to N$ and its discriminator $D_N$, we express the objective as:

$$\mathcal{L}_{adv}(G, D_N, R, N) = \frac{1}{2}\mathbb{E}_{n \sim p_{data}(n)}[(D_N(n))^2] + \frac{1}{2}\mathbb{E}_{r \sim p_{data}(r)}[(1 - D_N(n_r))^2]$$

$$= \frac{1}{2}\mathbb{E}_{n \sim p_{data}(n)}[(D_N(n))^2] + \frac{1}{2}\mathbb{E}_{r \sim p_{data}(r)}[(1 - D_N(G(r, m_0)))^2] \qquad (5)$$

where $G$ aims to minimize this objective so that $D_N$ cannot distinguish between clean image $n$ and deraining image $n_r$, while $D_N$ tries to maximize it.

Similarly, the adversarial loss used for the rain synthesis process can be defined as:

$$\mathcal{L}_{adv}(F, D_R, N, R) = \frac{1}{2}\mathbb{E}_{r \sim p_{data}(r)}[(D_R(r))^2] + \frac{1}{2}\mathbb{E}_{n \sim p_{data}(n)}[(1 - D_R(r_n))^2]$$

$$= \frac{1}{2}\mathbb{E}_{r \sim p_{data}(r)}[(D_R(r))^2] + \frac{1}{2}\mathbb{E}_{n \sim p_{data}(n)}[(1 - D_R((F(A(g, hm), n))^2] \qquad (6)$$

where $F$ aims to minimize this objective so that $D_R$ cannot distinguish between real rain image $r$ and synthetic rain image $r_n$, while $D_R$ tries to maximize it.

**Cycle-Consistency Loss.** Since there is no paired information in the unsupervised training of SAA-CycleGAN, cycle-consistency constraint [31] is adopted in two branches to avoid mode collapse. In branch one, given a rain image $r \in R$, after the sequential translations of the deraining process and the rain synthesis process, the reconstructed image $\tilde{r}$ is expected to be the same as the original rain image $r$. Similarly, $\tilde{n}$ is expected to be the same as $n$ in branch two. The cycle-consistency objective can be expressed as:

$$\mathcal{L}_{cc} = \mathbb{E}_{r \sim p_{data}(r)}\left[\|r - \tilde{r}\|_1\right] + \mathbb{E}_{n \sim p_{data}(n)}\left[\|n - \tilde{n}\|_1\right]$$

$$= \mathbb{E}_{r \sim p_{data}(r)}\left[\|r - F(G(r))\|_1\right] + \mathbb{E}_{n \sim p_{data}(n)}\left[\|n - G(F(A(g, hm), n), m_0)\|_1\right] \qquad (7)$$

**Identity Loss.** To ensure that the color distributions of the input image and the output image are similar, the identity consistency constraint is applied to the deraining process and the rain synthesis process. For a clean image $n \in N$, the image is better not to be changed after the translation of $n$ using the deraining process $G(n)$. The rain synthesis process has a similar situation as the deraining process. The identity loss is presented as follows:

$$\mathcal{L}_{idt} = \mathbb{E}_{r \sim p_{data}(r)}[\|n - G(n, m_0)\|_1] + \mathbb{E}_{n \sim p_{data}(n)}[\|r - F(A(g, hm), r)\|_1] \quad (8)$$

**Perceptual Loss.** To avoid unpleasant artificials in the generated images, the perceptual loss [26] is adopted to constrain the color and structure of rain image $r$ and deraining image $n_r$ in branch one and clean image $n$ and synthetic rain image $r_n$ in branch two:

$$\mathcal{L}_p = \mathbb{E}_{r \sim p_{data}(r)}[\|\phi_l(n_r) - \phi_l(r)\|_2^2] + \mathbb{E}_{n \sim p_{data}(n)}[\|\phi_l(r_n) - \phi_l(n)\|_2^2] \quad (9)$$

where $\phi_l(\cdot)$ is the feature extractor of the $l$-th layer of the VGG-16 network [24] pre-trained on ImageNet [2].

**Rain Model Loss.** Based on the rain model $R = M + N$ where $R$, $M$, and $N$ are rain image, rain mask and clean background image [26], we adopt the constraint named rain model loss to the RMA module and the RMR module to obtain natural rain masks:

$$\mathcal{L}_{rm} = \mathbb{E}_{r \sim p_{data}(r)}[\|r - m - n_r\|_2^2] + \mathbb{E}_{n \sim p_{data}(n)}[\|r_n - rm - n\|_2^2] \quad (10)$$

**Rain Mask-Consistency Loss.** In branch two, the refined rain mask $rm$ generated by the RMR module is expected to be the same as the rain mask generated by the RMA module $m_n$. Based on the constrain, we introduce the rain mask-consistency loss as:

$$\mathcal{L}_{rmc} = \mathbb{E}_{n \sim p_{data}(n)}[\|rm - m_n\|_2^2] \quad (11)$$

## 4    Experimental Results

In this part, we discuss the effectiveness of our SAA-CycleGAN in rain synthesis and deraining by exhaustive experiments. Based on the implementation details mentioned in Sect. 4.1 for training the SAA-CycleGAN, the comprehensive performance of our method in rain synthesis and deraining compared with other methods are illustrated in detail in Sect. 4.2 and Sect. 4.3. In order to investigate the influence of functional modules in our proposed SAA-CycleGAN, here we also complete the sufficient ablation studies at Sect. 4.4.

**Table 1.** FID comparison with datasets synthesized by photoshop and CycleGAN trained on the training set of RainCityscapes. The best result is highlighted in bold.

| Methods | Rain800 | Rain14000 | NYU-Rain | CycleGAN | SAA-CycleGAN |
|---------|---------|-----------|----------|----------|--------------|
| FID     | 250.16  | 261.86    | 218.96   | 89.45    | **85.91**    |

(a) Clean images

(b) Photoshop

(c) Ours

**Fig. 4.** The comparison of rain images generated by SAA-CycleGAN and synthesized by photoshop.

## 4.1 Implementation Details

Considering the visual effects in the real-world rainy environment, we adopt the RainCityscapes [10] as the dataset for the training and evaluation of SAA-CycleGAN without any paired data. In the training stage, we choose the Adam [16] algorithm as the optimizer while the learning rate is set as $1 \times 10^{-3}$. As for balancing the training process of rain synthesis and deraining, we empirically define the parameters $\lambda_{adv} = 1$, $\lambda_{cc} = 10$, $\lambda_p = 5$, $\lambda_{idt} = 0.5$, $\lambda_{rm} = 10$ and $\lambda_{rmc} = 5$. Here we resize the trainset images to $286 \times 286$, which is then cropped to $256 \times 256$ as the input of the network with the batch size of 1. We complete the training and testing task of our SAA-CycleGAN based on the PyTorch framework [22] in the Python3 environment where an NVIDIA GeForce GTX 2080Ti GPU with 12 GB memory on the 64-bit Ubuntu 18.04 LTS operating system has been used to run the experiments.

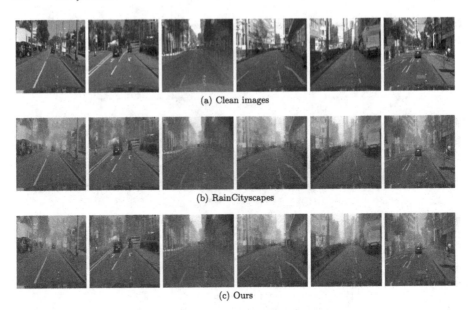

(a) Clean images

(b) RainCityscapes

(c) Ours

**Fig. 5.** The comparison of synthetic rain images between our SAA-CycleGAN and RainCityscapes.

## 4.2 Rain Synthesis Results

Here we analyze the rain synthesis ability of our proposed SAA-CycleGAN comparing with other different synthetic methods. The paired rain image datasets are divided into two parts, one only contains rain streaks synthesized by Photoshop (such as Rain800 [30] and Rain14000 [5] shown in Fig. 4(b)) and the other includes both rain streaks and rain mist (such as RainCityscapes [10] shown in Fig. 5(b)). With the reference of rain images from RainCityscapes in the test set, we utilize the perceptual metric FID to evaluate the rain synthesis result. The results of FID comparison of traditional methods (*i.e.*, Rain800, Rain14000 and NYU-Rain) and trained methods (*i.e.*, CycleGAN and our SAA-CycleGAN) are listed in the Table 1. It is obvious that comparing with traditional methods, CycleGAN and SAA-CycleGAN trained on the training set of RainCityscapes acquire conspicuous FID values and our SAA-CycleGAN achieves significant FID gains than CycleGAN.

Based on the comparison of FID, we also visualize some typical synthetic rain images in Fig. 4 and Fig. 5. Figure 4 presents the effect of rain images synthesized by our SAA-CycleGAN and Photoshop respectively, whose corresponding clean images are collected from the Internet. It can be seen that the rain image synthesized by Photoshop looks unreal comparing with our result. The rain images generated by the SAA-CycleGAN have a more natural and comfort visual effect, which are closer to the real rain environment. This means that SAA-CycleGAN has a better rain generalization ability than traditional methods. Meanwhile, we compare the synthetic rain images between our SAA-CycleGAN and RainCi-

**Table 2.** PSNR/SSIM comparison with the state-of-the-art image deraining methods on the test set of RainCityscapes. *Methods are supervised deraining networks while †methods are unsupervised ones.

| Methods | GMMLP* | DID-MDN* | RESCAN* | PReNet* | DAF-Net* | CycleGAN† | SAA-CycleGAN† |
|---------|--------|----------|---------|---------|----------|-----------|---------------|
| PSNR | 17.80 | 28.43 | 24.49 | 30.64 | 30.06 | 18.36 | 24.16 |
| SSIM | 0.8169 | 0.9530 | 0.8852 | 0.9789 | 0.9530 | 0.8341 | 0.8753 |

tyscapes based on the same environment. The rain images synthesized by both methods look natural. However, our method needs no human intervention for getting rain images while the RainCityscapes needs manual adjustment for improving the result.

### 4.3  Deraining Results

As for evaluating the deraining ability of our SAA-CycleGAN, we adopt the objective metrics PSNR and SSIM for quantitatively measuring the deraining result. This part we both compare the SAA-CycleGAN with several supervised deraining methods including GMMLP [19], DID-MDN [29], RESCAN [18], PReNet [23], DAF-Net [10] and unsupervised deraining method CycleGAN. The comparison result of deraining can be seen in Table 2 and Fig. 6. Results show that most of these supervised methods can achieve better quantitative results than our method. Considering that the SAA-CycleGAN is unsupervised, it is inevitable that our PSNR and SSIM are limited without using paired data for training. However, our SAA-CycleGAN still performs well in the deraining task and quantitative results are close to these supervised methods, which also outperforms the unsupervised deraining method CycleGAN. Meanwhile, the deraining images generated by our proposed SAA-CycleGAN achieve a good visual effect. Both visual and quantitative results prove that our SAA-CycleGAN has a great ability for dealing with the deraining task.

### 4.4  Ablation Study

In order to explore the effect of several functional modules i.e., asymmetry, hand-made rain mask and rain mask-consistency loss in our SAA-CycleGAN, here we define four variants of SAA-CycleGAN for the following ablation studies:

- Solution-1: This ablation model abandon all the functional module including asymmetry, hand-made rain mask and rain mask-consistency loss, also known as CycleGAN.
- Solution-2: This ablation model only incorporated with asymmetry by introducing the RMA module and the RMR module for verifying the influence of asymmetry structure.
- Solution-3: This ablation model incorporated with asymmetry and hand-made rain mask used as an additional input of the rain synthesis generator.

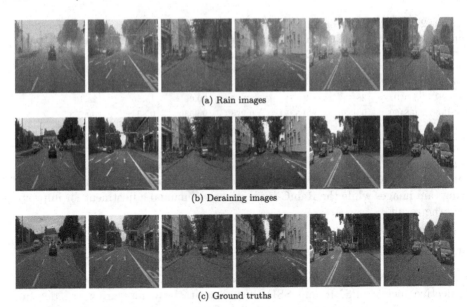

(a) Rain images

(b) Deraining images

(c) Ground truths

**Fig. 6.** The visual effect of deraining image generated by SAA-CycleGAN.

**Table 3.** FID comparison with different variants of SAA-CycleGAN on RainCityscapes. √ indicates the component is adopted while × means not. The best result is highlighted in bold.

|  | Asymmetry | Hand-made rain mask | Rain mask-consistency loss | FID |
|---|---|---|---|---|
| Solution-1 | × | × | × | 89.45 |
| Solution-2 | √ | × | × | 88.08 |
| Solution-3 | √ | √ | × | 87.90 |
| Solution-4 | √ | √ | √ | **85.91** |

- Solution-4: This ablation model incorporated with asymmetry, hand-made rain mask and rain mask-consistency loss, also known as SAA-CycleGAN.

We show the comparison result of perceptual metrics and visual effect of the four variants mentioned above. Table 3 shows the improvement of FID brought by these involving components. It can be seen that the adoption of each function module makes the model performs better while the complete SAA-CycleGAN achieves the best FID. This means that all the components of our SAA-CycleGAN have corresponding influence for improving the perceptual quality of rain synthesis. Also as shown in Fig. 7, the rain synthesis result is also visually more and more plausible as adopting each functional module. Rain streaks synthesized by Solution-1 are too sharp, while rain streaks synthesized by Solution-2 and Solution-3 are too sparse.

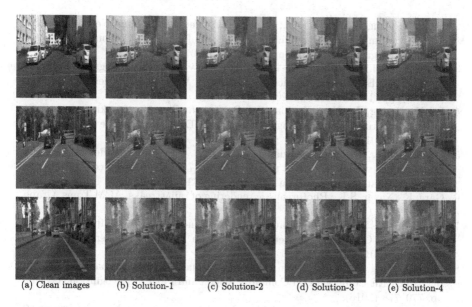

(a) Clean images     (b) Solution-1     (c) Solution-2     (d) Solution-3     (e) Solution-4

**Fig. 7.** Visual quality comparison of synthetic rain images from different variants of SAA-CycleGAN.

## 5    Conclusion

In this paper, a novel scene adaptive asymmetric CycleGAN is proposed for the rain synthesis task and the deraining task. We design different generators for the rain synthesis process and the deraining process according to the asymmetric information of these two processes. We train our SAA-CycleGAN on RainCityscapes and test it on real photos, and compare it with the state-of-the-art methods to demonstrate its superiority qualitatively. In the future, we plan to use SAA-CycleGAN to generate rain object detection datasets based on the existing object detection datasets obtained in good weather. We will train and test the object detection algorithms based on these synthetic rain object detection datasets to improve the accuracy of object detection on rainy days.

**Acknowledgement.** This work was supported by the National Natural Science Foundation of China (No. 62071500, 61701313), Shenzhen Science and Technology Program under Grant No. 2021A26.

## References

1. Choi, Y., Choi, M., Kim, M., Ha, J., Kim, S., Choo, J.: StarGAN: unified generative adversarial networks for multi-domain image-to-image translation. In: 2018 IEEE/CVF Conference on Computer Vision and Pattern Recognition (CVPR), pp. 8789–8797 (2018)

2. Deng, J., Dong, W., Socher, R., Li, L., Li, K., Fei-Fei, L.: ImageNet: a large-scale hierarchical image database. In: 2009 IEEE Conference on Computer Vision and Pattern Recognition (CVPR), pp. 248–255 (2009)

3. Deng, S., et al.: Detail-recovery image deraining via context aggregation networks. In: 2020 IEEE/CVF Conference on Computer Vision and Pattern Recognition (CVPR), pp. 14548–14557 (2020)

4. Fu, X., Huang, J., Ding, X., Liao, Y., Paisley, J.: Clearing the skies: a deep network architecture for single-image rain removal. IEEE Trans. Image Process. **26**(6), 2944–2956 (2017)

5. Fu, X., Huang, J., Zeng, D., Huang, Y., Ding, X., Paisley, J.: Removing rain from single images via a deep detail network. In: 2017 IEEE Conference on Computer Vision and Pattern Recognition (CVPR), pp. 1715–1723 (2017)

6. Garg, K., Nayar, S.K.: Photorealistic rendering of rain streaks. ACM Trans. Graph. **25**, 996–1002 (2006)

7. Goodfellow, I.J., et al.: Generative adversarial nets. In: Proceedings of the 27th International Conference on Neural Information Processing Systems (NIPS), pp. 2672–2680 (2014)

8. He, K., Zhang, X., Ren, S., Sun, J.: Deep residual learning for image recognition. In: 2016 IEEE Conference on Computer Vision and Pattern Recognition (CVPR), pp. 770–778 (2016)

9. Hochreiter, S., Schmidhuber, J.: Long short-term memory. Neural Comput. **9**, 1735–1780 (1997)

10. Hu, X., Fu, C., Zhu, L., Heng, P.: Depth-attentional features for single-image rain removal. In: 2019 IEEE/CVF Conference on Computer Vision and Pattern Recognition (CVPR), pp. 8014–8023 (2019)

11. Huang, G., Liu, Z., Van Der Maaten, L., Weinberger, K.Q.: Densely connected convolutional networks. In: 2017 IEEE Conference on Computer Vision and Pattern Recognition (CVPR), pp. 2261–2269 (2017)

12. Huang, X., Liu, M.-Y., Belongie, S., Kautz, J.: Multimodal unsupervised image-to-image translation. In: Ferrari, V., Hebert, M., Sminchisescu, C., Weiss, Y. (eds.) ECCV 2018. LNCS, vol. 11207, pp. 179–196. Springer, Cham (2018). https://doi.org/10.1007/978-3-030-01219-9_11

13. Iizuka, S., Simo-Serra, E., Ishikawa, H.: Globally and locally consistent image completion. ACM Trans. Graph. **36**(4), 1–14 (2017)

14. Isola, P., Zhu, J., Zhou, T., Efros, A.A.: Image-to-image translation with conditional adversarial networks. In: 2017 IEEE Conference on Computer Vision and Pattern Recognition (CVPR), pp. 5967–5976 (2017)

15. Junbo, J.Z., Michaël, M., Yann, L.: Energy-based generative adversarial network. CoRR (2016)

16. Kingma, D.P., Ba, J.: Adam: a method for stochastic optimization. In: International Conference on Learning Representations (ICLR) (2015)

17. Li, R., Cheong, L., Tan, R.T.: Heavy rain image restoration: integrating physics model and conditional adversarial learning. In: 2019 IEEE/CVF Conference on Computer Vision and Pattern Recognition (CVPR), pp. 1633–1642 (2019)

18. Li, X., Wu, J., Lin, Z., Liu, H., Zha, H.: Recurrent squeeze-and-excitation context aggregation net for single image deraining. In: Ferrari, V., Hebert, M., Sminchisescu, C., Weiss, Y. (eds.) ECCV 2018. LNCS, vol. 11211, pp. 262–277. Springer, Cham (2018). https://doi.org/10.1007/978-3-030-01234-2_16

19. Li, Y., Tan, R.T., Guo, X., Lu, J., Brown, M.S.: Rain streak removal using layer priors. In: 2016 IEEE Conference on Computer Vision and Pattern Recognition (CVPR), pp. 2736–2744 (2016)

20. Liu, M., Breuel, T., Kautz, J.: Unsupervised image-to-image translation networks. CoRR (2017)
21. Mao, X., Li, Q., Xie, H., Lau, R.Y., Wang, Z., Paul Smolley, S.: Least squares generative adversarial networks. In: 2017 IEEE International Conference on Computer Vision (ICCV), pp. 2794–2802 (2017)
22. Paszke, A., et al.: PyTorch: an imperative style, high-performance deep learning library. In: Advances in Neural Information Processing Systems, pp. 8026–8037 (2019)
23. Ren, D., Zuo, W., Hu, Q., Zhu, P., Meng, D.: Progressive image deraining networks: a better and simpler baseline. In: 2019 IEEE/CVF Conference on Computer Vision and Pattern Recognition (CVPR), pp. 3932–3941 (2019)
24. Simonyan, K., Zisserman, A.: Very deep convolutional networks for large-scale image recognition. In: International Conference on Learning Representations (ICLR) (2015)
25. Tero, K., Timo, A., Samuli, L., Jaakko, L.: Progressive growing of GANs for improved quality, stability, and variation. CoRR (2017)
26. Wei, Y., Zhang, Z., Wang, Y., Fan, J., Yan, S., Wang, M.: DerainCycleGAN: a simple unsupervised network for single image deraining and rainmaking (2019)
27. Wei, Y., Zhang, Z., Zhang, H., Hong, R., Wang, M.: A coarse-to-fine multi-stream hybrid deraining network for single image deraining. In: 2019 IEEE International Conference on Data Mining (ICDM), pp. 628–637 (2019)
28. Yang, W., Tan, R.T., Feng, J., Liu, J., Guo, Z., Yan, S.: Deep joint rain detection and removal from a single image. In: 2017 IEEE Conference on Computer Vision and Pattern Recognition (CVPR), pp. 1685–1694 (2017)
29. Zhang, H., Patel, V.M.: Density-aware single image de-raining using a multi-stream dense network. In: 2017 IEEE Conference on Computer Vision and Pattern Recognition (CVPR), pp. 695–704 (2018)
30. Zhang, H., Sindagi, V., Patel, V.M.: Image de-raining using a conditional generative adversarial network. IEEE Trans. Circ. Syst. Video Technol. 30(11), 3943–3956 (2020)
31. Zhu, J., Park, T., Isola, P., Efros, A.A.: Unpaired image-to-image translation using cycle-consistent adversarial networks. In: 2017 IEEE International Conference on Computer Vision (ICCV), pp. 2242–2251 (2017)

# Object Bounding Box-Aware Embedding for Point Cloud Instance Segmentation

Lixue Cheng, Taihai Yang, and Lizhuang Ma[✉]

East China Normal University, Shanghai, China
{clx_2021,thyang}@stu.ecnu.edu.cn,lzma@cs.ecnu.edu.cn

**Abstract.** In 2D image domain, recent researches have made significant progress in encoding context information for instance segmentation. While the counterpart in point cloud is still left far behind. Previous works mostly focus on leveraging semantic information and aggregating point local information through K-Nearest-Neighbor method. Such methods are unaware of object boundary information which is important to separating nearby objects. We propose a novel module to integrate object bounding box information into embedding for Point Cloud Instance Segmentation. The proposed module called Object Bounding Box-aware module (OBAM) boosts the instance segmentation performance by encoding Object Bounding Box information. Through attention mechanism, the module removes redundant boundary information. Comprehensive experiments on two popular benchmarks (S3DIS and ScanNetV2) show the effectiveness of our method. Our method achieves the State-of-the-art instance segmentation performance on S3DIS benchmark.

**Keywords:** 3D point cloud · Instance segmentation · Object bounding box-aware

## 1 Introduction

In computer vision, instance segmentation is a basic task for scene understanding. It is always regarded as an extension to semantic segmentation. The task of instance segmentation is to group pixels/points which have the identical semantic labels into different object instances. In 3D domain, instance segmentation has wild applications in robotics, autonomous driving. With the growth of 3D sensors, it has gained more researchers attention and some approaches have been proposed in some papers. However, it is far away from being solved.

Point cloud captured by 3D scanners is an important type of 3D data representation. It consists of collections of points in Euclidean space. In 3D point cloud, PointNet [5] is the pioneer deep-learning method directly using original point cloud as input. Subsequent method PointNet++ [6] abstracts local region information with PointNet to learn point features through a hierarchical structure. Methods like radius based ball query and K-Nearest-Neighbor are utilized

© Springer Nature Switzerland AG 2021
D. N. Pham et al. (Eds.): PRICAI 2021, LNAI 13033, pp. 182–194, 2021.
https://doi.org/10.1007/978-3-030-89370-5_14

for aggregating local region information. Our approach is building on Point-Net++ network.

In 3D point cloud area, approaches for instance segmentation are mostly composed of clustering-based approaches and proposal-based approaches. To tackle the task of instance segmentation on point clouds, clustering-based approaches group points through clustering algorithm and proposal-based approaches are mostly based on object proposal. Semantic-aware instance segmentation is in ASIS [12]. They put two tasks (instance segmentation and semantic segmentation) together so the two tasks can help each other. While achieving competitive performance, global information and object boundary information are not encoded into embedding. To address the problem, we notice the approach Bonet [13]. Yang proposed a new end-to-end network framework Bonet to learn the coarse object bounding box information for point cloud instance segmentation. Object bounding box information is crucial for separating adjacent objects. Bonet directly regresses coarse bounding box vertexes and corresponding scores from global features.

As object boundary information is important to separate nearby objects, we combine two kinds approaches through proposing object bounding box-aware module. Our backbone network PointNet++ maintains an encoder-decoder architecture. After abstracting point features, semantic segmentation branch, instance segmentation branch and bounding box prediction branch compose our network. With our proposed OBAM module, bounding box information is encoded into our instance discriminative embedding. Our approach outperforms previous approaches. As object bounding box information is supervised, our network gains more information about the scene.

Extensive experiments on popular benchmarks S3DIS and ScanNetV2 are conducted to validate the effectiveness of our approach. To summarize, our main contributions are as follows:

1) We propose a novel framework which combines clustering-based approaches and proposal-based approaches. Our approach successfully encodes object bounding box information for point cloud instance segmentation.
2) We propose object bounding box-aware module (OBAM). The module successfully encodes object boundary information. Redundant object boundary information is removed through attention element-wise manipulation in OBAM.
3) Extensive experiments demonstrate the effectiveness of our network. With the proposed module, our network outperforms previous approaches.

## 2   Related Work

Instance segmentation on point cloud has attracted the attention of researchers in recent years. In this section, we briefly review previous approaches related to this field.

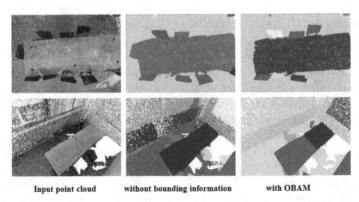

Input point cloud        without bounding information        with OBAM

**Fig. 1.** Comparison of the instance segmentation results. Our proposed OBAM model successfully encodes object boundary information which is crucial to separate adjacent object instances.

### 2.1    Deep Learning Methods on Point Cloud

Deep learning methods on point cloud are mostly divided into multi-view-based methods, voxel-based methods and point-based methods (Fig. 1).

As 2D convolution neural networks have gained considerable success, multi-view-based methods projected 3D point clouds onto 2D images and process with 2D CNNs. MVCNN [9] recognizes 3D shapes from different views of the shapes. Through a view-pool-layer, information can be accumulated into a single, compact descriptor. However, such multi-view-based methods may lose geometric details.

Voxel-based methods voxelize point cloud into spatial grids and utilize standard 3D convolution neural network framework to extract point features. In order to improve the voxelization efficiency of point clouds, Riegler [8] proposes a novel representation which uses a set of unbalanced Octrees. Pooled features representation is stored in the leaf nodes of Octrees. Their methods enable the network to be deep and high resolution. While achieving promising results, lower running speed still effects because of spatial sparsity of point cloud. Graham [3] proposes submanifold sparse convolution network to address the problem. With a hash table storing point features, their networks avoid nonsense computation cost and memory occupation of vacent voxels. Although achieving leading performance, Voxel-based methods are still limited by heavy computation cost when processing large-scale point clouds.

Unlike voxel-based and multiview-based methods, point-based methods directly process point cloud. The pioneer work PointNet [5] learns per-point encoding with Multilayer Perceptron. PointNet++ [6] is proposed to hierarchically extract local point features and maintains an encoder-decoder architecture. Hu comes up with a novel framework called Randlanet [4] to address the problem of efficient semantic segmentation. Instead of complex point selection algorithms, Random point sampling is utilized for its remarkable memory and computation efficiency. As random point sampling may discard key geometric details, They propose a novel local feature aggregation module to overcome the problem. In our work, we leverage PointNet++ as our backbone network to verify the validity of our approach.

## 2.2 Instance Segmentation on Point Cloud

Comparing with its counterpart on 2D images, the task of instance segmentation on point cloud is left far behind. Deep-learning approaches to the task can be divided into clustering-based approaches and proposal-based approaches.

SGPN [11] is the first work using deep learning technique in this field. With PointNet++ extracting global features and point features, the network learns feature space where points belonging to the same object have a close distance. They predict a similarity matrix yielding point-wise group proposals and a corresponding similarity map. They prune group proposals and generate point cloud groups through applying Non-Maximum Suppression. Due to the pair wise similarity matrix, the approach is heavily limited by computation and memory. In order to overcome the problem, clustering-based method ASIS [12] proposed by Wang removes the similarity matrix. Wang endorses that associative segmenting instances and semantics in point cloud are mutually beneficial to semantic segmentation task and instance segmentation task. Wang comes up with a method named mutual aid which enables the embedding of instance segmentation to benefit from point-level features of semantic segmentation. Semantic-aware embedding of instance segmentation achieves a huge breakthrough while it is unaware of the object bounding information. 3D Bonet [13] proposed by Yang directly predicts object bounding boxes. Better performance than ASIS is obtained through shared multi-layer perceptron without Non-Maximum Suppression algorithm. In our experiments, competitive performance are achieved through combining clustering-based methods and proposal-based methods.

## 3   Method

In this section, except semantic segmentation branch we mainly describe the other two branches (Bounding box branch and Instance segmentation branch). Details of our Object Bounding Box-aware module (OBAM) are presented below.

### 3.1   Network Framework

As shown in Fig. 2, our network is composed of a shared encoder and three parallel decoder branches. We apply PointNet++ as our backbone network to extract point features and global features. One of the branches handles semantic segmentation through decoding from point features. Another branch is to directly learn object bounding boxes from global features as 3D Bonet [13]. The other branch is to generate per-point embedding for instance segmentation. Backbone network encodes the input point cloud $P \in R^{N_p \times D}$ into point feature

$F_p \in R^{N_p \times D_f}$ matrix. Global point feature $F_g \in R^{D_f}$ is obtained by aggregation. $N_p$ refers to the total number of input points. $D$ denotes the dimension of input point cloud feature dimension and $D_f$ is the point feature dimension. Subsequently, per-point semantic results are generated by semantic segmentation branch. Bounding box coordinates $B_c \in R^{N_b \times 6}$ and corresponding score $B_s$ are obtained through bounding box branch. Two diagonal points coordinates refer to the rectangular bounding box. $N_b$ is a predefined hyper-parameter denoting the number of object bounding boxes. The instance segmentation branch outputs per-point instance embedding $E_{ins} \in R^{N_p \times D_e}$. $D_e$ is the embedding dimension. The embedding of points belonging to the same object should be close while the embedding of points belonging to different objects should be far away. Clustering algorithm mean-shift [7] is utilized to generate final group results during the inference.

To achieve the object bounding box-aware embedding, our proposed model OBAM is applied to encode the output of bounding box branch into instance segmentation branch. Besides, redundant object bounding box information is removed through an attention mechanism.

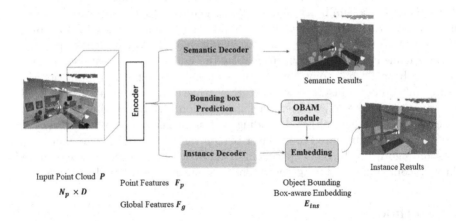

**Fig. 2.** The framework of our proposed method. Obviously, It is an encoder-decoder architecture. Point feature $F_p$ and global feature $F_g$ are obtained through a shared encoder. Three parallel decoders are applied. Semantic segmentation branch decodes from shared point features and classical cross entropy $L_{sem}$ is used to supervise. Bounding box prediction branch predicts object bounding box and corresponding score. Output of bounding box prediction branch is integrated into instance branch through OBAM module. Final instance embedding are generated from instance segmentation branch.

## 3.2   Bounding Box Prediction Branch

We utilize bounding box prediction branch in 3D bonet as it is lightweight and effective. It takes global vector $F_g$ as input. Bounding box $B_c \in R^{N_b \times 2 \times 3}$ and its corresponding score $B_s \in R^{N_b}$ are generated by the branch. For simplicity, the rectangular bounding boxes are parameterized as follows:

$$b_c = (x_{min}, y_{min}, z_{min} x_{max}, y_{max}, z_{max}) \in B_s \qquad (1)$$

The corresponding score $b_{score}$ ranges from 0 to 1. As the number of object instance is variable, the bounding box prediction branch generates predefined number $N_b$ of bounding boxes. We assume $N_b >= N_t$ where $N_t$ refers to the number of ground truth object bounding boxes.

Although there is no fixed order for ground truth bounding boxes. We formulate it as an optimal assignment problem to learn one-to-one match between predicted bounding box and ground truth bounding box. Boolean matrix $A$ denotes assignment where $A_{i,j} = 1$ refers to assign predicted box $b_i$ to the ground truth box $g_j$. Cost matrix $C$ is conducted where $C_{i,j}$ represents the cost between predicted bounding box $b_i$ and ground truth bounding box $g_j$. The more similar the two boxes, the less the cost $C_{i,j}$. Optimal problem is solved through the existing Hungarian algorithm [14]. We formulate the problem as follows:

$$A = \arg\min_{A} \sum_{i=1}^{N_b} \sum_{j=1}^{N_t} A_{i,j} C_{i,j} \text{ subject to } \sum_{i=1}^{N_b} A_{i,j} = 1 , \sum_{j=1}^{N_t} A_{i,j} \leq 1 \qquad (2)$$

$$C_{i,j} = C_{i,j}^{Ecu} + C_{i,j}^{SIou} + C_{i.j}^{cro} \qquad (3)$$

The association cost $C_{i,j}$ consists of three parts: Euclidean distance $C_{i,j}^{Ecu}$, soft intersection-over-union $C_{i,j}^{SIou}$ and point soft encoding cross-entropy $C_{i.j}^{cro}$ proposed in [13].

$b_{score}$ lies in the range (0, 1) which indicates the validity of predicted bounding box. After bounding box assignment, $N_t$ predicted bounding boxes of $N_b$ are assigned to the ground truth. The scores $b_{score}^t$ for the $N_t$ ground truth bounding boxes are all 1 while the remaining $N_b - N_t$ scores are '0'. $b_{score}^t$ refers to the scores for predicted bounding boxes which are assigned to the ground truth boxes while $b_{score}^f$ refers to the antithesis. The loss function of bounding box prediction branch is defined as follows:

$$L_{asso} = \frac{1}{N_t} \left( \sum_{i=1}^{N_b} \sum_{j=1}^{N_t} A_{i,j} C_{i,j} \right) \qquad (4)$$

$$L_{bscore} = -\frac{1}{N_b} \left( \sum_{1}^{N_t} \log b_{score}^t + \sum_{N_t+1}^{N_b} \log b_{score}^f \right) \qquad (5)$$

$$L_{box} = L_{asso} + L_{bscore} \qquad (6)$$

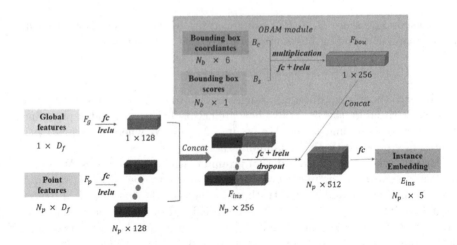

**Fig. 3.** The pipeline of our instance segmentation branch.

### 3.3 Instance Segmentation Branch

**Pipeline.** The instance segmentation branch fetches point feature matrix extracted by the backbone network and processes with the following predictions. Using efficient multilayer perceptrons (MLPs), the branch decodes the shared point feature matrix and global point feature is concatenated to the matrix. Applying Leaky Relu activation and Dropout technique, the intermediate feature matrix $F_{ins}$ is obtained. Object boundary information obtained by the object bounding box branch is integrated and fused through OBAM module. The final embedding $E_{ins}$ for instance segmentation can be represented as:

$$E_{ins} = \gamma_1 \left( F_{ins} \bigoplus F_{bou} \right) \tag{7}$$

Where $\gamma_1 : R^{D_m} \rightarrow \mathbb{R}^{D_e}$ ($D_m$ refers to the intermediate point feature dimension) and $\bigoplus$ means concatenating the features. Mixing up object instance bounding information generates more informative instance embedding. The pipeline is illustrated in Fig. 3.

**Object Bounding Box-Aware Module.** Benefiting from the bounding box branch described above, object bounding information is integrated into our instance branch through our proposed Object Bounding Box-aware Module. It takes the outputs $R_c$, $B_s$ of the bounding box branch as input. The higher validity of the predicted bounding box $b_c \in R_c$, the higher the corresponding score $b_{score} \in B_s$. Our module can be formulated as:

$$F_{bou} = \gamma_2 \left( \bar{R}_c \otimes B_s \right) \tag{8}$$

where $R_c \in R^{N_b \times 2 \times 3}$ is reshaped to $\bar{R}_c \in R^{N_b \times 6}$. $\otimes$ denotes element-wise multiplication, and $\gamma_2$ is a translation $R^{N_b \times 6} \rightarrow R^{N_b \times D_m}$ implemented by MLP. $D_m$ refers to the dimension of the intermediate point feature $F_{ins}$.

As described above, $B_s$ is supervised by $L_{bscore}$. Redundant predicted bounding boxes have scores close to '0'. Clearing up the effect of redundant predicted object bounding information, $B_s$ is also supervised by $L_{ins}$ (will be discussed in next section) through element-wise multiplication. The network selects helpful object bounding boxes information for instance embedding.

**Loss Function.** The informative embedding $E_{ins}$ for instance segmentation is to learn a distance metric that can measure the probability of points belonging to the same object. Intra-instance embedding should be pulled toward the corresponding cluster center and different instance centers should be pushed far away from each other. The loss function can be formulated as:

$$L_{push} = \frac{1}{N_t(N_t - 1)} \sum_{i=1}^{N_t} \sum_{j=1,j!=i}^{N_t} [2\sigma_d - \|\mu_i - \mu_j\|_1]_+^2 \qquad (9)$$

$$L_{pull} = \frac{1}{N_t} \sum_{i=1}^{N_t} \frac{1}{I_i} \sum_{j=1}^{I_i} [\|\mu_i - e_j\|_1 - \sigma_v]_+^2 \qquad (10)$$

$$L_{ins} = L_{push} + L_{pull} \qquad (11)$$

Where $\mu_i$ is the mean point embedding of instance $i$. $I_i$ is point number of instance $i$ and $e_j$ refers to an embedding of a point belonging to instance $i$. $\sigma_d$ and $\sigma_v$ are loose margins. $\|x\|_1$ is defined as the $l_1$ distance. $[x]_+$ denotes $[x]_+ = max(0, x)$

During the training, $L_{push}$ aims to make different instances repel each other and $L_{pull}$ is designed to pull point embedding toward the mean embedding of instance. During the inference, we adopt existing clustering algorithm mean-shift on instance embedding to obtain instance labels. As our instance embedding is class-agnostic, the semantic label of the points having the same instance label is assigned as the final instance category.

To summarize, our network is end-to-end trainable and supervised by three branches losses. The loss weights are all equals to 1 in our experiment.

$$L = L_{ins} + L_{sem} + L_{box} \qquad (12)$$

## 4    Experiments

In this section, we conduct quantitative and qualitative experiments to evaluate the effectiveness of our proposed approach. Ablation study and comparison with other approaches are reported below.

### 4.1    Experiment Settings

**Dataset.** We evaluate our approach on two public datasets: Stanford 3D Indoor Semantics Dataset (S3DIS) [1] and ScanNetV2 [2]. S3DIS consists of 3D scans in

6 large-scale indoor areas, covering total 272 rooms. S3DIS is a large-scale real indoor dataset containing more than 215 million points. Each point of S3DIS is associated with an instance label and a semantic label from 13 common semantic categories. Besides S3DIS, we further evaluate our approach on ScanNetV2. ScanNetV2 [2] contains about 1500 scans, divided into 1201, 300 and 100 scans, for training, validation and testing. We carry out our experiments on ScanNetV2 validation dataset.

**Evaluation Metrics.** We follow the 6-fold-cross-evaluation on S3DIS. Similar to ASIS [12] and Bonet [13], the performance on area 5 is also reported. Our instance segmentation performance is evaluated by four metrics: mean instance-wise coverage ($mCov$), mean weighted instance-wise coverage ($mWcov$), mean instance precision ($mPrec$), and mean recall ($mRec$). The experiments results are presented with IOU threshold of 0.5. For ScanNetV2, results on validation set are presented below.

**Implement Details.** For both S3DIS and ScanNetV2, each Scan contains a great deal of points, which makes it difficult to process all the points at one time. Each scene is split into 1 m × 1 m overlapped blocks. Each block contains 4096 points. Our experiment settings strictly follow Bonet [13], ASIS [12] and IAE [10]. $N_b$ is set as 24. The margins $\sigma_d, \sigma_v$ are set as $\sigma_d = 0.5$ and $\sigma_v = 1.5$. The embedding dimension $D_e$ is 5. The learning rate is set to 0.01 (0.001 for S3DIS) and divided by 2 every 20 epochs. We train the network 50 epochs for PointNet++. We adopt Adam optimizer with its default hyper-parameters to optimize the network. At test time, mean-shift [7] clustering with bandwidth 0.6 is used for inference. We use Blockmerging algorithm [11] to merge object instances from different blocks.

**Table 1.** Instance segmentation results on ScanNetV2 dataset (validation set). We report the metric of $mAP@0.25$. Categories of Sink, Sofa, Table, Toilet, and Window are not presented in the table.

| Method | mAP | bat | bed | she | cab | cha | cou | cur | des | doo | oth | pic | ref | shc |
|---|---|---|---|---|---|---|---|---|---|---|---|---|---|---|
| MaskRCNN [16] | 26.1 | 33.3 | 0.2 | 0.0 | 5.3 | 0.2 | 0.2 | 2.1 | 0.0 | 4.5 | 2.4 | 23.8 | 6.5 | 0.0 |
| SGPN [11] | 35.1 | 20.8 | 39.0 | 16.9 | 6.5 | 27.5 | 2.9 | 6.9 | 0.0 | 8.7 | 4.3 | 1.4 | 2.7 | 0.0 |
| ASIS [12] | 47.4 | 57.3 | 52.1 | 1.4 | 18.5 | 46.1 | 19.2 | 20.3 | 13.3 | 13.8 | 18.8 | 6.6 | 17.6 | 33.1 |
| **Ours** | 51.2 | 64.7 | 61.3 | 0.3 | 23.1 | 69.7 | 13.6 | 16.9 | 15.4 | 14.7 | 24.0 | 11.5 | 18.3 | 60.7 |

## 4.2    Ablation Study

We firstly build a baseline without OBAM module. The baseline is made up of two decoder branches: the semantic segmentation branch and the instance segmentation branch. The baseline is supervised by cross-entropy loss $L_{sem}$ for

**Table 2.** Instance segmentation results on the S3DIS. Experiment results on Area 5 and 6-fold are reported. **mCov**: average instance-wise coverage. **mWcov**: weighted average instance-wise coverage. **mPre**: mean precision. **mRec**: mean recall. Experiment performance is reported with IOU threshold of 0.5. For fair comparison, we carefully train the vanilla PointNet++ (without multi-scale grouping) as our backbone.

| Method | Year | mCov | mWcov | mPre | mRec |
|---|---|---|---|---|---|
| Test on area 5 | | | | | |
| SGPN [11] | 2018 | 32.7 | 35.5 | 36.0 | 28.7 |
| ASIS [12] | 2019 | 44.6 | 47.8 | 55.3 | 42.4 |
| 3D-BoNet [13] | 2019 | – | – | 57.5 | 40.2 |
| JSNet [15] | 2020 | 48.7 | 51.5 | 62.1 | 46.9 |
| IAE [10] | 2020 | 49.9 | **53.2** | 61.3 | 48.5 |
| **Ours** | – | **50.3** | 52.8 | **65.3** | **49.2** |
| Test on 6-fold | | | | | |
| SGPN [11] | 2018 | 36.0 | 28.7 | 31.2 | 38.2 |
| MV-CRF [15] | 2019 | – | – | 36.3 | – |
| ASIS [12] | 2019 | 51.2 | 55.1 | 63.6 | 47.5 |
| 3D-BoNet [13] | 2019 | – | – | 65.5 | 47.6 |
| PartNet[17] | 2019 | – | – | 56.4 | 43.4 |
| Ours | – | **54.7** | **57.1** | **68.4** | **52.9** |

semantic task and discriminative loss $L_{ins}$ for instance grouping. All ablation experiments we carry out are on the largest area 5 of S3DIS. The experiment results are shown in Table 3.

**OBAM.** We study the influence of our proposed OBAM and its components. Our proposed OBAM module with $l_{score}$ can improve the results by 9.1 for mPre and 3.4 for mRec. It indicates that encoding boundary information indeed boosts instance segmentation performance by a large margin.

**Manipulation.** We find out that bounding box scores $B_s$ supervised by $l_{score}$ are whether close to 1 or close to 0. As our OBAM module is based on multiple layer perceptron, we design the attention element-wise manipulation to remove the redundant boundary information and it further benefits instance segmentation performance. Comparing with the pipeline without attention element-wise manipulation, the full pipeline of our method improves the result by 5 for both $mPre$ and $mRec$.

**The Loss of Bounding Box Score.** Presented in [13], bounding box scores $B_s$ serve as a regularizer for bounding box prediction branch. After removing

**Table 3.** Ablation studies on the Area 5 of S3DIS. Both **mPre** and **mRec** metrics are reported. **OBAM:** using our proposed OBAM module. **Manipulation:** attention element-wise manipulation in Eq. (8). $l_{score}$: using $l_{score}$ to supervise the bounding boxes prediction branch.

| Method | OBAM | Manipulation | $l_{score}$ | mPre | mRec |
|--------|------|--------------|-------------|------|------|
| Baseline | | | | 51.2 | 40.7 |
| Ours1 | ✓ | | ✓ | 60.3 | 44.1 |
| Ours2 | ✓ | ✓ | | 60.5 | 46.1 |
| **Ours3** | ✓ | ✓ | ✓ | **65.3** | **49.2** |

Input Point Cloud          Instance ground truth          Ours

**Fig. 4.** Visualization of instance segmentation results on S3DIS. There are input point cloud, instance segmentation ground truth and our results from left to right. Through our proposed OBAM and discriminative embedding, our methods achieve sterling results of distinguishing adjacent objects.

bounding box score loss $l_{score}$ supervision, bounding box scores $B_s$ are only determined by attention element-wise manipulation. The instance segmentation performance drops significantly, primarily because of the difficulty to directly learn the score through attention mechanism.

### 4.3  Comparison with State-of-the-Art Approaches

In this section, Our comparison with other approaches is made on two popular benchmarks. Results on S3DIS and ScanNetV2 show the superiority of our approach.

**Quantitative Results on S3DIS.** Instance segmentation results testing on the area 5 of S3DIS and 6-fold validation are reported in Table 2. Our method is compared with other state-of-the-art methods which are also based on Point-Net++. Equipped with instance boundary information, our method achieve obvious improvement with metric mPre. Comparing with existing state-of-the-art methods, our method outperforms IAE [10] and JSNET [15], but not significantly. Both IAE and JSNET make a full use of point semantic information. IAE utilizes point semantic information and selects points from the instance to encode geometric information and instance context. JSNET jointly processes point cloud for Instance and Semantic Segmentation. Without leveraging semantic information, our approach achieves competitive performance. The effectiveness of our method and the importance of boundary information to instance segmentation are demonstrated. However, our approach is heavily affected by the bounding box prediction branch. We figure that more accurate bounding box prediction may boost the performance. Respectively, Fig. 4 shows our results of instance segmentation on the S3DIS dataset.

**Quantitative Results on ScanNetV2.** We conduct experiments on Scan-NetV2 validation set and the performance are reported in Table 1. Comparing with the previous state-of-the-art approach ASIS [12], our method achieves a significant improvement of metric mAP@0.25, by 3.8 from 47.4 to 51.2. Our bounding box-aware embedding shows great superiority on some categories. The instance segmentation results on ScanNetV2 demonstrate the superiority of our method.

## 5    Conclusion

In this paper, We presented a novel framework combining clustering-based and proposal-based approaches. Our proposed module OBAM integrates bounding box information into instance segmentation branch. Through OBAM, redundant bounding information is removed. Extensive experiments indicate the effectiveness of our method. Our bounding box-aware embedding indeed boots the instance segmentation performance on S3DIS and ScanNetV2. Our method achieves state-of-the-art performance on S3DIS dataset.

However, our method is limited by bounding box prediction. The limitation that directly learning object boundary information may lead to the future work.

**Acknowledgement.** The research is funded by National Natural Science Foundation of China (No. 61972157), National Key Research and Development Program of China (No. 2019YFC1521104) and Shanghai Municipal Science and Technology Major Project (2021SHZDZX0102).

## References

1. Armeni, I., et al.: IEEE: 3D semantic parsing of large-scale indoor spaces. In: Computer Vision & Pattern Recognition (2016)

2. Dai, A., Chang, A.X., Savva, M., Halber, M., Funkhouser, T., Niener, M.: ScanNet: richly-annotated 3D reconstructions of indoor scenes (2017)
3. Graham, B., Engelcke, M., Maaten, L.: 3D semantic segmentation with submanifold sparse convolutional networks. In: 2018 IEEE/CVF Conference on Computer Vision and Pattern Recognition (CVPR) (2018)
4. Hu, Q., Yang, B., Xie, L., Rosa, S., Markham, A.: RandLA-Net: efficient semantic segmentation of large-scale point clouds. In: 2020 IEEE/CVF Conference on Computer Vision and Pattern Recognition (CVPR) (2020)
5. Qi, C.R., Su, H., Mo, K., Guibas, L.J.: PointNet: deep learning on point sets for 3d classification and segmentation. In: Proceedings of the IEEE Conference on Computer Vision and Pattern Recognition (CVPR), July 2017
6. Qi, C.R., Yi, L., Su, H., Guibas, L.J.: PointNet++: deep hierarchical feature learning on point sets in a metric space. In: NIPS, pp. 5105–5114 (2017)
7. Comaniciu, D., Meer, P.: Mean shift: a robust approach toward feature space analysis. IEEE Trans. Pattern Anal. Mach. Intell. (2002)
8. Riegler, G., Ulusoy, A.O., Geiger, A.: OctNet: learning deep 3D representations at high resolutions. In: 2017 IEEE Conference on Computer Vision and Pattern Recognition (CVPR) (2017)
9. Su, H., Maji, S., Kalogerakis, E., Learned-Miller, E.: Multi-view convolutional neural networks for 3D shape recognition. IEEE (2015)
10. He, T., Liu, Y., Shen, C., Wang, X., Sun, C.: Instance-aware embedding for point cloud instance segmentation. In: Vedaldi, A., Bischof, H., Brox, T., Frahm, J.-M. (eds.) ECCV 2020. LNCS, vol. 12375, pp. 255–270. Springer, Cham (2020). https://doi.org/10.1007/978-3-030-58577-8_16
11. Wang, W., Yu, R., Huang, Q., Neumann, U.: SGPN: similarity group proposal network for 3D point cloud instance segmentation. In: Proceedings of the IEEE Conference on Computer Vision and Pattern Recognition (CVPR), June 2018
12. Wang, X., Liu, S., Shen, X., Shen, C., Jia, J.: Associatively segmenting instances and semantics in point clouds. In: 2019 IEEE/CVF Conference on Computer Vision and Pattern Recognition (CVPR) (2019)
13. Yang, B., et al.: Learning object bounding boxes for 3D instance segmentation on point clouds. In: Advances in Neural Information Processing Systems, pp. 6737–6746 (2019)
14. Yaw, H.: The Hungarian method for the assignment problem. Naval Res. Logist. Q. **2**, 83–97(1955)
15. Zhao, L., Tao, W.: JSNet: joint instance and semantic segmentation of 3D point clouds. In: Proceedings of the AAAI Conference on Artificial Intelligence, vol. 34, no. 7, pp. 12951–12958 (2020)
16. He, K., Gkioxari, G., Dollar, P., Girshick, R.: Mask R-CNN. In: Proceedings of the IEEE International Conference on Computer Vision (ICCV), October 2017
17. Mo, K., Zhu, S., Chang, A.X., Li, Y., Hao, S.: PartNet: a large-scale benchmark for fine-grained and hierarchical part-level 3D object understanding. In: 2019 IEEE/CVF Conference on Computer Vision and Pattern Recognition (CVPR) (2019)

# Objects as Extreme Points

Yang Yang[1,2], Min Li[1,2(✉)], Bo Meng[1,3], Zihao Huang[1,2], Junxing Ren[1,2], and Degang Sun[1,2]

[1] Institute of Information Engineering, Chinese Academy of Sciences, Beijing, China
{yangyang1995,limin,renjunxing,sundegang}@iie.ac.cn
[2] School of Cyber Security, University of Chinese Academy of Sciences, Beijing, China
[3] Beijing Institute of Technology, Beijing, China

**Abstract.** Object detection can be regarded as a pixel clustering task, and its boundary is determined by four extreme points (leftmost, top, rightmost, and bottom). However, most studies focus on the center or corner points of the object, which are conditional results of the extreme points. In this paper, we present an Extreme-Point-Prediction-Based object detector (EPP-Net), which directly regresses the relative displacement vector between each pixel and the four extreme points. We also propose a new metric to measure the similarity between two groups of extreme points, namely, Extreme Intersection over Union ($EIoU$), and incorporate this $EIoU$ as a new regression loss. Moreover, we propose a novel branch to predict the $EIoU$ between the ground-truth and the prediction results, and take it as the localization confidence to filter out poor detection results. On the MS-COCO dataset, our method achieves an average precision (AP) of 44.0% with ResNet-50 and an AP of 50.3% with ResNeXt-101-DCN. The proposed EPP-Net provides a new method to detect objects and achieves very competitive performance among the state-of-the-art anchor-free detectors.

**Keywords:** Object detection · Extreme points · Localization · Regression loss

## 1 Introduction

Object detection is a crucial prerequisite for many computer vision tasks, such as instance segmentation [4] and multi object tracking [21]. It also plays an essential role in many downstream technologies, such as intelligent video analysis and autonomous driving. Benefiting from the excellent performance of anchors, the detection accuracy of one-stage [15] and two-stage [16] object detectors has substantially improved. However, these detectors rely excessively on predefined anchors, thus requiring fine-tuning when training, and lead to poor generalization performance. Anchor-free detectors [7,19] have recently drawn much attention for their simple design, great accuracy, and high speed. Generally, anchor-free detectors can be classified into **key-point-based prediction** and **dense prediction**.

© Springer Nature Switzerland AG 2021
D. N. Pham et al. (Eds.): PRICAI 2021, LNAI 13033, pp. 195–208, 2021.
https://doi.org/10.1007/978-3-030-89370-5_15

**Fig. 1. Illustration of EPP-Net predictions.** As shown in this image, since the boundary of an object is determined by the extreme points, the bounding box (bbox) is actually a conditional result. Therefore, EPP-Net predicts four relative displacements, an 8D vector as the location of the object.

### 1.1   Key-Point-Based Prediction

The location of an object is usually represented by the smallest enclosing rectangle called the bounding box (bbox). Nevertheless, not all objects can perfectly fit into a rectangle, such as objects with a tilt angle. Therefore, bottom-up methods have been proposed to detect objects in a key-point-based fashion. Corner-Net [8] represents an object using a pair of corner points (top left and bottom right), whereas He et al. [3] also predicts the center point besides corner points. ExtremeNet [27] argues that corner points usually lie outside the object and lack appearance features. Therefore, it utilizes the four extreme points and the center points to represent the object. Free from the limitations of the rectangular box, these key-point-based detectors surpass anchor-based detectors for the first time. However, they require post-processing to group key-points to the same instance, which slows down the overall computing speed. Moreover, *the boundary of an object is determined by four extreme points, the corner points and the center point are both conditional results.* Therefore, the extreme regions have more substantial location features than the other ones.

### 1.2   Dense Prediction

FPN [10] powers various detectors to achieve high-precision dense prediction, such as FCOS [19] and FoveaBox [7]. In general, object detection algorithms process an image on the object level, whereas FCOS proves for the first time that the object detection task could also be solved in a per-pixel prediction fashion. This pixel-level-based detector provides a more fine-grained manner to understand an image. All these top-down methods represent the location of an object by a rectangular box. Compared with the four extreme points, such unified representation lacks the shape feature of an object, especially for those non-rigid objects with a large shape variance.

### 1.3 Motivation

Object detection involves classification and localization (bbox regression). However, there exists a misalignment between them. IoU-net [6] finds that some detection results with high classification confidence have coarse bbox predictions. *Therefore, taking classification confidence as the only criterion of detection results is not accurate enough.* BorderDet [13] utilizes border features to improve detection results. It also reveals that *the most important features for localization lie in the extreme point regions.*

In this paper, we provide **EPP-Net**, a simple yet effective fully convolutional one-stage object detection method, which densely predicts the relative displacement vector between each location and the four extreme points, as shown in Fig. 1. We also propose a new evaluation metric, namely, Extreme Intersection over Union ($EIoU$), to measure the similarity between two groups of extreme points, and a new loss function, namely, Extreme $IoU$ loss ($EIoU$ loss), tailored for this model. Moreover, we propose a new branch to predict the $EIoU$ between the extreme points and the matched ground-truth with the $EIoU$ servers as the localization confidence for each prediction result. By combining the predicted $EIoU$ with the classification confidence as the ranking keyword in non-maximum suppression (NMS), we show a considerable improvement in the detection results.

In summary, the contributions of this paper are as follows:

1. EPP-Net decomposes the detection task into extreme points prediction and classification. Compared with the bottom-up methods, EPP-Net does not need a subsequent grouping process.
2. We propose $EIoU$, a normalized and scale-invariant evaluation metric, to measure the similarity between any two groups of extreme points. By incorporating $EIoU$ as the regression loss, namely, $EIoU$ loss, the accuracy with $EIoU$ loss can easily exceed that of Smooth-$\ell_1$ loss by 1.4% without fine-tuning.
3. We present an $EIoU$ predictor to solve the misalignment problem between localization and classification. The predicted $EIoU$ serves as the localization confidence, and it is combined with the classification confidence as the ranking keyword in NMS. After appending this branch, the AP is improved by 0.5%.

## 2   Related Work

### 2.1   Anchor-Free Object Detection

Current anchor-free detectors can achieve the same accuracy as anchor-based ones, with fewer hyperparameters and no complicated $IoU$ calculations. Despite the fact that DenseBox [5] and YOLOv1 [14] are the earliest explorations of anchor-free models, DenseBox is not suitable for generic object detection, and the YOLO family added the anchor strategy in its subsequent versions. Therefore, these two methods are not included in the following discussions.

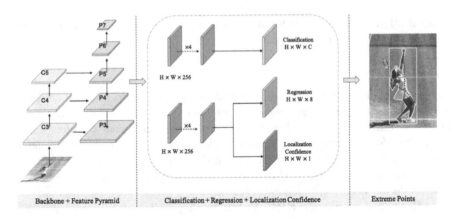

**Fig. 2. Architecture of EPP-Net.** This network consists of a backbone, a feature pyramid network, and two subnets, corresponding to classification and regression. For each pixel, EPP-Net outputs classification confidence, regression results, and the localization confidence.

**Key-Point-Based Prediction.** Key-point-based detectors detect an object as one or several key-points and utilize post-processing methods to group the key points. CornerNet outputs the heatmaps of the top-left and bottom-right corners and an embedding vector for each key-point. In its grouping process, embeddings that have smaller Euclidean distances are grouped as the same instance. Based on CornerNet, [3] adds center point prediction. In its grouping process, it also uses embedding vectors to group points. Each predicted bbox has a predefined central region and will be preserved only when the center point falls in this region. ExtremeNet predicts four extreme points and a center point for each object. In its grouping process, it uses a brute force method to enumerate all possible combinations. The box will be preserved only when the geometric center of the extreme points has a high response in the center point heatmap. The time complexities of these post-processing methods are $O(n^2)$, $O(n^2)$, and $O(n^4)$, respectively, which slow down the overall computing speed. Our EPP-Net is a top-down method so that it does not need a grouping process.

**Dense Prediction.** FSAF [28] employs an extra anchor-free module on the anchor-based detector for detection and feature selection. FSAF calculates the total loss for each instance and selects the pyramid level with the minimal loss to learn the instance. FoveaBox predicts category-sensitive semantic maps for the object's existing possibility and the bbox for each position that potentially contains an object. Our method outperforms them without the feature selection strategy and category-sensitive semantic maps. For FCOS, each location inside the object is a potential positive sample, and it directly predicts the relative distances from the four sides of the bbox to the location. It also utilizes a center-ness branch to suppress classification results far from the center region. Compared with it, our EPP-Net combines the localization and classification confidence to select the best detection results, which is more reasonable. Moreover, Instead of regressing the four bounds of the bbox, the way EPP-Net predicts is more precise.

## 2.2 Localization and Classification Spatial Misalignment

Localization is a position-sensitive task, whereas classification is not because of its translation and scale invariance properties; that is, the position or scale change of features does not affect the classification results. Therefore, a spatial misalignment exists between them. TSD [18] proves that localization is boundary-sensitive, whereas classification is salient-area-sensitive. IoU-net [6] utilizes an extra subnet to predict the $IoU$ between the detection results and ground-truth bboxes, and takes it as the ranking keyword in NMS. In contrast to IoU-net, first, IoU-Net is a two-stage, anchor-based detector while ours is a one-stage, and anchor-free detector. Second, The predicted $IoU$ in IoU-Net is class-aware, while our $EIoU$ predictor is unrelated to classes and the IoU-guided NMS is not used. Finally, our localization predictor is very light because it is only a branch of the regression subnet, while IoU-net requires a new head that is parallel with the classification and regression heads.

## 2.3 Regression Loss

$\ell_n$-norm-based losses are widely used in bbox regression. However, they suffer from the scale imbalance problem, which means the loss value is affected by the scale of the bbox. $IoU$ is an evaluation metric that measures the overlap between two bboxes. [24] proposes $IoU$ loss based on this metric, which also inherits $IoU$'s scale invariance. When the two bboxes do not overlap, $IoU$ becomes 0 and cannot be optimized. Therefore, $GIoU$ loss [17] is proposed to solve this problem. Standing on the shoulders of giants, we propose $EIoU$ loss to measure the similarity of two convex quadrilaterals.

# 3    Method

In this section, we briefly introduce the details of EPP-Net. We use FCOS from mmdetection [2] as the baseline and ResNet-50 as the basic backbone. In EPP-Net, an object is detected as four extreme points (leftmost, top, rightmost, and bottom) by predicting the relative displacement vector in a per-pixel prediction fashion. We propose $EIoU$ as well as $EIoU$ loss for extreme point regression. Finally, we propose a novel $EIoU$ predictor for accurate key-point prediction.

## 3.1 Positive Sampling with Dynamic Radius

The extreme points ground-truth is defined as $E$, where $E = (e_{xl}, e_{yl}, e_{xt}, e_{yt}, e_{xr}, e_{yr}, e_{xb}, e_{yb}) \in \mathbb{R}^8$. Given a location $(x, y)$, if it falls into the target area of the ground-truth box, it is considered as a positive sample; otherwise, a negative sample. Let $(c_x, c_y)$ be the center point of the ground-truth box, and $s_j$ [19] be the stride of feature map $j$. The target area is defined as $(c_x - s_j * r_x, c_y - s_j * r_y, c_x + s_j * r_x, c_y + s_j * r_y)$. $r_x$ and $r_y$ are the horizontal and vertical sampling radii, respectively. Considering the large difference of aspect ratio of different objects, it is improper if the sampling radii of different directions are set to be the same length. Therefore, we dynamically adjust the radius according to the aspect ratio, with the sampling radius on the longer side set to be larger, as shown in Fig. 3(b). Let $f = \frac{w}{h}$, where $w$ and $h$ are the width and height of the ground-truth box, respectively. $r_x$ and $r_y$ are defined as follows:

$$(r_x, r_y) = \begin{cases} (1.5 * f, 1.5), f > 1 \\ \left(1.5, \dfrac{1.5}{f}\right), f < 1 \end{cases} \tag{1}$$

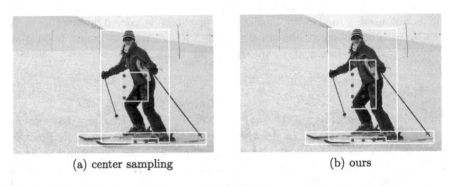

(a) center sampling                    (b) ours

**Fig. 3. Positive sampling.** The red points denote the positive samples. The center sampling strategy from FCOS takes the positive area as a square, whereas we dynamically adjust the sampling area according to the bbox shape. (Color figure online)

### 3.2  Network Outputs

As shown in Fig. 2, the classification subnet outputs the classification confidence with a shape as $H * W * C$, where $C$ is the number of MS-COCO categories [12]. The $C$ channels of the classification outputs correspond to $C$ binary classifiers.

The regression subnet consists of two branches, which output the $EIoU$ prediction results and the relative displacement vector, respectively, and their shapes are $H * W * 1$ and $H * W * 8$, respectively. Details of the $EIoU$ predictor are in Sect. 3.4. Given a positive sample $P(p_x, p_y)$ and the four extreme points coordinates, the relative displacement vector is $(e_{xl} - p_x, e_{yl} - p_y, \ldots, e_{yb} - p_y, )$.

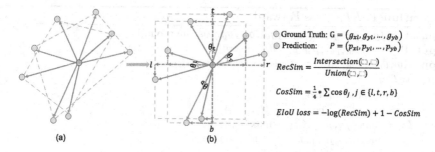

**Fig. 4. Illustration of EIoU loss.** The four extreme points are taken as a convex quadrilateral composed of four vectors. To simplify the calculation, the $IoU$ of the smallest enclosing rectangles and the cosine similarity between each paired vectors are used to measure the similarity of two groups of extreme points.

### 3.3   EIoU Loss

$\ell_n$-norm-based losses have the scale imbalance problem. Moreover, a gap exists between the $\ell_n$-norm and the evaluation metric $IoU$. The performances of $IoU$ loss and $GIoU$ loss prove the effectiveness of utilizing $IoU$ in regression loss. Compared with $IoU$ loss, $GIoU$ loss can optimize cases where bboxes have no overlap area. Therefore, we want to design a regression loss that inherits the scale-invariant property of $IoU$ and can compare any two convex quadrilaterals, even for non-overlapping cases.

As shown in Fig. 4(a), the four extreme points form an irregular convex quadrilateral. Thus, calculating the $IoU$ of these two quadrilaterals seems to be optimal. However, the calculation of $IoU$ with respect to non-axis-aligned quadrilaterals is very complicated. Therefore, we choose a compromise way to simplify the calculation. The features of a quadrilateral can be decomposed into position, scale, and shape. To compare the first two features, we calculate the similarity between the two smallest enclosing rectangles of these quadrilaterals (The dotted rectangles in Fig. 4(b)), and the similarity ($RecSim$) is defined as the $IoU$ between them. For the last feature, we use the mean value of the cosine similarity ($CosSim$) between each paired vectors to represent the overall shape difference, as shown in Eq. 2. The cosine similarity is equivalent to the angle between vectors, thus perfectly reflecting the shape difference.

$$CosSim = \frac{1}{4} * \sum \cos \theta_j, j \in \{l, t, r, b\} \tag{2}$$

Therefore, the similarity of any two convex quadrilaterals on the Euclidean plane can be measured by $EIoU$. If not specified, we use the $IoU$ between the two smallest enclosing rectangles as the $RecSim$ in all equations. The definition of $EIoU$ is shown in Eq. 3.

$$EIoU = \frac{1}{2} * (IoU + \frac{1 + CosSim}{2}) \tag{3}$$

The properties of $EIoU$ are as follows:

---

**Algorithm 1.** $EIoU$ loss Forward

---

**Input**: $G = (g_{xl}, g_{yl}, g_{xt}, g_{yt}, g_{xr}, g_{yr}, g_{xb}, g_{yb})$ as the ground-truth.
**Input**: $P = (p_{xl}, p_{yl}, p_{xt}, p_{yt}, p_{xr}, p_{yr}, p_{xb}, p_{yb})$ as the prediction.
**Input**: $\{\theta_l, \theta_t, \theta_r, \theta_b\}$ are the angles between paired vectors.
**Output**: $\mathcal{L}_{EIoU}$

1: **for** each prediction **do**
2:    $CosSim = \frac{1}{4} * \sum \cos \theta_j, j \in \{l, t, r, b\}$
3:    $\mathcal{I}_{x1} = \max(g_{xl}, p_{xl}), \mathcal{I}_{y1} = \max(g_{yt}, p_{yt})$
4:    $\mathcal{I}_{x2} = \min(g_{xr}, p_{xr}), \mathcal{I}_{y2} = \min(g_{yb}, p_{yb})$
5:    $\mathcal{A}_g = (g_{xr} - g_{xl}) * (g_{yb} - g_{yt})$
6:    $\mathcal{A}_p = (p_{xr} - p_{xl}) * (p_{yb} - p_{yt})$
7:    $\mathcal{I} = (\mathcal{I}_{x1} - \mathcal{I}_{x2}) * (\mathcal{I}_{y1} - \mathcal{I}_{y2})$
8:    **if** $\mathcal{I} > 0$ **then**
9:      $\mathcal{U} = \mathcal{A}_g + \mathcal{A}_p - \mathcal{I}$
10:     $IoU = \max\left(\frac{\mathcal{I}}{\mathcal{U}}, e^{-6}\right)$
11:     $\mathcal{L}_{EIoU} = -ln(IoU) + (1 - CosSim)$
12:   **else**
13:     $\mathcal{L}_{EIoU} = -ln(e^{-6}) + (1 - CosSim)$
14:   **end if**
15: **end for**

---

1. $IoU$ and cosine similarity are scale-invariant. Thus, $EIoU$ also inherits this property.
2. For any two convex quadrilaterals A and B. $A, B \subseteq \mathbb{S}, 0 \leq IoU(A, B) \leq 1, -1 \leq CosSim(A, B) \leq 1$, that $0 \leq EIoU(A, B) \leq 1$ can be easily obtained. Therefore, $EIoU$ is an normalized evaluation metric.
3. $IoU$ can be considered a special case of $EIoU$. When both convex quadrilaterals are axis-aligned rectangles, $EIoU$ is equivalent to $IoU$.

With $IoU$ ranges between 0 and 1, the cross-entropy of $IoU$ is $-1 * ln(IoU)$. The range of cosine similarity is between −1 and 1 and the cosine similarity difference is defined as $1 - CosSim$. Therefore, $\mathcal{L}_{EIoU}$ is defined as Eq. 4:

$$\mathcal{L}_{EIoU} = \mathcal{L}_{RecSim} + \mathcal{L}_{CosSim}$$
$$= -\ln(IoU) + (1 - CosSim) \tag{4}$$

The details of $EIoU$ loss are shown in Algorithm 1. $EIoU$ loss has the following properties:

1. $EIoU$ loss is invariant to scale changes.
2. The value range of $EIoU$ loss is $[0, 8]$. Its value will become 0 only when the two groups of extreme points completely coincide; otherwise, it will be positive. Consequently, $EIoU$ loss can optimize any two groups of extreme points.

## 3.4  EIoU Predictor

Here, we provide this *EIoU* predictor to deal with the misalignment problem between localization and classification. Object detection methods usually predict many bboxes with large overlapping areas. Therefore, the NMS algorithm is used to filter out poor prediction results with the classification confidence as the ranking keyword. However, this method may filter out the detection results with good bbox predictions but low classification confidence. Thus, our *EIoU* predictor scores each regression result by predicting the *EIoU* between each predicted bbox and its associated ground-truth. By doing so, we take the localization and classification confidence together as the evaluation criteria for prediction results.

During inference, we multiply the classification confidence and the *EIoU* prediction results as the final ranking keyword in NMS, as shown in Eq. 5.

$$\text{ranking} = EIoU * \text{cls-confidence} \tag{5}$$

## 3.5  Optimization

The total loss of this model is formulated as follows:

$$\mathcal{L} = \lambda_{cls}\mathcal{L}_{cls} + \lambda_{reg}\mathcal{L}_{reg} + \lambda_{eioup}\mathcal{L}_{eioup} \tag{6}$$

$\mathcal{L}_{cls}$ is focal loss for classification as in [11], and $\mathcal{L}_{reg}$ is defined in Eq. 4. $\mathcal{L}_{eioup}$ is BCE loss for *EIoU* predictions. To balance losses of all subtasks, hyperparameters $\lambda_{cls}$, $\lambda_{reg}$, and $\lambda_{eioup}$ are all set as 1.

# 4  Experiments

In this section, we perform several experiments on the MS-COCO dataset [12] to show the effectiveness of EPP-Net and its counterparts. EPP-Net is trained on the COCO train2017 split (115K images) and evaluated on the COCO val2017 split (5K images) for the ablation study. Visualization experiments are also conducted on the val2017 split. We also upload the detection results on the test-dev split (20K images) with different backbones to the MS-COCO server to compare our EPP-Net with the recent state-of-the-art detectors.

## 4.1  Implementation Details

Our implementation is based on mmdetection [2] with Pytorch 1.6. Extreme points are computed from the polygonal mask annotations following the extraction strategy from [27]. The hyperparameters in our model follow those in FCOS, and we use pre-trained models on ImageNet to initialize network weights. If not specified, we use ResNet-50 and the feature pyramid network as our basic network. We train this network with stochastic gradient descent and a total batch size of 16 images on 8 NVIDIA TITAN RTX GPUs for 90K iterations. We set the initial learning rate as 0.01, and the momentum and the weight decay as 0.9 and 0.0001, respectively. We decrease the learning rate by 10 at epochs 8 and epoch 11. The *IoU* threshold in NMS is set as 0.6.

## 4.2   Ablation Study

We perform several groups of ablation experiments to validate the effectiveness of different counterparts. All test results are reported on MS-COCO val2017 split.

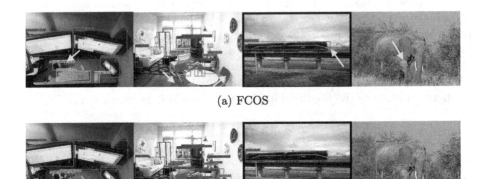

(a) FCOS

(b) EPP-Net

**Fig. 5. Qualitative results on the val2017 split.** Extreme points and bbox detection results of EPP-Net are shown on the same image. With ResNet-50, our model (The model with AP 39.5%) can achieve excellent detection results in various scenes.

**Table 1. EPP-Net *vs*. FCOS.** Comparisons on the val2017 split with ResNet-50-FPN as the backbone. "bbox" and "ex": representing objects by bounding boxes and extreme points. "loc": the localization confidence branch. "ctr-ness" and "ctr": centerness and center sampling in FCOS. "dr": our positive sampling strategy, details are in Sect. 3.1.

| Method | Reg | loc | Sampling | AP | AP$_{50}$ | AP$_{75}$ | AP$_S$ | AP$_M$ | AP$_L$ |
|--------|-----|-----|----------|-----|-----|-----|-----|-----|-----|
| FCOS [19] | $\mathcal{L}_{GIoU}$+bbox | ctr-ness | ctr | 38.6 | 57.4 | 41.4 | 22.3 | 42.5 | 49.8 |
| EPP-Net | $\mathcal{L}_{EIoU}$+ex | ctr-ness | ctr | 38.9 | 57.3 | 42.2 | 23.0 | 42.7 | 50.0 |
| EPP-Net | $\mathcal{L}_{EIoU}$+ex | $EIoU$ | ctr | 39.4 | 57.7 | **43.2** | **23.4** | **43.6** | 50.6 |
| EPP-Net | $\mathcal{L}_{EIoU}$+ex | $EIoU$ | dr | **39.5** | **58.1** | 42.9 | 23.1 | 43.4 | **51.1** |

**Overall Performance.** We compare our method with FCOS to evaluate the overall performance of EPP-Net. We use the control variable method to validate each counterpart in EPP-Net, which are *EIoU* loss, the *EIoU* predictor, and our positive sampling strategy. As shown in Table 1, the best model of EPP-Net outperforms FCOS with an AP of 39.5%. Compared with bounding boxes, the representation of extreme points can improve the AP by 0.3% (The model with AP 38.9). Our localization branch improves the AP@75 by 1.0%, which indicates the effectiveness of the $EIoU$ predictor. With our positive sampling strategy, we observe a considerable improvement of AP in large objects, namely, 0.5%. We explain as follows: First, large objects are more likely to sample more true positive samples. Second, the shape variance of large objects is larger than that of small objects, therefore, a dynamic sampling radius following the changes of object shapes is more appropriate. The visualization of the detection results are shown in Fig. 5 and one can see that our detection results are more accurate than that of FCOS.

**Table 2. EIoU loss *vs*. Smooth-$\ell_1$ loss.** Settings are the same as the EPP-Net in Table 1. The performance of $EIoU$ loss is much better than that of Smooth-$\ell_1$ loss.

| loss | AP | $AP_{50}$ | $AP_{75}$ | $AP_S$ | $AP_M$ | $AP_L$ |
|------|-----|-----|-----|-----|-----|-----|
| $EIoU$ | **39.5** | **58.1** | **42.9** | **23.1** | **43.4** | **51.1** |
| w/Smooth-$\ell_1$ | 38.1 | 57.5 | 40.7 | 21.5 | 42.2 | 49.9 |

**EIoU Loss.** The IoU-based losses require a 4D vector to represent the object which is incompatible with our regression task (8D vector). Therefore, we take Smooth-$\ell_1$ loss and $EIoU$ loss as the regression loss, respectively, to prove the effectiveness of $EIoU$ loss. The results are shown in Table 2. Smooth-$\ell_1$ loss achieves an AP of 38.1%, and our $EIoU$ loss outperforms it by 1.4%. $AP_S$, $AP_M$, and $AP_L$ are all raised considerably, which proves the importance of the scale invariance property of regression loss.

**Table 3. EIoU *vs*. other counterparts.** EIoU-branch denotes our $EIoU$ predictor. QFL denotes the joint representation of $IoU$ score and classification.

| Type | AP | $AP_{50}$ | $AP_{75}$ | $AP_S$ | $AP_M$ | $AP_L$ |
|------|-----|-----|-----|-----|-----|-----|
| EIoU-branch | **39.5** | **58.1** | **42.9** | **23.1** | **43.4** | **51.1** |
| Centerness-branch [19] | 38.6 | 57.4 | 41.4 | 22.3 | 42.5 | 49.8 |
| IoU-branch [6, 22] | 38.7 | 56.7 | 42.0 | 21.6 | 43.0 | 50.3 |
| QFL [9] | 39.0 | 57.8 | 41.9 | 22.0 | 43.1 | 51.0 |

**EIoU Predictor.** As shown in Table 3, we compare our localization confidence predictor with other strategies. The center-ness in FCOS is hand-crafted with the belief that the center area predicts better localization results. However, the geometric center of some objects does not fall in the foreground area, such as the crescent moon. Compared with center-ness, taking $IoU$ or $EIoU$ as the localization confidence is more generalized and has achieved better performance. The IoU-branch in IoU-Net and QFL in GFocal loss are class-aware, while our $EIoU$ branch is independent of classes. Our $EIoU$ outperforms all other counterparts with an AP of 39.5%. We can conclude that the $EIoU$ predictor can improve the detection accuracy by suppressing inaccurate localization results.

### 4.3   State-of-the-Art Comparisons

Table 4 shows the comparison results between EPP-Net and the state-of-the-art detectors. We use multi-scale training with the shorter side of input images randomly resized from 640 to 800 and the longer side less than 1333. The training process follows the 2× schedule in [2]. Test results are reported on the MS-COCO test-dev split by uploading the detection results to the MS-COCO server. Our model achieves a substantial improvement with different backbones. Compared with anchor-based RetinaNet, our model achieves an improvement of 5.0% in AP with backbone ResNeXt-101. EPP-Net also outperforms key-point-based detectors, CornerNet and ExtremeNet, with better accuracy and without the

**Table 4. EPP-Net *vs.* state-of-the-art detectors.** "†" indicates the multi-scale testing and settings are the same as in [20].

| Method | Backbone | AP | $AP_{50}$ | $AP_{75}$ | $AP_S$ | $AP_M$ | $AP_L$ |
|---|---|---|---|---|---|---|---|
| **Anchor-based** | | | | | | | |
| Faster R-CNN w/ FPN [10] | ResNet-101 | 36.2 | 59.1 | 39.0 | 18.2 | 39.0 | 48.2 |
| YOLOv4 [1] | CSPDarknet-53 | 43.5 | 65.7 | 47.3 | 26.7 | 46.7 | 53.3 |
| RetinaNet [11] | ResNeXt-101 | 40.8 | 61.1 | 44.1 | 24.1 | 44.2 | 51.2 |
| IoU-Net [6] | ResNet-101 | 40.6 | 59.0 | - | - | - | - |
| FSAF [28] | ResNeXt-101 | 42.9 | 63.8 | 46.3 | 26.6 | 46.2 | 52.7 |
| ATSS [25] | ResNeXt-101-DCN | 47.7 | 66.5 | 51.9 | 29.7 | 50.8 | 59.4 |
| GFL [9] | ResNeXt-101-DCN | 48.2 | 67.4 | 52.6 | 29.2 | 51.7 | 60.2 |
| **Anchor-free** | | | | | | | |
| CornerNet [8] | Hourglass-104 | 40.5 | 59.1 | 42.3 | 21.8 | 42.7 | 50.2 |
| ExtremeNet [27] | Hourglass-104 | 40.2 | 55.5 | 43.2 | 20.4 | 43.2 | 53.1 |
| CenterNet-HG [26] | Hourglass-104 | 42.1 | 61.1 | 45.9 | 24.1 | 45.5 | 52.8 |
| CenterNet511 [3] | Hourglass-104 | 44.9 | 62.4 | 48.1 | 25.6 | 47.4 | 57.4 |
| RepPoints [23] | ResNet-101 | 41.0 | 62.9 | 44.3 | 23.6 | 44.1 | 51.7 |
| FoveaBox-align [7] | ResNeXt-101 | 43.9 | 63.5 | 47.7 | 26.8 | 46.9 | 55.6 |
| FCOS-imprv [20] | ResNeXt-101 | 44.8 | 64.4 | 48.5 | 27.7 | 47.4 | 55.0 |
| FCOS-imprv†[20] | ResNeXt-101-DCN | 49.1 | 68.0 | 53.9 | 31.7 | 51.6 | 61.0 |
| EPP-Net† | ResNet-50 | 44.0 | 62.2 | 48.6 | 28.3 | 46.5 | 54.0 |
| EPP-Net | ResNeXt-101 | 45.8 | 65.1 | 49.9 | 28.1 | 49.0 | 56.4 |
| EPP-Net† | ResNeXt-101 | 48.1 | 66.7 | 53.0 | 31.8 | 50.9 | 58.8 |
| EPP-Net | ResNeXt-101-DCN | 48.3 | 67.5 | 52.5 | 29.0 | 51.6 | 61.6 |
| EPP-Net† | ResNeXt-101-DCN | **50.3** | **68.3** | **55.0** | **33.0** | **53.0** | **62.4** |

grouping process. Moreover, EPP-Net outperforms the FCOS baseline by 1.0% and achieves an AP of 45.8% with ResNeXt-101. Finally, the performance of the best model reaches 50.3% AP with ResNeXt-101-DCN as the backbone.

## 5 Conclusion

In this paper, we present EPP-Net as a new method to detect an object by predicting the relative displacement vector between each location and the four extreme points. We also propose $EIoU$, a novel evaluation metric, to measure the similarity between two groups of extreme points. Moreover, our proposed $EIoU$ loss can deal with the scale imbalance problem, which outperforms Smooth-$\ell_1$ loss. Furthermore, we propose the $EIoU$ predictor, which helps the detector obtain better localization results. The detection results on the MS-COCO reveal that our method can achieve the state-of-the-art accuracy.

## References

1. Bochkovskiy, A., Wang, C.Y., Liao, H.Y.M.: Yolov4: optimal speed and accuracy of object detection. arXiv preprint arXiv:2004.10934 (2020)
2. Chen, K., et al.: Mmdetection: open mmlab detection toolbox and benchmark. arXiv preprint arXiv:1906.07155 (2019)
3. Duan, K., Bai, S., Xie, L., Qi, H., Huang, Q., Tian, Q.: Centernet: keypoint triplets for object detection. In: Proceedings of the IEEE International Conference on Computer Vision, pp. 6569–6578 (2019)
4. He, K., Gkioxari, G., Dollár, P., Girshick, R.: Mask r-CAN. In: Proceedings of the IEEE International Conference on Computer Vision, pp. 2961–2969 (2017)
5. Huang, L., Yang, Y., Deng, Y., Yu, Y.: Densebox: unifying landmark localization with end to end object detection. arXiv preprint arXiv:1509.04874 (2015)
6. Jiang, B., Luo, R., Mao, J., Xiao, T., Jiang, Y.: Acquisition of localization confidence for accurate object detection. In: Proceedings of the European Conference on Computer Vision (ECCV). pp. 784–799 (2018)
7. Kong, T., Sun, F., Liu, H., Jiang, Y., Li, L., Shi, J.: Foveabox: beyound anchor-based object detection. IEEE Trans. Image Proces. **29**, 7389–7398 (2020)
8. Law, H., Deng, J.: Cornernet: detecting objects as paired keypoints. In: Proceedings of the European Conference on Computer Vision (ECCV), pp. 734–750 (2018)
9. Li, X., et al.: Generalized focal loss: learning qualified and distributed bounding boxes for dense object detection. arXiv preprint arXiv:2006.04388 (2020)
10. Lin, T.Y., Dollár, P., Girshick, R., He, K., Hariharan, B., Belongie, S.: Feature pyramid networks for object detection. In: Proceedings of the IEEE Conference on Computer Vision and Pattern Recognition, pp. 2117–2125 (2017)
11. Lin, T.Y., Goyal, P., Girshick, R., He, K., Dollár, P.: Focal loss for dense object detection. In: Proceedings of the IEEE International Conference on Computer Vision, pp. 2980–2988 (2017)
12. Lin, T.-Y., et al.: Microsoft COCO: common objects in context. In: Fleet, D., Pajdla, T., Schiele, B., Tuytelaars, T. (eds.) ECCV 2014. LNCS, vol. 8693, pp. 740–755. Springer, Cham (2014). https://doi.org/10.1007/978-3-319-10602-1_48

13. Qiu, H., Ma, Y., Li, Z., Liu, S., Sun, J.: BorderDet: border feature for dense object detection. In: Vedaldi, A., Bischof, H., Brox, T., Frahm, J.-M. (eds.) ECCV 2020. LNCS, vol. 12346, pp. 549–564. Springer, Cham (2020). https://doi.org/10.1007/978-3-030-58452-8_32
14. Redmon, J., Divvala, S., Girshick, R., Farhadi, A.: You only look once: unified, real-time object detection. In: Proceedings of the IEEE Conference on Computer Vision and Pattern Recognition, pp. 779–788 (2016)
15. Redmon, J., Farhadi, A.: Yolo9000: better, faster, stronger. In: Proceedings of the IEEE Conference on Computer Vision and Pattern Recognition, pp. 7263–7271 (2017)
16. Ren, S., He, K., Girshick, R., Sun, J.: Faster r-CNN: towards real-time object detection with region proposal networks. IEEE Trans. Patt. Anal. Mach. Intell. **39**(6), 1137–1149 (2016)
17. Rezatofighi, H., Tsoi, N., Gwak, J., Sadeghian, A., Reid, I., Savarese, S.: Generalized intersection over union: a metric and a loss for bounding box regression. In: Proceedings of the IEEE Conference on Computer Vision and Pattern Recognition, pp. 658–666 (2019)
18. Song, G., Liu, Y., Wang, X.: Revisiting the sibling head in object detector. In: Proceedings of the IEEE/CVF Conference on Computer Vision and Pattern Recognition, pp. 11563–11572 (2020)
19. Tian, Z., Shen, C., Chen, H., He, T.: Fcos: fully convolutional one-stage object detection. In: Proceedings of the IEEE/CVF International Conference on Computer Vision (ICCV), October 2019
20. Tian, Z., Shen, C., Chen, H., He, T.: Fcos: a simple and strong anchor-free object detector. In: IEEE Transactions on Pattern Analysis and Machine Intelligence (2020)
21. Wojke, N., Bewley, A., Paulus, D.: Simple online and realtime tracking with a deep association metric. In: 2017 IEEE International Conference on Image Processing (ICIP), pp. 3645–3649. IEEE (2017)
22. Wu, S., Li, X., Wang, X.: IoU-aware single-stage object detector for accurate localization. Image Vis. Comput. **97**, 103911 (2020)
23. Yang, Z., Liu, S., Hu, H., Wang, L., Lin, S.: Reppoints: point set representation for object detection. In: The IEEE International Conference on Computer Vision (ICCV), October 2019
24. Yu, J., Jiang, Y., Wang, Z., Cao, Z., Huang, T.: Unitbox: an advanced object detection network. In: Proceedings of the 24th ACM International Conference on Multimedia, pp. 516–520 (2016)
25. Zhang, S., Chi, C., Yao, Y., Lei, Z., Li, S.Z.: Bridging the gap between anchor-based and anchor-free detection via adaptive training sample selection. In: Proceedings of the IEEE/CVF Conference on Computer Vision and Pattern Recognition, pp. 9759–9768 (2020)
26. Zhou, X., Wang, D., Krähenbühl, P.: Objects as points. arXiv preprint arXiv:1904.07850 (2019)
27. Zhou, X., Zhuo, J., Krahenbuhl, P.: Bottom-up object detection by grouping extreme and center points. In: Proceedings of the IEEE Conference on Computer Vision and Pattern Recognition, pp. 850–859 (2019)
28. Zhu, C., He, Y., Savvides, M.: Feature selective anchor-free module for single-shot object detection. In: Proceedings of the IEEE Conference on Computer Vision and Pattern Recognition, pp. 840–849 (2019)

# Occlusion-Aware Facial Expression Recognition Based Region Re-weight Network

Xinghai Zhang[✉], Xingming Zhang, Jinzhao Zhou, and Yubei Lin

South China University of Technology, Guangzhou, China
cszhangxinghai@mail.scut.edu.cn

**Abstract.** Occlusion is a major obstacle for facial expression recognition (FER) in the wild, which can change facial appearance significantly. Current FER methods, although having achieved much progress in lab-constrained scenarios, suffers from partial occlusion remarkably. In this paper, we propose a novel Region Re-Weight Network (RRWN), to adaptively capture and emphasize the non-occluded areas of the face. RRWN contains two modules: Occlusion-Aware Module (OAM) and Block-Loss Module (BLM). More specifically, OAM works as an adaptive region selector in a convolutional neural network. It selects areas whose features made the best approximation to that of the whole face based on their feature similarity. BLM contains a region biased loss called Block-Loss to emphasize the role of key blocks. We validate our RRWN in four public expression datasets with occlusions: RAF-DB, FERPlus, Affect-Net, and SFEW. Experiments show that our RRWN largely improves the performance of FER with occlusion.

**Keywords:** Facial expression recognition · Occlusion · Sparse representation

## 1 Introduction

Facial expression recognition (FER) has been a popular research field for its potential applications in human-computer interaction, driver fatigue monitoring, mental health assessment, and other fields. Despite the high accuracy achieved under a standard environment, spatial occlusion has been the standing challenge to achieving robustness. Occlusions in real-life scenarios encompass a massive number of daily objects and occupy different positions of face images, which greatly affect the robustness of FER algorithms.

Earlier researchers mainly study the influence of occlusion positions on FER. Boucher et al. [4] occluded key areas of the face to learn which areas are the most important in human perception. Kotsia et al. [15] concluded that mouth occlusion causes a greater decrease in FER than the equivalent eyes occlusion. Then methods based on sparse representation are proposed. Cotter [7] presented the weighted voting method based on sparse representation classifier (SRC) for

© Springer Nature Switzerland AG 2021
D. N. Pham et al. (Eds.): PRICAI 2021, LNAI 13033, pp. 209–222, 2021.
https://doi.org/10.1007/978-3-030-89370-5_16

FER. Zhang *et al.* [31] extracted three typical facial features to evaluate the performance of the SRC method. Subsequently, with the emergence of large-scale datasets and robust novel network architectures, researchers carried out a combination of deep learning and sparse representation. Huang *et al.* [14] exploited the sparse representation and residual statistics to occlusion detection of video sequences. Zhong *et al.* [33] proposed a two-stage multi-task sparse learning framework to find dominant patches and learn specific facial patches for individual expression. Recently attention-based methods are proposed to address occlusions in FER [19,20,27], determined whether the facial block should be emphasized or not based on the importance score.

We are motivated to come up with a new mechanism to provide neural networks with the knowledge of occlusion for recognizing expressions with partial occlusion. When observing face images with occlusions, people will focus on the non-occluded areas and recognize expression based on the information of these non-occluded areas. Inspired by this, we propose a novel Region Re-Weight Network (RRWN) to capture and emphasize the non-occluded areas of the face. RRWN is mainly composed of two modules, Occlusion-Aware Module (OAM) and Block-Loss Module (BLM). OAM learns to pick out the non-occluded facial regions to facilitate recognition, which is compatible with the mainstream convolutional neural network (CNN) architecture. As depicted in Fig. 1, OAM works with a widely-used convolutional architecture, in which the feature maps of the holistic image are decomposed as the combination of feature maps from its local regions. Different from the most widely-used attention-based methods, OAM employs similarity measurements to capture the difference between facial and non-facial areas. After getting the non-occluded regions through OAM, the non-occluded regions will be highlighted in the latter network. In the meantime, we use the Block-Loss to emphasize the role of the key area among these non-occluded regions. Different from other occlusion-aware methods, our method guides the model to separate occlusions from the human face.

The major contributions of this work can be summarized in three aspects: 1) We propose OAM, a novel network structure to avoid facial blocks with occlusion and select non-occluded blocks. 2) A region biased loss (Block-Loss) is proposed to optimize the selection of crucial regions. 3) On four challenging datasets with occlusions, we demonstrate that our methods achieve superior performance.

## 2    Related Work

### 2.1    FER Methods Against Occlusions

Many FER methods consider using prior knowledge to strike a better performance both in lab-constraint and in-the-wild scenarios. Common options to incorporate such knowledge includes manually design refined segmentation based on detected facial landmarks since it is effective to constraint the model's input to only the regions where expression-related actions occur. According to the facial action coding system [10], action units are situated around the eyes, the forehead, and the mouth. Extracting those key areas accordingly reduces noise from hair, sunglasses, masks, and other occlusions. However, it works only if these key areas are not occluded.

When the location of occlusions is uncertain, dividing the whole facial image into smaller patches while applying some selection or weighting method over the patches is often more robust than the key-area segmentation approaches. Face partitioning methods varies from uniform partitioning [14], landmark-centered partitioning [19], to sampling-oriented [27]. Subsequently, the occluded patches are given smaller importance weights, or simply excluded from the recognition process.

Recent works following this principle prefer to generate an importance score for each block according to its contribution to the classification. For example, Li *et al.* [19] proposed to use a convolution neural network with attention mechanism to compute an adaptive weight from the region itself according to the unobstructedness and importance. Wang *et al.* [27] proposed a novel region attention network using the sigmoid value to represent the attention value and combining the overall and part features to enhance the ability of the network.

The above methods obtain the importance score through a designed deep neural network, and it is considered that the blocks with large importance scores should be focused on by the network. But in fact, the blocks with large importance scores are possible to be the occluded blocks. Different from these works, our method determines whether the block is occluded by the similarity between the facial block and the whole image, rather than simply using the important score. When the face image is partially obscured, its overall characteristics are still close to a face, so the blocks which are close to the face image are non-occluded blocks.

## 2.2 Sparse Representation

Inspired by the success of sparse approximation in the face recognition task [29], researchers proposed adaptations and variations of sparse encoding to the expression recognition task. Methods concerning sparse representation decompose a facial image as a linear combination of images from the same expression category. During the process, four typical facial features, *i.e.*, the raw pixels [31], Gabor wavelets representation [6], local binary patterns [2], and deep features extracted by a deep convolutional network [1] are used as the effective representations for the expression images.

However, the above methods suffer drastically from insufficient training sample size and variations included. To effectively represent an unseen image containing an occluded facial expression, they also require assistance from well-performing decorrelation technique, precise face alignment, and normalization which is far from reaching in many in-the-wild datasets to date. Although we also decompose the whole facial image as a linear combination, our method distinguishes itself from existing sparse representation methods since we measure how much content in each patch is related to the whole image.

## 3    Proposed Method

### 3.1    Overview of Region Re-weight Network

As depicted in Fig. 1, RRWN extends the traditional CNN architecture by the additional OAM and BLM. To begin with, the face image is fed into the first layer of the backbone network to obtain feature maps for the whole face image as well as each local block. Next, OAM selects the non-occluded blocks by measuring the similarity between local and global vectors. Finally, the non-occluded blocks will be highlighted in the latter CNN layers. In addition to OAM, we also introduce BLM which contains a loss function to emphasize the role of critical block, which comes from non-occluded blocks chosen by OAM. As a result, The whole RRWN can be trained in an end-to-end manner.

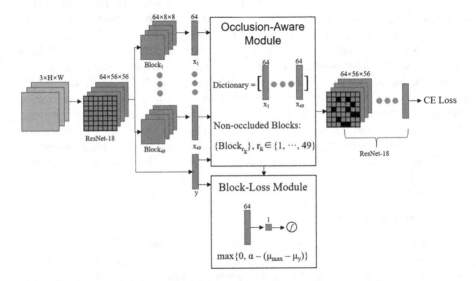

**Fig. 1.** The framework of our RRWN. A face image is fed into Resnet-18 and is represented as the global vector $y$ and local vectors $x_i$. The Occlusion-Aware Module takes $y$ and $x_i$ as input to find the non-occluded $\{Block_{r_k}\}$. Then the $\{Block_{r_k}\}$ will be re-weighted in the latter network (the corresponding black squares). The Block-Loss Modules emphasizes the role of key block among $\{Block_{r_k}\}$ through the Block-Loss function.

### 3.2    Occlusion-Aware Module

We hold the presumption that the overall characteristics of the face image are close to its components rather than the occlusions. In our case, the similarity is used as a mathematical measure to find the clear facial areas similar to the overall face image. In other words, the non-occluded blocks of the face image are located by the similarity measurement. Inspired by how the orthogonal matching pursuit (OMP) method finds the most similar component of a signal [24], we design OAM to find the non-occluded blocks.

As shown in Fig. 1, after getting feature maps that represent the whole facial image, we partition the feature maps to multiple sub-feature-maps uniformly to obtain diverse blocks of the same size. Next, an adaptive average pooling operation is utilized to encode the feature maps into a vector, i.e., each three-dimensional feature is mapped to a one-dimensional vector. Let $y$ denotes the global vector. We normalize $y$ for convenient calculation so that we have $||y|| = 1$. Similarly, $\chi = \{x_1, x_2, \cdots, x_n\}$ denotes local vectors and $||x_i|| = 1$. According to conventional sparse approximation methods, a dictionary is often created to store atomic vectors before finding the sparse representation of the global vector. In our method, the local vectors are used as the atomic vectors when building the dictionary $D = [x_1, x_2, \cdots, x_n] \in R^{n \times k}$, where $n$ is the number of atomic vectors and $k$ is the dimensionality of the atomic vectors.

After building the dictionary, the inner product of the global vector $y$ and each atomic vector $x_i$ is calculated. Then, the atomic vector with the largest absolute value of the inner product will be selected as the closest match-up to the $y$. This selection iterates until we obtain the maximum number of atomic vectors. In this way, $y$ is decomposed into the vertical projection in the direction of the chosen atomic vectors and the corresponding residual, which can be formulated as,

$$y = \langle y, x_{r_0} \rangle x_{r_0} + R_1, \tag{1}$$

where $\langle ., . \rangle$ is the inner product, $x_{r_0}$ is the closest match atomic vector, $r_0$ is the column index of $D$, $\langle y, x_{r_0} \rangle x_{r_0}$ is the vertical projection in the direction of $x_{r_0}$, and $R_1$ is the residual. Then we decompose the residual $R_1$ in the same way. After k iterations, we can get

$$y = \sum_{k=0}^{K} \langle R_k, x_{r_k} \rangle x_{r_k} + R_{k+1}, \tag{2}$$

where $K$ is a hyper-parameter served as the number of selected atomic vectors, and $R_0 = y$. If $K$ is too small, only a few non-occluded areas can be found. On the other hand, if $K$ is too large, the non-occluded area may also be selected. After several iterations, the linear representation of the target vector can be obtained, which is formulated as follows:

$$y = \sum_{k=0}^{K} c_k x_{r_k}$$

$$c_k = \langle R_k, x_{r_k} \rangle \tag{3}$$

Now that the non-occluded blocks and the corresponding weight are obtained, then we apply a re-weight operation on the original feature maps. The blocks corresponding to the selected atomic vectors are weighted as Eq. 4 while the unselected blocks remain unchanged, which can be defined as,

$$block_{r_k} = (c_k + c)block_{r_k},  \tag{4}$$

where $block_{r_k}$ denotes the $k^{th}$ selected block. The $c_k$ can be arbitrary in $(0,1)$. To strengthen the role of the non-occluded area, we increase the weight by $c$ times. If we overemphasize the key blocks and impose great weight on them, it will lead to a decrease of accuracy. We will analyze this in the later ablation studies. After OAM, the new feature maps continue to be input to the rest of ResNet-18.

OAM optimizes the latter network during the training by performing the weighting operation to the original feature maps. OAM can select the atom vector that is closest to the target vector. The weights describe how similar the atom vector is to the target vector. Even if the face is partially occluded, the face is still the dominant object in the image. In this way, OAM can select the non-occluded areas. However, when the occlusion is too large and occupies most of the face image, the overall feature of the image tends to be the occlusion rather than the face, OAM will perform poorly.

### 3.3  Block-Loss Module

After OAM, we find the non-occluded blocks. Among the non-occluded blocks, some blocks contribute to recognizing the expression more significantly than others [4]. To encourage high weights for the most important block among these non-occluded blocks. Inspired by [27], we propose the Block-Loss.

As can be seen in Fig. 1, BLM contains a fully-connected layer and a sigmoid function. After getting the global vector $y$ and the non-occluded local vectors $x_{r_k}$ chosen by OAM, they are fed to BLM. After the fully-connected layer and the sigmoid function, we get their importance value. Block-Loss can be formulated as,

$$\mathcal{L}_B = \max\{0, \alpha - (\mu_{max} - \mu_y)\},$$
$$\mu_{max} = \max\{f(x_{r_k}q)\},$$
$$\mu_y = f(yq),  \tag{5}$$

where $\alpha$ is a hyper-parameter served as a margin, $q$ is the parameter of the fully-connected layer, and $f$ denotes the sigmoid function. In the training process, the Cross-Entropy Loss is jointly optimized with the Block-Loss, which can be defined as,

$$\mathcal{L}_{All} = \mathcal{L}_{CE} + \mathcal{L}_B,  \tag{6}$$

where $\mathcal{L}_{CE}$ denotes the Cross-Entropy Loss.

BLM optimizes the former network during the training by the loss function. BLM enforces that one of the important values of non-occluded blocks should be larger than the face image with a margin so that RRWN can focus on the most important block among the non-occluded blocks.

# 4 Experiments

## 4.1 Datasets

**RAF-DB** [17] contains $30,000$ facial images annotated with basic or compound expressions by 40 trained human coders. In our experiment, only images with basic emotions(neutral, happiness, surprise, sadness, anger, disgust, fear) are used, including 12,271 images as training data and $3,068$ images as test data. **FERPlus** [3] contains $28,709$ training images, $3,589$ validation images, and $3,589$ test images collected by the Google search engine, and all images are resized to $48 \times 48$ pixels. FERPlus supplements a contempt emotion and is annotated by 10 labels. **AffectNet** [23] is the largest FER dataset that contains more than one million images collected by three search engines using expression-related keywords. About 400,000 images are manually annotated with eight discrete facial expressions as FERPlus. It has imbalanced training and test sets as well a balanced validation set. **SFEW** [8] contains 95 subjects and covers unconstrained facial expressions, a large range of ages, varied head poses, and real-word illumination. We use the newest version of SFEW [9] which has been divided into three sets: training (958 images), validation (436 images), and test (372 images), and all images are annotated with seven discrete facial expressions as RAF-DB.

**Table 1.** Values of hyper-parameters

| Parameter | Value |
|---|---|
| Number of blocks | 49 |
| Number of selected atomic vectors | 10 |
| Weight increment $c$ | 2 |
| Margin $\alpha$ | 0.01 |
| Ratio of the two loss functions | 1:1 |

## 4.2 Implementation Details

The proposed RRWN is implemented on the environment of Python 3.6 and the operating system of Windows 10. Preprocessing methods like image resizing are executed through OpenCV 3.4 for convenience. The proposed network involved in this work is run on Intel(R) Core(TM) i7-6700 3.4 GHz in CPU and NVIDIA RTX 1080 Ti with CUDA 9.0 in GPU. RRWN is implemented using the Pytorch platform and the backbone network is ResNet-18 [12]. By default, the ResNet-18 is pre-trained on MS-Celeb-1M face recognition dataset and we extract the feature maps after the first layer of ResNet-18.

Each face image is first resized to $224 \times 224$. Then the feature maps are partitioned into $7 \times 7$ blocks uniformly as depicted in Fig. 1. After adaptive average pooling operation, the feature maps are encoded as vectors of 64 dimensions. The number of selected atomic vectors is 10. The margin in Block-Loss is default as 0.01 and the whole network is jointly optimized with Block-Loss and Cross-Entropy Loss in training. The ratio of the two loss functions is empirically set at 1 : 1. Values of hyper-parameters are shown in Table 1. The batch-based stochastic gradient descent optimizer is used to train the model. On all datasets, the batch size is set to 64, the base learning rate was set as 0.01 and was reduced by the polynomial policy with the gamma of 0.1. Finally, the momentum was set as 0.9 and the weight decay was set as 0.0001.

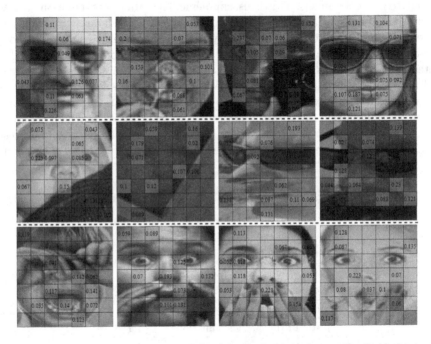

**Fig. 2.** Images with occlusions from RAF-DB. Each image is equally divided into 49 blocks. The orange squares represent the facial non-occluded areas, and the blue squares represent the occluded areas. Dark orange and dark blue squares represent the blocks selected by OAM. The number in the square is the coefficient of the linear combination obtained by OAM. (Color figure online)

### 4.3   Visualization of the Blocks Selected by OAM

OAM should be able to match the non-occluded areas of the face. To demonstrate the effect of OAM, non-occluded blocks selected by OAM are shown in Fig. 2. The occluded areas are covered by blue masks while the clear face areas are covered by orange masks. Areas selected by OAM are further highlighted with a darker color and the corresponding weights. It is clear that most of the selected blocks which OAM selects are non-occluded blocks. In addition, some non-occluded blocks play an important role in FER because they include key areas such as eyes, mouth, etc.

For the images in the first row, where the occlusion and the face have many differences, OAM can find the key blocks closest to the whole face, making it effective to avoid the blocks with occlusions. In the next row, where the occlusions occupy a relatively larger area of the face image, blocks containing occlusions will be selected because features of the face image in this situation include quite a lot of information of the occlusions. Down to the last row, if the occluded object is a hand, in which the color, texture, and other features are relatively similar to the face, OAM will be possible to select few blocks containing hands.

**Table 2.** Test accuracy(%) on real-world datasets.

| Pretrain | RRWN | RAF-DB | FERPlus | AffectNet |
|---|---|---|---|---|
| ✗ | ✗ | 72.00 | 82.40 | 46.58 |
| ✗ | ✓ | 76.83 | 82.68 | 48.63 |
| ✓ | ✗ | 84.20 | 86.80 | 58.50 |
| ✓ | ✓ | **85.82** | **87.70** | **58.70** |

## 4.4 Ablation Studies Evaluation

**Effectiveness of RRWN:** To evaluate the effectiveness of RRWN compared with the baseline (ResNet-18), we conduct experiments on real-world datasets. Results are shown in Table 2. When training from scratch, our proposed RRWN outperforms the baseline network by a margin of 4.83%, 0.28%, and 2.05% on RAF-DB, FERPlus, and AffectNet respectively. It shows that our method does improve the accuracy of the baseline. In addition, when using ResNet-18 pretrained on MS-Celeb-1M, our method obtains improvements of 1.62%, 0.9%, 0.2% on these datasets.

**Table 3.** Test accuracy(%) of the two modules on RAF-DB.

| OAM | BLM | ResNet-18 | ResNet-18 (pretrain) |
|---|---|---|---|
| ✗ | ✗ | 72.00 | 84.20 |
| ✗ | ✓ | 73.16 | 84.60 |
| ✓ | ✗ | 75.68 | 85.50 |
| ✓ | ✓ | **76.83** | **85.82** |

Furthermore, to explore the effectiveness of the two modules in improving accuracy, we conduct comparative experiments on RAF-DB. The result is shown in Table 3. By the way, when only BLM is added, the input vectors of BLM are directly from the vectors after the adaptive average pooling operation. When only adding OAM or BLM, we obtain improvements of 3.68% and 1.16% based on ResNet-18, 1.3% and 0.4% based on ResNet-18 (pretrain). This suggests that both OAM and BLM contribute to improving accuracy. In addition, OAM is the most contributed module for our RRWN.

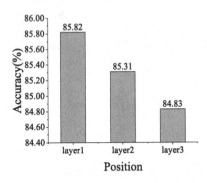

**Fig. 3.** Evaluation of the position on RAF-DB

**Position of OAM:** We study the impact of the different OAM positions. Since the backbone network is ResNet-18, which can be divided into four layers (we represent them as layer1, layer2, layer3, and layer4). Experiments are carried out with OAM being placed after the first, second, and third layers. Result on RAF-DB is shown in Fig. 3. The test result indicates that OAM works best when is placed after the first layer. And the further back it is placed, the worse the effect will be.

We analyze this phenomenon and concluded two major reasons for the declination. First, OAM represents the target vector linearly with a certain number of atomic vectors, so the greater the difference between the blocks, the more accurate OAM is to find the non-occluded blocks. Second, as CNN deepens and constantly carries out convolution, pooling, and other operations, the obtained feature maps become smaller, and the features become more abstract. The features of different blocks are mixed, which leads it more difficult to distinguish different blocks. Therefore, adding OAM after the first layer is appropriate.

**Evaluation of the Weight Increment** $c$: In OAM, we obtain the atomic vectors corresponding to the non-occluded blocks. The blocks corresponding to the selected atomic vectors are re-weighted, and the blocks that are not selected remain unchanged. We study the effect of the amount of weight increase, and the result is shown in Fig. 4(a).

As can be seen from Fig. 4(a), when we just multiply the coefficient $c_k$ to the non-occluded block, *i.e.*, $c = 0$, the result is poor because the coefficient $c_k$ is between 0 and 1, and the non-occluded blocks are weakened when we multiply them directly. On the other hand, the accuracy declined as $c$ increased. Because

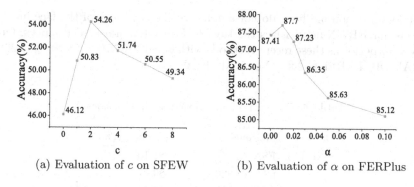

**Fig. 4.** Parameters evaluation

FER not only focuses on the partial key blocks but also the global features. We should combine local features and global features. As the article [19,27], the combination of global features and local features is more effective. If we focus too much on local features and ignore the global features, the weight increment $c$ is too large and the accuracy will decline.

**Evaluation of the Margin $\alpha$:** From Table 3, we can see that BLM further improves performance on RAF-DB.

The margin $\alpha$ in Block-Loss is set to 0.01 by default. We evaluate the $\alpha$ in FERPlus, the result is shown in Fig. 4(b). Increasing from 0 to 0.01 gradually improves the performance while larger $\alpha$ leads to fast degradation, which indicates the features of the overall face image are also important for FER. It also further confirms that we need to combine local features and global features. We mainly carry out the combination of local features and global features in two aspects. One is to input the global vector into BLM, and the other is to appropriately emphasize the key blocks selected by OAM.

### 4.5 Results and Comparison

We compare our RRWN to several methods on RAF-DB, FERPlus, Affect-Net, and SFEW including attention-based methods [19,20,27] and loss-function methods [5,18,21]. The result is shown in Table 4.

pACNN [20] re-weights each patch according to the attention mechanism. gACNN [19] leverages a patch-based attention network and a global network. RAN-ResNet18 [27] captures the importance of facial regions and aggregates region features into a compact representation. These attention-based methods are time-consuming due to the carefully designed deep neural networks. Our RRWN does not increase much computational expense by simply adding two modules to the existing network architecture. DLP-CNN [18] uses a locality-preserving loss for network training. Island Loss [5] proposes the island loss which combines the Center Loss [28] and an inter-class loss. IACNN [21] proposes an identity-sensitive contrastive loss to achieve identity-invariant FER.

These loss-function methods do not emphasize the key block of the face image, whereas our RRWN emphasizes the key block in the non-occluded blocks. Our RRWN outperforms these recent methods with 85.80%, 87.70%, 58.70%, 54.26% on RAF-DB, FERPlus, AffectNet, and SFEW.

**Table 4.** Comparison on datasets with occlusions

| Datasets | Methods | Accuracy(%) |
|---|---|---|
| RAF-DB | FSN [32] | 81.10 |
| | pACNN [20] | 83.27 |
| | DLP-CNN [18] | 84.13 |
| | ALT [11] | 84.50 |
| | gACNN [19] | 85.07 |
| | Our RRWN | **85.82** |
| FERPlus | TFE-JL [16] | 84.30 |
| | PLD [3] | 85.10 |
| | SHCNN [22] | 86.54 |
| | ESR-9 [25] | 87.15 |
| | DTAGN [13] | 87.40 |
| | Our RRWN | **87.70** |
| AffectNet | Up-Sampling [23] | 47.00 |
| | pACNN [20] | 55.33 |
| | IPA2LT [30] | 55.71 |
| | IPFR [26] | 57.40 |
| | Weighted-Loss [23] | 58.00 |
| | Our RRWN | **58.70** |
| SFEW | IACNN [21] | 50.98 |
| | Island Loss [5] | 52.52 |
| | RAN-ResNet18 [27] | 54.19 |
| | Our RRWN | **54.26** |

## 5    Conclusion

In this work, we propose RRWN to address facial expression recognition in the presence of occlusions. Our RRWN uses the Occlusion-Aware module (OAM) to adaptively capture and emphasize the uncovered area of the face. In addition, we design a region biased loss (Block-Loss) function to encourage high weight for the most important region. We evaluate our method on real-world datasets. Experiments show that our proposed method has substantial improvement on RAF-DB, FERPlus, AffectNet, and SFEW compared with other methods.

# References

1. Abavisani, M., Patel, V.M.: Deep sparse representation-based classification. IEEE Sig. Proces. Lett. **26**(6), 948–952 (2019)
2. Ashir, A.M., Eleyan, A.: Facial expression recognition based on image pyramid and single-branch decision tree. Sig. Image Video Process. **11**(6), 1017–1024 (2017). https://doi.org/10.1007/s11760-016-1052-9
3. Barsoum, E., Zhang, C., Ferrer, C.C., Zhang, Z.: Training deep networks for facial expression recognition with crowd-sourced label distribution. In: Proceedings of the 18th ACM International Conference on Multimodal Interaction, pp. 279–283 (2016)
4. Boucher, J.D., Ekman, P.: Facial areas and emotional information. J. Commun. **25**, 21–29 (1975)
5. Cai, J., Meng, Z., Khan, A.S., Li, Z., O'Reilly, J., Tong, Y.: Island loss for learning discriminative features in facial expression recognition. In: 2018 13th IEEE International Conference on Automatic Face & Gesture Recognition (FG 2018), pp. 302–309. IEEE (2018)
6. Cotter, S.F.: Sparse representation for accurate classification of corrupted and occluded facial expressions. In: 2010 IEEE International Conference on Acoustics, Speech and Signal Processing, pp. 838–841. IEEE (2010)
7. Cotter, S.F.: Weighted voting of sparse representation classifiers for facial expression recognition. In: 2010 18th European Signal Processing Conference, pp. 1164–1168. IEEE (2010)
8. Dhall, A., Goecke, R., Lucey, S., Gedeon, T.: Static facial expression analysis in tough conditions: data, evaluation protocol and benchmark. In: 2011 IEEE International Conference on Computer Vision Workshops (ICCV Workshops), pp. 2106–2112. IEEE (2011)
9. Dhall, A., Ramana Murthy, O., Goecke, R., Joshi, J., Gedeon, T.: Video and image based emotion recognition challenges in the wild: Emotiw 2015. In: Proceedings of the 2015 ACM on International Conference on Multimodal Interaction, pp. 423–426 (2015)
10. Ekman, R.: What the Face Reveals: Basic and Applied Studies of Spontaneous Expression Using the Facial Action Coding System (FACS). Oxford University Press, Oxford (1997)
11. Florea, C., Florea, L., Badea, M.S., Vertan, C., Racoviteanu, A.: Annealed label transfer for face expression recognition. In: BMVC, p. 104 (2019)
12. He, K., Zhang, X., Ren, S., Sun, J.: Deep residual learning for image recognition. In: Proceedings of the IEEE Conference on Computer Vision and Pattern Recognition, pp. 770–778 (2016)
13. Huang, C.: Combining convolutional neural networks for emotion recognition. In: 2017 IEEE MIT Undergraduate Research Technology Conference (URTC), pp. 1–4. IEEE (2017)
14. Huang, X., Zhao, G., Zheng, W., Pietikäinen, M.: Towards a dynamic expression recognition system under facial occlusion. Patt. Recogn. Lett. **33**(16), 2181–2191 (2012)
15. Kotsia, I., Buciu, I., Pitas, I.: An analysis of facial expression recognition under partial facial image occlusion. Image Vis. Comput. **26**(7), 1052–1067 (2008)
16. Li, M., Xu, H., Huang, X., Song, Z., Liu, X., Li, X.: Facial expression recognition with identity and emotion joint learning. IEEE Trans. Affect. Comput. **12**, 544–550 (2018)

17. Li, S., Deng, W.: Reliable crowdsourcing and deep locality-preserving learning for unconstrained facial expression recognition. IEEE Trans. Image Process. **28**(1), 356–370 (2018)
18. Li, S., Deng, W., Du, J.: Reliable crowdsourcing and deep locality-preserving learning for expression recognition in the wild. In: Proceedings of the IEEE Conference on Computer Vision and Pattern Recognition, pp. 2852–2861 (2017)
19. Li, Y., Zeng, J., Shan, S., Chen, X.: Occlusion aware facial expression recognition using CNN with attention mechanism. IEEE Trans. Image Proces. **28**(5), 2439–2450 (2018)
20. Li, Y., Zeng, J., Shan, S., Chen, X.: Patch-gated CNN for occlusion-aware facial expression recognition. In: 2018 24th International Conference on Pattern Recognition (ICPR), pp. 2209–2214. IEEE (2018)
21. Meng, Z., Liu, P., Cai, J., Han, S., Tong, Y.: Identity-aware convolutional neural network for facial expression recognition. In: 2017 12th IEEE International Conference on Automatic Face & Gesture Recognition (FG 2017), pp. 558–565. IEEE (2017)
22. Miao, S., Xu, H., Han, Z., Zhu, Y.: Recognizing facial expressions using a shallow convolutional neural network. IEEE Access **7**, 78000–78011 (2019)
23. Mollahosseini, A., Hasani, B., Mahoor, M.H.: Affectnet: a database for facial expression, valence, and arousal computing in the wild. IEEE Trans. Affect. Comput. **10**(1), 18–31 (2017)
24. Pati, Y.C., Rezaiifar, R., Krishnaprasad, P.S.: Orthogonal matching pursuit: recursive function approximation with applications to wavelet decomposition. In: Proceedings of 27th Asilomar Conference on Signals, Systems and Computers, pp. 40–44. IEEE (1993)
25. Siqueira, H., Magg, S., Wermter, S.: Efficient facial feature learning with wide ensemble-based convolutional neural networks. In: Proceedings of the AAAI Conference on Artificial Intelligence, vol. 34, pp. 5800–5809 (2020)
26. Wang, C., Wang, S., Liang, G.: Identity-and pose-robust facial expression recognition through adversarial feature learning. In: Proceedings of the 27th ACM International Conference on Multimedia, pp. 238–246 (2019)
27. Wang, K., Peng, X., Yang, J., Meng, D., Qiao, Y.: Region attention networks for pose and occlusion robust facial expression recognition. IEEE Trans. Image Process. **29**, 4057–4069 (2020)
28. Wen, Y., Zhang, K., Li, Z., Qiao, Y.: A Discriminative feature learning approach for deep face recognition. In: Leibe, B., Matas, J., Sebe, N., Welling, M. (eds.) ECCV 2016. LNCS, vol. 9911, pp. 499–515. Springer, Cham (2016). https://doi.org/10.1007/978-3-319-46478-7_31
29. Wright, J., Yang, A.Y., Ganesh, A., Sastry, S.S., Ma, Y.: Robust face recognition via sparse representation. IEEE Trans. Patt. Anal. Mach. Intell. **31**(2), 210–227 (2008)
30. Zeng, J., Shan, S., Chen, X.: Facial expression recognition with inconsistently annotated datasets. In: Proceedings of the European Conference on Computer Vision (ECCV), pp. 222–237 (2018)
31. Zhang, S., Zhao, X., Lei, B.: Robust facial expression recognition via compressive sensing. Sensors **12**(3), 3747–3761 (2012)
32. Zhao, S., Cai, H., Liu, H., Zhang, J., Chen, S.: Feature selection mechanism in CNNs for facial expression recognition. In: BMVC, p. 317 (2018)
33. Zhong, L., Liu, Q., Yang, P., Liu, B., Huang, J., Metaxas, D.N.: Learning active facial patches for expression analysis. In: 2012 IEEE Conference on Computer Vision and Pattern Recognition, pp. 2562–2569. IEEE (2012)

# Online Multi-Object Tracking with Pose-Guided Object Location and Dual Self-Attention Network

Xin Zhang, Shihao Wang, Yuanzhe Yang, Chengxiang Chu,
and Zhong Zhou[✉]

State Key Laboratory of Virtual Reality Technology and Systems,
Beihang University, Beijing, People's Republic of China
zz@buaa.edu.cn

**Abstract.** The recent trend in Multi-Object Tracking (MOT) is heading towards using deep learning to detect objects and extract features. Although tracking frameworks using detection network have achieved outstanding performance in object locating on MOT, it is still challenging for crowded occlusion. In this paper, we propose to alleviate this difficulty by combining bounding boxes from outputs of both object detection and pose estimation. The motivation behind generating redundant candidates is that object detection and pose estimation can complement each other in tracking scenes. In order to get optimal tracking objects from candidates, we present Soft-Pose-NMS. For similarity calculation, we design a Dual Self-Attention Network (DSAN) with the self-attention mechanism. The network generates the self-attention map that enables the network to focus on the object area of detection and tracklet images. Simultaneously, the network can extract the temporal self-attention feature map to suppress noisy images in the tracklet. Experiments are conducted on the MOT benchmark datasets. Results show that our tracker achieves competitive results and is state-of-the-art in half of the metrics.

**Keywords:** Multi-object tracking · Person re-identification · Dual self-attention network

## 1 Introduction

Multi-object tracking (MOT) is one of the most fundamental computer vision tasks, aiming to generate the trajectory information of all interested objects across video frames. It has attracted much attention because of its broad application such as intelligent video analysis, autonomous driving and smart city. The current MOT studies mainly adopt the "tracking-by-detection" strategy that applies the detector to locate objects in each frame and associates objects among the different frames to generate object trajectories [5,25,31].

Despite the encouraging progress made in the past few years, there are two significant problems with "tracking-by-detection" strategy. One is that tracking

© Springer Nature Switzerland AG 2021
D. N. Pham et al. (Eds.): PRICAI 2021, LNAI 13033, pp. 223–235, 2021.
https://doi.org/10.1007/978-3-030-89370-5_17

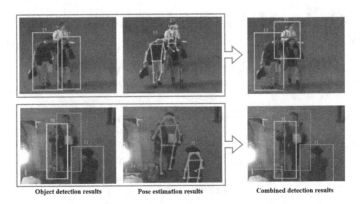

**Fig. 1.** Object locating with pose guiding. In applying only one kind of detection result, the bounding boxes are mislabeled due to heavy occlusion. Object detection result and pose estimation result can complement each other to locate objects correctly.

results heavily rely on the quality of object detection, which by itself is hard to generate reliable results across frames. Taking the tracking scenes in the MOT16 dataset as examples, during the crowd scenes, the bounding boxes based on one kind of detection method of the occluded objects is usually unreliable, posing drifting and ID-switching in tracking, as shown in Fig. 1. To alleviate such issues, recent research [24] introduces the object location information from an instance segmentation method to locate the tracking objects. In this paper, we combine the merits of multi-person pose estimation and object detection in a unified framework to introduce object joint points information. We use the pedestrian joint points information to assist in locating the object and alleviate unreliable detection.

On the other hand, for similarity computation in MOT, we need to compare the current detect object with a sequence of previous observations in the trajectory. One of the most commonly track objects in MOT is pedestrians, so the re-identification [16,22] is commonly used for similarity calculation with challenging factors including occlusion, partial loss and pose variation [31], as shown in Fig. 1. To alleviate such issues, [7,31] propose the feature extraction network that introduces attention mechanism [27] to extract detection and tracklet appearance features. Additionally, inspired by [29], we introduce the self-attention mechanism, which calculates the self-attention map for detection image and tracklet images, respectively. Moreover, our network is end-to-end, which can alleviate training complexity and extract more robust features.

The main contributions of this paper can be summarized as follows.

1. A new detection strategy is proposed to combine object detection and pose estimation results. The strategy takes advantage of both object detection and pose estimation to handle unreliable detection in online MOT.

2. We design a Dual Self-Attention Network (DSAN), introducing the self-attention mechanism to allocate different attention values to each location in the object image and exploit self-attention temporal feature from the tracklet.
3. Experimental results demonstrate that our tracker achieves competitive performance on the MOT benchmark dataset and is state-of-the-art in half of the metrics.

## 2  Related Work

In recent years there has been an explosion of technological progress in MOT driven primarily by object detection strategy. Sanchez-Matilla et al. [20] exploited multiple detectors to improve detection performance in MOT. Chen et al. [5] combined detection and predicted bounding boxes by Kalman filter as tracking candidate set for quality evaluation and used different strategies for data association. Although these methods alleviate the unreliable detection results, they still use one kind of detection information. Hence these methods cannot effectively alleviate the issue of missing detection. There are also several works that use other category location information to determine the coordinates of the tracking candidates [6,10,13,24]. Voigtlaender et al. [24] proposed MOTS task and TrackR-CNN network to merge segmentation and multi-object tracking. The network employed top-down segmentation information instead of detection information to locate the object. Nevertheless, the top-down object location information introduced in the above methods still depends on the quality of the object detection results [8,24]. On the contrary, we propose the Soft-Pose-NMS detection strategy to introduce object joint points information from the bottom-up pose estimation method. The bottom-up object location information is not affected by the object detection performance and can provide additional object position information, and thereby it can effectively improve the object detection results in MOT.

For object feature extraction and similarity computation, Mahmoudi et al. [17] applied CNN extracted appearance features along with position features to calculate more accurate similarity score. Chu et al. [7] introduced a Spatial-Temporal Attention Mechanism (STAM) to handle the tracking drift caused by the occlusion and interaction among objects. Zhu et al. [31] proposed a Dual Matching Attention Networks (DMAN) with both spatial and temporal attention mechanisms to perform the tracklet data association. In this paper, we integrate both spatial and temporal self-attention mechanisms into the proposed MOT framework. Our framework differs from the state-of-the-art DMAN [31] method. First, the spatial attention in the DMAN corresponds to the detection image and trajectory images. Since the attention map is affected by different trajectory images, it becomes unreliable when other objects appear in the trajectory image. In contrast, we exploit the image itself to generate the self-attention map, which is demonstrated to be more robust to inter-object occlusion and noisy detection. Second, the DMAN needs to be divided into two steps to train the model, while our spatial and temporal self-attention map can be end-to-end trained.

## 3    Proposed Method

Our online tracking framework consists of three tasks, object detection, similarity calculation and trajectory management. We first measure all tracking objects by the proposed Soft-Pose-NMS detection strategy that introduces object pose information. Then we use the Dual Self-Attention Networks (DSAN) to extract feature and compute the similarity score of the detection image and tracklet images. Finally, we update the tracking state of objects and trajectories.

### 3.1    Soft-Pose-NMS Object Detection Strategy

Given a new frame, we get the joint points of each object through the pose estimation network [15]. Nonetheless, there are abnormal points in these joint points, as shown in Fig. 2. Therefore, the Soft-Pose-NMS detection strategy is designed to generate accurate joint points-based bounding boxes with pose estimation results and determine tracking candidates by screening two types of bounding boxes. These bounding boxes are adopted to alleviate detection failures in crowded scenes.

First, we obtain the primary detection-based bounding box set $PB_{det}$ by object detection method. It is necessary to generate a sufficient number of detection bounding boxes to filter and obtain accurate tracking bounding boxes. Therefore, we set a lower confidence threshold $T_{detcon}$ to generate the detection-based bounding box set $B_{det}$ form $PB_{det}$.

(a)                    (b)                    (c)

**Fig. 2.** The bounding box results based on pose estimation. (a) shows the result missing part of the object joint points. (b) shows the results of abnormal joint points with large offsets. (c) shows the result of abnormal joint points with small offsets. Red points and blue points are the clustering result of the object joint points and $W_i$ is the width of two point-groups.

Second, a primary joint points-based bounding box $PB_{jpi}$ is generated by expanding the coordinates of the joint points. Here we define $NP_{PBjpi}$ as the number of joint points and $AR_{PBjpi}$ as the aspect ratio for the $PB_{jpi}$. Then the primary joint points-based bounding boxes set $PB_{jp}$ can be defined as:

$$PB_{jp} = \{PB_{jp1}...PB_{jpi}\}, NP_{jpi} > T_{njp} \, and \, AR_{jpi} < T_{ratio} \qquad (1)$$

where $T_{njp}$ is threshold for the number of joint points, $T_{ratio}$ is threshold of the aspect ratio. We set $T_{njp} = 8$ and $T_{ratio} = 0.6$ to generate $PB_{jp}$. However, the joint points-based bounding box coordinate shifting still exists in $PB_{jp}$, as shown in Fig. 2(c). We observe that this shifting only appears on the abscissa. In order to deal with this joint points drift issue to get exact width value for joint points-based bounding box. First, we use the clustering algorithm to cluster the joint points of each bounding box $PB_{jpi}$ in $PB_{jp}$ into two point groups. Then we calculate the width ratio of the two points groups. Here we define $w_1$ and $w_2$ as the width of two point group width, respectively, as shown in Fig. 2(c). We define $R_w$ as the width ratio of $w_1$ and $w_2$. Therefore, the width of $i$th joint points-based bounding box $W_{PBjpi}$ can be generated by the following formula:

$$W_{PBjpi} = \begin{cases} w_1 & R_w > Tw_{ratio} \\ w_2 & R_w \leq Tw_{ratio} \end{cases} \tag{2}$$

where $Tw_{ratio}$ as the threshold of the width ratio. We analyse the position of the drift joint point and set $Tw_{ratio}$ to 2.

After recalculating the width of each joint point-based bounding box, we get the final joint point-based bounding box set $B_{jp}$. In order to combine detection based bounding boxes and screen unreliable bounding boxes, we need to calculate a reasonable confidence score to the $i$th joint points-bounding box $B_{jpi}$ in $B_{jp}$. Directly using the average score of each joint point in joint points-based bounding box $B_{jpi}$ as corresponding confidence value will cause confidence bias. Therefore, we propose a function to explicitly encode pose information of each joint point into the confidence maps. We expand the total variance and make the scoring probability distribution distance of different pedestrians farther. The confidence of $B_{jpi}$ is defined as:

$$CB_{jpi} = \frac{1}{n} \sum_n^{i=1} \tan h \frac{s_i}{\sigma} \tag{3}$$

where $CB_{jpi}$ is the confidence of $i$th joint points-based bounding box $B_{jpi}$, $\sigma$ is a data-driven parameter used to control the degree of score suppression and $s_i$ is the score of each joint point. The scores are averaged after $\tan h$ function mapping to generate the confidence $CB_{jpi}$ and the final joint points-based bounding box set $B_{jp}$.

In order to measure tracking objects bounding box set $B_{track}$. First, we fuse the detection-based bounding box set $B_{det}$ and the joint points-based bounding box set $B_{jp}$ to generate the all candidates bounding box set $B_{can}$ of current frame. Second, we sort all the bounding boxes according to the confidence and output the bounding box $B_{max}$ with the maximum confidence as tracking objects. Then, we re-assign the confidence of remaining bounding boxes as:

$$CB_{cani} = \begin{cases} CB_{cani} & IoU_{mi} < T_{IoU} \\ CB_{cani}(1 - IoU_{mi}) & IoU_{mi} > T_{IoU} \end{cases} \tag{4}$$

where $CB_{cani}$ indicates the confidence of $i$th bounding box $B_{cani}$ in candidates bounding box set $B_{can}$, $IoU_{mi}$ indicates the IoU of bounding box $B_{max}$ and

$B_{cani}$, $T_{IoU}$ indicates the threshold of IoU. Finally, we delete the candidates that confidence less than the confidence threshold $T_{con}$, until $B_{can}$ is empty.

---

**Algorithm 1 :** The Soft-Pose-NMS detection strategy

---

**Input:** The primary detection-based bounding box set $PB_{det}$ and the primary joint points-based bounding box set $PB_{jp}$ of current frame in tracking video.

**Output:** Tracking objects bounding box set $B_{track}=\{B_{track1},...,B_{tracki}\}$ of the current frame.

1: Generate detection-based bounding box set $B_{det} = \{B_{det1},...,B_{detj}\}$, $CB_{detj} >$ $T_{detcon}$ ($CB_{detj}$ is confidence of detection-based bounding box $B_{detj}$);
2: Generate joint points-based bounding box set $PB_{jp}$ by Ep.(1);
3: // Calculate the coordinates of joint points-based bounding boxes
4: **for** each $PB_{jpi}$ in $PB_{jp}$ **do**
5:     Cluster the joint points of $PB_{jpi}$ into two groups;
6:     Calculate the width $W_{PB_{jpi}}$ for $PB_{jpi}$ by Ep.(2);
7: **end for**
8: $B_{jp} = PB_{jp}$
9: **for** each $B_{jpi}$ in $B_{jp}$ **do**
10:     Calculate the confidence $CB_{jpi}$ for $PB_{jpi}$ by EP.(3);
11: **end for**
12: $B_{can} = B_{det} \cup B_{jp}$;
13: $B_{track} \leftarrow \{\}$
14: **while** $B_{can}$ is not empty **do**
15:     $B_{can} = \text{Sort}(B_{can})$
16:     $B_{max} = B_{can}[0]$
17:     $B_{track}.\text{append}(B_{mix})$
18:     $B_{can} = B_{can} - B_{mix}$
19:     **for** each $B_{cani}$ in $B_{can}$ **do**
20:         Update confidence of bounding box in $B_{can}$ by Ep.(4);
21:         **if** $CB_{cani} < T_{con}$ **then:**
22:             delete $B_{cani}$
23:         **end if**
24:     **end for**
25: **end while**
26: **return** $B_{track}$;

---

## 3.2 Feature Extraction with Dual Self-Attention Network

Extracting more discriminative appearance feature is the critical component of calculating accurate similarity scores. Moreover, the challenge is that object and tracklet images may undergo occlusion and noise in the tracking scene. To alleviate such issues, we design a Dual Self-Attention Network (DSAN) with self-attention mechanisms. Figure 3 illustrates the architecture of our network.

In this work, we use the DenseNet-101 [12] as backbone network and introduce the self-attention mechanism to extract tracking object and tracklet feature

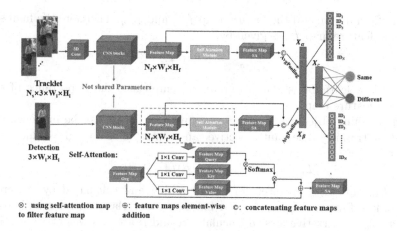

**Fig. 3.** The architecture of the proposed DSAN. It contains two branches. Given an image of tracking object bounding box and sequence of object tracklet images as inputs. The network extracts the detection and tracklet self-attention feature maps and predicts the probability that the detection and the tracklet are the same object by the combined feature map $X_c$.

map. The self-attention mechanism can enlarge the receptive field and get contextual information which enables the network to pay more attention to the object area in the detection and tracklet images. We convolve the tracklet image in the temporal direction by the 3D convolutional layer to exploit the temporal feature of the object. The self-attention map is applied to the feature maps from the last convolutional layer of the DenseNet-101 to compute the self-attention feature map. We apply the detection self-attention feature map $X_\alpha$ and tracklet self-attention feature map $X_\beta$ for re-identification training and combined feature $X_c$ for binary classifier training to predict whether detection and tracklet are the same object. Furthermore, we will apply the similarity probability $P_{same}$ that predicted by the network to calculate the similarity score between the detection and trajectory.

To infer the self-attention maps of the detection and tracklet, we transform the backbone network feature maps into query feature map $f_q$, key feature map $f_k$ and value feature map $f_v$ respectively. After that, we use the feature map $f_q$ and $f_k$ to calculate the attention map as the following formula:

$$\beta_{i,j} = \frac{exp(S_{ij})}{\sum_{i=1}^{N} exp(S_{ij})}, S_{ij} = f_q(x_i)^T f_k(x_j) \tag{5}$$

where $\beta_{i,j}$ indicates the attention value of the other $j$th position in the image on the $i$th pixel. Then we multiply $\beta_{i,j}$ with $f_v$ to get the self-attention masked feature map $f_{org}^{att}$ that weight by the self-attention map, where:

$$f_{org}^{att} = \sum_{i=1}^{N} \beta_{ij} f_v \tag{6}$$

Additionally, we add the feature map $f_{org}^{att}$ and $f_{org}$. Therefore the final self-attention feature map $f_{sa}$ is given by:

$$f_{sa} = \theta f_{org}^{att} + f_{org} \tag{7}$$

where $\theta$ is a learnable scalar, to gradually emphasize the importance of self-attention feature map.

The training objective of each feature map in DSAN can be modelled as a multi-task training. The joint objective can be written as a weighted linear sum of losses:

$$L_{total} = \alpha L_{sig} + (1 - \alpha)L_{seq} + \beta L_{same} \tag{8}$$

where $L_{sig}$ and $L_{seq}$ are used for re-id training and calculated by the cross-entropy loss function. $L_{same}$ is used for the binary classification training and applying the contrastive loss to calculate. $\alpha$ and $\beta$ are loss weights. We utilize the ground-truth bounding boxes and objects identity provided in the MOT16 training set to generate detection images and object trajectories for training the network.

### 3.3    Data Association and Trajectory Management

For data association, we calculate the similarity score between the detection and tracklet feature map firstly, by the following formula:

$$S_{dt} = w_1 dist(f_\alpha, f_\beta) + w_2 P_{same} \tag{9}$$

where $w_1$ and $w_2$ are similar score weights, $S_{dt}$ is the final similar score of detection and tracklet. Then tracker generates affinity matrix with the similar scores. Meanwhile, we apply the Hungarian algorithm and affinity matrix to associate the detection and tracklet. Last, the tracker associates the remaining detection with unassociated tracklet based on IoU between detection and tracklets, with a threshold $T_{IoUa}$. For trajectory management, we initial the trajectory for detection, which is not associated with any trajectory in any of the first $T_{init}$ frames. Trajectories are terminated if they are not associated for $T_{term}$ frames.

## 4    Experiments

### 4.1    Implementation Details

To validate the effectiveness of the proposed online tracking approach, we design experiments on popular MOT datasets, MOT16 and MOT17 [18]. We employ Pifpaf in [15] to estimate the objects pose information, and use SDP [28] detection results that officially provided by MOT16 and MOT17 as the object detection results. We set $T_{IoU} = 0.95$ and $T_{con} = 0.5$ for filtering repetitive bounding box to generate the tracking object set $B_{track}$ and select 5 observations from the 20 most recent frames as tracklet input for DSAN. We set $T_{IoUa} = 0.7$ for data association. For trajectory management, we set the threshold $T_{init} = 3$ for trajectory initialization and $T_{term} = 10$ for trajectory termination.

## 4.2   Performance on MOT Benchmark Datasets

In order to measure the accuracy of tracking results, we adopt multiple metrics used in the MOT benchmark [2] to evaluate the proposed tracking method, including Multiple Object Tracking Accuracy (MOTA), ID F1 score (IDF, the ratio of correct detections over the average number of ground-truth and computed detections), MT (the ratio of Mostly Tracked objects), Ml (the ratio of Mostly Lost objects), the number of False Negatives (FN), the number of False Positives (FP), the number of ID Switches (IDS), the number of fragments (Frag). Table 1 and Table 2 present the tracking performance on the MOT16 and MOT17 datasets, respectively.

**Table 1.** Tracking performance on MOT16 dataset. The arrow each metric indicates that the higher (↑) or lower (↓) value is better.

| Method | Mode | MOTA↑ | IDF1↑ | MT↑ | ML↓ | FP↓ | FN↓ | IDs↓ | Frag↓ |
|---|---|---|---|---|---|---|---|---|---|
| EDMT [4] | Batch | 45.3 | 47.9 | 17.0% | 39.9% | 11122 | 87899 | 639 | 946 |
| QuadMOT [21] | Batch | 44.1 | 38.3 | 14.6% | 44.9% | 6388 | 94775 | 745 | 1096 |
| LMP [23] | Batch | 48.8 | 51.3 | 18.2% | 40.1% | 6654 | 86245 | 481 | 595 |
| DMAN [31] | Online | 46.1 | 54.8 | 17.4% | 42.7% | 7909 | 89874 | 744 | 1616 |
| Tracktor++ [1] | Online | 56.2 | 54.9 | 20.7% | 35.8% | **2394** | 76844 | 617 | 1068 |
| CNNMTT [17] | Online | 65.2 | 62.2 | 32.4% | 21.3% | 6578 | 55896 | 946 | 2283 |
| TrctrD16 [26] | Online | 54.8 | 53.4 | 19.1% | 37.0% | 2955 | 78765 | 645 | 1515 |
| RAR16wVGG [9] | Online | 63.0 | 63.8 | **39.9%** | 22.1% | 13663 | 53248 | 482 | 1251 |
| MPNTrack [3] | Online | 58.6 | 61.7 | 27.3% | 34.0% | 4949 | 70252 | 354 | **684** |
| Tube_TK_POL [19] | Online | 66.9 | 62.2 | 39.0% | **16.1%** | 11544 | 47520 | 1236 | 1444 |
| Ours | Online | **67.7** | **66.4** | 37.9% | 18.6% | 11453 | 42494 | **334** | 902 |

**Table 2.** Tracking performance on MOT17 dataset.

| Method | Mode | MOTA↑ | IDF1↑ | MT↑ | ML↓ | FP↓ | FN↓ | IDs↓ | Frag↓ |
|---|---|---|---|---|---|---|---|---|---|
| EDMT [4] | Batch | 50.0 | 51.3 | 21.6% | 36.3% | 32279 | 247297 | 2264 | 3260 |
| MHT_DAM [14] | Batch | 50.7 | 47.2 | 20.8% | 36.9% | 22875 | 252889 | 2314 | 2865 |
| Tube_TK_POI [19] | Online | 63.0 | 58.6 | 31.2% | **19.9%** | 27060 | 177483 | 4137 | 5727 |
| CTTrack17 [30] | Online | **67.8** | 64.7 | 34.6% | 24.6% | **18498** | 160332 | 3039 | 6102 |
| Ours | Online | 67.3 | **65.9** | **37.9%** | 20.7% | 20574 | 195176 | **2031** | **2681** |

Quantitative results and comparison with the other tracking methods are shown in Table 1 and Table 2. As shown in Table 1, our tracking method achieves a comparable MT, ML, FP, Frag score and performs favourably against the state-of-the-art methods in terms of MOTA, IDF1, FN and IDs on the MOT16 dataset. Our tracker upgrades MOTA to 67.7, IDF1 to 66.4 and reduces FN to 42494, IDs to 334. Meanwhile, our tracker achieves the best performance in IDF1 and IDs among online and batch methods, demonstrating the merits of our tracker in object identity matching and the stability of multi-object tracking. MOTA and FN correspond to the object detection capability. Therefore, the improvement of

MOTA and FN demonstrates the merits of our Soft-Pose-Nms detection strategy in object locating for MOT. Similarly, Table 2 shows that our tracker outperforms existing online trackers on half of the metrics and achieves the best performance in terms of IDF1, MT, IDs and Frag on the MOT17 dataset.

In addition, as shown in Table 1, our tracker has a high FP. According to this phenomenon, the detection strategy proposed in this paper is combining the object detection results and pose estimation results. This can alleviate unreliable detection and complement missing object. Second, we find that only the moving pedestrians are recorded as tracking object ground-truth in MOT16 and MOT17. Nevertheless the detection strategy proposed in this paper can detect and track these small-scale pedestrians, occluded pedestrians, stationary pedestrians and pedestrians who are not recorded as tracking objects. Therefore, our detection strategy will cause the phenomenon of high FP, and the similar situation exists in [4,5] too. This phenomenon also reflects the effectiveness of the detection strategy proposed in this paper.

### 4.3  Ablation Studies

In order to verify the effectiveness of the proposed detection strategy and evaluate its contribution, we use different object detection results and conduct ablation experiments in the MOT16 dataset. We choose Mask R-CNN [11] and SDP [28] as bounding box-based object detection method and PifPaf [15] as pose estimation method. In addition, to exclude the disturbance of other factors, we use DeepSORT [25], the more common method in MOT, for tracking.

**Table 3.** Evaluation tracking results on MOT16 dataset with different detection method. Ours (M+P) indicates combining Mask R-CNN detection results and PifPaf pose estimation results. Ours (S+P) indicates combining SDP detection results and PifPaf pose estimation results.

| Method | MOTA↑ | IDF1↑ | MT↑ | ML↓ | FP↓ | FN↓ | IDs↓ |
|---|---|---|---|---|---|---|---|
| Mask R-CNN [11] | 40.2 | 52.6 | 21.5% | 26.9% | 14266 | 51234 | 528 |
| SDP [28] | 60.7 | 62.4 | 31.3% | 20.9% | **3417** | 38041 | 462 |
| PifPaf [15] | 37.6 | 51.8 | 14.5% | 32.1% | 14652 | 53729 | 537 |
| Ours (M+P) | 43.8 | 55.8 | 22.6% | 22.8% | 15226 | 46270 | 511 |
| Ours (S+P) | **64.3** | **65.9** | **34.4%** | **15.6%** | 5115 | **35732** | **433** |

The experiment results are shown in Table 3. The comparison between our detection strategy and object detection methods and pose estimation method confirms that our detection strategy performs best. Our detection strategy improves 3.6 in MOTA, 3.5 in IDF1, 3.1% in MT with the second best detection method and effectively reduced FN demonstrating the merits of our detection strategy in locating the objects. By combining object detection results and pose

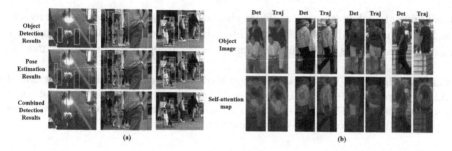

**Fig. 4.** Visualization of pose-guided object locating results and self-attention maps.

**Table 4.** Evaluation results on MOT16 with different feature representations.

| Method | MOTA↑ | IDF1↑ | IDs↓ |
|---|---|---|---|
| DenseNet121 [12] | 61.7 | 63.1 | 548 |
| PCB [22] | 62.6 | 64.3 | 482 |
| Ours (TBSAN) | **65.7** | **68.7** | **455** |

estimation results, our detection strategy can reduce unreliable detections and alleviate missing detections, as shown in Fig. 4(a).

To demonstrate the contribution of the proposed DSAN network in our method, we compare representations learned by DSAN with PCB, DenseNet-121. Moreover, we use SDP [28] detection result, provide by MOT16 officially, for tracking. The experiment results are shown in Table 4. It can be seen that the IDF1, IDs and MOTA of DSAN are better than other methods. Our tracker upgrades MOTA to 65.7, IDF1 to 68.7 and reduces IDs to 455, which demonstrates the effectiveness of our feature extraction network.

Figure 4(b) shows the visualization results of the self-attention feature map from DSAN. In Fig. 4(b), each group consists of four images. The top row of each group shows an image pair from the same object, while the bottom row presents corresponding self-attention feature maps. It can be seen that our self-attention feature map focus more explicitly on object regions and suppress noise and occlusion, which enhances the power of extracting discriminative features.

## 5   Conclusions

This paper presents a detection strategy and a feature extraction network to improves two main components of most online trackers, detection and feature extraction. The tracker locates joint points of objects with pose estimation results. Then generating optimal object bounding boxes by proposed Soft-Pose-NMS method, which also helps alleviate typical difficulties in tracking such as occlusion handling and track drifting. In this paper, the tracker learns the discriminative self-attention maps from the MOT dataset with the Self-Attention mechanism to calculate more accurate similarity scores. The experimental results on MOT Challenge datasets demonstrated that the proposed tracking framework leads to competitive performance improvement through extensive experiments.

**Acknowledgment.** This work was supported by National Key R&D Program of China (Grant No. 2018YFB2100603) and National Natural Science Foundation of China (Grant No. 61872024). The authors would like to thank the anonymous reviewers for their critical and constructive comments and suggestion.

# References

1. Bergmann, P., Meinhardt, T., Leal-Taixe, L.: Tracking without bells and whistles. In: Proceedings of the IEEE International Conference on Computer Vision, pp. 941–951 (2019)
2. Bernardin, K., Stiefelhagen, R.: Evaluating multiple object tracking performance: the clear mot metrics. EURASIP J. Image Video Process. **2008**, 1–10 (2008)
3. Brasó, G., Leal-Taixé, L.: Learning a neural solver for multiple object tracking. In: Proceedings of the IEEE/CVF Conference on Computer Vision and Pattern Recognition, pp. 6247–6257 (2020)
4. Chen, J., Sheng, H., Zhang, Y., Xiong, Z.: Enhancing detection model for multiple hypothesis tracking. In: Proceedings of the IEEE Conference on Computer Vision and Pattern Recognition Workshops, pp. 18–27 (2017)
5. Chen, L., Ai, H., Zhuang, Z., Shang, C.: Real-time multiple people tracking with deeply learned candidate selection and person re-identification. In: 2018 IEEE International Conference on Multimedia and Expo (ICME), pp. 1–6 (2018)
6. Choi, W.: Near-online multi-target tracking with aggregated local flow descriptor. In: Proceedings of the IEEE International Conference on Computer Vision, pp. 3029–3037 (2015)
7. Chu, Q., Ouyang, W., Li, H., Wang, X., Liu, B., Yu, N.: Online multi-object tracking using CNN-based single object tracker with spatial-temporal attention mechanism. In: Proceedings of the IEEE International Conference on Computer Vision, pp. 4836–4845 (2017)
8. Fang, H.S., Xie, S., Tai, Y.W., Lu, C.: Rmpe: regional multi-person pose estimation. In: Proceedings of the IEEE International Conference on Computer Vision, pp. 2334–2343 (2017)
9. Fang, K., Xiang, Y., Li, X., Savarese, S.: Recurrent autoregressive networks for online multi-object tracking. In: 2018 IEEE Winter Conference on Applications of Computer Vision (WACV), pp. 466–475. IEEE (2018)
10. Fragkiadaki, K., Shi, J.: Detection free tracking: Exploiting motion and topology for segmenting and tracking under entanglement. In: CVPR 2011, pp. 2073–2080. IEEE (2011)
11. He, K., Gkioxari, G., Dollár, P., Girshick, R.: Mask r-CNN. In: Proceedings of the IEEE International Conference on Computer Vision, pp. 2961–2969 (2017)
12. Huang, G., Liu, Z., Van Der Maaten, L., Weinberger, K.Q.: Densely connected convolutional networks. In: Proceedings of the IEEE Conference on Computer Vision and Pattern Recognition, pp. 4700–4708 (2017)
13. Keuper, M., Tang, S., Andres, B., Brox, T., Schiele, B.: Motion segmentation & multiple object tracking by correlation co-clustering. IEEE Trans. Patt. Anal. Mach. Intell. **42**(1), 140–153 (2018)

14. Kim, C., Li, F., Ciptadi, A., Rehg, J.M.: Multiple hypothesis tracking revisited. In: IEEE International Conference on Computer Vision (2015)
15. Kreiss, S., Bertoni, L., Alahi, A.: Pifpaf: Composite fields for human pose estimation. In: Proceedings of the IEEE Conference on Computer Vision and Pattern Recognition, pp. 11977–11986 (2019)
16. Luo, H., Gu, Y., Liao, X., Lai, S., Jiang, W.: Bag of tricks and a strong baseline for deep person re-identification. In: Proceedings of the IEEE Conference on Computer Vision and Pattern Recognition Workshops, pp. 1487–1495 (2019)
17. Mahmoudi, N., Ahadi, S.M., Rahmati, M.: Multi-target tracking using CNN-based features: Cnnmtt. Multimedia Tools Appl. $78(6)$, 7077–7096 (2019)
18. Milan, A., Leal-Taixe, L., Reid, I., Roth, S., Schindler, K.: MOT16: a benchmark for multi-object tracking. arXiv e-prints arXiv:1603.00831 (Mar 2016)
19. Pang, B., Li, Y., Zhang, Y., Li, M., Lu, C.: Tubetk: adopting tubes to track multi-object in a one-step training model. In: Proceedings of the IEEE/CVF Conference on Computer Vision and Pattern Recognition, pp. 6308–6318 (2020)
20. Sanchez-Matilla, R., Poiesi, F., Cavallaro, A.: Online multi-target tracking with strong and weak detections. In: European Conference on Computer Vision. pp. 84–99. Springer (2016)
21. Son, J., Baek, M., Cho, M., Han, B.: Multi-object tracking with quadruplet convolutional neural networks. In: Proceedings of the IEEE conference on computer vision and pattern recognition. pp. 5620–5629 (2017)
22. Sun, Y., Zheng, L., Yang, Y., Tian, Q., Wang, S.: Beyond part models: person retrieval with refined part pooling (and a strong convolutional baseline). In: Proceedings of the European Conference on Computer Vision (ECCV), pp. 480–496 (2018)
23. Tang, S., Andriluka, M., Andres, B., Schiele, B.: Multiple people tracking by lifted multicut and person re-identification. In: Proceedings of the IEEE Conference on Computer Vision and Pattern Recognition, pp. 3539–3548 (2017)
24. Voigtlaender, P., et al.: Mots: multi-object tracking and segmentation. In: Proceedings of the IEEE Conference on Computer Vision and Pattern Recognition, pp. 7942–7951 (2019)
25. Wojke, N., Bewley, A., Paulus, D.: Simple online and realtime tracking with a deep association metric. In: 2017 IEEE International Conference on Image Processing (ICIP), pp. 3645–3649. IEEE (2017)
26. Xu, Y., Osep, A., Ban, Y., Horaud, R., Leal-Taixé, L., Alameda-Pineda, X.: How to train your deep multi-object tracker. In: Proceedings of the IEEE/CVF Conference on Computer Vision and Pattern Recognition, pp. 6787–6796 (2020)
27. Yan, C., et al.: Stat: spatial-temporal attention mechanism for video captioning. IEEE Trans. Multimedia $22(1)$, 229–241 (2019)
28. Yang, F., Choi, W., Lin, Y.: Exploit all the layers: fast and accurate CNN object detector with scale dependent pooling and cascaded rejection classifiers. In: Proceedings of the IEEE Conference on Computer Vision and Pattern Recognition, pp. 2129–2137 (2016)
29. Zhang, H., Goodfellow, I., Metaxas, D., Odena, A.: Self-attention generative adversarial networks. In: International Conference on Machine Learning, pp. 7354–7363. PMLR (2019)
30. Zhou, X., Koltun, V., Krhenbühl, P.: Tracking objects as points. arXiv arXiv:2004.01177 (2020)
31. Zhu, J., Yang, H., Liu, N., Kim, M., Zhang, W., Yang, M.H.: Online multi-object tracking with dual matching attention networks. In: Proceedings of the European Conference on Computer Vision (ECCV), pp. 366–382 (2018)

# Random Walk Erasing with Attention Calibration for Action Recognition

Yuze Tian[1], Xian Zhong[1,2]([✉]) [ID], Wenxuan Liu[1] [ID], Xuemei Jia[1], Shilei Zhao[1], and Mang Ye[3] [ID]

[1] School of Computer and Artificial Intelligence, Wuhan University of Technology, Wuhan 430070, China
zhongx@whut.edu.cn
[2] Hubei Key Laboratory of Transportation Internet of Things, Wuhan University of Technology, Wuhan 430070, China
[3] School of Computer Science, Wuhan University, Wuhan 430072, China

**Abstract.** Action recognition in videos has attracted growing research interests because of the explosive surveillance data in social security applications. In this process, due to the distraction and deviation of the network caused by occlusions, human action features usually suffer different degrees of performance degradation. Considering the occlusion scene in the wild, we find that the occluded objects usually move unpredictably but continuously. Thus, we propose a random walk erasing with attention calibration (RWEAC) for action recognition. Specifically, we introduce the random walk erasing (RWE) module to simulate the unknown occluded real conditions in frame sequence, expanding the diversity of data samples. In the case of erasing (or occlusion), the attention area is sparse. We leverage the attention calibration (AC) module to force the attention to stay stable in other regions of interest. In short, our novel RWEAC network enhances the ability to learn comprehensive features in a complex environment and make the feature representation robust. Experiments are conducted on the challenging video action recognition **UCF101** and **HMDB51** datasets. The extensive comparison results and ablation studies demonstrate the effectiveness and strength of the proposed method.

**Keywords:** Action recognition · Random walk erasing · Data augmentation · Attention calibration · Siamese network

## 1 Introduction

Action recognition has enjoyed great success in recent years owing to the development of deep neural networks. It aims at analyzing an ongoing action from an unknown video or image sequence automatically. Recent action recognition methods have achieved promising results. Generally, these methods extract the most representative action features in the monotonous environment, but they

© Springer Nature Switzerland AG 2021
D. N. Pham et al. (Eds.): PRICAI 2021, LNAI 13033, pp. 236–251, 2021.
https://doi.org/10.1007/978-3-030-89370-5_18

**Fig. 1.** Illustration of the effects of occlusion in action recognition. A complete moving subject may be occluded by other subjects in the real world, thus losing helpful information and causing attention confusion. The blue color in the figure is the occluded action objects that need to be identified. We can see that the critical information is occluded, and the model's attention may be disturbed by other objects, resulting in an inaccurate recognition effect. (Color figure online)

do not meet the standards of practical applications. Optimizing semantic information in complex scenes is an elusive challenge [19].

As real-world video has complex motion information and a complex environment, many entities will move in unpredictable ways. Occlusion happens when the background disturbs, or the action actor is hidden by another object of the same type, and it will significantly interfere with the correct judgment of the network for the action, as shown in Fig. 1, and this phenomenon is unpredictable. Previous methods [1,3,16,26] mainly focused on searching for more efficient and robust architectures. [1,3] incomplete key-points and feed them to 3D temporal convolution networks to handle the occlusion conditions. [16] introduces the radio frequency (RF) signals as input. [26] discusses the background disturbing by adding the background in the image. However, with the change of the position of the camera or scene, the moving subject will change the occluded object or degree. The above lacks enough persuasiveness for reality to separate humans from the background. In this way, the random occlusion is lost, and even the interaction between persons and objects, persons, and background is ignored. The addition of another modal increases the amount of calculation and also brings the alignment problem between modals. In addition, the above-mentioned occlusion-based method does not consider the diversity and authenticity of occlusion in the video, and there is no associated spatio-temporal characteristic between video sequences, which does not meet the random walk of occluded objects in a natural scene.

This paper aims to enhance the robustness of recognizing actions in complex scenes by proposing random walk erasing (RWE). The difference from the random erasing algorithm is shown in Fig. 3. In the continuous frame sequence of each epoch, an RWE module is introduced to simulate the actual situation. As we all know, action recognition may be affected by background information [26]. Due to the random erasing, we can treat persons and backgrounds equally without losing the connection between the actors and the appropriate environment. If there is no additional modal noise, we should make the occlusion area continue to occur in multiple frames and have a temporal and spatial correlation between the previous and next frames. This operation makes the two connected frames in the video more coherent, and at the same time, increases the generalization ability of convolutional neural networks (CNNs).

However, the only branch cannot provide a precise and holistic description of the whole video due to the occluded semantic information. The spatial-temporal erasing branch deletes some region expressions and mistakenly gets rid of some informative cues, especially under the circumstances of self-occlusion. Hence, the Siamese inputs are introduced for obtaining more robust and informative feature representations. On the one hand, the erased one pays more attention to small-scale information after erasing some areas, which helps learn richer details. On the other hand, the original path can retain useful features, preventing the erased vital information.

Intuitively, visual semantic information, i.e., the actor, the interaction, and the scene, is essential for action recognition. Semantics together with motion trajectories reveal the implication of human action. Two different regions of the same video frames would deliver various semantics. For example, for a region in clear frames, the focus of this action is likely to be the objects related but not the action itself. It might obstruct the machine from distinguishing the specific features of videos. According to the drawback, we leverage the attention mechanism to exclude the interference of occlusions. Here, we introduce the attention mechanism to obtain attention map. Compared with previous attention mechanisms [25] used in action recognition, attention map employed here is to find more comprehensive and purposeful features. However, the existence of the occlusion confuses the network to make the right decisions and hesitate around the area of occlusion. Therefore, we introduced an attention calibration (AC) module in our network to solve this problem. Through the AC module, the acquisition error or scattered characterization information caused by occlusion can be corrected again, and the impact of occlusion can be weakened so that the attention mechanism can turn to find other regions of interest.

In this work, we propose an RWEAC network to improve the model's ability to recognize actions in complex video scenes with occlusion. Specifically, we use the RWE module to simulate accurate occlusion and the AC module to correct the attention confused by the occluded object. Given a video, we randomly select an area, and then according to the randomness of the movement of the occluded object relative to the moving object in the video, we randomly add a moving direction and move a certain distance for each frame. After the occlusion, the original information and the information are added to learn global and local features through the Siamese network. By adding AC modules and fusing features, different identification information of the same video can be aggregated. Using attention calibration can reduce the distraction caused by occlusion and force the attention mechanism to find other places of interest, thereby improving the robustness of recognition tasks in complex scenes.

The paper has threefold contributions:

- We introduce the random walk erasing (RWE) module to simulate the random occlusion problem in reality. Meanwhile, the module can simulate occlusion drift under natural conditions and concerns the data augmentation for the videos.
- We present an attention calibration (AC) module to exploit semantic correlations of the erasing feature and original feature. The AC module may calibrate the attention under the occlusion shift condition.
- We introduce the RWEAC network to improve the robustness to partially occluded samples. When we randomly add occlusion to the benchmark testing dataset, extensive experiments significantly show that our methods outperform the baseline model.

## 2    Related Work

### 2.1    Video Action Recognition

Advances in action recognition are primarily driven by the success of 2D ConvNets in image recognition. Two-stream models and 3D convolution models are two representative streams of neural network methods for action recognition. Two-stream methods [8,22,29] train spatial (RGB) and temporal (optical) flows separately, and the final prediction is obtained by averaging the outputs of the two classifiers. However, these types of methods mainly suffer from two limitations. First, these methods need pre-compute optical flow, which is expensive in both time and space. Second, the learned feature and final prediction from multiple segments are fused simply using weighted or average sum, making it inferior to temporal relationship modeling.

Another type of method tries to learn spatio-temporal features from videos directly with 3D CNN [2,4,7,24], which could only rely on RGB information and achieve impressive performance in end-to-end ways. C3D [24] is the first work to learn spatio-temporal features using deep 3D CNN. However, Its performance on standard benchmarks is not satisfactory. I3D [2] inflated the filters and pooling kernels of 2D ConvNet pre-trained on ImageNet into 3D to capture spatio-temporal features. After pre-training on Kinetics, I3D has achieved very competitive performance in benchmark datasets. Since most traditional 3D networks only use the local correlation along the input channels, STCNet [4] inserts its STC block into 3D ResNet to model the spatial-temporal correlation between 3D CNN channels, to improve the performance of 3D networks. The Slowfast [7] model is an inspiring architecture, which uses a slow path to capture actual spatial semantics, and a fast path to capture motion at acceptable temporal resolution.

### 2.2    Motion Occlusion in Video

Erasing algorithm has been widely used in the field of person and vehicle re-identification [30,33] to simulate occlusion and has been gradually applied to the field of action recognition in recent years. [34] propose an occlusion-aware Siamese network, which uses attention mechanism to predict the attention heat map of recognizable occlusion, and performs feature reconstruction to recover the information destroyed by occlusion excessively. By employing estimated 2D confidence heatmaps of key-points and optical-flow consistency constraint, [3] filter out the unreliable estimations of occluded key-points to enforce temporal smoothness to produce a full 3D pose. [1] presented the ActionX Pose algorithm for 2D pose-based Human Action Recognition, which proposed high-level features to improve accuracy and robustness to occlusions and missing data in comparison with the low-level features-based method. [16] is the first model to generate a 3D human skeleton using RF signal as input, which proves that the model can recognize the behavior and interaction under occlusion or extreme lousy light conditions. To mitigate the model reliance towards the background, [26] proposed a background erasing (BE) method, which forces the model to draw closer to the features of the interfering video and the original video so that the model is limited to resist the influence of the background and pay more attention to the action.

Unlike these works that only consider the spatial information of the occlusion region, our proposed RWE method more dynamically adapts to the occlusion situation in the actual video scene, adding spatio-temporal correlations to the inter-frame occlusion, and obtains more robust representation information.

## 3   Approach

This section presents the RWEAC network in three aspects in detail. We first elaborate on the overall network architecture. Then, the RWE module and the AC module are introduced.

### 3.1   Network Overview

The core idea of RWEAC mainly includes two parts. The RWE dynamically fits the state of the unpredictable occluded area in the actual scene to obtain more robust representation information. Moreover, the AC module is used to correct the problem of attention wandering in the erasing area after RWE. As shown in Fig. 2, we use the two-stream 3D CNN model, and each path uses the same network structure. The network takes the original video as the input, and the two paths sample video frames at different rates. The slow path of processing spatial semantics takes $T$ frames as the input, and the other path takes $\alpha T$ frame as the input. In particular, the slow path is divided into two branches: the branch processing the original data and the branch adding RWE information. The specific RWE module is shown in Subsect. 3.2, and then the weight information is shared in the way of Siamese input so that the local information erased matches the global information of the original data. Then, the AC module is used to make the network get more accurate and refined representation information for training. The fast path adopts a structure similar to Slowfast,

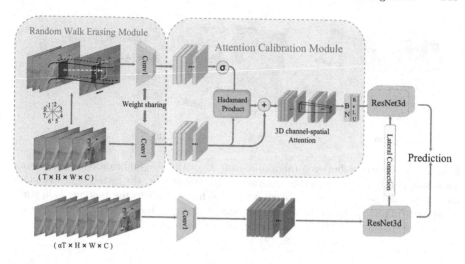

**Fig. 2.** Architecture diagram of our proposed approach. The RWEAC network includes two paths, both of which use ResNet3D-50 as the backbone network. The RWE module has the Siamese input and fused by the AC module after the conv1 of ResNet.

shares data with the network of the slow path using horizontal links, and finally carries out prediction and classification together.

## 3.2   Random Walk Erasing Module

This paper uses Random Walk Erasing data with temporal information to simulate occluded objects with unpredictable spatio-temporal features in natural complex scenes and consider the consistency between frames and unknown occluded motion features. In this section, we describe the implementation of the RWE algorithm and the use of Siamese input structure.

**Random Walk Erasing Processing of Video.** By adding random walk spatio-temporal association information between frames in the erasing area, each frame will move in a certain range relative to the previous frame, which can more accurately simulate the occlusion movement in the video. The specific methods are as follows:

During training, the video $V$ is cut into $T$ frames using a video decoder during each round of training. The area $S_e$ and aspect ratio $r_e$ of an erasing region are initialized randomly for each video, and then the length and width of the erased area can be initialized randomly:

$$h = \sqrt{S_e * r_e}$$
$$w = \sqrt{S_e / r_e} \tag{1}$$

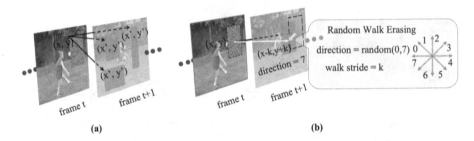

**Fig. 3.** The difference between random erasing algorithm (a) and random walk erasing algorithm (b). It can be seen that compared with the former, the latter adds a random motion process to the occlusion block itself, which is similar to the random walk state of non moving subjects in the real scene, and is more in line with the characteristics of complex spatio-temporal characteristics of occlusion in video.

For the first frame of each video sequence $T$, the coordinates of the erasing region are initialized randomly:

$$
\begin{aligned}
x_0 &= \mathrm{random}(0, W - w) \\
y_0 &= \mathrm{random}(0, H - h)
\end{aligned}
\tag{2}
$$

For the remaining $i-1$ frames, $k$ units are moved in the direction of $Direction$ based on the $(x_{i-1}, y_{i-1})$ of previous frame. $Direction$ is initialized randomly to determine the movement angle of the occlusion area. A total of 8 directions are taken, and the function $\Psi$ as shown in Fig. 3.

$$
Direction = random(0, 7)
\tag{3}
$$

$$
(x_i, y_i) = \Psi(Direction, x_{i-1}, y_{i-1}, k)
\tag{4}
$$

Finally, random pixel values are processed for each frame erasing region:

$$
P(x, y) = \mathrm{random}(0, 255)
\tag{5}
$$

Thus, the video frame sequence after erasing $T_{re}$ is obtained.

**Siamese Input.** The entire network is divided into two main pathways, and we choose the spatial way to learn feature semantic representation in the video. There exist two branches that take the randomly occluded frames as input in the spatial pathway. The sharing mechanism between the two branches reduces the number of parameters and improves network efficiency.

Because the spatial semantic information in the video is redundant, the same input may obtain different representations. To make the spatial path obtain more valuable features, it is thought of using the teacher-student model, *i.e.* distillation to perform the instructional program. Teacher models with more comprehensive and reliable information provide more confident supervision for student models.

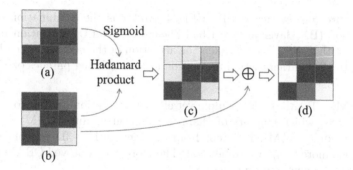

**Fig. 4.** Attention Calibration Algorithm. It can be seen that the feature (d) obtained by the AC model corrects the salient points in (a) and weakens the influence of occlusion.

In our method, we take the branch of the spatial path input original information as the teacher and the branch input as the added occlusion information as the student.

In this paper, we abandon the usage of distillation and propose a teacher-student model to simulate the process. As shown in Fig. 2, the structure of Siamese input is used to capture the representation information of different branches in the spatial path.

### 3.3   Attention Calibration Module

**Attention Calibration Algorithm.** Adding attention mechanism after RWE can enhance the most comprehensive features of the not occluded part and improve the accuracy of action recognition in complex scenes. A single attention mechanism may lead to the oscillation of the region of interest, thus reducing the recognition accuracy of the network. Therefore, we propose an AC module, as shown in Fig. 4.

The two branches of the spatial path get $F_s$ and $F_{re}$, through the conv1 layer of ResNet-50. The information lost in $F_{re}$ may affect the overall performance, and $F_s$ itself still carries enormous distractive information. Therefore, we fuse features in the following ways:

Firstly, normalize the feature $F_{re}$ extracted from occlusion information to get $F'_{re}$:

$$F'_{re} = \frac{1}{1 + e^{-F_{re}}} \tag{6}$$

$F_c$ is obtained by Hadamard product of the feature $F_s$ and $F'_{re}$, which as (c) showed in Fig. 4:

$$F_c = F'_{re} \odot F_s \tag{7}$$

so we can use the features of $F'_{re}$ to guide $F_s$ to pay attention to the common useful representation information.

Finally, we combine $F_s$ and $F_c$ by elements addition:

$$F_{AC} = \varphi(F_s \oplus F_c) \tag{8}$$

To get feature $F_{AC}$, which is (d) in Fig. 4, And $\varphi$ is the combination of batch normalization (BN) layer and rectified linear unit (ReLU) activation function. Compared with $F_s$, $F_{AC}$ can weaken the attention of the corresponding location according to the characteristic information of the occluded patches of $F_{re}$.

**3D-CBAM.** CBAM [32] is a simple yet effective attention module for 2D feed-forward CNNs, which consists of channel attention module (CAM) and space attention module (SAM). Different from 2D convolution, 3D convolution network has one more temporal dimension. Therefore, we improved CBAM to work effectively in 3D convolutional networks.

For the feature map $F_{3d} \in \mathbb{R}^{C \times T \times H \times W}$ ($T$ is the number of video frames) after 3D convolution in this paper, we first get the one-dimensional feature map $M_{CAM_{3d}} \in \mathbb{R}^{C \times 1 \times 1 \times 1}$ through the CAM, and then multiply it with $F_{3d}$ to get $F'_{3d}$. Then the two-dimensional feature map $M_{SAM_{3d}} \in \mathbb{R}^{C \times 1 \times 1 \times 1}$ is obtained by SAM, and the final accurate output $F''_{3d}$ is obtained by multiplying with $F'_{3d}$. The formula of the whole process is as follows:

$$\begin{aligned} F'_{3d} &= M_{CAM_{3d}}(F_{3d}) \otimes F_{3d} \\ F''_{3d} &= M_{SAM_{3d}}(F'_{3d}) \otimes F'_{3d} \end{aligned} \tag{9}$$

where $\otimes$ denotes element-wise multiplication.

The channel attention module uses the feature relationship between channels to select the features that play a decisive role in prediction. We first aggregate spatial information of a feature map by using both average-pooling and max-pooling operations and get the $F^c_{avg}$ and $F^c_{max}$, then forward to a shared network multi-Layer perceptron (MLP). After passing through the shared network, we use element-wise summation and the sigmoid function to generate channel attention feature map $M_{CAM_{3d}}$. In short, the channel attention is computed as:

$$\begin{aligned} M_{CAM_{3D}}(F_{3D}) &= \sigma(\text{MLP}(\text{AvgPool3D}(F_{3D}))) + \text{MLP}(\text{MaxPool3D}(F_{3D})) \\ &= \sigma(W_1(W_0(F^c_{avg})) + W_1(W_0(F^c_{max}))) \end{aligned} \tag{10}$$

where $\sigma$ denotes the sigmoid function, $W_0$ and $W_1$ are MLP weights that are shared for both inputs.

SAM focuses on which pixels in RGB images play a decisive role in network prediction. Firstly, The channel attention feature map and input feature map are element-wise multiplied to generate the input features $F'_{3d}$ of the SAM. After that, we aggregate channel information of a feature map by using two pooling operations, generating two feature maps: $F^s_{avg}$ and $F^s_{max}$. Then they are concatenated and convoluted by standard convolution layer. After dimensionality reduction, the sigmoid function is used to generate the 3D spatial attention map. The formula is as follows:

$$\begin{aligned} M_{S3D}(F'_{3D}) &= \sigma(f^{Conv}[\text{AvgPool3D}(F'_{3D}); \text{MaxPool3D}(F'_{3D})]) \\ &= \sigma(f^{Conv}[F^s_{avg}; F^s_{max}]) \end{aligned} \tag{11}$$

# 4   Experiments

## 4.1   Datasets and Implementations

**Datasets.** We evaluate our approach on two widely applied benchmark datasets, **UCF101** [23] and **HMDB51** [13]. **UCF101** is a realistic video dataset that contains 13,320 videos from YouTube, and each source video usually corresponds to an action type. It has great diversity in action acquisition, including appearance change, attitude change, object proportion change, background change, *etc.* **HMDB51** contains 6,849 videos in 51 action categories, most of which are edited from movies clips. Moreover, it eliminates the interference caused by camera motion and uses standard image stitching technology to align video clips. We follow the provided evaluation protocol and adopt standard different training/testing splits for both of them. We use the same data format as Slowfast [7] and resize the video to the short edge size of 256 via FFmpeg.

**Metrics.** The **UCF101** and **HMDB51** dataset has three official splits. We calculate the accuracy of the three classifications and report the average. Moreover, we report the top-1 classification accuracy on the average accuracy over three splits.

**Implementations.** The backbone network we used is ResNet-50. We pre-train the model on Kinetics400 [12] and fine-tune it on the two datasets. Two 1080Ti GPUs are used to train the whole model, with a batch size of 16 and an initial learning rate of 0.025. We adopt stochastic gradient descent (SGD) as our optimizer with momentum of 0.9 and weight decay of 1e−5. For each input video, it is processed in the temporal domain and spatial domain. We randomly sample an $\alpha T \times \tau$ ($\alpha = 4$, $T = 8$, $\tau = 8$) frame clip of a full-length video along the time axis for processing in the temporal domain, and the input of the two pathways are respectively $T$ and $\alpha T$ frames. For the spatial domain, we stochastically crop $224 \times 224$ pixels from a video, or its horizontal flip, with a shorter side sampled in [256, 320] pixels [56, 56]. And then, we randomly flip and jitter all inputs during the training phase for data enhancement, same as other 3D CNN methods [31].

Following the conventional method of evaluating the accuracy of action recognition in 3D-CNN, we sampled 10 clips uniformly along the time axis of the video, and scale the shorter spatial side to 256 pixels, and take 3 crops of $256 \times 256$ (instead of $224 \times 224$ for training) to cover the spatial dimensions. The inference-time spatial size is $256^2$ and 10 temporal clips each with 3 spatial crops are used (30 views). Then get the final prediction by averaging the scores of all clips.

## 4.2   Main Results

In this section, to verify the effectiveness of the algorithm, we compare our method with other methods in the standard datasets **UCF101** and **HMDB51**. We use the train and test settings reported in Sect. 4.1 and report top-1 and

**Table 1.** Comparison of top-1 accuracy (%) performances with the state-of-the-arts on **UCF101** and **HMDB51**. **Bold** numbers are the best results. Blue numbers is the second best result. † indicates that method is reproduced by us.

| Method | Venue | Flow | Backbone | UCF101 | HMDB51 |
|---|---|---|---|---|---|
| Two-stream [22] | NeurIPS '14 | ✓ | CNN | 88.0 | 59.4 |
| LRCN [6] | CVPR '15 | ✓ | CNN | 82.3 | - |
| TDD [28] | CVPR '15 | ✓ | CNN | 90.3 | 63.2 |
| Fusion [8] | CVPR '16 | ✓ | VGG-16 | 92.5 | 65.4 |
| TSN [29] | ECCV '16 | ✓ | BN-Inception | 94.0 | 68.5 |
| TLE [5] | CVPR '17 | ✓ | BN-Inception | 95.6 | 71.1 |
| C3D [24] | ICCV '15 | × | VGG-16 | 82.3 | 56.8 |
| P3D [21] | ICCV '17 | × | ResNet-50 | 88.6 | - |
| I3D-RGB [2] | CVPR '17 | × | BN-Inception | 95.6 | 74.8 |
| ARTNET [27] | CVPR '18 | × | ResNet-18 | 94.3 | 70.9 |
| ResNet3D [10] | CVPR '18 | × | ResNetXt-101 | 94.5 | 70.2 |
| ECO [35] | ECCV '18 | × | ResNet-18 | 94.8 | 72.4 |
| TSM [20] | ICCV '19 | × | ResNet-50 | 95.9 | 73.5 |
| STM [11] | ICCV '19 | × | ResNet-50 | 96.2 | 72.2 |
| SIFP [14] | ACM MM '20 | × | ResNet-50 | 94.0 | 72.3 |
| CIDC [17] | ECCV '20 | × | ResNet-50 | 95.3 | 74.5 |
| TEA [18] | CVPR '20 | × | ResNet-50 | **96.9** | 73.3 |
| SPL [15] | AAAI '21 | × | ResNet-50 | 94.6 | 67.6 |
| SMART [9] | AAAI '21 | × | BN-Inception | 95.8 | 74.6 |
| Slowfast [7] † | ICCV '19 | × | ResNet-50 | 95.7 | 75.7 |
| RWEAC | | × | ResNet-50 | 96.4 | **76.1** |

top-5 accuracy. The results in Table 1 show that our proposed method achieves encouraging results. Typical neural network models currently used for original video action recognition include two-stream methods and 3D convolution methods. Following the chronology, we will compare these two methods and the state-of-the-art methods.

The 2D two-stream methods use the original RGB video and computationally complex optical flow for motion recognition. Our proposed method uses only the original RGB video for recognition, and according to the comparison results on the two datasets shown in Table 1, our method has higher recognition accuracy than most 2D two-stream algorithms. This proves the advantages and competitiveness of our RWEAC method. In the second part of the table, we only compare methods of 3D convolution using RGB video as input. The results show that our results on the two datasets have reached the best compared to some classic methods. We compare state-of-the-art methods in the past two years, and the experimental results prove that our method is better than most. Among

**Table 2.** The respective ablation experiments of the two components and their influence in the overall framework on **UCF101**.

| Method | top-1 | top-5 |
|---|---|---|
| Baseline | 95.7 | 99.4 |
| Baseline w RE | 95.9 | 99.6 |
| Baseline w RWE ($k = 0$) | 96.0 | 99.7 |
| Baseline w RWE ($k = 1$) | 96.2 | 99.7 |
| Baseline w RWE ($k = 2$) | 95.7 | 99.7 |
| Baseline w RWE ($k = 1$) & CBAM | 95.8 | 99.6 |
| Baseline w RWE ($k = 1$) & AC | **96.4** | **99.8** |

them, the result on **UCF101** dataset is second only to TEA which used the motion exception module to process adjacent frames, and uses the multiple temporal aggregation module to process distant frames, so as to identify actions with strong time correlation, such as the long jump actions in **UCf101** dataset, which is more accurate than our method. However, the accuracy rate on **HMDB51** dataset has reached state-of-the-art. That is because compared with the former, the interaction between the action objects of **HMDB51** dataset and persons, objects, and scenes are more frequent than that of **UCF101** dataset, and there are more occlusions. This further shows that our method improves the accuracy and robustness of behavior recognition when occlusion occurs in complex scenes.

### 4.3    Ablation Studies

In this section, we investigate how the various components of our approach contribute to its final performance and then use the accuracy of top-1 and top-5 on the **UCF101** dataset to comprehensively evaluate our proposed RWEAC. All ablation experiments use the reasoning setting of Sect. 4.1.

**Network Structures.** Our RWEAC framework contains two key structure designs: the RWE module and the AC module. As shown in Table 2, we conducted overall ablation experiments to verify the effect of these components and the complete framework combined with components.

It can be seen that the addition of the RWE allows the network to learn more about the action information when there is an occlusion in the video scene, brings about 0.5% top-1 and 0.3% top-5 accuracy improvement compared to the baseline. Moreover, the RWE module increases the Complexity of spatial and temporal domains in video data and improves recognition. Therefore, the addition of AC enables the network to pay attention to the critical information after joining RWE, enhances the robustness of recognition, and improves the top-1 of 0.7% and the top-5 of 0.4% compared with the baseline. From the experimental results, it can be concluded that the two components are practical and improve the overall framework's recognition accuracy.

**Effect of RWE.** Firstly, it can be seen from Table 2 that compared with the baseline and its addition of the classic random erasing used in the image, it proves that insufficient data with occlusion will limit the accuracy of action recognition to a certain extent. At the same time, the RWE we proposed has a higher accuracy rate, which shows that the random walk of erasure block is more suitable for simulating the unpredictable dynamic occlusion information in video than the classical RE method. Moreover, we also implement a parameter comparison experiment on the stride $k$ in RWE. The experimental results show that the best effect is obtained when the $k = 1$ is more consistent with the average moving speed of the occlusion area in the video scene, so it is more suitable to simulate the dynamic occlusion information in the video.

**Effect of AC.** The results in the second part of Table 2 show that the effect of adding attention mechanism after using erasing algorithm is worse than that of using erasing algorithm alone, which indicates that after adding occlusion information, attention will be distracted and inaccurate focus will be obtained. So we need to correct attention so that the proper attention can pay more attention to the right place. Our method is to send the features of the two branches into the attention mechanism after calibration and fusion. The results show that adding AC is better than only using attention mechanism and improves the accuracy after adding RWE, which indicates that our AC model can eliminate the problem of distraction in the erased area. By fusing the two branches of the spatial path, we can find features with high reliability in the residual information after erasing, the robustness of occlusion recognition is enhanced.

## 5   Conclusion

This paper constructed a novel random walk erasing with attention calibration (RWEAC) network to learn the comprehensive video representation. We introduced the random walk erasing (RWE) module to simulate the occlusion of the natural environment. In addition, as a data expansion, the RWE module increased the diversity of samples and improves the difficulty of identification. All experiments demonstrated that our novel RWEAC achieved excellent accuracy on benchmark video datasets, and the accuracy of top-1 on **HMDB51** dataset reaches the state-of-the-art result in 3D-CNN models. In the future, we intend to improve the random walk erasure model and look forward to proposing a data enhancement algorithm that better fits the complex scenes in the real world.

**Acknowledgements.** This work was supported in part by the Fundamental Research Funds for the Central Universities of China under Grant 191010001 and in part by the Hubei Key Laboratory of Transportation Internet of Things under Grant 2020III026GX.

# References

1. Angelini, F., Fu, Z., Long, Y., Shao, L., Naqvi, S.M.: 2D pose-based real-time human action recognition with occlusion-handling. IEEE Trans. Multimedia **22**(6), 1433–1446 (2020)
2. Carreira, J., Zisserman, A.: Quo vadis, action recognition? A new model and the kinetics dataset. In: Proceedings IEEE/CVF Conference Computing Vision Pattern Recognition (CVPR), pp. 4724–4733 (2017)
3. Cheng, Y., Yang, B., Wang, B., Wending, Y., Tan, R.T.: Occlusion-aware networks for 3D human pose estimation in video. In: Proceedings IEEE/CVF International Conference Computing Vision (ICCV) (2019)
4. Diba, A., et al.: Spatio-temporal channel correlation networks for action classification. In: Ferrari, V., Hebert, M., Sminchisescu, C., Weiss, Y. (eds.) ECCV 2018. LNCS, vol. 11208, pp. 299–315. Springer, Cham (2018). https://doi.org/10.1007/978-3-030-01225-0_18
5. Diba, A., Sharma, V., Gool, L.V.: Deep temporal linear encoding networks. In: Proceedings IEEE/CVF Conference Computing Vision Pattern Recognition (CVPR) (2017)
6. Donahue, J., et al.: Long-term recurrent convolutional networks for visual recognition and description. In: Proceedings IEEE/CVF Conference Computing Vision Pattern Recognition (CVPR) (2015)
7. Feichtenhofer, C., Fan, H., Malik, J., He, K.: Slowfast networks for video recognition. In: Proceedings IEEE/CVF International Conference Computing Vision (ICCV), pp. 6201–6210 (2019)
8. Feichtenhofer, C., Pinz, A., Zisserman, A.: Convolutional two-stream network fusion for video action recognition. In: Proceedings IEEE/CVF Conference Computing Vision Pattern Recognition (CVPR), pp. 1933–1941 (2016)
9. Gowda, S.N., Rohrbach, M., Sevilla-Lara, L.: SMART frame selection for action recognition. arxiv:2012.10671 (2020)
10. Hara, K., Kataoka, H., Satoh, Y.: Can spatiotemporal 3D CNNs retrace the history of 2D CNNs and ImageNet? In: Proceedings IEEE/CVF Conference Computing Vision Pattern Recognition (CVPR), pp. 6546–6555 (2018)
11. Jiang, B., Wang, M., Gan, W., Wu, W., Yan, J.: STM: spatiotemporal and motion encoding for action recognition. In: Proceedings IEEE/CVF International Conference Computing Vision (ICCV), pp. 2000–2009 (2019)
12. Kay, W., et al.: The kinetics human action video dataset. arxiv:1705.0695 (2017)
13. Kuehne, H., Jhuang, H., Garrote, E., Poggio, T.A., Serre, T.: HMDB: a large video database for human motion recognition. In: Proceedings IEEE/CVF International Conference Computing Vision (ICCV), pp. 2556–2563 (2011)
14. Li, J., Wei, P., Zhang, Y., Zheng, N.: A slow-i-fast-p architecture for compressed video action recognition. In: Proceedings ACM International Conference Multimedia (ACM MM), pp. 2039–2047 (2020)
15. Li, K., et al.: Learning from weakly-labeled web videos via exploring sub-concepts. arxiv:2101.03713 (2021)
16. Li, T., Fan, L., Zhao, M., Liu, Y., Katabi, D.: Making the invisible visible: action recognition through walls and occlusions. In: Proceedings IEEE/CVF International Conference Computing Vision (ICCV), pp. 872–881 (2019)
17. Li, X., Shuai, B., Tighe, J.: Directional temporal modeling for action recognition. In: Vedaldi, A., Bischof, H., Brox, T., Frahm, J.-M. (eds.) ECCV 2020. LNCS, vol. 12351, pp. 275–291. Springer, Cham (2020). https://doi.org/10.1007/978-3-030-58539-6_17

18. Li, Y., Ji, B., Shi, X., Zhang, J., Kang, B., Wang, L.: TEA: temporal excitation and aggregation for action recognition. In: Proceedings IEEE/CVF Conference Computing Vision Pattern Recognition (CVPR) (2020)
19. Liao, L., Xiao, J., Wang, Z., Lin, C., Satoh, S.: Uncertainty-aware semantic guidance and estimation for image inpainting. IEEE J. Sel. Top. Sig. Process. 15(2), 310–323 (2021)
20. Lin, J., Gan, C., Han, S.: TSM: temporal shift module for efficient video understanding. In: Proceedings IEEE/CVF International Conference Computing Vision (ICCV), pp. 7082–7092 (2019)
21. Qiu, Z., Yao, T., Mei, T.: Learning spatio-temporal representation with pseudo-3D residual networks. In: Proceedings IEEE/CVF International Conference Computing Vision (ICCV) (2017)
22. Simonyan, K., Zisserman, A.: Two-stream convolutional networks for action recognition in videos. In: Proceedings Advanced Neural Information Processing System (NIPS), pp. 568–576 (2014)
23. Soomro, K., Zamir, A.R., Shah, M.: UCF101: a dataset of 101 human actions classes from videos in the wild. arxiv:1212.0402 (2012)
24. Tran, D., Bourdev, L.D., Fergus, R., Torresani, L., Paluri, M.: Learning spatiotemporal features with 3D convolutional networks. In: Proceedings IEEE/CVF International Conference Computing Vision (ICCV), pp. 4489–4497 (2015)
25. Ulutan, O., Rallapalli, S., Srivatsa, M., Torres, C., Manjunath, B.S.: Actor conditioned attention maps for video action detection. In: Proceedings IEEE Workshop/Winter Conference Application Computing Vision (WACV), pp. 516–525 (2020)
26. Wang, J., Gao, Y., Li, K., Lin, Y., Ma, A.J., Sun, X.: Removing the background by adding the background: towards background robust self-supervised video representation learning. arXiv:2009.05769 (2020)
27. Wang, L., Li, W., Li, W., Gool, L.V.: Appearance-and-relation networks for video classification. In: Proceedings IEEE/CVF Conference Computing Vision Pattern Recognition (CVPR), pp. 1430–1439 (2018)
28. Wang, L., Qiao, Y., Tang, X.: Action recognition with trajectory-pooled deep-convolutional descriptors. In: Proceedings IEEE/CVF Conference Computing Vision Pattern Recognition (CVPR) (2015)
29. Wang, L., et al.: Temporal segment networks: towards good practices for deep action recognition. In: Leibe, B., Matas, J., Sebe, N., Welling, M. (eds.) ECCV 2016. LNCS, vol. 9912, pp. 20–36. Springer, Cham (2016). https://doi.org/10.1007/978-3-319-46484-8_2
30. Wang, X., et al.: $S^3$d: scalable pedestrian detection via score scale surface discrimination. IEEE Trans. Circuits Syst. Video Technol. 30(10), 3332–3344 (2020)
31. Wang, X., Girshick, R.B., Gupta, A., He, K.: Non-local neural networks. In: Proceedings IEEE/CVF Conference Computing Vision Pattern Recognition (CVPR), pp. 7794–7803 (2018)
32. Woo, S., Park, J., Lee, J.-Y., Kweon, I.S.: CBAM: convolutional block attention module. In: Ferrari, V., Hebert, M., Sminchisescu, C., Weiss, Y. (eds.) ECCV 2018. LNCS, vol. 11211, pp. 3–19. Springer, Cham (2018). https://doi.org/10.1007/978-3-030-01234-2_1
33. Xu, X., Liu, L., Zhang, X., Guan, W., Hu, R.: Rethinking data collection for person re-identification: active redundancy reduction. Pattern Recognit. 113, 107827 (2021)

34. Zhou, L., Chen, Y., Gao, Y., Wang, J., Lu, H.: Occlusion-Aware Siamese network for human pose estimation. In: Vedaldi, A., Bischof, H., Brox, T., Frahm, J.-M. (eds.) ECCV 2020. LNCS, vol. 12365, pp. 396–412. Springer, Cham (2020). https://doi.org/10.1007/978-3-030-58565-5_24

35. Zolfaghari, M., Singh, K., Brox, T.: ECO: efficient convolutional network for online video understanding. In: Ferrari, V., Hebert, M., Sminchisescu, C., Weiss, Y. (eds.) ECCV 2018. LNCS, vol. 11206, pp. 713–730. Springer, Cham (2018). https://doi.org/10.1007/978-3-030-01216-8_43

# RGB-D Based Visual Navigation Using Direction Estimation Module

Chao Luo[1], Sheng Bi[1,2(✉)], Min Dong[1,2], and Hongxu Nie[1]

[1] School of Computer Science and Engineering, South China University
of Technology, Guangzhou 510006, Guangdong, China
{picy,hollymin}@scut.edu.cn
[2] Key Laboratory of Big Data and Intelligent Robot, Ministry of Education,
Guangzhou 510006, Guangdong, China

**Abstract.** Target-driven visual navigation without mapping works to solve navigation problems that given a target object, mobile robots can navigate to the target object. Recently, visual navigation has been researched and improved largely by learning-based methods. However, their methods lack depth information and spatial perception, using only single RGB images. To overcome these problems, two methods are presented in this paper. Firstly, we encode visual features of objects by dynamic graph convolutional network and extract 3D spatial features for objects by 3D geometry, a high level visual feature for agent to easily understand object relationship. Secondly, as human beings, they solve this problem in two steps, first exploring a new environment to find the target object and second planning a path to arrive. Inspired by the way of humans navigation, we propose direction estimation module (DEM) based on RGB-D images. DEM provides direction estimation of the target object to our learning model by a wheel odometry. Given a target object, first stage, our agent explores an unseen scene to detect the target object. Second stage, when detected the target object, we can estimate current location of the target object by 3D geometry, after that, each step of the agent, DEM will estimate new location of target object, and give direction information of the target object from a first-view image. It can guide our agent to navigate to the target object. Our experiment results outperforms the result of state of the art method in the artificial environment AI2-Thor.

**Keywords:** Visual navigation · Mobile robot · Direction estimation module · Reinforcement learning

## 1 Introduction

Target-driven visual navigation aims to help a agent to solve object-based goal navigation problem based on its first-perspective visual observation. Given a target object, an agent can explore unseen environment and navigate to the target object based on visual inputs. Because of complex environment and a lack of

© Springer Nature Switzerland AG 2021
D. N. Pham et al. (Eds.): PRICAI 2021, LNAI 13033, pp. 252–264, 2021.
https://doi.org/10.1007/978-3-030-89370-5_19

location information of the target object and agent itself, it is a challenging task for agent to achieve without mapping. A series of deep learning based methods and deep reinforcement learning methods [4,7,17,20,21,24] have been proposed to tackle this problem. Their techniques bring large improvement of visual navigation task in simulation environment. However, two problems need to be solved. Firstly, lack of depth information and spatial perception makes it easier for the agent to collide with other objects. Secondly, these methods ignore some complex situations in the real world. For example, after the agent finds the target object, it may lose field of view of the target object due to obstacles and perspective reasons. In fact, once the agent finds the target object, it can estimate approximate direction of each step for the target object by a wheel odometry. Since the action spaces for our agent is limited, the agent has a fixed rotation angle and moving distance. We present two methods to handle these questions. First of all, we train our agent to explore an unseen environment to detect objects by employing object detector from RGB-D images, encode spatial relationship of objects by dynamic graph convolutional network and compute 3D coordinate of detected objects as high level features by 3D geometry. We extract the high level object relation features for our model to strengthen spatial awareness of the agent. Moreover, when human beings try to navigate to a target object in an unseen environment, they usually catch sight of the target, and then they know its approximate location in their head for each step. Inspired by human navigation, we design a new module called direction estimation module (DEM). We compute coordinate of the detected target object by 3D geometry and then project it to 2D space. After that, we take direction information of the target object as additional input to train agent using DEM.

Like [20], we adopt LSTM [8] and Asynchronous Advantage Actor-critic (A3C) architecture [15] to study navigation policy for agent in the 3D simulation environment AI2-Thor [11]. Experiment results shows that our method outperforms the state of the art method. Most notably, our method improves 5.5% of success rate (SR) and 3% of success weighted by path length (SPL) for all length path.

Overall, the main contributions of this paper are as follows:

- We extract object detection information and employ dynamic GCN module to encode visual features of objects from images and then we generate 3D spatial features using RGB-D frame to get relationship of current objects. It helps agent to easily perceive spatial relationship of objects in complex environments.
- We design direction estimation module (DEM) to generate direction information of target objects as input for our network, once the agent detected the target object, it will accept direction feature of the target object as input for each step which can guide the agent to navigate to the target object. The direction information is not relevant to the environment, so it will improve the generalization ability of our network.

- We introduce a new reward strategy to train our model which efficiently improves performance of navigation task. Owing to enhanced capability of 3D spatial perception and direction estimation module, our model can converge more quickly than other methods.

## 2    Related Works

Visual navigation is an important technique for indoor intelligent robots. Indoor navigation is full of challenge because of complex and unseen environment. Mapping, navigation method and end-to-end visual navigation without mapping method have been proposed by researchers to solve this problem. Traditional navigation mainly focus on building a map and planning on the map. Feder et al. [5]; Cummins et al. [3]; Oriolo et al. [16] propose traditional mapping and planning methods for mobile robots. Sebastian et al. [19] proposed metric-topological maps for indoor mobile robot navigation. Learning-based mapping and navigation have been employed in [7] by Gupta et al. However, these techniques rely on accuracy of mapping and can not work in dynamic semantic scenes and unseen environment.

The navigation problem without prior information can be defined as a state space search problem. Howard et al. [9]; Krose et al. [13] propose state space search methods to solve navigation problems. Reinforcement learning method can also solve some state search problems. Recently, reinforcement learning (RL) based visual navigation has attracted many researchers to study. Piotr Mirowski et al. [14] propose jointly learning and deep estimation to navigate in 3D mazes. Zhu et al. [24] propose RL-based approach for agent to navigate taking only with a target image and first-view images as input. These works [21,22] pay attention to semantic scene and knowledge graph of objects for navigation. Wu, Yi et al. [21] propose Bayesian Relational Memory for semantic visual navigation. Wei Yang et al. [22] use Graph Convolutional Networks (GCN) with prior knowledge from Visual Genome [12] dataset to encode 3D spatial relationship. Wortsman et al. [20] propose meta-reinforcement learning method [6] to navigate.

Recently, many 3d simulation environments and datasets have been proposed to solve navigation problem of embodied agent. AI2-Thor [11] environment is designed to solve reinforcement learning and indoor visual navigation problem. Matterport3D [2] is a cross-scene datasets, The authors of this article propose visual and language navigation problem, meanwhile, they introduce a baseline method for this problem. Habitat [18] is a modular high-level library for end-to-end development for embedded robot to complete different navigation tasks. In this paper, we focus on indoor visual navigation using AI2-Thor environment.

## 3    Method

We aim to improve spatial perception of mobile robot using RGB-D based method. With only RGB image input, agent can not construct 3D spatial relationship of scenes efficiently. To achieve this goal, we construct a deep learning reinforcement architecture to learn navigation policy. Firstly, given first perspective RGB-D images of our agent as input, we use object detection method to detect objects and 3d geometry methods to compute 3d coordinate of the objects as high level spatial features. Following [4], we use dynamic graph convolutional network to encode object visual features. An agent can navigate to a target object in two stages. First stage, the agent explore novel environment to find target object. Second stage, the agent plans a path to get to the target object. The agent may lose field of view for the target object from first-view due to the complexity of the unseen environment. To help the agent to avoid losing the target object, we employ direction estimation module (DEM) to estimate direction of current target object from first-view. We train our network to learn navigation policy in AI2-Thor simulation environment.

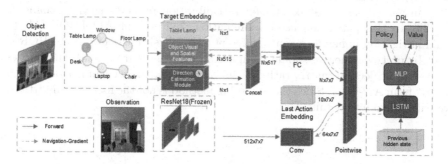

**Fig. 1. Model overview.** We use object information detected by object detector and frozen ResNet18 feature map extracted from images as model input. We encode object visual features by dynamic graph convolutional network and compute 3D coordinate of objects using 3D geometry. Specifically, we estimate direction of a target object using DEM each step, concatenate inputs and feed them to LSTM module. We adopt A3C architecture to train our model.

### 3.1   Task Definition

Our task is that given a target object from set $O = \{AlarmClock, ..., Toaster\}$ represented by word embedding and a scene random chosen from set $S = \{S_1, ..., S_n\}$, the agent can navigate to positions near the target. The distance between the target and the ending position should be less than threshold (e.g. 1.5 m). The agent takes egocentric images as input, and the sensor input of agent is RGB-D image in this paper. The action spaces for the agent are RotateLeft, RotateRight, MoveAhead, Lookup, LookDown, Done. For each step, the agent can choose an action to execute from action spaces.

We define a complete episode that once the agent executes action "Done" or steps of agent exceeds a threshold, the episode ends. When the agent signals "Done" and the target object appears in current first-view image and meanwhile the actual distance from the target object to the agent is less than threshold (e.g. 1.5 m), we define this episode is successful, otherwise, the episode fails.

## 3.2    3D Geometry

Without distance information, the agent can not understand spatial relationship efficiently. To solve this problem, we use RGB-D images as input so that the agent can enhance ability of spatial perception of the surrounding environment. We can reconstruct 3d coordinate of any pixel point by 3d geometry with a RGB-D image. Given an point $(x, y, z)$ on camera coordinate system, we can calculate pixel coordinate $(u, v, 1)$ by using camera intrinsic matrix as follow:

$$z \begin{pmatrix} u \\ v \\ 1 \end{pmatrix} = \begin{pmatrix} f_x & 0 & c_x \\ 0 & f_y & c_y \\ 0 & 0 & 1 \end{pmatrix} \begin{pmatrix} x \\ y \\ z \end{pmatrix} \tag{1}$$

Similarly, we can compute 3d coordinate of pixel by inverse intrinsic matrix. We can get intrinsic matrix by camera calibration methods such as zhang et al. [23]. In this paper, we use 3d simulation environment AI2-THOR [11] to train navigation policy for agent. Different from physical camera, AI2-THOR is built by unity engine, we should compute 3d coordinate from rendering images by inverse projection matrix rather than intrinsic matrix, we can get projection matrix from AI2-Thor. Since the rendering method is not the focus of this article, we will not go into details here.

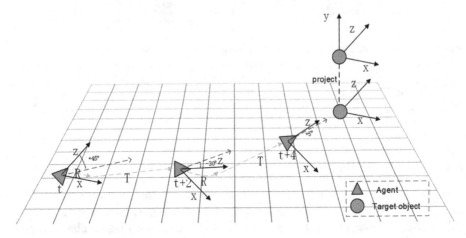

**Fig. 2. Example of DEM.** As the graph shown, our agent detected the target object in t-th step and calculate direction of the target object. After that, in t+2, t+4 step, we use DEM to compute the new direction of the target object from first view. Direction information can guide the agent get to the target object.

## 3.3    Visual and Spatial Features of Objects

We detect objects from an egocentric image and compute corresponding 3d coordinate of objects on camera coordinate system. To get relative visual features for objects of interest, We perform Faster R-CNN network [17] to detect objects of interest, extract information from the second ResBlock layer of the network and project bounding box positions to the layer to get 512 dimensions of local detection feature. We concatenate local detection features of all objects to $N \times 512$ features represented by $L$, where N is the number of different types of objects. We extract bounding box position, confidence and labels information of objects, concatenate them to $N \times 5$ feature as 2d spatial feature map. Following [4], we use dynamic graph convolutional module to encode 2d spatial relationship of objects using the 2d spatial feature map as input. We can represent it as follow:

$$H^{(l+1)} = f(A \cdot H^l \cdot W^l) \tag{2}$$

where A is adjacent matrix and $W^l$ is the parameters of l-th GCN layer, the final layer $H$ encodes spatial relationship of objects. $f$ is ReLU activate function. Different from traditional GCNs, we do not use pre-defined adjacent matrix. We represent $A$ and $W$ parameters by linear layers and our network learn $A$ and $W$ parameters by training. After that, we encode 2d spatial feature map to $N \times N$ feature represented by $D$. To get visual features of objects, we also employ graph attention layer to focus on visual features for objects of interest. We use feature $D$ as our attention map. The formula as follow:

$$\hat{F} = f(D \cdot L) \tag{3}$$

$\hat{F}$ represents our visual features of objects. We compute the $(x_{center}, y_{center})$ center of bounding box for each category. If corresponding category of objects do not exist in current perspective, we represent it as 0. We can obtain Z value from depth image from $(x_{center}, y_{center})$ position. Then, we calculate 3D coordinate for objects detected from first-view image and concatenate them as $N \times 3$ features. At last, we concatenate visual features of objects and 3D spatial features to $N \times 515$ matrix as our features of objects. Since our GCN network encode features without prior knowledge, It can adapt new environment well. And we directly encode 3D spatial relationship as input so that our model can easily perceive spatial relationship which is helpful for our agent to make decision to navigate in complex environment.

### 3.4   Direction Estimation Module

When human beings navigate to a target object in an unseen environment, they usually try to explore environment to catch sight of the target object and plan a path to get to the target object. We know approximate orientation after we saw the target object. We design Direction Estimation Module to estimate direction estimation of target object each step after agent firstly caught sight of target. Firstly, if object detector detect target object successfully, we can compute 3D coordinate of target object on camera coordinate system. To simplify estimation procedure, we project $(x, y, z)$ to $(x, z)$ from 3D coordinate system to 2D coordinate system. Assume that our mobile robot has a perfect odometry, we can compute rotation matrix and translation vector of action for mobile robot each step. The deduction of odometry system of mobile robot is omitted, because this is not our primary focus. After finding the target object, we can calculate its 3D coordinate $(x, y, z)$ and project it to a 2D coordinate $(x, z)$ on 2D coordinate system. We can deduce position of target object relative to the agent any step, the equation as follows:

$$
\begin{pmatrix} x_{t+1} \\ z_{t+1} \end{pmatrix} = \begin{pmatrix} cos\theta & sin\theta & \beta \\ -sin\theta & cos\theta & \gamma \\ 0 & 0 & 1 \end{pmatrix} \begin{pmatrix} x_t \\ z_t \\ 1 \end{pmatrix} \tag{4}
$$

$(x_t, z_t)$ and $(x_{t+1}, z_{t+1})$ are the positions of the target object relative to the agent at t and t+1 step. $(\beta, \gamma)$ is translation vector and $\theta$ is rotation angle from t step to t+1 step. When getting relative position of target object of last step, we compute direction of target object as follows.

$$
\theta = arctan(\frac{z}{x}) \tag{5}
$$

We convert the angle to direction of first-view for agent, for example, $+45°$ means $45°$ to right of agent, similarly, $-45°$ means to $45°$ to left of agent. The example is shown in Fig. 2. We feed the direction information as input to model to guide agent make rational decision each step. The reason why we do not give accurate position to model is that existing error from odometry system and object detection. Above all, we give rough direction rather than precise position to avoid overfitting of model, a slight change in direction caused by existing error has little effect on decision making for agent. We only need to know its approximate direction. Meanwhile, to avoid cumulative error, once target object detected by object detector again, we update its position again and reset transform matrix.

### 3.5    Actor-Critic Policy Network

We employ Asynchronous Advantage Actor-Critic (A3C) [15] architecture to learn policy for our agent. As the Fig. 1 shown, we extract global visual features from egocentric image using Resnet18 backbone pre-trained on ImageNet, concatenate object visual features from GCN module and 3d spatial features from 3d geometry as inputs for our model. To estimate location of the target object, we use DEM module proposed above to compute possible direction of the target object. Meanwhile, we encode our target object and last action as word embedding, concatenate with visual features mentioned above. Then we perform pointwise convolution to the inputs and feed the inputs to a Long Short-Term Memory module (LSTM). Finally we utilize A3C architecture to get policy and value for our agent.

We consider a reward function to minimize the trajectory length of agent for visual navigation. When our agent navigates to near of target object within numbers of steps, we will give the agent a large positive reward 5. Each step, the agent will receive $-0.005$ negative reward so that the agent can learn to reduce the number of steps. Moreover, to improve efficiency of navigation and avoid status of dead lock which the agent is always repeating same actions. We penalize the agent $-0.005$ when it steps to location where it has been arrived. This can activate our agent to explore unknown location for complex environment.

## 4    Experiment

Our target in this section is to evaluate our model and compare with other methods, to demonstrate that our method is more effective to accomplish navigation task and analyse how our method improve performance by ablation experiment.

### 4.1    Dataset and Evaluation

We train our model in AI2-Thor [11] which includes four types of 3D scenes. They are living room, bedroom, kitchen and bathroom. Each of them has 30 rooms with different layout, texture and furniture. Following [20], we choose 22 types of objects from all rooms as our navigation targets. Each type of room has over four different targets. We use Success Rate (SR) and Success weighted by Path Length (SPL) as our performance evaluation for visual navigation. The success rate is defined as $\frac{1}{N}\sum_{i=1}^{N} S_i$, SPL proposed by [1] evaluates navigation efficiency of agent, defined as $\frac{1}{N}\sum_{i=1}^{N} S_i \frac{L_i}{max(P_i,L_i)}$, where $N$ is number of episodes, $S_i$ represents binary indicator (success or fail), $L_i$ is the length of the optimal trajectory from initial position to target position and $P_i$ denotes the length of actual trajectory of navigation of the i-th episode. We evaluate our model on all length path and length over 5, we use $L \geq 5$ to represent it.

### 4.2    Experiment Setup and Comparison Methods

We adopt training and evaluation methods using AI2-Thor following [1]. Similarly, we choose 20 rooms for training, 5 rooms for validation from each type of scene. To evaluate generalization of our model, we use 20 remaining unseen scenes to test.

**Random Policy.** We use random strategy to sample action from action space for agent.

**Scene Prior.** [22] uses prior knowledge of object relation learned from additional database to train a deep reinforcement learning model.

**Self-adaptive Visual Navigation Method (SAVN).** [20] proposes meta-learning based visual navigation in unseen environments.

**Learning Object Relation Graph and Tentative Policy for Visual Navigation.** [4] proposes object relation graph (ORG), tentative policy (TPN) and imitation learning (IL) for visual navigation in unseen environment. It is state of the art method so far in visual navigation field. The method did not use depth feature of images. For fair comparison, we replace its input features with our input features information encoding as new input called D-(ORG+IL).

### 4.3   Training Details

We train our model with 12 asynchronous workers, each worker trains navigation gradient with random state in different scenes and transfer gradients to shared model. We employ Adam optimizer [10] to update our parameters of navigation policy. For learning rate, we choose $10^{-4}$. For evaluation, we perform 1000 episodes in different scenes, 250 episodes for each type of scene. For reward function, we give a positive reward 5 when agent get to target object and signal "Done", and each step we penalize agent $-0.005$. To reduce duplicate steps, the agent will receive $-0.005$ when it repeats same action. We retrain our object detector Faster R-CNN with dataset from AI2-Thor scenes. To avoid overfitting, we only use images from half of scenes to train our object detector.

**Table 1. Quantitative results**. We compare our performance of model with above methods. We use success rate (%) denoted by Success and SPL as our evaluation metrics. As a result, our method shows major improvement in both SR and SPL.

| Method | ALL | | L $\geq= 5$ | |
|---|---|---|---|---|
| | Success | SPL | Success | SPL |
| Random | 8.0 | 0.036 | 0.3 | 0.001 |
| SP [22] | 15.5 | 0.351 | 22.2 | 0.114 |
| SAVN [20] | 40.8 | 0.161 | 28.7 | 0.139 |
| ORG+IL+TPN [4] | 69.3 | 0.394 | 60.7 | 0.386 |
| D-(ORG+IL) [4] | 70.8 | 0.397 | 62.2 | 0.402 |
| Ours | **76.3** | **0.421** | **69.0** | **0.446** |

### 4.4   Results and Analysis

Table 1 summarizes the results of our approach and the baselines. Our method outperforms other technologies listed in the table both on Success Rate (SR) and Success weighted by Path Length (SPL) metrics. Scene Prior [22] extracts object spatial relationship from extra database using graph convolutional network. However, the spatial relationship between objects from different scenes is changing. Thus, directly learning from additional database can not adapt complex unseen environment. For this reason, we use object detector to detect position of object and employ 3d geometry to compute 3d position of detected object, encode local object spatial relationship by dynamic graph convolutional network. Our model only pay attention to current object spatial relationship, it stimulates our agent to select appropriate action by spatial perception rather than using fixed object relation. Thus, our method can adapt new environment well even without prior knowledge. SAVN [20] proposes meta learning based method to visual navigation. The article uses glove embedding to encode target object and ResNet18 (frozen) feature as input. But visual feature and word feature are characteristics from different dimension, it is difficult for network

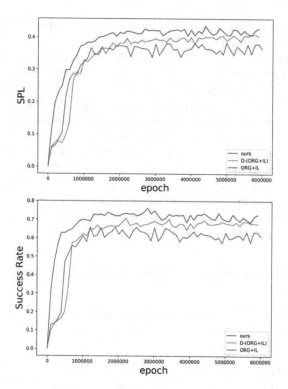

**Fig. 3. SPL and Success Rate on testing set.** The graph shows that our method outperform other methods both on spl and success rate, and achieves the state of art. Our approach has faster convergence speed than other methods.

to map target glove embedding to corresponding visual feature. To tackle this problem, following [4] we encode target object to $N \times 1$ one-hot embedding, extract all object information and map them to $N \times M$ matrix, N is categories of object, M is dimension of visual information encoded. It helps model to find the relation between target object and visual features. Different from method (ORG+IL+TPN) [4], we not only extract object relation from egocentric image but compute 3d spatial relation of them rather than only information from object detector. Thus, our model can more easily perceive the three-dimensional spatial relationship. The agent may loses view of target object from first-view because of avoiding obstacles or complex environment, these methods are not consider how to handle this problem, our direction estimation module can solve this problem by estimating direction of target of first-view to guide agent to navigate. Since our method utilises depth information of image and TPN module can not train end to end, It needs extra 2M episodes to train from (ORG+IL) trained model. So, for fair comparison, we feed our 3d spatial relation features to model (ORG+IL), called D-(ORG+IL). As shown from tables, our method improves

5.5% of success rate, 2.4% of SPL for all path and 6.8% of success rate, 4.4% for at least 5 length path than state of art method.

Figure 3 compares the performance for SPL and Success Rate of above methods in 6 million epoches. We see that our method performs better than other methods both on SPL and Success Rate. Above all, our method can fastly converge and get higher success rate only within 1 million epoches than other methods and each epoch our method outperforms than other methods. Our direction estimation module can guide our agent to navigate to target even encountering obstacles or losing target from view. Meanwhile, in order to improve the efficiency of our agent in navigation, we try to reduce duplicate actions to a same position for the agent by designing corresponding reward function, when it steps to the same position, we penalize our agent with a little negative value. It both improves our Success Rate and SPL since our agent learn to plan an optimal path to get more positive reward.

**Table 2. Comparison of our modules.** The comparison of performance for our different methods.

| Method | | w/o 3d features | w/o DEM | w/o our reward | Ours |
|--------|---------|-----------------|---------|----------------|------|
| ALL | Success | 68.1 | 72.3 | 74.3 | **76.3** |
| | SPL | 0.352 | 0.402 | **0.435** | 0.421 |
| L >= 5 | Success | 60.0 | 63.7 | 67.7 | **69.0** |
| | SPL | 0.368 | 0.408 | **0.448** | 0.446 |

### 4.5 Ablation Study

Our main contributions in this paper are that we proposed 3d spatial features, direction estimation module and a new reward strategy for agent, to clearly compare effects of our different methods, we perform an ablation on our methods for our navigation task.

**Ablation of 3d Spatial Features.** To improve capability of spatial perception for our agent, we introduce 3d spatial features so that the agent can understand complex environment. We verify the effect of this module by ablation experiment. As indicated in Table 2, the performance of our method with 3d spatial features improves efficiently compared with (w/o 3d feature). This demonstrate that high level spatial features can enhance ability of understanding spatial relationship of unseen environment.

**Impact of Direction Estimation Module.** We propose DEM method inspired by visual navigation of human in corresponding circumstance. Since the agent may lose view of target object because of complicated environment or path planning, we introduce DEM method to calculate direction of target object which the agent have found in first-view image. As shown in Table 2, our DEM method outperforms than (w/o DEM) method both on SPL and Success Rate. A rough direction information of target object can guide our agent to plan a better path and avoid duplicate steps. Another advantage of DEM is that it's independent of navigation environment, this means the method can adapt complex environment and has good generalization capability.

**Modifying Reward Function.** We adjust reward strategy based on reward function from SAVN [20] method. To avoid deadlock or duplicate steps for our agent, we design reward function proposed above. As illustrated in Table 2, there is an increase in Success Rate. We penalise a negative reward when the agent falls into status of duplicate position. The experiment shows that our reward strategy can improve success rate of navigation. We can see that the performance for SPL using normal reward strategy is better than ours, because difficult tasks need more steps to explore, when some complex object-based navigation tasks are accomplished by our methods, it will reduce complete SPL metrices.

## 5   Conclusion

In this paper, we propose employing 3d geometry to compute high level visual features and introduce a new method called direction estimation module to estimate direction of target object. Our high level visual features improve ability for spatial perception of agent, It helps agent fastly understand an unseen and complex environment. When our agent navigates to a target object, it may lose view of the target object. To avoid lose position of detected target object, we use DEM to estimate a real-time direction for the target object, so that our agent can quickly arrive to target object. Since DEM method is independent of the environment, it has high generalization capability in other unseen environment. To improve efficiency for path planning of our agent, we design a new reward function to avoid duplicate actions. Our experiments results demonstrate our method outperforms other methods and achieves state of art. Our next work will focus on visual navigation of cross-scene.

**Acknowledgements.** This research work is supported by Guang dong province science and technology plan projects (2020A0505100015). National Natural Science Foundation of China (61703168).

## References

1. Anderson, P., et al.: On evaluation of embodied navigation agents. CoRR abs/1807.06757 (2018). arXiv:1807.06757
2. Anderson, P., et al.: Vision-and-language navigation: interpreting visually-grounded navigation instructions in real environments. In: Proceedings of the IEEE Conference on Computer Vision and Pattern Recognition, pp. 3674–3683 (2018)
3. Cummins, M., Newman, P.: Probabilistic appearance based navigation and loop closing. In: Proceedings 2007 IEEE International Conference on Robotics and Automation, pp. 2042–2048. IEEE (2007)
4. Du, H., Yu, X., Zheng, L.: Learning object relation graph and tentative policy for visual navigation. In: Vedaldi, A., Bischof, H., Brox, T., Frahm, J.-M. (eds.) ECCV 2020. LNCS, vol. 12352, pp. 19–34. Springer, Cham (2020). https://doi.org/10.1007/978-3-030-58571-6_2

5. Feder, H.J.S., Leonard, J.J., Smith, C.M.: Adaptive mobile robot navigation and mapping. Int. J. Robot. Res. **18**(7), 650–668 (1999)
6. Finn, C., Abbeel, P., Levine, S.: Model-agnostic meta-learning for fast adaptation of deep networks. arXiv preprint arXiv:1703.03400 (2017)
7. Gupta, S., Davidson, J., Levine, S., Sukthankar, R., Malik, J.: Cognitive mapping and planning for visual navigation. In: Proceedings of the IEEE Conference on Computer Vision and Pattern Recognition, pp. 2616–2625 (2017)
8. Hochreiter, S., Schmidhuber, J.: Long short-term memory. Neural Comput. **9**(8), 1735–1780 (1997)
9. Howard, T.M., Green, C.J., Kelly, A., Ferguson, D.: State space sampling of feasible motions for high-performance mobile robot navigation in complex environments. J. Field Robot. **25**(6–7), 325–345 (2008)
10. Kingma, D., Ba, J.: Adam: a method for stochastic optimization. Computer Science (2014)
11. Kolve, E., et al.: AI2-THOR: an interactive 3D environment for visual AI. arXiv e-prints arXiv:1712.05474, December 2017
12. Krishna, R., et al.: Visual genome: connecting language and vision using crowd-sourced dense image annotations. Int. J. Comput. Vis. **123**(1), 32–73 (2017)
13. Krose, B.J., Van Dam, J.W.: Adaptive state space quantisation for reinforcement learning of collision-free navigation. In: Proceedings of the IEEE/RSJ International Conference on Intelligent Robots and Systems, vol. 2, pp. 1327–1332. IEEE (1992)
14. Mirowski, P., et al.: Learning to navigate in complex environments (2017)
15. Mnih, V., et al.: Asynchronous methods for deep reinforcement learning. In: International Conference on Machine Learning, pp. 1928–1937 (2016)
16. Oriolo, G., Vendittelli, M., Ulivi, G.: On-line map building and navigation for autonomous mobile robots. In: Proceedings of 1995 IEEE International Conference on Robotics and Automation, vol. 3, pp. 2900–2906. IEEE (1995)
17. Ren, S., He, K., Girshick, R., Sun, J.: Faster R-CNN: towards real-time object detection with region proposal networks. IEEE Trans. Pattern Anal. Mach. Intell. **39**(6), 1137–1149 (2017)
18. Savva, M., et al.: Habitat: a platform for embodied AI research. In: Proceedings of the IEEE/CVF International Conference on Computer Vision (ICCV) (2019)
19. Thrun, S.: Learning metric-topological maps for indoor mobile robot navigation. Artif. Intell. **99**, 21–71 (1998)
20. Wortsman, M., Ehsani, K., Rastegari, M., Farhadi, A., Mottaghi, R.: Learning to learn how to learn: self-adaptive visual navigation using meta-learning. In: Proceedings of the IEEE Conference on Computer Vision and Pattern Recognition, pp. 6750–6759 (2019)
21. Wu, Y., Wu, Y., Tamar, A., Russell, S., Gkioxari, G., Tian, Y.: Bayesian relational memory for semantic visual navigation. In: Proceedings of the IEEE/CVF International Conference on Computer Vision (ICCV), October 2019
22. Yang, W., Wang, X., Farhadi, A., Gupta, A., Mottaghi, R.: Visual semantic navigation using scene priors (2018)
23. Zhang, Z.: Flexible camera calibration by viewing a plane from unknown orientations. In: Seventh IEEE International Conference on Computer Vision (1999)
24. Zhu, Y., et al.: Target-driven visual navigation in indoor scenes using deep reinforcement learning. In: 2017 IEEE International Conference on Robotics and Automation (ICRA), pp. 3357–3364. IEEE (2017)

# Semi-supervised Single Image Deraining with Discrete Wavelet Transform

Xin Cui[1], Wei Shang[2], Dongwei Ren[2(✉)], Pengfei Zhu[1], and Yankun Gao[3]

[1] Tianjin University, Tianjin 300350, China
2019216101@tju.edu.cn
[2] Harbin Institute of Technology, Harbin 150001, China
[3] Beijing Institute of Computer Technology and Application, Beijing, China

**Abstract.** In recent years, single image deraining has received considerable research interests. Supervised learning is widely adopted for training
dedicated deraining networks to achieve promising results on synthetic
datasets, while limiting in handling real-world rainy images. Unsupervised and semi-supervised learning-based deranining methods have been
studied to improve the performance on real cases, but their quantitative
results are still inferior. In this paper, we propose to address this crucial
issue for image deraining in terms of backbone architecture and the strategy of semi-supervised learning. First, in terms of network architecture,
we propose an attentive image deraining network (AIDNet), where residual attention block is proposed to exploit the beneficial deep feature from
the rain streak layer to background image layer. Then, different from
the traditional semi-supervised method by enforcing the consistency of
rain pattern distribution between real rainy images and synthetic rainy
images, we explore the correlation between the real clean images and the
predicted background image by imposing adversarial losses in wavelet
space $I_{HH}$, $I_{HL}$, and $I_{LH}$, resulting in the final AID-DWT model. Extensive experiments on both synthetic and real-world rainy images have
validated that our AID-DWT can achieve better deraining results than
not only existing semi-supervised deraining methods qualitatively but
also outperform state-of-the-art supervised deraining methods quantitatively. All the source code and pre-trained models are available at
https://github.com/cuiyixin555/DeRain-DWT.

**Keywords:** Single image deraining · Semi-supervised learning ·
Attention · Discrete wavelet transform

## 1 Introduction

Single image deraining is a challenging task, and has a board application prospect
in object detection, outdoor recognition and automatic driving [4,11] when fac-
ing bad weather condition. Image deraining can be regarded as an image decomposition problem that rainy image can be separated into rain pattern space $\mathcal{R}$
and clean background image space $\mathcal{X}$. Previously, traditional optimization algorithms, *e.g.* low-rank model, sparse code model, and Gaussian mixture model

© Springer Nature Switzerland AG 2021
D. N. Pham et al. (Eds.): PRICAI 2021, LNAI 13033, pp. 265–278, 2021.
https://doi.org/10.1007/978-3-030-89370-5_20

[1,15,18,21,25], etc., are adopted as the priors of rain streak layer and background image layer. However, these handcrafted designed priors are limited in modeling the complicated composition pattern of real-world rainy images, and also they are very time-consuming. With the rapid development of deep learning in recent years, learning-based deraining methods have achieved great progress. Supervised learning is introduced to address image deraining problem, and many Convolutional Neural Networks (CNNs)-based methods for single image deraining have been proposed [6,8,24,26,28–30,33,41]. These methods employ deep networks to automatically extract features of layers, enabling them to model more complex mappings from rainy images to clean images. Albeit great quantitative results on synthetic datasets, they cannot well deal with real-world rainy images. Then, unsupervised learning and semi-supervised learning are suggested to exploit real-world rainy images, leading to better generalization in practical applications. But unsupervised deraining method is quantitatively inferior to supervised deraining methods. In [31,35], transfer learning is introduced to transfer deraining model trained on synthetic images to real rainy images. As for heavy rainy image, these semi-supervised deraining methods can not process it, and there is leeway to improve deraining visual quality.

In this paper, we adopt semi-supervised strategy that we design a residual attention image deraining network and introduce real clean images to make our network learn the similarity of image texture in discrete wavelet space. In particular, we design the main network into two parts, where one is used to extract rainy streak layer, and the other is used to recover clean background image. As training iterations increasing, each convolution attention block is used as a coefficient unit for rainy pattern feature aggregation in image space. As for semi-supervised stage, to make the predicted clean background more natural, we design a discriminator which contains multiple convolutional layers to calculate adversarial losses between real-world clean images and predicted clean images in three subband $f_{HH}$, $f_{HL}$ and $f_{LH}$. As for residual attention modules, we adopt 4 kinds of attention modules to explore its performance advantages in our deraining backbone.

Extensive experiments have been conducted on both synthetic and real-world rainy benchmark datasets. Our model quantitatively outperforms not only semi-supervised deraining method qualitatively but also state-of-the-art supervised deraining methods quantitatively.

Our contributions can be summarized from three aspects:

- We propose a simple yet effective semi-supervised deraining approach by Discrete Wavelet Transform (DWT), via which real-world clean images can be easily used to benefit the generalization ability of trained deraining model.
- We design a residual attention-based image deraining model to enhance the separation of the rain streak layer and the corresponding background layer; We use a ordinary convolution attention block for rain streak feature extraction, and compare with the other three attention modules, such as self-calibration block [17], attention feature fusion block [36] and self-attention block [39].

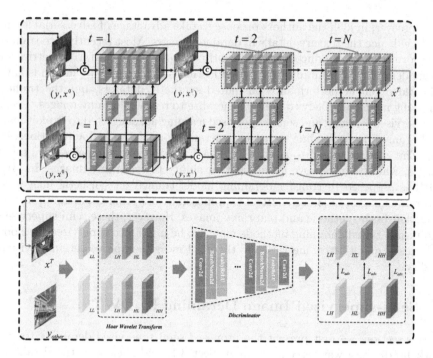

**Fig. 1.** The architecture of Semi-supervised deraining with Haar Wavelet Transform.

- Extensive experiments on synthetic and real-world rainy images have been conducted to validate that our model is superior to both supervised and semi-supervised deraining methods.

## 2    Related Works

Deep learning-based image deraining has been widely studied with the supervised learning manner, where various network architectures are designed to learn the mapping from rainy image to clean background image. In pioneer works [5,6], CNN and ResNet are first adopted to predict clean background image, outperforming conventional deraining methods. Subsequently, more complicated network architectures are proposed to better extract deep features from rainy images. In [28,30], multi-scale strategy can help model learn image features under different scales and enhance its robustness; Especially the application of dilation convolution is proposed, which is benefited in detecting and removing rain streaks simultaneously. In [14,26], recurrent networks are proposed to handle heavy rain streak accumulation. In [29,37], densely connected CNN is adopted for jointly estimating rain density and removing rain streaks. Besides, there are several works to incorporate lightweight networks in a cascaded scheme [3] or in a Laplacian pyramid framework [7].

Moreover, in [38], the authors propose to take advantage of adversarial learning to enhance the texture details in derained images. Most recently, pre-trained transformer [8] is introduced to significantly improve the quantitative metrics for image deraining. To sum up, supervised learning-based deraining methods have achieved excellent performance on paired synthetic datasets, but the trained deraining model are likely to poorly generalize to real-world rainy images. Then, unsupervised learning and semi-supervised learning are suggested to exploit real-world rainy images, leading to better generalization in practical applications. In [42], Zhu et al. proposed to adopt CycleGAN [43] to exploit unpaired real rainy images, which can improve generalization ability to real rainy images. In [31], SIRR is proposed to transfer deraining model trained on synthetic images to real rainy images. In [35], Syn2Real is proposed by adopting Gaussian processes to exploit both synthetic and real rainy images. However, these semi-supervised and unsupervised deraining methods may also be inferior to supervised methods in terms of quantitative metrics, and there is leeway to improve deraining visual quality.

## 3   Semi-supervised Image Deraining by DWT

In this section, we first present the proposed semi-supervised deraining framework by discrete wavelet transform in Sect. 3.1, and then give the details of residual attention framework in Sect. 3.2, finally the realization of our semi-supervised training method on the discrete wavelet transform is explained in Sect. 3.3.

### 3.1   Methodology Overview

As shown in Fig. 1, we propose to exploit real-world rainy images without paired ground-truth when training deraining networks, which is a semi-supervised approach. Different from [31,35], we propose a simple yet effective discriminative learning strategy by DWT to enforce the feature consistency of clean background from synthetic and real-world clean images on three subband $f_{HH}$, $f_{HL}$ and $f_{LH}$. As shown in Fig. 1, the entire network structure is divided into two parts; One is LSTM followed by 5 resblocks for background prediction, and the other is LSTM followed by 3 resblocks to rain streak extracted. Between the upper and lower parts, the residual attentive blocks is applied to converge rain pattern feature removal in image space. Formally, the procedure is described as

$$Res_{r_i}^t = F_{res_i}(h_r^{t-1}), i = 1, 2, 3$$
$$Res_{x_j}^t = F_{res_j}(h_x^{t-1}), j = 1, 2, 3, 4, 5 \tag{1}$$
$$Rab_{x_k}^t = F_{rab_k}(res_{r_i}^t) \times res_{x_j}^t + res_{x_j}^t, k = 1, 2, 3$$

where hidden state $h_r$ is from LSTM in space $\mathcal{R}$, hidden state $h_x$ is from LSTM in space $\mathcal{X}$, $res_{r_i}^t$ indicates the residual map of $i$-th ResBlock in space $\mathcal{R}$, $res_{x_j}^t$ denotes the residual map of $j$-th ResBlock in space $\mathcal{X}$. And thus there are three

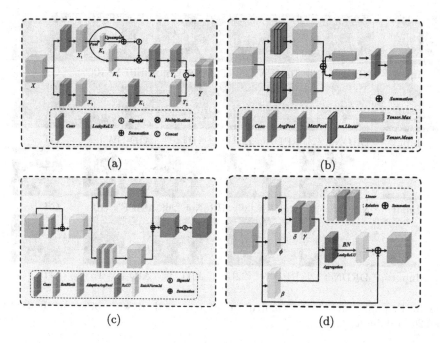

**Fig. 2.** *Top row*: (a) self-calibrated attention, (b) convolutional attention. *Bottom row*: (c) feature fusion attention, (d) self-attention.

RAB modules, where $rab_{x_k}^t$ connects the $i$-th ResBlock in $\mathcal{R}$ and $j$-th ResBlock in $\mathcal{X}$, exploiting the beneficial deep features between $\mathcal{R}$ and $\mathcal{X}$. The last crucial issue is how to determine the connections of $i$ and $j$. To answer this question, we conducted experiments on Rain200H datasets [28] to validate the effectiveness of different connections. We will explain it specificly.

Finally, the predicted background $X^g$ is used to initialize discrete wavelet transform discriminator network. When training deraining model shown on bottom row by only using real-world clean images, adversarial losses calculated in predicted background $X^g$ and real clean image $X_c$ in $f_{HH}$, $f_{HL}$ and $f_{LH}$ that is adopted to enforce its the consistency of feature distribution. Our model AID-DWT can achieve better results than existing semi-supervised and supervised deraining methods.

Overall, AID-DWT model consists of three parts: (i) Recurrent training for rain streak extracted and clean background image predicted with ResLSTM framework; (ii) Applying attention block for extracting rainy pattern feature strongly in image space; (iii) Calculating three subband adversarial losses on $f_{HH}$ and $f_{HL}$ and $f_{LH}$.

## 3.2 Residual Attentive Network Architecture

The good design of attention block can describe the rain pattern feature to the maximum extent. With the structure of deep CNNs becoming more and more

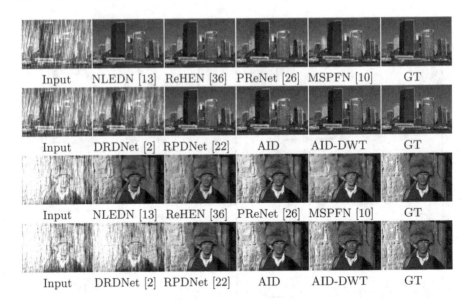

**Fig. 3.** Examples about the comparison of our method with other methods on Rain200H dataset.

complicated, extracting mean feature and max feature by average pool and max pool is not enough to achieve satisfactory results. Thanks to variety of attention module [17, 32, 36, 39], as shown in Fig. 2, we will explain them respectively.

**Self-Calibrated Block (SC):** Different from the traditional attention mechanism, its usually performs operations in the dimension of the feature to obtain the average feature and the maximum feature. SC block has four parts of filters, i.e., $[K_1, K_2, K_3, K_4]$. Through splitting filters, the input $X$ with channel C is split into $X_1$ and $X_2$ through $1 \times 1$ convolution with the channel C/2. Reviewing the entire self-calibrated convolution, it enables each spatial position to adaptively encode the context, which make difference between it and traditional attention block (CA).

**Self-Attention Block (SAN):** In [39], Zhao *et al.* firstly introduce feature aggregation into pairwise self-attention block. The whole procedure is describe as

$$y_i = \sum_{j \in R(i)} \alpha(x_i, x_j) \odot \beta(x_j), \tag{2}$$

where $x_i$ and $x_j$ are feature maps with indexes i and j, $\odot$ is the Hadamard product called aggregated with R(i). In order to utilize more surrounding pixels, the size of footprint is set $5 \times 5$.

**Attention Feature Fusion Block (AFF):** Similar to traditional convolution attention block (CA), AFF block [36] extracts the key pixels, as well as processes the residual information further. The whole process can be described as

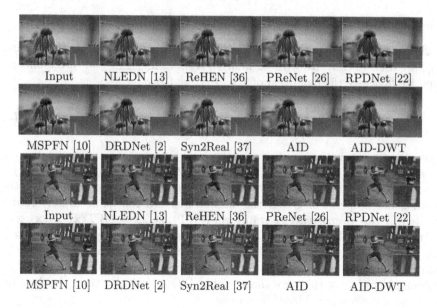

**Fig. 4.** Examples about the comparison of our method with other methods on real-world datasets.

$$\alpha_i = Local(x_i) + Global(x_i), \tag{3}$$

$$y_i = x_i \times \alpha + Res(x_i) \times (1 - \alpha), \tag{4}$$

where $\alpha_i$ is a attentional factor that is realized through a local attention block and a global attention block; A local attention block include multi-layer convolution that help model to learn feature based on dimension, while a global attention contains global average pool to extracted feature on space. Finally, the original feature $x_i$ and the residual feature $Res(x_i)$ are proportionally distributed through attentional factor, which effectively solves the problem of information decreased as the number of convolution layers increases.

**Convolution Attention Block (CA):** As a traditional attention block, CA is widely used in feature extraction. As for input feature map F (H×W×C), it will be dealt with global max pooling and global average pooling, respectively to obtain two $1 \times 1 \times C$ features. And then, its will be sent to a two-layer neural network (MLP) that the number of neurons in the first layer is C/r (r is the reduction rate), the activation function is Relu, and the number of neurons in the second layer is C; The two-layer neural network is shared. After that, the MLP output features are subjected to an element-wise addition operation, as well as the sigmoid activation operation is performed to generate the final channel attention feature, namely $M_c$. Finally, the $M_c$ and the input feature map F are subjected to an element-wise multiplication operation to generate the input features required by the Spatial attention module.

### 3.3    Discriminator by DWT for Semi-supervised Method

In 2D Discrete wavelet transform (DWT), four filters, i.e. $f_{LL}$, $f_{LH}$, $f_{HL}$, and $f_{HH}$, are used to convolve with an image $x$ [19]. To illustrate the three subband filter, we first give the definition of $f_{LH}$, $f_{HL}$, and $f_{HH}$,

$$\mathbf{f}_{LH} = \begin{bmatrix} -1 & -1 \\ 1 & 1 \end{bmatrix}, \mathbf{f}_{HL} = \begin{bmatrix} -1 & 1 \\ -1 & 1 \end{bmatrix}, \mathbf{f}_{HH} = \begin{bmatrix} 1 & -1 \\ -1 & 1 \end{bmatrix}. \tag{5}$$

Given an image $\mathbf{x}$ with size of $m \times n$, the $(i,j)$-th value of $\mathbf{x}_1$ after 2D discrete transform can be written as $\mathbf{x}_1(i,j) = \mathbf{x}(2i-1,2j-1) + \mathbf{x}(2i-1,2j) + \mathbf{x}(2i,2j-1) + \mathbf{x}(2i,2j)$. Even though the downsampling operation is deployed, due to the biorthogonal property of DWT, the original image $\mathbf{x}$ can be accurately reconstructed by the inverse wavelet transform (IWT), i.e., $\mathbf{x} = IWT(\mathbf{x}_1, \mathbf{x}_2, \mathbf{x}_3, \mathbf{x}_4)$.

In order to make our predicted clean background image have similar texture distribution with real-world clean image, we introduce adversarial loss in the three subband image $f_{HH}$, $f_{HL}$, $f_{LH}$. First, we achieve $X_{hh}$, $X_{hl}$ and $X_{lh}$ by Hadamard product with above three subband. Our goal is to train the discriminator with the above subband images as

$$L_{hh} = Adv(X_{hh}^i, X_{hh}^c), \tag{6}$$

$$L_{hl} = Adv(X_{hl}^i, X_{hl}^c), \tag{7}$$

$$L_{lh} = Adv(X_{lh}^i, X_{lh}^c), \tag{8}$$

where $Adv$ is WGAN-GP Loss, as well as $X^i$ and $X^c$ are denoted as a predicted background and a real-world clean image, respectively. So, we can treat $X_{hh}^c$, $X_{hl}^c$ and $X_{lh}^c$ as pseudo label for corresponding predicted output.

## 4    Experimental Results

In this section, we conduct extensive experiments to demonstrate the effectiveness of the proposed method on widely used four synthetic datasets and two real-world datasets. Eight state-of-the-art baseline are compared in this paper. Next, we will introduce the datasets and measurements in details as in Sect. 4.1, implementation details in Sect. 4.2, results on synthetic datasets and real-world datasets in Sect. 4.3 and ablation study in Sect. 4.4, respectively.

### 4.1    Datasets and Measurements

Our experiment is verified on four synthetic datasets and two real-world datasets, such as Rain200H [28], Rain1200 [37], Rain1400 [6] and Rain12 [16] for synthetic, as well as SPADatasets [27] and $Real_{275}$ for real-world datasets. Rain200H has heavy rain with different shapes, directions and sizes, which is the most challenging dataset including 1800 images for training and 200 images for testing. Rain200L contains the same number of pictures, which has light rain and easy to trained. Rain1200 has three different level of rain images, including heavy rain, medium rain and light rain, which contains 12000 training images and 1200 testing images. Rain1400 has medium level rain images, which includes 12600 images for training and 1400 images for testing. Rain12 has 12 images for testing. SPA Datasets include 1000 testing images with labels. In addition, we has achieve 275 real rainy images from Internet. We has trained our proposed model on different datasets for verifying its robustness.

**Table 1.** The values of PSNR, SSIM and NIQE on two real datasets. **Red**, blue and cyan colors are used to indicate top **1**st, 2nd and 3rd rank, respectively.

| | NLEDN [13] | | ReHEN [34] | | PReNet [26] | | RPDNet [22] | | AID | | AID-HWT | |
|---|---|---|---|---|---|---|---|---|---|---|---|---|
| Dataset | PSNR | SSIM | PSNR | SSIM | PSNR | SSIM | PSNR | SSIM | PSNR | SSIM | PSNR | SSIM |
| SPA | 30.596 | 0.9363 | 32.652 | 0.9297 | 32.720 | 0.9317 | 32.803 | 0.9337 | 31.721 | 0.9359 | **33.263** | **0.9375** |
| Dataset | Derain | GT | Derain | GT | Derain | GT | Derain | GT | Derain | GT | Derain | GT |
| $Real_{275}$ | 3.5554 | – | 3.7355 | – | 3.7745 | – | 3.8957 | – | 3.6013 | – | **3.5519** | – |
| | MSPFN [10] | | DRDNet [2] | | SIRR [31] | | Syn2Real [35] | | AID | | AID-HWT | |
| Dataset | PSNR | SSIM | PSNR | SSIM | PSNR | SSIM | PSNR | SSIM | PSNR | SSIM | PSNR | SSIM |
| SPA | 29.538 | 0.9193 | 28.083 | 0.9126 | 22.666 | 0.7474 | 31.824 | 0.9307 | 31.721 | 0.9359 | **33.263** | **0.9375** |
| Dataset | Derain | GT | Derain | GT | Derain | GT | Derain | GT | Derain | GT | Derain | GT |
| $Real_{275}$ | 3.8616 | – | 3.6634 | – | 3.5592 | – | 4.0372 | – | 3.6013 | – | **3.5519** | – |

## 4.2   Implementation Details

Our AID-DWT networks are implemented using Pytorch [23] framework, adopt ADAM [12] algorithm for optimization, and are trained on PC equipped with two NVIDIA GTX 2080Ti GPUs. In our experiments, all the network shared the same training setting. We trained the network for 100 epochs. Each pair of training of samples will be randomly cropped $100 \times 100$ pixels. Adam optimizer is used with a learning rate of 0.001 which is divided by 5 after the 30th epochs, 50th epochs and 80th epochs.

## 4.3   Results and Analysis

**Quantitative Comparsion.** We compare our proposed model with NLEDN [13], ReHEN [34], PReNet [26], RPDNet [22], MSPFN [10] and DRDNet [2], which baseline models adopted supervised pattern, and SIRR [31], Syn2Real [35] with semi-supervised methods under the three metrics of PSNR [9], SSIM [40] and NIQE [20]. We trained our models on the synthetic datasets Rain200H, Rain1200 and Rain1400, and compare the quantitative results obtained with the training methods under the corresponding dataset, respectively. The metric results are presented on Table 2 and Table 1. Our proposed method has achieved the highest PSNR, SSIM and NIQE in all datasets.

**Qualitative Comparsion.** Figure 3 exhibits some synthetic examples on Rain200H dataset. We can see that we proposed model can achieve the best

**Table 2.** The values of PSNR and SSIM on four synthetic datasets. **Red**, blue and cyan colors are used to indicate top $1^{st}$, $2^{nd}$ and $3^{rd}$ rank, respectively.

| | NLEDN [13] | | ReHEN [34] | | PReNet [26] | | AID-HWT | |
|---|---|---|---|---|---|---|---|---|
| Dataset | PSNR | SSIM | PSNR | SSIM | PSNR | SSIM | PSNR | SSIM |
| Rain200H | 27.315 | 0.8904 | 27.525 | 0.8663 | 27.883 | 0.8908 | **28.903** | **0.9074** |
| Rain1200 | 30.799 | 0.9127 | 30.456 | 0.8702 | 27.307 | 0.8712 | **31.960** | **0.9136** |
| Rain1400 | 30.808 | 0.9181 | 30.984 | 0.9156 | 30.609 | 0.9181 | **31.001** | **0.9246** |
| Rain12 | 33.028 | 0.9615 | 35.095 | 0.9400 | 34.7912 | 0.9644 | **35.587** | **0.9679** |
| | RPDNet [22] | | MSPFN [10] | | DRDNet [2] | | AID-HWT | |
| Dataset | PSNR | SSIM | PSNR | SSIM | PSNR | SSIM | PSNR | SSIM |
| Rain200H | 27.909 | 0.8923 | 25.554 | 0.8039 | 22.825 | 0.7114 | **28.903** | **0.9074** |
| Rain1200 | 26.486 | 0.8401 | 30.390 | 0.8862 | 28.386 | 0.8275 | **31.960** | **0.9136** |
| Rain1400 | 30.772 | 0.9178 | 30.016 | 0.9164 | 28.360 | 0.8574 | **31.001** | **0.9246** |
| Rain12 | 35.055 | 0.9657 | 34.253 | 0.9469 | 25.199 | 0.8497 | **35.587** | **0.9679** |

results, while other baseline models also are left some artifacts or remaining rain streaks. Especially, DRDNet [2] fails to work on Rain200H datasets. In addition, we also provide some examples shown in Fig. 4 of real-world datasets to prove the superiority of the proposed algorithm comparing with others. Expecially the rainy scene in forth column, our method can well recognize the cropped area that presents interspace between a trunk and the other, while the RPDNet [22] model removed it and regard it as a rain streak; In addition, our model can remove most of the rain streaks in the background while MSPFN [10] and DRDNet [2] even leaves behind traces of rain streaks. To sum up, our proposed model can adapt various rainy condition and restore image details and texture information better.

### 4.4   Ablation Study

In this section, we analyse the proposed model by conducting various experiments on Rain200H [28] datasets.

We analyze the network designment that consist of different attention modules, different location for residual attention connection, different recurrent stage numbers, different unsupervised losses. The experiment results are illustrated in Table 3, Table 4 and Table 5;

We adopt four attention block in ablation experiments on condition of the residual attention location fixed on $j = 1, 3, 5$, such as SAN block [39], AFF block [36], SC block [17] and CA block [32]; Further more, as for different combinations of location for residual attentive connection (RC), we set four experiments on different location, such as $j = 1, 2, 3$, $j = 2, 3, 4$, $j = 3, 4, 5$ and $j = 1, 3, 5$; To explore whether unsupervised losses with HWT can play a key role in the clean background predication, we set four experiments with $L_{HH}$, $L_{HL}$, $L_{LH}$ and without HWT operation.

**Table 3.** The results of different modules on Rain200H. The best results are highlighted in boldface.

| Experiments | E1 | E2 | E3 | E4 | E5 | E6 | E7 | E8 |
|---|---|---|---|---|---|---|---|---|
| Single SAN Block | ✓ | | | | | | | |
| Single AFF Block | | ✓ | | | | | | |
| Single SC Block | | | ✓ | | | | | |
| Single CA Block | | | | ✓ | ✓ | ✓ | ✓ | ✓ |
| RA Connection on Location 1, 2, 3 | | | | | ✓ | | | |
| RA Connection on Location 2, 3, 4 | | | | | | ✓ | | |
| RA Connection on Location 3, 4, 5 | | | | | | | ✓ | |
| RA Connection on Location 1, 3, 5 | ✓ | ✓ | ✓ | ✓ | | | | ✓ |
| PSNR | 28.871 | 27.423 | 28.581 | 28.903 | 28.646 | 28.587 | 28.398 | **28.903** |
| SSIM | 0.9066 | 0.8882 | 0.9027 | 0.9074 | 0.9054 | 0.9046 | 0.9042 | **0.9074** |

**Table 4.** The results of different stage numbers on Rain200H. The best results are highlighted in boldface.

| Experiments | E9 | E10 | E11 | E12 | E13 | E14 | E15 | E16 | E17 |
|---|---|---|---|---|---|---|---|---|---|
| 1 Recurrent Stage | ✓ | | | | | | | | |
| 2 Recurrent Stage | | ✓ | | | | | | | |
| 3 Recurrent Stage | | | ✓ | | | | | | |
| 4 Recurrent Stage | | | | ✓ | | | | | |
| 5 Recurrent Stage | | | | | ✓ | | | | |
| 6 Recurrent Stage | | | | | | ✓ | | | |
| 7 Recurrent Stage | | | | | | | ✓ | | |
| 8 Recurrent Stage | | | | | | | | ✓ | |
| 9 Recurrent Stage | | | | | | | | | ✓ |
| PSNR | 25.753 | 26.392 | 27.501 | 27.761 | 28.073 | 28.277 | 28.346 | **28.903** | 28.760 |
| SSIM | 0.8732 | 0.8817 | 0.8914 | 0.8949 | 0.8986 | 0.8991 | 0.9006 | **0.9074** | 0.9062 |

**Analysis on Single Attentive Block.** We adopted four different blocks, such as self-attention block [39] (SAN), attention fusion feature block [36] (AFF), self-calibrated block [17] (SC) and convolution attention block [32] (CA); When the residual attention position is fixed on $j = 1, 3, 5$, the experiment results proves that CA block can achieve better performance.

**Analysis on Different Residual Attentive Connection.** In order to explore the connection of residual attention output from rain space to image space, we conducted experiments on Rain200H to validate the effectiveness of different connections. We set four experiments on different connection location, namely $j = 1, 2, 3$, $j = 2, 3, 4$, $j = 3, 4, 5$ and $j = 1, 3, 5$. The experimental results show that the location $j = 1, 3, 5$ can achieve best results on Table 3.

**Analysis on the Number of Recurrent Stage.** As the number of recurrent stage increasing, the separation of a background layer and its rain streak layer

Input     $L_{HH}$     $L_{HL}$     $L_{LH}$     AID     AID-HWT

**Fig. 5.** Examples about the comparison of different unsupervised losses on $Real_{275}$.

tends to be obvious. In order to discover the optimal value of the recurrent stage number, we set the stage $T = 1, 2, 3, 4, 5, 6, 7, 8, 9$; The experiments results verified that the stage $T = 8$ achieve the best performance in terms of PSNR and SSIM, whose specific results are shown on Table 4.

**Analysis on Unsupervised Losses.** At the stage of semi-supervised training, in order to show the effectiveness of DWT discriminative loss, we conduct experiments with $Loss_{HH}$, $Loss_{HL}$, $Loss_{LH}$ and No-DWT that is our AID model. As shown in Table 5, we set four different experiments to verify the unsupervised losses effectiveness on $Real_{275}$ datasets. Our final results also confirm that calculating the adversial losses of $f_{HH}$, $f_{HL}$ and $f_{LH}$ between real-world clean image and the generated clean background are more beneficial to image restoration.

**Table 5.** The analysis on unsupervised losses.

| Experiments | $L_{HH}$ | $L_{HL}$ | $L_{LH}$ | AID | AID-DWT |
|---|---|---|---|---|---|
| PSNR | 28.557 | 28.574 | 28.491 | 28.548 | **28.903** |
| SSIM | 0.9040 | 0.9030 | 0.9028 | 0.9042 | **0.9074** |

## 5   Conclusion

In this work, we proposed a semi-supervised approach with residual attention based on Haar wavelet transform to tackle image deraining, i.e., AID-DWT. We design two sets of multi-layer residual block combined with the LSTM network to divide the rainy image into streak layer space and image layer space, and connect the two spaces through the residual attention block to accelerate the convergence and removal of rain features in image layer space. Moreover, we simultaneously calculate the adversarial losses on $f_{HH}$, $f_{HL}$ and $f_{LH}$ between real-world clean image and restored background image to better predict clean background image. Extensive experiments on synthetic and real-world benchmark datasets have validated the effectiveness of our AID-DWT, which quantitatively and qualitatively outperforms existing semi-supervised deraining methods and state-of-the-art supervised deraining methods. In future work, the proposed semi-supervised framework has the potential to be extended to other relevant low-level vision tasks, e.g., blind image denoising.

# References

1. Chen, Y., Hsu, C.: A generalized low-rank appearance model for spatio-temporally correlated rain streaks. In: IEEE ICCV (2013)
2. Deng, S., et al.: Detail-recovery image deraining via context aggregation networks. In: IEEE CVPR, pp. 14548–14557 (2020)
3. Fan, Z., Wu, H., Fu, X., Hunag, Y., Ding, X.: Residual-guide feature fusion network for single image deraining. In: ACM MM, pp. 1751–1759 (2018)
4. Fu, X., Liang, B., Huang, Y., Ding, X., Paisley, J.: Lightweight pyramid networks for image deraining. In: IEEE TNNLS (2020)
5. Fu, X., Huang, J., Ding, X., Liao, Y., Paisley, J.: Clearing the skies: a deep network architecture for single-image rain removal. IEEE TIP $26(6)$, 2944–2956 (2017)
6. Fu, X., Huang, J., Zeng, D., Huang, Y., Ding, X., Paisley, J.: Removing rain from single images via a deep detail network. In: IEEE CVPR, pp. 1715–1723 (2017)
7. Fu, X., Liang, B., Huang, Y., Ding, X., Paisley, J.: Lightweight pyramid networks for image deraining. IEEE TNNLS $31(6)$, 1–14 (2019)
8. Chen, H., et al.: Pre-trained image processing transformer. arXiv:2012.00364 (2021)
9. Huynh-Thu, Q., Ghanbari, M.: Scope of validity of PSNR in image/video quality assessment. Electron. Lett. $44(13)$, 800–801 (2008)
10. Jiang, K., et al.: Multi-scale progressive fusion network for single image deraining. In: IEEE CVPR, pp. 8343–8352 (2020)
11. Kang, L., Lin, C., Fu, Y.: Automatic single-image-based rain streaks removal via image decomposition. In: IEEE TIP (2012)
12. Kingma, D.P., Ba, J.: Adam: a method for stochastic optimization. In: ICLR (2015)
13. Li, G., He, X., Zhang, W., Chang, H., Dong, L., Lin, L.: Non-locally enhanced encoder-decoder network for single image de-raining. In: ACM MM, pp. 1056–1064 (2018)
14. Li, X., Wu, J., Lin, Z., Liu, H., Zha, H.: Recurrent squeeze-and-excitation context aggregation net for single image deraining. In: Ferrari, V., Hebert, M., Sminchisescu, C., Weiss, Y. (eds.) ECCV 2018. LNCS, vol. 11211, pp. 262–277. Springer, Cham (2018). https://doi.org/10.1007/978-3-030-01234-2_16
15. Li, Y., Tan, R.T., Guo, X., Lu, J., Brown, M.S.: Rain streak removal using layer priors. In: IEEE CVPR, pp. 2736–2744 (2016)
16. Li, Y., Tan, R.T., Guo, X., Lu, J., Brown, M.S.: Rain streak removal using layer priors (2016)
17. Liu, J.J., Hou, Q., Cheng, M.M., Wang, C., Feng, J.: Improving convolutional networks with self-calibrated convolutions. In: IEEE CVPR, pp. 10093–10102 (2020)
18. Luo, Y., Xu, Y., Ji, H.: Removing rain from a single image via discriminative sparse coding. In: IEEE ICCV (2015)
19. Mallat, S.G.: A theory for multiresolution signal decomposition: the wavelet representation. IEEE TPAMI $11(7)$, 674–693 (1989)
20. Mittal, A., Soundararajan, R., Bovik, A.C.: Making a "completely blind" Image quality analyzer. IEEE Sig. Process. Lett. $20$, 209–212 (2013)
21. Pan, J., Hu, Z., Su, Z., Yang, M.: $l_0$-regularized intensity and gradient prior for deblurring text images and beyond. In: IEEE TPAMI (2017)

22. Pang, B., Zhai, D., Jiang, J., Liu, X.: Single image deraining via scale-space invariant attention neural network. In: ACM MM, pp. 375–383 (2020)
23. Paszke, A., et al.: Automatic differentiation in pytorch. In: NIPS Autodiff Workshop The Future of Gradient-based Machine Learning Software and Techniques
24. Ren, D., Shang, W., Zhu, P., Hu, Q., Meng, D., Zuo, W.: Single image deraining using bilateral recurrent network. IEEE TIP **29**, 6852–6863 (2020)
25. Ren, D., Zuo, W., Zhang, D., Zhang, L., Yang, M.: Simultaneous fidelity and regularization learning for image restoration. IEEE TPAMI **43**(1), 284–299 (2019)
26. Ren, D., Zuo, W., Hu, Q., Zhu, P., Meng, D.: Progressive image deraining networks: a better and simpler baseline. In: IEEE CVPR (2019)
27. Wang, T., et al.: Spatial attentive single-image deraining with a high quality real rain dataset. In: IEEE CVPR (2019)
28. Yang, W., et al.: Deep joint rain detection and removal from a single image. In: IEEE CVPR, pp. 1357–1366 (2017)
29. Wang, C., Wu, Y., Su, Z., Chen, J.: Joint self-attention and scale-aggregation for self-calibrated deraining network. In: ACM MM, pp. 2517–2525 (2019)
30. Wang, C., Xing, X., Wu, Y., Su, Z., Chen, J.: DCSFN: deep cross-scale fusion network for single image rain removal. In: ACM MM, pp. 1643–1651 (2019)
31. Wei, W., Meng, D., Zhao, Q., Xu, Z., Wu, Y.: Semi-supervised transfer learning for image rain removal. In: IEEE CVPR, pp. 3872–3881 (2019)
32. Woo, S., Park, J., Lee, J.-Y., Kweon, I.S.: CBAM: convolutional block attention module. In: Ferrari, V., Hebert, M., Sminchisescu, C., Weiss, Y. (eds.) ECCV 2018. LNCS, vol. 11211, pp. 3–19. Springer, Cham (2018). https://doi.org/10.1007/978-3-030-01234-2_1
33. Li, X., et al.: Recurrent squeeze-and-excitation context aggregation net for single image deraining. In: ECCV, pp. 2736–2744 (2016)
34. Yang, Y., Lu, H.: Single image deraining via recurrent hierarchy enhancement network. In: ACM MM, pp. 1814–1822 (2019)
35. Yasarla, R., Sindagi, V.A., Patel, V.M.: Syn2real transfer learning for image deraining using gaussian processes. In: IEEE CVPR, pp. 2723–2733 (2020)
36. Dai, Y., Gieseke, F., Oehmcke, S., Wu, Y., Barnard, K.: Attentional feature fusion. In: IEEE WACV (2021)
37. Zhang, H., Patel, V.M.: Density-aware single image de-raining using a multi-stream dense network. In: IEEE CVPR, pp. 695–704 (2018)
38. Zhang, H., Sindagi, V., Patel, V.M.: Image de-raining using a conditional generative adversarial network. IEEE TCSVT **30**(11), 3943–3956 (2019)
39. Zhao, H., Jia, J., Koltun, V.: Exploring self-attention for image recognition. In: IEEE CVPR (2020)
40. Wang, Z., Bovik, A.C., Sheikh, H.R., Simoncelli, E.P.: Image quality assessment: from error visibility to structural similarity. IEEE TIP **13**(4), 600–612 (2004)
41. Zhu, H., Wang, C., Zhang, Y., Su, Z., Zhao, G.: Physical model guided deep image deraining. In: IEEE ICME, pp. 1–6 (2020)
42. Zhu, H., et al.: Singe image rain removal with unpaired information: a differentiable programming perspective. In: AAAI, pp. 9332–9339 (2019)
43. Zhu, J., Park, T., Isola, P., Efros, A.A.: Unpaired image-to-image translation using cycle-consistent adversarial networks. In: IEEE ICCV, pp. 2242–2251 (2017)

# Simple Light-Weight Network for Human Pose Estimation

Bin Sun[1] and Mingguo Zhao[2]([✉])

[1] Beijing Research Institute of UBTECH, Beijing, China
[2] Department of Automation, Center for Brain-Inspired Computing Research (CBICR), Tsinghua University, Beijing, China
mgzhao@mail.tsinghua.edu.cn

**Abstract.** Human pose estimation has achieved significant improvement. However, most existing methods mainly consider how to improve the model performance using complex architecture or computationally expensive model, ignoring the deployment costs in practice, especially in human-robot interaction. In this paper, we investigate a highly efficient pose estimation model with comparable accuracy. We propose an adaptive convolution, which can adaptively generate one or more feature maps with desired channels. Since redundant information in the feature map is an important characteristic, to preserve the redundant information while taking only a few numbers of FLOPs and parameters, we propose a light-weight block based on adaptive convolution, which is performed with two parallel convolution operations. And then, to further reduce the FLOPs, we propose heterogeneous filters based light-weight block, which contains two different kinds of filters in each layer. Finally, three light-weight units are designed to stack light-weight block, and a simple light-weight pose estimation network (SLPE) can be easily established. Extensive evaluations demonstrate the advantages of SLPE over state-of-the-art methods in terms of model cost-effectiveness on the standard benchmark datasets, MPII and COCO dataset.

**Keywords:** Pose estimation · Adaptive convolution · Light-weight network

## 1 Introduction

Human pose estimation (HPE) is an important research issue in the field of human-robot interaction, which can better understand human behavior and recognize activity [6,22,23,25]. The aim of HPE is to accurately locate the positions of human keypoints (e.g., elbow, wrist, etc.) or parts from images. Similar to many vision tasks, deep learning technology makes significant progress in HPE [8,10,13,15]. The improvement of model performance comes from more complex and deeper network architecture and a large number of parameters and floating point operations (FLOPs). However, these models have poor scalability,

D. N. Pham et al. (Eds.): PRICAI 2021, LNAI 13033, pp. 279–292, 2021.
https://doi.org/10.1007/978-3-030-89370-5_21

and cannot be applied to mobiles and robots. Thus, it is an inevitable trend to explore a light-weight human pose estimation.

The existing methods for exploring the light-weight model can be divided into two categories. The first approach is to use model compression, such as quantization [9], pruning [11], etc. Quantization based methods can map multiple weights to the same value for weight sharing. However, during inference shared weights need to be restored to their original positions, it cannot save run-time memory. Pruning based methods can reduce redundant connections in a pre-trained model, and the model is usually finetuned to maintain its performance, which requires expensive training and is a costly process.

The second approach is to establish an efficient architecture by designing efficient convolution operation [7,12,27]. We observe that AlexNet [16] first proposed group convolution, which distributes the model over two GPUs. As a special form, depthwise convolution was proposed in Xception [7], which has been well demonstrated its effectiveness in MobileNet [12]. Depthwise convolution requires the same input and output channels, so a $1 \times 1$ pointwise convolution is usually added before or after this layer. In this case, it is inevitable to decompose a convolutional layer into two or three sequential layers. For example, a unit in MobileNet splits each standard convolutional layer into two layers sequentially, which first use depthwise convolution and then pointwise convolution. The strategy reduces parameters and FLOPs, but latency[1] occurred.

In this paper, to improve the efficiency of pose estimation with comparable accuracy results, we propose a new simple light-weight human pose estimation method. Specifically, combining the advantages of depthwise convolution (DWC) and groupwise convolution (GWC), we propose adaptive convolution, which can adaptively obtain features with desired channels. Based on the new convolution form, a light-weight block (LWB) is presented. Different from MobileNet, which decomposes a convolutional layer into two sequential layers, we decompose a convolutional layer into two parallel layers, which are responsible for the information exchange of several channels and all channels, respectively. This light-weight block can well reduce FLOPs and parameters with low latency. To further reduce FLOPs and parameters, we propose a heterogeneous filter based light-weight block (HFLWB). Different from traditional methods, which contain the same filter in each layer, heterogeneous filters based HFLWB contain different filters in each layer. Our proposed LWB/HFLWB is a generic way, which can be easily deployed as a plug-and-play block to replace standard convolution, without the need of changing network architectures. Based on two different light-weight blocks, we establish an efficient neural architecture for pose estimation. Experimental results show that the proposed light-weight pose estimation model can decrease computational costs while preserving comparable performance. Our contributions can be summarized as follows:

---

[1] If one parallel step is converted to multiple sequential steps, it means increasing the latency. Because all computations have to be done sequentially across layers, the latter layer needs to be executed after the previous layer is executed.

- We propose adaptive convolution, which can adaptively obtain features with desired channels.
- We propose a light-weight block, which decomposes a convolutional layer into two parallel layers, one of which is the layer of information exchange between channels, and the other is the layer of information exchange within channels.
- We propose heterogeneous filters based light-weight block (HFLWB), which contains two different kinds of filters in each layer.

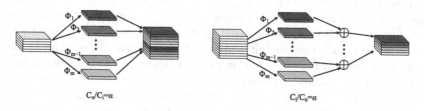

**Fig. 1.** The illustration of adaptive convolution.

## 2   Methodology

In this section, we first introduce the adaptive convolution, and then describe two different light-weight blocks. Finally, we describe network architecture details, and show how to integrate light-weight block into pose estimation architecture.

### 2.1   Adaptive Convolution

For standard convolutional layer, we assume the size of input feature map $\mathbf{X}$ is $H_i \times W_i \times C_i$, where $H_i$ and $W_i$ is the height and width of input feature map, and $C_i$ is the number of input channels. The operation of convolutional layer is as follows:

$$\mathbf{Y} = \mathbf{W} * \mathbf{X} \tag{1}$$

where $*$ is the convolution operation, the bias term is omitted for simplicity, $\mathbf{Y} \in R^{H_o \times W_o \times C_o}$ is output feature map, $H_o$ and $W_o$ is the height and width of output feature map, $C_o$ is the number of output channels, $\mathbf{W} \in R^{C_i \times K \times K \times C_o}$ is convolution filters, $K$ the size of kernel. Therefore, the total computational cost is $H_o \times W_o \times K \times K \times C_i \times C_o$. Since the number of channels ($C_i$) and convolution filters ($C_o$) are very large, the computational cost of standard convolution is as large as hundreds of thousands.

To reduce the computational cost, we propose adaptive convolution (AC), which can use linear operation on each input feature map to adaptively generate multiple feature maps from one input feature map or merge multiple input feature maps into one feature map. Adaptive convolution can be formulated as

$$\mathbf{Y}_{[m]} = \sum_{j=m\alpha}^{m\alpha+\alpha-1} \mathbf{\Phi}_m\left(\mathbf{X}_{[j]}\right), if \ \ C_i/C_o = \alpha$$

$$\mathbf{Y}_{[(m\alpha):(m\alpha+\alpha-1)]} = \mathbf{\Phi}_m\left(\mathbf{X}_{[m]}\right), if \ \ C_o/C_i = \alpha \tag{2}$$

where $\alpha > 0$ represents scaling factor, $\mathbf{X}$ and $\mathbf{Y}$ represents input feature map and output feature map, respectively. $\mathbf{Y}_{[m]}$ represents feature of channel $m$, $\mathbf{Y}_{[(m\alpha):(m\alpha+\alpha-1)]} = [\mathbf{Y}_{[m\alpha]}, \mathbf{Y}_{[m\alpha+1]}, \mathbf{Y}_{[m\alpha+2]}, \ldots, \mathbf{Y}_{[m\alpha+\alpha-1]}]$ represents a set of multiple feature maps. $\mathbf{\Phi}_m$ represents $m$-th linear operation for generating feature map. Thus, we can obtain $C_o$ output feature maps from $C_i$ input feature maps by Eq. 2 as shown in Fig. 1. By using linear operations, the total computational cost of adaptive convolution is $H_o \times W_o \times K \times K \times C_i \times C_o)/min(C_i, C_o)$. We can observe that the computational cost of adaptive convolution is much less than the standard convolution. In practice, there could be several different linear operations in adaptive convolution, e.g. $3 \times 3$ and $5 \times 5$ linear kernels. In this paper, we use $3 \times 3$ linear kernels. Compared with DWC and GWC, adaptive convolution does not need to manually set the group number of each layer like GWC, nor does it require the same input and output channels as DWC. Furthermore, adaptive convolution has large diversity and has adaptive feature mapping.

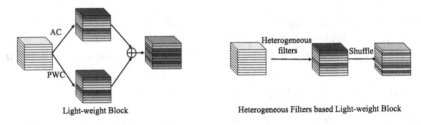

**Fig. 2.** The illustration of two different light-weight block.

## 2.2  Light-Weight Block

In this section, based on adaptive convolution, we propose a light-weight block (LWB) to replace the standard convolution. As we all know, redundant information in the feature map can better understand the input data. Thus, our light-weight block preserves the advantage while taking only a few FLOPs and parameters. For light-weight block, the feature map will perform two parallel convolution operations. For one convolution operation, adaptive convolution is utilized, which describes the spatial feature of each channel and the information exchange within adjacent feature maps. For the other convolution operation, pointwise convolution (PWC) is utilized, which describes the features of each point and the information exchange across channels. The light-weight block is illustrated in Fig. 2, and the formula is as follows:

$$\mathbf{Y} = \mathbf{W}' * \mathbf{X} + \mathbf{\Phi}(\mathbf{X}) \tag{3}$$

where $\mathbf{W}'$ is $1 \times 1$ convolution filters. Since our light-weight block is a plug-and-play block, we can easily replace the standard convolution or other convolution with the light-weight block in existing neural architectures. Here we further analyze the profit on memory usage and theoretical speed-up when using light-weight block. The theoretical speed-up ratio of standard convolution with the light-weight block is

$$
\frac{H_o \times W_o \times K \times K \times C_i \times C_o}{H_o \times W_o \times C_i \times C_o + H_o \times W_o \times K \times K \times C_i \times C_o / min(C_i, C_o)}
$$
$$
= \frac{K \times K}{1 + K \times K / min(C_i, C_o)} = \frac{K \times K \times min(C_i, C_o)}{min(C_i, C_o) + K \times K} \approx K^2 \tag{4}
$$

where $K \ll min(C_i, C_o)$. The compression ratio in parameters is equal to the speed-up ratio, since they are proportional to each other.

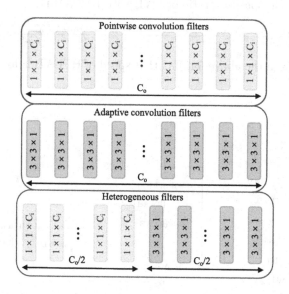

**Fig. 3.** Comparison between the proposed heterogeneous filters with other filters.

## 2.3    Heterogeneous Filters Based Light-Weight Block

In light-weight block, each layer uses the same filter. To further reduce the number of FLOPs and parameters, we propose heterogeneous filters based light-weight block (HFLWB), which contains two different kinds of filters in each layer. Figure 3 shows pointwise convolution filters, adaptive convolution filters and heterogeneous filters. From the figure we can see that our proposed heterogeneous filter consists of pointwise convolution filters and adaptive convolution filters, each of which contains $C_o/2$ filters. Based on heterogeneous filters, the architecture of HFLWB is shown in Fig. 2. HFLWB operates using heterogeneous filters. However, the operation is limited to respective filters, the information flow of the model is restricted to the respective filter. In other words, there is no information exchange between feature maps using adaptive convolution filters and feature maps using pointwise convolution filters. Therefore, it is necessary to introduce a mechanism for information exchange. To tackle the problem, channel shuffle is used. Thus, the formula of HFLWB is as follows:

$$\mathbf{Y} = \mathbf{\Gamma}(\mathbf{\Psi}(\mathbf{X})) \tag{5}$$

where $\mathbf{\Psi}$ is heterogeneous filters, $\mathbf{\Gamma}$ is shuffle operation. The theoretical speed-up ratio of standard convolution with HFLWB is

$$\frac{H_o \times W_o \times K \times K \times C_i \times C_o}{(H_o \times W_o \times C_i \times C_o)/4 + H_o \times W_o \times K \times K \times C_i \times C_o/4\,min(C_i,C_o)}$$
$$= \frac{4K \times K}{1 + K \times K/min(C_i,C_o)} = \frac{4\,K \times K \times min(C_i,C_o)}{min(C_i,C_o) + K \times K} \approx 4K^2 \tag{6}$$

and the theoretical speed-up ratio of LWB with HFLWB is

$$\frac{H_o \times W_o \times C_i \times C_o + H_o \times W_o \times K \times K \times C_i \times C_o/min(C_i,C_o)}{(H_o \times W_o \times C_i \times C_o)/4 + H_o \times W_o \times K \times K \times C_i \times C_o/4\,min(C_i,C_o)} = 4 \tag{7}$$

It can be seen from the above formula that speed of HFLWB is four times faster than LWB.

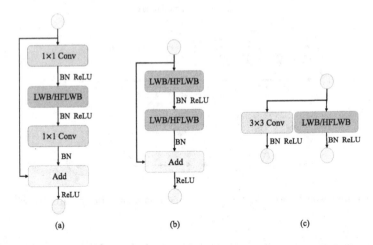

**Fig. 4.** Detail light-weight units. a) Light-weight residual unit; b) Light-weight basic unit; c) Light-weight interface unit.

## 2.4   Network Architecture

The common pipeline to predict human keypoints is composed of a stem consisting of two strided convolutions decreasing the resolution, the main body with input and output feature maps of the same resolution, and a regressor estimating the heatmaps where the keypoint positions are chosen and transformed to the full resolution. We mainly focus on the light-weight of the main body. We follow the main body of HRNet [20] for its superiority. We describe the HRNet here, and more details can be found in [20]. HRNet starts with a high resolution branch in the 1st stage, and maintains high-resolution representations through the whole process. In every following stage, a new branch is added to current branches in parallel with 1/2 of the lowest resolution in current branches. The network starts from a stem that consists of two strided 3 × 3 convolutions decreasing the resolution to 1/4. The 1st stage contains 4 residual units where each unit is formed by a bottleneck with the width 64, and followed by one 3 × 3 convolution reducing the width of feature maps to 32. The 2nd, 3rd, 4th stages contain 1, 4, and 3 multi-resolution blocks, respectively. The widths of the convolutions of the four resolutions are 32, 64, 128, and 256, respectively. Each multi-resolution block has 4 basic units and each unit has two 3 × 3 convolutions in each resolution.

We adopt HRNet backbone as our baseline. Following its design principles, we present a simple light-weight pose estimation network (SLPE). Different from HRNet, we replace the three units used in HRNet backbone with our proposed three light-weight units based on LWB or HFLWB. The three units are residual units in the 1st stage, basic units in the 2nd, 3rd and 4th stages, and interface units between two adjacent stages. We will take LWB as an example to introduce these three units. For residual unit, we do not directly replace it with light-weight block, and embed our light-weight block in residual units as shown in Fig. 4(a). Similarly, we embed our light-weight block in basic unit as shown in Fig. 4(b). For interface unit, we only replace convolution outputting the feature maps with the same resolution as its input feature maps as shown in Fig. 4(c). HFLWB can also be directly replaced with the corresponding position of light-weight block. It must be noted that our proposed lightweight block can be applied to any arbitrary pose estimation model according to the needs.

## 3   Experiments

### 3.1   Experiment Setup

We evaluate the proposed method on two public available human pose benchmark datasets: MPII dataset [1] and COCO dataset [17]. In our experiments, we study two different pose estimation networks. One is based on LWB, and the other one is based on HFLWB. For the convenience of description, the former is called SLPE and the latter is called SLPE-light.

**MPII Dataset.** The MPII dataset consists of around 25K images with 40K subjects (12K subjects for testing and the remaining subjects for training) labeled with 16 keypoints. The test annotations are not provided. So in all of our experiments, we train on a subset of training images while evaluating on a heldout validation set of around 3000 samples. These images are taken from a wide-range of real-world activities with full-body pose annotations. The standard evaluation metric is based on the PCKh (head-normalized probability of correct keypoint) score. The PCKh@0.5 ($\alpha = 0.5$) score is reported. During training, following [20], we crop the human detection box from the image, which is resized to a fixed size, $256 \times 256$, and use data augmentation, which includes random rotation ($[-45°;$ $45°]$), random scale ($[0.65, 1.35]$), and flipping. We use the Adam optimizer [14]. The base learning rate is set to 1e−3, and dropped to 1e−4 and 1e−5 at the 170th and 200th epochs, respectively. We train the model for a total of 210 epochs.

**COCO Dataset.** The COCO dataset consists of over 200,000 images and 250,000 person instances labeled with 17 keypoints. We train our model on COCO train2017 dataset, including 57K images and 150K person instances, and evaluate our method on the val2017 set containing 5000 images. The standard evaluation metric is based on Object Keypoint Similarity (OKS): $OKS = \frac{\sum_i \exp\left(-d_i^2/2s^2k_i^2\right)\delta(v_i>0)}{\sum_i \delta(v_i>0)}$. Here $d_i$ is the Euclidean distance between the detected keypoint and the corresponding ground truth, $v_i$ is the visibility flag of the ground truth, $s$ is the object scale, and $k_i$ is a per-keypoint constant that controls falloff. We report standard average precision and recall scores: $AP^{50}$ (AP at OKS = 0.50), $AP^{75}$, AP (the mean of AP scores at 10 positions, OKS = 0.50, 0.55, ..., 0.90, 0.95; $AP^M$ for medium objects, $AP^L$ for large objects, and AR at OKS = 0.50, 0.55, ..., 0.90, 0.955. The data augmentation and the training strategy are the same as MPII, except that the input size is cropped to $256 \times 192$.

**Table 1.** Comparisons on the MPII validation set (PCKh@0.5).

| Method | Hea | Sho | Elb | Wri | Hip | Kne | Ank | Total | #Params | GFLOPs |
|---|---|---|---|---|---|---|---|---|---|---|
| Large networks | | | | | | | | | | |
| 8-stage Hourglass | 96.5 | 96.0 | 90.3 | 85.4 | 88.8 | 85.0 | 81.9 | 89.2 | 25.1M | 19.1 |
| PRM [26] | 96.8 | 96.0 | 90.4 | 86.0 | 89.5 | 85.2 | 82.3 | 89.6 | 28.1M | 21.3 |
| DLCM [21] | 95.6 | 95.9 | 90.7 | 86.5 | 89.9 | 86.6 | 82.5 | 89.8 | 15.5M | 15.6 |
| SimpleBaseline [24] | 97.0 | 95.9 | 90.3 | 85.0 | 89.2 | 85.3 | 81.3 | 89.6 | 68.6M | 20.9 |
| HRNet-W32 [20] | 97.1 | 95.9 | 90.3 | 86.4 | 89.1 | 87.1 | 83.3 | 90.3 | 28.5M | 9.5 |
| Small networks | | | | | | | | | | |
| MobileNetV2 [29] | – | – | – | – | – | – | – | 85.4 | 9.6M | 1.97 |
| MobileNetV3 [28] | – | – | – | – | – | – | – | 84.3 | 8.7M | 1.82 |
| ShuffleNetV2 [18] | – | – | – | – | – | – | – | 82.8 | 7.6M | 1.70 |
| BCLL [2] | – | – | – | – | – | – | – | 85.5 | 6M | – |
| **SLPE** | 96.8 | 95.7 | 89.8 | 85.3 | 88.7 | 85.2 | 81.1 | 89.5 | 11.8M | 2.7 |
| **SLPE-light** | 96.6 | 95.2 | 88.5 | 82.8 | 88.0 | 82.7 | 78.3 | 88.1 | 4.6M | 1.6 |

**Table 2.** Comparisons on the COCO validation set. Pretrain = pretrain the backbone on the ImageNet classification task.

| Method | Backbone | Pretrain | #Params | GFLOPs | AP | $AP^{50}$ | $AP^{75}$ | $AP^M$ | $AP^L$ | AR |
|---|---|---|---|---|---|---|---|---|---|---|
| Large networks | | | | | | | | | | |
| 8-stage Hourglass [19] | 8-stage Hourglass | N | 25.1M | 14.3 | 66.9 | – | – | – | – | – |
| CPN [4] | ResNet-50 | Y | 27.0M | 6.20 | 68.6 | – | – | – | – | – |
| CPN + OHKM [4] | ResNet-50 | Y | 27.0M | 6.20 | 69.4 | – | – | – | – | – |
| Simple Baseline [24] | ResNet-50 | Y | 34.0M | 8.90 | 70.4 | 88.6 | 78.3 | 67.1 | 77.2 | 76.3 |
| Simple Baseline [24] | ResNet-101 | Y | 53.0M | 12.4 | 71.4 | 89.3 | 79.3 | 68.1 | 78.1 | 77.1 |
| Simple Baseline [24] | ResNet-152 | Y | 68.6M | 15.7 | 72.0 | 89.3 | 79.8 | 68.7 | 78.9 | 77.8 |
| HRNet-W32 [20] | HRNet-W32 | N | 28.5M | 7.10 | 73.4 | 89.5 | 80.7 | 70.2 | 80.1 | 78.9 |
| HRNet-W32 [20] | HRNet-W32 | Y | 28.5M | 7.10 | 74.4 | 90.5 | 81.9 | 70.8 | 81.0 | 79.8 |
| Small networks | | | | | | | | | | |
| Mobile NetV2 [29] | MobileNetV2 | Y | 9.6M | 1.48 | 64.6 | 87.4 | 72.3 | 61.1 | 71.2 | 70.7 |
| Shuffle NetV2 [18] | ShuffleNetV2 | Y | 7.6M | 1.28 | 59.9 | 85.4 | 66.3 | 56.6 | 66.2 | 66.4 |
| Small HRNet | HRNet-W16 | N | 1.3M | 0.54 | 55.2 | 83.7 | 62.4 | 52.3 | 61.0 | 62.1 |
| DY-Mobile NetV2 [30] | DY-MobileNetV2 | Y | 16.1M | 1.01 | 68.2 | 88.4 | 76.0 | 65.0 | 74.7 | 74.2 |
| DY-ReLU [31] | MobileNetV2 | Y | 9.0M | 1.03 | 68.1 | 88.5 | 76.2 | 64.8 | 74.3 | – |
| **SLPE** | SLPE | N | 11.8M | 2.06 | 72.2 | 89.2 | 79.5 | 68.5 | 78.9 | 77.7 |
| **SLPE-light** | SLPE | N | 4.6M | 1.22 | 67.7 | 87.6 | 75.8 | 64.2 | 74.2 | 73.8 |

## 3.2 Results

**Results on MPII.** We report the PCKh@0.5 accuracy results, the model size and the FLOPs of our method and other state-of-the-art methods in Table 1. It can be seen from the table that the proposed model has much fewer parameters and cost much fewer FLOPs with comparable results (better than 88.1%). Specifically, compared with the best method [20], the proposed model only requires 16.8%–28.4% (1.6/9.5–2.7/9.5) computational cost but gains 97.6%–99.1% (88.1/90.3–89.5/90.3) performance in mean PCKh accuracy. This leads to a 3.5×–5.8× (99.1/28.4–97.6/16.8) cost-effective advantage. Compared with other light-weight methods, it is obvious that SLPE-light outperforms others, which means that the method is efficient and has good generalization capability.

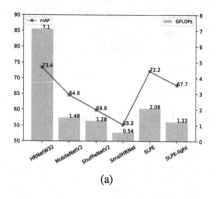
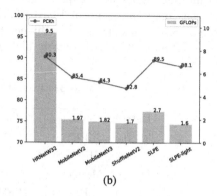

(a)                              (b)

**Fig. 5.** Illustration of the GFLOPs and accuracy comparison on the COCO val and MPII val sets. (a) Comparison on COCO val with 256 × 192 input size. (b) Comparison on MPII val with 256 × 256 input size.

**Results on COCO.** Table 2 shows the accuracy results, the model size and the FLOPs of the proposed method and state-of-the-art methods on the validation set of MSCOCO. Where Small HRNet simply reduces the depth and the width of the original HRNet. From the results, we can see that SLPE trained from scratch with the input size $256 \times 192$, achieves a 72.2 AP score, outperforming many methods, which pretrain the backbone on the ImageNet classification task. Compared to CPN and SimpleBaseline, SLPE trained from scratch, has much fewer model sizes and lower complexity, achieves 1.8–3.6 points gain. Compared to baseline HRNet, though our method has slightly worse performance, the number of the parameters and the FLOPs of ours are only 41.4% and 29% of HRNet, respectively. Our lighter network, SLPE-light, can further reduce the size of model and FLOPs with acceptable performance. Compared to Hourglass, which is also trained from scratch, SLPE-light improves AP by 0.8 points, and reduces 20.5M parameters, and the GFLOPs of SLPE-light are much lower and less than 10%. Compared to small networks, our methods are significantly better.

It can be seen from experiments on two datasets that SLPE-light is more suitable for MPII dataset. There are fewer people on each image in this dataset, and it is easier to estimate the pose, so a lighter model is enough. While COCO dataset is more challenging, so the performance of our large model, SLPE, will be more stable. Figure 5 shows the comparison of GFLOPs and accuracy. Our models achieve a better balance between accuracy and computational complexity.

### 3.3   Ablation Study

We perform some ablation study to analyze the proposed method on MPII validation set and COCO2017 validation set.

**Effect of Light Weight Block.** We test the effect of light-weight block, which consists of two parallel convolution operations. The contrast method is HRNet with sequential convolution operations (HRNet-SCO), i.e., depthwise followed by pointwise convolution. Similar to SLPE, we replace residual units, basic units, and interface units with sequential convolution. As shown in Table 3, HRNet-SCO has only 88.9% mean PCKh@0.5 on MPII, and 70.3% AP on COCO, whereas SLPE has significantly higher 89.5% mean PCKh@0.5 on MPII, and 72.2% AP on COCO with slightly higher model size and GFLOPs. The results

**Table 3.** Effect of light-weight block.

| Dataset | Method | #Params | GFLOPs | PCKh@0.5 |
|---------|-----------|---------|--------|----------|
| MPII    | SLPE      | 11.8M   | 2.7    | 89.5     |
|         | HRNet-SCO | 9.1M    | 2.4    | 88.9     |

| Dataset | Method | #Params | GFLOPs | AP |
|---------|-----------|---------|--------|------|
| COCO    | SLPE      | 11.8M   | 2.06   | 72.2 |
|         | HRNet-SCO | 9.1M    | 1.79   | 70.3 |

**Table 4.** Effect of adaptive convolution.

| Dataset | Method | #Params | GFLOPs | PCKh@0.5 |
|---------|--------|---------|--------|----------|
| MPII | Ours-GWC | 5.1M | 1.7 | 87.9 |
| | Ours-AC | 4.6M | 1.6 | 88.1 |

| Dataset | Method | #Params | GFLOPs | AP |
|---------|--------|---------|--------|----|
| COCO | Ours-GWC | 5.1M | 1.3 | 67.4 |
| | Ours-AC | 4.6M | 1.2 | 67.7 |

**Table 5.** Effect of shuffle (PCKh@0.5).

| Method | Shuffle | Hea | Sho | Elb | Wri | Hip | Kne | Ank | Total |
|--------|---------|-----|-----|-----|-----|-----|-----|-----|-------|
| Ours | × | 96.2 | 94.8 | 87.5 | 82.2 | 87.6 | 81.9 | 77.4 | 87.4 |
| Ours | √ | 97.0 | 94.9 | 87.8 | 82.4 | 88.1 | 82.6 | 78.2 | 87.9 |

mean that the fusion of information between and within channels in parallel layer is helpful for feature acquisition.

**Effect of Adaptive Convolution.** To evaluate the effect of adaptive convolution, we further test the performance of GWC based model, whose group number is 16. The results in Table 4 show that adaptive convolution is a better choice in comparison to GWC. Adaptive convolution with fewer parameters and GFLOPs can achieve slightly better performance. The plausible reason is that adaptive convolution can divide feature maps into as many groups as possible, allows for more channel information.

**Effect of Shuffle.** We further evaluate the effect of shuffle operation. Table 5 compares the performance of our method with/without channel shuffle. We can see that channel shuffle improves the performance, which shows the information exchange between the two branches can bring gain.

**Cost Effectiveness Analysis of the Depth.** We finally evaluate the effect of the depth. Table 6 shows the results of SLPE-light with different stages on MPII dataset. From the table we can see that removing more stages leads to performance degradation. When the 3rd, 4th stages and even 2nd stage were removed, performance deteriorated significantly. This indicates that multi-scale fusion is helpful and more fusions lead to better performance. If the 4th stage was removed, it leads to quite limited performance degradation, which is also an acceptable result.

### 3.4 Qualitative Results

To visualize the results, Fig. 6 shows qualitative evaluations on COCO. We can observe that our method can achieve reliable and robust pose estimation in arbitrary images with various background clutters and different human poses.

**Table 6.** Cost-effectiveness analysis of the depth on MPII dataset.

| Stage | #Params | GFLOPs | PCKh@0.5 |
|-------|---------|--------|----------|
| 4 | 4.6M | 1.6 | 88.1 |
| 3 | 1.6M | 1.5 | 86.3 |
| 2 | 0.5M | 1.2 | 71.6 |
| 1 | 0.2M | 0.7 | 46.8 |

**Fig. 6.** Qualitative results of some example images in COCO dataset.

## 4   Conclusion

In this paper, we propose a novel simple light-weight pose estimation network (SLPE). Different from most of the methods, which only focus on the performance of models and ignore the practicality, SLPE aims to improve the efficiency of pose estimation with comparable accuracy results. We have carried out extensive experiments on two datasets with the results suggesting the superiority of SLPE in comparison to state-of-the-art methods. Moreover, we have also conducted some ablation study to provide detailed analysis about the gains. Our proposed light-weight block is sufficiently generic to replace the regular convolution operation in-place without model architecture adjustment. It can be applied not only to HRNet, but also to other deep learning based pose estimation models, and even to deep learning methods in other fields. In future work, we will apply the light-weight block to other tasks, e.g., semantic segmentation, object detection, and design more efficient architectures.

## References

1. Andriluka, M., Pishchulin, L., Gehler, P., Schiele, B.: 2d human pose estimation: new benchmark and state of the art analysis. In: CVPR, pp. 3686–3693 (2014)

2. Bulat, A., Tzimiropoulos, G.: Binarized convolutional landmark localizers for human pose estimation and face alignment with limited resources. In: ICCV, pp. 3706–3714 (2017)
3. Cao, Z., Simon, T., Wei, S.-E., Sheikh, Y.: Realtime multi-person 2d pose estimation using part affinity fields. In: CVPR, pp. 7291–7299 (2017)
4. Chen, Y., Wang, Z., Peng, Y., Zhang, Z., Yu, G., Sun, J.: Cascaded pyramid network for multi-person pose estimation. In: CVPR, pp. 7103–7112 (2018)
5. Chen, Y., et al.: Drop an octave: reducing spatial redundancy in convolutional neural networks with octave convolution. In: ICCV, pp. 3435–3444 (2019)
6. Chéron, G., Laptev, I., Schmid, C.: P-CNN: pose-based CNN features for action recognition. In: ICCV, pp. 3218–3226 (2015)
7. Chollet, F.: Xception: deep learning with depthwise separable convolutions. In: CVPR, pp. 1251–1258 (2017)
8. Fang, H.-S., Xie, S., Tai, Y.-W., Lu, C.: RMPE: regional multi-person pose estimation. In: ICCV, pp. 2334–2343 (2017)
9. Han, S., Mao, H., Dally, W.J.: Deep compression: compressing deep neural networks with pruning, trained quantization and Huffman coding. In: ICLR, pp. 1–14 (2016)
10. He, K., Gkioxari, G., Dollár, P., Girshick, R.: Mask R-CNN. In: ICCV, pp. 2961–2969 (2017)
11. He, Y., Kang, G., Dong, X., Fu, Y., Yang, Y.: Soft filter pruning for accelerating deep convolutional neural networks. In: IJCAI, pp. 2234–2240 (2018)
12. Howard, A.G., et al.: MobileNets: efficient convolutional neural networks for mobile vision applications. arXiv preprint arXiv:1704.04861 (2017)
13. Huang, S., Gong, M., Tao, D.: A coarse-fine network for keypoint localization. In: ICCV, pp. 3028–3037 (2017)
14. Kingma, D.P., Ba, J.: Adam: a method for stochastic optimization. In: ICLR, pp. 1–15 (2015)
15. Kocabas, M., Karagoz, S., Akbas, E.: MultiPoseNet: fast multi-person pose estimation using pose residual network. In: Ferrari, V., Hebert, M., Sminchisescu, C., Weiss, Y. (eds.) ECCV 2018. LNCS, vol. 11215, pp. 437–453. Springer, Cham (2018). https://doi.org/10.1007/978-3-030-01252-6_26
16. Krizhevsky, A., Sutskever, I., Hinton, G.E.: ImageNet classification with deep convolutional neural networks. In: NIPS, pp. 1097–1105 (2012)
17. Lin, T.-Y., et al.: Microsoft COCO: common objects in context. In: Fleet, D., Pajdla, T., Schiele, B., Tuytelaars, T. (eds.) ECCV 2014. LNCS, vol. 8693, pp. 740–755. Springer, Cham (2014). https://doi.org/10.1007/978-3-319-10602-1_48
18. Ma, N., Zhang, X., Zheng, H.-T., Sun, J.: ShuffleNet V2: practical guidelines for efficient CNN architecture design. In: Ferrari, V., Hebert, M., Sminchisescu, C., Weiss, Y. (eds.) Computer Vision – ECCV 2018. LNCS, vol. 11218, pp. 122–138. Springer, Cham (2018). https://doi.org/10.1007/978-3-030-01264-9_8
19. Newell, A., Yang, K., Deng, J.: Stacked hourglass networks for human pose estimation. In: Leibe, B., Matas, J., Sebe, N., Welling, M. (eds.) ECCV 2016. LNCS, vol. 9912, pp. 483–499. Springer, Cham (2016). https://doi.org/10.1007/978-3-319-46484-8_29
20. Sun, K., Xiao, B., Liu, D., Wang, J.: Deep high-resolution representation learning for human pose estimation. In: CVPR, pp. 5693–5703 (2019)
21. Tang, W., Yu, P., Wu, Y.: Deeply learned compositional models for human pose estimation. In: Ferrari, V., Hebert, M., Sminchisescu, C., Weiss, Y. (eds.) ECCV 2018. LNCS, vol. 11207, pp. 197–214. Springer, Cham (2018). https://doi.org/10.1007/978-3-030-01219-9_12

22. Wan, B., Zhou, D., Liu, Y., Li, R., He, X.: Pose-aware multi-level feature network for human object interaction detection. In: ICCV, pp. 9469–9478 (2019)

23. Wang, C., Wang, Y., Yuille, A.L.: An approach to pose-based action recognition. In: CVPR, pp. 915–922 (2013)

24. Xiao, B., Wu, H., Wei, Y.: Simple baselines for human pose estimation and tracking. In: Ferrari, V., Hebert, M., Sminchisescu, C., Weiss, Y. (eds.) ECCV 2018. LNCS, vol. 11210, pp. 472–487. Springer, Cham (2018). https://doi.org/10.1007/978-3-030-01231-1_29

25. Yan, S., Xiong, Y., Lin, D.: Spatial temporal graph convolutional networks for skeleton-based action recognition. In: AAAI, pp. 7444–7452 (2018)

26. Yang, W., Li, S., Ouyang, W., Li, H., Wang, X.: Learning feature pyramids for human pose estimation. In: ICCV, pp. 1281–1290 (2017)

27. Zhang, X., Zhou, X., Lin, M., Sun, J.: ShuffleNet: an extremely efficient convolutional neural network for mobile devices. In: CVPR, pp. 6848–6856 (2018)

28. Howard, A., et al.: Searching for mobilenetv3. In: ICCV, pp. 1314–1324 (2019)

29. Andrew, H., Andrey, Z., Liang-Chieh, C., Mark, S., Menglong, Z.: Inverted residuals and linear bottlenecks: mobile networks for classification, detection and segmentation. In: CVPR, pp. 122–138 (2018)

30. Chen, Y., Dai, X., Liu, M., Chen, D., Yuan, L., Liu, Z.: Dynamic convolution: attention over convolution kernels. In: CVPR, pp. 11030–11039 (2020)

31. Chen, Y., Dai, X., Liu, M., Chen, D., Yuan, L., Liu, Z.: Dynamic ReLU. In: Vedaldi, A., Bischof, H., Brox, T., Frahm, J.-M. (eds.) ECCV 2020. LNCS, vol. 12364, pp. 351–367. Springer, Cham (2020). https://doi.org/10.1007/978-3-030-58529-7_21

# SIN: Superpixel Interpolation Network

Qing Yuan[1], Songfeng Lu[2,3]([✉]), Yan Huang[1], and Wuxin Sha[1]

[1] School of Computer Science and Technology, Huazhong University of Science and Technology, Wuhan, China
[2] School of Cyber Science and Engineering, Huazhong University of Science and Technology, Wuhan, China
[3] Shenzhen Huazhong University of Science and Technology Research Institute, Shenzhen, China
{yuanqing,lusongfeng,m201372777,d201980975}@hust.edu.cn

**Abstract.** Superpixels have been widely used in computer vision tasks due to their representational and computational efficiency. Meanwhile, deep learning and end-to-end framework have made great progress in various fields including computer vision. However, existing superpixel algorithms cannot be integrated into subsequent tasks in an end-to-end way. Traditional algorithms and deep learning-based algorithms are two main streams in superpixel segmentation. The former is non-differentiable and the latter needs a non-differentiable post-processing step to enforce connectivity, which constraints the integration of superpixels and downstream tasks. In this paper, we propose a deep learning-based superpixel segmentation algorithm SIN which can be integrated with downstream tasks in an end-to-end way. Owing to some downstream tasks such as visual tracking require real-time speed, the speed of generating superpixels is also important. To remove the post-processing step, our algorithm enforces spatial connectivity from the start. Superpixels are initialized by sampled pixels and other pixels are assigned to superpixels through multiple updating steps. Each step consists of a horizontal and a vertical interpolation, which is the key to enforcing spatial connectivity. Multi-layer outputs of a fully convolutional network are utilized to predict association scores for interpolations. Experimental results show that our approach runs at about 80 fps and performs favorably against state-of-the-art methods. Furthermore, we design a simple but effective loss function which reduces much training time. The improvements of superpixel-based tasks demonstrate the effectiveness of our algorithm. We hope SIN will be integrated into downstream tasks in an end-to-end way and benefit the superpixel-based community. Code is available at: https://github.com/yuanqqq/SIN.

**Keywords:** Superpixel · Spatial connectivity · Deep learning

© Springer Nature Switzerland AG 2021
D. N. Pham et al. (Eds.): PRICAI 2021, LNAI 13033, pp. 293–307, 2021.
https://doi.org/10.1007/978-3-030-89370-5_22

# 1  Introduction

Superpixels are small clusters of pixels that have similar intrinsic properties. Superpixels provide a perceptually meaningful representation of image data and reduce the number of image primitives for subsequent tasks. Owing to their representational and computational efficiency, superpixels are widely applied to computer vision tasks such as object detection [20,25], saliency detection [9,26,29], semantic segmentation [7,8,18] and visual tracking [24,27].

In common, superpixel-based tasks first generate superpixels of input images. Afterwards, features of superpixels are extracted and fed into subsequent steps. Since most superpixel algorithms cannot ensure spatial connectivity directly, we need to enforce spatial connectivity through a post-processing step before extracting superpixel features. Recently, deep neural networks and end-to-end framework have been widely adopted in computer vision owing to their effectiveness. However, existing superpixel segmentation algorithms cannot be combined with downstream tasks in an end-to-end way, which constrains the application of superpixels and the performance of superpixel-based tasks. We will demonstrate the limitations of existing superpixel segmentation algorithms in the following.

Existing superpixel segmentation algorithms can be divided into traditional and deep learning-based branches. Traditional superpixel segmentation algorithms [1,2,4,6,13,16] mainly rely on hand-crafted features. They are not trainable and cannot be integrated to subsequent deep learning methods in an end-to-end way obviously. Not to mention that most traditional algorithms run at a low speed, which affects the speed of downstream tasks heavily. While few attempts have been made [10,23,28], utilizing deep networks to extract superpixels remains challenging. [10,23] use a deep network to extract pixel features, followed by a superpixel segmentation module. FCN [28] proposes a network to directly generate superpixels and enforce connectivity as a post-processing step. All these methods need a post-processing step to handle orphan pixels and the step is non-differentiable. The post-processing step hinders existing deep learning-based algorithms to be combined with superpixel-based tasks in an end-to-end way. In fact, most traditional algorithms also need post-process to enforce spatial connectivity.

In this paper, we aim to propose a superpixel segmentation algorithm which can be integrated into downstream tasks in an end-to-end way. The speed of generating superpixels is also very important, because some downstream tasks such as visual tracking require real-time speed. Since the post-processing step is the main obstacle of existing deep learning-based methods, we enforce spatial connectivity from the start to remove the step. Without the post-processing step, not only the algorithm becomes a whole trainable network, but also the speed is faster. Our initial superpixels are initialized with sampled pixels and remaining pixels are assigned to superpixels through multiple similar steps. Each step consists of a horizontal and a vertical interpolation. According to current pixel-superpixel map and association scores, the interpolations assign partial pixels to superpixels. The pixel-superpixel map represents the map between pixels and superpixels, and the association scores are predicted by the multi-layer outputs of a fully convolutional network. The rule of interpolations is the key to enforcing spatial connectivity and we will prove it in Sect. 3.3. Furthermore, we design a simple but effective loss function that can reduce training time and fully utilize segmentation labels.

Extensive experiments have been conducted to evaluate SIN. Our method is the fastest compared to existing deep learning-based algorithms(running at about 80 fps), which means it satisfies the instantaneity of downstream tasks. For superpixel segmentation, experimental results on public benchmarks such as BSDS500 [3] and NYUv2 [21] demonstrate that our method performs favorably against the state-of-the-art in a variety of metrics. For semantic segmentation and saliency object detection, we replace superpixels in the original BI [7] and SO [29] with ours. The results on PascalVOC 2012 test set [5] and ECSSD dataset [19] show that SIN superpixels benefit these downstream vision tasks.

In summary, the main contributions of this paper are:

- We propose a superpixel segmentation network which can be integrated into downstream tasks in an end-to-end way, which does not need post-processing to handle orphan pixels. Our algorithm enforces spatial connectivity from the first instead of using a non-differentiable post-processing step. To the best of our knowledge, we are the first to develop a deep learning-based method to be integrated into superpixel-based tasks in an end-to-end way.
- We analyze the runtime of deep learning-based superpixel algorithms and our model has the fastest speed. When utilizing our SIN superpixels in subsequent tasks, the instantaneity will not be destroyed. Extensive experiments show that our method performs well in superpixel segmentation especially in generating more compact superpixels.
- We design a simple but effective loss function that fully utilizes the segmentation label. The loss function is computational efficiency and shortens plenty of training time.

## 2   Related Work

### 2.1   Traditional Superpixel Segmentation

Traditional superpixel segmentation algorithms can be roughly categorized as graph-based and clustering-based algorithms. Graph-based algorithms treat image pixels as graph nodes and pixel affinities as graph edges. Usually, superpixel segmentation problems are solved by graph-partitioning. [16] applies the Normalized Cuts algorithm to produce the superpixel map. FH [6] defines an adaptive segmentation criterion to capture global image properties. ERS [13] proposes an objective function for superpixel segmentation, which consists of the entropy rate and the balancing term.

Clustering-based algorithms utilize clustering methods such as $k$-means for superpixel segmentation. SEEDS [4] starts from an initial superpixel partitioning and continuously exchanges pixels on the boundaries between neighboring superpixels. SLIC [1] adopts a $k$-means clustering approach to generate super-pixels based on a 5-dimensional positional and *Lab* color features. Owing to its simplicity and high performance, there are many variants [2,11,14] of SLIC. LSC [11] projects the 5-dimensional features to a 10-dimensional space and per-forms weighted $k$-means in the projected space. Manifold-SLIC [14] maps the image to 2-dimensional manifold feature space for superpixel clustering. SNIC [2] proposes a non-iterative scheme for superpixel segmentation. Traditional super-pixel algorithms are mainly based on hand-crafted features, which often fail to preserve weak object boundaries. Most traditional algorithms are computed on CPU, so it is hard to achieve real-time speed. What's more, we cannot integrate traditional methods into subsequent tasks in an end-to-end way because they are non-differentiable.

### 2.2 Superpixel Segmentation Using DNN

Recently, some researchers have focused on integrating deep networks into superpixel segmentation algorithms [10,23,28]. [10,23] use a deep network to extract pixel features, which are then fed to a superpixel segmentation module. SEAL [23] develops the Pixel Affinity Net for affinity prediction and defines a new loss function which takes the segmentation error into account. These affinities are then passed to a graph-based algorithm to generate superpixels. To form an end-to-end trainable network, SSN [10] turns SLIC into a differentiable algorithm by relaxing the nearest neighbors' constraints. FCN [28] combines feature extraction and superpixel segmentation into a single step. The proposed method employs a fully convolutional network to predict association scores between image pixels and regular grid cells. When utilizing superpixels generated by existing deep learning-based methods, a post-processing step is needed to handle orphan pix-els. The step is not trainable and can only be computed on CPU, so existing deep learning-based methods cannot be integrated into downstream tasks in an end-to-end approach.

### 2.3 Spatial Connectivity

Most superpixel algorithms [1,6,10,11,14,23,28] do not explicitly enforce con-nectivity and there may exist some "orphaned" pixels that do not belong to the same connected components. To correct this, SLIC [1] assigns these pixels the label of the nearest cluster. [10,28] also apply a component connection algo-rithm to merge superpixels that are smaller than a certain threshold with the surrounding ones. These algorithms enforce connectivity using a post-processing step, whereas SNIC [2] enforces connectivity explicitly from the start. SNIC uses a priority queue to choose the next pixel to be assigned, and the queue is popu-lated with pixels which are 4 or 8-connected to a currently growing superpixel. As far as we know, there is no method which utilizes learned features and enforces connectivity explicitly.

# 3   Superpixel Segmentation Method

In this section, we introduce our superpixel segmentation method SIN. The framework of our proposed method is illustrated in Fig. 1. We first present our idea of superpixel initialization and updating scheme. After that, we introduce our network architecture and loss function design. Finally, we will explain why our method can enforce spatial connectivity from the start.

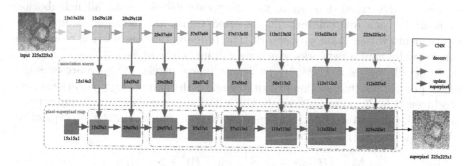

**Fig. 1. Illustration of our proposed method.** The SIN model takes the image as input, and predicts association scores for each updating step. In the training stage, association scores are utilized to compute loss. In the testing stage, new pixel-superpixel maps are obtained from current pixel-superpixel maps and association scores.

## 3.1   Learn Superpixels by Interpolation

Our superpixels are obtained by initializing pixel-superpixel map and updating the map multiple times. Similar to the commonly adopted strategy in [1,2,4], we generate the initial superpixels by sampling the image $I \in \mathbb{R}^{H \times W \times 3}$ with a regular step $S$. By assigning each pixel to a unique superpixel, we get the initial pixel-superpixel map $M_0 \in \mathbb{Z}^{h_0 \times w_0}$. The values of $M_0$ denote ID of superpixels to which sampled pixels are assigned.

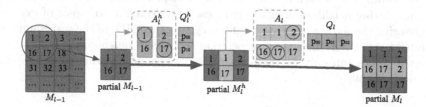

**Fig. 2. Illustration of expanding pixel-superpixel map.** Each expanding step consists of a horizontal interpolation followed by a vertical interpolation. The horizontal interpolation inserts values in each row and the vertical interpolation inserts values in each column. The inserted values are determined by association scores and neighboring superpixels.

Superpixel segmentation is to find the final pixel-superpixel map $M \in \mathbb{Z}^{H \times W}$, which assigns all pixels to superpixels. The problem of finding $M$ can be seemed as expanding $M_0$ to $M$. Inspired by resizing image, we use interpolation to expand the matrix. The rule of interpolation is carefully designed to enforce spatial connectivity from the start and to be computed on GPU in parallel. As depicted in Figure 1, the process of expanding $M_0$ to $M$ can be divided into multiple similar steps and each step consists of a horizontal interpolation and a vertical interpolation. As shown in Fig. 2, when we expand pixel-superpixel map in horizontal/vertical dimension, we interpolate values among all neighboring elements in each row/column. The inserted values are the same as neighboring elements with certain probability. The probabilities (association scores) are computed by neural networks which we will introduce in Sect. 3.2.

In detail, we use $P \in \mathbb{R}^{H \times W}$ to denote image pixels. $P(i, j)$ represents the image pixel at the intersection of $i$-th row and $j$-th column. $M(i, j)$ is the superpixel to which $P(i, j)$ is assigned. In the initial step, we find partial connections between image pixels $P$ and superpixels. $M_0(i, j)$ represents the superpixel to which $P(i * S, j * S)$ is assigned.

$$h_0 = (H + S - 1)/S, \quad w_0 = (W + S - 1)/S. \tag{1}$$

To obtain $M$, we need to expand $M_0$ multiple times. At $l$-th expansion, we use $M_l^h \in \mathbb{Z}^{h_{l-1} \times w_l}$ and $M_l \in \mathbb{Z}^{h_l \times w_l}$ to denote pixel-superpixel maps after horizontal and vertical interpolation.

$$h_l = 2 * h_{l-1} - 1, \quad w_l = 2 * w_{l-1} - 1. \tag{2}$$

Figure 2 has shown a part of interpolation at $l$-th expansion. At $l$-th horizontal/vertical interpolation step, the inserted values are confirmed by association scores $A_l^h \in \mathbb{R}^{h_{l-1} \times (w_{l-1}-1) \times 2}/A_l \in \mathbb{R}^{(h_{l-1}-1) \times w_l \times 2}$ and neighboring superpixels $Q_l^h \in \mathbb{Z}^{h_{l-1} \times (w_{l-1}-1) \times 2}/Q_l \in \mathbb{Z}^{(h_{l-1}-1) \times w_l \times 2}$. $A_l^h(i, j, k)$ and $A_l(i, j, k)$ denote the probability of $i$-th row, $j$-th column inserted value is the same with its $k$-th neighbor. All association scores are obtained from multi-layer outputs of the neural network described in Sect. 3.2. $Q_l^h(i, j, k)$ and $Q_l(i, j, k)$ denote the $k$-th neighbor's value of $i$-th row, $j$-th column inserted element. Neighboring superpixels are obtained from current pixel-superpixel map. We interpolate new elements among existing neighboring elements at each row/column, so a pair of existing neighboring elements' values are neighboring superpixel IDs of the corresponding inserted element. According to association scores and neighboring superpixels, inserted values can only be same with one of their neighboring elements with certain probability.

## 3.2   Network Architecture and Loss Function

We use a convolutional neural network similar to [28] to extract image feature $F_0 \in \mathbb{R}^{h_0 \times w_0 \times c_0}$. We stack module *deconv_h* and *deconv_v* multiple times to extract multi-layer features $F_l^h \in \mathbb{R}^{h_{l-1} \times w_l \times c_l}$ and $F_l \in \mathbb{R}^{h_l \times w_l \times c_l}$, where $c_l$ denotes feature channels. *deconv_h* and *deconv_v* are transposed convolutional neural networks, in which stride are $(1,2)$ and $(2,1)$ respectively. Specially, *deconv_h* will reduce feature channels by half. *conv* is a convolutional neural network, which transforms the multi-layer features to 2-dimensional association scores.

Our model is trained with ground truth segmentation labels $T \in \mathbb{Z}^{H \times W}$ from BSDS500. Every interpolation is to find partial connections between pixels and superpixels. To get loss of all connections, we need to compute partial loss at every interpolation. We define $s_l = S/2^l$ to simplify descriptions. The inserted values at $l$-th step in horizontal/vertical dimension are ID of superpixels to which pixels $U_l^h$ and $U_l$ are assigned. $U_l^h$ denotes the subtraction of pixels sampled by stride $(s_{l-1}, s_l)$ and $(s_{l-1}, s_{l-1})$. $U_l$ denotes the subtraction of pixels sampled by stride $(s_l, s_l)$ and $(s_{l-1}, s_l)$. Partial ground truth connections $T_l^h$ and $T_l$ are segmentation labels of pixels $U_l^h$ and $U_l$. To speed up training process, we do not generate pixel-superpixel maps to compute loss. Instead, we utilize association scores to compute loss directly. Association scores $A_l^h$ and $A_l$ denote the probabilities of pixels assigned to neighboring superpixels. Inspired by tasks of classification, the ground truth labels $G_l^h$ and $G_l$ are defined as the indexes of neighboring superpixels to which pixels should be assigned. $G_l^h$ and $G_l$ can be inferred from $T_l^h$ and $T_l$. Owing to each inserted element has two neighbors, the ground truth labels are 0 or 1. If the neighboring superpixels ID of an inserted element are same, we will ignore it when computing loss. We define $\mathbb{I}_l^h$ and $\mathbb{I}_l$ to represent whether to consider the elements when computing loss. Loss of each interpolation at $l$-th step can be computed by:

$$L_l^h = \mathcal{C}_{\mathbb{I}_l^h}(G_l^h, A_l^h), \quad L_l^v = \mathcal{C}_{\mathbb{I}_l}(G_l, A_l) \tag{3}$$

where $L_l^h$ and $L_l$ denote the loss of horizontal and vertical at $l$-th step. $\mathcal{C}_{\mathbb{I}_l^h}$ and $\mathcal{C}_{\mathbb{I}_l}$ denote cross entropy loss functions, which only consider partial elements according to the values of $\mathbb{I}_l^h$ and $\mathbb{I}_l$.

Total loss $\mathcal{L}$ can be computed by:

$$\mathcal{L} = -\sum_l \left( w_l^h L_l^h + w_l^v L_l^v \right) \tag{4}$$

where $w_l^h$ and $w_l^v$ denote weights of horizontal and vertical interpolation loss at $l$-th step.

### 3.3 Illustration of Spatial Connectivity

Thanks to removing the post-processing step, our method can be integrated into subsequent tasks in an end-to-end way. The key to enforcing spatial connectivity from the start is the rule of interpolation. An expanding step consists of a horizontal interpolation and a vertical interpolation. The design ensures spatial connectivity of pixel-superpixel maps will not be destroyed by interpolations. Owing to initial pixel-superpixel map has spatial connectivity and interpolations preserve the property, the final pixel-superpixel map $M$ remains spatial connectivity. $M$ assigns all pixels to superpixels, so $M$ has spatial connectivity equals our SIN superpixels have spatial connectivity. In the following, we will first explain why the spatial connectivity of $M$ and superpixels are equivalent. Afterwards, we illustrate how interpolations preserve spatial connectivity of pixel-superpixel maps.

The fact that a superpixel has spatial connectivity means the set of all pixels in the superpixel is a connected set. We use $X_i$ to denote a set where elements have same value $i$ in $M$ and $X = \{X_1, X_2, \ldots, X_n\}$ to denote all such sets. If all elements in $X$ are connected sets, $M$ has spatial connectivity. Spatial information of elements in $X_i$ equals spatial information of pixels assigned to superpixel $i$, so $X_i$ is a connected set represents superpixel $i$ has spatial connectivity. Evidently, $M$ has spatial connectivity equals all superpixels have spatial connectivity. All sets in $M_0$ only has one element, so $M_0$ has spatial connectivity definitely. If interpolations can preserve spatial connectivity, we can infer that $M$ has spatial connectivity.

Our scheme of interpolation is to insert elements among existing neighboring elements at each row/column. When we insert a element between a pair of neighbors, only sets including these three elements will be taken into consideration. If existing neighboring elements are in a same set, the inserted element will be added to the set and the set is still connected. If existing neighboring elements belong to different sets, the inserted element will be added to one of the sets, and the other will not change. The added set is still connected and spatial connectivity of the other will not be affected. We want to address that it is the design of interpolation preserves spatial connectivity. If we interpolate once at an expanding step and the inserted value is same with its 8-neighborhood, spatial connectivity of pixel-superpixel map will be destroyed. Above all, our method can enforce spatial connectivity explicitly through the delicate design of interpolation.

## 4   Experiments

To be integrated into subsequent tasks in an end-to-end way without impeding their instantaneity, we analyze the runtime of deep learning-based models. To demonstrate the effectiveness of SIN in superpixel segmentation, we train and test our model on the standard benchmark BSDS500 [3]. We also report its performance without fine-tuning on the benchmark NYUv2 [21] to evaluate the generalizability of our model. We use protocols and codes provided by [22] to evaluate all methods on two benchmarks. SNIC [2], SEAL [23], SSN [10] and FCN [28] are tested with the original implementations from the authors. SLIC [1] and ERS [13] are tested with the codes provided in [22]. For SLIC and ERS, we use the best parameters reported in [22], and for the rest, we use the default parameters recommended in the original papers. Figure 3 shows the visual results of some state-of-the-art methods and ours.

## 4.1   Comparison with the State-of-the-Arts

*Implementation Details.* We implement our model with PyTorch and use Adam with $\beta_1 = 0.9$ and $\beta_2 = 0.999$ to optimize it. For training, we randomly crop the images to size $225 \times 225$ as input and perform horizontal/vertical flipping for data augmentation. The initial learning rate is set to $5 \times 10^{-5}$ and is reduced by half after 200k iterations. It takes us about 3 h to train the model for 300k iterations on 1 NVIDIA RTX 2080Ti GPU device.

| Input | GT | SNIC | SEAL | SSN | FCN | Ours |
|-------|----|----|----|----|----|----|

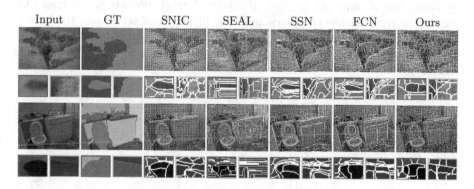

**Fig. 3. Visual results.** Compared to SEAL, SSN and FCN, our method is competitive or better in terms of object boundary adherence while generating more compact superpixels. Top rows: BSDS500. Bottom rows: NYUv2.

We set the regular step $S$ as 16 and we can get $15 \times 15(225)$ superpixels through 4 expanding steps when training. We set $w^h$ and $w^v$ as $[20, 10, 5, 2.5]$ and $[8, 4, 2, 1]$ respectively. To generate the varying number of superpixels when testing, we simply resize the input image to the appropriate size. For example, if we want to generate $30 \times 20$ superpixels, we can resize the image to $(30 * 16 - 15) \times (20 * 16 - 15)$ *i.e.* $465 \times 305$.

*Runtime Analysis.* We compare the runtime difference between deep learning-based methods. Figure 4 reports the average runtime *w.r.t* the number of generated superpixels on a NVIDIA RTX 2080Ti GPU device. Our method runs about 1.5 to 2 times faster than FCN, 12 to 33 times faster than SSN, and more than 70 times faster than SEAL. Note that existing deep learning-based methods need a post-processing step which takes 2.5 ms to 8 ms [17] and runtime in Fig. 4 does not include the time. The reason of our method has the fastest speed is that we use a novel interpolation method to generate superpixels. What's more, our method saves plenty of training time compared to FCN due to the

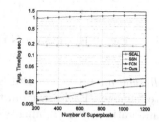

**Fig. 4. Runtime analysis.** Average runtime of different DL methods *w.r.t* number of superpixels. Note that *y*-axis is plotted in the logarithmic scale.

simple and effective loss function. For training, we spend about 3 h on a single GPU, while FCN spends about 20 h.

*Evaluation Metrics.* To demonstrate the effectiveness of SIN, we use the achievable segmentation accuracy (ASA), boundary recall and precision (BR-BP), and compactness (CO) to evaluate the superpixels. ASA evaluates superpixels by measuring the total effective segmentation area of a superpixel representation concerning the ground truth segmentation map. BR and BP measure the boundary adherence of superpixels given the ground truth boundary, whereas CO assesses the compactness of superpixels. The higher these scores are, the better the superpixel segmentation result is. As in [22], for BR and BP evaluation, the boundary tolerance is 0.0025 times the image diagonal rounded to the closest integer.

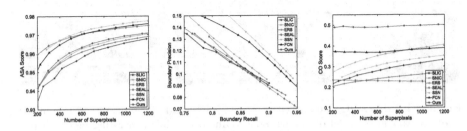

**Fig. 5. Results on BSDS500.** From left to right: ASA, BR-BP, and CO.

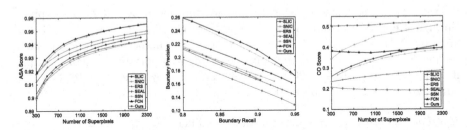

**Fig. 6. Results on NYUv2.** From left to right: ASA, BR-BP, and CO.

*Results on BSDS500.* BSDS500 contains 200 training, 100 validation, and 200 test images. Each image in this dataset is provided with multiple ground truth annotations. For training, we follow [10,23,28] and treat each annotation as an individual sample. With this dataset, we have 1633 training/validation samples and 1063 testing samples. We train our model using both the training and validation samples.

Figure 5 reports the performance of all methods on BSDS500 test set. Our method outperforms all traditional methods on all evaluation metrics, except SNIC in terms of BR-BP. Comparing to the other deep learning-based methods, our method achieves competitive results in terms of ASA and BR-BP, and significantly higher scores in terms of CO. With high CO, our method can better capture spatially coherent information and avoids paying too much attention to image details and noises. As shown in Fig. 3, when handling fuzzy boundaries, our method can generate smoother superpixels.

*Results on NYUv2.* NYUv2 is an RGB-D dataset containing 1499 images with object instance labels, which is originally proposed for indoor scene understanding tasks. [22] removes the unlabelled regions near the image boundary and develops a benchmark on a subset of 400 test images with size 608 × 448 for superpixel evaluation. We directly apply the models of SEAL, SSN, FCN, and our method trained on BSDS500 to this dataset without any fine-tuning.

Figure 6 shows the performance of all methods on NYUv2. In general, these deep learning-based algorithms achieve competitive or better performance against the traditional algorithms, which demonstrate that they can extract high-quality superpixels on other datasets. Also, our method outperforms all other methods in terms of CO. As the visual results shown in Fig. 3, our method handles the fuzzy boundary better than other deep learning-based methods.

*Illustration of High CO Score.* The experimental results on BSDS500 and NYUv2 show that our method has lower ASA and BR-BP scores, while a higher CO score. We will illustrate the reason in the following.

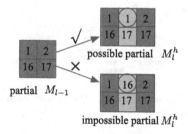

**Fig. 7. Illustration of high CO score.** According to the rule of interpolation, the above is a possible new pixel-superpixel map and the below is an impossible one.

To enforce spatial connectivity from the first, we expand pixel-superpixel map in horizontal and vertical dimensions. The horizontal/vertical interpolation constrains the inserted value can only be same with its horizontal/vertical neighbors. As Fig. 7 shown, the black circled value can be 1/2 and cannot be 16/17. However, if the ground truth of the value is 16, our method cannot interpolate the same value. That is the reason our ASA and BR-BP scores are lower than other deep learning-based methods. Meanwhile, the constraint results in pixels in a superpixel are 4-neighborhood connected which is more compact than 8-neighborhood connected. Owing to the high CO score, our method generates smoother superpixels on the fuzzy boundaries as Fig. 3 shown. The importance of compactness has been demonstrated in [28]. To extract more useful features in downstream tasks, it is important to capture spatial coherence in the local region in our superpixel method. In our view, it is worthy to enforce spatial connectivity from the start and get a higher CO score while sacrificing slight ASA and BR-BP scores.

## 4.2 Ablation Study

We present an ablation study where we evaluate different design choices of the image feature extraction and loss sum. Unlike [28], we do not take image features from previous layers into account to predict association scores. Our total loss is the sum of horizontal and vertical loss at each step, so we can compute average or weighted sum. In our final model, we choose weighted sum to compute total loss. For comparison, we include a baseline model which uses the previous features and current features(concat) to predict scores and simply sums the loss values averagely. We evaluate each of these design options of the network. Figure 8 shows that each of the 2 alternatives in our model performs better.

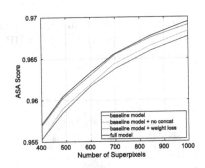

**Fig. 8. Ablation study.** We show the effectiveness of each design choice in the SIN model in improving accuracy.

## 5 Application

In this section, we evaluate whether our SIN superpixels can improve the performance of downstream vision tasks which utilize superpixels. For this study, we choose existing semantic segmentation and salient object detection algorithms and substitute the original superpixels with our superpixels. For the following two tasks, our superpixels are generated by the network fine-tuned on PascaVOC 2012 training and validation datasets.

*Semantic Segmentation.* For semantic segmentation, CNN models [12,15] achieve the state-of-the-art performance. However, most CNN architectures generate lower resolution outputs and then upsample them using post-processing techniques. To alleviate the need for post-processing CRF techniques, [7] propose the Bilateral Inception (BI) networks to utilize SLIC superpixels for long-range and edge-aware propagation across CNN units. We use SNIC and our super-pixels to substitute SLIC superpixels and set the number of superpixels as 600. We evaluate the generated semantic segmentation on the PascalVOC 2012 test set [5]. Table 1 shows the standard Intersection over Union (IoU) scores. The results indicate that we can obtain significant IoU improvements when using SIN superpixels.

*Salient Object Detection.* Superpixels are widely used in salient object detection algorithms. We experiment with Saliency Optimization(SO) [29] and report standard Mean Absolute Error (MAE) scores on the ECSSD dataset [19]. To demonstrate the potential of our SIN Superpixels, we replace SLIC superpixels used in SO with ours, SNIC, and ERS superpixels and set the number of super-pixels as 200 and 400. Experimental results in Table 2 show that the use of our 200/400 superpixels consistently improves the performance of SO.

The above results on semantic segmentation and salient object detection demonstrate the effectiveness of integrating our superpixels into downstream vision tasks.

**Table 1. Superpixels for semantic segmentation.** We compute semantic segmentation using the BI network with different types of superpixels and compare the IoU scores on the PascalVOC 2012 test set.

| Method | DeepLab [12] | +CRF [12] | +BI (SLIC) [7] | +BI (ERS) | +BI (Ours) |
|--------|-------------|-----------|----------------|-----------|------------|
| IoU    | 68.9        | 72.7      | 73.5           | 74.0      | **74.4**   |

**Table 2. Superpixels for salient object detection.** We run the SO algorithm with different types of superpixels and evaluate on the ECSSD dataset.

| Method | SLIC | SNIC | ERS | Ours |
|--------|------|------|-----|------|
| # of superpixels 200 | 0.1719 | 0.1714 | 0.1686 | **0.1657** |
| # of superpixels 400 | 0.1675 | 0.1654 | 0.1630 | **0.1616** |

# 6   Conclusion

In this paper, we present a superpixel segmentation network SIN which can be integrated into downstream tasks in an end-to-end way. To extract superpixels, we initialize superpixels and expand pixel-superpixel map multiple times. By dividing an expanding step into a horizontal and a vertical interpolation, we enforce spatial connectivity explicitly. We utilize multi-layer outputs of a fully convolutional network to predict association scores for interpolations. To speed up training process, association scores are used to compute loss instead of pixel-superpixel maps. Owing to our interpolation constrains the number of neighbors of inserted elements, SIN has the fastest speed compared to existing deep learning-based methods. The high speed of our method ensures it can be integrated into downstream tasks requiring real-time speed. Our model performs favorably against several existing state-of-the-art superpixel algorithms. SIN can generate more compact superpixels thanks to the design of interpolation, which is important to downstream tasks. What's more, visual results illustrate that our method outperforms when handling fuzzy boundaries. Furthermore, we apply our superpixels in downstream tasks and make progress. We will integrate SIN into downstream tasks in an end-to-end way in the future and we hope SIN can benefit superpixel-based computer vision tasks.

**Acknowledgments.** This work is supported by the Hubei Provincinal Science and Technology Major Project of China under Grant No. 2020AEA011, the Key Research & Development Plan of Hubei Province of China under Grant No. 2020BAB100, the project of Science, Technology and Innovation Commission of Shenzhen Municipality of China under Grant No. JCYJ20210324120002006 and the Fundamental Research Funds for the Central Universities, HUST: 2020JYCXJJ067.

# References

1. Achanta, R., Shaji, A., Smith, K., Lucchi, A., Fua, P., Süsstrunk, S.: Slic superpixels compared to state-of-the-art superpixel methods. IEEE Trans. Pattern Anal. Mach. Intell. **34**(11), 2274–2282 (2012)
2. Achanta, R., Susstrunk, S.: Superpixels and polygons using simple non-iterative clustering. In: CVPR, pp. 4651–4660, July 2017
3. Arbelaez, P., Maire, M., Fowlkes, C., Malik, J.: Contour detection and hierarchical image segmentation. IEEE Trans. Pattern Anal. Mach. Intell. **33**(5), 898–916 (2010)
4. Van den Bergh, M., Boix, X., Roig, G., de Capitani, B., Van Gool, L.: SEEDS: superpixels extracted via energy-driven sampling. In: Fitzgibbon, A., Lazebnik, S., Perona, P., Sato, Y., Schmid, C. (eds.) ECCV 2012. LNCS, vol. 7578, pp. 13–26. Springer, Heidelberg (2012). https://doi.org/10.1007/978-3-642-33786-4_2
5. Everingham, M., Eslami, S.A., Van Gool, L., Williams, C.K., Winn, J., Zisserman, A.: The pascal visual object classes challenge: a retrospective. Int. J. Comput. Vision **111**(1), 98–136 (2015)
6. Felzenszwalb, P.F., Huttenlocher, D.P.: Efficient graph-based image segmentation. Int. J. Comput. Vision **59**(2), 167–181 (2004)
7. Gadde, R., Jampani, V., Kiefel, M., Kappler, D., Gehler, P.V.: Superpixel convolutional networks using bilateral inceptions. In: Leibe, B., Matas, J., Sebe, N., Welling, M. (eds.) ECCV 2016. LNCS, vol. 9905, pp. 597–613. Springer, Cham (2016). https://doi.org/10.1007/978-3-319-46448-0_36
8. Gould, S., Rodgers, J., Cohen, D., Elidan, G., Koller, D.: Multi-class segmentation with relative location prior. Int. J. Comput. Vision **80**(3), 300–316 (2008)
9. He, S., Lau, R.W., Liu, W., Huang, Z., Yang, Q.: SuperCNN: a superpixelwise convolutional neural network for salient object detection. Int. J. Comput. Vision **115**(3), 330–344 (2015)

10. Jampani, V., Sun, D., Liu, M.-Y., Yang, M.-H., Kautz, J.: Superpixel sampling networks. In: Ferrari, V., Hebert, M., Sminchisescu, C., Weiss, Y. (eds.) ECCV 2018. LNCS, vol. 11211, pp. 363–380. Springer, Cham (2018). https://doi.org/10.1007/978-3-030-01234-2_22

11. Li, Z., Chen, J.: Superpixel segmentation using linear spectral clustering. In: CVPR, pp. 1356–1363 (2015)

12. Liang-Chieh, C., Papandreou, G., Kokkinos, I., Murphy, K., Yuille, A.: Semantic image segmentation with deep convolutional nets and fully connected CRFs. In: ICLR (2015)

13. Liu, M.Y., Tuzel, O., Ramalingam, S., Chellappa, R.: Entropy rate superpixel segmentation. In: CVPR, pp. 2097–2104. IEEE (2011)

14. Liu, Y.J., Yu, C.C., Yu, M.J., He, Y.: Manifold slic: a fast method to compute content-sensitive superpixels. In: CVPR, pp. 651–659 (2016)

15. Long, J., Shelhamer, E., Darrell, T.: Fully convolutional networks for semantic segmentation. In: CVPR, pp. 3431–3440 (2015)

16. Ren, M.: Learning a classification model for segmentation. In: ICCV, pp. 10–17, vol. 1 (2003). https://doi.org/10.1109/ICCV.2003.1238308

17. Ren, C.Y., Reid, I.: gSLIC: a real-time implementation of slic superpixel segmentation. University of Oxford, Department of Engineering, Technical report, pp. 1–6 (2011)

18. Sharma, A., Tuzel, O., Liu, M.Y.: Recursive context propagation network for semantic scene labeling. In: NeurIPS, pp. 2447–2455 (2014)

19. Shi, J., Yan, Q., Xu, L., Jia, J.: Hierarchical image saliency detection on extended CSSD. IEEE Trans. Pattern Anal. Mach. Intell. 38(4), 717–729 (2015)

20. Shu, G., Dehghan, A., Shah, M.: Improving an object detector and extracting regions using superpixels. In: CVPR, pp. 3721–3727 (2013)

21. Silberman, N., Hoiem, D., Kohli, P., Fergus, R.: Indoor segmentation and support inference from RGBD images. In: Fitzgibbon, A., Lazebnik, S., Perona, P., Sato, Y., Schmid, C. (eds.) ECCV 2012. LNCS, vol. 7576, pp. 746–760. Springer, Heidelberg (2012). https://doi.org/10.1007/978-3-642-33715-4_54

22. Stutz, D., Hermans, A., Leibe, B.: Superpixels: an evaluation of the state-of-the-art. Comput. Vis. Image Underst. 166, 1–27 (2018)

23. Tu, W.C., et al.: Learning superpixels with segmentation-aware affinity loss. In: CVPR, pp. 568–576 (2018)

24. Wang, S., Lu, H., Yang, F., Yang, M.H.: Superpixel tracking. In: ICCV, pp. 1323–1330. IEEE (2011)

25. Yan, J., Yu, Y., Zhu, X., Lei, Z., Li, S.Z.: Object detection by labeling superpixels. In: CVPR, pp. 5107–5116 (2015)

26. Yang, C., Zhang, L., Lu, H., Ruan, X., Yang, M.H.: Saliency detection via graph-based manifold ranking. In: CVPR, pp. 3166–3173 (2013)

27. Yang, F., Lu, H., Yang, M.H.: Robust superpixel tracking. IEEE Trans. Image Process. 23(4), 1639–1651 (2014)

28. Yang, F., Sun, Q., Jin, H., Zhou, Z.: Superpixel segmentation with fully convolutional networks. In: CVPR, pp. 13964–13973 (2020)

29. Zhu, W., Liang, S., Wei, Y., Sun, J.: Saliency optimization from robust background detection. In: CVPR, pp. 2814–2821 (2014)

# SPANet: Spatial and Part-Aware Aggregation Network for 3D Object Detection

Yangyang Ye[(✉)]

Zhejiang University, 866 Yuhangtang Road, Hangzhou, Zhejiang, China
yeyangyang@zju.edu.cn

**Abstract.** 3D object detection is a fundamental technique in autonomous driving. However, current LiDAR-based single-stage 3D object detection algorithms do not pay sufficient attention to the encoding of the inhomogeneity of LiDAR point clouds and the shape encoding of each object. This paper introduces a novel 3D object detection network called the spatial and part-aware aggregation network (SPANet), which utilizes a spatial aggregation network to remedy the inhomogeneity of LiDAR point clouds, and embodies a part-aware aggregation network that learns the statistic shape priors of objects. SPANet deeply integrates both 3D voxel-based features and point-based spatial features to learn more discriminative point cloud features. Specifically, the spatial aggregation network takes advantage of the efficient learning and high-quality proposals by providing flexible receptive fields from PointNet-based networks. The part-aware aggregation network includes a part-aware attention mechanism that learns the statistic shape priors of objects to enhance the semantic embeddings. Experimental results reveal that the proposed single-stage method outperforms state-of-the-art single-stage methods on the KITTI 3D object detection benchmark. It achieved a bird's eye view (BEV) average precision (AP) of 91.59%, 3D AP of 80.34%, and heading AP of 95.03% in the detection of cars.

**Keywords:** 3D object detection · Spatial aggregation · Part-aware aggregation · Single-stage method

## 1 Introduction

3D object detection has received increasing attention in recent years from both industry and academia in various fields such as autonomous driving, unmanned aerial vehicles, and robotics. It commonly uses data from range sensors such as LiDAR sensors, time-of-flight cameras, and stereo cameras to predict accurate 3D bounding boxes from objects in the real world. LiDAR sensors have become the preferred type of sensor for the perception of outdoor scenes owing to accurate distance information.

However, there are two critical problems involved in LiDAR-based 3D object detection. The first is the need to generate low-level descriptive features against

© Springer Nature Switzerland AG 2021
D. N. Pham et al. (Eds.): PRICAI 2021, LNAI 13033, pp. 308–320, 2021.
https://doi.org/10.1007/978-3-030-89370-5_23

the sparse and inhomogeneous point clouds sampled from the LiDAR sensor. There are more points within a short distance than at a large distance. In addition, the non-uniform distributions of the point cloud will decrease the performance of the detector. To handle this problem, most existing 3D object detection methods utilize grid-based and point-based approaches to encode point clouds. The grid-based methods transform the irregular point clouds into 3D voxels or bird's eye view (BEV) maps to obtain a regular representation. 3D or 2D convolutional neural networks (CNNs) can be efficiently applied to these methods. Point-based methods directly learn discriminative features from raw point clouds and easily achieve a larger receptive field through the set abstraction module [15]. Both of the aforementioned methods have weaknesses. Grid-based methods are only suitable for describing the local features of objects because the expanded receptive field through downsampling will cause information loss. Meanwhile, point-based methods have a higher computation cost associated with creating a large receptive field. PV-RCNN [16] incorporates the advantages of both the point-based and voxel-based feature learning methods to boost 3D detection performance. However, this method consists of two stages. The first stage is only dependent on a voxel-based network to predict coarse detection results, and then the second stage uses the detected results to fuse the point-based and voxel-based features. This type of architecture cannot be used in a single-stage detector, and the voxel-based branch has a scarcity of larger receptive fields and therefore lacks the encoding of the object as a whole.

Another problem is achieving efficient encoding of the shape of objects for greater discrimination. Two-stage detectors use a region proposal network (RPN) to predict coarse detection results and then apply the 2D or 3D ROI pooling [3] technique to aggregate the features within a shape-specific box that eventually encodes each instance to be detected. However, due to the working principle of LiDAR, these methods ignore the fact that point clouds are only distribution on parts of the surface of the object. In other words, the features of the LiDAR point cloud region need to be enhanced. Part-aware aggregation module [18] is proposed to handle this problem. It applies 3D ROI pooling technique and 3D sparse convolution to encode each instance, and then converts the encode features into full connected features. However, the part-aware aggregation information using 3D sparse convolution may disappear during this process. In addition, the ROI pooling operation increases the processing time of these algorithms. Because of the lack of ROI pooling operation, the single-stage detectors is faster than the two-stage detectors. To improve the lack of shape encoding in the single-stage method, SARPNET [20] extends this type of BEV-based shape prior to 3D by redesigning the LiDAR encoding layers and adding a vertical attention branch. SA-SSD [6] proposes a part-sensitive warping (PSWarping) operation to solve the misalignment between the predicted bounding boxes and corresponding confidence maps. PSWarping can provide more accurate object features, but it lacks the important attribute of encoding of the shape of the objects.

This paper proposes a novel 3D object detection solution called the spatial and part-aware aggregation network (SPANet) to address the aforementioned issues. SPANet introduces a spatial aggregation network to extract the point-based and voxel-based features to improve the limitations of single encoding features. It incorporates point-based and voxel-based features through a spatial attention module to enhance the representation ability of the features. In addition, a part-aware aggregation network is proposed to encode the importance of each object part to improve the recognition ability of the detector. The proposed method is evaluated using the KITTI [2] 3D object detection benchmark. The contributions of this study are as follows: A spatial aggregation network is developed to handle the limitations of encoding features in current 3D object detectors. A part-aware aggregation network is integrated into a single-stage detector to learn the shape information of objects.

## 2   Related Work

There are roughly two types of methods for 3D object detection with LiDAR point clouds.

### 2.1   Single-Stage Approaches

To enhance the computational efficiency, this type of object detector processes the point cloud in a fully convolutional network and predicts the 3D detection information immediately. VoxelNet [21] utilizes PointNet [14] to encode each voxel, extracts spatial information using 3D dense convolutional network, and applies a 2D detector head to predict 3D objects. SECOND [19] adopts 3D sparse convolutional networks and introduces a heading classification branch to accelerate the inference of the network and improve the performance of the detector. PointPillars [9] enlarges the voxel size, upgrades the encoder of each LiDAR point, and simplifies the above networks, thereby enabling it to be a more rapid and efficient method. Because all the aforementioned methods lack large receptive fields, Voxel-FPN [8] applies multi-scale voxel feature aggregation to improve the performance of the detector. Point-based detectors can easily obtain larger receptive field. VoteNet [12] uses PointNet++ networks to extract point cloud features, applies the vote module to predict the offset from each seed point to the object center point, and adopts clustering to obtain object candidate regions. However, these methods cause a decline in performance and unstable detection results because single-stage detectors ignore the shape prior for each object. Unlike two-stage methods, single-stage methods lack ROI pooling-based technology, which makes it difficult to encode the instance characteristics of objects. To introduce the shape prior into single-stage detectors, SARPNET [20] generates a 3D shape prior by modifying the feature encoding layers and extending a vertical attention branch. SA-SSD [6] proposes a PSWarping module to mimic the operation of ROI pooling and applies an auxiliary network with point-level supervision to guide the intermediate features from different scales of backbone 3D sparse CNN. However, the PSWarping module does not consider the importance of each part overall.

## 2.2 Two-Stage Approaches

To improve the detection performance of 3D object detectors, these methods usually use ROI pooling-based technology to further optimize the results. By designing LiDAR features based on the top view to predict the proposal, MV3D [1] applies 2D convolution to encode LiDAR features and combines the features extracted from the camera view and front view for 3D object detection. AVOD [7] utilizes 3D anchors and fewer channels to enhance the detector's efficiency. F-PointNet [13] applies a 2D image detector to extract corresponding frustums in the 3D point cloud, and then uses PointNet to predict 3D object information. PointRCNN [17] generates 3D proposals by segmenting the point cloud of the entire scene into background and foreground points and then, refines these proposals using 3D ROI pooling. Part-A2 [18] consists of a part-aware stage and a part-aggregation stage. The part-aware stage estimates the intra-object part locations and generates 3D proposals, and the part-aggregation stage conducts ROI-aware point cloud pooling operations to group the part features and predict object information. PV-RCNN [16] utilizes the advantages of both the point-based and voxel-based feature learning methods to boost 3D detection performance. However, the voxel-based detector in the first stage affects detection performance. Benefiting from the detected results of the 2D or 3D bounding boxes (shape priors) in the first stage, two-stage detectors achieve better performance than single-stage detectors.

# 3   SPANet

In this section, we describe the proposed SPANet in detail. As shown in Fig. 1, it consists of four main components: (1) a voxel-based backbone, (2) a spatial aggregation network, (3) a RPN, and (4) a part-aware aggregation network.

## 3.1   Voxel-Based Backbone

Voxel-based 3D detectors [18–20] apply 3D sparse convolution [4,5] to efficiently encode point clouds. We utilize it as the backbone of our framework for feature encoding. The procedure for generating voxel representation from LiDAR point clouds follows SA-SSD [6]. Supposing the LiDAR point cloud includes a 3D space with range $H$, $W$, $D$ which represents height in the vertical direction, position in the horizontal direction, and distance from the sensor, respectively. Each voxel has a size $\Delta_H$, $\Delta_W$, $\Delta_D$. The size of the entire voxel grid is $H/\Delta_H$, $W/\Delta_W$, $D/\Delta_D$. Let $\{p_i = (x_i, y_i, z_i, r_i), i = 1, ..., N\}$ be the coordinates and the reflectivity of the point cloud, which is the input data representation. The backbone network consists of four 3D sparse convolutional blocks. Except for the first block, all the other three blocks have a downsampling layer. Each convolution layer is followed by a batch normalization layer and ReLU. The size of the output for each voxel is $\Delta_H \times 8$, $\Delta_W \times 8$, $\Delta_D \times 8$.

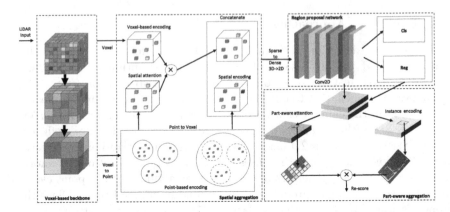

**Fig. 1.** The structure of SPANet. The detector takes a raw LiDAR point cloud as input, utilizes 3D sparse convolutional layers to learn voxel-based features, and then applies an aggregation module to encode spatial features. Finally, the RPN predicts the 3D information of objects and a part-aware aggregation module to refine the results.

### 3.2 Spatial Aggregation Network

This network improves the encoding features of the network by aggregating the spatial features and spatial attention. It includes a voxel-based encoding branch, a point-based encoding branch and an aggregation module. Figure 2 shows the comparison of the two encoding methods.

**Voxel-Based Encoding Branch.** This branch is mainly used to retain voxel-based encoding features. The branch utilizes a 3D sparse convolutional layer with a kernel size of $(3, 3, 3)$ to encode the voxel-based features.

**Point-Based Encoding Branch.** It provides spatial information to the network using a larger receptive field. This branch takes voxel-based features as input, and each voxel is viewed as a point, PointNet++ is used to generate spatial attention and spatial encoding features. A PointNet++ block consists of a sampling layer, a grouping layer and a PointNet layer. The sampling stage adopts the iterative furthest point sampling (FPS) algorithm to choose a small number of $N$ key points $KP = \{p_1, ..., p_n\}$ from the voxel-based features. This strategy can easily and efficiently generate a lager receptive field than voxel-based convolution. In the grouping stage, the ball query method is used to generate $N'$ local areas. This ball query algorithm finds points within a sphere of a certain radius $R$, and sets the upper number limit to $K$. The output of the grouped features has a size of $N' \times K \times (d + C)$. $C$ is the dimension of the features, and $d$ represents the coordinates. In the PointNet learning stage, it sets the features to be a size of $N' \times (d + C)$. Suppose the input voxels have a shape $(M, d + C_{in})$, M is the number of voxels, $C_{in}$ is the dimension of the features, and d represents the coordinates. We apply two PointNet++ blocks to learn $N'_1 = 512$ and $N'_2 = 128$

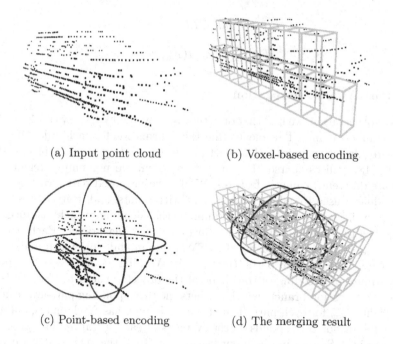

(a) Input point cloud          (b) Voxel-based encoding

(c) Point-based encoding        (d) The merging result

**Fig. 2.** The diagram of voxel-based encoding and point-based encoding.

key points, respectively. The radius are set to $R_1 = 1.0\,\mathrm{m}$ and $R_2 = 1.6\,\mathrm{m}$, and the upper number limits $K$ are set to 32 and 16, respectively. Such a processing method can not only obtain larger receptive fields, but also avoid the computational burden caused by utilizing PointNet++ from raw LiDAR point cloud.

**Aggregation Module.** The module is used to integrate local features from the voxel-based encoding branch and global features from the point-based encoding branch. The point-based encoding branch applies a lager respective field to learn spatial features $F_{sf}$ and spatial attention $F_{sa}$. The voxel-based encoding branch utilizes normal convolution to learn local features $F_{lf}$. The spatial attention $F_{sa}$ and local features $F_{lf}$ are used to generate guided local features $F_{gl}$ using Eq. 1. PV-RCNN [16] applies both the point-based and voxel-based features to boost 3D detection performance. But the point-based branch is only used in the second stage. We employ a feature propagation $FP$ layer [15] to interpolate $F_{sf}$ and $F_{sa}$, which sets these features to have the same voxel position as $F_{lf}$. We apply $Tanh$ instead of $Sigmoid$ activity function to obtain the effect from both positive and negative values. Then, we combine the guided local and spatial by using a concatenate operation (Eq. 2).

$$F_{gl} = Tanh(FP(F_{sa})) * F_{lf} \tag{1}$$

$$F_{spa} = Concat(F_{gl}, F_{sf}) \tag{2}$$

### 3.3 Part-Aware Aggregation

Through observation, we find that only the area covered by the rays in the LiDAR point cloud has points. This means that the information for each object depends on the regions with points. The part-aware aggregation module proposed by Part-A$\hat{2}$ [18] utilizes sparse 3D convolution to encode non-empty regions and aggregate different Semantic features. While, the proposed part-aware aggregation module is used to enhance the regions with points, and it attributes higher attention weights to these regions to improve the encoding of each instance. The module has two branches. One is the instance encoding branch. Each instance feature $F_{ins}$ is obtained by using the PSWarping module [6], which makes each instance generate $N = 28$ parts. However, PSWarping module lacks the important attribute of encoding of the shape of the objects. The other branch is the part-aware attention branch, which predicts the corresponding part-aware attention weights $F_{aw}$ for each part. The attention branch has $N$ channels, and each foreground anchor corresponds to the $N$ parts of each instance. The process is shown in Fig. 3. Supposing the input features $F_{in}$ from the 2D encoder, we apply Eq. 3 to obtain the attention encoding $F_{att}^{ins}$ for each detected object. However, the size of $F_{att}^{ins}$ is based on region, which cannot be used for pixel-wise prediction. We adopt a sum operation to obtain the re-score value for each object.

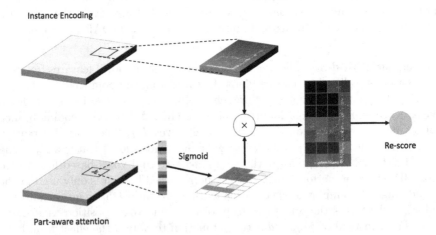

**Fig. 3.** The structure of part-aware aggregation network.

$$F_{ins} = PSWarping(Conv2D(F_{in}))$$
$$F_{aw} = Conv2D(F_{in}) \tag{3}$$
$$F_{att}^{ins} = F_{ins} \times Sigmoid(F_{aw})$$

## 3.4   Loss Function

For the 3D object proposal generation, we use classification and regression losses followed [19]. It consists of three branches, a classification loss for type, a classification loss for direction, and a regression loss for position, size and heading.

**Classification Loss Function.** To solve the problem of an extreme imbalance between foreground and background classes during training, the focal loss [10] (Eq. 4) is applied.

$$\mathcal{L}_{cls} = -\alpha_t (1 - p_t)^{\gamma_t} \log(p_t) \tag{4}$$

$$p_t = \begin{cases} p, & y = 1, \\ 1 - p, & \text{otherwise.} \end{cases} \tag{5}$$

where the $p$ is the estimated probability of the model for the class with label $y = 1$. The $\alpha_t$ and $\gamma_t$ are the parameters of the focal loss. We set $\alpha_t = 0.25$ and $\gamma_t = 2$ in our experiments.

**Direction Classification Loss Function.** Direction classification is used to further strengthen the ability of the model to estimate yaw rotation. Because the yaw will cause a large loss when the angle of the box is 0 or $\pi$ radian. We apply $\mathcal{L}_{dir}$ to indicate the direction classification loss.

**Regression Loss Function.** For anchor-based regression, supposing a 3D ground truth bounding box as $x_g, y_g, z_g, l_g, w_g, h_g, \theta_g$, where $x, y, x$ are the central location, $l, w, h$ represent the length, width, and height of the 3D bounding box, and $\theta$ is the yaw rotation around the z-axis. The positive anchor parameterized as $*_a, \{* \in (x, y, z, l, h, w, \theta)\}$. Then, we use $\Delta*$ to represent the corresponding residual. The residual can be viewed as Eq. 6. The SmoothL1 [11] function is used to compute the regression loss.

$$\Delta x = \frac{x_g - x_a}{d_a}, \Delta y = \frac{y_g - y_a}{d_a}, \Delta z = \frac{z_g - z_a}{h_a},$$
$$\Delta l = \log(\frac{l_g}{l_a}), \Delta w = \log(\frac{w_g}{w_a}), \Delta h = \log(\frac{h_g}{h_a}), \tag{6}$$
$$\Delta \theta = sin(\theta_g - \theta_a).$$

where $d_a = \sqrt{l_a^2 + w_a^2}$ is the diagonal of the base of the anchor.

**Total Loss.** The overall loss function of our SPANet for end-to-end training is calculated as:

$$\mathcal{L}_{total} = \beta_{loc}\mathcal{L}_{loc} + \beta_{cls}\mathcal{L}_{cls} + \beta_{dir}\mathcal{L}_{dir} \tag{7}$$

where $\beta_{loc} = 2$, $\beta_{cls} = 1$, and $\beta_{dir} = 0.2$ in our experiments.

## 4   Experiments

### 4.1   Dataset

**Kitti Dataset.** KITTI [2] is one of the most popular datasets used in 3D detection for autonomous driving. It consists of 7,481 training samples and 7,518 test samples, in which the training samples are generally divided into train split (3,712 samples) and val split (3,769 samples). The splitting of the sets follows the approach proposed in MV3D [1].

### 4.2   Implementation Details

**Network Architecture.** The size of $\Delta_H$, $\Delta_W$, $\Delta_D$ is (0.05, 0.05, 0.1) m and the range of $\{H, W, D\}$ is $\{(0, 70.4), (-40, 40), (-3, 1)\}$ m for both training and testing on KITTI dataset. The anchor size is (1.6, 3.9, 1.5) m for width, length, and height respectively. The anchors are assigned to the positive objects when intersection-over-unions (IOU) is above 0.6 and assigned to the negative when IOU is less than 0.45. The rest of the anchors are ignored during training.

**Training Parameters.** The network was trained for 50 epochs using an SGD optimizer. We set the batch size to 2, the learning rate to 0.01, and the weight decay to 0.001. The learning rate was decayed with a cosine annealing strategy. In the inference, we filter out the low-confidence bounding box by a threshold of 0.3. The non-maximum suppression set an IoU threshold of 0.1.

**Data Augmentation.** Data augmentation is critical to prevent over-fitting for achieving good performance. Inspired from SECOND [19], the strategy of augmentation of ours is as follows. First, a lookup table is used to records all the ground truth 3D boxes and the corresponding LiDAR point clouds. For each LiDAR sample, we randomly select 15, 30 ground truth samples for cars on KITTI dataset and vehicles on Waymo open dataset respectively and place them into the current LiDAR sample to increase the number of objects. Second, for each ground truth bounding box, we randomly rotate it from $[-\pi/4, \pi/4]$ and the center of box randomly shift from $\mathcal{N}(0, 0.5)$. Third, the scaling noise is drawn from the uniform distribution [0.95, 1.05]. Fourth, a global rotation is applied to the whole LiDAR sample from $[-\pi/4, \pi/4]$.

**Table 1.** The comparison of performances in bird's eye view (BEV) detection, 3D object detection and object orientation estimation: AP(%) on KITTI test set for the class of Car.

| | Method | Modality | Times(s) | BEV | | | 3D | | | Orientation | | |
|---|---|---|---|---|---|---|---|---|---|---|---|---|
| | | | | Easy | Mod. | Hard | Easy | Mod. | Hard | Easy | Mod. | Hard |
| Two-stage | MV3D | LiDAR & Img | 0.36 | 86.62 | 78.93 | 69.80 | 74.97 | 63.63 | 54.00 | N/A | N/A | N/A |
| | F-PointNet | LiDAR & Img | 0.17 | 91.17 | 84.67 | 74.77 | 82.19 | 69.79 | 60.59 | N/A | N/A | N/A |
| | AVOD | LiDAR & Img | 0.10 | 90.99 | 84.82 | 79.62 | 83.07 | 71.76 | 65.73 | 94.65 | 88.61 | 83.71 |
| | STD | LiDAR | 0.08 | 94.74 | 89.19 | 86.42 | 87.95 | 79.71 | 75.09 | N/A | N/A | N/A |
| | PointRCNN | LiDAR | 0.10 | 92.13 | 87.39 | 82.72 | 86.96 | 75.64 | 70.70 | 95.90 | 91.77 | 86.92 |
| | PartA2 | LiDAR | 0.08 | 91.70 | 87.79 | 84.61 | 87.81 | 78.49 | 73.51 | 95.00 | 91.73 | 88.86 |
| | PV-RCNN | LiDAR | 0.08 | 94.98 | 90.65 | 86.14 | 90.25 | 81.43 | 76.82 | 98.15 | 94.57 | 91.85 |
| Single-stage | ContFuse | LiDAR & Img | 0.06 | 94.07 | 85.35 | 75.88 | 83.68 | 68.78 | 61.67 | N/A | N/A | N/A |
| | SECOND | LiDAR | 0.05 | 91.38 | 85.63 | 78.60 | 83.66 | 73.07 | 68.12 | 95.99 | 90.04 | 84.70 |
| | PointPillars | LiDAR | 0.016 | 90.07 | 86.56 | 82.81 | 82.58 | 74.31 | 68.99 | 93.84 | 90.70 | 87.47 |
| | SARPNET | LiDAR | 0.05 | 92.21 | 86.92 | 81.68 | 85.63 | 76.64 | 71.31 | 95.82 | 92.58 | 87.33 |
| | TANET | LiDAR | 0.035 | 91.58 | 86.54 | 81.19 | 84.39 | 75.94 | 68.82 | 93.52 | 90.11 | 84.61 |
| | SA-SSD | LiDAR | 0.04 | 95.03 | 91.03 | 85.96 | 88.75 | 79.79 | 74.16 | 39.40 | 38.30 | 37.07 |
| | 3DSSD | LiDAR | 0.04 | 92.66 | 89.02 | 85.86 | 88.36 | 79.57 | 74.55 | N/A | N/A | N/A |
| | Point-GNN | LiDAR | 0.60 | 93.11 | 89.17 | 83.90 | 88.33 | 79.47 | 72.29 | 38.66 | 37.20 | 36.29 |
| | **SPANet** | LiDAR | 0.06 | **95.59** | **91.59** | **86.53** | **91.05** | **80.34** | **74.89** | **96.31** | **95.03** | **89.99** |

**Table 2.** The comparison of performances in bird's eye view (BEV) detection and 3D object detection: AP(%) on KITTI validation set for the class of Car.

| Method | Spatial | Part-aware | BEV | | | 3D | | |
|---|---|---|---|---|---|---|---|---|
| | | | Easy | Mod. | Hard | Easy | Mod. | Hard |
| Baseline | ✗ | ✗ | 96.40 | 90.27 | 87.53 | 92.87 | 83.79 | 78.96 |
| Type1 | ✗ | ✓ | 96.51 | 90.45 | 87.87 | 93.48 | 84.52 | 81.68 |
| Type2 | ✓ | ✗ | 96.63 | 90.36 | 87.69 | 93.36 | 84.15 | 79.36 |
| SPANet | ✓ | ✓ | **96.88** | **90.74** | **88.06** | **93.95** | **84.93** | **81.97** |

## 4.3 Results

We evaluate our model on the KITTI dataset to validate the effectiveness of the proposed method. We use an NVIDIA GTX 1080 Ti GPU for the inference of our experiments. We evaluate the proposed SPANet on the KITTI benchmark for bird's eye view detection, 3D object detection, and orientation estimation for the class of *Car*. The comparison results are shown in Table 1. The upper part of Table 1 shows the results of two-stage methods, and the lower part shows the results of single-stage methods. When compared with the single-stage methods, SPANet achieves the best performance for bird's eye view detection, 3D object detection and orientation estimation. The SPANet shows 0.5–0.6 AP points improvement over the best results on bird's eye view detection, 0.6–2.7 AP points improvement over the best results on 3D object detection, and 0.5–2.5 AP points improvement over the best results on orientation estimation. Some detected results on KITTI dataset are shown in Fig. 4.

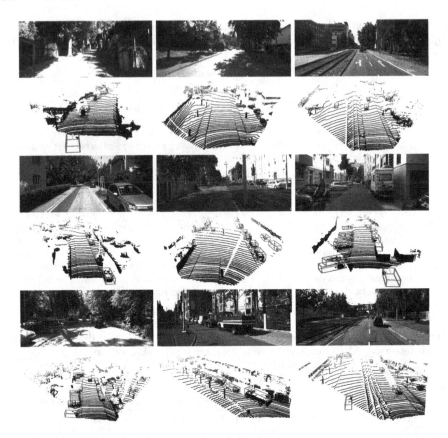

**Fig. 4.** Results of the 3D object detection on the KITTI test set. 3D boxes are projected on to the RGB images and LiDAR point cloud. The results of orientation estimation are drawn in the LiDAR point cloud using green.

### 4.4    Ablation Studies

In this section, we conduct extensive ablation experiments to analyze the effectiveness of different components of the SPANet on KITTI 3D object detection. All the ablation experiments were trained on the train set and tested on the validation set [1]. All the ablation studies were conducted on the car class because the relatively large amount of data to make system run stably. To analyze the effects of the proposed spatial aggregation and the part-aware attention modules, we tested the performance of each module separately. All results are shown in Table 2. The **Spatial** indicates the spatial aggregation module. This module improves 0.36 AP points for the performance of 3D. The **Part-aware** represents the part-aware aggregation module. This module improves 0.73 AP points for the performance of 3D. When we apply these two modules at the same time, the performance of 3D is improved by 1.14 AP points. And the performance of

BEV is improved by 0.52 AP points. The results prove the effectiveness of the two proposed modules.

## 5 Conclusion

We have presented the SPANet framework, a novel method for accurate 3D object detection from point clouds. SPANet integrates both the 3D voxel-based features and the point-based features using the proposed spatial aggregation module, which learns more discriminative features. In addition, the proposed part-aware aggregation module integrates fine-grain shape priors into the detector to improve the performance of 3D object detection significantly. Experimental results on the KITTI dataset demonstrate that the proposed method achieved state-of-the-art performance for single-stage 3D object detectors.

## References

1. Chen, X., Ma, H., Wan, J., Li, B., Xia, T.: Multi-view 3D object detection network for autonomous driving. In: IEEE CVPR, vol. 1, p. 3 (2017)
2. Geiger, A., Lenz, P., Urtasun, R.: Are we ready for autonomous driving? the kitti vision benchmark suite. In: 2012 IEEE Conference on Computer Vision and Pattern Recognition (CVPR), pp. 3354–3361. IEEE (2012)
3. Girshick, R.: Fast r-cNN. In: Proceedings of the IEEE International Conference on Computer Vision, pp. 1440–1448 (2015)
4. Graham, B., Engelcke, M., Van Der Maaten, L.: 3D semantic segmentation with submanifold sparse convolutional networks. In: Proceedings of the IEEE Conference on Computer Vision and Pattern Recognition, pp. 9224–9232 (2018)
5. Graham, B., van der Maaten, L.: Submanifold sparse convolutional networks. arXiv preprint arXiv:1706.01307 (2017)
6. He, C., Zeng, H., Huang, J., Hua, X.S., Zhang, L.: Structure aware single-stage 3d object detection from point cloud. In: CVPR (2020)
7. Ku, J., Mozifian, M., Lee, J., Harakeh, A., Waslander, S.: Joint 3D proposal generation and object detection from view aggregation. arXiv preprint arXiv:1712.02294 (2017)
8. Kuang, H., Wang, B., An, J., Zhang, M., Zhang, Z.: Voxel-FPN: multi-scale voxel feature aggregation for 3d object detection from lidar point clouds. Sensors 20(3), 704 (2020)
9. Lang, A.H., Vora, S., Caesar, H., Zhou, L., Yang, J., Beijbom, O.: Pointpillars: fast encoders for object detection from point clouds. arXiv preprint arXiv:1812.05784 (2018)
10. Lin, T.Y., Goyal, P., Girshick, R., He, K., Dollár, P.: Focal loss for dense object detection. IEEE Trans. Patt. Anal. Mach. Intell. 42, 318–327(2018)
11. Liu, W., et al.: SSD: single shot multibox detector. In: Leibe, B., Matas, J., Sebe, N., Welling, M. (eds.) ECCV 2016. LNCS, vol. 9905, pp. 21–37. Springer, Cham (2016). https://doi.org/10.1007/978-3-319-46448-0_2
12. Qi, C.R., Litany, O., He, K., Guibas, L.J.: Deep hough voting for 3d object detection in point clouds. In: Proceedings of the IEEE International Conference on Computer Vision, pp. 9277–9286 (2019)

13. Qi, C.R., Liu, W., Wu, C., Su, H., Guibas, L.J.: Frustum pointnets for 3D object detection from rgb-d data. arXiv preprint arXiv:1711.08488 (2017)
14. Qi, C.R., Su, H., Mo, K., Guibas, L.J.: Pointnet: deep learning on point sets for 3D classification and segmentation. In: Proceedings of the Computer Vision and Pattern Recognition (CVPR), vol. 1, p. 4. IEEE (2017)
15. Qi, C.R., Yi, L., Su, H., Guibas, L.J.: Pointnet++: deep hierarchical feature learning on point sets in a metric space. In: Advances in Neural Information Processing Systems, pp. 5099–5108 (2017)
16. Shi, S., et al.: Pv-RCNN: Point-voxel feature set abstraction for 3D object detection. In: CVPR (2020)
17. Shi, S., Wang, X., Li, H.: Pointrcnn: 3D object proposal generation and detection from point cloud. arXiv preprint arXiv:1812.04244 (2018)
18. Shi, S., Wang, Z., Shi, J., Wang, X., Li, H.: From points to parts: 3D object detection from point cloud with part-aware and part-aggregation network. In: IEEE Transactions on Pattern Analysis and Machine Intelligence (2020)
19. Yan, Y., Mao, Y., Li, B.: Second: sparsely embedded convolutional detection. Sensors **18**(10), 3337 (2018)
20. Ye, Y., Chen, H., Zhang, C., Hao, X., Zhang, Z.: Sarpnet: shape attention regional proposal network for lidar-based 3D object detection. Neurocomputing **379**, 53–63 (2020). https://doi.org/10.1016/j.neucom.2019.09.086
21. Zhou, Y., Tuzel, O.: Voxelnet: end-to-end learning for point cloud based 3D object detection. arXiv preprint arXiv:1711.06396 (2017)

# Subspace Enhancement and Colorization Network for Infrared Video Action Recognition

Lu Xu[1], Xian Zhong[1,2(✉)] [iD], Wenxuan Liu[1] [iD], Shilei Zhao[1], Zhengwei Yang[1], and Luo Zhong[1,2]

[1] School of Computer and Artificial Intelligence, Wuhan University of Technology, Wuhan 430070, China
zhongx@whut.edu.cn
[2] Hubei Key Laboratory of Transportation Internet of Things, Wuhan University of Technology, Wuhan 430070, China

**Abstract.** Human action recognition is an essential area of research in the field of computer vision. However, existing methods ignore the essence of infrared image spectral imaging. Compared with the visible modality with all three channels, the infrared modality with approximate single-channel pays more attention to the lightness contrast and loses the channel information. Therefore, we explore channel duplication and tend to investigate more appropriate feature presentations. We propose a subspace enhancement and colorization network ($S^2$ECNet) to recognize infrared video action recognition. Specifically, we apply the subspace enhancement ($S^2$E) module to promote edge contour extraction with subspace. Meanwhile, a subspace colorization ($S^2$C) module is utilized for better completing missing semantic information. What is more, the optical flow provides effective supplements for temporal information. Experiments conducted on the infrared action recognition dataset **InfAR** demonstrates the competitiveness of the proposed method compared with the state-of-the-arts.

**Keywords:** Infrared video action recognition · Subspace enhancement · Subspace colorization · Optical flow · Feature fusion

## 1 Introduction

Human action recognition in many vital applications *e.g.* surveillance, health monitoring, video recording, and human-computer interaction, has made remarkable progress in the past few years [1–4]. Most research only focuses on action recognition in the visible spectrum, providing rich color information and texture information.

However, visible spectrum can be limited in surveillance and may not capture useful appearance information under poor illumination conditions. Due to that, infrared cameras are used frequently in the place which may suffer low

© Springer Nature Switzerland AG 2021
D. N. Pham et al. (Eds.): PRICAI 2021, LNAI 13033, pp. 321–336, 2021.
https://doi.org/10.1007/978-3-030-89370-5_24

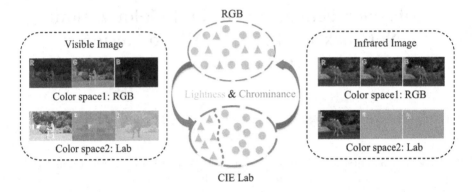

**Fig. 1.** Illustration of Subspace, which exists between visible image and infrared image. **Color space1: RGB** and **Color space2: Lab** represent the three-channel images of visible image and infrared image in RGB color space and Lab color space. It should be noted that channel a and channel b of the infrared image in the Lab color subspace has little valuable information, proving that the infrared image is approximate single-channel image and pays more attention to the lightness contrast. In addition, triangles represent lightness, and circles represent chrominance.

light environment. Thus, action recognition in infrared modality has attracted extensive attention as its immunity to visual influence.

Most of the existing methods leverage the multi-stream network to obtain different modality features. However, they ignore a characteristic of infrared images. As an approximate single-channel image, infrared modality pays more attention to the contrast of lightness and loses the chrominance channel information. A series of the problem has been observed. Some existing methods tend to use the infrared sequences without any background, making it susceptible to variations in background [5]. What is worse, the infrared images can hardly capture the interior motion [6], which motivates a rising trend to break through the single modality limitation. Inspired by cross-modality tasks in image retrieval [7–9], we find the vast performance gap to be bridged. It is an essential part of handling mentioned problem to elaborate the subspace relationship between modalities. To better explore the critical issue of our method, we visually illustrate it in Fig. 1. Image can be expressed through chrominance and lightness channels. The infrared image only has lightness information. Thus, we find that the subspace containing the common points of the two modalities can be integrated to express the feature.

According to the characteristics of human vision, humans perceive color from hue, saturation, and lightness. The most common red-green-blue (RGB) color subspace for human beings is expressed through the combination and super-position of the three primary colors of red (R), green (G), and blue (B). The disadvantage is that the uniform lightness change in human visual perception cannot be reflected in the data. Infrared image expression tends to be a way of separating lightness and color information. This inspired us to find a subspace to solve the above problem. Some of the satisfying condition color subspaces we shall briefly discuss are HSV, HSL, Lab. It should be noted that there is no proportional linear relationship between human vision's perception of uniform changes in color and the uniform change of light wavelength in the true physical sense. Therefore, the Lightness data designed in the color subspace of HSV and HSL does not conform to the actual physical meaning. The data is evenly distributed. This also results in the HSV and HSL color subspaces being more suitable for art design applications and cannot meet the demand for uniform data distribution required by the machine. In the varieties of color subspaces, CIE Lab comprises three channels as L, a, and b. L represents the lightness/luminance, whereas a and b are the chrominance. In the investigation process, we found that the Lab color subspace is a subspace that has nothing to do with equipment and expresses a broader color gamut. Further, color subspaces (essentially transformations of original RGB images) can significantly affect classification accuracy and commission Internationale de l'Eclairage (CIE) Lab obtain the best accuracy [10].

In the research process, we find that the imaging of infrared images and the Lightness channel showed a high correlation trend, and the reflection of infrared rays by different types of objects is different. If the background information can be appropriately subtracted from the infrared Lightness information to enhance the edge contour information of the human body in the background, the performance of infrared video action recognition can be improved to a certain extent. Thus, it is necessary to use the lightness information to suppress the effect of background clutter. Inspired by the Simple Linear Iterative Clustering (SLIC) [11] in image segmentation, we enhance the information of similar pixels in the same area, expand the distance between the human body and the background noise generated by the background clutter in the infrared image. We propose the subspace enhancement (S²E) model by re-fusing the lightness channels to obtain the edge contour and relatively suppress the effect of background noise from background clutter.

Automatically converting an infrared image to a plausible color image is an exciting way to obtain plentiful information. However, predicting two missing channels from a given near single-channel image is inherently an illposed problem. Previous works have utilized the colorization net to predict the color, which goal is to minimize Euclidean error between an estimate and the ground truth [10]. CIE Lab is a perceptually linear colorspace as it establishes a mapping between the colors in Euclidean space and the colors in human perception. Therefore, it is more suitable than other colorspaces for our colorization task. In this paper, we introduce the subspace colorization (S²C) module to our network.

In this paper, we propose a novel three-stream subspace enhancement and colorization network (S²ECNet) network based on the CIE Lab latent space, as Fig. 2 shows. Specifically, S²ECNet is naturally decomposed into spatial and temporal components. In the form of individual frame appearance, the spatial part carries information about scenes and objects depicted in the video. The S²E model superimposes the channels with contrast information from single-channel to dual-channel, that is, $X_i^{Lab} \rightarrow X_i^{LaL}$. Then the S$^2$C module achieves the purpose of filling the color in the lab image.

In the form of motion across the frames, the temporal part conveys the observer's movement (the camera) and the objects. The objects with strong reflectance to infrared light still exist in the video, so the immobile objects can be further filtered through optical flow so that the network pays more attention to the moving human body. Particularly, to better complement the spatial-temporal information, we share the weighting. In theory, our method is to process the data before it enters the deep convolutional network so that we can extend this method to other action recognition techniques for infrared video.

Our main contributions are summarized threefold:

- We propose a three-stream S$^2$ECNet and interpolate, which can provide a subspace between infrared modality and visible modality. Besides, the network has considered weight sharing to complement the spatial and temporal information.
- We propose a new S$^2$E module. The influence of background clutter in infrared images is suppressed, and the contrast is improved to enhance the profile information.
- We use the S$^2$C module to bridge the modal gap between visible data and infrared data and supplement the details of infrared video to improve the video action recognition under infrared spectrum.

## 2   Related Work

### 2.1   Visible-Based Action Recognition

In the visible domain, with the significant progress of deep learning techniques, various deep learning architectures have also been proposed. The deep learning methods for RGB-based action recognition can be divided into two-stream 2D CNN, 3D CNN-based methods, and recurrent neural network (RNN). Simonyan et al. [1] proposed a two-stream CNN model consisting of a spatial network and a temporal network. More specifically, given a video, each individual RGB frame and multi-frame-based optical flows were fed to the spatial stream and temporal stream, respectively, and fused their scores for final prediction. Wang et al. [3] divided each video into three segments and processed each segment with a two-stream network. Then the classification scores of the three segments were then fused by an average pooling method to produce the video-level prediction. However, the two-stream CNN model had limitations in effectively modeling the video-level temporal information. Many researchers have extended 2D CNNs to 3D structures to simultaneously model the spatial and temporal context information in videos crucial for action recognition. Tran et al. [2] proposed to model spatial-temporal information using 3D CNNs.

To decrease the computation, R(2+1)D [12] decomposed the 3D filters into a spatial filter and a temporal filter. Carreira et al. [13] inflated the weights from pre-trained 2D CNNs, which can leverage both the successful design and solid parameters of deep image classification architecture. Lin *et al.* [14] proposed a temporal shift module (TSM) for 3D CNN, which shifts the channels along the temporal dimension both forward and backward. Thus the information is exchanged between adjacent frames, and the complexity is maintained to the level of 2D CNNs. More recently, RNN based approaches [4] and [15] were also popular to model the spatial-temporal representation in videos.

## 2.2 Infrared-Based Action Recognition

With the maturity of infrared technology, some action recognition methods for infrared video are gradually proposed. For the early research, Han *et al.* [16] firstly applied infrared images in human contour detection and clipping by using a hierarchical genetic algorithm (HGA). Zhu *et al.* [17] extracted the distribution histogram features of infrared image and used an SVM classifier trained by visible data to classify. The classification result was only a little higher than that of random. Gao *et al.* [18] complemented the gap of undisclosed infrared video datasets. Moreover, they proposed a new infrared action dataset, **InfAR** dataset. On this dataset, Gao *et al.* evaluated some hand-made features *e.g.* STIP [19], HOG3D [20], 3DSIFT [21], followed by feature encoding using Fisher vector (FV) [22] and vector of locally aggregated descriptors (VLAD) [23]. In terms of individual feature performance, DT gives the best result of 68.66% on **InfAR** dataset using VLAD encoding with linear kernel.

For the infrared video, it is crucial to learn informative and efficient feature representations. Since infrared frames are insufficient for texture detail, it is natural to adopt multi-stream architecture. Gao *et al.* further proposed a two-stream framework based on 2D CNNs to extract extra features like optical flow and optical flow-Motion history image (OF-MHI) [24], and this method achieved 76.66% results. Some later methods adopted deeper networks than the previous works. Hilsenbeck *et al.* [25] used Hoff forest and integral channel features (ICF) to identify violent and non-violent actions in infrared images. Jiang *et al.* [26] proposed a two-stream network using convolutional 3D (C3D) [2] to learn spatial-temporal features from infrared images and optical flows. Wang *et al.* [27,28] proposed a GAN network to generate information missing from the infrared data. Ali *et al.* [29] applied the Beta-Liouville Hidden Markov Models (BLHMM) for the first time in action recognition of infrared data. That model overcomes overfitting and under-fitting, and optimized the generalization ability. Riva *et al.* [30] investigated Bayesian 3D ConvNets for action recognition when training infrared video examples were scarce. Bayesian 3D ConvNets have been shown effective regularizers for deep networks. Liu *et al.* [31] sent optical flow motion history image, optical flow, and superimposed difference image of optical flow image to a third-stream CNN network for action recognition, respectively. Inspired by this, Imran *et al.* [32] proposed a four-stream architecture that uses two CNN pathways to learn the global temporal information, while two CNN-BiLSTM pathways to capture local spatial-temporal features. Chen *et al.* [33] explored an effective way to generate optical flow and obtained discriminative features automatically, with only input the single infrared stream.

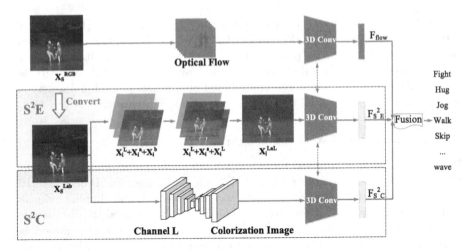

**Fig. 2.** Overview of the proposed method. Given an Infrared sequence $X_S^{RGB}$ as input, our model starts with converting the color subspace from RGB to CIE Lab. We then extract temporal feature $F_{flow}$ via Optical flow and use S²E and S²C stream to extract spatial feature $F_{S^2E}$ and $F_{S^2C}$ via $X_S^{Lab}$ image. In addition, S²E replaces one of the channels of $X_S^{Lab}$ image and refuses to obtain $X_i^{LaL}$. S²C uses colorization network to colorize $X_S^{Lab}$ and obtain globally consistent colorization results **Colorization Image**. Finally, we propose to fuse all the features $F_{flow}$, $F_{S^2E}$, and $F_{S^2C}$ in the last layer network.

## 3   Method

### 3.1   Framework

In this section, we introduce our proposed method in detail. An overview of the framework is presented in Fig. 2. We adopt an S²ECNet to learn informative and efficient feature representations. In this architecture, we input a sequence of infrared video frames $X_S^{RGB}$ into the network. Moreover, the temporal feature is extracted by the first stream, the spatial feature is extracted by the second and the third streams. The first stream is to use the optical flow to solve temporal modeling. The second stream is S²E stream, in which the channels of the image are recombined and pay more attention to the lightness information of the infrared image. The third stream of the proposed network is S²C stream, and we use it to complete the missing color details of the infrared image. Finally, we use an inflated 3D ConvNet (I3D) [13] network to extract these features respectively and fuse these three features and use the softmax function to classify human action.

First of all, we use (1), (2), and (3) to transfer the color subspace of the infrared video frame from RGB to CIE Lab color subspace. We convert the RGB image to XYZ image. And then, we set a frame in video as $X_i^{RGB}$, and the network input is a sequence of frames $X_S^{RGB} \in \mathbb{R}^{N \times T \times H \times W \times C}$, which can be obtained by (4).

$$\begin{bmatrix} R \\ G \\ B \end{bmatrix} = \begin{bmatrix} 3.240479 & -1.537150 & -0.498535 \\ -0.969256 & 1.875992 & 0.041556 \\ 0.055648 & -0.204043 & 1.057311 \end{bmatrix} \begin{bmatrix} X \\ Y \\ Z \end{bmatrix} \quad (1)$$

$$L^* = 116\, f\left(\frac{Y}{Y_n}\right) - 16,$$

$$a^* = 500\left[f\left(\frac{X}{X_n}\right) - f\left(\frac{Y}{Y_n}\right)\right], \quad (2)$$

$$b^* = 200\left[f\left(\frac{Y}{Y_n}\right) - f\left(\frac{Z}{Z_n}\right)\right]$$

$$f(t) = \begin{cases} t^{\frac{1}{3}}, & \text{if } t > \left(\frac{6}{29}\right)^3 \\ \frac{1}{3}\left(\frac{29}{6}\right)^2 t + \frac{4}{29}, & \text{otherwise} \end{cases} \quad (3)$$

$$X_S^{RGB} = \{X_0^{RGB}, X_1^{RGB}, X_2^{RGB}, \dots, X_i^{RGB}\} \quad (4)$$

### 3.2  Subspace Enhancement

As we all know, the imaging of infrared images is mainly determined by the strength of the object's ability to reflect light. Therefore, compared to visible imaging, background clutter has a more significant impact on infrared images. Through the result of channel matrix and channel visualization output, as shown in Fig. 1, as we can easily conclude that the imaging in infrared has the most significant amount of information in the $X_i^L$ (Lightness) channel, and there is no comparative and helpful information in the color channel $X_i^a$ and $X_i^b$. Thus, to suppress the effect of background clutter, in the S²E, the lightness channels of the images are superimposed, such that the contour information of the human is amplified and the contrast between the background noise and the human body is increased. Finally, it has positive implications on the performance of the action recognition model. As shown in Fig. 2, we propose a S²E module. Given a sequences of infrared image $X_S^{RGB}$ in RGB color subspace, S²E starts with extracting the infrared frame $X_S^{RGB}$. We then obtained three channels of image ($X_i^L$, $X_i^a$, and $X_i^b$) in Lab color subspace by converting the color subspace of $X_S^{RGB}$ from RGB to Lab and split the channel of $X_S^{Lab}$. We utilize $X_i^L$ to replace the color channel (i.e. $X_i^a$ and $X_i^b$) and merge these new three channels. Finally, we have a new image in Lab space, i.e. $X_i^{Lab} \rightarrow X_i^{LaL}$ (or $X_i^{LLb}$) $\rightarrow X_i^{LLL}$. Based on the previous ablation experimental results, we select the configuration $X_i^{LaL} \in \mathbb{R}^{N \times T \times 224 \times 224 \times C}$.

From Fig. 2, we can see that the boundary between the human and the background in image $X_i^{LaL}$ is more evident than in image $X_S^{RGB}$, and the background noise in $X_i^{LaL}$ is also less. All of these factors cause the network to pay more attention to the human. One of the reasons that make the $X_i^{LaL}$ has a background color that the channel $X_i^L$ is used to replace the $X_i^b$ channel, which represents the chrominance. An image is nothing but numbers to a computer. Hence, transformations of these images should be viewed as a completely new image to a computer. Essentially transferring an image into different color sub-spaces should generate new images in the view of the computer, but for the image after compositing the channels, it is giving inappropriate color information to the infrared image. However, for the network, the lightness channel $X_i^L$ is superimposed, and the contrast between the human and the background is increased. At last, we resize the cropped images to a resolution of $224 \times 224$ after channel fusion and input a sequence of $X_i^{LaL}$.

### 3.3 Subspace Colorization

To bridge the modality gap between infrared and visible, we propose an S²C module, which uses partial mode (infrared image) to generate full mode (color image). Moreover, the network can obtain complementary but heterogeneous information conveyed by different spectrums of data, which can improve the model performance of infrared video action recognition.

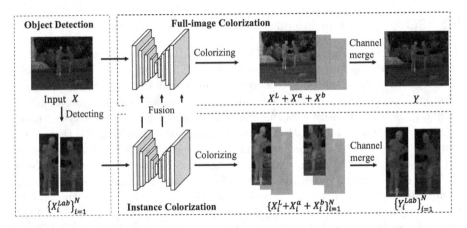

**Fig. 3.** Overview of the proposed S²C module. Given an infrared image $X$ as input, our model detects the object bounding boxes using an off-the-shelf object detection model. Then we crop out every detected instance of $\{X_i^L\}_{i=1}^N$ and use instance colorization network to colorize single-channel image $X_i^L$. We obtain a three-channel (L, a, b) image result $Y_i^{Lab}$. However, as the color of instance may not be compatible concerning the predicted background colors, features of instance maps in every layer are fused with the extracted full-image feature maps by using the proposed fusion module. We obtain globally consistent colorization results $Y$.

Referring to the method [34], as shown in Fig. 3, our colorization network is also divided into two stages, object detection and colorization. The colorization stage consists of two parts, one for coloring the instance images and the other for coloring the full image. Before colorization, we employ an off-the-shelf pre-trained network, Mask R-CNN [35], as our object detector. We crop the instances $X_i^{Lab}$ in the image according to the size of the bounding box. We feed each instance image $X_i^{Lab}$ and original $X$ to the instance colorization network and full-image colorization network, respectively. Moreover, S²C module follows [36] to train the model on COCO-Stuff dataset and fine-tune it. S²C module using channel $X_i^L$ of $X_i^{Lab}$ to predict a couple of chrominance $\{X_i^a, X_i^b\}$ then merge these three channels. Finally, we get the color instance image $Y_i^{Lab}$ and the color full image $Y^{Lab}$, then optimize the feature fusion to obtain these smooth colorization results by a fusion module. Specifically, we resize the instance feature $Y_i^{Lab}$ as well as the weight map $W_i^I$ to match the size of full-image and exploit zero paddings on both of them. We denote the resized instance feature and weight map as $\bar{Y}_{X_i}^{Lab}$ and $\bar{W}_i^I$. After that, we stack all the weight maps, apply softmax on each pixel, and obtain the fused feature using a weighted sum as (5), where $Y^{Lab}$ is a full-image feature, $\bar{Y}_i^{Lab}$ is a bunch of instance features, and $N$ is the number of instances. These two features are given different weights, $W_F$ and $W_i^I$, and each instance feature $Y_i^{Lab}$ is integrated into the corresponding full-image feature $Y^{Lab}$. We utilize the input bounding box, which defines the size and location of the instance $Y_i^{Lab}$. The final fused image is image $Y$.

$$Y = Y^{Lab} \circ W_F + \sum_{i=1}^{N} \bar{Y}_i^{Lab} \circ \bar{W}_i^I \tag{5}$$

### 3.4  Fusion

Fusion refers to the integration of information from two or more modalities for training and inference. Therefore, it is natural to use the complementary advantages of different data patterns through fusion to achieve higher performance. There are two common multi-modal fusion methods in human action recognition: score fusion and feature fusion. Our method will use feature fusion to integrate modalities for training. In the S²ECNet, $F_{S^2E}$ is generated by S²E module, $F_{S^2C}$ feature generated by S²C module, and $F_{flow}$ feature extracted by optical flow. We fuse these three features in the Logits layer after the last perception module. The concatenate operation is as follows:

$$Y^S = W_{S^2E} \cdot F_{S^2E} \oplus W_{S^2C} \cdot F_{S^2C} \oplus W_{flow} \cdot F_{flow} \tag{6}$$

where $\oplus$ is the concatenate operation, $W_{S^2E}$, $W_{S^2C}$, and $W_{flow}$ are the weight factors of the three features. $Y^S$ is the final fusion feature. Before feature fusion, three kinds of features need to be normalized.

## 4  Experiment and Metrics

### 4.1  Datasets

**InfAR** dataset consists of 12 action classes. Each class consists of 90 videos recorded at a resolution of 293 × 256. Each class has 75 videos as training set and 25 videos as testing set. All action instances are displayed in Fig. 4. **InfAR**

**Fig. 4.** Video samples for 12 action classes on **InfAR** action dataset.

dataset includes one-hand wave (wave1), multiple-hand wave (wave2), handclap, jog, jump, walk, skip, hug, push, handshake, punch, and fighting action, with 25 frames per second (FPS) and resolution of 293 × 256. Each video clip lasts about 4 s on average. Some of these videos illustrate interactions between multiple actors. We use Top-1% accuracy as our network metrics.

## 4.2   Experimental Settings

We conducted our experiments on video action recognition tasks by following the same strategy mentioned in I3D, given an input video, then we randomly selected frames to obtain a clip with $T$ frames. The size of the shorter side of these frames is fixed to 256, and cropping is utilized for data augmentation. We use random cropping, both spatially resizing the smaller video side to 256 pixels, then randomly cropping a 224 × 224, when picking the starting frame among those early enough to guarantee a desired number of frames. The input fed to the model is of the size $N \times T \times 224 \times 224 \times 3$, where $N$ is the batch size, $T$ is the number of frames in each clip. We looped the video as many times as necessary to satisfy each model's input interface for shorter videos. During testing, the model is applied convolutionally over the whole video taking 224 × 224 center crops, and the predictions are averaged. We briefly try spatially-convolutional testing on the 256 × 256 videos but do not observe improvement. Better performance could be obtained by also considering left-right flipped videos at test time and adding additional augmentation during training. It is worth mentioning that we verified the results when $T = 64, 25, 16$. The best performance of the model is obtained by $T = 16$, so we set $T = 16$ by default in the other experiment.

During training, the models were trained with two GPUs and were implemented using TensorFlow library and accelerated by CUDA 10.0. We use I3D [13] network as backbone, which uses ImageNet pre-trained Inception-V1 as baseline. We follow each convolutional layer by a batch normalization layer and a rectified linear unit (ReLU) activation function for all architectures, except for the last convolutional layers, which produce the class scores for each network. Same as I3D method, we adopted Adam optimization algorithm, and we set the initial learning rate at $1 \times 10^{-4}$. Meanwhile, we train S$^2$E stream and S$^2$C stream models on **InfAR** for 10k steps with the learning rate decreases by 0.1 every 2k steps, while optical flow stream for 20k steps with the learning rate decreases by 0.1 every 5k steps. We followed the I3D method of model fusion, the weight of the appearance feature and the motion feature are equally distributed. Since S$^2$E stream and S$^2$C stream are included in the appearance features, our method also distributes the weights of S$^2$E stream and S$^2$C stream equally. Finally, we choose $W_{S^2E} = 0.25$, $W_{S^2C} = 0.25$, and $W_{flow} = 0.5$. There are two common multi-modal fusion methods in human action recognition: score fusion and feature fusion. However, due to lack of time and space, we will seek a better model fusion method in future work.

**Table 1.** Comparison of top-1 accuracy (%) performances with the state-of-the-arts on **InfAR** dataset. **Bold** numbers are the best results.

| Method | Venue | Flow | Accuracy |
|---|---|---|---|
| STIP [19] | IJCV '05 | × | 49.16 |
| 3DSIFT [21] | ACM MM '07 | × | 49.50 |
| Dense-Traj [37] | CVPR '11 | × | 68.66 |
| Two-stream 2D-CNN [18] | Neurocomputing '16 | ✓ | 76.66 |
| TSTDD [31] | SPL '18 | ✓ | 79.25 |
| Global + Local SSDI [32] | IPT '19 | × | 69.25 |
| Global SSDI + Local SDFDI [32] | IPT '19 | ✓ | 83.50 |
| IR net 3D-CNN [26] | CVPR '17 | × | 54.58 |
| Two-stream 3D-CNN [26] | CVPR '17 | ✓ | 77.50 |
| PM-GANs [27] | ECCV '18 | ✓ | 78.00 |
| Bayesian 3D ConvNets [30] | ICCV '19 | × | 45.00 |
| Filter-OF 3D CNN [38] | CEAI '19 | ✓ | 88.19 |
| FEN [33] | TMM '21 | ✓ | 84.25 |
| I3D-RGB [13] (baseline) | CVPR '17 | × | 82.67 |
| S$^2$ECNet w/o Flow (ours) | | × | **86.00** |
| S$^2$ECNet w Flow (ours) | | ✓ | **92.33** |

## 4.3   Comparisons with Other Methods

We evaluate the performance comparison of our proposed $S^2$ECNet against other state-of-the-art methods on **InfAR** [18] dataset. In Table 1, the first compartment contains the methods based on handcrafted features, the methods in the second compartment are all based on 2D CNNs or 2D CNNs + RNN, and the methods in the third compartment are all based on 3D CNNs. It can be observed that methods based on 3D CNNs or 3D CNNs + GAN (except Bayesian 3D ConvNets [30]) average outperform methods based on 2D-CNN architecture. One reason is that the 3D-CNN architecture is better in modeling temporal variations. In addition, we also find that the unpredictability of Bayesian 3D ConvNets model may be due to the use of a small number of 3D CNN layers. Moreover, the main reason why Global SSDI-Local SDFDI [32] performs so well is that it learns the temporal feature of infrared video through bi-directional long short-term memory (BiLSTM) + 2D CNN network.

Our propose $S^2$ECNet outperforms the best-handcrafted techniques by more than 23% (68.66% vs. 92.33%). Compared with the method based on 2D CNN, the performance of our proposed $S^2$ECNet is increased by a significant margin, about 8.83% (83.50% vs. 92.33%). Furthermore, our method also outperforms the best method Filter-OF 3D CNN [38] by 4.14% (88.19% vs. 92.33%). The superiority of our $S^2$E and $S^2$C modules on **InfAR** dataset is quite impressive. It confirms the remarkable ability of $S^2$E and $S^2$C modules for spatial and temporal modeling. Our method uses I3D for feature extraction, where optical flow is used to capture temporal information. Moreover, considering the proposed three-stream network has impact both in spatial and temporal receptive fields, it is necessary to ascertain the independent impact of the two aspects. To this end, we compare the method without using optical flow, as shown in Table 1. The "I3D-RGB" is our baseline, which only uses video frames in RGB color subspace as input. The "$S^2$ECNet w/o Flow" can be obtained by fusing $S^2$E stream and $S^2$C stream. Our method "$S^2$ECNet w Flow" contains $S^2$E stream, $S^2$C stream, and optical flow stream. Compared with the method without optical flow, we can see that the accuracies of $S^2$ECNet w/o Flow all outperform the best techniques without optical flow and even by more than 16% (69.25% vs. 86.00%). It proves that such improvement is not entirely brought about by using optical flow information.

**Table 2.** Comparison of top-1 accuracy (%) performances with different variants of our method on **InfAR** dataset. **Bold** numbers are the best results.

| Baseline | $S^2$C | $S^2$E | Flow | Accuracy |
|----------|--------|--------|------|----------|
| ✓ | × | × | × | 82.67 |
| ✓ | ✓ | × | × | 84.00 |
| ✓ | ✓ | ✓ | × | 86.00 |
| ✓ | ✓ | ✓ | ✓ | **92.33** |

### 4.4   Ablation Studies

In order to verify the effectiveness of different modules in our method, we conducted ablation experiments, as shown in Table 2. We compare the first row and the second row, and it can be seen that our S²C module improves the model's ability to represent the appearance information of the infrared video (82.67% vs. 84.00%). The third row adds the S²E and attains higher accuracy (84.00% vs. 86.00%). Finally, we fuse all of the modules, the accuracy of our S²ECNet can be further improved to 92.33%.

To select the most suitable channel fusion method, we also perform a set of ablation experiments on S²E stream. In this set of experiments, channel $X_i^a$ and channel $X_i^b$ in the three-channel infrared image $X_i^{Lab}$ are replaced with lightness channel $X_i^L$ respectively. In this way, four types of combinations are obtained: Lab, LaL, LLb, and LLL. The best channel combination is LaL, with an accuracy rate of 84.00%. However, our experiments show that the model's performance does not increase with the number of L channels. One possible reason for this may be that when the image is overlayed with too much light information, some background clutter is magnified along with the human body. So the influence of background clutter on the network is also amplified, resulting in a decline in the result. Therefore, a moderate two-channel stacking method is selected on the channel fusion.

## 5   Conclusion

We propose a subspace enhancement and colorization network (S²ECNet) to solve the infrared video action recognition problem. In detail, the S²E module enhances the edge contour of human by using channel duplication. Besides, the S²C module is utilized to better complete missing semantic information, reducing the modality gap between the infrared and visible images. What is more, optical flow has made significant contributions to temporal modeling. Good experiments prove that our proposed method has apparent competitiveness compared with other existing methods on **InfAR** dataset. It would be of great value to extend this method to other techniques of action recognition for infrared video, which will be explored in our future work.

**Acknowledgements.** This work was supported in part by the Fundamental Research Funds for the Central Universities of China under Grant 191010001, in part by the Hubei Key Laboratory of Transportation Internet of Things under Grant 2020III026GX.

## References

1. Simonyan, K., Zisserman, A.: Two-stream convolutional networks for action recognition in videos. In: Proceedings of the Advances in Neural Information Processing Systems (NeurIPS), pp. 568–576 (2014)

2. Tran, D., Bourdev, L.D., Fergus, R., Torresani, L., Paluri, M.: Learning spatiotemporal features with 3D convolutional networks. In: Proceedings of the IEEE/CVF International Conference on Computer Vision (ICCV), pp. 4489–4497 (2015)
3. Wang, L., et al.: Temporal segment networks: towards good practices for deep action recognition. In: Leibe, B., Matas, J., Sebe, N., Welling, M. (eds.) ECCV 2016. LNCS, vol. 9912, pp. 20–36. Springer, Cham (2016). https://doi.org/10.1007/978-3-319-46484-8_2
4. Fan, Z., Zhao, X., Lin, T., Su, H.: Attention-based multiview re-observation fusion network for skeletal action recognition. IEEE Trans. Multimed. **21**(2), 363–374 (2019)
5. Lee, E.J., Ko, B.C., Nam, J.Y.: Recognizing pedestrian's unsafe behaviors in far-infrared imagery at night. Infrared Phys. Technol. **76**, 261–270 (2016)
6. Akula, A., Shah, A.K., Ghosh, R.: Deep learning approach for human action recognition in infrared images. Cogn. Syst. Res. **50**, 146–154 (2018)
7. Huang, Z., Wang, Z., Tsai, C.C., Satoh, S., Lin, C.W.: DotSCN: group re-identification via domain-transferred single and couple representation learning. IEEE Trans. Circ. Syst. Video Technol. **31**(7), 2739–2750 (2021)
8. Kansal, K., Subramanyam, A.V., Wang, Z., Satoh, S.: SDL: spectrum-disentangled representation learning for visible-infrared person re-identification. IEEE Trans. Circ. Syst. Video Technol. **30**(10), 3422–3432 (2020)
9. Zhong, X., Lu, T., Huang, W., Ye, M., Jia, X., Lin, C.: Grayscale enhancement colorization network for visible-infrared person re-identification. IEEE Trans. Circ. Syst. Video Technol. (2021). https://doi.org/10.1109/TCSVT.2021.3072171
10. Gowda, S.N., Yuan, C.: ColorNet: investigating the importance of color spaces for image classification. In: Jawahar, C.V., Li, H., Mori, G., Schindler, K. (eds.) ACCV 2018. LNCS, vol. 11364, pp. 581–596. Springer, Cham (2019). https://doi.org/10.1007/978-3-030-20870-7_36
11. Achanta, R., Shaji, A., Smith, K., Lucchi, A., Fua, P., Süsstrunk, S.: SLIC superpixels compared to state-of-the-art superpixel methods. IEEE Trans. Pattern Anal. Mach. Intell. **34**(11), 2274–2282 (2012)
12. Tran, D., Wang, H., Torresani, L., Ray, J., LeCun, Y., Paluri, M.: A closer look at spatiotemporal convolutions for action recognition. In: Proceedings of the IEEE/CVF Conference on Computer Vision and Pattern Recognition (CVPR), pp. 6450–6459 (2018)
13. Carreira, J., Zisserman, A.: Quo vadis, action recognition? A new model and the kinetics dataset. In: Proceedings of the IEEE/CVF Conference on Computer Vision and Pattern Recognition (CVPR), pp. 4724–4733 (2017)
14. Lin, J., Gan, C., Han, S.: TSM: temporal shift module for efficient video understanding. In: Proceedings of the IEEE/CVF International Conference on Computer Vision (ICCV), pp. 7082–7092 (2019)
15. Wu, H., Ma, X., Li, Y.: Convolutional networks with channel and STIPs attention model for action recognition in videos. IEEE Trans. Multimed. **22**(9), 2293–2306 (2020)
16. Han, J., Bhanu, B.: Fusion of color and infrared video for moving human detection. Pattern Recogn. **40**(6), 1771–1784 (2007)
17. Zhu, Y., Guo, G.: A study on visible to infrared action recognition. IEEE Sig. Process. Lett. **20**(9), 897–900 (2013)
18. Gao, C., et al.: Infar dataset: infrared action recognition at different times. Neurocomputing **212**, 36–47 (2016)
19. Laptev, I.: On space-time interest points. Int. J. Comput. Vis. **64**(2–3), 107–123 (2005). https://doi.org/10.1007/s11263-005-1838-7

20. Kläser, A., Marszalek, M., Schmid, C.: A spatio-temporal descriptor based on 3D-gradients. In: Proceedings of the BMVA British Machine Vision Conference (BMVC), pp. 1–10 (2008)
21. Scovanner, P., Ali, S., Shah, M.: A 3-dimensional sift descriptor and its application to action recognition. In: Proceedings of the ACM International Conference on Multimedia (ACM MM), pp. 357–360 (2007)
22. Shi, Y., Tian, Y., Wang, Y., Zeng, W., Huang, T.: Learning long-term dependencies for action recognition with a biologically-inspired deep network. In: Proceedings of the IEEE/CVF International Conference on Computer Vision (ICCV), pp. 716–725 (2017)
23. Jégou, H., Douze, M., Schmid, C., Pérez, P.: Aggregating local descriptors into a compact image representation. In: Proceedings of the IEEE/CVF Conference on Computer Vision and Pattern Recognition (CVPR), pp. 3304–3311 (2010)
24. Tsai, D.-M., Chiu, W.-Y., Lee, M.-H.: Optical flow-motion history image (OF-MHI) for action recognition. SIViP 9(8), 1897–1906 (2014). https://doi.org/10.1007/s11760-014-0677-9
25. Hilsenbeck, B., Münch, D., Grosselfinger, A., Hübner, W., Arens, M.: Action recognition in the longwave infrared and the visible spectrum using hough forests. In: Proceedings of the IEEE International Symposium on Multimedia (ISM), pp. 329–332 (2016)
26. Jiang, Z., Rozgic, V., Adali, S.: Learning spatiotemporal features for infrared action recognition with 3D convolutional neural networks. In: Proceedings of the IEEE/CVF Conference on Computer Vision and Pattern Recognition Workshops (CVPR), pp. 309–317 (2017)
27. Wang, L., Gao, C., Yang, L., Zhao, Y., Zuo, W., Meng, D.: PM-GANs: discriminative representation learning for action recognition using partial-modalities. In: Ferrari, V., Hebert, M., Sminchisescu, C., Weiss, Y. (eds.) ECCV 2018. LNCS, vol. 11210, pp. 389–406. Springer, Cham (2018). https://doi.org/10.1007/978-3-030-01231-1_24
28. Wang, L., Gao, C., Zhao, Y., Song, T., Feng, Q.: Infrared and visible image registration using transformer adversarial network. In: Proceedings of the IEEE International Conference on Image Processing (ICIP), pp. 1248–1252 (2018)
29. Ali, S., Bouguila, N.: Variational learning of beta-liouville hidden Markov models for infrared action recognition. In: Proceedings of the IEEE/CVF Conference on Computer Vision and Pattern Recognition Workshops (CVPR), pp. 898–906 (2019)
30. de la Riva, M., Mettes, P.: Bayesian 3D convnets for action recognition from few examples. In: Proceedings of the IEEE/CVF International Conference on Computer Vision Workshops (ICCV), pp. 1337–1343 (2019)
31. Liu, Y., Lu, Z., Li, J., Yang, T., Yao, C.: Global temporal representation based CNNs for infrared action recognition. IEEE Sig. Process. Lett. 25(6), 848–852 (2018)
32. Imran, J., Raman, B.: Deep residual infrared action recognition by integrating local and global spatio-temporal cues. Infrared Phys. Technol. 102, 103014 (2019)
33. Chen, X., Gao, C., Li, C., Yang, Y., Meng, D.: Infrared action detection in the dark via cross-stream attention mechanism. IEEE Trans. Multimed. (2021). https://doi.org/10.1109/TMM.2021.3050069
34. Zhang, R., Isola, P., Efros, A.A.: Colorful image colorization. In: Leibe, B., Matas, J., Sebe, N., Welling, M. (eds.) ECCV 2016. LNCS, vol. 9907, pp. 649–666. Springer, Cham (2016). https://doi.org/10.1007/978-3-319-46487-9_40
35. He, K., Gkioxari, G., Dollár, P., Girshick, R.B.: Mask R-CNN. IEEE Trans. Pattern Anal. Mach. Intell. 42(2), 386–397 (2020)

36. Su, J., Chu, H., Huang, J.: Instance-aware image colorization. In: Proceedings of the IEEE/CVF Conference on Computer Vision and Pattern Recognition (CVPR), pp. 7965–7974 (2020)
37. Wang, H., Kläser, A., Schmid, C., Liu, C.: Action recognition by dense trajectories. In: Proceedings of the IEEE/CVF Conference on Computer Vision and Pattern Recognition (CVPR), pp. 3169–3176 (2011)
38. Khebli, A., Meglouli, H., Bentabet, L., Airouche, M.: A new technique based on 3D convolutional neural networks and filtering optical flow maps for action classification in infrared video. Control Eng. Appl. Inform. **21**(4), 43–50 (2019)

# Thinking in Patch: Towards Generalizable Forgery Detection with Patch Transformation

Xueqi Zhang[1,2(✉)], Shuo Wang[1], Chenyu Liu[3], Min Zhang[1,2], Xiaohan Liu[3], and Haiyong Xie[1,2(✉)]

[1] University of Science and Technology of China, Hefei 230026, China
{xqzhang7,minz}@mail.ustc.edu.cn, {shuowangcv,hxie}@ustc.edu.cn
[2] Key Laboratory of Cyberculture Content Cognition and Detection,
Ministry of Culture and Tourism, Anhui 230027, China
[3] National Engineering Laboratory for Public Safety Risk Perception
and Control by Big Data, Beijing 100040, China
liuxiaohan@cetc.com.cn, 2011010090@bupt.cn

**Abstract.** Nowadays, synthetic faces can completely trick human eyes, which raises social concerns for malicious dissemination of such fake content. As a result, face forgery detection has become a significant research topic. Due to the different distributions of synthetic data in different generation algorithms, it is a great challenge to improve the generalization ability of the face forgery detection algorithm. To address this challenge, we propose a general two-stream patch-based face forgery detection network (*FDPT*), which introduces a patch transformation to encourage the model to focus on stable information in different data. Specifically, a random transformation is designed to help CNN stream extract local subtle artifacts from images. Meanwhile, a sequence transformation is employed to enhance the global spatial representation ability of the image through the CNN-GRU stream. Finally, a fusion strategy is used to improve the detection accuracy. We conduct extensive experiments to show that FDPT achieves state-of-the-art performance on two popular benchmarks. Moreover, FDPT outperforms the recently proposed generalization methods when applied to forgery generated by unseen face manipulation techniques (*e.g.*, 84.39% → 95.53% on Face2Face dataset).

**Keywords:** Face forgery detection · Generalization · Patch transforamtion

## 1 Introduction

With the development of artificial intelligence technologies, researchers have proposed various deep-learning-based generation algorithms to synthesize images and videos. Since a Reddit user first used such algorithms in 2017 [11], fake content generation has gradually penetrated into politics, media, and many other fields. It has become a serious problem that abusing fake images for malicious

D. N. Pham et al. (Eds.): PRICAI 2021, LNAI 13033, pp. 337–352, 2021.
https://doi.org/10.1007/978-3-030-89370-5_25

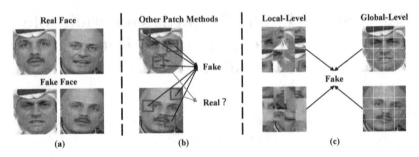

**Fig. 1.** Comparisons between our method and other patch-based methods. (a) There are two fake faces (bottom) generated by DeepFakes [1] based on the two real faces (top). (b) Other methods based on patch learning assume all patches cropped from a fake image as fake (black line), but some patches may come from the real part (green line). (c) Our method is trained with the global label instead of the aforementioned assumption. FDPT uses patch transformation to capture the local subtle artifacts and global spatial features of the image. (Color figure online)

purposes (*e.g.*, influencing public opinions) will bring negative impacts on the society, economics, and even politics. Therefore, it is necessary to study algorithms for image forgery detection, especially for face forgery detection.

Researchers have made numerous attempts in order to address the challenge of face forgery detection. For instance, a series of earlier works classify an image into a real/fake category by using handcrafted features [7,12,25]. However, they require high-resolution images and exhaustive feature tuning. In the past few years, convolutional neural networks (CNNs) have shown a powerful ability in a number of visual tasks. Therefore, recent works have begun to use deep learning methods to achieve forgery detection [4,15,22,26,31]. However, most of these methods are trained with known face manipulation techniques and have the problem of insufficient generalizability.

Generalizability is highly desired in face forgery detection; in other words, models should perform well not only on the face data used in training (*i.e.*, known face manipulation datasets), but also on other unseen face forgery datasets (*i.e.*, generated by unknown face manipulation techniques). Due to the lack of generalizability, most existing methods for face forgery detection are effective on seen datasets (known face manipulation techniques) and can achieve a detection accuracy up to 98%. However, they tend to suffer from over-fitting and perform poorly (50% or even lower) on unseen datasets. Therefore, forgery detection methods without sufficient generalizability are unsuitable for practical applications.

There exists many challenges in the process of improving generalizability, for example, large-scale dataset dependence, and forged class limitation [14,21,30]. To address such challenges, Chai *et al.* extract the local features from small patches to improve the representation of the image [8]. Compared with the global features of the whole image, the local and subtle features are more stable in different datasets. However, Chai *et al.* assume that all patches cropped from a forgery face are considered fake (as shown in Fig. 1(a) and (b)). It is clearly not suitable to apply such method to forgery images that consist of many real face parts where some belong to a real one and some do not (as shown in Fig. 1(b)). Therefore, although it has excellent generalization performance within the entire face forgery datasets, it is not effective across different partial face forgery datasets (*e.g.*, the four manipulations of FaceForensics++ [27]).

Inspired by [8], we find that local information learning is a good method to solve the lack of generalizability. To remove the assumption in [8] that degrades the generalizability, we use a patch transformation strategy to help the model focus on stable artifacts, rather than limiting model learning to a local patch. The model can be trained with the global label without the aforementioned assumption (*i.e.*, a real/fake image corresponds to a real/fake label). Specifically, we randomly shuffle the image patches to help the CNN stream emphasize local artifacts from the image. In addition, we convert the image into a patch sequence and capture the global spatial features by using CNN-GRU stream. Compared to the method proposed in [8], our method not only focuses on the local subtle artifacts (local-level) by the CNN stream but also learns global spatial features (global-level) from the CNN-GRU stream (shown in Fig. 1(c)). Finally, we fuse different levels of features to further improve the performance and generalizability of the model.

We summarize our contributions as follows. Firstly, we propose a patch random transformation strategy to help the CNN stream focus on the local subtle artifacts of the image. It provides a solution to distinguish the differences between real and fake faces. Secondly, we employ a patch sequence transformation strategy to enrich the global representation of images by the CNN-GRU stream, which firstly introduces spatial features between patches in face forgery detection task. Lastly, we conduct extensive experiments to show the effectiveness of our proposed method; moreover, we achieve meaningful gains in many generalizability experiments.

## 2   Related Work

### 2.1   Fake Face Generation

The studies on Face forgery can be divided into two categories: entire face forgery and partial face forgery.

**Entire Face Forgery.** The generative adversarial networks (GANs) are usually used to synthesize images [6,16]. PGGAN [18] and StyleGAN [19] are proposed to focus on the high-level attributes (*e.g.*, pose and identity when trained on human faces) in an image and generate a high-resolution image. Glow is a flow-based generation model by using modified $1 \times 1$ invertible convolutions and achieves excellent results in interpolation generation [20].

**Partial Face Forgery.** It usually contains many meticulous sub-tasks, such as identity swap, expression swap, and attributes manipulation. For this category,

StarGAN [9] and FaceApp [2] are proposed to achieve face attributes manipulation by modifying the partial attributes of the face image (*e.g.*, hair, gender, age, *etc.*) during the training stage. Similar work includes recently proposed FaceSwap [3], Face2Face [29], DeepFakes [1], and NeuralTextures [28]. Rossler *et al.* collect the fake face videos from four popular generation methods [1,3,28,29] and propose a dataset named FaceForensic++ to facilitate the evaluation of detection methods [27].

## 2.2 Forgery Detection

We divide the studies on forgery detection into two categories: generalizable forgery detection and patch based forgery detection.

**Generalizable Forgery Detection.** Recently, many methods achieve a high accuracy on known datasets in forgery detection. However, their accuracies on unseen datasets decrease significantly. To solve the generalizability problem, recent works [8,14,21,30] have been proposed. Specifically, Du *et al.* employ a locality aware strategy to enhance the representation of images [14] and achieve incremental improvement. Wang *et al.* improve the generalizability by adding blur and random noise during the training phase [30]. However, this method relies on a large training set. Li *et al.* propose the Face X-Ray [21], which uses noise as well as error level analysis to extract the blending boundary of fake faces. Although it can achieve a certain level of generalizability, it is only applicable to specific manipulation types of fake faces; in other words, it achieves high generalizability between different face swap technologies, but is not suitable for detecting fake faces in the entire face synthesis.

**Forgery Detection with Patches.** Most of recent excellent face forgery detection methods are based on an overall image [13,21,26,30]. But they often ignore key local details in the image. To avoid this problem, many methods leverage the local perspectives instead of global detection [22–24,32]. Specifically, Zhou *et al.* propose a model to learn local features from patches [32]. Mayer *et al.* use the similarity between patches to judge whether the image is forgery [23,24]. Chai *et al.* propose a patch-based classifier to focus on local artifacts and obtain excellent generalization on the entire face forgery dataset [8]. They all assume that all patches cropped from an image belong to the same class as the input image, which is not consistent with reality (as shown in Fig. 1(b)).

## 3    Approach

### 3.1    FDPT Architecture for Face Forgery Detection

As shown in Fig. 2, FDPT is a two-stream face forgery detection network (*i.e.*, a CNN stream and a CNN-GRU stream). It benefits from two different but complementary visual features. Specifically, the CNN stream learns on local subtle artifacts through the pre-processing of patch random transformation, and the

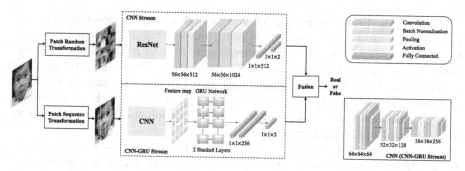

**Fig. 2.** FDPT architecture. The CNN stream focuses on local subtle artifacts through a patch random transformation. The CNN-GRU stream first obtains the global spatial features by passing input image through the patch sequence transformation. The CNN module of CNN-GRU stream is expanded in the lower right corner.

CNN-GRU stream learns global spatial features between patches through patch sequence transformation. Then, a fusion strategy is used to improve the accuracy and generalization ability.

### 3.2  Local Subtle Artifacts Learning

The process of our local subtle artifacts learning stream (*i.e.*, the CNN stream) can be divided into four steps. First, we utilize a traditional data augmentation strategy to enrich the training set by randomly cropping the images in batch data. Second, a cropped image is self-shuffled by a patch random transformation method. Third, we use a CNN module to learn and extract the subtle artifacts of these shuffled images. In our method, the CNN stream is generic and could be implemented on any backbone feature extractor (*e.g.*, ResNet [17]). Finally, two convolution blocks and fully connected layers are employed to predict the authenticity of the input image, where the prediction is normalized by the Sigmoid function and we denote the normalized result as the prediction forgery score.

**Fig. 3.** Patch random transformation with different $n$.        **Fig. 4.** Hilbert curves.

**Patch Random Transformation.** Most forgery detection methods extract global artifacts in an entire image to distinguish real from fake. However, there are different global artifacts in data generated by different face generators. As a result, most of the face forgery detection methods cannot be generalized across different generators. We leverage the patch random transformation to disturb the global artifacts existing in an entire image, thus to retain the local subtle artifacts and represent the face image in a more stable fashion. In patch random transformation, we divide the input image into patches, then randomly shuffle and assemble these patches into a new image. The purpose of these operations is to generate a new image after random transformation and force the stream to focus on local subtle features in the training stage.

Denote an input image by $I \in \mathbb{R}^{W \times H \times 3}$ and the split parameter by $n$, where $W$ and $H$ are the width and the height of the image, respectively. The image is divide into $n \times n$ non-overlapped patches. The size of each patch is $\frac{W}{n} \times \frac{H}{n} \times 3$. These patches are reconstructed into a new image. Figure 3 illustrates an original image and the transformed new image.

Note that there is no need to pre-process that in the training stage during the inference (*i.e.*, patch random transformation). The input image is randomly cropped and put into the CNN stream to get a prediction forgery score. If given a video, we extract multiple frames randomly and average the predictions.

### 3.3 Global Spatial Features Learning

As shown in Fig. 2, we employ a hybrid CNN-GRU module to extract global spatial features between patches. Given the patches split from an image, we organize patches in a specific order and expect GRU to capture the dependency among patches. Note that if patches are organized vertically or horizontally, sequential learning can not correlate them well due to long-distance between adjacent patches [5]. Inspired by the work in [5], we leverage the Hilbert curve to organize the patches and maintain the local correlation in the spatial domain. Then, we use a sequential module GRU to extract spatial features from the reordered patch images.

**Patch Sequence Transformation.** The patch sequence transformation consists of two steps: (1) we first split an image into several local patches on average and connecting patches in order, (2) we then adopt a sequential learning method (*i.e.*, GRU) to capture the global spatial features between the patches. Note that it is important to determine the order of patches fed to GRU. A common solution is to organize the patches either horizontally or vertically; however, such sequences do not better capture local information. For instance, if we connect patches horizontally, the adjacent patches in the vertical direction will be separated by an entire line of patches. Thus, it is difficult to learn the correlation characteristics between patches due to long-distance interval. To solve this problem, the space-filling curve is proposed. It maps data in multi-dimensional space to one-dimensional space and keeps the relevance of adjacent parts. We leverage the Hilbert curve to reconstructed patches in our method. Compared with other curves, the Hilbert curve maintains a better spatial local property, which is more favorable for sequential learning. The second-order Hilbert curve that we used is shown in Fig. 4.

The CNN-GRU stream works in a similar way as the CNN stream. More specifically, given an image $I \in \mathbb{R}^{W \times H \times 3}$, we first divide it into $n \times n$ non-overlapped patches and the size of each patch is $\frac{W}{n} \times \frac{H}{n} \times 3$. We then transform the feature learning from a multi-dimensional to one-dimensional sequence by using a space-filling curve (*i.e.*, connect $n \times n$ patches into a sequence according to Hilbert curve). After that, we put each patch into a CNN module to extract the patch feature, where the CNN module can be any excellent backbone feature extractor. In our method, we simplified the CNN module to reduce the parameters during the training. Therefore, the CNN module in the CNN-GRU stream contains three calculation blocks and each block has two convolution layers, two activation layers, one batch normalization layer, and one max pooling layer. More detailed structure is shown in Fig. 2. Last, we feed the features of patches into the GRU module in the order of Hilbert curve to capture the correlation between patches. Our GRU module has two stacked GRU layers and three fully connected layers, and we normalize the outputs of the last layer using the Sigmoid function to predict the authenticity of the input image. As a result of these steps, the CNN-GRU stream can describe the correlation between patches and capture the global spatial representation by the space-filling curve.

### 3.4  Fusion Strategy

As mentioned in Sect. 3.2 and Sect. 3.3, the proposed CNN and CNN-GRU streams mine the local subtle artifacts and the global spatial features respectively. The two patch-related forgery features are different but complementary. Therefore, we adopt a fusion strategy to promote the final performance.

More specifically, we consider the prediction forgery score set $P = \{P_C, P_G\}$ in the evaluation phase, where $P_C \in [0,1]$ and $P_G \in [0,1]$ means the prediction forgery scores of the CNN stream and the CNN-GRU stream, respectively. The final forgery score $P_{fusion}$ is calculated by Eq. (1), where the closer $P_{fusion}$ is to 1, the more likely the input image is a forgery.

$$P_{fusion} = \frac{P_C + P_G}{2} \tag{1}$$

## 4  Evaluation

### 4.1  Experiment Setting

***Dataset.*** We evaluate our method on two benchmark datasets: the entire face forgery detection dataset and the partial face forgery detection dataset. For the entire face forgery detection dataset, the real images come from FFHQ and the fake images are generated by StyleGAN/PGGAN (labeled as Style-GAN and PGGAN in corresponding datasets in the sequel). For the partial face forgery detection dataset, we use FaceForensics++ collected by [8]. FaceForensics++ contains 1,000 real videos and 4,000 manipulated fake videos, where these manipulated videos are generated by four face manipulation algorithms, namely, DeepFakes (DF), Face2Face (F2F), FaceSwap (FS), and NeuralTexture (NT). Similarly, we refer to the corresponding datasets using the DF, F2F, FS, and NT labels in the sequel.

*Evaluation Metrics.* For fair comparisons with other methods, we use the Accuracy score (ACC) to evaluate different methods. In addition, to evaluate the effectiveness of each component of FDPT, we also calculate the Area Under the Receiver Operating Characteristic Curve (AUC) in our ablation study.

*Implementation.* In our experiments, the input size of the CNN stream is $448 \times 448 \times 3$. Then, we train the CNN stream using the stochastic gradient descent (SGD) method, where the learning rate is $10^{-3}$ and the number of epochs is 20. For the CNN-GRU stream, the input size is $256 \times 256 \times 3$ and we train the CNN-GRU stream using SGD with the learning rate being $10^{-2}$. We stop the training stage of the CNN-GRU stream at the 50th epoch. For more details, the code is available at https://github.com/xihe7/PatchT/.

During the training stage, we evaluate different parameters $n$ in patch transformation and find that the results of $n = 4$ perform better. Thus, we set $n = 4$ in our remaining experiments.

## 4.2 Ablation Study

In order to evaluate the effectiveness of each component of FDPT, we conduct experiments on the entire face forgery and partial face forgery datasets separately and summarize results in Table 1.

Note that ID 1 and 2 in Table 1 represent the CNN stream without and with patch random transformation respectively, while ID 3 and 4 mean the CNN-GRU stream without and with patch sequence transformation respectively. We also apply the fusion strategy on different components to attempt to improve the detection results. The fusion results are shown in ID 5−7. Specifically, ID 5 refers to the fusion of two streams without any patch transformation. ID 6 and 7 respectively indicate only one of the patch transformation methods used in the weighted fusion two-stream network.

**Table 1.** Ablation study of FDPT.

| ID | Stream | Patch random transformation | Patch sequence transformation | Entire face forgery | | Partial face forgery | |
|---|---|---|---|---|---|---|---|
| | | | | ACC | AUC | ACC | AUC |
| 1 | CNN | × | | 94.10 | 0.9352 | 93.23 | 0.9277 |
| 2 | | ✓ | | 98.25 | 0.9904 | 99.00 | 0.9932 |
| 3 | CNN-GRU | | × | 98.17 | 0.9864 | 98.44 | 0.9805 |
| 4 | | | ✓ | 99.00 | 0.9941 | 99.17 | 0.9921 |
| 5 | Fusion | × | × | 95.03 | 0.9416 | 95.83 | 0.9524 |
| 6 | | × | ✓ | 95.35 | 0.9456 | 96.50 | 0.9673 |
| 7 | | ✓ | × | 98.53 | 0.9887 | 99.17 | 0.9940 |
| 8 | FDPT | ✓ | ✓ | **99.87** | **0.9996** | **99.83** | **0.9989** |

We observe that ACC and AUC are significantly improved due to patch random transformation; more specifically, the detection ACC increases by 4% and AUC is improved by 0.06 on the entire face forgery dataset. In addition, the ACC increases by more than 5% and AUC increases by 0.06 on FaceForensics++. Therefore, the effect of local artifacts on forgery detection is noticeable.

We also observe that ACC and AUC scores have slight improvement after using the Hilbert curve to organize patches. Although the improvement of quantitative results is relatively small, it is a meaningful improvement for face forgery detection. These results suggest that using the Hilbert sequence is conductive to improving detection results.

Furthermore, after the application of the fusion strategy, we observed that the results of ID 5–6 are not as good as one of the two streams. In the two-stream network, when the performance of one stream is poor, the effect of simple fusion is not obvious. On the contrary (compared ID 7 with ID 2 and 3), when the network effect of both two streams is excellent, the final fusion performance is improved. Further as shown in ID 8, both ACC and AUC scores of FDPT are higher than its variants (*i.e.*, ID 1–7). This suggests that the two features are complementary to each other. We can draw a conclusion that local artifacts play a key role in improving detection results, and the global representation is excellent in detection.

## 4.3   Comparison with Existing Methods

We train and evaluate existing methods including full MesoInception4 [4], MesoNet [4], ResNet [17], Xception [10], and a classifier proposed in [30] (CNNp) on the same datasets as the datasets FDPTuses. In addition, we also compare FDPT with the latest patch-based method [8] (PatchW).

Note that ResNet and Xception are advanced classification networks. Xception draws on the idea of depth-wise separable convolution and combines with the idea of ResNet. It is the leading classification network at present. On the other hand, MesoInception4, MesoNet, and CNNp of [30] are open-source face forgery detection algorithms. In particular, CNNp is one of the most recent works and is trained to detect CNN artifacts via blurring and compression augmentations. PatchW is the latest face forgery detection using patches. To better compare with it, we directly take the experimental results in [8].

### 4.3.1   Comparison Results on Entire Face Forgery Dataset   We divide the fake face testing set into three types: PGGAN, StyleGAN, and their mixture. The results are shown in the left of Table 2. We observe that the accuracy (*i.e.*, ACC) of FDPT in three cases are 99.85%, 99.80%, 99.87%, respectively, with a noticeable improvement compared against the current methods and excellent classification networks (except PatchW). PatchW achieves almost 100% accuracy on known datasets; however, it is more likely to suffer from over-fitting. The significant performance gains mainly benefit from the two sets of complementary discriminative information learnt from patches, which contributes to FDPT's capability of learning more local details of face images.

**Table 2.** Accuracy results (%) on entire face forgery and partial face forgery dataset.

| Methods | Entire face forgery | | | Partial face forgery | | | | |
|---|---|---|---|---|---|---|---|---|
| | StyleGAN | PGGAN | Mix | DF | FS | F2F | NT | FF++ |
| ResNet [17] | 91.65 | 97.01 | 94.10 | 95.53 | 92.77 | 93.02 | 96.92 | 93.23 |
| Xception [10] | 98.00 | 96.49 | 98.52 | 99.27 | 98.87 | 98.17 | 98.00 | 98.30 |
| MesoNet [4] | 91.90 | 98.70 | 94.17 | 92.19 | 93.75 | 90.62 | 88.97 | 86.67 |
| MesoInception4 [4] | 95.00 | 98.40 | 96.67 | 90.62 | 92.19 | 89.27 | 87.52 | 90.17 |
| CNNp ($p = 0.1$) [30] | 98.85 | 99.70 | 99.63 | 82.07 | 96.77 | 97.13 | 77.50 | 89.88 |
| CNNp ($p = 0.5$) [30] | 98.00 | 99.40 | 99.78 | 81.33 | 91.63 | 89.13 | 80.77 | 85.40 |
| PatchW [8] | **100.0** | **100.0** | - | 99.27 | 96.56 | 97.66 | 92.23 | - |
| **FDPT** | 99.85 | 99.80 | **99.87** | **99.83** | **99.83** | **99.00** | **98.67** | **99.53** |

**4.3.2    Comparison Results on Partial Face Forgery Dataset** Furthermore, we evaluate FDPT on different face manipulation techniques. We mix four face manipulation techniques of FaceForensics++ for training and evaluating together (*i.e.*, DF, FS, F2F, NT). They are all fake face video datasets, and we extract frames as fake face images in the experiments. We then train the model and evaluate it in four types of face manipulated dataset respectively. When training, in order to balance the proportion of real and fake datasets, the number of frames extracted from original videos is four times that of each face manipulation video. We summarize the results in the right of Table 2.

We observe that FDPT achieves a high detection accuracy and performs much better than other methods. FDPT achieves an accuracy of nearly 100% in all testing sets. Note that due to the two-stream structure, our FDPT model extracts multiple frames from each video, and each frame is detected by the CNN stream and CNN-GRU stream. The two streams complementarily make corrections to the error and make the final results perform better.

**4.3.3    Analysis** By comparing the results in Sect. 4.3.1 and Sect. 4.3.2, we observe that the performance of both CNNp and PatchW degrade significantly on fake faces of FaceForensics++. Note that CNNp focuses on CNN-synthesized images and detects CNN artifacts to distinguish real and fake. However, the FaceForensics++ dataset lacks sufficient CNN artifacts, which is completely different from the entire face forgery dataset. Therefore, the accuracy results of the classifier methods drop significantly. In terms of PatchW, it assumes that all patches cropped from a fake image are considered as fake. Therefore, it has excellent detection accuracy in the task of entire face forgery detection. However, the detection results drop on the FaceForensics++ dataset due to the incorrectness which may be introduced by the assumption mentioned above.

The experimental results suggest that FDPT can be applied to all fake face image datasets, such as StyleGAN, PGGAN, and FaceForensics++, and consistently achieves state-of-the-art performances. Note that CNNp [30] and PatchW [8] are the latest face forgery detection methods. Both can only perform well on

**Table 3.** Generalization ability evaluation on entire face forgery dataset. Each model is trained on one dataset and evaluated on another unseen dataset.

| Training set | StyleGAN | | PGGAN | |
| Testing set | StyleGAN | PGGAN | PGGAN | StyleGAN |
|---|---|---|---|---|
| ResNet [17] | 91.65 | 62.18 | 97.01 | 52.37 |
| Xception [10] | 98.00 | 65.87 | 96.49 | 74.33 |
| MesoInception4 [4] | 95.00 | 76.23 | 98.40 | 71.27 |
| CNNp (p = 0.1) [30] | 99.85 | 86.92 | 99.70 | 85.27 |
| CNNp (p = 0.5) [30] | 98.00 | 85.28 | 99.40 | 56.34 |
| PatchW [8] | - | - | **100.0** | 95.85 |
| **FDPT** | **99.85** | **93.95** | 99.80 | **96.85** |

a specific type of fake face image. The results suggests that FDPT can achieve good universality and is suitable for various types of fake faces.

## 4.4 Generalizability

Forgery generation algorithms have been constantly evolving. Therefore, it is crucial to explore forgery detection methods that can achieve great generalizability; in other words, the detection model trained with one face forgery dataset can be generalized to images generated by other new forgery manipulated techniques. We next investigate the generalizability performance of FDPT.

We first evaluate the generalizability on the entire face forgery dataset and summarize the results in Table 3. We train each model with one face forgery dataset and evaluate it on another one (unseen). Because there are many similarities between StyleGAN and PGGAN, it is relatively easy to implement generalization between them. We observe from Table 3 that many methods are prone to over-fitting and perform poorly on the unseen dataset. PatchW performs better than some other methods. The reason is that it utilizes small patches to ignore global differences between real from fake images and focus on shared generator artifacts. Our method FDPT achieves an accuracy of nearly 100% on the seen dataset, and is superior to all other methods on the unseen dataset. Even though our accuracy is a little less than PatchW on PGGAN (seen), we have significantly improved the generalizability on StyleGAN (unseen).

We then evaluate the generalizability of FDPT across four different generators of FaceForensics++. We train on each of the four manipulations and evaluate on the remaining three datasets. We summarize in Table 4 the results in terms of ACC with respect to each type of manipulated video. We observe that ACC of most methods is up to 99% on seen manipulation dataset (in gray); however, it drops drastically for unseen manipulations (in black). This is because the model learns the specific artifacts quickly and suffers from over-fitting. Therefore, it performs well on a given dataset and has poor generalizability on unseen datasets.

**Table 4.** Generalizability on FaceForensics++. Each model is trained on one dataset and evaluated on the remaining datasets. ACC on the testing set corresponding to training images is colored in gray.

| | Train on DF | | | | Train on FS | | | |
|---|---|---|---|---|---|---|---|---|
| | DF | FS | F2F | NT | DF | FS | F2F | NT |
| ResNet [17] | 95.53 | 52.43 | 53.15 | 52.42 | 58.83 | 92.77 | 53.16 | 51.04 |
| Xception [10] | 99.27 | 47.12 | 53.57 | 58.15 | 54.26 | 98.87 | 53.42 | 51.28 |
| MesoInception4 [4] | 94.32 | 51.34 | 60.17 | 58.27 | 51.64 | 96.19 | 55.32 | 49.46 |
| CNNp (p = 0.1) [30] | 92.64 | 51.23 | 57.66 | 59.29 | 55.24 | 96.72 | 61.32 | 52.88 |
| CNNp (p = 0.5) [30] | 91.46 | 55.99 | 56.06 | 54.02 | 57.29 | 97.65 | 60.04 | 51.16 |
| PatchW [8] | 99.14 | 58.74 | **71.74** | 74.99 | **61.77** | 97.13 | 62.00 | 53.44 |
| FDPT | 99.84 | **61.05** | 68.32 | **75.63** | 55.58 | 98.46 | **73.43** | **53.81** |
| | Train on F2F | | | | Train on NT | | | |
| | DF | FS | F2F | NT | DF | FS | F2F | NT |
| ResNet [17] | 54.32 | 53.08 | 93.02 | 52.86 | 65.76 | 50.14 | 55.23 | 89.56 |
| Xception [10] | 66.08 | 53.15 | 96.17 | 55.07 | 69.67 | 48.55 | 56.79 | 93.60 |
| MesoInception4 [4] | 64.43 | 55.16 | 94.37 | 54.42 | 63.72 | 55.83 | 62.25 | 86.87 |
| CNNp (p = 0.1) [30] | 66.24 | 59.04 | 97.83 | 62.97 | 69.27 | 49.88 | 67.04 | 88.50 |
| CNNp (p = 0.5) [30] | 66.86 | 64.52 | 93.42 | 62.17 | 67.08 | 51.63 | 69.45 | 90.88 |
| PatchW [8] | 84.39 | 63.10 | 97.66 | 79.72 | 70.32 | 52.37 | 65.04 | 86.93 |
| FDPT | **95.53** | **67.91** | 98.15 | **82.42** | **98.78** | **65.71** | **96.30** | 98.92 |

As shown in Table 4, our approach FDPT has better generalizability than PatchW in most cases, and performs better than other methods in all cases. Specifically, training on NT and F2F images can still achieve satisfactory generalizability on remaining datasets, and generalization to FS images is the hardest. PatchW is the latest patch-based forgery detection method, which focuses on local patches. The assumption PatchW used will bring errors when training on partial face forgery dataset; therefore, the generalizability of PatchW on FaceForensics++ is not as good as that on the entire face forgery dataset (as shown in Table 3).

Compared with PatchW, FDPT achieves higher generalizability. More specifically, FDPT achieves face forgery detection from more general evidences available from both local subtle artifacts and global spatial features. It is clear that the improved generalizability comes from the design of FDPT, namely, detecting discriminative information from local patch space instead of paying attention to the global features of specific manipulation artifacts.

### 4.5   Impacts of Image Quality

Images and videos in practical scenarios may be of lower quality (*e.g.*, due to compression), and many methods with good performance on high-quality images may suffer from low image quality.

Note that different quality is available in FaceForensics++. More specifically, FaceForensics++ provides the original output video dataset (RAW). Addition-

**Table 5.** Accuracy results (%) of FDPT on FaceForensics++ with different quality.

| | HQ (High quality) | | | | LQ (Low quality) | | | |
|---|---|---|---|---|---|---|---|---|
| | DF | FS | F2F | NT | DF | FS | F2F | NT |
| ResNet [17] | 97.33 | 98.50 | 97.67 | 86.17 | 88.89 | 81.95 | 82.17 | 69.50 |
| Xception [10] | 97.17 | 96.33 | 95.67 | 88.50 | 90.57 | 82.35 | 83.67 | 73.83 |
| MesoInception4 [4] | 91.42 | 87.78 | 88.13 | 68.33 | 83.18 | 77.67 | 76.83 | 60.94 |
| CNNp (p = 0.1) [30] | 96.29 | 93.58 | 94.66 | 75.15 | 90.95 | 86.53 | 81.62 | 64.27 |
| CNNp (p = 0.5) [30] | 96.58 | 94.03 | 93.17 | 86.25 | 91.13 | 84.32 | 80.87 | 61.33 |
| **FDPT** | **98.33** | **98.17** | **98.00** | **94.17** | **91.17** | **88.33** | **88.67** | **81.50** |

ally, FaceForensics++ provides two different compression datasets: low-quality videos (LQ) and high-quality videos (HQ). HQ is produced with a light compression which is almost visually lossless (*i.e.*, constant rate quantization parameter equal to 23), while LQ produced with the quantization parameter being 40 [27].

We evaluate FDPT on FaceForensics++ with different image quality. The models are trained and evaluated on the HQ and LQ datasets for each of the four face manipulation scenarios. We summarize the results in Table 5.

We observe that FDPT outperforms other methods. First, FDPT performs well on the HQ datasets. More specifically, FDPT achieves 98.33%, 98.17%, 98.00%, and 94.17% accuracy on DF, FS, F2F, and NT, respectively. The accuracy of FDPT on the DF, FS and F2F datasets is close to 100.0%. This suggests that FDPT can still perform excellent detection even when the light compression degrades the image quality. We also observe that the performance of FDPT drops on LQ dataset; more specifically, FDPT achieves 91.17%, 88.33%, 88.67%, and 81.50% accuracy on DF, FS, F2F, and NT, respectively. Although FDPT suffers from heavily compressed images, it can still achieve a high detection accuracy.

Note that compared with videos generated by DF, FS and F2F, fake videos generated by NT is a great challenge to detection models, due to its generated faces without noticeable forgery artifacts. Therefore, the accuracy results on the NT datasets are not as good as the results on the other three datasets. But, the accuracy of FDPT on NT is more than 90% in HQ and 80% in LQ, and FDPT still plays an excellent detection effect. This is consistent with the research results in [26] which proposed a forgery detection method specifically optimized for compressed videos.

## 5   Conclusion

In this paper, we propose FDPT, a general two-stream face forgery detection network based on patch transformation, to achieve higher generalizability. Specifically, FDPT consists of a CNN stream and a CNN-GRU stream. The first CNN stream enhances the capture of local subtle artifacts and avoids introducing the pseudo labels used in other methods. Then, the second CNN-GRU stream captures global spatial features between patches to strength the representation of the image. Finally, the fusion of these two streams improves the performance and generalization of our proposed models. The extensive experiments have shown that our model achieves state-of-the-art results on two different face forgery datasets. Moreover, FDPT remains effective when applied on unseen forgery datasets and achieves superior performance in the generalizability experiments.

**Acknowledgments.** This work is supported in part by the Natural Science Foundation of China (NSFC) under Grant U19B2036.

# References

1. DeepFakes (2019). https://www.github.com/deepfakes/faceswap
2. FaceApp (2019). https://faceapp.com/app
3. FaceSwap (2019). https://www.github.com/MarekKowalski/FaceSwap
4. Afchar, D., Nozick, V., Yamagishi, J., Echizen, I.: MesoNet: a compact facial video forgery detection network. In: 2018 IEEE International Workshop on Information Forensics and Security (WIFS), pp. 1–7 (2018)
5. Bappy, J.H., Simons, C., Nataraj, L., Manjunath, B., Roy-Chowdhury, A.K.: Hybrid LSTM and encoder-decoder architecture for detection of image forgeries. IEEE Trans. Image Process. **28**(7), 3286–3300 (2019)
6. Berthelot, D., Schumm, T., Metz, L.: BEGAN: Boundary Equilibrium Generative Adversarial Networks. arXiv e-prints arXiv:1703.10717 (2017)
7. Bianchi, T., De Rosa, A., Piva, A.: Improved DCT coefficient analysis for forgery localization in jpeg images. In: 2011 IEEE International Conference on Acoustics, Speech and Signal Processing (ICASSP), pp. 2444–2447 (2011)
8. Chai, L., Bau, D., Lim, S.-N., Isola, P.: What makes fake images detectable? Understanding properties that generalize. In: Vedaldi, A., Bischof, H., Brox, T., Frahm, J.-M. (eds.) ECCV 2020. LNCS, vol. 12371, pp. 103–120. Springer, Cham (2020). https://doi.org/10.1007/978-3-030-58574-7_7
9. Choi, Y., Choi, M., Kim, M., Ha, J.W., Kim, S., Choo, J.: StarGAN: unified generative adversarial networks for multi-domain image-to-image translation. In: Proceedings of the IEEE Conference on Computer Vision and Pattern Recognition (CVPR), pp. 8789–8797, June 2018
10. Chollet, F.: Xception: deep learning with depthwise separable convolutions. In: Proceedings of the IEEE Conference on Computer Vision and Pattern Recognition (CVPR), pp. 1251–1258, July 2017
11. Cole, S.: AI-assisted fake porn is here and we're all fucked. Motherboard Tech by Vice, December 2017
12. Cozzolino, D., Poggi, G., Verdoliva, L.: Recasting residual-based local descriptors as convolutional neural networks: an application to image forgery detection. In: Proceedings of the 5th ACM Workshop on Information Hiding and Multimedia Security, pp. 159–164 (2017)
13. Dang, H., Liu, F., Stehouwer, J., Liu, X., Jain, A.K.: On the detection of digital face manipulation. In: Proceedings of the IEEE/CVF Conference on Computer Vision and Pattern Recognition (CVPR), pp. 5781–5790, June 2020
14. Du, M., Pentyala, S., Li, Y., Hu, X.: Towards generalizable deepfake detection with locality-aware autoencoder. In: Proceedings of the 29th ACM International Conference on Information and Knowledge Management, pp. 325–334 (2020)

15. Durall, R., Keuper, M., Pfreundt, F.J., Keuper, J.: Unmasking DeepFakes with simple Features. arXiv e-prints arXiv:1911.00686 (2019)
16. Goodfellow, I., et al.: Generative adversarial nets. Adv. Neural Inf. Process. Syst. **27**, 2672–2680 (2014)
17. He, K., Zhang, X., Ren, S., Sun, J.: Deep residual learning for image recognition. In: Proceedings of the IEEE Conference on Computer Vision and Pattern Recognition (CVPR). pp. 770–778, June 2016
18. Karras, T., Aila, T., Laine, S., Lehtinen, J.: Progressive growing of GANs for improved quality, stability, and variation. In: Proceedings of International Conference on Learning Representations (ICLR) (2018)
19. Karras, T., Laine, S., Aila, T.: A style-based generator architecture for generative adversarial networks. In: Proceedings of the IEEE/CVF Conference on Computer Vision and Pattern Recognition (CVPR), pp. 4401–4410, June 2019
20. Kingma, D.P., Dhariwal, P.: Glow: generative flow with invertible $1 \times 1$ convolutions. In: Advances in Neural Information Processing Systems NeurIPS 2018, pp. 10236–10245 (2018)
21. Li, L., et al.: Face x-ray for more general face forgery detection. In: Proceedings of the IEEE/CVF Conference on Computer Vision and Pattern Recognition (CVPR), pp. 5001–5010, June 2020
22. Liu, Z., Luo, P., Wang, X., Tang, X.: Deep learning face attributes in the wild. In: Proceedings of the IEEE International Conference on Computer Vision (ICCV), pp. 3730–3738, December 2015
23. Mayer, O., Stamm, M.C.: Exposing fake images with forensic similarity graphs. IEEE J. Sel. Top. Sig. Process. **14**(5), 1049–1064 (2020)
24. Mayer, O., Stamm, M.C.: Forensic similarity for digital images. IEEE Trans. Inf. Forensics Secur. **15**, 1331–1346 (2020)
25. Nataraj, L., et al.: Detecting GAN generated fake images using co-occurrence matrices. Electron. Imag. **2019**(5), 532-1–532-7 (2019)
26. Qian, Y., Yin, G., Sheng, L., Chen, Z., Shao, J.: Thinking in frequency: face forgery detection by mining frequency-aware clues. In: Vedaldi, A., Bischof, H., Brox, T., Frahm, J.-M. (eds.) ECCV 2020. LNCS, vol. 12357, pp. 86–103. Springer, Cham (2020). https://doi.org/10.1007/978-3-030-58610-2_6
27. Rossler, A., Cozzolino, D., Verdoliva, L., Riess, C., Thies, J., Niessner, M.: Faceforensics++: Learning to detect manipulated facial images. In: Proceedings of the IEEE/CVF International Conference on Computer Vision (ICCV), pp. 1–11, October 2019
28. Thies, J., Zollhöfer, M., Nießner, M.: Deferred neural rendering: image synthesis using neural textures. ACM Trans. Graph. (TOG) **38**(4), 1–12 (2019)
29. Thies, J., Zollhöfer, M., Stamminger, M., Theobalt, C., Nießner, M.: Face2face: real-time face capture and reenactment of RGB videos. In: Proceedings of the IEEE Conference on Computer Vision and Pattern Recognition (CVPR), pp. 2387–2395, June 2016
30. Wang, S.Y., Wang, O., Zhang, R., Owens, A., Efros, A.A.: CNN-generated images are surprisingly easy to spot... for now. In: Proceedings of the IEEE/CVF Conference on Computer Vision and Pattern Recognition (CVPR), pp. 8695–8704, June 2020

31. Zhang, X., Karaman, S., Chang, S.F.: Detecting and simulating artifacts in GAN fake images. In: 2019 IEEE International Workshop on Information Forensics and Security (WIFS), pp. 1–6 (2019)

32. Zhou, P., Han, X., Morariu, V.I., Davis, L.S.: Two-stream neural networks for tampered face detection. In: 2017 IEEE Conference on Computer Vision and Pattern Recognition Workshops (CVPRW), pp. 1831–1839 (2017)

# When Distortion Meets Perceptual Quality: A Multi-task Learning Pipeline

Jing Wen and Qianyu Guo[✉]

Shanxi University, Taiyuan, China

**Abstract.** Most of the existing studies about image quality assessment (IQA) focus on predicting image quality score without adequately considering image distortion clues, which is very significant in IQA tasks. To improve the performance of current IQA algorithms, we propose a novel multi-task learning-based deep convolutional neural network for predicting image quality score and recognizing distortion type simultaneously. Furthermore, to explore the significance of utilizing multiple layers of image features, we introduce a multi-layer feature fusion strategy to exploit the effect of image features fully. By utilizing a shared network to learn the commonalities and differences between two tasks, we can achieve state-of-the-art performance on IQA tasks and a superior result on distortion classification. The introduced framework is trained on three different public IQA datasets LIVE, TID2013 and CSIQ, to verify the effectiveness of the designed approach. Compared with current SOTA hand-crafted-based and deep learning-based approaches, our pipeline achieves a great improvement on both aforementioned tasks by a noteworthy margin.

**Keywords:** Multi-task learning · Image quality assessment · Distortion classification

## 1 Introduction

Over the past years, image quality assessment (IQA) has been an active topic for researchers since it can be used as an auxiliary function in several computer vision tasks, such as super-resolution [30], image segmentation [7], image inpainting [11], etc. IQA aims to design an effective model to automatically evaluate a given image's perceptual quality score, which should be consistent with the human subjective score as much as possible. Generally speaking, image quality assessment tasks can be roughly classified into three categories: full-reference IQA (FR-IQA), reduced-reference IQA (RR-IQA), and no-reference IQA (NR-IQA), depending on the usability of the reference image information [9]. Unlike RR-IQA and NR-IQA methods, FR-IQA is able to sufficiently utilize useful information from the reference images and can dig out the extracted pixel-level information in reflecting the distortion degree of the images, which often achieves the highest prediction accuracy. Hence, in this paper, we mainly focus on the research of FR-IQA method.

Multi-task learning (MTL) [19,23,31] intends to improve the performance of multiple related learning tasks by taking advantage of available information among them.

© Springer Nature Switzerland AG 2021
D. N. Pham et al. (Eds.): PRICAI 2021, LNAI 13033, pp. 353–365, 2021.
https://doi.org/10.1007/978-3-030-89370-5_26

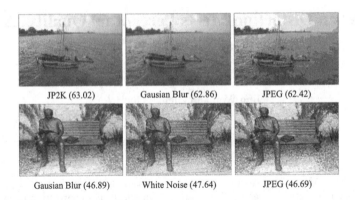

JP2K (63.02)          Gausian Blur (62.86)          JPEG (62.42)

Gausian Blur (46.89)     White Noise (47.64)          JPEG (46.69)

**Fig. 1.** Sample images from the LIVE dataset with different distortion types and similar quality scores. Lower scores indicate better perceptual quality.

Despite numerous IQA methods proposed throughout these years, there are still many characteristics to be exploited. In the prior approaches, few attentions have been put to the distortion type of the image, which is crucial in image quality evaluation. When the human observers evaluate the visual quality level of an image, apart from evaluating the degree of distortion, it is necessary to pay enough attention to the type of image distortion. For example, as shown in Fig. 1, the distorted images in each row have similar scores. However, they have different distortion levels, attributing to their different kinds of distortion. To dig into this clue, in this paper, we propose a novel MTL architecture, which can predict the quality score of a given image and identify the distortion type simultaneously. Rather than treating the loss weights of multiple tasks equally or based on attempts, we introduce a novel strategy to automatically assign the weights for the two tasks above.

In this work, we propose a novel multi-task learning architecture for full reference image quality assessment and distortion classification simultaneously, codenamed **MTL-IQA**. Given an image and the corresponding reference image, our model is able to predict the quality score and identify the distortion type of the image, as illustrated in Fig. 2. The most significant contributions can be summarized as follows:

(1) We propose an efficient multi-task learning architecture for image quality assessment and distortion classification, which leads to more accurate predictions and robust generalization compared with single-task learning only.
(2) We introduce an enhanced edge fusion module into the proposed network, which helps the edge information be better preserved during the feature extraction stage.
(3) We propose to fuse multi-layer feature outputs to compute the final image quality score. Experimental results on diverse IQA datasets demonstrate that the fused feature learning surpasses the score computation using the final feature output only.
(4) Instead of manually assigning, we automatically assign applicable loss weights to the score prediction task and the distortion classification task to achieve the best performance for both of them.

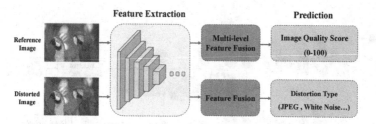

**Fig. 2.** Our method conducts image quality assessment and distortion type classification from distorted image and reference image during the testing stage.

## 2  Related Work

**Full-Reference IQA:** For full reference image quality assessment, the earliest traditional methods compute the pixel differences between distorted images and their corresponding reference images, such as PSNR [25] and MSE [10], which are the most commonly used FR-IQA algorithms. However, these error sensitivity-based methods constantly analyze the image differences mathematically, ignoring critical factors related to characteristics of the human eye. As a result, the prediction results of this kind of method often differ significantly from the human visual perception results. Structural similarity (SSIM) index is proposed in [27], it treats the degradation of images as a perceptual change in structural information. Comparing with error sensitivity-based methods, SSIM considers luminance, contrast, and structure features to evaluate the quality of images. Since then, a series of SSIM-based algorithms are proposed, for instance, Gradient Magnitude Similarity Deviation (GMSD) [28], Feature Similarity (FSIM) [29], Information Content Weighting Structural Similarity (IW-SSIM) [26]. The traditional FR-IQA methods are easy to use, however, since the neglect of advanced semantic feature information, the improvement of prediction accuracy is minimal. In recent years, deep learning has been widely utilized in FR-IQA tasks, which use a neural network and a large number of image data to train out a reliable IQA model. In order to reflect the distorted image's prediction quality score, DeepQA [15] uses convolutional neural networks to learn the perceptual sensitivity map of the difference between the distorted image and the reference image. DeepSim [8] and PAVIF [21] work in a similar way which calculates the similarity of feature maps extracted from each convolutional layer in feature extraction operations of the two input images, the quality score of the distorted image is then computed by average pooling these values. WaDIQaM-FR [3] randomly selects 32 patches from each image and predicts the quality scores of them. The final score is obtained by weighted average pooling these patches' values.

**Distortion Classification:** Distortion classification is one of the branches of image classification, it is a crucial step for lots of image processing tasks. Identifying the distortion type of image is able to help the model learn other image attributes, such as image quality evaluation, image inpainting, distortion restoration, etc. Several distortion classification methods have been proposed these years. Bandawi proposes a classification method bases on the generalized Benford's law, which extracts features from the distribution of the first digit of the transformation coefficient of an image, and uses

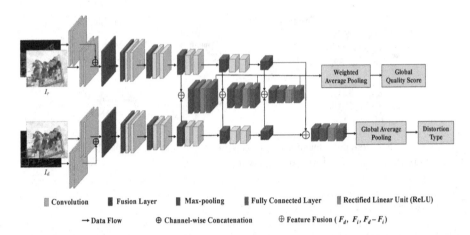

**Fig. 3.** The overall architecture of our MTL-IQA. The multi-task learning-based method can evaluate image quality and identify distortion type simultaneously. Several patches are selected randomly from input distorted and reference images. The designed feature extractor is applied to learn image information, and then they are fused as input for quality score and distortion type prediction.

generalized Benford's law to simulate distribution [2]. Deep learning is also be employed in the distortion classification research, such as [1,4], which both use convolutional neural networks to detect and identify image distortion.

Multi-task learning (MTL) pipeline is popular in deep learning networks. However, to our best knowledge, seldom IQA methods have employed MTL into their models. Among them, IQA-CNN++ [13] first proposes to utilize a shared network to estimate image quality score and identify distortion type simultaneously. MGCN [12] uses a convolutional neural network with an encoder module to transform and extract features, and then predicts image quality and distortion.

## 3    Our MTL-IQA Framework

Figure 3 depicts the overall network architecture of our **MTL-IQA**. As a multi-task learning network, we use a shared convolutional neural network to learn the characteristics of each of the two tasks and the commonalities between them. As an FR image quality assessment model, the inputs of this network are distorted images $I_d$ and their corresponding reference images $I_r$, we use a siamese network to learn the relationship between the inputs. Specifically, Each image is divided into small patches of size 32 × 32 to calculate the global image score based on the weighted score of the local patch. Furthermore, a number of small patches also rich the training data for CNN. We set our feature extraction network with 10 convolutional layers and 5 max-pooling layers. During the extraction process, in order to preserve more useful edge information, we introduce an enhanced edge fusion module for both two input brands. After the feature extraction, we leverage different feature fusion methods to compute the final outputs of the two tasks. We demonstrate that our model helps to achieve the best performance for both distortion type classification and quality score estimation tasks.

## 3.1 Enhanced Edge Fusion Module

The human's eye is sensitive to object's contour or edge, however, as a low-level feature, edge information is lost as the network goes deeper. To address this problem, we propose an enhanced edge fusion module to preserve edge information as much as possible. For edge detector, we directly choose Canny [5] detector to extract edge feature and then use the edge map as input together with the raw image. It is worth mentioning that for edge map, we use the first two layers of the same feature extraction network to learn the edge information, which would output edge feature vector $F_e$, then fuse it with the main branch after the second convolutional layer. To verify the effectiveness of the enhanced edge fusion module, we show the ablation experiment results in Table 5.

## 3.2 Multi-layer Feature Fusion

The feature extractor is designed to learn the informative features of the input, which is composed of convolutional neural networks. Compared with other conventional IQA methods which only employ the feature vectors from the end of the network, we propose to utilize multi-layer features to learn the image perceptual quality, which can provide more informative and significant features. Hence, we assign three sets of fully connected layers after the mid-level and high-level feature extraction process. To learn the relationship between two output feature vectors, we explicitly provide useful relation information which can help to improve prediction accuracy. In this way, the deviation of the feature maps of distorted image patch $F_{d_l}$ ($l = 1, 2, 3$), feature maps of reference image patch $F_{r_l}$ ($F_{d_l} - F_{r_l}$) are fused. Then the branch outputs the fused vector $F_{i_l}$ for layer $l$, patch $i$. A rectified linear unit (ReLU) is used to activate $F_{i_l}$, afterwards output $\beta_{i_l}$. Since our model tends to weight local patch quality score $q_i$ for global score $Q$, we express the weight $\omega$ of layer $l$ as:

$$\omega_{i_l} = \frac{\beta_{i_l}}{\sum_i^N \beta_{i_l}} \tag{1}$$

where $N$ is the total amount of local patches.

## 3.3 Multi-task Learning for IQA and Classification

As a multi-task learning framework, in order to achieve the best performance on both tasks simultaneously, it is crucial to decide where to branch the backbone into independent tasks. In our method, for quality prediction task, we fuse the output of three sets of fully connected layers for the final quality score computation. Then the global image perceptual quality score $Q$ can be computed as:

$$Q = \sum_i^N \omega_i q_i = \sum_i^N (\sum_1^{l=3} \omega_{i_l} q_{i_l}) = \sum_i^N (\sum_1^{l=3} \frac{\beta_{i_l} q_{i_l}}{\sum_i^N \beta_{i_l}}) \tag{2}$$

$q_i$ and $q_{i_l}$ denote the quality score of patch $i$ and the layer $l$ of patch $i$, respectively. And for classification task, we only utilize one set of fully connected layers at the end of the network, and we use a different feature fusion scheme from quality score prediction task. By concatenating $(F_{d_l}, F_{r_l}, F_{d_l} - F_{r_l})$ as feature vector, we experimentally find that this strategy helps obtain best prediction accuracy for classification. Then we average the local distributions to global.

The design of loss function is crucial for multi-task learning, which influences the final prediction accuracy directly. As a regression task, mean absolute error (MAE) is utilized as the quality prediction loss, which is expressed as:

$$L_{quality} = \frac{1}{N} \sum_i^N |q_i - S| \tag{3}$$

where $S$ represents the ground-truth quality score of distorted image $I_d$. And for the distortion classification task, we use cross entropy loss as $L_{class}$.

$$L_{class} = -\sum_{c=1}^M y_c \log P_c \tag{4}$$

where $M$ indicates the number of distortion types. The label value $c$ is the index in the range of $[1, M]$, which is the true distortion type label of the distorted image. $y_c$ is the indicator variable, and $P_c$ means the prediction probability of class $c$.

### 3.4   Bayesian Uncertainty-Based Automatically Loss Weighting

Generally, the performance of multi-task learning system heavily depends on the inter-task loss weights. However, manually adjusting the weights is time and labor consuming. In our method, a Bayesian uncertainty-based method for automatically loss weighting is introduced. Assume the overall loss function for two tasks is minimized as:

$$L = \lambda_1 L_{quality} + \lambda_2 L_{class} \tag{5}$$

where $\lambda_1$ and $\lambda_2$ weigh importance between the two tasks. Different from other methods that tune weights manually, we set the regularization parameter by learning a relative weighting, motivated by [14]. More specifically, we introduce a Gaussian likelihood maximization loss function with homoscedastic uncertainty, which is given as:

$$L(W, \sigma1, \sigma2) = \frac{1}{2\sigma_1^2} L_{quality}(W) + \frac{1}{\sigma_2^2} L_{class}(W) + \log \sigma1 + \log \sigma2 \tag{6}$$

where $W$ is parameter matrix, $\sigma1$ and $\sigma2$ are observation noise parameters of quality score prediction task and distortion type classification task, respectively. By optimizing $W$, $\sigma1$, $\sigma2$, and adjusting the weighted parameters in the loss function based on "uncertainty", the loss function in each task achieves a similar range of scale. Finally, $\lambda_1$ and $\lambda_2$ are determined to be 0.83 and 0.17 for LIVE and CSIQ database, and 0.80 and 0.20 for TID2013 database, respectively.

# 4   Experiments

In this section, we first briefly introduce datasets, evaluation metrics in our experiment. Then we compare the performance of our method with other single-task or multi-task methods. Ablation studies are also conducted to demonstrate the effectiveness of each proposed component.

**Table 1.** Summary of the databases used in our experiments.

| Databases | # of reference images | # of distorted images | # of distortion types | Score type | Score range |
|---|---|---|---|---|---|
| LIVE [24] | 29 | 779 | 5 | DMOS | [1,100] |
| TID2013 [22] | 25 | 3000 | 24 | MOS | [0,9] |
| CSIQ [18] | 30 | 866 | 6 | DMOS | [0,1] |

## 4.1   Experimental Protocol

**Datasets:** We train and test the proposed model on three standard image quality assessment datasets: LIVE [24], TID2013 [22], and CSIQ [18], as summarized in Table 1. The LIVE dataset includes 779 distorted images, which are degenerated from 29 super-resolution images. It contains 5 distortion types: Gaussian blur, JPEG compression, JPEG2000 compression, white noise, and simulated fast-fading Rayleigh channel. The difference mean opinion scores (DMOS) of the images lie in the range of 0 to 100. It should be noted that lower score value means better image quality degree. The TID2013 dataset contains 25 reference images and 3,000 distorted images with 24 types of distortion at 5 degrees of degradation. The mean opinion score (MOS) of each image is provided, which ranges from 0 to 9, higher value indicates better image visual quality. It is worth mentioning that different with numerous IQA approaches which only use a part of TID2013, we use the full dataset and do not ignore any distortion type. And the CSIQ dataset includes 866 distortion images. 30 high-resolution reference images are distorted by Gaussian white noise, Gaussian pink noise, Gaussian blur, contrast change, JPEG compression, or JPEG2000 compression. After a series of normalization processes, the DMOS of CSIQ lies in the range of 0 to 1, lower value corresponds to better perceptual quality.

**Evaluation Metrics:** To verify the IQA performance of the proposed model, we use four metrics: Pearson linear correlation coefficient (PLCC), Kendall rank-order correlation coefficient (KROCC), Spearman rank correlation coefficient (SROCC), and root mean square error (RMSE). KROCC and SROCC reflect the monotonicity of the objective evaluation method to predict image quality, while PLCC and RMSE reflect the prediction accuracy. The higher PLCC, KROCC, SROCC and lower RMSE means better performance. For distortion classification, overall accuracy is used for evaluation.

## 4.2 Training Strategy

In the implementation, we train and test the introduced model on the three aforementioned datasets. In experiments, each dataset is randomly divided by reference images into a training set, a validation set and a testing set in the ratio of 60%, 20% and 20%. The random division of the dataset by reference image strategy ensures that no distorted or original images used for testing or validation are used during training. For LIVE, there are 17 reference images used for training, 6 for validation and testing. For TID2013, the training set bases on 15 reference images, both the validation and testing sets are based on 5 images. Similarly, CSIQ is divided into 18 training, 6 validation and 6 test images. We train the models by using Adam optimizer with the learning rate starts as 0.0001, the batch size is set of 4 for each dataset. Models are trained for 1000 epochs. We repeat the experiment for 10 times, finally report the median performance for each evaluation metrics.

**Table 2.** Performance comparison of different IQA models on three datasets LIVE, CSIQ, and TID2013. Higher PLCC, SROCC, KROCC and lower RMSE indicate better performance. The best results are bolded.

| Class | Methods | LIVE | | | | TID2013 | | | | CSIQ | | | |
|---|---|---|---|---|---|---|---|---|---|---|---|---|---|
| | | PLCC | SROCC | KROCC | RMSE | PLCC | SROCC | KROCC | RMSE | PLCC | SROCC | KROCC | RMSE |
| NR | IQA-CNN++ [13] | 0.950 | 0.950 | – | – | – | – | – | – | – | – | – | – |
| | MEON [20] | – | – | – | – | 0.912 | 0.912 | – | – | 0.944 | 0.932 | – | – |
| | DIQaM-NR [3] | 0.972 | 0.960 | – | – | 0.855 | 0.835 | – | – | – | – | – | – |
| | DIQA [16] | 0.977 | 0.975 | – | – | 0.850 | 0.825 | – | – | 0.915 | 0.884 | – | – |
| FR | PSNR [25] | 0.865 | 0.873 | 0.680 | 13.716 | 0.677 | 0.687 | 0.496 | 0.912 | 0.819 | 0.810 | 0.601 | 0.154 |
| | SSIM [27] | 0.945 | 0.948 | 0.797 | 8.946 | 0.790 | 0.742 | 0.559 | 0.761 | 0.861 | 0.876 | 0.691 | 0.133 |
| | FSIM [29] | 0.960 | 0.963 | 0.834 | 7.678 | 0.859 | 0.802 | 0.629 | 0.635 | 0.912 | 0.924 | 0.757 | 0.108 |
| | GMSD [28] | 0.960 | 0.960 | 0.827 | 7.694 | 0.855 | 0.804 | 0.634 | 0.642 | 0.954 | 0.957 | 0.812 | 0.079 |
| | VIF [24] | 0.960 | 0.964 | 0.828 | 7.614 | 0.772 | 0.677 | 0.515 | 0.788 | 0.928 | 0.920 | 0.754 | 0.098 |
| FR-DL | WaDIQaM-FR [3] | 0.977 | 0.968 | 0.846 | 5.101 | 0.958 | 0.947 | 0.802 | 0.387 | 0.953 | 0.961 | 0.829 | 0.083 |
| | DISTS [6] | 0.954 | 0.954 | 0.811 | 8.214 | 0.855 | 0.830 | 0.639 | 0.643 | 0.928 | 0.929 | 0.767 | 0.098 |
| | DRF-IQA [17] | 0.983 | **0.983** | – | – | 0.944 | 0.942 | – | – | 0.964 | 0.960 | – | – |
| | MGCN-weight [12] | 0.967 | 0.966 | – | – | 0.942 | 0.934 | – | – | – | – | – | – |
| Ours | MTL-IQA | **0.985** | 0.979 | **0.882** | **4.302** | **0.961** | **0.961** | **0.837** | **0.369** | **0.970** | **0.973** | **0.868** | **0.067** |

## 4.3 Evaluation for IQA Task

As shown in Table 2, we compare ours with four NR-IQA methods IQA-CNN++ [13], MEON [20], DIQaM-NR [3] and DIQA [16], five traditional IQA methods, PSNR [25], SSIM [27], FSIM [29], GMSD [28], VIF [24], and four deep learning-based IQA methods, WaDIQaM-FR [3], DISTS [6], DRF-IQA [17], and MGCN-weight [12]. IQA-CNN++, MEON, and MGCN-weight are MTL methods, which also predict perceptual quality and identify distortion type simultaneously. Experimental results demonstrate that the proposed method outperforms almost all other methods on three datasets. Especially, we achieve superior results in PLCC (0.985 on LIVE dataset), which indicates the effectiveness of our model. Compared with the state-of-the-art method DRF-IQA, our MTL-IQA outperforms all other methods on almost each dataset and evaluation metric except the SROCC on LIVE database.

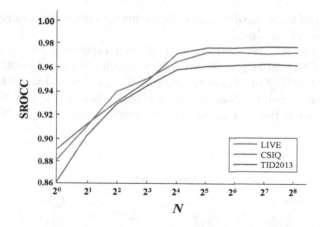

**Fig. 4.** With the proposed MTL-IQA, SROCC evaluated on LIVE, CSIQ and TID2013 is given, with x-coordinate referring to the different numbers of sampled patches. When $N = 32$, the model on all of the three datasets can achieve best prediction performance.

**Table 3.** Comparison of distortion classification testing results of different MTL methods IQA-CNN++ [13], MEON [20], MGCN-ave [12], and MGCN-weight [12]. Higher value means better classification performance.

| Class | Methods | LIVE | TID2013 | CSIQ |
|-------|---------|------|---------|------|
| NR | IQA-CNN++ [13] | 0.951 | – | – |
|    | MEON [20] | – | 0.940 | – |
| FR | MGCN-ave [12] | 0.950 | 0.979 | – |
|    | MGCN-weight [12] | 0.958 | 0.972 | – |
|    | MTL-IQA (Ours) | **0.980** | **0.982** | **0.977** |

### 4.4   Evaluation for Classification Task

Our model also obtains superior accuracy for classification task. We compare our method with four advanced multi-task learning models: IQA-CNN++ [13], MEON [20], MGCN-ave [12] and MGCN-weight [12]. As shown in Table 3, MTL-IQA achieves the highest performance for classification task. Compared with the state-of-the-art method MGCN-weight, the accuracy of our method has a 2.2% improvement on the LIVE database, while on the TID2013 database, our model improves 0.3% over MGCN-ave. The superior performance can be attributed to our deeper feature extraction network, which outputs more efficient feature information.

### 4.5   Convergence Evaluation

In the experiments, we choose the number of local patches $N$ as 32, which means we randomly select 32 patches from each input image to predict a local quality score. We find that the selection of $N$ is able to significantly influence the prediction accuracy of the model. Therefore, we design a series of experiments to show the influence of $N$ and the reasonability of our choice.

We train and test this convergence evaluation experiment on datasets LIVE, TID2013 and CSIQ, then report SROCC values of each set of experimental results. As we see in Fig. 4, MTL-IQA tends to be saturated when $N = 32$ and almost achieves the best performance for all the three databases. Though when $N > 32$ may have slightly better results, considering the reasonable use of computing resources, finally we choose $N$ as 32.

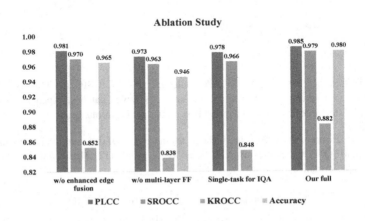

**Fig. 5.** Ablation study of the proposed components. To validate the contributions of the proposed enhanced edge fusion module, multi-layer feature fusion, and multi-task learning pipeline, we conduct ablation experiments on LIVE dataset.

### 4.6  Ablation Study

Furthermore, we conduct a series of ablation experiments on the LIVE database. To validate the effectiveness of our contributions, we list ablation tests with regard to enhanced edge fusion module, multi-layer feature fusion scheme and single-task learning for FR-IQA. The results are shown in Fig. 5. By adding enhanced edge information and utilizing multi-layer feature fusion, the PLCC and classification accuracy values enjoy 0.4% and 1.2%, 1.5% and 3.4% improvements, respectively. Compared with single-task learning for IQA, the multi-task learning helps to improve PLCC, SROCC, and KROCC for 0.7%, 1.3% and 3.4%, respectively.

Finally, we design an experiment to depict the results on several sets of different loss weight assignments. From Fig. 6 we are capable of observing that learning multiple tasks simultaneously improves the performance of each task. And by using uncertainty weights for the two tasks, we can find an improved performance for both of them. Figure 6 demonstrates the higher accuracy of our setting (0.83 for IQA and 0.17 for classification on LIVE, 0.8 for IQA and 0.2 for classification on TID2013) than other experience-based settings.

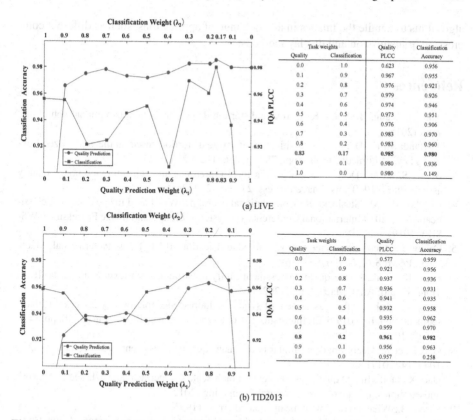

| Task weights | | Quality | Classification |
|---|---|---|---|
| Quality | Classification | PLCC | Accuracy |
| 0.0 | 1.0 | 0.623 | 0.956 |
| 0.1 | 0.9 | 0.967 | 0.955 |
| 0.2 | 0.8 | 0.976 | 0.921 |
| 0.3 | 0.7 | 0.979 | 0.926 |
| 0.4 | 0.6 | 0.974 | 0.946 |
| 0.5 | 0.5 | 0.973 | 0.951 |
| 0.6 | 0.4 | 0.976 | 0.906 |
| 0.7 | 0.3 | 0.983 | 0.970 |
| 0.8 | 0.2 | 0.983 | 0.960 |
| 0.83 | 0.17 | 0.985 | 0.980 |
| 0.9 | 0.1 | 0.980 | 0.936 |
| 1.0 | 0.0 | 0.980 | 0.149 |

(a) LIVE

| Task weights | | Quality | Classification |
|---|---|---|---|
| Quality | Classification | PLCC | Accuracy |
| 0.0 | 1.0 | 0.577 | 0.959 |
| 0.1 | 0.9 | 0.921 | 0.956 |
| 0.2 | 0.8 | 0.937 | 0.936 |
| 0.3 | 0.7 | 0.936 | 0.931 |
| 0.4 | 0.6 | 0.941 | 0.935 |
| 0.5 | 0.5 | 0.932 | 0.958 |
| 0.6 | 0.4 | 0.935 | 0.962 |
| 0.7 | 0.3 | 0.959 | 0.970 |
| 0.8 | 0.2 | 0.961 | 0.982 |
| 0.9 | 0.1 | 0.956 | 0.963 |
| 1.0 | 0.0 | 0.957 | 0.258 |

(b) TID2013

**Fig. 6.** Comparing the performance of different loss weight assignments when learning image quality and distortion type on datasets LIVE and TID2013. These figures and tables indicate the advantages of using a multi-task learning pipeline for IQA and distortion classification, also show the importance of learning adaptive loss weights. Finally, We set $\lambda_1$ and $\lambda_2$ as 0.83, 0.17 for LIVE, $\lambda_1$ and $\lambda_2$ as 0.8, 0.2 for TID2013, respectively.

## 5 Conclusion

In this work, we have proposed a novel approach to the FR-IQA and distortion classification problems using multi-task learning architecture. By introducing an enhanced edge fusion module, designing a multi-layer feature fusion scheme and dynamically assigning loss weights automatically, the robustness and performance of the two tasks both improve by a large margin. The experimental results on the LIVE, CSIQ and TID2013 datasets demonstrate the state-of-the-art performance of our proposed method.

Under the current trend that digital imaging and display technologies have greatly changed the way how we capture, store, perceive and post images, our method has performed remarkable results at predicting image quality like human judgments, and has the capability of discerning the image and video quality and analyzing the distortion reason in a short time. Future work will be put on to design more advanced IQA algorithms to handle the images in a wide range of applications, such as different compression, transmission and display methods.

# References

1. Ahn, N., Kang, B., Sohn, K.A.: Image distortion detection using convolutional neural network (2018)
2. Al-Bandawi, H., Deng, G.: Classification of image distortion based on the generalized Benford's law. Multimedia Tools Appl. **78**(18), 25611–25628 (2019)
3. Bosse, S., et al.: Deep neural networks for no-reference and full-reference image quality assessment. IEEE Trans. Image Process. **27**, 206–219 (2018)
4. Buczkowski, M., Stasinski, R.: Convolutional neural network-based image distortion classification. In: 2019 International Conference on Systems, Signals and Image Processing (IWSSIP) (2019)
5. Canny, J.: A computational approach to edge detection. IEEE Trans. Pattern Anal. Mach. Intell. PAMI **8**(6), 679–698 (1986)
6. Ding, K., et al.: Image quality assessment: unifying structure and texture similarity. IEEE Trans. Pattern Anal. Mach. Intell. (2020)
7. Feng, Y., et al.: Quality assessment of synthetic fluorescence microscopy images for image segmentation. In: 2019 IEEE International Conference on Image Processing (ICIP), pp. 814–818 (2019)
8. Gao, F., et al.: DeepSim: deep similarity for image quality assessment. Neurocomputing **257**, 104–114 (2017)
9. Gao, X., et al.: Image quality assessment - a multiscale geometric analysis-based framework and examples. In: Handbook of Natural Computing (2012)
10. Girod, B.: What's wrong with mean-squared error? (1993)
11. Hu, W., et al.: A new method of thangka image inpainting quality assessment. J. Vis. Commun. Image Represent. **59**, 292–299 (2019)
12. Huang, C., Jiang, T., Jiang, M.: Encoding distortions for multi-task full-reference image quality assessment. In: 2019 IEEE International Conference on Multimedia and Expo (ICME), pp. 1864–1869 (2019)
13. Kang, L., et al.: Simultaneous estimation of image quality and distortion via multi-task convolutional neural networks. In: 2015 IEEE International Conference on Image Processing (ICIP), pp. 2791–2795 (2015)
14. Kendall, A., Gal, Y., Cipolla, R.: Multi-task learning using uncertainty to weigh losses for scene geometry and semantics. In: 2018 IEEE/CVF Conference on Computer Vision and Pattern Recognition, pp. 7482–7491 (2018)
15. Kim, J., Lee, S.: Deep learning of human visual sensitivity in image quality assessment framework. In: IEEE Conference on Computer Vision & Pattern Recognition, pp. 1969–1977 (2017)
16. Kim, J., Nguyen, A., Lee, S.: Deep CNN-based blind image quality predictor. IEEE Trans. Neural Netw. Learn. Syst. **30**, 11–24 (2019)
17. Kim, W., et al.: Dynamic receptive field generation for full-reference image quality assessment. IEEE Trans. Image Process. **29**, 4219–4231 (2020)
18. Larson, E.C., Chandler, D.: Most apparent distortion: full-reference image quality assessment and the role of strategy. J. Electron. Imag. **19**, 011006 (2010)
19. Liu, S., Johns, E., Davison, A.: End-to-end multi-task learning with attention. In: 2019 IEEE/CVF Conference on Computer Vision and Pattern Recognition (CVPR), pp. 1871–1880 (2019)

20. Ma, K., et al.: End-to-end blind image quality assessment using deep neural networks. IEEE Trans. Image Process. **27**, 1202–1213 (2018)
21. Ma, X., Jiang, X.: Multimedia image quality assessment based on deep feature extraction. Multimedia Tools Appl. **79**(6), 1–12 (2020)
22. Ponomarenko, N., et al.: Color image database TID2013: peculiarities and preliminary results. In: European Workshop on Visual Information Processing (EUVIP), pp. 106–111 (2013)
23. Ruder, S.: An overview of multi-task learning in deep neural networks. ArXiv abs/1706.05098 (2017)
24. Sheikh, H., Bovik, A.: Image information and visual quality. IEEE Trans. Image Process. **15**, 430–444 (2006)
25. Wang, Y., et al.: Image quality evaluation based on image weighted separating block peak signal to noise ratio. In: International Conference on Neural Networks & Signal Processing (2003)
26. Wang, Z., Li, Q.: Information content weighting for perceptual image quality assessment. IEEE Trans. Image Process. **20**(5), 1185–1198 (2011)
27. Wang, Z., et al.: Image quality assessment: from error visibility to structural similarity. IEEE Trans. Image Process. **13**, 600–612 (2004)
28. Xue, W., et al.: Gradient magnitude similarity deviation: a highly efficient perceptual image quality index. IEEE Trans. Image Process. **23**, 684–695 (2014)
29. Zhang, L., et al.: FSIM: a feature similarity index for image quality assessment. IEEE Trans. Image Process. **20**, 2378–2386 (2011)
30. Zhang, W., et al.: RankSRGAN: generative adversarial networks with ranker for image super-resolution. In: 2019 IEEE/CVF International Conference on Computer Vision (ICCV), pp. 3096–3105 (2019)
31. Zhang, Y., Yang, Q.: A survey on multi-task learning. IEEE Trans. Knowl. Data Eng. (2021)

# Feature Adaption with Predicted Boxes for Oriented Object Detection in Aerial Images

Minhao Zou, Ziye Hu, Yuxiang Guan, Zhongxue Gan$^{(\boxtimes)}$, Chun Guan$^{(\boxtimes)}$, and Siyang Leng$^{(\boxtimes)}$

Academy for Engineering and Technology, Fudan University, Shanghai 200433, China
{ganzhongxue,chunguan,syleng}@fudan.edu.cn

**Abstract.** Object detection is a fundamental research field in computer vision. Arbitrary-oriented objects inevitably appear in face, natural scene text, and aerial image detection, which have attracted widespread attention recently. However, existing rotation detectors still suffer from the feature misalignment problem, due to the fixed convolution kernel adopted in detecting arbitrary-oriented and deformed objects. In this paper, we propose a novel method, One-stage Feature Adaption Network (OFA-Net), for oriented object detection in aerial images. A feature adaption module, implemented by the deformable convolution and the align convolution, is proposed to refine the feature maps according to the predicted offsets and decoded boxes. Furthermore, specific to the long-existing periodic angle regression problem in the detection, the box regression branch is decoupled into the size branch and the angle branch, with a new periodic loss in the angle regression branch to leverage the periodic orientation of the object. Extensive experiments demonstrate the effectiveness of our approach, achieving promising results compared with state-of-the-art methods in three benchmark datasets, DOTA, HRSC2016, and UCAS-AOD.

**Keywords:** Deep learning · Computer vision · Object detection

## 1 Introduction

Object detection based on deep learning is a topic of paramount importance in image processing and computer vision with broad applications. Specifically, the goal of object detection is to locate objects with rectangle boxes and further classify them from images or videos. Traditional object detection methods with axis-aligned bounding boxes fail in accurately detecting the ubiquitous rotated objects, such as planes, ships, vehicles and harbors from aerial images, which bring background information as noise [8]. In recent years, arbitrary-oriented object detection with rotatable rectangular boxes has played a considerable role in aerial image processing [4,21,25], natural scene text detection [10], face recognition [16], and robot grasping [26], etc. A series of advanced

D. N. Pham et al. (Eds.): PRICAI 2021, LNAI 13033, pp. 366–378, 2021.
https://doi.org/10.1007/978-3-030-89370-5_27

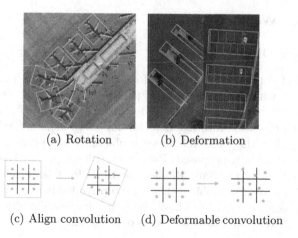

(a) Rotation          (b) Deformation

(c) Align convolution     (d) Deformable convolution

**Fig. 1.** Causes and solutions of feature misalignment problem.

rotation detectors based on deep learning have been proposed, concentrating on the representation of bounding boxes [20], small objects [23], and densely distributed objects [21,23]. Although these rotation detectors have achieved satisfactory performance, the accurate object detection in an arbitrary-oriented (Fig. 1(a)) and deformed (Fig. 1(b)) circumstance remains a challenging problem, limited by the use of axis-aligned and fixed convolution kernels, which can not capture the essential information of different shaped objects and leads to the feature misalignment problem.

To this end, we design a new feature adaption module that extracts information from predicted offsets and decoded boxes to refine the feature maps by jointly introducing the align convolution [6] and the deformable convolution [3].

The main contributions of this work are as follows:

- To alleviate the feature misalignment problem due to the fixed convolution kernel adopted in detecting arbitrary-oriented and deformed objects, a feature adaption module, implemented by the deformable convolution and the align convolution, is proposed to refine the feature maps with respect to the predicted offsets and decoded boxes.
- To adapt the periodic angle regression, the box regression branch is decoupled into the size branch and the angle branch, and a new periodic loss in angle regression branch is proposed to alleviate the inconsistency in calculating the regressing loss, improving the overall performance.
- Combining the above feature adaption module and the decoupled regression branch with angle loss, a universal method, One-stage Feature Adaption Network (OFA-Net), is proposed to generate well-adapted feature maps and high-quality bounding boxes enabling accurate oriented object detection.

## 2    Related Work

### 2.1    Oriented Object Detection

Oriented object detection is a research focus. Yang et al. [25] design a sampling fusion network, which fuses multi-layer feature maps to improve the detection sensitivity for arbitrary-oriented small objects. Yang et al. [23] design an accurate and fast One-stage rotating detector for large aspect ratio objects with high accuracy. For the class imbalance problem, a two-phase Feature Refinement Module (FRM) is proposed. Pan et al. [12] propose a Feature Selection Module (FSM) and a Dynamic Refinement Head for Classification/Regression (DRH-C/R) to solve the problem that all receptive fields of convolution kernels are arranged along the axis and have the same shape while objects usually are arranged in different directions and have different shapes.

### 2.2    Feature Adaption

Some methods have been proposed to deal with the feature misalignment problem. For example, deformable convolution [3] uses an extra convolution layer to learn offsets from input feature maps and adjusts the input feature maps. Yang et al. [23] design a feature refinement module to reconstruct the feature maps using the information of refined anchor obtained by feature interpolation. However, these deformable-based feature adaption methods are implicit and often get offsets from the extra structure without supervised information. Han et al. [6] propose an explicit way, which is artificial design and can not able to express the real feature adaption process. Our method can combine the implicit and explicit information of predicted offsets and decoded boxes to realize feature alignment compared to these methods.

### 2.3    Regression Loss

For the most current oriented bounding box methods, an additional angle variable is added based on the horizontal bounding box, and the distance-based loss is used to optimize the angle. IoU Smoothing L1 loss [25] and modular rotation loss [14] replace the calculation method of regression loss using the IoU factor and RIoU, respectively. However, these methods are complex and not always effective in different scenarios. The most commonly used method is still the Smooth L1 loss [5] based on five parameters (x-coordinate, y-coordinate, width, height, and angle), but the mismatch between angle periodicity and loss function of the rotation box are still not solved, due to two different bounding boxes would be predicted and the same loss value would be obtained in the same position in some cases [25]. Therefore, we propose a new periodic angle loss function, which can adapt to the periodicity of the angle and converge faster.

## 3  Proposed Methods

We give an overview of our method in Fig. 2. The framework consists of three components, a feature extraction backbone, a feature pyramid network, and a regression and classification head. The baseline is a One-stage rotation detector based on the RetinaNet. The feature adaption module is added in the head to reconstruct the feature maps. To realize rotation detection, we use five parameters $(x, y, w, h, \theta)$ to represent the rectangle with different orientations. $\theta$ refers to the acute angle with the x-axis, and the other side corresponds to $w$. The angle ranges in $[-\frac{\pi}{2}, 0)$. The regression targets are as follows:

$$
\begin{aligned}
t_x &= (x - x_a)/w_a, t_y = (y - y_a)/h_a, \\
t_w &= \log(w/w_a), t_h = \log(h/h_a), t_\theta = \theta - \theta_a, \\
t'_x &= (x' - x_a)/w_a, t'_y = (y' - y_a)/h_a, \\
t'_w &= \log(w'/w_a), t'_h = \log(h'/h_a), t'_\theta = \theta' - \theta_a,
\end{aligned} \tag{1}
$$

where $x, y, w, h, \theta$ represents the center x-coordinate, center y-coordinate, width, height, and angle of the box, respectively. The variables $x, x_a, x'$ are used for the ground truth box, anchor box, and prediction box (also for $y, w, h, \theta$). The loss of our method consists of the first phase loss and the second phase one. We assign a class label to each anchor or refined anchor for each phase and regress the position. The loss function is defined as follows:

$$
\begin{aligned}
L = & \frac{\lambda_1}{N} \sum_{n=1}^{N} t_n \sum_{j \in \{x,y,w,h\}} L_r \left(v'_{nj}, v_{nj}\right) + \frac{\lambda_2}{N} \sum_{n=1}^{N} t_n L_\theta \left(\theta'_n, \theta_n\right) \\
& + \frac{\lambda_3}{N} \sum_{n=1}^{N} L_c \left(p'_n, p_n\right),
\end{aligned} \tag{2}
$$

where $N$ indicates the number of anchors, $t_n$ is a binary variable ($t_n = 1$ for foreground and $t_n = 0$ for background). $v'_{nj}$ represents the predicted offset vectors, $v_{nj}$ represents the targets vector of groundtruth. $\theta'_n$ represents the predicted angle offset, $\theta_n$ represents the targets angle of groundtruth. $p_n$ is the probability of predicted object category, $p'_n$ represents the label of object. The Focal loss, Smooth L1 loss and Theta loss are adopted as the classification loss $L_c$, the regression loss $L_r$ and the angle regression loss $L_\theta$, respectively. The hyper-parameter $\lambda_1$, $\lambda_2$, and $\lambda_3$ are set as 1.

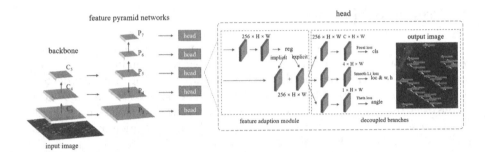

**Fig. 2.** The architecture of One-stage Feature Adaption Network (OFA-Net).

### 3.1 Feature Adaption Module

As shown in Fig. 3, we design different structures of the feature adaption module. The implicit structure uses the deformable convolution [3] with the offsets learned from the predicted offset by a 3 × 3 convolution. The explicit way uses the decoded predicted box information, which is fed into the align convolution [6], to refine the feature map. Our method combine the implicit and explicit way by using the information of predicted offsets and decoded boxes in a parallel or series way to achieve the purpose of feature alignment. The parallel structure concatenates the refined feature maps with 3 × 3 convolution kernels and the series structure gets the explicit refined feature maps from the implicit refined ones, the details are in Fig. 4.

### 3.2 Decoupled Branch

Considering that angle is a periodic variable and different from other regression variables, but all predicted variables are shared the same feature maps, the regression branch is decoupled into the size and the angle branch to fit various regression tasks. The three-branch structure is in the head part (Fig. 2).

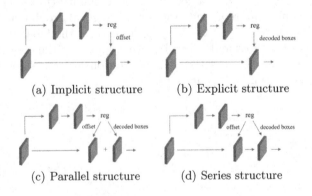

**Fig. 3.** Different adaption structures with predicted boxes.

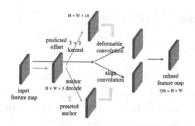

**Fig. 4.** Detailed series and parallel feature adaption module.

## 3.3  Angle Regression Loss

The simulation result of matching two oriented boxes (Fig. 5(a)) shows that the relationship of the two radian is not entirely linear distribution (the darker the color of the point, and the more data is located in), which means two predicted oriented bounding boxes would be regard as the same one even their angle are total different. Aiming to handle this problem, a new angle loss function is designed to apply to angle regression. The Theta loss function is based on Smooth L1 loss and is calculated as follow:

$$\text{Theta Loss }(x) = \begin{cases} 0.5t^2, & \text{if } t < 2 \\ t - 0.5, & \text{otherwise} \end{cases}, \text{where} \quad t = 2 - 2|\cos(x)|. \quad (3)$$

Compared with Smooth L1 loss (Fig. 5(b)), the Theta loss is periodic, and its gradient is larger when $x$ is far away from zero in a period near the zero-point, which means that the loss value will decline faster.

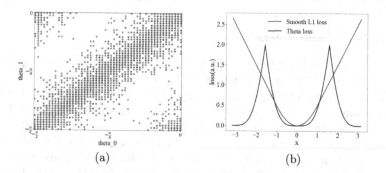

(a)                                    (b)

**Fig. 5.** Analysis and comparison on the proposed Theta loss. (a) The angle distribution of two oriented bounding boxes when IoU > 0.7. (b) The function graph of Smooth L1 loss and the proposed Theta loss.

## 4    Experiments and Analysis

### 4.1    Datasets

Our experiments are conducted on three oriented datasets DOTA [18], HRSC2016 [9]and UCAS-AOD [27]. All objects in these datasets are arbitrary-oriented, and the ground-truth boxes are converted into oriented bounding boxes.

**DOTA** is a challenging benchmark and one of the largest datasets for horizontal and orientated object detection in aerial images. We focus on the task of detection with oriented bounding boxes. There are 15 common object categories, including plane (PL), baseball diamond (BD), bridge (BR), ground field track (GTF), small vehicle (SV), large vehicle (LV), ship (SH), tennis court (TC), basketball court (BC), storage tank (ST), soccer-ball field (SBF), roundabout (RA), harbor (HA), swimming pool (SP), and helicopter (HC). The dataset consists of the training set, validation set, and test set. Both the training and validation sets are used for training, with a total of 1869 pictures.

**UCAS-AOD** is an aerial image dataset of two categories: airplanes and vehicles. It contains 1510 images in total, with 1000 images of airplanes and 510 images of cars. The image shapes range from $1,280 \times 685$ to $1,372 \times 941$. We follow the paper [11] and divide it into the training set, validation set, and test set with a ratio of 5:2:3. In detail, we use the training set and validation set to train.

**HRSC2016** is a challenging remote sensing images detection dataset with arbitrary-oriented and high aspect ratio ship objects. The dataset contains 1061 pictures ranging from $300 \times 300$ to $1,500 \times 900$ pixels. All images are divided into the training set, validation set, and test set, officially, including 436, 181, and 444 images. In detail, we use the training set and validation set to train, and all images are resized to $800 \times 800$ without changing the aspect ratio.

### 4.2    Implementation Details

The methods are implemented with PyTorch [13] based on the mmdetection [2] project. We use the One-stage detector RetinaNet as baseline. If not specified, We use ResNet-50 with FPN, initialize the pre-trained model from PyTorch [13] as the experimental backbone network, and train the network on RTX 2080Ti or RTX 3090, with a total batch size of 2. The training schedule is adopted the same as mmdetection [2]. We train all models with 16 epochs for DOTA, 36 epochs for UCAS-AOD and 72 epochs for HRSC2016. The Stochastic Gradient Descent (SGD) method is adopted with an initial learning rate of 0.004, and the learning rate is reduced by 10 at each decay step. The weight decay and momentum are 0.0001 and 0.9, respectively. The loss weight parameters $\lambda_1, \lambda_2, \lambda_3$ are set as 1. The hyperparameters of Focal loss $L_c$ are set as $\alpha = 0.25$ and $\gamma = 1.0$. Finally, a rotated Non-Maximum Suppression (NMS) with a threshold of 0.05 is applied to the results for post-processing. All the performance is evaluated by the mean Average Precision (mAP, VOC07 metric) method. The random rotation and random HSV (Hue, Saturation and Value) are adopted for data augmentation.

### 4.3    Ablation Studies

**Effectiveness of Decoupled Branch.** RetinaNet is a One-stage detector, which can achieve competitive performance and better speed-accuracy trade-off. Besides, most existed One-stage rotated detectors are based on it. To compare with other existed methods fairly, we choose the RetinaNet as the baseline, and the depth of the head is set as 4 in this ablation experiment. As the results shown in Table 1, we decouple the regression branch into the size branch and the angle branch, the mAP increases 0.29%, which means the decoupled branch could adapt the angle regression and make a slight increase in performance by generating adaption feature maps.

**Table 1.** Ablation experiments under different settings of network.

| Methods | Backbone | Branches | mAP |
|---------|----------|----------|-------|
| Baseline | ResNet50 | 2 | 68.77 |
| Baseline | ResNet50 | 3 | 69.06 |

**Effectiveness of Feature Adaption Module.** Results are given in Table 2. We compare the effect of different settings of the feature adaption module on the effectiveness of the adaption module. Without adaption structure, the detector only achieves 68.93% mAP (the depth of head is set as 2). The implicit structure could improve about 2.76% mAP. And the mAP of the explicit structure could increase to 73.43%. Furthermore, we design a series and a parallel structure that combines the implicit and explicit way as depicted in Fig. 4, where the mAP could reach 73.53% and 74.06%, respectively.

**Effectiveness of Theta Loss.** The results in Table 3 are based on baseline, the input image size is 600 × 600 and resized to 800 × 800. The epochs are set as 12, while the epochs in other experiments in this paper are set as 16, s & s means the angle loss in two phases are Smooth L1 loss and Smooth L1 loss. Likewise, t & t mean Theta loss and Theta loss. As the results shown, the Theta loss could help converge faster and achieve about 73.40% mAP. Further studies show that the Theta loss in phase 1 could achieve higher mAP, which means

**Table 2.** Ablation experiments under different settings of feature adaption module.

| Methods | mAP |
|---------|-------|
| w/o adaption | 68.93 |
| Implicit | 71.69 |
| Explicit | 73.43 |
| Series | 73.53 |
| Parallel | 74.06 |

that Theta loss could help converge faster. If Theta loss is set in phase 2, it will lose generality as indicated in Table 4.

**Table 3.** Ablation experiments of loss based on baseline.

| Input size | Loss function | mAP |
|---|---|---|
| 600->800 | s & s | 72.80 |
| 600->800 | t & t | 73.40 |

**Table 4.** Ablation experiments under different settings of loss.

| | Angle regression loss | (a) | (b) | (c) | (d) |
|---|---|---|---|---|---|
| Phase 1 | Theta loss | | | ✓ | ✓ |
| | Smooth L1 loss | ✓ | ✓ | | |
| Phase 2 | Theta loss | ✓ | | | ✓ |
| | Smooth L1 loss | | ✓ | ✓ | |
| mAP | | 73.32 | 73.61 | 74.06 | 74.07 |

**Comparisons with the State-of-the-Art.** This section compares our proposed methods with other state-of-the-art methods on three aerial image datasets, DOTA, UCAS-AOD, and HRSC2016. The settings and implementation details have been introduced in Sect. 4.2.

**Results on DOTA.** We compare our results with the state-of-the-art methods in DOTA as depicted in Table 5. The DOTA results reported here are obtained by submitting the predicted text file to the official DOTA evaluation server. The latest two-stage detection methods, such as HSP [19] and ReDet [6], perform well. However, they use a complex model structure in exchange for performance improvement, which is highly inefficient in detection. The One-stage detection method proposed in this paper has almost the same performance as the most advanced two-stage detection method. In detail, our multi-scale testing results are fused from tested results of different scales. In terms of overall performance, our method can achieve the best performance so far on One-stage detectors, about 79.52% mAP.

**Results on UCAS-AOD.** Experimental results in Table 6 show that our method achieves the best performance compared with other methods, reaching the mAP of 90.21% and getting the best results in detecting both the cars

**Table 5.** Comparisons with state-of-the-art methods on DOTA, R-101 stands for ResNet-101 (also R-50), H-104 for hourglass 104. † denotes multi-scale training with data augmentation. ‡ means multi-scale training and testing.

| Method | Backbone | PL | BD | BR | GTF | SV | LV | SH | TC | BC | ST | SBF | RA | HA | SP | HC | mAP |
|---|---|---|---|---|---|---|---|---|---|---|---|---|---|---|---|---|---|
| *Two-stage* | | | | | | | | | | | | | | | | | |
| FR-O [18] | R-101 | 79.09 | 69.12 | 17.17 | 63.49 | 34.20 | 37.16 | 36.20 | 89.19 | 69.60 | 58.96 | 49.4 | 52.52 | 46.69 | 44.80 | 46.30 | 52.93 |
| ICN [1] | R-101 | 81.40 | 74.30 | 47.70 | 70.30 | 64.90 | 67.80 | 70.00 | 90.80 | 79.10 | 78.20 | 53.60 | 62.90 | 67.00 | 64.20 | 50.20 | 68.20 |
| SCRDET [25] | R-101 | 89.98 | 80.65 | 52.09 | 68.36 | 68.36 | 60.32 | 72.41 | 90.85 | 87.94 | 86.86 | 65.02 | 66.68 | 66.25 | 68.24 | 65.21 | 72.61 |
| CSL [24] | R-152 | **90.25** | **85.53** | 54.64 | 75.31 | 70.44 | 73.51 | 77.62 | 90.84 | 86.15 | 86.69 | 69.60 | 68.04 | 73.83 | 71.10 | 68.93 | 76.17 |
| ReDet [7] | ReR50-ReFPN | 88.81 | 82.48 | **60.83** | 80.82 | 78.34 | **86.06** | 88.31 | 90.87 | **88.77** | 87.03 | 68.65 | 66.90 | 79.26 | **79.71** | **74.67** | **80.10** |
| *One-stage* | | | | | | | | | | | | | | | | | |
| O²-DNET [17] | H-104 | 89.31 | 82.14 | 47.33 | 61.21 | 71.32 | 74.03 | 78.62 | 90.76 | 82.23 | 81.36 | 60.93 | 60.17 | 58.21 | 66.98 | 61.03 | 71.04 |
| DRN [12] | H-104 | 89.71 | 82.34 | 47.22 | 64.10 | 76.22 | 74.43 | 85.84 | 90.57 | 86.18 | 84.89 | 57.65 | 61.93 | 69.30 | 69.63 | 58.48 | 73.23 |
| R³DET [23] | R-152 | 89.80 | 83.77 | 48.11 | 66.77 | 78.76 | 83.27 | 87.84 | 90.82 | 85.38 | 85.51 | 65.67 | 62.68 | 67.53 | 78.56 | 72.62 | 76.47 |
| R³DET-DCL [22] | R-152 | 89.26 | 83.60 | 53.54 | 72.76 | 79.04 | 82.56 | 87.31 | 90.67 | 86.59 | 86.98 | 67.49 | 66.88 | 73.29 | 70.56 | 69.99 | 77.37 |
| S²ANet [6] | R-50 | 88.89 | 83.60 | 57.74 | **81.95** | **79.94** | 83.19 | **89.11** | 90.78 | 84.87 | 87.81 | **70.30** | 68.25 | **78.30** | 77.01 | 69.58 | 79.42 |
| Baseline | R-50 | 81.26 | 74.43 | 41.03 | 71.67 | 65.13 | 74.29 | 77.55 | 90.87 | 85.19 | 72.42 | 56.84 | 64.17 | 56.83 | 68.13 | 51.67 | 68.77 |
| OFA-Net w/da (ours) | R-50 | 88.49 | 79.82 | 54.23 | 77.60 | 76.92 | 80.78 | 87.57 | 90.89 | 85.41 | 85.54 | 59.56 | 62.77 | 67.85 | 70.71 | 54.83 | 74.86 |
| OFA-Net (ours) † | R-50 | 87.91 | 82.21 | 55.27 | 74.18 | 77.78 | 83.88 | 88.58 | 90.75 | 85.85 | 87.79 | 66.05 | 70.54 | 76.59 | 72.87 | 68.18 | 77.89 |
| OFA-Net (ours) ‡ | R-101 | 88.75 | 82.75 | 57.14 | 81.37 | 78.83 | 85.45 | 88.63 | **90.90** | 86.60 | **87.97** | 66.46 | **70.66** | 77.35 | 78.82 | 71.55 | **79.52** |

and airplanes. The detection performance indicates that our approach is robust to arbitrary-oriented objects.

**Table 6.** Comparison with state-of-the-art methods on UCAS-AOD.

| Methods | Backbone | Input size | Car | Airplane | mAP |
|---|---|---|---|---|---|
| Faster RCNN [15] | ResNet50 | 800 × 800 | 89.52 | 89.86 | 88.36 |
| RRetinaNet (ours) | ResNet50 | 800 × 800 | 88.11 | 90.50 | 89.31 |
| DAL [11] | ResNet50 | 800 × 800 | 89.25 | 90.49 | 89.87 |
| S²ANet [6] | ResNet50 | 800 × 800 | 89.56 | 90.42 | 89.99 |
| **OFA-Net (ours)** | ResNet50 | 800 × 800 | **89.88** | **90.54** | **90.21** |

**Table 7.** Comparison with state-of-the-art methods on HRSC2016.

| Methods | Backbone | Input size | mAP |
|---|---|---|---|
| R³Det [23] | ResNet101 | 800 × 800 | 89.26 |
| DCL [22] | ResNet101 | 800 × 800 | 89.46 |
| DAL [11] | ResNet101 | 800 × 800 | 89.77 |
| S²ANet [6] | ResNet101 | **512 × 800** | **90.17** |
| **OFA-Net (ours)** | ResNet50 | 800 × 800 | **89.80** |

**Results on HRSC2016.** The HRSC2016 contains a large number of ships with large aspect ratio and arbitrary direction, which poses a significant challenge to the detector's accuracy. Note that our methods are evaluated under PASCAL VOC2007 metrics. S²ANet achieves the state-of-the-art performance based on ResNet101 and the input image size is 512 × 800, which is closer to the aspect ratio of the original images. Under ResNet50 backbone, our model can achieve the best mAP among the detector based on the input image size of 800 × 800 with smaller backbone structure, and the results are in Table 7.

### 4.4  Visualization on DOTA

We visualize the detection results of our method on the DOTA test dataset, the results are shown in Fig. 6. The visualization shows that our approach is robust to different categories and could obtain high-quality bounding boxes.

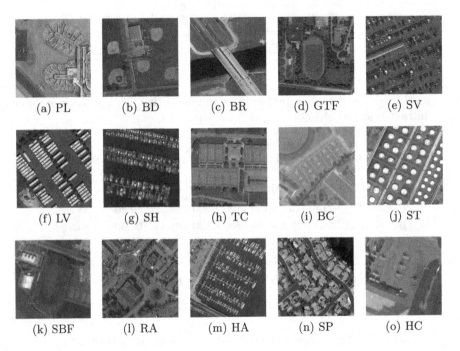

| (a) PL | (b) BD | (c) BR | (d) GTF | (e) SV |

| (f) LV | (g) SH | (h) TC | (i) BC | (j) ST |

| (k) SBF | (l) RA | (m) HA | (n) SP | (o) HC |

**Fig. 6.** Detection results on the Oriented Bounding Boxes (OBB) task on DOTA.

## 5  Conclusion

This paper proposes a One-stage Feature Adaption Network (OFA-Net), which enables us to generate well-adapted feature maps and high-quality bounding boxes for accurate arbitrary-oriented object detection. Considering the feature misalignment problem, we design a new feature adaption module, integrating the advantages of the deformable convolution and the align convolution, to refine the feature maps. Existing frameworks always encounter the periodic angle problem, recently many efforts have been devoted by techniques such as extending the representations of the bounding boxes. Without adding complexity of bounding box representations, we alternatively focus on the angle loss and replace it by a periodic one, effectively improving the detection accuracy. Promising results compared with state-of-the-art methods in the DOTA, UCAS-AOD, HRSC2016 benchmarks demonstrate the broad applicability of our OFA-Net.

**Acknowledgments.** This work is sponsored by Shanghai Municipal Science and Technology Major Project (No.2021SHZDZX0103) and supported by the Shanghai Engineering Research Center of AI & Robotics, Fudan University, China, and the Engineering Research Center of AI & Robotics, Ministry of Education, China. S. Leng is sponsored by Shanghai Sailing Program (No. 21YF1402300).

# References

1. Azimi, S.M., Vig, E., Bahmanyar, R., Körner, M., Reinartz, P.: Towards multi-class object detection in unconstrained remote sensing imagery. In: Jawahar, C.V., Li, H., Mori, G., Schindler, K. (eds.) ACCV 2018. LNCS, vol. 11363, pp. 150–165. Springer, Cham (2019). https://doi.org/10.1007/978-3-030-20893-6_10
2. Chen, K., et al.: MMDetection: open MMlab detection toolbox and benchmark. arXiv preprint arXiv:1906.07155 (2019)
3. Dai, J., et al.: Deformable convolutional networks. In: Proceedings of the IEEE International Conference on Computer Vision, pp. 764–773 (2017)
4. Ding, J., Xue, N., Long, Y., Xia, G.S., Lu, Q.: Learning RoI transformer for oriented object detection in aerial images. In: Proceedings of the IEEE/CVF Conference on Computer Vision and Pattern Recognition, pp. 2849–2858 (2019)
5. Girshick, R.: Fast R-CNN. In: Proceedings of the IEEE International Conference on Computer Vision, pp. 1440–1448 (2015)
6. Han, J., Ding, J., Li, J., Xia, G.S.: Align deep features for oriented object detection. IEEE Trans. Geosci. Remote Sens. (2021)
7. Han, J., Ding, J., Xue, N., Xia, G.S.: ReDet: a rotation-equivariant detector for aerial object detection. arXiv preprint arXiv:2103.07733 (2021)
8. Liu, L., Pan, Z., Lei, B.: Learning a rotation invariant detector with rotatable bounding box. arXiv preprint arXiv:1711.09405 (2017)
9. Liu, Z., Yuan, L., Weng, L., Yang, Y.: A high resolution optical satellite image dataset for ship recognition and some new baselines. In: International Conference on Pattern Recognition Applications and Methods, vol. 2, pp. 324–331. SCITEPRESS (2017)
10. Ma, J., et al.: Arbitrary-oriented scene text detection via rotation proposals. IEEE Trans. Multimedia **20**(11), 3111–3122 (2018)
11. Ming, Q., Zhou, Z., Miao, L., Zhang, H., Li, L.: Dynamic anchor learning for arbitrary-oriented object detection. arXiv preprint arXiv:2012.04150 (2020)
12. Pan, X., et al.: Dynamic refinement network for oriented and densely packed object detection. In: Proceedings of the IEEE/CVF Conference on Computer Vision and Pattern Recognition, pp. 11207–11216 (2020)
13. Paszke, A., et al.: PyTorch: an imperative style, high-performance deep learning library. arXiv preprint arXiv:1912.01703 (2019)
14. Qian, W., Yang, X., Peng, S., Guo, Y., Yan, J.: Learning modulated loss for rotated object detection. arXiv preprint arXiv:1911.08299 (2019)
15. Ren, S., He, K., Girshick, R., Sun, J.: Faster R-CNN: towards real-time object detection with region proposal networks. arXiv preprint arXiv:1506.01497 (2015)

16. Shi, X., Shan, S., Kan, M., Wu, S., Chen, X.: Real-time rotation-invariant face detection with progressive calibration networks. In: Proceedings of the IEEE Conference on Computer Vision and Pattern Recognition, pp. 2295–2303 (2018)
17. Wei, H., Zhang, Y., Chang, Z., Li, H., Wang, H., Sun, X.: Oriented objects as pairs of middle lines. ISPRS J. Photogram. Remote. Sens. **169**, 268–279 (2020)
18. Xia, G.S., et al.: DOTA: a large-scale dataset for object detection in aerial images. In: Proceedings of the IEEE Conference on Computer Vision and Pattern Recognition, pp. 3974–3983 (2018)
19. Xu, C., Li, C., Cui, Z., Zhang, T., Yang, J.: Hierarchical semantic propagation for object detection in remote sensing imagery. IEEE Trans. Geosci. Remote Sens. **58**(6), 4353–4364 (2020)
20. Xu, Y., et al.: Gliding vertex on the horizontal bounding box for multi-oriented object detection. IEEE Trans. Pattern Anal. Mach. Intell. (2020)
21. Yang, F., Fan, H., Chu, P., Blasch, E., Ling, H.: Clustered object detection in aerial images. In: Proceedings of the IEEE/CVF International Conference on Computer Vision, pp. 8311–8320 (2019)
22. Yang, X., Hou, L., Zhou, Y., Wang, W., Yan, J.: Dense label encoding for boundary discontinuity free rotation detection. arXiv preprint arXiv:2011.09670 (2020)
23. Yang, X., Liu, Q., Yan, J., Li, A., Zhang, Z., Yu, G.: R3Det: refined single-stage detector with feature refinement for rotating object. arXiv preprint arXiv:1908.05612 (2019)
24. Yang, X., Yan, J.: Arbitrary-oriented object detection with circular smooth label. In: Vedaldi, A., Bischof, H., Brox, T., Frahm, J.-M. (eds.) ECCV 2020. LNCS, vol. 12353, pp. 677–694. Springer, Cham (2020). https://doi.org/10.1007/978-3-030-58598-3_40
25. Yang, X., et al.: SCRDet: towards more robust detection for small, cluttered and rotated objects. In: Proceedings of the IEEE/CVF International Conference on Computer Vision, pp. 8232–8241 (2019)
26. Zhang, H., Lan, X., Bai, S., Zhou, X., Tian, Z., Zheng, N.: RoI-based robotic grasp detection for object overlapping scenes. In: 2019 IEEE/RSJ International Conference on Intelligent Robots and Systems (IROS), pp. 4768–4775. IEEE (2019)
27. Zhu, H., Chen, X., Dai, W., Fu, K., Ye, Q., Jiao, J.: Orientation robust object detection in aerial images using deep convolutional neural network. In: 2015 IEEE International Conference on Image Processing (ICIP), pp. 3735–3739. IEEE (2015)

# Few-Shot Crowd Counting via Self-supervised Learning

Jiefeng Long, Chun Li, and Lin Shang[✉]

State Key Laboratory for Novel Software Technology, Nanjing University,
Nanjing 210023, China
{longjf,lichun}@smail.nju.edu.cn,shanglin@nju.edu.cn

**Abstract.** Crowd counting has been developed significantly, attributing to the booming of deep learning. However, deep learning based methods are extreme data consuming, and labeling dataset for crowd counting is a sophisticated task. Both the number and the density of people in an image can be very large while the resolution is too low. Meanwhile, collecting crowd pictures without label is much easier. In this paper, we propose a few-shot crowd counting method based on self-supervised learning to leverage these unlabeled data. We firstly collect and clean an unlabeled dataset consisting of crowd images. And two self-supervised assistant tasks are designed with the purpose of training a backbone model to extract the crowd-related features from those unlabeled images. The parameters of the backbone model are then utilized as an initialization for the crowd counting model, which is further fine-tuned with only very few annotated images. We conduct experiments with different amounts of annotated data. Results have demonstrated the effectiveness of the proposed approach.

**Keywords:** Crowd counting · Self-supervised learning · Few-shot learning

## 1 Introduction

In modern society, there are many large-scale crowd gathering scenarios, such as community activities, concerts, sports events, etc., which will cause large crowds to gather in a short time. Crowd counting, which can help with the security issues, has attracted significant attention. A large amount of deep models have been proposed to address this challenging task, from directly predicting the number of people to estimating the crowd density [8,18,19].

However, deep neural networks acquire sufficient data for training, while obtaining high-quality datasets can be extremely costly both temporally and financially, especially for crowd counting. Thus, few-shot learning has become a hot topic, which aims to leverage only few labeled data to train a model with high capacity. In few-shot learning, a typical method is to train a model in a two-stage manner. At the first stage, the model is trained on a source task with

© Springer Nature Switzerland AG 2021
D. N. Pham et al. (Eds.): PRICAI 2021, LNAI 13033, pp. 379–390, 2021.
https://doi.org/10.1007/978-3-030-89370-5_28

sufficient data, e.g. pre-training a CNN on the ImageNet. At the second stage, the model is further fine-tuned on a target task, generally with few data. The parameters of the model are partially or totally migrated from the for source-task as a better initialization. Sometimes finding an appropriate source task for pre-training can also be a tough problem. The targets of different tasks may vary greatly and domain shifts of different datasets can be large. Thus, it is significant to mine latent labels from in-domain unlabeled data and leverage them for model training, for which self-supervised learning can be taken into consideration.

In crowd counting task, the burden of annotating is heavy due to the large number and density of people in an image and the low resolution. Meanwhile, with the popularity of cameras and smart phones, a great many of crowd images are taken and uploaded to the Internet. Collecting unlabeled crowd data can be accomplished easily with technologies such as search engines and web crawlers. Therefore, it is valuable to find out how to leverage the large amount of unlabeled data to boost deep learning based models.

In this paper, we propose a self-supervised learning based few-shot crowd counting method. Specifically, two self-supervised assistant tasks are designed to help with learning how to extract the crowd-related features. The first one is a crowd count ranking task, which aims to guide the model to extract crowd related features by ranking crowd counts of different images, instead of predicting accurate counts directly. The other one is a crowd distance ranking task, in which the model attempts to rank the distance between the crowd and the camera based on perspective theory. A backbone model is trained on these tasks and its parameters are transferred to the crowd counting model as an initialization. Therefore, the crowd counting model is initialized with the ability to capture crowd-related features before training and is further fine-tuned with few labeled images for better performance.

We collect and clean an unlabelled dataset containing crowd images for the self-supervised learning tasks. We conduct experiments with different amounts of labeled data, results have demonstrated the effectiveness of the proposed method and visualizations have further proved the benefits of the self-supervised learning tasks.

## 2    Related Work

Most early works of crowd counting are detection-based approaches, which employ a sliding window detector to detect people for counting [3,7]. Among them, body-based approaches extract features from full bodies while part-based approaches detect particular body parts such as head or shoulder. Besides, regression-based methods are proposed to deal with occlusions, through learning a mapping between extracted features and crowd counts [1,13]. Some of them propose to learn a mapping from local patch features to corresponding density maps to utilize spatial information in crowd images [6,11]. In recent years, a variety of deep learning based methods have been proposed for crowd counting. They either predict the crowd counts directly [18], or estimate a density map firstly and then compute the crowd counts based on it [8,14,16,19,21]. Density estimation based methods tend to outperform since a density map contains more information than a simple crowd count number. Our model for the crowd counting task is also a density estimating network.

Self-supervised learning, which attempts to mine annotations from unlabeled data to reduce labeling burden, has attracted much attention recently. In [2], an image is split into nine blocks, and the model is trained to predict the positions of each block. In [10], part of the image is cut off and the model learns to recover a complete image with the rest parts. Since most images are colorful, [20] proposes a coloration task by converting all images into gray mode and the model is trained to colorizing it. Besides, in [5], an image is rotated and the model is trained to predict the rotation angle. Only few works has been done to introduce self-supervised to crowd counting [9]. We try to move a step forward and designed 2 unique tasks to leverage unlabeled data.

Few-shot learning is proposed to train a model with limited examples for a task. There are 3 main ways to solve this problem: model-based, metric-based and optimization-based respectively. Model-based methods tend to employ a memory to store useful information [15]. Metric-based methods tend to learn a distance to measure the differences between examples [17]. Optimization-based methods intend to find a better initialization parameters through multiple tasks [4,12]. It is believed that optimization-based methods can help alleviate the difficulty for searching the best hypothesis in the large hypothesis space. Based on this theory, we propose our two-stage method for few-shot crowd counting.

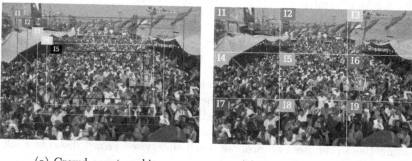

(a) Crowd count ranking          (b) Crowd distance ranking

**Fig. 1.** An illustration of how we generate training examples for crowd count ranking task (a) and crowd distance ranking task (b).

## 3   Our Method

Data labeling for crowd counting is an extremely onerous task due to the denseness of individuals in crowd images and their low resolution. Whereas, collecting crowd images can be much easier. Thus, we attempt to leverage the images without annotations. Specifically, we turn to self-supervised learning to utilize these data with efficiency.

We propose two self-supervised tasks to mine latent information in the unlabeled data.

### 3.1  Crowd Count Ranking

When confronting with several images, we can rank them easily according to their approximate crowd counts without accurate estimations. Inspired by this, we design a self-supervised crowd count ranking task.

For each image, we acquire five image blocks from it, each of which covers different areas of the original image. The height and width of these blocks are respectively 8/25, 2/5, 1/2, 5/8 and 25/32 of the raw image while sharing a common center, which is presented in Fig. 1(a). It is natural that blocks with larger areas retain larger or equal crowd counts when compared to smaller ones, the smaller ones are contained by them. Thus, we can obtain the ranking labels of these blocks according to their areas.

While training, each input image is processed as aforementioned and all the image crops are scaled into the same size. Then each block is fed into the network which predicts a crowd count value for it. The blocks are ranked according to these predicted values, and losses can be calculated with the ranking labels. For each raw image, five values are predicted corresponding to the five blocks. Each block is compared with each other without duplication, so finally 10 ranking results can be obtained.

### 3.2  Crowd Distance Ranking

Assuming that all the crowd photos are taken by cameras, we can find that the sizes of the human bodies are highly related to their distances from cameras. Specifically, the closer to the camera, the larger the body size is in the picture. Therefore, in most cases, obtaining the size information of human bodies in different positions is homogeneous to extracting the distance information of them. Following these premises, we propose a self-supervised crowd distance ranking task.

For each image, we divide it into nine picture blocks, as presented in Fig. 1(b). According to the perspective principle, in general, the distance between the objects on the bottom side of the picture and the camera tend to be smaller than that between the objects on the upper side and the camera. Accordingly, we divide these blocks into three groups based on their distances from the camera. The first group includes picture blocks I1, I2, I3, which is the farthest away from the camera. The second one includes picture blocks I4, I5, I6. And the third group, which is supposed to be the closest to the camera, consists of picture blocks I7, I8, I9. Similar to the crowd count ranking task, we rank these blocks in accordance with their distance away from the camera.

During training, we only take use of the blocks in the second and third group. As for blocks in the first group, we find that they tend to be filled with large areas of sky and trees instead of crowds, so we drop them. The rest blocks are fed into the network which predicts the distance of each block away from the camera. Then we rank these blocks and calculate the loss based on the ranking labels. Note that we only compare blocks from different groups as we assume that crowds in the same group share a common distance away from the camera. In summary, for each raw image, 6 values will be predicted corresponding to each block in 2 groups, and 9 ranking results will be obtained.

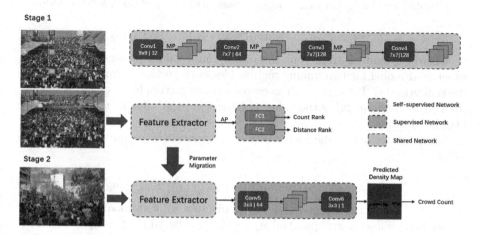

**Fig. 2.** An overview of our proposed method. A backbone model is firstly trained on the designed self-supervised tasks. The parameters of its features extractor are migrated to the crowd counting model as an initialization. The crowd counting model is then fine-tuned with few labeled data.

### 3.3   Model

We devise a simple but efficient model for our experiments. As is shown in Fig. 2, the model can be split into 2 parts: public feature extracting layers and private task-specific layers.

For self-supervised learning tasks, each image is passed by 4 convolutional layers, which are combined by max pooling layers. Then the extracted features are average pooled and fed into a fully connected layer, which projects the features into a value standing for the crowd count or the distance away from the camera. Note that these values are not expected to be precise but only used for comparing and ranking.

After the first stage of self-supervised training, this backbone model has gained the ability to extract features of the crowd. The parameters of its feature extractor are migrated to the crowd counting model, hence it is able to extract .

crowd-related features before further training. The fully connected layer of the backbone model is replaced by 2 convolutional layers to generate a density map.

Finally, we take use of only a small number of labeled crowd pictures to train the crowd counting network in a supervised manner. The model can further learn to extract essential features which are more related to crowd counting, thereby obtaining a more accurate crowd density map.

### 3.4 Training

For self-supervised learning tasks, we apply Margin Ranking Loss for training. Specifically, for the crowd count ranking task, its loss $L_c$ is calculated as follows:

$$L_c(x1_c, x2_c, y_c) = max(0, -y_c * (x1_c - x2_c) + m_c) \tag{1}$$

where $x1_c$ and $x2_c$ represent the crowd count values predicted by the self-supervised model for two unique picture blocks respectively. And $y_c$ represents the ranking label. If the area of the corresponding picture block of $x1_c$ is greater than that of $x2_c$, $y_c$ takes the value 1. Otherwise, the value of $y_c$ is -1. $m_c$ is a margin constant.

Similarly, we define the loss function of crowd distance ranking task $L_d$ as follows:

$$L_d(x1_d, x2_d, y_d) = max(0, -y_d * (x1_d - x2_d) + m_d) \tag{2}$$

where $x1_d$ and $x2_d$ represent the crowd distance values for two unique picture blocks from different groups. And $y_d$ represents the label of comparing result similar to $y_c$ while $m_d$ is similar to $m_c$.

To collaboratively train the self-supervised model on 2 tasks, we add 2 losses together to form up an overall loss $L_{ss}$ as follows:

$$L_{ss} = \alpha * L_c + \beta * L_d \tag{3}$$

where $\alpha$ and $\beta$ are the weight hype-parameters over two parts.

As for the second training stage, we apply Euclidean distance to measure the differences between ground-truth maps and generated maps as follows:

$$L_{fs} = \frac{1}{2N} \sum_{i=1}^{N} \left\| D_i^* - D_i^{GT} \right\|^2 \tag{4}$$

where $N$ is the size of training batch, $D_i^*$ represents the estimated density map and $D_i^{GT}$ represents the ground-truth density map.

## 4    Experiments

### 4.1    Dataset

We use both unlabeled and labeled data in our experiments, the former for self-supervised learning tasks and the latter for fine-tuning the model.

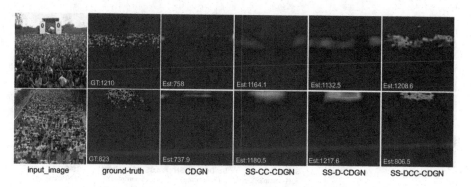

**Fig. 3.** Density maps generated by each baseline and our method.

## Unlabeled Data Collection

We collect unlabeled crowd images through search engine on Internet, based on queries such as *Street   Crowd*. Considering the noises, we conduct manual check to filter out duplicate images and unnatural images(*e.g.* paintings and comics). To this end, 2400 crowd pictures are reserved without. And we use them for our proposed self-supervised tasks. Each image is processed as introduced in Sects. 3.1 and 3.2, producing 11 image blocks. Each block is scaled into 512x512 before feeding into models.

**Labeled Dataset.** We employed the widely used datasets ShanghaiTech [21] and UCF_CC_50 for fine-tuning and testing our model. ShanghaiTech contains 1198 annotated images with a total of 330165 annotated people. It is divided into two parts named Part A and Part B. We use Part A, which contains 482 images with highly congested scenes. We use the train-test splits provided in the original paper [21]. UCF_CC_50, which contains 50 images from the Internet, is a very challenging dataset due to the limited number of images and large variance in crowd counts. The number of annotated persons ranges from 94 to 4543 with an average of 1280 per image. We select the last 30 pictures for testing, and the rest are split as training set.

## 4.2   Settings

Our goal is to measure the performance of the crowd density map generation model under few-shot settings. Thus, we only select a few pictures from the training set randomly to fine-tune crowd count models. In order to alleviate influences of the picture selection process, we repeated the selection and the subsequent experiments for 5 times. The final result is the average of the 5 experimental results. We apply the nearest neighbor distance method to generate the ground-truth crowd density maps and each density map is scaled to a size of 128x128. We use Adam for optimization in both training stages and the learning rate is set to 1e-4. All the trainable parameters of each layer are initialized with a Gaussian distribution with a standard deviation of 0.01. Each convolution layer is followed by a ReLU layer.

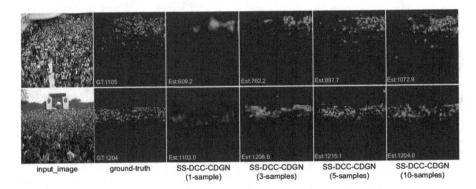

**Fig. 4.** Density maps generated by SS-DCC-CDGN fine-tuned with different numbers of labeled crowd images.

As for evaluation, we employ mean absolute error(MAE), which is defined as follows:

$$MAE = \frac{1}{N} \sum_{i=1}^{N} \left\| C_i - C_i^{GT} \right\| \tag{5}$$

where $N$ is the number of test images, $C_i^{GT}$ is the actual number of people in the $i$th image and $C_i$ is the estimated number of people in the $i$th image.

### 4.3   Comparing Methods

Since we focus on the effects of self-supervised learning tasks, we employ a simple model as our baseline and try 2 tasks both respectively and collaboratively on it. But note that our method can be compatible with any models with few modifications.

**CDGN**: We do not pre-train the Crowd Density Generation Network with any self-supervised tasks. The parameters of this model are all directly initialized with a Gaussian distribution with a standard deviation of 0.01.

**SS-CC-CDGN**: For this model, we engage the Self-Supervised Crowd Count(SS-CC) ranking task to get a better parameter initialization.

**SS-D-CDGN**: Similarly to SS-CC-CDGN, we engage the Self-Supervised Distance(SS-D) ranking task for pre-training.

**SS-DCC-CDGN**: Both tasks are employed and the self-supervised models are trained with 2 parts of losses, setting $\alpha$ and $\beta$ to be equal as 1.

### 4.4   Results

Experimental results on ShanghaiTech Part A and UCF_CC_50 are presented at Table 1. $k$ indicates the number of labeled images used to train or fine-tune each model.

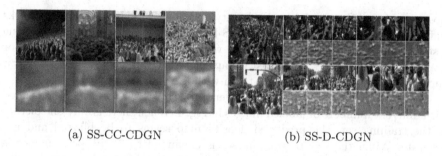

(a) SS-CC-CDGN                    (b) SS-D-CDGN

Fig. 5. Visualizations of extracted features of the last convolutional layer.

On ShanghaiTech Part A, SS-DCC-CDGN outperforms all other baselines while CDGN performs much worse than all other methods. Specifically, when k is set to 5, MAE is reduced from 183 of CDGN to 152 of SS-DCC-CDGN, improving around 17%.

Similarly, on UCF_CC_50, SS-DCC-CDGN achieves best results when $k$ is set to 3, 5 and 10 while CDGN still performs worst under all conditions. Besides, as $k$ grows larger, the improvement of SS-DCC-CDGN against CDGN increases as well. This may be caused by the diversity and complexity of this challenging dataset. More data is required for fine-tuning and our method can leverage them with more efficiency. When $k$ is set to 10, SS-DCC-CDGN reduces MAE from 399 to 338, which improves over 15%.

As for SS-CC-CDGN and SS-D-CDGN, which applies only one self-supervised task, they both achieve better results than CDGN, which implies that both self-supervised tasks are effective for leveraging unlabeled data to optimize crowd counting network.

Table 1. MAE results on ShangHaiTech Part A and UCF_CC_50.

| Model | ShangHaiTech Part A | | | | UCF_CC_50 | | | |
|---|---|---|---|---|---|---|---|---|
| | $k=1$ | $k=3$ | $k=5$ | $k=10$ | $k=1$ | $k=3$ | $k=5$ | $k=10$ |
| CDGN | 218 | 193 | 183 | 153 | 596 | 402 | 383 | 399 |
| SS-CC-CDGN | 204 | 167 | 164 | **144** | **575** | 376 | 373 | 371 |
| SS-D-CDGN | 203 | 182 | 163 | 148 | 585 | 384 | 370 | 344 |
| SS-DCC-CDGN | **197** | **163** | **152** | **144** | 576 | **371** | **356** | **338** |

We visualize the density map generated by each baseline and our model in Fig. 3. It can be found that CDGN has significantly underestimated the density of densely populated areas, resulting in a low crowd count prediction. This is mainly due to the fact that the training set is too small, leading to its lack of feature extraction capabilities for crowds, especially for dense crowds. The predicted values of SS-CC-CDGN and SS-D-CDGN in high-density areas are larger and closer to the real situation, but the density maps predicted by these two networks suffer from excessive blur. Meanwhile, SS-DCC-CDGN can better reflect the true distribution of people in crowd scenes, whether in densely populated areas or sparsely populated areas. The density map can be activated with higher accuracy, and it is the closest to the ground-truth with less blur.

We also present the density maps generated by SS-DCC-CDGN fine-tuned with different numbers of labeled images in Fig. 4. When there is only one picture in the training set, the predicted density map seems to be blurred and not accurate. When the size of training set is expanded to 3, the performance is significantly improved. With the further enrichment of training samples, the density map obtained is more refined and accurate. When the training set size is 10, the crowd counting network has achieved very high counting accuracy on the two images shown.

Overall, it can be concluded that our proposed self-supervised tasks can benefit crowd counting, both separately and collaboratively.

### 4.5    Feature Visualization

We use CAM [22] to visualize the output features of the last convolutional layer of SS-CC-CDGN, as shown in Fig. 5(a). The areas where the crowd exist are activated and appear yellow, which proves that the outputs are formed of the features extracted from these yellow parts, i.e., the network has the ability to capture the location of the crowd to a certain extent.

Similarly, we do the visualizations for SS-D-CDGN, as shown in Fig. 5(b). It can be found that in the parts farther from the camera (i.e., I4, I5, I6), the extracted highlight features are denser. Thus, it can be inferred that the network distinguishes the distance based on the denseness of the crowd features. Denser crowd features tend to be corresponding to smaller body size of individuals in the area, which is more likely to be farther from the camera. It can be concluded that the model has the ability to capture the size information of human body.

In summary, both tasks are effective and can guide the network to capture features related with crowd and thus beneficial for the crowd counting task.

## 5    Conclusion

In this paper, we propose a self-supervised learning based method for few-shot crowd counting. Two different self-supervised tasks are devised to guide the backbone model to extract crowd features with large amounts of unlabeled data. Afterwards, parameters are partly migrated to another model for crowd counting, provides a better initialization and thereby reducing the difficulty of subsequent tasks and improving the performance. Extensive experiments and visualizations have proved the effectiveness of our proposed self-supervised auxiliary tasks.

**Acknowledgments.** This work is supported by the National Natural Science Foundation of China (No. 51975294).

# References

1. Chen, K., Loy, C.C., Gong, S., Xiang, T.: Feature mining for localised crowd counting. In: Bowden, R., Collomosse, J.P., Mikolajczyk, K. (eds.) British Machine Vision Conference, BMVC 2012, Surrey, 3–7 September, pp. 1–11. BMVA Press (2012)
2. Doersch, C., Gupta, A., Efros, A.A.: Unsupervised visual representation learning by context prediction. In: 2015 IEEE International Conference on Computer Vision, ICCV 2015, Santiago, 7–13 December, pp. 1422–1430. IEEE Computer Society (2015)
3. Dollár, P., Wojek, C., Schiele, B., Perona, P.: Pedestrian detection: an evaluation of the state of the art. IEEE Trans. Pattern Anal. Mach. Intell. **34**(4), 743–761 (2012)
4. Finn, C., Abbeel, P., Levine, S.: Model-agnostic meta-learning for fast adaptation of deep networks. In: Precup, D., Teh, Y.W. (eds.) Proceedings of the 34th International Conference on Machine Learning, ICML 2017, Sydney, 6–11 August, vol. 70, pp. 1126–1135. PMLR (2017)
5. Gidaris, S., Singh, P., Komodakis, N.: Unsupervised representation learning by predicting image rotations. In: 6th International Conference on Learning Representations, ICLR 2018, Vancouver, April 30 - May 3, Conference Track Proceedings, OpenReview.net (2018)
6. Lempitsky, V.S., Zisserman, A.: Learning to count objects in images. In: Lafferty, J.D., Williams, C.K.I., Shawe-Taylor, J., Zemel, R.S., Culotta, A. (eds.) Advances in Neural Information Processing Systems 23: 24th Annual Conference on Neural Information Processing Systems 2010, Proceedings of a meeting held 6–9 December, Vancouver, pp. 1324–1332. Curran Associates, Inc. (2010)
7. Li, M., Zhang, Z., Huang, K., Tan, T.: Estimating the number of people in crowded scenes by MID based foreground segmentation and head-shoulder detection. In: 19th International Conference on Pattern Recognition (ICPR 2008), Tampa, 8–11 December, pp. 1–4. IEEE Computer Society (2008)
8. Li, Y., Zhang, X., Chen, D.: Csrnet: Dilated convolutional neural networks for understanding the highly congested scenes. In: 2018 IEEE Conference on Computer Vision and Pattern Recognition, CVPR 2018, Salt Lake City, 18–22 June, pp. 1091–1100. IEEE Computer Society (2018)
9. Liu, X., van de Weijer, J., Bagdanov, A.D.: Leveraging unlabeled data for crowd counting by learning to rank. In: 2018 IEEE Conference on Computer Vision and Pattern Recognition, CVPR 2018, Salt Lake City, 18–22 June, pp. 7661–7669. IEEE Computer Society (2018)
10. Pathak, D., Krähenbühl, P., Donahue, J., Darrell, T., Efros, A.A.: Context encoders: Feature learning by inpainting. In: 2016 IEEE Conference on Computer Vision and Pattern Recognition, CVPR 2016, Las Vegas, 27–30 June, pp. 2536–2544. IEEE Computer Society (2016)
11. Pham, V., Kozakaya, T., Yamaguchi, O., Okada, R.: COUNT forest: Co-voting uncertain number of targets using random forest for crowd density estimation. In: 2015 IEEE International Conference on Computer Vision, ICCV 2015, Santiago, 7–13 December, pp. 3253–3261. IEEE Computer Society (2015)
12. Ravi, S., Larochelle, H.: Optimization as a model for few-shot learning. In: 5th International Conference on Learning Representations, ICLR 2017, Toulon, 24–26 April, Conference Track Proceedings, OpenReview.net (2017)

13. Ryan, D., Denman, S., Fookes, C., Sridharan, S.: Crowd counting using multiple local features. In: DICTA 2009, Digital Image Computing: Techniques and Applications, Melbourne, 1–3 December, pp. 81–88. IEEE Computer Society (2009)
14. Sam, D.B., Surya, S., Babu, R.V.: Switching convolutional neural network for crowd counting. In: 2017 IEEE Conference on Computer Vision and Pattern Recognition, CVPR 2017, Honolulu, 21–26 July, pp. 4031–4039. IEEE Computer Society (2017)
15. Santoro, A., Bartunov, S., Botvinick, M., Wierstra, D., Lillicrap, T.P.: Meta-learning with memory-augmented neural networks. In: Balcan, M., Weinberger, K.Q. (eds.) Proceedings of the 33nd International Conference on Machine Learning, ICML 2016, New York City, 19–24 June, JMLR Workshop and Conference Proceedings, vol. 48, pp. 1842–1850. JMLR.org (2016)
16. Sindagi, V.A., Patel, V.M.: Generating high-quality crowd density maps using contextual pyramid cnns. In: IEEE International Conference on Computer Vision, ICCV 2017, Venice, 22–29 October, pp. 1879–1888. IEEE Computer Society (2017)
17. Vinyals, O., Blundell, C., Lillicrap, T., Kavukcuoglu, K., Wierstra, D.: Matching networks for one shot learning. In: Lee, D.D., Sugiyama, M., von Luxburg, U., Guyon, I., Garnett, R. (eds.) Advances in Neural Information Processing Systems 29: Annual Conference on Neural Information Processing Systems 2016, Barcelona, 5–10 December, pp. 3630–3638 (2016)
18. Wang, C., Zhang, H., Yang, L., Liu, S., Cao, X.: Deep people counting in extremely dense crowds. In: Zhou, X., Smeaton, A.F., Tian, Q., Bulterman, D.C.A., Shen, H.T., Mayer-Patel, K., Yan, S. (eds.) Proceedings of the 23rd Annual ACM Conference on Multimedia Conference, MM 2015, Brisbane, 26–30 October, pp. 1299–1302. ACM (2015)
19. Zhang, C., Li, H., Wang, X., Yang, X.: Cross-scene crowd counting via deep convolutional neural networks. In: IEEE Conference on Computer Vision and Pattern Recognition, CVPR 2015, Boston, 7–12 June, pp. 833–841. IEEE Computer Society (2015)
20. Zhang, R., Isola, P., Efros, A.A.: Colorful image colorization. In: Leibe, B., Matas, J., Sebe, N., Welling, M. (eds.) ECCV 2016. LNCS, vol. 9907, pp. 649–666. Springer, Cham (2016). https://doi.org/10.1007/978-3-319-46487-9_40
21. Zhang, Y., Zhou, D., Chen, S., Gao, S., Ma, Y.: Single-image crowd counting via multi-column convolutional neural network. In: 2016 IEEE Conference on Computer Vision and Pattern Recognition, CVPR 2016, Las Vegas, 27–30 June, pp. 589–597. IEEE Computer Society (2016)
22. Zhou, B., Khosla, A., Lapedriza, À., Oliva, A., Torralba, A.: Learning deep features for discriminative localization. In: 2016 IEEE Conference on Computer Vision and Pattern Recognition, CVPR 2016, Las Vegas, 27–30 June, pp. 2921–2929. IEEE Computer Society (2016)

# Low-Rank Orthonormal Analysis Dictionary Learning for Image Classification

Kun Jiang$^{(\boxtimes)}$, Zhaoli Liu, and Qindong Sun

School of Computer Science and Engineering, Xi'an University of Technology,
Xi'an, China
{jk_365,zhaoliliu,sqd}@xaut.edu.cn

**Abstract.** Sparse representation of images by analysis dictionary learning (ADL) has been an active topic in pattern classification as samples can be transformed into sparse representation efficiently. However, learning a discriminative and compact analysis dictionary (ADL) has not been well addressed when the samples are corrupted with noises. In this paper, we propose a low-rank orthonormal analysis dictionary learning (LR-OADL) model. Specially, the low-rank constraint is firstly imposed on the analysis representation to handle the possible noises in the samples. With orthonormal constraint and off-block diagonal supressing term, the analysis dictionary atoms from different classes are incoherent from each other, leading to discriminative block-diagonal representations. Furthermore, a novel locality constraint is exploited to promote the discriminative within class representation similarity. Finally, we employ an alternating minimization algorithm to solve this problem. Experiments on benchmark image datasets demonstrate the efficacy of the proposed LR-OADL model.

**Keywords:** Low-rank representation · Analysis dictionary · Orthonormal constraint

## 1 Introduction

Recent years, sparse representation has been widely applied to many data mining areas across signal processing and pattern recognition, by which signals can be represented as a linear combination of a relatively small number of atoms of an over-complete dictionary [1]. Then, sparse representation models can be classified into two categories by the learning method, synthesis dictionary learning (SDL) and analysis dictionary learning (ADL) [1,9]. A typical SDL model expects to learn the over-completed dictionary by minimizing the reconstruction errors such that it can linearly represent the original signals. Instead of learning an over-complete representation dictionary in SDL, the ADL model mainly focuses on learning a transformation matrix, and constructing sparse analyzed coefficients. The ADL model has aroused much attention since it has a more

© Springer Nature Switzerland AG 2021
D. N. Pham et al. (Eds.): PRICAI 2021, LNAI 13033, pp. 391–402, 2021.
https://doi.org/10.1007/978-3-030-89370-5_29

intuitive illustration for the role of analysis atoms and high classification efficiency by a simple multiplication of analysis dictionary and the new sample.

However, images often include severe illumination, pose, expression and occlusion changes that can destroy the subspace structures of data in reality, which will inevitably affect the analysis representation and classification accuracy. Low-rank representation (LRR) has been widely used in computer vision and pattern recognition due to its strong robustness to the noise of the corrupted data [5,7]. However, the current LRR model are commonly combined with SDL model for spanning the multiple subspaces, and learning representations for test samples is a quite time-consuming procedure [2]. Furthermore, the traditional ADL model views the signal transformation problem as a pure approximation task, which may overlook signal intrinsic attributes, such as structural and discriminative capability [9]. Thus, the discriminative ability of the analysis dictionary is not fully exploited only with the label matrix of training samples [3,17].

To remedy these deficiencies, several sparse coding models incorporating the geometrical structures of the image space have been proposed. They are based on the locally invariant idea, which assumes that two close points in the original space are likely to have similar representations [21]. Motivated by recent progress in sparse representation, we present a novel orthonormal ADL model with manifold learning, called low-rank and orthonormal ADL model(LR-OADL). Then, we incorporate a novel weighted locality regularization characterizing the similarity of nearby samples. Furthermore, the off-block suppressing term is also imposed on analysis representations to enhance the inter-class samples discrimination. Finally, a novel alternation direction method based on the linearized alternating direction method with adaptive penalty(LADMAP) is proposed to solve the LR-OADL model.

The rest of this paper is organized as follows. The related works are presented in Sect. 2. The proposed LR-OADL model is presented in Sect. 3. The optimization algorithm is introduced in Sect. 4. Experimental results are presented in Sect. 5 and conclusions are given in Sect. 6.

## 2    Related Work

### 2.1    Dictionary Learning

Given signals $X = [x_1, x_2, \cdots, x_n] \in R^{m \times n}$, let $D = [d_1, d_2, \cdots, d_k] \in R^{m \times k}$ be a synthesis dictionary with a serials of atom $d_i$, and $Z = [z_1, z_2, \cdots, z_n] \in R^{k \times n}$ be the sparse coefficient matrix. Synthesis dictionary learning (SDL) is to approximately reconstruct the original signals $X$ by the combination of dictionary atoms $d_i(1 \leq i \leq k)$ with respective weight factors or coefficients $Z$. The sparse optimization problem of SDL can be formulated as follows.

$$\min_{D,Z}(\|X - DZ\|_F^2 + \lambda \sum_{i=1}^{M} \|z_i\|_0) \tag{1}$$

where $\|X - DZ\|_F^2$ is the reconstruction error term, $\|z_i\|_0$ is the sparse constraint term and $\lambda$ is a scalar weight parameter [1].

The analysis dictionary learning (ADL) model aims to learn a projective matrix (i.e., analysis dictionary) $\Omega \in R^{k \times m}$ with $k > m$ to implement the approximately sparse representation $Z \in R^{k \times n}$ in transformed domain [8,9]. Specifically, it assumes that the product of $\Omega$ and $x_i$ is sparse, i.e., $z_i = \Omega x_i$ with $\|z_i\|_0 = k - l$, where $0 \leq l \leq k$ is the number of zeros in $z_i \in R^k$. The sparse optimization problem can be formulated as follows.

$$\min_{\Omega, Z}(\|Z - \Omega X\|_F^2 + \lambda \sum_{i=1}^{M} \|z_i\|_0) \tag{2}$$

where $\|Z - \Omega X\|_F^2$ is the representation error term which shows the disparity between sparse representation in the transformed space and the coefficients with target sparsity level explicitly constrained by the $\|z_i\|_0$ term.

## 2.2 Low-Rank Representation

Robust PCA (RPCA) is the first representative work of low-rank representation for maintaining the global structure of training data [15]. It seeks to decompose corrupted observations $X$ into a low-rank matrix $A$ and the associated sparse error matrix $E$. RPCA minimizes the single low-rank of matrix $A$ while reducing the $l_0$-norm of $E$. As the optimization of rank function and $l_0$-norm is highly nonconvex, we can get the following tractable convex optimization surrogate by replacing the rank function with nuclear norm $\|A\|_*$ and the $l_0$-norm with the $l_1$-norm,

$$\min_{A,E} \|A\|_* + \lambda_1 \|E\|_1, \; s.t. \; X = A + E \tag{3}$$

where $\lambda_1$ is a scale parameter.

However, the practical images are approximately drawn from a union of multiple subspaces. Samples of one subject may be drawn from the same subspace, while samples of different subjects are from different subspaces. Thus, Liu et al. [7] presented a more general low-rank representation (LRR) minimization problem, defined as follows,

$$\min_{Z,E} \|Z\|_* + \lambda_1 \|E\|_1, \; s.t. \; X = DZ + E \tag{4}$$

where $D$ is a dictionary that linearly spans the data space into multiple subspaces. The low-rank presentation of the training samples can be used as the input features for training the classifier, but the representation of the test samples should also go through another time-consuming LRR processing. The alternating direction method has been used to solve the LRR problem [6,7].

## 3 The LR-OADL Model

In this section, we propose a novel low-rank orthonormal analysis dictionary learning (LR-OADL) model and an efficient image classifier. The proposed

LR-OADL model considers three parts, including low-rank analysis representation [5], off-block diagonal discrimination and locality constrained representation [20].

First, as the analysis dictionary can generate sparse representation more efficiently than SDL for test samples. To generate a robust analysis dictionary, we combine conventional ADL model and low-rank representation into one unified framework with orthonormal dictionary constraint [2] as

$$\min_{\Omega, Z, E} \|Z\|_* + \lambda_1 \|E\|_1$$
$$s.t. \ \Omega(X - E) = Z, \Omega^T \Omega = I$$

(5)

The above basic model means that samples without sparse noises can be transformed into a low-rank subspace with a compact orthonormal analysis dictionary $\Omega$.

Second, in order to enhance the discriminative capability of the analysis coefficients, we propose the discriminative off-block diagonal regularization·term $\|Z \odot S\|_F^2$ to the coefficients $Z$, where $\odot$ means the element-wise multiplication operator [18]. The $S \in R^{k \times n}$ is defined as

$$S = \begin{cases} 0, \ if \ \omega_i \ and \ x_j \ belong \ to \ the \ same \ class \\ 1, \qquad\qquad\quad otherwise \end{cases}$$

(6)

where $\omega_i$ is the $i$th row of the dictionary $\Omega$, and $x_j$ is the $j$th column of training samples matrix $X$. This off-block diagonal term can proved to be equal to the Fisher discrimination constraint on representation [3].

Third, motivated by the recent progress in manifold learning [16,17], we employ a locality constrained term which explicitly considers the local geometrical structure representation sparsity of samples.

$$\|Z \odot R\|_1$$

(7)

where the weight matrix $R$ is defined as $R_{ij} = \|x_i - x_j\|_2^2$. As such, with the minimization of $\|Z \odot R\|_1$, the samples that are far from $x_i$ will have a smaller coefficient in $Z$. Furthermore, the $l_1$-norm in term $\|Z \odot R\|_1$ will also enforce the reconstructed coefficient matrix $Z$ to be sparse.

In brief, the proposed low-rank orthonomal analysis dictionary learning model (LR-OADL) is defined as follows,

$$\min_{\Omega, Z, E} \|Z\|_* + \lambda_1 \|E\|_1 + \lambda_2 \|Z \odot S\|_F^2 + \lambda_3 \|Z \odot R\|_1$$
$$s.t. \ \Omega(X - E) = Z, \ \Omega^T \Omega = I$$

(8)

where the first and second term provide the robust analysis dictionary model, the third term enhance the discrimination ability for representation, and the fourth term can be seen as a weighted sparsity constraint which simultaneously enables more locality and sparsity ability.

The linear ridge multivariate classifier is trained on the analysis representation and utilized in the following experiments as that in previous study [3,18].

## 4    Optimization

In order to optimize problem (5), an auxiliary variable $J$ and $L$ are introduced, and the optimization problem is rewritten as

$$\min_{\Omega,Z,E,J,L} \|Z\|_* + \lambda_1\|E\|_1 + \lambda_2\|J \odot S\|_F^2 + \lambda_3\|L \odot R\|_1$$

$$s.t.\ \Omega(X-E) = Z, \Omega^T\Omega = I, Z = J, Z = L$$

(9)

which can be solved based on LADMAP method with the iterative following steps [6]. The augmented Lagrangian function of Eq. (4) is

$$L(\Omega, Z, E, J, L, A, B, C, \mu)$$
$$= \|Z\|_* + \lambda_1\|E\|_1 + \lambda_2\|J \odot S\|_F^2 + \lambda_3\|L \odot R\|_1$$
$$+ <A, \Omega(X-E) - Z> + <B, Z-J> + <C, Z-L>$$
$$+ \frac{\mu}{2}\left(\|\Omega(X-E) - Z\|_F^2 + \|Z-J\|_F^2 + \|Z-L\|_F^2\right)$$
$$s.t.\ \Omega^T\Omega = I$$

(10)

where $<A, B> = Tr(A, B)$ denotes the trace of $A^T B$, $A$, $B$ and $C$ are Lagrange multipliers and $\mu > 0$ is a scalar parameter. The optimization of (10) can be solved iteratively by updating $\Omega$, $Z$, $E$, $J$ and $L$ one at a time. The updating scheme is as follows.

**Updating $\Omega$:** Fix the other variables and the minimization of Eq. (5) can be deduced to

$$\min_{\Omega}\left\|\Omega(X-E) - Z + \frac{A}{\mu}\right\|_F^2$$

$$s.t.\ \Omega^T\Omega = I$$

(11)

which is a quadratic form of $\Omega$. Let the first partial derivative w.r.t. $\Omega$ be zero, and $\Omega$ is updated as

$$\Omega^{(t+1)} = (Z^{(t)} - \frac{A^{(t)}}{\mu})(X - E^{(t)})^T((X - E^{(t)})(X - E^{(t)})^T)^{-1}$$

(12)

then the Gram-Schmidt method is used to orthonormalize the rows vectors of $\Omega$ after updating.

**Updating $Z$:** Fix the other variables and update $Z$ by solving the following problem

$$\min_Z \left(\|Z\|_* + \frac{\mu}{2}\left(\left\|Z - \Omega(X-E) - \frac{A}{\mu}\right\|_F^2 + \left\|Z - J + \frac{B}{\mu}\right\|_F^2 + \left\|Z - L + \frac{C}{\mu}\right\|_F^2\right)\right)$$

(13)

The quadratic term of $Z$ can be replaced by its first order Taylor approximation at the previous iteration step $Z^{(t)}$. Thus, the representation $Z$ is updated by solving

$$Z^{t+1} = \underset{Z}{argmin} \left( \|Z\|_* + \frac{\mu\eta}{2} \|Z - F\|_F^2 \right)$$

$$= US_{\frac{1}{\mu\eta}}[\Sigma]V^T \tag{14}$$

where $F = (1 - 3/\eta)Z + (\Omega(X - E) + \frac{A}{\mu} + J - \frac{B}{\mu} + L - \frac{C}{\mu})/\eta$, and $\eta$ is a parameter, and $(U, \Sigma, V^T) = SVD(F)$ and $S_\varepsilon[\cdot]$ is the shrinkage operator defined as follows [6]

$$S_\varepsilon[x] = \begin{cases} x - \varepsilon, & if \ x > \varepsilon \\ x + \varepsilon, & if \ x < \varepsilon \\ 0, & otherwise \end{cases} \tag{15}$$

**Updating $E$:** Fix the other variables and update $E$ by solving the following problem

$$E^{t+1} = \underset{E}{argmin} \left( \lambda_1 \|E\|_1 + \frac{\mu}{2} \left\| \Omega(X - E) - Z + \frac{A}{\mu} \right\|_F^2 \right) \tag{16}$$

With the orthonormal constraint term $\Omega^T\Omega = I$, the above equation can be further deduced as.

$$E^{t+1} = \underset{E}{argmin} \left( \lambda_1 \|E\|_1 + \frac{\mu}{2} \left\| E - F' \right\|_F^2 \right)$$

$$= S_{\frac{\lambda_1}{\mu}}[F'] \tag{17}$$

where $F' = X - \Omega^T Z + \frac{\Omega^T A}{\mu}$, and $S_\varepsilon[\cdot]$ is the magnitude shrinkage operator.

**Updating $J$:** Fix the other variables and update $J$ by solving the following problem

$$J^{t+1} = \underset{J}{argmin} \left( \lambda_2 \|J \odot S\|_F^2 + \frac{\mu}{2} \left\| Z - J + \frac{B}{\mu} \right\|_F^2 \right) \tag{18}$$

which can be updated column-wisely as follows

$$J_j^{t+1} = (\mu^t x_j^{t+1} + b_j^t)M^{-1}$$

$$M = \lambda_2 diag(s_j) + \mu^t I \tag{19}$$

where $I \in R^{N \times N}$ is the identity matrix, $diag(s_j)$ returns a diagonal matrix with $s_j$ as the main diagonal elements, $s_j$, $h_j$ and $b_j$ represent the $j$th row of $S$, $H$ and $B$, respectively.

**Updating $L$:** Fix the other variables and update $L$ by solving the following problem

$$L^{t+1} = \underset{L}{argmin} \left( \lambda_3 \|L \odot R\|_1 + \frac{\mu}{2} \left\| L - (Z + \frac{C}{\mu}) \right\|_F^2 \right) \tag{20}$$

which can be solved by elementwise strategy. For the element $L_{ij}$, the optimal solution of $L$ is

$$L_{ij}^{t+1} = \underset{L_{ij}}{argmin}\, \lambda_3 R_{ij}|L_{ij}| + \frac{\mu^t}{2}\|L_{ij} - M_{ij}\|_F^2$$
$$= S_{\frac{\lambda_3 R_{ij}}{\mu^t}}(M_{ij}) \tag{21}$$

where $M_{ij} = Z_{ij}^{k+1} + \frac{C_{ij}^k}{\mu^t}$, and $S_{\varepsilon}[.]$ is the magnitude shrinkage operator.

The analysis sub-dictionary $\Omega_i$ can be initialized as random matrix, and the whole dictionary $\Omega^{(0)}$ is obtained by combing all the sub-dictionaries as $\Omega^{(0)} = [\Omega_1, \Omega_2, \cdots, \Omega_c]$, where $c$ is the number of class in training samples. After the orthonormalization of the initialized dictionary $\Omega^{(0)}$, the representations $Z^{(0)}$ is initialized by the orthogonal matching pursuit. The error $E^{(0)}$ and the auxiliary variable $J^{(0)}$ and $L^{(0)}$ are initialized as zeros. Thus, the above training procedure is summarized in Algorithm 1.

---

**Algorithm 1.** Solving Eq. (5) by LADMAP method

---

**Input:** Training data $X$, off-block diagonal supressing matrix $S$, weight matrix $R$, model parameter $\lambda_1, \lambda_2$ and $\lambda_3$.

1: Initialize $\Omega^{(0)}$, $Z^{(0)}$, $E^{(0)}$, $J^{(0)}$, $L^{(0)}$ as described above, and $A^{(0)} = B^{(0)} = C^{(0)} = 0$, $\mu_{max} = 10^8$, $\varepsilon = 10^{-6}$, $\rho = 1.15$.

2: **while** not converge **do**

3:    fix the others and update $\Omega$ by Eq. (12)

4:    fix the others and update $Z$ by Eq. (14)

5:    fix the others and update $E$ by Eq. (17)

6:    fix the others and update $J$ by Eq. (18)

7:    fix the others and update $L$ by Eq. (21)

8:    update the multipliers:
$$A^{(t+1)} = A^{(t)} + \mu^{(k)}(Z^{(t+1)} - \Omega^{(t+1)}(X - E^{(t+1)}))$$
$$B^{(t+1)} = B^{(t)} + \mu^{(k)}(Z^{(t+1)} - J^{(t+1)})$$
$$C^{(t+1)} = C^{(t)} + \mu^{(k)}(Z^{(t+1)} - L^{(t+1)})$$

9:    update $\mu$:
$$\mu^{(t+1)} = min(\mu_{max}, \rho\mu^{(t)})$$

10:   check the convergence condition:

11:   $\left\|Z^{(t+1)} - J^{(t+1)}\right\|_\infty < \varepsilon$, $\left\|Z^{(t+1)} - L^{(t+1)}\right\|_\infty < \varepsilon$ and
$\left\|Z^{(t+1)} - \Omega^{(t+1)}(X - E^{(t+1)})\right\|_\infty < \varepsilon$

12: **end while**

**Output:** $\Omega$, $Z$ and $E$.

---

## 5    Experiments

In this section, we evaluate our LR-OADL model on five image datasets for sparse representation-based classification, i.e., Extended YaleB (EYaleB), AR,

Scene15, UCF50 and CALTECH101. The features are provided by [4] and [10]. On EYaleB and AR datasets, random features are generated by the projection with a randomly generated matrix. AR face database contains illumination, expression, and occlusions variations. We choose a subset consisting of 2600 face images from 50 males and 50 females. On Scene15 datasets, features are achieved by extracting SIFT descriptors, max pooling in spatial pyramid and reducing dimensions by PCA. UCF50 is a large-scale and challenging action recognition database. It has 50 action categories and 6680 realistic human action videos collected from YouTube. The Caltech101 dataset are used to contains 9,144 images from 102 categories, and 30 samples per category of the 3000 dimensional spatial pyramid features are used to train the models.

With the above common used image classification features, we compare our method with some state-of-the-art approaches: SRC [15], CRC, K-SVD [1], D-KSVD [19], LC-KSVD [4], ADL-SVM [11], CADL [13], SLC-ADL [12] and SK-DADL [14]. Strictly speaking, SRC and CRC are not dictionary learning methods, as they use the full set of training samples as the dictionary for classification. For fair comparison, the experiment settings we follow are in accordance with [4] and [14]. The sparsity is set as 45 in all the methods, and the dictionary atom is set between 500 and 600 which is the integral multiple of the number of classes in different datasets. There are four parameters in LR-OADL model, i.e., $\lambda_1$, $\lambda_2$, $\lambda_3$ and $\delta$, where $\delta = 0.001$ is preset and the optimal $\lambda_1$, $\lambda_2$ and $\lambda_3$ in the training phase are obtained by 5-fold cross validation and optimized by using grid search strategy. The best parameters we set in each database are listed in Table 1. We repeat the experiments 5 times on different selected training and testing image features, and the mean accuracies are reported.

**Table 1.** Parameter selection in the best performance for parameter $\lambda_1$, $\lambda_2$ and $\lambda_3$.

|             | EYaleB | AR   | Scene15 | UCF50 | CALTECH101 |
|-------------|--------|------|---------|-------|------------|
| $\lambda_1$ | 25     | 15   | 20      | 10    | 30         |
| $\lambda_2$ | 0.01   | 0.05 | 0.11    | 0.01  | 0.5        |
| $\lambda_3$ | 0.001  | 0.01 | 0.01    | 0.001 | 0.03       |

### 5.1  Results and Analysis

Table 2 shows the mean classification accuracy results on different datasets. As can be seen, our method achieves notably higher accuracy than SRC and LC-KSVD on all four databases. This is mainly due to the low-rank constraint and structured discrimination ability achieved in our method for ADL model, which is a further improvement on the LC-KSVD that only considers the label-consistent term and classification error term on SDL model. The SRC model that directly uses all training samples as the dictionary will introduce noise for the sparse representation. The low-rank and locality constraint on representation coefficients

**Table 2.** Classification accuracy (%) comparison on different image datasets.

|            | EYaleB | AR   | Scene15 | UCF50 | CALTECH101 |
|------------|--------|------|---------|-------|------------|
| SRC (full) | 96.5   | 97.5 | 91.8    | 68.4  | 70.7       |
| CRC (full) | 97.0   | 98.0 | 92.0    | 68.6  | 68.2       |
| K-SVD      | 93.1   | 86.5 | 86.7    | 51.5  | 73.0       |
| D-KSVD     | 94.1   | 88.8 | 89.1    | 57.8  | 73.2       |
| LC-KSVD    | 96.7   | 97.5 | 92.9    | 70.1  | 73.6       |
| ADL-SVM    | 95.4   | 96.1 | 91.8    | 72.3  | 64.5       |
| CADL       | 96.7   | 97.3 | 97.6    | 78.0  | 75.0       |
| SK-DADL    | 96.9   | 97.7 | 97.4    | 74.6  | 74.4       |
| LR-OADL    | 97.2   | 97.9 | 98.5    | 78.5  | 74.7       |

can boost the selection of representative analysis atoms, enhance the atom similarity of homogeneous samples while weakening the coherence of heterogeneous samples, and this may help to overcome the above sample noise disadvantage. Our method also achieves favorable results compared with all three ADL-based methods. This proves the availability of adding off-block diagonal structured constraint can further enhance the discriminative representation ability of the conventional ADL models.

**Table 3.** The time (ms) for classifying one testing image.

|         | EYaleB | AR    |
|---------|--------|-------|
| SRC     | 39.93  | 41.24 |
| LC-KSVD | 0.426  | 0.442 |
| SK-DADL | 0.029  | 0.078 |
| LR-OADL | 0.025  | 0.073 |

As for the testing efficiency, Table 3 shows the time for classifying one testing image on databases EYaleB (dictionary size = 570) and AR (dictionary size = 600). As can be seen, our LR-OADL method is approximately 15 times faster than LC-KSVD method, which indicates that it can be applied in practical scenarios. This mainly owns to the simple projection and low classification complexity of ADL which uses feature transformation with analysis dictionary and the jointly learned classifier, without the time-consuming reconstruction processing in SDL. Also, our LR-OADL method performs slightly better than SK-DADL, due to the locality and off-block constraints on sparse coding, which enhance the discriminative capability of the learned analysis dictionary. The accuracies and time costs in tables can demonstrate that analysis dictionary learning has huge potential in pattern classification tasks.

Figure 1 shows the confusion matrix for our LR-OADL method on Scene15 dataset. It presents proportion of images in each category classified to all categories. We can observe that most images can be classified into the right category, with some class even getting all right classification. From the figures, we can conclude that the desired effect of our LR-OADL method is reached.

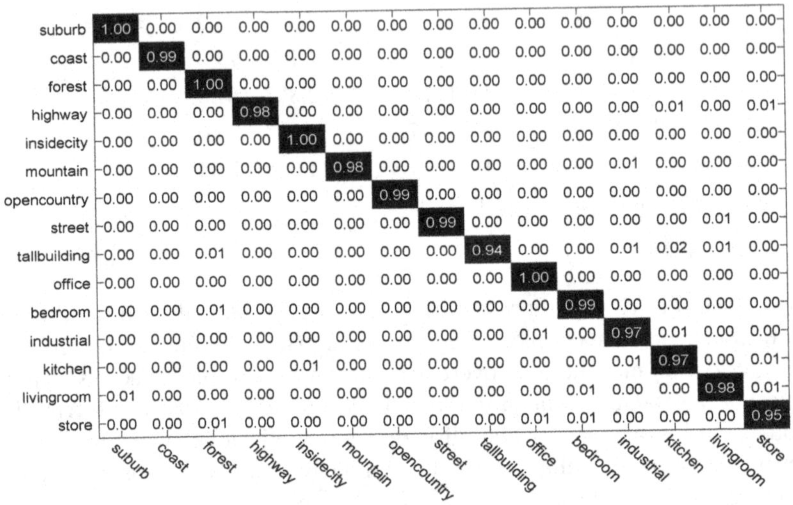

**Fig. 1.** Confusion matrix of the ground truth on Scene 15 dataset.

## 6    Conclusions

In this paper, we proposed a novel discriminative analysis dictionary learning model with low-rank constraint on representation for robust image classification. By introducing the off-block diagonal suppressing term and a locality constraint term into robust low-rank analysis representation model, the proposed approach could capture the intrinsic manifold structure of the training data, and leads to discriminative and sparse representation. Moreover, the orthonormal constraint on analysis dictionary atoms yields further discrimination for classification. The experimental results on benchmark databases demonstrate the efficacy of the proposed LR-OADL model.

**Acknowledgments.** This work is supported by the Natural Science Basic Research Plan in Shaanxi Province of China (Grant No. 2021JM-339).

## References

1. Aharon, M., Elad, M., Bruckstein, A.: K-SVD: an algorithm for designing overcomplete dictionaries for sparse representation. IEEE Trans. Sig. Process. **54**(11), 4311–4322 (2006). https://doi.org/10.1109/TSP.2006.881199

2. Chen, C.F., Wei, C.P., Wang, Y.C.F.: Low-rank matrix recovery with structural incoherence for robust face recognition. In: 2012 IEEE Conference on Computer Vision and Pattern Recognition, pp. 2618–2625 (2012). https://doi.org/10.1109/CVPR.2012.6247981
3. Dong, Z., Pei, M., Jia, Y.: Discriminative orthonormal dictionary learning for fast low-rank representation. In: Arik, S., Huang, T., Lai, W.K., Liu, Q. (eds.) Neural Information Processing, pp. 79–89. Springer International Publishing, Cham (2015)
4. Jiang, Z., Lin, Z., Davis, L.S.: Label consistent K-SVD: learning a discriminative dictionary for recognition. IEEE Trans. Pattern Anal. Mach. Intell. 35(11), 2651–2664 (2013). https://doi.org/10.1109/TPAMI.2013.88
5. Li, Z., Zhang, Z., Qin, J., Li, S., Cai, H.: Low-rank analysis-csynthesis dictionary learning with adaptively ordinal locality. Neural Netw. 119, 93–112 (2019). https://doi.org/10.1016/j.neunet.2019.07.013, https://www.sciencedirect.com/science/article/pii/S0893608019302011
6. Lin, Z., Chen, M., Ma, Y.: The augmented lagrange multiplier method for exact recovery of corrupted low-rank matrices. ArXiv http://arxiv.org/abs/1009.5055 (2009)
7. Liu, G., Lin, Z., Yan, S., Sun, J., Yu, Y., Ma, Y.: Robust recovery of subspace structures by low-rank representation. IEEE Trans. Pattern Anal. Mach. Intell. 35(1), 171–184 (2013). https://doi.org/10.1109/TPAMI.2012.88
8. Ravishankar, S., Bresler, Y.: Learning sparsifying transforms. IEEE Trans. Sig. Process. 61(5), 1072–1086 (2013). https://doi.org/10.1109/TSP.2012.2226449
9. Rubinstein, R., Peleg, T., Elad, M.: Analysis K-SVD: a dictionary-learning algorithm for the analysis sparse model. IEEE Trans. Sig. Process. 61(3), 661–677 (2013). https://doi.org/10.1109/TSP.2012.2226445
10. Sadanand, S., Corso, J.J.: Action bank: a high-level representation of activity in video. In: 2012 IEEE Conference on Computer Vision and Pattern Recognition, pp. 1234–1241 (2012). https://doi.org/10.1109/CVPR.2012.6247806
11. Shekhar, S., Patel, V.M., Chellappa, R.: Analysis sparse coding models for image-based classification. In: 2014 IEEE International Conference on Image Processing (ICIP), pp. 5207–5211 (2014). https://doi.org/10.1109/ICIP.2014.7026054
12. Wang, J., Guo, Y., Guo, J., Li, M., Kong, X.: Synthesis linear classifier based analysis dictionary learning for pattern classification. Neurocomputing 238, 103–113 (2017). https://doi.org/10.1016/j.neucom.2017.01.041, https://www.sciencedirect.com/science/article/pii/S0925231217301157
13. Wang, J., Guo, Y., Guo, J., Luo, X., Kong, X.: Class-aware analysis dictionary learning for pattern classification. IEEE Sig. Process. Lett. 24(12), 1822–1826 (2017). https://doi.org/10.1109/LSP.2017.2734860
14. Wang, Q., Guo, Y., Guo, J., Kong, X.: Synthesis K-SVD based analysis dictionary learning for pattern classification. Multimedia Tools Appl. 77(13), 17023–17041 (2018). https://doi.org/10.1007/s11042-017-5269-6
15. Wright, J., Yang, A.Y., Ganesh, A., Sastry, S.S., Ma, Y.: Robust face recognition via sparse representation. IEEE Trans. Pattern Anal. Mach. Intell. 31(2), 210–227 (2009). https://doi.org/10.1109/TPAMI.2008.79
16. Yi, Y., Wang, J., Zhou, W., Zheng, C., Kong, J., Qiao, S.: Non-negative matrix factorization with locality constrained adaptive graph. IEEE Trans. Circuits Syst. Video Technol. 30(2), 427–441 (2020). https://doi.org/10.1109/TCSVT.2019.2892971
17. Yin, H., Wu, X., Kittler, J.: Face recognition via locality constrained low rank representation and dictionary learning. CoRR abs/1912.03145 http://arxiv.org/abs/1912.03145 (2019)

18. Yin, H., Wu, X., Kittler, J., Feng, Z.: Learning a representation with the block-diagonal structure for pattern classification. Pattern Anal. Appl. **23**(3), 1381–1390 (2020). https://doi.org/10.1007/s10044-019-00858-4
19. Zhang, Q., Li, B.: Discriminative K-SVD for dictionary learning in face recognition. In: 2010 IEEE Computer Society Conference on Computer Vision and Pattern Recognition, pp. 2691–2698 (2010). https://doi.org/10.1109/CVPR.2010.5539989
20. Zhang, Z., Xu, Y., Shao, L., Yang, J.: Discriminative block-diagonal representation learning for image recognition. IEEE Trans. Neural Netw. Learn. Syst. **29**(7), 3111–3125 (2018). https://doi.org/10.1109/TNNLS.2017.2712801
21. Zheng, M., et al.: Graph regularized sparse coding for image representation. IEEE Trans. Image Process. **20**(5), 1327–1336 (2011). https://doi.org/10.1109/TIP.2010.2090535

# MRAC-Net: Multi-resolution Anisotropic Convolutional Network for 3D Point Cloud Completion

Sheng Liu[1]([⊠]), Dingda Li[1], Wenhao Huang[1], Yifeng Cao[1], and Shengyong Chen[2]

[1] Zhejiang University of Technology, HangZhou, China
edliu@zjut.edu.cn
[2] Tianjin University of Technology, Tianjin, China

**Abstract.** Point cloud completion aims to infer the missing parts of the 3D object from incomplete point clouds. Previous methods usually use Multi-layer Perceptrons to directly extract latent features from incomplete point clouds. However, these latent features usually suffer from the loss of information about the structural details of the local area of incomplete point clouds. To solve this problem, we propose a new Multi-Resolution Anisotropic Convolutional Network (MRAC-Net). It could effectively extract latent features from incomplete point clouds through a series of 3D convolutions, which contain the structure and context information of point clouds. Also, we design a combined pyramid generation network to concatenate the feature vectors of different layers, which could better estimate the missing point clouds hierarchically. Extensive experiments on the ShapeNet benchmark show that the proposed approach outperforms the previous state-of-the-art baselines by remarkable margins.

**Keywords:** Point cloud completion · 3D convolution · Anisotropic convolutional

## 1 Introduction

With the increasing popularity of low-cost sensors (such as LiDARs), 3D data has attracted widespread attention in the vision and robotics community. 3D data can usually be represented in different formats, including depth images, point clouds, grids, and volume grids. As a commonly used format, point clouds are the preferred representation for describing the 3D shape of objects. However, due to occlusion, light reflection, surface material transparency, sensor resolution and viewing angle limitations, etc., the point cloud is usually incomplete. This will cause the geometric and semantic information of the point clouds to be lost so that it cannot be used in practical applications directly.

Due to the disorder and unstructured nature of 3D point clouds, deep networks cannot be applied to 3D point clouds as simply as convolutional networks

© Springer Nature Switzerland AG 2021
D. N. Pham et al. (Eds.): PRICAI 2021, LNAI 13033, pp. 403–414, 2021.
https://doi.org/10.1007/978-3-030-89370-5_30

are applied to 2D images. There are also other ways of expressing point clouds, such as GRNet [27], which proposed a gridding-based method that retrieves structural context by performing cubic feature sampling per grid and complete the output with "Gridding Reverse" layers and MLPs. These methods may cause irreversible loss of geometric information. Thanks to the previous PointNet [22] proposal, which pioneered the use of Multi-layer Perceptrons to directly process point clouds, PCN [29] is the first framework to work on raw point clouds in a coarse to fine way. Recently, PF-Net [11] retained the spatial structure of the original incomplete point cloud and predicted the hierarchical missing points of a multi-scale generation network. However, these methods use MLPs modules to extract features and do not fully consider the connectivity across points and the context of neighboring points.

In order to solve these problems, we propose a new network framework to predict missing point clouds from incomplete point clouds in two stages. In the first stage, we designed a novel multi-resolution anisotropic convolutional encoder to better extract the latent features of 3D objects from incomplete point clouds. These latent features contain not only local and global features but also low-level features and high-level features. In the second stage, we design a novel decoder to better infer the missing point cloud from the feature map.

The contributions of our paper can be summarized as follows:

- We propose a novel learning-based point cloud completion architecture, which has better performance in detail preservation and potential shape prediction through a multi-resolution feature aggregation strategy.
- We design a multi-resolution Anisotropic Convolutional Encoder (ACE) that can better extract the local and global features of 3D objects to improve the network's ability to extract semantic and geometric information.
- We design a Combined Pyramid Decoder (CPD) to better infer the missing point cloud from the feature map. It can output hierarchically point clouds of different resolutions by layering to preserve the structure of the complete shape in layers with different resolutions.
- Extensive experiments demonstrate that our proposed network outperforms state-of-the-art 3D point cloud completion methods.

## 2    Related Work

### 2.1    3D Shape Completion

The traditional methods of 3D shape completion mainly include geometry-based approaches and example-based approaches. The geometry-based approaches fill in the partially broken parts by generating a smooth interpolation algorithm [2] or repairs the shape by identifying symmetric and repetitive structures [21]. Example-based approaches are to match the input structure with the complete structure in the database to obtain the complete structure [16]. However, this approach is expensive to optimize in the inference and iteration process, which makes it unsuitable for real-time tasks. Currently, 3D shape completion is mainly

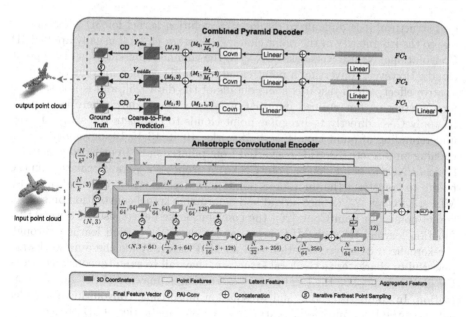

**Fig. 1.** The architecture of MRAC-Net. With input point clouds, it predicts additional parts of sparse and partial data by an Anisotropic Convolutional Encoder (ACE) and a Combined Pyramid Decoder (CPD).

based on learning-based methods such as 3D voxel grids or point clouds. Methods based on 3D voxels, such as the work of GRNet [27], have been proposed to reconstruct the complete 3D voxels in a coarse-to-fine manner. However, for the method based on the voxel grid [4], it is limited by its resolution, because as the resolution increases, the computational cost will increase sharply. Without loss of geometric information, the point cloud can become a more effective representation. Deep learning poses great challenges to the disorder and unstructured nature of point clouds. L-GAN [1] introduced the first deep learning model with Encoder-Decoder architecture on the point cloud. PCN [29] proposed a coarse-to-fine program to synthesize dense and complete data through a specially designed decoder. RL-GAN-Net [23] proposed a GAN controlled by a reinforcement learning agent to speed up the inference stage. PF-Net [11] recovers the point cloud through multi-scale generation of the network layer based on the latent features of the point cloud. Although these MLPs-based methods are effective, we claim that MLPs-based methods would impair the capacity of the feature extraction, and our network can effectively improve this.

## 2.2 Convolution-Based Networks

The convolution-based method follows the conventional convolution mechanism in 2D image processing. However, compared with the kernel defined on the 2D grid structure, it is difficult to design a convolution kernel for 3D point clouds due to the irregularity of the point cloud. Early work [4,8,14] usually applied 3D Convolutional Neural Networks (CNN) to the volume representation of 3D point clouds. However, converting a point cloud into a 3D volume introduces a quantitative effect, which discards some details of the data [25], and is not suitable for representing fine-grained information. As far as we know, there is no work to apply CNN directly to irregular point clouds to complete the shape. In the understanding of point clouds, several works [10,12,13,15,19] developed CNNs running on discrete 3D grids converted from point clouds. In order to generalize typical CNNs to point clouds, PointCNN [15] proposes a $\chi$ transformation on the points to transform the unordered points into a potentially canonical order by MLPs. KPConv [24] defines a rigid and deformable kernel convolution on several kernel points. In PointConv [26], the convolution kernel consists of a weighting function learned through MLP layers and a density function learned through the kernelized density estimation and an MLP layer. While these networks are powerful to characterize the local structure, they fail to simultaneously consider the global shape, i.e., the local feature extraction is unaware of the global information. In comparison, our multi-resolution anisotropic convolutional encoder enhances the local and global feature extraction capabilities of 3D objects.

## 3    Approach

In this section, we will introduce our MRAC-Net, which predicts the missing region of the point cloud from its incomplete known configuration. Figure 1 shows the complete architecture of MRAC-Net. The overall architecture of MRAC-Net is composed of two fundamental building blocks, named Anisotropic Convolutional Encoder (ACE) and Combined Pyramid Decoder (CPD).

### 3.1    Anisotropic Convolutional Encoder

The input to Anisotropic Convolutional Encoder is an $N \times 3$ unordered point cloud $P = \{p_1, p_2, ..., p_N\}$ . Each point contains 3D coordinates $p_i = [x_i, y_i, z_i]^\top$ in the Euclidean space. For each point, its neighboring points are gathered by the simple K-nearest neighbors (KNN) algorithm based on the point-wise Euclidean distances for efficiency. We denote the $i$th point's K-nearest neighbors as $N_i = \{p_i, p_{i,1}, ..., p_{i,k-1}\}$. It is first downsampled to obtain two more views of smaller resolutions (size: $\frac{N}{k} \times 3$ and $\frac{N}{k^2} \times 3$) by iterative farthest point sampling (IFPS). Three point clouds with different resolutions pass through three independent anisotropic convolutional networks to extract the latent features of this point cloud.

In the anisotropic convolutional network, we use permutable anisotropic convolutional(PAI-Conv) [7] to encode each point into multiple dimensions [64-64-128-256]. The Fibonacci lattice is first mapped to the surface of the sphere by equal area projection to generate a set of kernel points $K = \{k_0, k_1, ..., k_{l-1}\}(k_0 = [0, 0, 0]^\top$ is at the origin and $l$ is the number of kernel points), so that the kernel points are evenly distributed on the sphere. For the $i$th point, we obtain the local neighboring positions of the neighbors as $\tilde{p}_{i,j} = p_i - p_{i,j}$, where $p_{i,j} \in N_i$ and $\tilde{p}_{i,0} = [0,0,0]^\top$ is at the origin. The soft-permutation matrix is simply calculated by the dot product between the local neighboring positions and the kernel points followed by sparsemax [20], expressed as

$$M_i = f\left(\tilde{P}_i K^\top\right), \tag{1}$$

where $\tilde{P}_i \in \mathbb{R}^{k \times 3}$, $K \in \mathbb{R}^{l \times 3}$, $M_i \in \mathbb{R}^{k \times l}$, and $f(\cdot)$ is sparsemax.

For each kernel point, the dot product ensures a local neighboring position with a smaller angle to the kernel point has a larger weight. Sparsemax ensures the soft-permutation matrix is sparse and only those points with small angles to a kernel point are selected and give the corresponding weight otherwise the weight is zero. Inspired by RandLA-Net [9], we first encode the relative point position of the point cloud as

$$r_{i,j} = MLP\left(concat\left(p_i, (p_i - p_{i,j}), \|p_i - p_{i,j}\|\right)\right), \tag{2}$$

where $\|\cdot\|$ Calculate the Euclidean distance between point $p_i$ and its neighbors. The relative point position and feature of each point are concatenated as follows to obtain the point feature, $x_{i,j} = concat\left(r_{i,j}, f_{i,j}\right)$, where $f_{i,j}$ is the intermediate feature learned from the network structure, $x_{i,j} \in \mathbb{R}^{D_{in}}$, and $D_{in}$ is the feature dimension. For each point, we construct $X_i = \{x_{i,0}, x_{i,1}, ..., x_{i,k-1}\} \in \mathbb{R}^{D_{in} \times k}$ for the convolutional operation.

Since the order and orientation of each point's neighbors vary from one to another, directly applying an anisotropic filter on unordered neighbors diminishes the representation power. While training, the anisotropic filter might struggle to adapt to the large variability of the unordered coordinate systems, and the possibility of learning rotation invariant filter increases. In this paper, we resample each point's neighbors using the soft-permutation matrix in (1). The resampled convolutional neighbors of each point can be obtained by $\tilde{X}_i = X_i M_i$, where $\tilde{X}_i \in \mathbb{R}^{D_{in} \times l}$. Since the point's neighbors are rearranged according to the canonical order of the fixed kernel points, we can apply a shared anisotropic filter on each point of a point cloud. This operation is the same as the conventional convolution and can be expressed as

$$y_i = g(vec(\tilde{X}_i)^\top W + b), \tag{3}$$

where $W \in \mathbb{R}^{(D_{in} \times l) \times D_{out}}$, $b \in \mathbb{R}^{D_{out}}$ is the bias, $y_i \in \mathbb{R}^{D_{out}}$ is the output feature point corresponding to the input feature point $x_i \in \mathbb{R}^{D_{in}}$, $vec(\cdot)$ is a vectorization function which converts a matrix into a column vector, and $g(\cdot)$ is an activation function, e.g., ELU [3], to introduce non-linearity. Resample the latent features generated by four anisotropic convolutions through IFPS, concatenate them (size: $\frac{N}{64} \times 512$) and use MLP to form new latent features (size: $1 \times 1024$). Three latent features generated at different resolutions are concatenated, and the final feature vector is generated by using MLP.

## 3.2  Combined Pyramid Decoder

The encoder aims to complete the missing part of the point cloud from the final feature vector. Inspired by Feature Pyramid Network (FPN) [18] and PF-Net [11], we designed a combined pyramid decoder (CPN) from coarse to fine. Three feature layers $FC_1$, $FC_2$, $FC_3$ (size: 1024, 512, 256) are calculated by passing the final feature vector through the fully connected layers, each of which is responsible for predicting the point cloud in different resolutions. The coarse center points $Y_{coarse}$ are predicted by $FC_1$, which are of the size of $M_1 \times 3$. The relative coordinates of the middle center point $Y_{middle}$ are predicted by the concatenate of $FC_1$ and $FC_2$. Each point in $Y_{coarse}$ serves as the center of the $\frac{M_2}{M_1}$ point that generates $Y_{middle}$. Therefore, the size of $Y_{middle}$ is $M_2 \times 3$. The fine points of $Y_{fine}$ will be predicted by connecting the three feature layers that contain both low-level and high-level feature information, and the size is $M \times 3$.

## 3.3  Loss Function

Fan [5] has proposed two permutation-invariant metrics to compare unordered point clouds which are Chamfer Distance (CD) and Earth Mover's Distance (EMD). In this work, we choose Chamfer Distance as our completion loss since it is differentiable and more efficient to compute compared to EMD. The Chamfer Distance be expressed as

$$d_{CD}(S_1, S_2) = \frac{1}{S_1} \sum_{x \in S_1} \min_{y \in S_2} \|x - y\|_2^2 + \frac{1}{S_2} \sum_{x \in S_2} \min_{y \in S_1} \|y - x\|_2^2 \qquad (4)$$

It measures the average nearest squared distance between the predicted point set $S_1$ and the ground truth $S_2$. Sine the Combined Pyramid Decoder will predict three point cloud in different resolution, the multi-level completion loss an be expressed as

$$L = d_{CD1}(Y_{fine}, Y_{gt}) + \alpha \, d_{CD2}(Y_{middle}, Y'_{gt}) + 2\alpha \, d_{CD3}(Y_{coarse}, Y''_{gt}), \qquad (5)$$

where $d_{CD1}$, $d_{CD2}$, $d_{CD3}$ are weighted and $\alpha$ is a hyperparameter. We obtain $Y'_{gt}$ and $Y''_{gt}$ by applying IPFS from $Y_{gt}$, $Y'_{gt}$ and $Y''_{gt}$ to be the same size as $Y_{middle}$, $Y_{coarse}$, respectively. Then, the squared distances between the predicted values of the three different resolutions and the ground truth of the corresponding resolutions are calculated and assigned different weights.

## 4  Experiments

In this section, we subsequently present experimental evaluation, containing datasets and implementation details, results, and ablation studies.

## 4.1   Data Generation

We conduct experiments on 13 categories of different objects in the benchmark data set ShapeNet-Part [28]. The total number of shapes totals 14473 (11705 for training and 2768 for testing). We follow PF-Net, all input point cloud data are centered on the origin, and their coordinates are standardized to $[-1, 1]$. Creating ground truth point cloud data by uniformly sampling 2048 points on each shape. Incomplete point cloud data is generated by randomly selecting a viewpoint among multiple viewpoints as the center and deleting points within a certain radius from the complete data. We control the radius to obtain different numbers of missing points. When comparing our method with other methods, the incomplete point cloud is set to lack 25% of the original data for training and testing.

## 4.2   Implementation Detail

Our network is trained on 2 TITAN RTX GPUs using PyTorch. By using the ADAM optimizer to alternately train all two components, the initial learning rate is 0.0001 and the batch size is 32. We use batch normalization (BN) and RELU activation units on ACE, but only use RELU activation units (except for the last layer). In ACE, we set $k = 2$. In CPD, we only change $M$ to control the size of the final prediction, and set $M_1 = 64$ and $M_2 = 128$ according to the number of points of each shape.

**Table 1. Point cloud completion results of overall point cloud.** The training data consists of 13 categories of different objects [28]. The numbers shown are [Pred $\rightarrow$ GT error/GT $\rightarrow$ Pred error], scaled by 1000. We compute the mean values across all categories and show them in the last row of the table.

| Category | LGAN-AE | PCN | 3D-Capsule | PF-Net | MRAC-Net (ours) |
|---|---|---|---|---|---|
| Airplane | 0.856/0.722 | 0.800/0.800 | 0.826/0.881 | 0.263/0.238 | **0.143/0.125** |
| Bag | 3.102/2.994 | 2.954/3.063 | 3.228/2.722 | 0.926/0.772 | **0.615/0.449** |
| Cap | 3.530/2.823 | 3.466/2.674 | 3.439/2.844 | 1.226/1.169 | **0.581/0.449** |
| Car | 2.232/1.687 | 2.324/1.738 | 2.503/1.913 | 0.599/0.424 | **0.448/0.264** |
| Chair | 1.541/1.473 | 1.592/1.538 | 1.678/1.563 | 0.487/0.427 | **0.295/0.216** |
| Guitar | 0.394/0.354 | 0.367/0.406 | 0.298/0.461 | 0.108/0.091 | **0.068/0.065** |
| Lamp | 3.181/1.918 | 2.757/2.003 | 3.271/1.912 | 1.037/0.640 | **0.703/0.297** |
| Laptop | 1.206/1.030 | 1.191/1.155 | 1.276/1.254 | 0.301/0.245 | **0.223/0.174** |
| Motorbike | 1.828/1.455 | 1.699/1.459 | 1.591/1.664 | 0.522/0.389 | **0.345/0.212** |
| Mug | 2.732/2.946 | 2.893/2.821 | 3.086/2.961 | 0.745/0.739 | **0.549/0.387** |
| Pistol | 1.113/0.967 | 0.968/0.958 | 1.089/1.086 | 0.252/0.244 | **0.182/0.127** |
| Skateboard | 0.887/1.020 | 0.816/1.206 | 0.897/1.262 | 0.225/0.172 | **0.220/0.166** |
| Table | 1.694/1.601 | 1.604/1.790 | 1.870/1.749 | 0.525/0.404 | **0.348/0.273** |
| Mean | 1.869/1.615 | 1.802/1.662 | 1.927/1.713 | 0.555/0.458 | **0.363/0.247** |

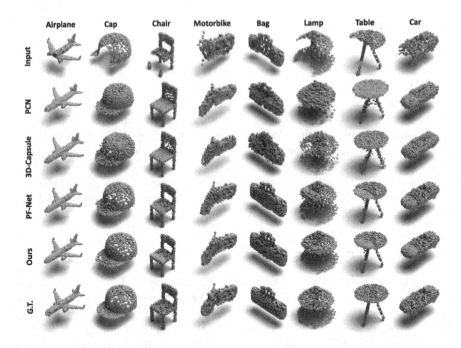

**Fig. 2.** Visualized completion comparison on ShapeNet. From top to bottom: Input, PCN [29], 3D-Capsule [30], PF-Net [11], our method, and the ground truth. Our method retains more detailed structural information, and predicts less noise and distortion.

## 4.3    Results

We compare our method with several representative baselines running directly on 3D point clouds, including L-GAN [1], PCN [29], 3D Point Capsule Networks [30], PF-Net [11]. Since these existing methods mentioned above are all trained in different data sets, we train and test them in the same data set in order to better quantitatively evaluate them. It should be noted that all methods are trained in an unsupervised method, which means that no label information will be provided. In order to evaluate the above methods, we use the evaluation metric by [6,17]. It contains two indexes: Pred → GT (prediction to ground truth) error and GT → Pred (ground truth to prediction) error. The Pred → GT error calculates the average squared distance from each point in the prediction to the nearest point in the ground truth. It can measure the difference between the forecast and the actual situation. GT → Pred error calculates the average square distance from each point in the ground truth to the closest point in the prediction. Indicates the extent to which the real surface of the ground is covered by the predicted shape.

We first connect the prediction of the network with the input point cloud to calculate the Pred → GT error and GT → Pred error on the entire complete point cloud. Table 1 shows the results. On Pred → GT and GT → Pred error, our method outperforms the other methods mentioned above in all categories.

**Table 2. Point cloud completion results of the missing point cloud.** The numbers shown are [Pred → GT error/GT → Pred error], scaled by 1000. In this table, We compute those two metrics in the missing region of point cloud.

| Category | LGAN-AE | PCN | 3D-Capsule | PF-Net | MRAC-Net (ours) |
|---|---|---|---|---|---|
| Airplane | 3.357/1.130 | 5.060/1.243 | 2.676/1.401 | 1.091/1.070 | **0.775/0.742** |
| Bag | 5.707/5.303 | 3.251/4.314 | 5.228/4.202 | 3.929/3.768 | **2.893/2.524** |
| Cap | 8.968/4.608 | 7.015/4.240 | 11.040/4.739 | 5.290/4.800 | **2.832/2.541** |
| Car | 4.531/2.518 | 2.741/2.123 | 5.944/3.508 | 2.489/1.839 | **2.286/1.474** |
| Chair | 7.359/2.339 | 3.952/2.301 | 3.049/2.207 | 2.074/1.824 | **1.532 /1.256** |
| Guitar | 0.838/0.536 | 1.419/0.689 | 0.625/0.662 | 0.456/0.429 | **0.399/0.365** |
| Lamp | 8.464/3.627 | 11.610/7.139 | 9.912/5.847 | 5.122/3.460 | **4.589/2.305** |
| Laptop | 7.649/1.413 | 3.070/1.422 | 2.129/1.733 | 1.247/0.997 | **1.106/0.907** |
| Motorbike | 4.914/2.036 | 4.962/1.922 | 8.617/2.708 | 2.206/1.775 | **1.910/1.324** |
| Mug | 6.139/4.735 | 3.590/3.591 | 5.155/5.168 | 3.138/3.238 | **2.722/2.224** |
| Pistol | 3.944/1.424 | 4.484/1.414 | 5.980/1.782 | 1.122/1.055 | **1.039/0.843** |
| Skateboard | 5.613/1.683 | 3.025/1.740 | 11.490/2.044 | **1.136 / 1.337** | 1.232/1.066 |
| Table | 2.658/2.484 | 2.503/2.452 | 3.929/3.098 | 2.235/1.934 | **1.869/1.650** |
| Mean | 5.395/2.603 | 4.360/2.661 | 5.829/3.008 | 2.426/2.117 | **1.937/1.479** |

Because PF-Net noticed that the error of the overall complete point cloud comes from two parts: the prediction error of the missing area and the change of the original local shape. Our method takes part of the shape as input and only outputs the missing area, so it does not change the original part of the shape. To ensure that our evaluation is reasonable, we also calculate the Pred → GT error and GT → Pred error on the missing region. Table 2 shows the results. In terms of Pred → GT error and GT → Pred error, our method outperforms existing methods in 12 of 13 categories. In addition, in terms of the mean values of all 13 categories, our method has considerable advantages in both indicators. The results in Table 1 and Table 2 show that our method can generate more high-precision point clouds, while the distortion in the entire point cloud and the point cloud in the missing area is smaller. The qualitative results in Fig. 2 further confirm the perceptual advantage of our method. In comparison, our method can generate fine structures with shapes, while other methods are prone to produce fuzzy results. It is also possible to generate realistically detailed structures, such as where the front piece of the hat intersects with the visor. In general, our completed result looks less noisy and visually pleasing.

### 4.4 Ablation Study

In this section, we will explore the effects of the two modules. We use PF-Net [11] as the baseline, replace our related modules, and train on the ShapeNet-Part data set. All models are trained with the same training parameters.

**Analysis of ACE.** In order to evaluate the effectiveness of our ACE module, we choose the MRE module in PF-Net to replace. The results are shown in Table 3. In terms of Pred → GT error and GT → Pred error, the network with the ACE

**Table 3. Quantitative comparisons for the ablation study.** The numbers shown are [Pred → GT error/GT → Pred error], scaled by 1000. In this table, the influence of different modules on the two index values of the point cloud is shown.

| Category | Baseline | w/o CPD | w/o ACE | Ours full |
|---|---|---|---|---|
| Airplane | 0.952/0.960 | 0.902/0.859 | 0.894/0.952 | **0.775/0.742** |
| Bag | 3.542/4.278 | 3.332/2.899 | 3.556/3.587 | **2.893/2.524** |
| Cap | 8.549/5.467 | 3.590/2.968 | 3.482/3.026 | **2.832/2.541** |
| Car | 2.491/1.718 | 2.431/1.632 | 2.383/1.782 | **2.286/1.474** |
| Chair | 2.268/2.116 | 1.748/1.411 | 1.783/1.660 | **1.532/1.256** |
| Guitar | 0.395/0.383 | 0.450/0.382 | 0.499/0.513 | **0.399/0.365** |
| Lamp | 4.695/3.864 | 4.663/2.490 | **4.399** / 3.312 | 4.589/**2.305** |
| Laptop | 1.308/1.087 | 1.187/1.049 | 1.230/1.299 | **1.106/0.907** |
| Motorbike | 2.453/1.883 | 2.049/1.474 | 2.146/1.592 | **1.910/1.324** |
| Mug | 3.642/4.603 | 2.862/2.381 | 2.871/3.304 | **2.722/2.224** |
| Pistol | 1.313/1.241 | 1.075/0.817 | 1.148/1.020 | **1.039/0.843** |
| Skateboard | 1.383/1.661 | 1.247/0.985 | 1.232/1.301 | **1.232/1.066** |
| Table | 2.751/2.741 | 1.998/1.704 | 2.213/1.954 | **1.869/1.650** |
| Mean | 2.749/2.462 | 2.118/1.619 | 2.141/1.946 | **1.937/1.479** |

module is better than the network without the ACE module in 12 of the 13 categories. Therefore, the anisotropic convolutional encode can better extract the latent features of 3D objects, thereby better improving the extraction of geometric and semantic information of the network.

**Analysis of CPD.** In order to prove the effectiveness of our CPD module, we choose the PDD module in PF-Net to replace. The results are shown in Table 3. In terms of Pred → GT error and GT → Pred error, the network with CPD module is in 13 categories Both are better than the network without CPD module. Therefore, it can be seen that the CPD module can better express and map the latent features, so as to better infer the missing point cloud.

## 5    Conclusion

We present a novel framework MRAC-Net for point cloud completion. It includes an anisotropic convolutional encoder for extracting local and global features for 3D objects to enhance the network's extraction ability of latent features. In addition, the combined pyramid encoder generates high-quality missing point clouds by combining various feature vectors. Extensive experiments on ShapeNet have verified the state-of-the-art performance of MRAC-Net and the effectiveness of each suggested component.

**Acknowledgments.** This work was supported by the National Key R&D Program of China (No. 2018YFB1305200) and Science Technology Department of Zhejiang Province (No. LGG19F020010).

# References

1. Achlioptas, P., Diamanti, O., Mitliagkas, I., Guibas, L.: Learning representations and generative models for 3D point clouds. In: Dy, J., Krause, A. (eds.) Proceedings of the 35th International Conference on Machine Learning. Proceedings of Machine Learning Research, vol. 80, pp. 40–49. PMLR, Stockholmsmässan, Stockholm Sweden, 10–15 July 2018. http://proceedings.mlr.press/v80/achlioptas18a.html

2. Berger, M., et al.: State of the art in surface reconstruction from point clouds. In: Eurographics 2014 - State of the Art Reports. EUROGRAPHICS Star Report, Strasbourg, France, vol. 1, pp. 161–185, April 2014. https://doi.org/10.2312/egst.20141040. https://hal.inria.fr/hal-01017700

3. Clevert, D.A., Unterthiner, T., Hochreiter, S.: Fast and Accurate Deep Network Learning by Exponential Linear Units (ELUs) (2016)

4. Dai, A., Qi, C.R., Nießner, M.: Shape completion using 3D-encoder-predictor CNNs and shape synthesis. In: Proceedings of Computer Vision and Pattern Recognition (CVPR). IEEE (2017)

5. Fan, H., Su, H., Guibas, L.: A point set generation network for 3D object reconstruction from a single image. In: 2017 IEEE Conference on Computer Vision and Pattern Recognition (CVPR), pp. 2463–2471 (2017). https://doi.org/10.1109/CVPR.2017.264

6. Gadelha, M., Wang, R., Maji, S.: Multiresolution tree networks for 3D point cloud processing. In: Ferrari, V., Hebert, M., Sminchisescu, C., Weiss, Y. (eds.) ECCV 2018. LNCS, vol. 11211, pp. 105–122. Springer, Cham (2018). https://doi.org/10.1007/978-3-030-01234-2_7

7. Gao, Z., Zhai, G., Yan, J., Yang, X.: Permutation matters: anisotropic convolutional layer for learning on point clouds (2020)

8. Han, X., Li, Z., Huang, H., Kalogerakis, E., Yu, Y.: High-resolution shape completion using deep neural networks for global structure and local geometry inference. In: 2017 IEEE International Conference on Computer Vision (ICCV), pp. 85–93 (2017). https://doi.org/10.1109/ICCV.2017.19

9. Hu, Q., et al.: RandLA-Net: efficient semantic segmentation of large-scale point clouds. In: Proceedings of the IEEE Conference on Computer Vision and Pattern Recognition (2020)

10. Hua, B., Tran, M., Yeung, S.: Pointwise convolutional neural networks. In: 2018 IEEE/CVF Conference on Computer Vision and Pattern Recognition, pp. 984–993 (2018). https://doi.org/10.1109/CVPR.2018.00109

11. Huang, Z., Yu, Y., Xu, J., Ni, F., Le, X.: PF-Net: point fractal network for 3D point cloud completion. In: Proceedings of the IEEE/CVF Conference on Computer Vision and Pattern Recognition (CVPR), June 2020

12. Lan, S., Yu, R., Yu, G., Davis, L.S.: Modeling local geometric structure of 3D point clouds using Geo-CNN. In: Proceedings of the IEEE/CVF Conference on Computer Vision and Pattern Recognition (CVPR), June 2019

13. Lei, H., Akhtar, N., Mian, A.: Octree guided CNN with spherical kernels for 3D point clouds. In: IEEE Conference on Computer Vision and Pattern Recognition (2019)

14. Li, D., Shao, T., Wu, H., Zhou, K.: Shape completion from a single RGBD image. IEEE Trans. Vis. Comput. Graph. **23**(7), 1809–1822 (2017). https://doi.org/10.1109/TVCG.2016.2553102

15. Li, Y., Bu, R., Sun, M., Wu, W., Di, X., Chen, B.: PointCNN: convolution on x-transformed points. In: Advances in Neural Information Processing Systems, pp. 820–830 (2018)

16. Li, Y., Dai, A., Guibas, L., Nießner, M.: Database-assisted object retrieval for real-time 3D reconstruction. In: Computer Graphics Forum, vol. 34. Wiley Online Library (2015)

17. Lin, C.H., Kong, C., Lucey, S.: Learning efficient point cloud generation for dense 3D object reconstruction. In: AAAI Conference on Artificial Intelligence (AAAI) (2018)

18. Lin, T., Dollár, P., Girshick, R., He, K., Hariharan, B., Belongie, S.: Feature pyramid networks for object detection. In: 2017 IEEE Conference on Computer Vision and Pattern Recognition (CVPR), pp. 936–944 (2017). https://doi.org/10.1109/CVPR.2017.106

19. Mao, J., Wang, X., Li, H.: Interpolated convolutional networks for 3D point cloud understanding. In: Proceedings of the IEEE/CVF International Conference on Computer Vision (ICCV), October 2019

20. Martins, A.F.T., Astudillo, R.F.: From softmax to sparsemax: a sparse model of attention and multi-label classification. In: Proceedings of the 33rd International Conference on International Conference on Machine Learning, ICML 2016, vol. 48, pp. 1614–1623 (2016). JMLR.org

21. Mitra, N.J., Guibas, L., Pauly, M.: Partial and approximate symmetry detection for 3D geometry. ACM Trans. Graph. (SIGGRAPH) **25**(3), 560–568 (2006)

22. Qi, C.R., Su, H., Mo, K., Guibas, L.J.: PointNet: deep learning on point sets for 3D classification and segmentation. In: Proceedings of the IEEE Conference on Computer Vision and Pattern Recognition (CVPR), July 2017

23. Sarmad, M., Lee, H.J., Kim, Y.M.: RL-GAN-Net: a reinforcement learning agent controlled GAN network for real-time point cloud shape completion. In: The IEEE Conference on Computer Vision and Pattern Recognition (CVPR), June 2019

24. Thomas, H., Qi, C.R., Deschaud, J.E., Marcotegui, B., Goulette, F., Guibas, L.J.: KPConv: flexible and deformable convolution for point clouds. In: Proceedings of the IEEE International Conference on Computer Vision, pp. 6411–6420 (2019)

25. Wang, Z., Lu, F.: VoxSegNet: volumetric CNNs for semantic part segmentation of 3D shapes. IEEE Trans. Vis. Comput. Graph. **26**(9), 2919–2930 (2020). https://doi.org/10.1109/TVCG.2019.2896310

26. Wu, W., Qi, Z., Fuxin, L.: PointConv: deep convolutional networks on 3D point clouds. In: Proceedings of the IEEE Conference on Computer Vision and Pattern Recognition, pp. 9621–9630 (2019)

27. Xie, H., Yao, H., Zhou, S., Mao, J., Zhang, S., Sun, W.: GRNet: gridding residual network for dense point cloud completion. In: Vedaldi, A., Bischof, H., Brox, T., Frahm, J.-M. (eds.) ECCV 2020. LNCS, vol. 12354, pp. 365–381. Springer, Cham (2020). https://doi.org/10.1007/978-3-030-58545-7_21

28. Yi, L., et al.: A scalable active framework for region annotation in 3D shape collections. SIGGRAPH Asia (2016)

29. Yuan, W., Khot, T., Held, D., Mertz, C., Hebert, M.: PCN: point completion network. In: 2018 International Conference on 3D Vision (3DV) (2018)

30. Zhao, Y., Birdal, T., Deng, H., Tombari, F.: 3D point capsule networks. In: Conference on Computer Vision and Pattern Recognition (CVPR) (2019)

# Nonlinear Parametric Transformation and Generation of Images Based on a Network with the CWNL Layer

Slawomir Golak[✉]

Department of Industrial Informatics, Silesian University of Technology,
Gliwice, Poland
slawomir.golak@polsl.pl

**Abstract.** Correlated weights neural layers (CWNL) extend the concept of weight sharing present in the convolution layers by using neural subnetworks that dynamically calculate multiple weights and biases as a function of the position of a neuron and its inputs. By using, in contrast to the convolutional layer, absolute coordinates of the neuron and inputs and a universal approximator instead of a static kernel matrix, this type of layer allows for global, parametric, and nonlinear operations on the image. The article presents a mathematical model of such a layer and the methodology of its training. The advantage of networks using CWNL layers was demonstrated on the example of the nonlinear transformation of images from the MNIST set and generation of synthetic images based on Bezier curves.

**Keywords:** Neural network architecture · Overfitting prevention · Image transformation · Image generation

## 1   Introduction

Convolutional layers are the core of deep networks, which are currently triumphing in many areas, such as, for example, image and video processing [1,2] and strategy games [3]. One of the main reasons for the strength of this type of neural layer is the reduced amount of parameters that have to be determined during a learning process. Figure 1 shows a well-known diagram of the convolution layer. For simplicity, we will analyze the layer generating a single feature map.

The layer performs the convolution operation using data from the weight matrix - the kernel. A weight of a single connection between a neuron and its input in the convolutional layer can be defined as a function of the relative position of the neuron and the input:

$$w = f(\boldsymbol{P}^{(I)} - \boldsymbol{P}^{(O)}) \tag{1}$$

where: $\boldsymbol{P}^{(O)}$ - vector of a neuron spatial coordinates, $\boldsymbol{P}^{(I)}$ - vector of spatial coordinates of a neuron input.

This research was supported by grants of Silesian University of Technology (11/040/RGJ20/0017 and 11/040/BK21/0023) and by PLGrid Infrastructure.

D. N. Pham et al. (Eds.): PRICAI 2021, LNAI 13033, pp. 415–425, 2021.
https://doi.org/10.1007/978-3-030-89370-5_31

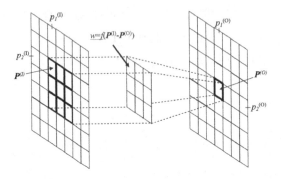

**Fig. 1.** Schematic diagram of a convolution layer.

In the case of the most commonly used CNN structures, two-dimensional patterns are processed (for spatial dimensions), therefore the dimension of the spatial coordinate vectors is 2, although it may be much larger in some applications. With such a definition of weight, the range of values $min(\boldsymbol{P}^{(I)} - \boldsymbol{P}^{(O)})$ and $max(\boldsymbol{P}^{(I)} - \boldsymbol{P}^{(O)})$ means the size and shift of the neuron receptive field in the CNL layer. Since the value of $\boldsymbol{P}^{(I)} - \boldsymbol{P}^{(O)}$ occurs many times for each neuron in the layer, we obtain weight sharing - the main advantage of the CNL layer is that it strongly reduces the number of parameters describing this layer. The function $f()$ itself is actually a kernel matrix indexed by difference $\boldsymbol{P}^{(I)} - \boldsymbol{P}^{(O)}$. Its parameters are discontinuous and limited by the kernel size.

As shown by the experience of recent years, such a function defining weights based on relative coordinates works very well in local transformations of patterns - e.g. the most common detection of local features. Unfortunately, the architecture of the layer in which weights are a function of relative coordinates can not perform global transformations of patterns (e.g. affine transformations of images). Basing weights on relative coordinates means a loss of information about the complete position of a neuron and its inputs and blocks the implementation of global pattern transformations. The only exception is the image translation that can be performed by such a layer. However, you need to be aware of the increase of the required size of the kernel with increasing the translation vector. The new network structure initially proposed in the paper [4] and presented in a more mature form in the paper [5] is based on a description of a weight of a connection between a neuron and its input by a function using absolute spatial coordinates of the neuron and its input:

$$\omega = f(\boldsymbol{P}^{(I)}, \boldsymbol{P}^{(O)}) \tag{2}$$

The implementation of the function was based on a universal approximator - a neural subnetwork, which in the learning process discovers the correlation between the spatial, absolute coordinates of the neuron, its input, and the weight value. Both the CNL layer and the original version of the CWNL layer perform a static transformation. The modification of the CWNL layer, by extending the definition of the weight function and including additional parameters, external to the layer, controlling the work of the layer (3), allows you to build information flow paths in the network architecture that are not available in existing solutions.

$$\omega = f(\boldsymbol{P}^{(I)}, \boldsymbol{P}^{(O)}, \boldsymbol{S}^{(E)}) \tag{3}$$

where: $\boldsymbol{S}^{(E)}$-vector of external signals.

The space of control parameters $\boldsymbol{S}^{(E)}$ is continuous as opposed to the discrete space of $\boldsymbol{P}^{(I)}$ and $\boldsymbol{P}^{(O)}$ limited by the finite resolution of the processed patterns.

The concept of contextual control of the method of data processing in the neural network has already been proposed in the paper [6]. The proposed network structure includes a module based on the parameterised sampling grid. The points of this grid are delivered through a separate network processing path. The proposed module is able to perform some limited range of transformations of patterns. The CWNL layer, on the other hand, is based on a universal approximator (neural network) and can perform any nonlinear, parametric transformations. The work presents the mathematical model and methodology of teaching the CWNL layer with external control. The paper describes the research on the ability of a network with this type of neural layer to implement nonlinear image transformations acquired in the learning process using a very limited size of the training set. In addition, studies were carried out on a truncated version of the CWNL layer used for the generation of images with a nonlinear structure based on a set of parameters.

## 2  Mathematical Model of the CWNL Layer with External Control

The structure of the correlated weights neural layer with external control is shown in Fig. 2. The position of each layer input is described by the spatial coordinates vector $\boldsymbol{P}^{(I)}$, which size is compatible with the dimensionality of the input data. The topology of the CWNL layer is compatible with dimensionality and the size of its output pattern. Each of its neurons also has its own spatial, absolute coordinates $\boldsymbol{P}^{(O)}$. The output of the CWNL neuron is determined based on the standard equation (4). The difference is that in the equation, instead of the constant weights and the bias, their values are calculated dynamically by dedicated neural subnets.

$$y_i^{(O)} = f(s_i) \quad \& \quad s_i = \sum_{j=1}^{N^{(O)}} \omega_{ij0}\left(\boldsymbol{P}_i^{(O)}, \boldsymbol{P}_j^{(I)}, \boldsymbol{S}^{(E)}\right) y_j^{(I)} + \beta_{i0}\left(\boldsymbol{P}_i^{(O)}, \boldsymbol{S}^{(E)}\right) \tag{4}$$

where: $f()$ - activation function of the CWNL layer, $y_i^{(O)}$ - output of $i$-th neuron in the layer (output of the layer), $y_j^{(I)}$ - $j$-th input of the layer, $\omega_{ij0}()$ - dynamically calculated weight, $\beta_{i0}()$ - dynamically calculated bias, $\boldsymbol{P}_i^{(O)}$ - vector of $i$-th neuron spatial coordinates, $\boldsymbol{P}_j^{(I)}$ - vector of spatial coordinates of $j$-th layer

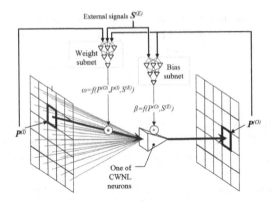

**Fig. 2.** Schematic diagram of a correlated weights neural layer with external control.

input, $S^{(E)}$ - vector of external signals. The function $\omega()$ that dynamically calculates the value of weights based on the coordinates of the neuron and the input is implemented by a neural subnetwork with standard fully connected layers:

$$\omega_{ijk}^{(m)} = \phi^{(\omega,m)}\left(\sigma_{ijk}^{(\omega,m)}\right) \tag{5}$$

$$\sigma_{ijk}^{(\omega,m)} = \sum_{l=1}^{N^{(\omega,m-1)}} w_{kl}^{(\omega,m)}\omega_{ijl}^{(m-1)} + b_k^{(\omega,m)} \tag{6}$$

where: $\omega_{ijk}^{(m)}$- processed by the subnetwork signal of the dynamically calculated weight for $i$-th neuron and $j$-th input (of the CWNL layer) in $m$-th subnet layer, $\phi^{(m)}()$ - activation function of $m$-th subnetwork layer, $w_{kl}^{(\omega,m)}$- weight of $l$-th input of $k$-th neuron (of the subnet layer), $b_k^{(\omega,m)}$ - bias of $k$-th subnet neuron.

The input of the subnetwork calculating weights is the union of the vector of the neuron coordinates $P^{(O)}$, the vector of the layer input coordinates $P^{(I)}$ and the vector of external control signals $S^{(E)}$:

$$\omega_{ijk}^{(0)} = \{P_i^{(O)} \cup P_j^{(I)} \cup S^{(E)}\}_k \tag{7}$$

A bias in a neural layer can be defined as a weight of an input with a constant value of 1. In the case of a convolution layer, for one feature map, a single value of the bias is repeatedly used for each neuron of this layer. The layer CWNL allows to dynamically calculate the bias value based on the coordinates of the neuron supplemented with external control signals. This task is performed by the second dedicated subnet. Since each neuron has only one bias value, the subnet does not use the coordinates of the inputs:

$$\beta_{ik}^{(m)} = \phi^{(\beta,m)}\left(\sigma_{ik}^{(\beta,m)}\right) \tag{8}$$

$$\sigma_{ik}^{(\beta,m)} = \sum_{l=1}^{N^{(\beta,m-1)}} w_{kl}^{(\beta,m)}\beta_{il}^{(m-1)} + b_k^{(\beta,m)} \tag{9}$$

$$\beta_{ik}^{(0)} = \{\boldsymbol{P}_i^{(O)} \cup \boldsymbol{S}^{(E)}\}_k \tag{10}$$

## 2.1   Training Methodology of the CWNL Layer

If activation functions of the CWNL layer and subnets layers are continuous and differentiable, a learning process can be carried out based on any gradient optimization technique. After determining error values for neurons of the CWNL layer by backpropagation of loss function gradient in the main neural network of which this layer is a component the error for the output layer of the subnetwork providing weights can be calculated:

$$\epsilon_{ij0}^{(\omega,M)} = e_i y_j^{(I)} f'(s_i) \tag{11}$$

where: $e_i$ - error for $i$-th neuron of the CWNL layer, $y_j^{(I)}$ - $j$-th input of the layer, $f'()$ - derivative of the activation function.

The determined error is then propagated through successive layers of the weight subnet:

$$\epsilon_{ijk}^{(\omega,m)} = \sum_{l=1}^{N^{(\omega,m+1)}} \left( \epsilon_{ijl}^{(m+1)} w_{lk}^{(m+1)} \phi'^{(\omega,m+1)} \left( \sigma_{ijl}^{(\omega,m+1)} \right) \right) \tag{12}$$

Based on the error determined in all layers of the subnetwork, the partial derivative of the loss function for all the subnet parameters (for single pattern processing) can be calculated:

$$\frac{\partial E}{\partial w_{kl}^{(\omega,m)}} = \sum_{i=1}^{N^{(O)}} \sum_{j=1}^{N^{(I)}} \epsilon_{ijk}^{(\omega,m)} \omega_{ijl}^{(m-1)} \quad \& \quad \frac{\partial E}{\partial b_k^{(\omega,m)}} = \sum_{i=1}^{N^{(O)}} \sum_{j=1}^{N^{(I)}} \epsilon_{ijk}^{(\omega,m)} \tag{13}$$

The CWNL neuron error is also propagated to the output layer of the subnet for calculating biases (one bias error for one neuron of the CWNL):

$$\epsilon_{i0}^{(\beta,M)} = e_i f'(s_i) \tag{14}$$

The error backpropagation in the bias subnet layers is carried out in the same way as in the weight subnet. Using this error, the partial derivatives of the loss function for the parameters of this subnetwork are calculated:

$$\frac{\partial E}{\partial w_{kl}^{(\beta,m)}} = \sum_{i=1}^{N^{(O)}} \epsilon_{ik}^{(\beta,m)} \beta_{il}^{(m-1)} \quad \& \quad \frac{\partial E}{\partial b_k^{(\beta,m)}} = \sum_{i=1}^{N^{(O)}} \epsilon_{ik}^{(\beta,m)} \tag{15}$$

# 3   Experiments

## 3.1   Nonlinear Transformation

The first experiment concerned the ability of the CWNL layer to implement nonlinear image transformations. An example of such a transformation was the wave deformation of the image based on trigonometric functions (Fig. 3, the first section). The transformation is controlled by two parameters: the amplitude and the deformation period. Based on the MNIST set, synthetic training and test sets were generated, in which the input data was an original image of the digit and the transformation parameters. The output was a deformed image.

The CWNL layer in the main network used a sigmoidal activation function. The structure of the subnet calculating values of weights was $I4$-$H32$-$H16$-$H8$-$O1$ (the ELU activation function in hidden layers, the linear output neuron). The subnet calculating biases had layers $I4$-$H8$-$H4$-$O1$ (the ELU function in hidden layers, the linear function in the output neuron). The learning process was based on the minimization of the binary entropy loss function. The classic RProp learning algorithm [7] was used, which proved to be much more effective for the developed network architecture than the currently used algorithms (e.g. SGD, Adam, RMSProp). The early stopping based on validation error was applied.

The third section of Fig. 3 shows images provided by the network with the single CWNL layer. For only 96 examples in the training set, the obtained quality of the transformed images is satisfactory and confirms the ability of the developed network to implement this exemplary nonlinear transformation.

The same experiment was also carried out for a network with fully connected layers. The structure of the network was modeled on the structures of autoencoders using FC layers [8]. The input of the autoencoder was supplemented with additional inputs for control parameters (period and amplitude). Applied neural network structure consisted of 5 hidden layers with the ELU activation function and a sigmoid output layer, its layout: $I(28*28+4)$-$H128$-$H64$-$H32$-$H64$-$H128$-$O(28*28)$. The analysis of the obtained results (Fig. 3, the fourth section) shows that the proposed network with FC layers can implement the expected onlinear transformation subject to an increase in the required size of the training (two orders of magnitude).

A network with convolutional layers is dedicated to image processing but the great challenge is to introduce external control signals into such a layer. The implementation of this task is impossible in the case of a single convolutional layer. Therefore, a modified convolutional autoencoder structure [8] was used for this task. The external signals were delivered to the middle layers starting the block of the pattern decoder (Fig. 4). Using the network configured in this way, slightly better results (Fig. 3, the last section) were obtained than the network using only FC layers. Figure 5 presents a comparison of the obtained binary cross-entropy loss levels for the three analyzed networks depending on the number of training cases.

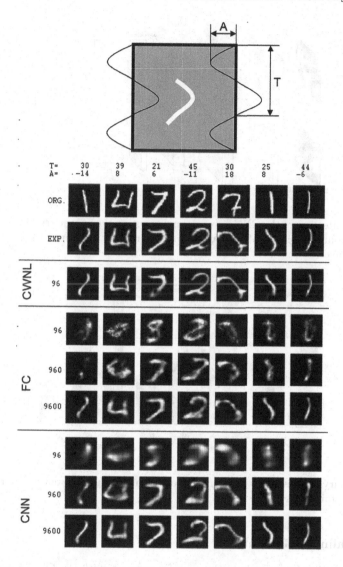

**Fig. 3.** Nonlinear transformation using networks based on the CWNL layer, full connect layers and convolutional layers: input control parameters (period and amplitude), input (orginal) image; expected images from testing set and images after learning on the training set containing 96–9600 examples.

Summarizing the results of this experiment, it can be stated that, at least in terms of the required size of the training set, the network with FC layers only and the mixed network with CNL and FC layers turned out to be clearly weaker than the network with CWNL layer.

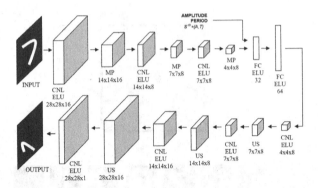

**Fig. 4.** Architecture of the CNN network implementing the parametric transformation: CNL - convolutional layer, MF - max pooling layer, US - Upsampling layer, FC - fully connected layer.

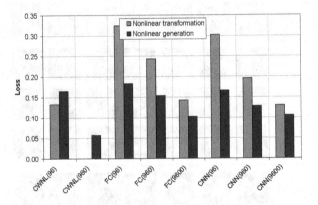

**Fig. 5.** Binary cross-entropy loss for both experiments and different number of examples in the training set.

## 3.2   Nonlinear Generation

The second, simple example of the use of a network with the CWNL layer is the generation of an image only based on the numerical parameters that describe it. This task may be defined as the network performing a decoder function in an auto-encoder or a generator in a generative network. For the purposes of the research, an artificial training set was generated, in which the input data are the coordinates of four points defining the Bezier curve, and the output data is the image of this curve. Since the network does not process the input pattern, in this case, the CWNL layer is only implemented in a simplified form - the neuron

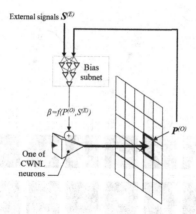

**Fig. 6.** Schematic diagram of CWNL layer with external control and without multidimensional pattern input.

output is determined only based on the bias value (Fig. 6). The network consisted of a single CWNL layer (sigmoid activation function) controlled by 8 external signals. The subnet computing biases had the structure $I4$-$H32$-$H24$-$H16$-$O1$ with the ELU activation function in hidden layers and a linear output layer. As shown in Fig. 7, the network with such a structure achieved a satisfactory generation quality for the training set containing 960 cases.

The result was compared with the results obtained for the network with only FC layers (with the structure of $I4$-$H64$-$H128$-$O(28*28)$, the ELU activation function in hidden layers, the sigmoid output). This network was able to obtain an acceptable quality of transformation (Fig. 7, the third section) based on the training set containing 9600 examples.

The third of the networks used in this experiment had only the decoding section of the CNN autoencoder (Fig. 8). The generation quality visually comparable to the network with the CWNL layer was obtained after training with the use of 9600 examples (Fig. 7, the last section). However, a comparison of the error measures (Fig. 5) shows that for 10 times as many examples, the generation quality is significantly worse.

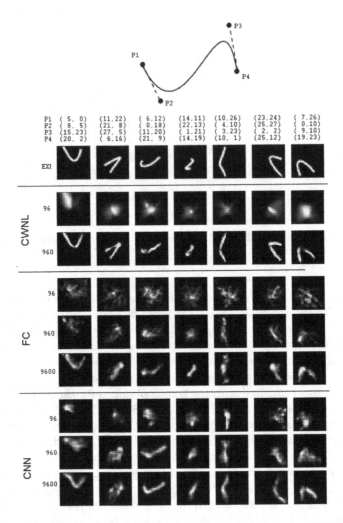

**Fig. 7.** Bezier curve image generation using networks based on the CWNL layer, full connect layers, and convolutional layers: input parameters, expected images from testing set and images after learning on the training set containing 96–9600 examples.

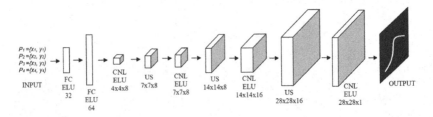

**Fig. 8.** Architecture of the CNN network implementing the parametric generation: CNL - convolutional layer, US - Upsampling layer, FC - fully connected layer.

# 4   Conclusions

The conducted studies have shown that networks using the CWNL layer can effectively implement parameterized, nonlinear image transformations. It has been shown that due to the small number of parameters describing such a layer (repeatedly used weights of subnets instead of direct weight values of the main layer), related to the complexity of a pattern content (not to its size), small data sets are enough to train a network with the CWNL layer. The ability of the CWNL network to generate images with a nonlinear structure also demonstrated during the research, gives a chance to use them, such as output parts of autoencoders and auto-generative solutions.

The conducted analysis, confirmed by experiments, suggests that the CWNL layer controlled by external signals can be an interesting component of more complex network structures used in popular applications such as image classification (especially in terms of reducing the influence of nonlinear pattern deformations) or generation of synthetic images and videos.

An issue that requires extensive research is the computational complexity of the CWNL layers. In contrast to the CNL layers in which it is proportional to the product of the number of neurons and the size of the kernel, in the case of the CWNL layer, it is associated with a much higher value of the product of the number of neurons, the size of the input pattern and the subnet size.

# References

1. Dhillon, A., Verma, G.K.: Convolutional neural network: a review of models, methodologies and applications to object detection. Prog. Artif. Intell. **9**(2), 85–112 (2020)
2. Yao, G., Lei, T., Zhong, J.: A review of convolutional-neural-network-based action recognition. Pattern Recogn. Lett. **118**, 14–22 (2019)
3. Silver, D., et al.: Mastering the game of go without human knowledge. Nature **550**(7676), 354–359 (2017)
4. Golak, S.: Induced weights artificial neural network. In: Duch, W., Kacprzyk, J., Oja, E., Zadrożny, S. (eds.) ICANN 2005. LNCS, vol. 3697, pp. 295–300. Springer, Heidelberg (2005). https://doi.org/10.1007/11550907_47
5. Golak, S., Jama, A., Blachnik, M., Wieczorek, T.: New architecture of correlated weights neural network for global image transformations. In: Kůrková, V., Manolopoulos, Y., Hammer, B., Iliadis, L., Maglogiannis, I. (eds.) ICANN 2018. LNCS, vol. 11140, pp. 56–65. Springer, Cham (2018). https://doi.org/10.1007/978-3-030-01421-6_6
6. Jaderberg, M., Simonyan, K., Zisserman, A., Kavukcuoglu, K.: Spatial transformer networks. In: NIPS 2015 (Spotlight), vol. 2, pp. 2017–2025 (2015)
7. Riedmiller, M., Braun, H.: RPROP-a fast adaptive learning algorithm. In: Proceedings of ISCIS VII), Universitat (1992)
8. Chollet, F.: Building autoencoders in keras. The Keras Blog 14 (2016)

# PupilFace: A Cascaded Face Detection and Location Network Fusing Attention

Xiang Li$^{(\boxtimes)}$ and Jiancheng Zou

Image Processing and Pattern Recognition Laboratory, North China University
of Technology, Beijing 100000, China
zjc@ncut.edu.cn

**Abstract.** Although the development of uncontrolled face detection and
location technology have made great progress, there are some problems
needing to be solved in more complicated situation, such as massive
occlusion and pose variation. In this paper, we propose a robust one-
stage face detection and location network named PupilFace. It can locate
faces of different sizes at the pixel level in complex scenarios. Specifically, we have made contributions in the following three aspects: (1)
Using a lightweight backbone, we can not only detect images of dense
faces, but also mark facial landmarks in pictures of various scale. In this
paper, the pictures are difficult to detect because of massive occlusion
or tiny faces. On the WIDER FACE hard test set, PupilFace performs
better than other state-of-the-art networks. (2) The addition of the attention module–Hard Efficient Channel Attention (HECA), proposed by us,
enhances the connection between the feature channels and improves the
detection performance without reducing the dimension. The parameters
and computations of HECA, against the parameters and computations
of MobileNetV2 are 9 vs. 3.34M and 5.1e−4 GFLOPs vs. 0.32 GFLOPs.
(3) We can employ varying-depths backbones accordingly to different
detection and location tasks, so the model can be popularized in different fields. Extra annotations and code have been made available at:
https://github.com/Ideal-maths/PupilFace.

**Keywords:** Face location · Attention module · Hard Efficient Channel
Attention (HECA) · MobileNetV2 · Feature pyramid networks (FPN)

## 1 Introduction

Face detection and location are hot issues, however how to extract the facial key
points is a perplexing problem. As for the definition of face location, the narrow
definition can refer to the traditional face detection [24]. In a broad sense, it
includes four aspects: face detection, face alignment, pixel painting face analysis
and 3D intensive correspondence and regression.

In recent years, the application of convolutional neural network helps to solve
this problem well. In face position, it could be simply divided into methods based
on cascaded shape regression, such as Cascaded Pose Regression (CPR) [21],

© Springer Nature Switzerland AG 2021
D. N. Pham et al. (Eds.): PRICAI 2021, LNAI 13033, pp. 426–437, 2021.
https://doi.org/10.1007/978-3-030-89370-5_32

based deep learning method, such as Multi-task Convolutional Neural Network (MTCNN) [2], RetinaFace [1] and so on.

At present, based deep learning methods do not consider the relationship between channels enough, and regard channels as isolated things, which misses important features. We introduce an attention module, Hard Efficient Channel Attention (HECA), similar to Efficient Channel Attention (ECA), to solve this problem. We can automatically obtain the weight of each feature channel by learning, then enhance the useful character, and confine the useless character for current task.

This greatly reduces the model complexity while maintaining the same effect. Some studies have improved the attention module by capturing more complex channel dependencies or incorporating additional spatial attention. Although these methods achieve high accuracy, they often have high model computation complexity. Unlike them, this paper pays attention to whether channel attention can be learned in a more effective way. We want to employ a backbone being light-weight network whose results are better than before, and the detecting and locating speed is not reduced as much as possible, through the introduction of attention module. For face detection, this architecture can effectively identify and locate various size faces.

To summarize, the main contributions of this paper are as follows:

- Introduced the attention module, which enhanced the feature interaction between channels and improved the detection performance. Especially in the detection of difficult samples, performance was greatly improved.
- We propose a network that can replace the backbone as needed, and it could solve a variety of practical problems, such as fatigue detection, facial expression recognition.
- Code and comments have been published to facilitate communication with peers.

## 2   Related Work

We focused on the following parts to achieve our face positioning.

**Feature Pyramid.** The previous development of the feature pyramid took three forms: a) Featurized image pyramid [12]: The feature pyramid consists of images of different sizes, which are then convolved and predicted separately. This way is too computationally heavy. b) Single feature map [15]: Convolution is carried out on the image and prediction is made on the final feature map. This method has a receptive field problem: the receptive field is larger in the more abstract feature map, so the small feature may not be detected. c) Pyramidal feature hierarchy [17,21]: We make prediction on the each layer feature map. The large-sized feature maps at the bottom of pyramidal feature hierarchy have little semantic information.

**Attention Module.** The basic idea of attention is to teach the system to pay attention to be able to ignore irrelevant information and focus on important information. Squeeze-and-Excitation Networks (SE-Net) [9] uses both the squeeze and excitation operations to learn the channel attention for each convolution block. ECA-Net [20] considering every channel and their K neighbors to capture the local cross channel information, their author could avoid reducing the dimension and maintain the efficiency.

**Context Model.** Context modelling is divided into two types: rigid and non-rigid. Rigid means expansion, while non-rigid means deformation. Single Stage Headless face detector [11] and Pyramid-box [16] output the feature map of feature pyramid to context modules to expand the receptive field. The work enhances rigid context modelling capacity.

## 3   PupilFace

Our network, PupilFace, is based on RetinaFace [1], which is composed of the backbone (MobileNet [8] or ResNet [5]) with Feature Pyramid Networks(FPN) [10]. The feature maps go through the context module similar to SSH, finally output five facial landmarks (i.e. mouth corners, nose tip and eye centers) and loss. As an improvement of Retinaface, we use a light-weight backbone, improved MobileNetV2. The specific method is to add the attention module, Hard Efficient Channel Attention (HECA), to MobileNetV2 to enhance non-linear cross-channel interaction. The structure of our network is briefly shown in Fig. 1.

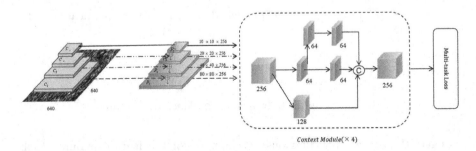

**Fig. 1.** 640 × 640 images with dense faces are input into our network. The last feature map, at the backbone different stages, will output to Feature pyramid networks (FPN) after adjusting the channels number. Then the output of FPN is processed by the context module in turn. The multi-task loss is obtained after calculation at the end of the network.

## 3.1 Nonlinearities and Multi-task Loss

**Nonlinearities.** A nonlinearity, called swish, is imported in [3,6,13]. When this nonlinearity is used as a direct substitute for ReLU, it can improve the accuracy of the neural network significantly. Swish's formula is as follows:

$$swish x = x \cdot \sigma(x) \tag{1}$$

We replace the sigmoid function with other activation functions, for example $\frac{ReLU6(x+3)}{6}$, which is very similar to [7]. The minor difference is that we use ReLU6 instead of a custom clipping constant. H-swish's formula is as follows:

$$H - swish[x] = x\frac{ReLU6(x+3)}{6} \tag{2}$$

In quantitative mode, H-swish reduces the numerical precision loss due to the approximately sigmoid function.

**Multi-task Loss.** We propose multi-task loss, and i denotes training anchor.

$$L = L_{cla}(n_i, n_i^*) + \varphi_1 p_i^* L_{box}(c_i, c_i^*) + \varphi_2 p_i^* L_{pfl}(m_i, m_i^*) \tag{3}$$

(1) Face classification loss $L_{cla}(n_i, n_i^*)$, $n_i$ is the predictive probability of anchor i being a human face. When $n_i^*$ is 1, it means that the anchor is positive and 0 presents negative anchor. Since only images with and without human faces are considered in this paper, it is a binary classification problem when considering classification loss.

(2) Face box regression loss $L_{box}(c_i, c_i^*)$, here, $c_i = \{c_x, c_y, c_w, c_h\}, c_i^* = \{c_x^*, c_y^*, c_w^*, c_h^*\}$ respectively represent the coordinates of prediction box and ground-truth box related to the positive anchor. We normalize the target of the regression box (central coordinates, width and height). And we use $R(c_i, c_i^*) = L_{box}(c_i, c_i^*)$, where R is smooth$-L_1$ loss function.

(3) Facial landmark regression loss $L_{pfl}(m_i, m_i^*)$, here $l_i = \{m_{x_1}, m_{y_1}, \ldots, m_{x_5}, m_{y_5}\}$, $l_i^* = \{l_{x_1}^*, l_{y_1}^*, \ldots, l_{x_5}^*, l_{y_5}^*\}$ represent the predicted five human facial landmarks and ground-truth. The regression of the five facial landmarks also adapts the target normalization based on anchor center. In this paper, we set the loss-balancing parameters $\varphi_1, \varphi_2$ to 0.25 and 0.1.

## 3.2 Design of Fusing Attention Networks

**Efficient Mobile Building Blocks.** At present, the model applicable to face detection and facial landmarks is based on increasingly efficient structure blocks. MobileNet was a light-weight network proposed by Google. MobileNet had three versions. MobileNetV1 [8] introduced Depthwise Separable Convolution to replace the traditional convolution layer, which reduced quantities of parameters while ensuring the effect as much as possible. MobileNetV2 [14] combined the residual network with the Depthwise Separable Convolution. Compared with MobileNetV2, MobileNetV3 [7] added Squeeze-and-Excite (SE) at Bottleneck, which enhanced the feature connection between channels. The structure of MobileNetV3 is briefly shown in Fig. 2.

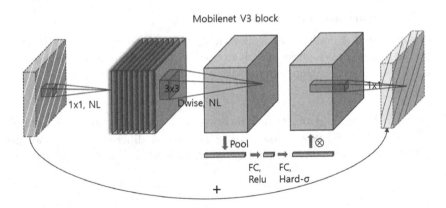

**Fig. 2.** MobileNetV2 + Squeeze-and-Excite [9]. FC denotes Fully Connected Layers, Hard-$\sigma$ denotes Hard-sigmoid activation.

**Attention Module.** About channel attention module, some researchers used a novel method, Efficient Channel Attention (ECA), to capture local cross-channel information interaction. Some author also substituted the Global Average Pooling (GAP) for Fully Connected Layers (FC) and compressed the feature map into a $1 \times 1 \times C$ feature map. And then went through the activation function, character multiplied the corresponding elements in the feature diagram before passing GAP. This article only considered the information interaction between the weights and its K neighbors,

$$y_i = \sigma(\sum_{j=1}^{k} \omega_i^j y_i^j), \qquad \omega_i^j \in \varphi_i^k \tag{4}$$

To further improve performance, it is also possible to let all channels share weight information, that is

$$y_i = \sigma(\sum_{j=1}^{k} \omega_i^j y^j), \qquad \omega_i^j \in \varphi_i^k \tag{5}$$

Based on these analyses, the original author proposed a novel approach that enables information interaction between channels with a one - dimensional convolution, C1D, whose core size is K:

$$y = \sigma(C1D_k(\omega)) \tag{6}$$

In experiments, we set K being 3.

The standard sigmoid is slow to compute because of computing the exp() function. In many cases the high-precision exp() results aren't needed, and an approximation will suffice.

$$Hard - sigmoid = \begin{cases} 0 & \text{if } x < -2.5, \\ 0.25x + 0.5 & \text{if } -2.5 \leq x \leq 2.5, \\ 1 & \text{if } x > 2.5. \end{cases} \tag{7}$$

Hard-sigmoid is a piecewise linear approximation of Logistic Sigmoid activation function. It's easy to differentiate, and Hard-sigmoid computes faster than sigmoid. In this paper, we replace the sigmoid with the Hard-sigmoid. If the activation function is sigmoid function, this method will be called ECA. So we call the attention module HECA. The structure of MobileNetV3 adding HECA is shown in Fig. 3.

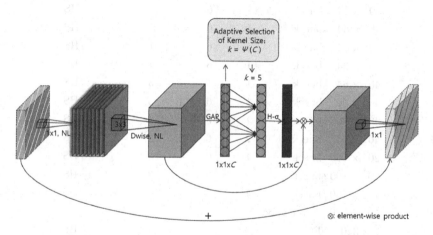

**Fig. 3.** MobileNetV2 + Hard Efficient Channel Attention (HECA). HECA uses Global Average Pooling (GAP) to transform the feature map into 1×1×C, replacing the role of Fully Connected Layers (FC). Fast 1D convolution is used to obtain local cross-channel interaction information. The one-dimensional convolution kernel size, K, is proportional to the channel dimension, C.

**Redesigning the Net's Backbone.** As is mentioned above, we introduced Feature Pyramid Networks, Attention Module–HECA and Context Model. We choose MobileNetV2-HECA as our backbone, whose structure data are shown in Table 1. As our networks go deeper, the cost of nonlinearity will be lower. In our experiments, we find that H-swish alone in deeper layers could achieve most benefits.

**Table 1.** Specification for MobileNetV2-HECA. HECA denotes whether there is Efficient Channel Attention with Hard-sigmoid activation in that block. T is the input channels multiplier (that is, the channels number in the middle is t times the channels number in the input). NL means the type of nonlinearity, used. HS is H-swish and RE represents ReLU.

| Input | Operator | Stride | Exp ratio | ksize | HECA | NL |
|---|---|---|---|---|---|---|
| $640^2 \times 3$ | conv2d | 2 | – | 1 | – | HS |
| $320^2 \times 32$ | bneck | 1 | 1 | 1 | – | RE |
| $320^2 \times 16$ | bneck | 2 | 6 | 1 | – | RE |
| $160^2 \times 24$ | bneck | 1 | 6 | 1 | – | RE |
| $160^2 \times 24$ | bneck | 2 | 6 | 1 | – | RE |
| $80^2 \times 32$ | bneck | 1 | 6 | 1 | – | RE |
| $80^2 \times 32$ | bneck | 1 | 6 | 1 | Yes | RE |
| $80^2 \times 32$ | bneck | 2 | 6 | 1 | – | HS |
| $40^2 \times 64$ | bneck | 1 | 6 | 1 | – | HS |
| $40^2 \times 64$ | bneck | 1 | 6 | 1 | – | HS |
| $40^2 \times 64$ | bneck | 1 | 6 | 1 | – | HS |
| $40^2 \times 64$ | bneck | 1 | 6 | 3 | – | HS |
| $40^2 \times 96$ | bneck | 1 | 6 | 3 | – | HS |
| $40^2 \times 96$ | bneck | 1 | 6 | 3 | Yes | HS |
| $40^2 \times 96$ | bneck | 2 | 6 | 3 | – | HS |
| $20^2 \times 160$ | bneck | 1 | 6 | 3 | – | HS |
| $20^2 \times 160$ | bneck | 2 | 6 | 3 | Yes | HS |
| $10^2 \times 160$ | bneck | 1 | 6 | 3 | Yes | HS |
| $10^2 \times 320$ | ada-avgpool | – | – | – | – | – |
| $1 \times 320$ | FC | – | – | – | – | HS |

## 4  Experiments

### 4.1  Dataset

We use a large-scale face detection dataset, the WIDER FACE dataset [22], which is made up of 32,203 images and 393,703 labeled faces. For event classes, the WIDER FACE dataset can be divided into 60 categories. For each category, author randomly divide the images into a 4:1:5 ratio of the training, validation and the test subsets. Based on the detection rate of Edgebox [27], the WIDER FACE dataset is set to three levels, Easy, Medium and Hard.

**Extra Annotations.** As shown in Fig. 4, Retinaface divided the pictures in the WIDER FACE dataset into five levels, according to the difficulty of marking landmarks on the faces in images. It marked five facial landmarks (i.e. mouth corners, nose tip and eye centers).

## 4.2   Implementation Details

*Feature Pyramid.* The PupilFace feature pyramid has four layers, P2-P5. And they are all made from the last feature map, C2-C5, for each stage in the backbone. Then they adjust the channel number with convolution layers. In C2-C5, we add HECA to the inverted residual, which enhanced the information interaction between channels.

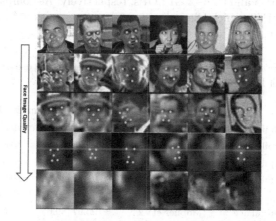

**Fig. 4.** RetinaFace added extra annotations of five facial landmarks.

*Anchor Settings.* As shown in Table 2, we take specific scale anchors on P2-P5, like [19]. In order to recognize tiny faces, we use plenty of small anchors in P2. This results in more computation complexity and a little false positive. In this paper, the size of our picture is . The ratio of positive and negative samples is more than 4:1.

**Table 2.** The details of feature pyramid, stride size, anchor in PupilFace.

| Feature pyramid | Stride | Anchor |
|---|---|---|
| $P_2$ ($80 \times 80 \times 256$) | 8 | 16,32 |
| $P_3$ ($40 \times 40 \times 256$) | 16 | 32,64 |
| $P_4$ ($20 \times 20 \times 256$) | 32 | 64,128 |
| $P_5$ ($10 \times 10 \times 256$) | 64 | 128,256 |

*Training Details.* We trained the PupilFace on two NVIDIA RTX 3080 (20 GB) GPUs using the Adam optimizer (weight decay at 0.0005, batch size of 32).

*Testing Details.* As for the WIDER FACE test subsets, we did the same like [11] with different sizes images. Using an IoU threshold of 0.35, we apply Box voting [4] on the union set of predicted face boxes.

### 4.3   Experimental Results

**Experimental Results and Analyses.** According to Table 3, we can see that PupilFace has achieved good results in choosing light-weight backbone. Compared with the backbone, the attention module in our network has a small amount of parameters and computation. For example, for MobileNetV2 with 3.34M parameters and 0.32 GFLOPs, the additional parameters and computations of HECA are 9 and 5.1e−4 GFLOPs, respectively; As compared in Table 3, it adds MobileNetV2, which has a significant improvement on Average Precision (AP) of hard test set.

**Table 3.** WiderFace Value Performance in single scale when we use different networks as the backbone of PupilFace and other popular networks.

|                 | Backbone          | Easy  | Medium | Hard  |
|-----------------|-------------------|-------|--------|-------|
| PupilFace       | MobileNet         | 90.92 | 89.17  | 79.62 |
| PupilFace       | MobileNetV2       | 91.33 | 89.96  | 80.03 |
| PupilFace       | MobileNetV2-ECA   | 91.60 | 90.28  | 80.57 |
| PupilFace (ours)| MobileNetV2-HECA  | 91.82 | 90.65  | 80.94 |
| RetinaFace      | MobileNet         | 90.63 | 89.02  | 79.37 |
| RetinaFace      | MobileNetV2       | 90.97 | 89.65  | 79.59 |

As shown in Fig. 5, we plot the Precision-recall curves of the PupilFace on the WIDER FACE test subsets. They are drawn in three difficult levels: Easy, Medium and Hard(The WIDER FACE dataset is set to three levels, based on the detection rate of Edgebox [11]). And we could see the pictures that our

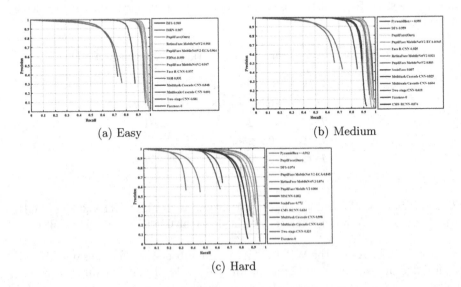

(a) Easy                    (b) Medium

(c) Hard

**Fig. 5.** The WIDER FACE test subsets' Precision-recall curves.

light-weight face detection and location network, PupilFace, works better than quantities of the state-of-the-art networks. Here we compare our networks with pyramid-box [17], DFS [18], Multitask Cascade CNN [25], ScaleFace [23], CMS-RCNN [26] and Two-stage CNN [22].

In Fig. 6, we show our PupilFace on two pictures of dense faces. In the top picture, it's clear that we detect almost all the faces in the picture and mark facial landmarks, except that the faces were covered by a hat (which means massive occlusion). Even this image has a low pixel size and is a bit blurry, the performance still looks good. The other is a high resolution image of the person in different position, some of the faces being dim and wearing hats but can still be detected and located. These performances are great for our light-weight face detection and location network, PupilFace.

**Fig. 6.** Typical results on the WIDER FACE test subsets.

# 5    Conclusion

We study how to simultaneously locate tiny faces and align faces with any scale in the picture. The conventional method requires two-stage, but we proposed a lightweight one-stage network called PupilFace. PupilFace shows excellent performance in face detection in cases with massive occlusion and pose variations. In addition, by employing different backbones it could adapt to more cumbersome tasks. The model is available for further research on this topic. In the future, we will apply the model to actual scenes. For example, we can increase the facial landmarks number, and then use facial landmarks to determine whether the driver is fatigue driving.

# References

1. Deng, J., Guo, J., Zhou, Y., Yu, J., Kotsia, I., Zafeiriou, S.: RetinaFace: single-stage dense face localisation in the wild. arXiv preprint arXiv:1905.00641 (2019)
2. Dollár, P., Welinder, P., Perona, P.: Cascaded pose regression. In: 2010 IEEE Computer Society Conference on Computer Vision and Pattern Recognition, pp. 1078–1085. IEEE (2010)
3. Elfwing, S., Uchibe, E., Doya, K.: Sigmoid-weighted linear units for neural network function approximation in reinforcement learning. Neural Netw. **107**, 3–11 (2018)
4. Gidaris, S., Komodakis, N.: Object detection via a multi-region and semantic segmentation-aware CNN model. In: Proceedings of the IEEE International Conference on Computer Vision, pp. 1134–1142 (2015)
5. He, K., Zhang, X., Ren, S., Sun, J.: Deep residual learning for image recognition. In: Proceedings of the IEEE Conference on Computer Vision and Pattern Recognition, pp. 770–778 (2016)
6. Hendrycks, D., Gimpel, K.: Bridging nonlinearities and stochastic regularizers with gaussian error linear units (2016)
7. Howard, A., et al.: Searching for MobileNetV3. In: Proceedings of the IEEE/CVF International Conference on Computer Vision, pp. 1314–1324 (2019)
8. Howard, A.G., et al.: MobileNets: efficient convolutional neural networks for mobile vision applications. arXiv preprint arXiv:1704.04861 (2017)
9. Hu, J., Shen, L., Sun, G.: Squeeze-and-excitation networks. In: Proceedings of the IEEE Conference on Computer Vision and Pattern Recognition, pp. 7132–7141 (2018)
10. Lin, T.Y., Dollár, P., Girshick, R., He, K., Hariharan, B., Belongie, S.: Feature pyramid networks for object detection. In: Proceedings of the IEEE Conference on Computer Vision and Pattern Recognition, pp. 2117–2125 (2017)
11. Najibi, M., Samangouei, P., Chellappa, R., Davis, L.S.: SSH: single stage headless face detector. In: Proceedings of the IEEE International Conference on Computer Vision, pp. 4875–4884 (2017)
12. Pang, Y., Wang, T., Anwer, R.M., Khan, F.S., Shao, L.: Efficient featurized image pyramid network for single shot detector. In: Proceedings of the IEEE/CVF Conference on Computer Vision and Pattern Recognition, pp. 7336–7344 (2019)
13. Ramachandran, P., Zoph, B., Le, Q.V.: Searching for activation functions. arXiv preprint arXiv:1710.05941 (2017)

14. Sandler, M., Howard, A., Zhu, M., Zhmoginov, A., Chen, L.C.: MobileNetV2: inverted residuals and linear bottlenecks. In: Proceedings of the IEEE Conference on Computer Vision and Pattern Recognition, pp. 4510–4520 (2018)

15. Shi, L., Xu, X., Kakadiaris, I.A.: SSFD: a face detector using a single-scale feature map. In: 2018 IEEE 9th International Conference on Biometrics Theory, Applications and Systems (BTAS), pp. 1–10. IEEE (2018)

16. Shrivastava, A., Gupta, A., Girshick, R.: Training region-based object detectors with online hard example mining. In: Proceedings of the IEEE Conference on Computer Vision and Pattern Recognition, pp. 761–769 (2016)

17. Tang, X., Du, D.K., He, Z., Liu, J.: PyramidBox: a context-assisted single shot face detector. In: Ferrari, V., Hebert, M., Sminchisescu, C., Weiss, Y. (eds.) ECCV 2018. LNCS, vol. 11213, pp. 812–828. Springer, Cham (2018). https://doi.org/10.1007/978-3-030-01240-3_49

18. Tian, W., et al.: Learning better features for face detection with feature fusion and segmentation supervision. arXiv preprint arXiv:1811.08557 (2018)

19. Wang, J., Yuan, Y., Yu, G.: Face attention network: an effective face detector for the occluded faces. arXiv preprint arXiv:1711.07246 (2017)

20. Wang, Q., Wu, B., Zhu, P., Li, P., Zuo, W., Hu, Q.: ECA-Net: efficient channel attention for deep convolutional neural networks. In: 2020 IEEE CVF Conference on Computer Vision and Pattern Recognition (CVPR). IEEE (2020)

21. Wu, Q., et al.: Lattice materials with pyramidal hierarchy: systematic analysis and three dimensional failure mechanism maps. J. Mech. Phys. Solids 125, 112–144 (2019)

22. Yang, S., Luo, P., Loy, C.C., Tang, X.: Wider face: a face detection benchmark. In: Proceedings of the IEEE Conference on Computer Vision and Pattern Recognition, pp. 5525–5533 (2016)

23. Yang, S., Xiong, Y., Loy, C.C., Tang, X.: Face detection through scale-friendly deep convolutional networks. arXiv preprint arXiv:1706.02863 (2017)

24. Zafeiriou, S., Zhang, C., Zhang, Z.: A survey on face detection in the wild: past, present and future. Comput. Vis. Image Underst. 138, 1–24 (2015)

25. Zhang, K., Zhang, Z., Li, Z., Qiao, Y.: Joint face detection and alignment using multitask cascaded convolutional networks. IEEE Signal Process. Lett. 23(10), 1499–1503 (2016)

26. Zhu, C., Zheng, Y., Luu, K., Savvides, M.: CMS-RCNN: contextual multi-scale region-based CNN for unconstrained face detection. In: Bhanu, B., Kumar, A. (eds.) Deep Learning for Biometrics. ACVPR, pp. 57–79. Springer, Cham (2017). https://doi.org/10.1007/978-3-319-61657-5_3

27. Zitnick, C.L., Dollár, P.: Edge boxes: locating object proposals from edges. In: Fleet, D., Pajdla, T., Schiele, B., Tuytelaars, T. (eds.) ECCV 2014. LNCS, vol. 8693, pp. 391–405. Springer, Cham (2014). https://doi.org/10.1007/978-3-319-10602-1_26

# Author Index

Printed in the United States
by Baker & Taylor Publisher Services